Winston's War

WINSTON'S WAR

CHURCHILL, 1940–1945

Max Hastings

Alfred A. Knopf · New York

2010

THIS IS A BORZOI BOOK
PUBLISHED BY ALFRED A. KNOPF

Copyright © 2009 by Max Hastings
All rights reserved. Published in the United States by Alfred A. Knopf,
a division of Random House, Inc., New York
www.aaknopf.com

Originally published in Great Britain as *Finest Years: Churchill as Warlord, 1940–45*
by HarperPress, an imprint of HarperCollins*Publishers*, London, in 2009.

Knopf, Borzoi Books and the colophon are
registered trademarks of Random House, Inc.

Library of Congress Cataloging-in-Publication Data
Hastings, Max.
Winston's war : Churchill, 1940–1945 / Max Hastings. —1st American ed.
p. cm.
ISBN 978-0-307-26839-6
"Originally published in Great Britain by HarperPress, an imprint of
HarperCollinsPublishers, London, in 2009"—T.p. verso.
"This is a Borzoi book"—T.p. verso.
Includes bibliographical references and index.
1. Churchill, Winston, 1874–1965—Military leadership.
2. World War, 1939–1945—Great Britain.
3. Great Britain—Politics and government—1936–1945.
4. Great Britain—History, Military—20th century.   I. Title.
DA566.9.C5H274   2009
940.53'41092—dc22
[B]
2009038836

Manufactured in the United States of America
First United States Edition

In memory of Roy Jenkins,
and our Indian summer friendship

It may well be that the most glorious chapters of our history have yet to be written. Indeed, the very problems and dangers that encompass us and our country ought to make English men and women of this generation glad to be here at such a time. We ought to rejoice at the responsibilities with which destiny has honoured us, and be proud that we are guardians of our country in an age when her life is at stake.

—*Winston Spencer Churchill, April 1933*

History with its flickering lamp stumbles along the trail of the past, trying to reconstruct its scenes, to revive its echoes, and kindle with pale gleams the passion of former days.

—*Winston Spencer Churchill, November 1940*

Contents

List of Maps   xi

Introduction   3

1. The Battle of France   11

2. The Two Dunkirks   40

3. Invasion Fever   59

4. The Battle of Britain   74

5. Greek Fire   99

6. Comrades   130

7. The Battle of America   147

8. A Glimpse of Arcadia   182

9. "The Valley of Humiliation"   198

10. "Second Front Now!"   230

11. Camels and the Bear   255

12. The Turn of Fortune   270

13. Out of the Desert   297

14. Sunk in the Aegean   323

15. Tehran   341

16. Setting Europe Ablaze   364

17. Overlord   384

18. Bargaining with an Empty Wallet   398

19. Athens: "Wounded in the House of Our Friends"   422

20. Yalta   441

21. The Final Act   450

    Acknowledgements and References   485

    Notes   487

    Select Bibliography   517

    Index   525

Maps

Europe   xii

The Mediterranean   xiv

May 1940 Deployments   17

The German Advance   29

The Dunkirk Perimeter   35

Operation Sealion   86

Operation Compass   108

The North African Campaign   274

Operation Torch   276

The Italian Campaign   310

The Dodecanese   328

Overlord and Anvil   401

ATLANTIC
OCEAN

IRELAND
Dublin

NORTH
SEA

DENMARK

GREAT
BRITAIN
London

B

G R
G E

Brest

Paris

F R A N C E

Vichy

ITALY

Bay
of
Biscay

La Spezia

Menton

Marseilles

Toulon

PORTUGAL

Madrid

SPAIN

Barcelona

Corsica

Rome

Anzio

Lisbon

Sardinia

Naples

Gibraltar

Rabat

SPANISH
MOROCCO

Casablanca

Oran

Algiers

Palermo

Bizerta

N

Bône

Si

Safi

Tunis

Sousse

MOROCCO

Hajjerat M'Guil

TUNISIA

Sfax

M

A L G E R I A

Gabès

Médenine

Tripoli

TRIPOLITANIA

THE MEDITERRANEAN

0   200 miles

0   300 km.

L I

WINSTON'S WAR

Introduction

CHURCHILL was the greatest Englishman and one of the greatest human beings of the twentieth century, indeed of all time. Yet, beyond that bald assertion, there are infinite nuances in considering his conduct of Britain's war between 1940 and 1945, which is the theme of this book. It originated nine years ago, when Roy Jenkins was writing his biography of Churchill. Roy flattered me by inviting my comments on the typescript, chapter by chapter. Some of my suggestions he accepted; many he sensibly ignored. When we reached the Second World War, his patience expired. Exasperated by the profusion of my strictures, he said: "You're trying to get me to do something which you should write yourself, if you want to!" By that time, his health was failing. He was impatient to finish his own book, which achieved triumphant success before his death.

In the years which followed, I thought much about Churchill and the war, mindful of some Boswellian lines about Samuel Johnson: "He had once conceived the thought of writing The Life Of Oliver Cromwell . . . He at length laid aside his scheme, on discovering that all that can be told of him is already in print; and that it is impracticable to procure any authentick information in addition to what the world is already possessed of." Among the vast Churchillian bibliography, I was especially apprehensive about venturing anywhere near the tracks of David Reynolds's extraordinarily original and penetrating 2005 *In Command of History*. The author dissected successive drafts of Churchill's war memoirs, exposing contrasts between judgements on people and events which the old statesman initially proposed to make, and those which he finally deemed it prudent to publish. Andrew Roberts has painted a striking portrait of wartime Anglo-American relations in his 2009 *Masters and Commanders*. We have been told more about Winston Churchill than any other human being. Tens of thousands of people of many nations have recorded even trifling encounters, noting every word which they heard him utter. The most vivid wartime memory of one soldier of Britain's Eighth Army derived from a day in 1942 when he found the prime minister his neighbour in a North African desert latrine. Churchill's speeches and writings fill many volumes.

Yet much remains opaque, because he wished it thus. Always mindful of his role as a stellar performer upon the stage of history, he became supremely so after May 10, 1940. He kept no diary because, he observed, to do so would be to expose his follies and inconsistencies to posterity. Within months of his ascent to the premiership, however, he told his staff that he had already schemed the chapters of the book which he would write as soon as the war was over. The outcome was a ruthlessly partial six-volume work which is poor history, if sometimes peerless prose. We shall never know with complete confidence what he thought about many personalities—for instance Roosevelt, Eisenhower, Brooke, King George VI, his Cabinet colleagues—because he took good care not to tell us.

Churchill's wartime relationship with the British people was much more complex than is often acknowledged. Few denied his claims upon the premiership. But between the end of the Battle of Britain in 1940 and El Alamein in November 1942, not only many ordinary citizens, but also some of his closest colleagues wanted operational control of the war machine to be removed from his hands, and some other figure appointed to his role as minister of defence. It is hard to overstate the embarrassment and even shame of the British people, as they perceived the Russians playing a heroic part in the struggle against Nazism, while their own army seemed incapable of winning a battle. To understand Britain's wartime experience, it appears essential to recognise, as some narratives do not, the sense of humiliation which afflicted Britain amid the failures of its soldiers, contrasted—albeit often on the basis of wildly false information—with the achievements of Stalin.

Churchill was dismayed by the performance of the British Army, even after victories began to come at the end of 1942. Himself a hero, he expected others likewise to show themselves heroes. In 1940, the people of Britain, together with their navy and air force, wonderfully fulfilled his hopes. Thereafter, however, much of the story of Britain's part in the war seems to me that of the prime minister seeking more from his nation's warriors than they could deliver. The failure of the army to match the prime minister's aspirations is among the central themes of this book.

Much discussion of Britain's military effort in World War II focuses upon Churchill's relationship with his generals. In my view, this preoccupation is overdone. The difficulties of fighting the Germans and Japanese went much deeper than could be solved by changes of commanders. The

British were beaten again and again between 1940 and 1942, and continued to suffer battlefield difficulties thereafter, in consequence of failures of tactics, weapons, equipment and culture even more significant than lack of mass or inspired leadership. The gulf between Churchillian aspiration and reality extended to the peoples of occupied Europe, hence his faith in "setting Europe ablaze" through the agency of Special Operations Executive, which had malign consequences that he failed to anticipate. SOE armed some occupied peoples to fight more energetically against one another in 1944–45 than they had done earlier against the Germans.

It is a common mistake to suppose that those who bestrode the stage during momentous times were giants, set apart from the personalities of our own humdrum society. I have argued in earlier books that we should instead see 1939–45 as a period when men and women not much different from ourselves strove to grapple with stresses and responsibilities which stretched their powers to the limit. Churchill was one of a tiny number of actors who proved worthy of the role in which destiny cast him. Those who worked for the prime minister, indeed the British people at war, served as a supporting cast, seeking honourably but sometimes inadequately to play their own parts in the wake of a titan.

Sir Edward Bridges, then cabinet secretary, wrote of Churchill between 1940 and 1942: "Everything depended upon him and him alone. Only he had the power to make the nation believe that it could win." This remains the view of most of the world, almost seventy years later. Yet there is also no shortage of iconoclasts. In a recent biography Cambridge lecturer Nigel Knight writes contemptuously of Churchill: "He was not mad or simple; his misguided decisions were a product of his personality—a mixture of arrogance, emotion, self-indulgence, stubbornness and a blind faith in his own ability." Another modern biographer, Chris Wrigley, suggests that Sir Edward Bridges's tribute to Churchill "may overstate his indispensability."

Such strictures seem otiose to those of us convinced that, in his absence, Britain would have made terms with Hitler after Dunkirk. Thereafter, beyond his domestic achievement as war leader, he performed a diplomatic role of which only he was capable: as suitor of the United States on behalf of the British nation. To fulfil this, he was obliged to overcome intense prejudices on both sides of the Atlantic. So extravagant was Churchill's—and Roosevelt's—wartime rhetoric about the Anglo-American alliance that even today the extent of mutual suspicion and indeed dislike between the two peoples is often underestimated. The British ruling class, in particular, condescended amazingly towards Americans.

In 1940–41, Winston Churchill perceived, with a clarity which eluded some of his fellow countrymen, that only American belligerence might open a path to victory. Pearl Harbor, and not the prime minister's powers of seduction, eventually brought Roosevelt's nation into the war. But no other statesman could have conducted British policy towards the United States with such consummate skill, nor have achieved such personal influence upon the American people. This persisted until 1944, when his standing in the United States declined precipitously, to revive only when the onset of the Cold War caused many Americans to hail Churchill as a prophet. His greatness, which had come to seem too large for his own impoverished country, then became perceived as a shared Anglo-American treasure.

From June 1941 onwards, Churchill saw much more clearly than most British soldiers and politicians that Russia must be embraced as an ally. But it seems important to strip away legends about aid to the Soviet Union, and acknowledge how small this was in the decisive 1941–42 period. Stalin's nation saved itself with little help from the Western Allies. Only from mid-1943 onwards did supplies to Russia gain critical mass, and Anglo-American ground operations absorb a significant part of the Wehrmacht's attention.

The huge popularity of the Soviet Union in wartime Britain was a source of dismay, indeed exasperation, to the small number of people at the top who knew the truth about the barbarity of Stalin's regime, its implacable hostility to the West and its imperialistic designs on eastern Europe. The divide between the sentiments of the public and those of the prime minister towards the Soviet Union became a chasm in May 1945. One of Churchill's most astonishing acts, in the last weeks of his premiership, was to order the Joint Planning Staff to produce a draft for Operation Unthinkable. The resulting document considered the practicability of launching an Anglo-American offensive against the Russians, with forty-seven divisions reinforced by the remains of Hitler's Wehrmacht, to restore the freedom of Poland. Though Churchill acknowledged this as a remote contingency, it is remarkable that he caused the Chiefs of Staff to address it at all.

I am surprised how few historians seem to notice that many things which the British and Americans believed they were concealing from the Soviets—for instance, Bletchley Park's penetration of Axis ciphers and Anglo-American arguments about launching a Second Front—were well-known to Stalin, through the good offices of Communist sympathisers and traitors in Whitehall and Washington. The Soviets knew vastly more about their allies' secret policy making than did the British and Americans about that of the Russians.

It is fascinating to study public mood swings through wartime British, American and Russian newspapers and the diaries of ordinary citizens. These often give a very different picture from that of historians, with their privileged knowledge of how the story ended. As for sentiment at the top, some men who were indifferent politicians or commanders contributed much more as contemporary chroniclers. The diaries of such figures as Hugh Dalton, Leo Amery and Lt. Gen. Henry Pownall make them more valuable to us as eyewitnesses and eavesdroppers than they seemed to their contemporaries as players in the drama.

Maj. Gen. John Kennedy, for much of the war the British Army's director of military operations, kept a diary which arguably ranks second only to that of Gen. Sir Alan Brooke for its insights into the British military high command. On January 26, 1941, in the darkest days of the conflict, Kennedy expressed a fear that selective use of accounts of the meetings of Britain's leaders might mislead posterity:

> It would be easy by a cunning or biased selection of evidence to give the impression for instance that the P.M.'s strategic policy was nearly always at fault, & that it was only by terrific efforts that he is kept on the right lines—and it would be easy to do likewise with all the chiefs of staff. The historian who has to deal with the voluminous records of this war will have a frightful task. I suppose no war has been so well documented. Yet the records do not often reveal individual views. It is essentially a government of committees . . . Winston is of course the dominating personality & he has in his entourage and among his immediate advisers no really strong personality. Yet Winston's views do not often prevail if they are contrary to the general trend of opinion among the service staffs. Minutes flutter continually from Winston's typewriter on every conceivable subject. His strategic imagination is inexhaustible and many of his ideas are wild and unsound and impracticable . . . but in the end they are killed if they are not acceptable.

These observations, made in the heat of events, deserve respect from every historian of the period. Another banal and yet critical point is that circumstances and attitudes shifted. The prime minister often changed his mind, and deserves more credit than he sometimes receives for his willingness to do so. Meanwhile, others vacillated in their views of him. Some who revered Churchill in the first months of his premiership later became bitterly sceptical, and vice versa. After Dunkirk, Britain's middle classes were considerably more staunch than some members of its traditional ruling caste, partly because they knew less about the full horror of the country's predicament. History perceives as pivotal Britain's survival through 1940, so that the weariness and cynicism which pervaded the country by 1942, amid continuing defeats, are often underrated. Industrial unrest, manifested through strikes especially in the coalfields and in the aircraft and shipbuilding industries, revealed fissures in the fabric of national unity which are surprisingly seldom acknowledged.

This book does not seek to retell the full story of Churchill at war, but rather to present a portrait of his leadership from the day on which he became prime minister, May 10, 1940, set in the context of Britain's national experience. It is weighted towards the first half of the conflict, partly because Churchill's contribution was then much greater than it became later, and partly because I have sought to emphasise issues and events about which there seem new things to be said.

I have written relatively little in this book about the strategic air offensive, having addressed this earlier in *Bomber Command* and *Armageddon*. I have here confined myself to discussion of the prime minister's personal role in key bombing decisions. I have not described land and naval campaigns in detail, but instead considered the institutional cultures which influenced the performance of the British Army, the Royal Navy and the Royal Air Force (RAF), and the three services' relationships with the prime minister.

To maintain coherence, it is necessary to address some themes and episodes which are familiar, though specific aspects deserve reconsideration. There was, for instance, what I have called the second Dunkirk, no less miraculous than the first. Churchill's biggest misjudgement of 1940 was his decision to send more troops to France in June after the rescue of the British Expeditionary Force (BEF) from the beaches. Only the stubborn insistence of their commander, Lt. Gen. Sir Alan Brooke, made it possible to overcome the rash impulses of the prime minister and evacuate almost 200,000 men who would otherwise have been lost.

The narrative examines some subordinate issues and events in which the prime minister's role was crucial, such as the strategic contribution of SOE (as distinct from romantic tales of its agents' derring-do), the Dodecanese campaign and Churchill's Athens adventure in December 1944. I have attempted little original research in his own papers. Instead, I have explored the impression he made upon others—generals, soldiers, citizens, Americans and Russians. Moscow's closure of key archives to foreign researchers has curtailed the wonderful bonanza of the post–Cold War period. But much important material has now been published in Russian documentary collections.

It seems mistaken to stint on quotation from Alan Brooke, John Colville and Charles Wilson (Lord Moran), merely because their records have been long in the public domain. Recent research on Moran's manuscript suggests that, rather than being a true contemporary record, much of it was written up afterwards. Yet most of his anecdotes and observations appear credible. The diaries of Churchill's military chief, junior private secretary and doctor provide, for all their various limitations, the most intimate testimony we shall ever have about Churchill's wartime existence.

He himself, of course, bestrides the tale in all his joyous splendour. Even at the blackest periods, when his spirits sagged, flashes of exuberance broke through, which cheered his colleagues and contemporaries, but caused some people to recoil from him. They were dismayed, even disgusted, that he so conspicuously thrilled to his own part in the greatest conflict in human history. "Why do we regard history as of the past and forget we are making it?" he exulted to Australian prime minister Robert Menzies in 1941. It was this glee which caused such a man as the aesthete and diarist James Lees-Milne to write fastidiously after it was all over: "Churchill so evidently enjoyed the war that I could never like him. I merely acknowledge him, like Genghis Khan, to have been great."

Lees-Milne and like-minded critics missed an important aspect of Churchill's attitude to conflict in general, and to the Second World War in particular. He thrilled to the cannon's roar, and rejoiced in its proximity to himself. Yet never for a moment did he lose his sense of dismay about the death and destruction which war visited upon the innocent. "Ah, horrible war, amazing medley of the glorious and the squalid, the pitiful and the sublime," he wrote as a correspondent in South Africa in January 1900. "If modern men of light and leading saw your face closer simple folk would see it hardly ever." Hitler was indifferent to the sufferings his policies imposed upon mankind. Churchill never flinched from the necessity to pay in blood for the defeat of Nazi tyranny. But his sole purpose was to enable the guns to be silenced, the peoples of the world restored to their peaceful lives.

Appetite for the fray was among Churchill's most convincing credentials for national leadership in May 1940. Neville Chamberlain had many weaknesses as prime minister, but foremost among them was a revulsion from the conflict to which his country was committed, shared by many members of his government. One of them, Rob Bernays, said: "I wish I were twenty. I cannot bear this responsibility." A nation which found itself committed to a life-and-death struggle against one of the most ruthless tyrannies in history was surely wise to entrust its leadership to a man eager to embrace the role, rather than one who shrank from it. This book discusses Churchill's follies and misjudgements, which were many and various. But these are as pimples upon the mountain of his achievement. It is sometimes said that the British and American peoples are still today, in the twenty-first century, indecently obsessed with the Second World War. The reason is not far to seek. We know that here was something which our parents and grandparents did well, in a noble cause that will forever be identified with the person of Winston Churchill, warlord extraordinary.

Chilton Foliat, Berkshire
January 2009

ONE

The Battle of France

FOR SEVEN MONTHS after the Second World War began in September 1939, many British people deluded themselves that it might gutter out before there was a bloodbath in the west. On April 5, 1940, while the armed but passive confrontation between the Wehrmacht and Anglo-French forces which had persisted since the fall of Poland still prevailed on the Franco-German border, Prime Minister Neville Chamberlain told a Conservative Party meeting: "Hitler has missed the bus." Less than five weeks later, however, on May 7, he addressed the House of Commons, to explain the disastrous outcome of Britain's campaign to frustrate the German occupation of Norway. Beginning with a tribute to British troops who had "carried out their task with magnificent gallantry," in halting tones he continued:

> I hope that we shall not exaggerate the extent or the importance of the check we have received. The withdrawal from southern Norway is not comparable to the withdrawal from Gallipoli . . . There were no large forces involved. Not much more than a single division . . . Still, I am quite aware . . . that some discouragement has been caused to our friends, and that our enemies are crowing. . . . I want to ask hon. Members not to form any hasty opinions on the result of the Norwegian campaign so far as it has gone . . . A minister who shows any sign of confidence is always called complacent. If he fails to do so, he is labelled defeatist. For my part I try to steer a middle course [Interruption]— neither raising undue expectations [Hon. Members: "Hitler missed the bus"] which are unlikely to be fulfilled, nor making people's flesh creep by painting pictures of unmitigated gloom. A great many times some hon. Members have repeated the phrase "Hitler missed the bus"— [Hon. Members: "You said it"] . . . While I retain my complete confidence in our ultimate victory, I do not think that the people of this

country yet realise the extent or the imminence of the threat which is impending against us [An Hon. Member: "We said that five years ago"].

When the debate ended the following night, thirty-three Tories voted against their own party, and a further sixty abstained. Though Chamberlain retained a parliamentary majority, it was plain that his Conservative government had lost the nation's confidence. This was not merely the consequence of the Norway campaign, but because through eight fumbling months it had exposed its lack of stomach for war. An all-party coalition was indispensable. Labour would not serve under Chamberlain. Winston Churchill became Britain's prime minister following a meeting between himself, Chamberlain, Foreign Secretary Lord Halifax and Tory chief whip David Margesson on the afternoon of May 9, at which Halifax declared his own unsuitability for the post, as a member of the House of Lords who would be obliged to delegate direction of the war to Churchill in the Commons. In truth, some expedient could have been adopted to allow the foreign secretary to return to the Commons. But Halifax possessed sufficient self-knowledge to recognise that no more than Neville Chamberlain did he possess the stuff of a war leader.

While much of the ruling class disliked and mistrusted the new premier, he was the overwhelming choice of the British people. With remarkably sure instinct, they perceived that if they must wage war, the leadership of a warrior was needed. David Reynolds has observed that when the Gallipoli campaign failed in 1915, many people wished to blame Churchill—then, as in 1940, first lord of the Admiralty—while after Norway nobody did. "It was a marvel," Churchill wrote in an unpublished draft of his war memoirs. "I really do not know how— I survived and maintained my position in public esteem while all the blame was thrown on poor Mr. Chamberlain." He may also have perceived his own good fortune in not having achieved the highest office in earlier years, or even in the earlier months of the war. Had he done so, it is likely that by May 1940 his country would have tired of the excesses which he would surely have committed, while being no more capable than Chamberlain of stemming the tide of fate on the continent. Back in 1935, Stanley Baldwin explained to a friend his unwillingness to appoint Churchill to his own Cabinet: "If there is going to be a war—and who can say there is not—we must keep him fresh to be our war Prime Minister." Baldwin's tone was jocular and patronising, yet there proved to be something in what he said.

In May 1940 only generals and admirals knew the extent of Churchill's responsibility for Britain's ill-starred Scandinavian deployments. Nonetheless the familiar view, that he was the sole architect of disaster, seems overstated. Had British troops been better trained, motivated and led, they would have made a better showing against Hitler's forces, which repeatedly worsted them in Norway while often inferior in numbers. The British Army's failure reflected decades of neglect, together with institutional weaknesses which would influence the fortunes of British arms through the years which followed. These were symbolically attested to by a colonel who noticed among officers' baggage being landed at Namsos, on the central Norwegian coast, "several fishing rods and many sporting guns." No German officer would have gone to war with such frivolous accoutrements.

Now, Halifax wrote disdainfully to a friend, "I don't think WSC will be a very good PM though . . . the country will think he gives them a fillip." The foreign secretary told his junior minister R. A. Butler, when they discussed his own refusal to offer himself for the premiership: "It's all a great pity. You know my reasons, it's no use discussing that—but the gangsters will shortly be in complete control." Humbler folk disagreed. Lancashire housewife Nella Last wrote in her diary on May 11: "If I had to spend my whole life with a man, I'd choose Mr. Chamberlain, but I think I would sooner have Mr. Churchill if there was a storm and I was shipwrecked. He has a funny face, like a bulldog living in our street who has done more to drive out unwanted dogs and cats . . . than all the complaints of householders." London correspondent Mollie Panter-Downes told *New Yorker* readers: "Events are moving so fast that England acquired a new Premier almost absent-mindedly . . . It's paradoxical but true that the British, for all their suspicious dislike of brilliance, are beginning to think they'd be safer with a bit of dynamite around." National Labour MP Harold Nicolson, a poor politician but fine journalist and diarist, wrote in the *Spectator* of Churchill's "Elizabethan zest for life . . . His wit . . . rises high in the air like some strong fountain, flashing in every sunbeam, and renewing itself with ever-increasing jets and gusts of image and association."

Though Churchill's appointment was made by the king on the advice of Chamberlain, rather than following any elective process, popular acclaim bore him to the premiership—and to the role as minister of defence which he also appropriated. Tory MP Leo Amery was among those sceptical that Churchill could play so many parts: "How Winston thinks that he can be Prime Minister, co-ordinator of defence and leader of the House all at once, is puzzling, and confirms my belief that he really means the present arrangement to be temporary. Certainly no one can coordinate defence properly who is not prepared to be active head of the three Chiefs of Staff and in fact directly responsible for plans." Critics were still expressing dismay about Churchill's joint role as national leader and defence minister three years later. Yet Churchill's dispositions were prompted not by mere personal conceit, but by dismay at the shocking lack of coordination between the services which characterised the Norway campaign. And posterity perceives, as did he at the time, that beyond his own eagerness to run Britain's war machine, there was no other political or military figure to whom delegation of such power would have been appropriate.

In one of the most famous and moving passages of his memoirs, Churchill declared himself on May 10 "conscious of a profound sense of relief. At last I had the authority to give directions over the whole scene. I felt as if I were walking with destiny, and that all my past life had been but a preparation for this hour and this trial." He thrilled to his own ascent to Britain's leadership. Perhaps he allowed himself a twitch of satisfaction, now that he could at last with impunity smoke cigars through Cabinet meetings, a habit which had annoyed his predecessor. If, however, he cherished a belief that it would be in his gift to shape strategy, events immediately disabused him.

At dawn on May 10, a few hours before Churchill was summoned to Buckingham Palace, Hitler's armies stormed across the frontiers of neutral Holland, Belgium and Luxembourg. Capt. David Strangeways, serving with the British Expeditionary Force near Lille, just inside the French border, bridled at the impertinence of an orderly-room clerk who rushed into the quarters where he lay abed shouting: "David, sir, David!" Then the officer realised that the clerk was passing the order for Operation David, the BEF's advance from the fortified line which it had held since the previous autumn deep into Belgium to meet the advancing Germans. Though the Belgians since 1936 had declared themselves neutrals, Allied war planning felt obliged to anticipate an imperative need to offer them aid if Germany violated their territory.

Operation David perfectly fulfilled Hitler's predictions and wishes. On May 10 the British, together with the French First and Seventh armies, hastened to abandon laboriously prepared defensive positions. They mounted their trucks and armoured vehicles, then set off in long columns eastward towards the proffered "matador's cloak," in Basil Liddell Hart's phrase, which the Germans flourished before them in Belgium. Farther south, in the Ardennes forest, panzer columns thrashed forward to launch one of the war's great surprises, a thrust at the centre of the Allied line, left inexcusably weak by the deployments of the Allied supreme commander, France's General Maurice Gamelin. Heinz Guderian's and Georg Reinhardt's tanks, racing for the Meuse, easily brushed aside French cavalry posturing in their path. Luftwaffe paratroops and glider-borne forces burst upon the Dutch and Belgian frontier fortresses. Stukas and Messerschmitts poured bombs and machine-gun fire upon bewildered formations of four armies.

No more than his nation did the prime minister grasp the speed of approaching catastrophe. The Allied leaders supposed themselves at the beginning of a long campaign. The war was already eight months old, but thus far neither side had displayed impatience for a decisive confrontation. The German descent on Scandinavia was a sideshow. Hitler's assault on France promised the French and British armies the opportunity, so they supposed, to confront his legions on level terms. The paper strengths of the two sides in the west were similar—about 140 divisions apiece, of which just ten on the Allied side were British. Allied commanders and governments believed that weeks, if not months, would elapse before the critical clash came. Churchill retired to bed on the night of May 10 knowing that the Allies' strategic predicament was grave, but bursting with thoughts and plans, and believing that he had time to implement them.

Events which tower in the perception of posterity must at the time compete for attention with trifles. The BBC radio announcer who told the nation of the German invasion of Belgium and Holland followed this by reporting, "British troops have landed in Iceland," as if the second news item atoned for the first. The *Times* of May 11, 1940, reported the issue of an arrest warrant at Brighton bankruptcy court for a playwright named Walter Hackett, said to have fled to America. An army court-martial was described, at which a colonel was charged with "undue familiarity" with a sergeant in his searchlight unit. What would soldiers think, demanded the prosecutor, on hearing a commanding officer address a sergeant as "Eric"? Advertisements for Player's cigarettes exhorted smokers: "When cheerfulness is in danger of disturbance, light a Player . . . with a few puffs put trouble in its proper place." The Irish Tourist Association promised, "Ireland will welcome you." On the front page, a blue Persian cat was offered for sale at £2 10.s: "house-trained; grandsire Ch. Laughton Laurel; age 7 weeks—Bachelor, Grove Place, Aldenham." Among "Business Offers," a "Gentleman with extensive experience wishes join established business, Town or Country, capital available." A golf report on the sports page was headed, "What the public want." There was a poem by Walter de la Mare: "O lovely England, whose ancient peace / War's woful dangers strain and fret."

The German blitzkrieg was reported under a double-column headline: HITLER STRIKES AT THE LOW COUNTRIES. Commentaries variously asserted: BELGIANS CONFIDENT OF VICTORY; TEN TIMES AS STRONG AS IN 1914; THE

SIDE OF HOLLAND'S ECONOMIC LIFE OF GREATEST INTEREST TO HITLER IS DOUBTLESS HER AGRICULTURAL AND ALLIED ACTIVITIES; THE MILITARY OUTLOOK: NO SURPRISE THIS TIME. The *Times*'s editorial column declared: "It may be taken as certain that every detail has been prepared for an instant strategic reply . . . The Grand Alliance of our time for the destruction of the forces of treachery and oppression is being steadily marshalled."

A single column at the right of the main news, on page 6, proclaimed: NEW PRIME MINISTER. MR. CHURCHILL ACCEPTS. The newspaper's correspondence was dominated by discussion of parliament's Norway debate three days earlier, which had precipitated the fall of Chamberlain. Mr. Geoffrey Vickers urged that Lord Halifax was by far the best-qualified minister to lead a national government, assisted by a Labour leader of the Commons. Mr. Quintin Hogg, Tory MP for Oxford, noted that many of those who had voted against the government were serving officers. Mr. Henry Morris-Jones, Liberal MP for Denbigh, deplored the vote that had taken place, observing complacently that he himself had abstained. The news from France was mocked by a beautiful spring day, with bluebells and primroses everywhere in flower.

Henry "Chips" Channon, American-born Tory MP, diarist, millionaire and consummate ass, wrote on May 10: "Perhaps the darkest day in English history . . . We were all sad, angry and felt cheated and out-witted." His distress was inspired by the fall of Chamberlain, not the blitzkrieg in France. Churchill himself knew better than anyone how grudgingly he had been offered the premiership, and how tenuous was his grasp on power. Much of the Conservative Party hated him, not least because he had twice in his life "ratted"—changed sides in the House of Commons. He was remembered as the architect of the disastrous 1915 Gallipoli campaign, the 1919 sponsor of war against the Bolsheviks in Russia, the 1933–34 opponent of Indian self-government, the 1936 supporter of King Edward VIII in the abdication crisis, and the savage back-bench critic of both Baldwin and Chamberlain, Tory prime ministers through his own "wilderness years."

In May 1940, while few influential figures questioned Churchill's brilliance or oratorical genius, they perceived his career as wreathed in misjudgements. Robert Rhodes James subtitled his biography of Churchill before he ascended to the premiership *A Study in Failure*. As early as 1914, the historian A. G. Gardiner wrote an extraordinarily shrewd and admiring assessment, which concluded equivocally: " 'Keep your eye on Churchill' should be the watchword of these days. Remember, he is a soldier first, last and always. He will write his name big on our future. Let us take care he does not write it in blood."

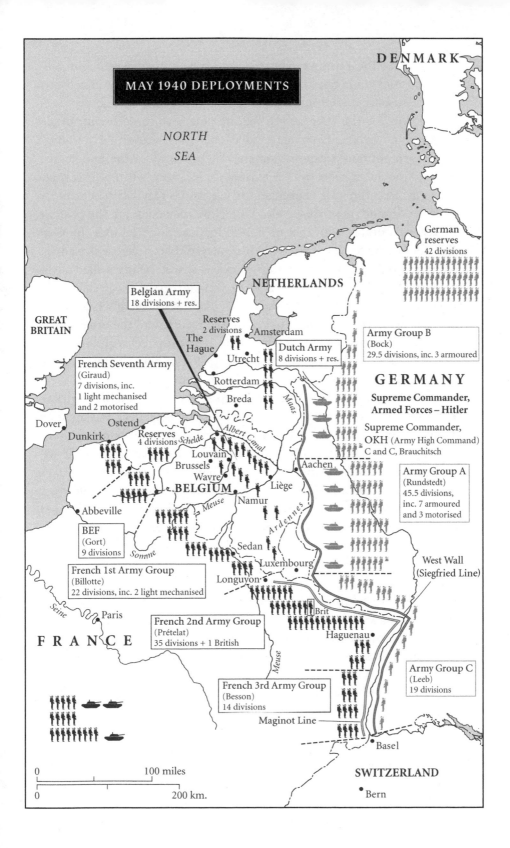

MAY 1940 DEPLOYMENTS

NORTH SEA

DENMARK

German reserves
42 divisions

NETHERLANDS

Belgian Army
18 divisions + res.

GREAT BRITAIN

Reserves
2 divisions · Amsterdam
The Hague
Utrecht

Dutch Army
8 divisions + res.

Army Group B
(Bock)
29.5 divisions, inc. 3 armoured

GERMANY

Supreme Commander, Armed Forces – Hitler

Supreme Commander, OKH (Army High Command)
C and C, Brauchitsch

French Seventh Army
(Giraud)
7 divisions, inc.
1 light mechanised
and 2 motorised

Dover

Ostend

Dunkirk

Reserves
4 divisions

Louvain
Brussels
Wavre
BELGIUM

Liège

Namur

Aachen

Army Group A
(Rundstedt)
45.5 divisions,
inc. 7 armoured
and 3 motorised

Abbeville

BEF
(Gort)
9 divisions

Meuse

Somme

Sedan

Luxembourg

West Wall
(Siegfried Line)

French 1st Army Group
(Billotte)
22 divisions, inc. 2 light mechanised

Seine

Paris

French 2nd Army Group
(Prételat)
35 divisions + 1 British

Longuyon

Brit

Haguenau

FRANCE

Meuse

Army Group C
(Leeb)
19 divisions

French 3rd Army Group
(Besson)
14 divisions

Maginot Line

Basel

0   100 miles

0   200 km.

SWITZERLAND

· Bern

Now, amid the crisis precipitated by Hitler's blitzkrieg, Churchill's contemporaries could not forget that he had been wrong about much even in the recent past, and even in the military sphere in which he professed expertise. During the approach to war, he described the presence of aircraft over the battlefield as a mere "additional complication." He claimed that modern antitank weapons neutered the powers of "the poor tank," and that "the submarine will be mastered . . . There will be losses, but nothing to affect the scale of events." On Christmas Day 1939, he wrote to Sir Dudley Pound, the first sea lord: "I feel we may compare the position now very favourably with that of 1914." He had doubted that the Germans would invade Scandinavia. When they did so, Churchill told the Commons on April 11: "In my view, which is shared by my skilled advisers, Herr Hitler has committed a grave strategic error in spreading the war so far to the north . . . We shall take all we want of this Norwegian coast now, with an enormous increase in the facility and the efficiency of our blockade." Even if some of Churchill's false prophecies and mistaken expressions of confidence were unknown to the public, they were common currency among ministers and commanders.

His claim upon his country's leadership rested not upon his contribution to the war since September 1939, which was equivocal, but upon his personal character and his record as a foe of appeasement. He was a warrior to the roots of his soul, who found his being upon battlefields. He was one of the few British prime ministers to have killed men with his own hand—at Omdurman in 1898. Now, he wielded a sword symbolically, if no longer physically, amid a body politic dominated by men of paper, creatures of committees and conference rooms. "It may well be," he enthused, six years before the war, "that the most glorious chapters of our history have yet to be written. Indeed, the very problems and dangers that encompass us and our country ought to make English men and women of this generation glad to be here at such a time. We ought to rejoice at the responsibilities with which destiny has honoured us, and be proud that we are guardians of our country in an age when her life is at stake." Leo Amery had written back in March 1940: "I am beginning to come round to the idea that Winston with all his failings is the one man with real war drive and love of battle." So he was, of course. But widespread fears persisted that this erratic genius might lead Britain in a rush towards military disaster.

Few of the ministers whom he invited to join his all-party coalition were equal to the magnitude of their tasks. If this is true of all governments at all times, it was notably unfortunate now. Twenty-one out of thirty-six senior officeholders were, like Halifax, David Margesson,

Kingsley Wood and Chamberlain himself, veterans of the previous discredited administration. "Winston has not been nearly bold enough with his changes and is much too afraid of the [Conservative] Party," wrote Amery, who had led the Commons charge against Chamberlain.

Of the Labour recruits—notably Clement Attlee, A. V. Alexander, Hugh Dalton, Arthur Greenwood and Ernest Bevin—only Bevin was a personality of the first rank, though Attlee as deputy prime minister would provide a solid bulwark. Sir Archibald Sinclair, the Liberal leader who had served as an officer under Churchill in France in 1916 and now became secretary for air, was described by those contemptuous of his subservience to the new prime minister as "head of school's fag." Churchill's personal supporters who received office or promotion, led by Anthony Eden, Lord Beaverbrook, Brendan Bracken and Amery, were balefully regarded not only by Chamberlain loyalists but also by many sensible and informed people who were willing to support the new prime minister but remained sceptical of his associates.

Much of the political class thought Churchill's administration would be short-lived. "So at last that man has gained his ambition," an elderly Tory MP, Cuthbert Headlam, noted sourly. "I never thought he would. Well—let us hope that he makes good. I have never believed in him. I only hope that my judgement . . . will be proved wrong." The well-known military writer Captain Basil Liddell Hart wrote gloomily on May 11: "The new War Cabinet appears to be a group devoted to "victory" without regard to its practical possibility." Lord Hankey, veteran Whitehall éminence grise and a member of the new government, thought it "perfectly futile for war" and Churchill himself a "rogue elephant."

Even as Hitler's panzer columns drove for Sedan and pushed onwards through Holland and Belgium, Churchill was filling lesser government posts, interviewing new ministers, meeting officials. On the evening of May 10 Sir Edward Bridges, the shy, austere Cabinet secretary, called at Admiralty House, where Churchill still occupied the desk from which he had presided as first lord. Bridges decided that it would be unbecoming for an official who until that afternoon had been serving a deposed prime minister obsequiously to welcome the new one. He merely said cautiously: "May I wish you every possible good fortune?" Churchill grunted, gazed intently at Bridges for a moment, then said: "Hum. 'Every good fortune!' I like that! These other people have all been congratulating me. Every good fortune!"

At Churchill's first meeting with the Chiefs of Staff as prime minister on May 11, he made two interventions, both trifling: he asked whether the police should be armed when sent to arrest enemy aliens; and he pondered the likelihood of Sweden joining the war on the Allied side. Even this most bellicose of men did not immediately attempt to tinker with the movements of Britain's army on the Continent. When Eden, the new secretary for war, called on the prime minister that day, he noted in his diary that Churchill "seemed well satisfied with the way events were shaping." If these words reflected a failure to perceive the prime minister's inner doubts, it is also certainly true that he did not perceive the imminence of disaster.

Churchill cherished a faith in the greatness of France, the might of her armed forces, most touching in a statesman of a nation traditionally wary of its Gallic neighbour. "In Winston's eyes," wrote his doctor later, "France is civilisation." Even after witnessing the German conquest of Poland, Norway and Denmark, Churchill understood little about the disparity between the relative fighting powers of Hitler's Wehrmacht and Luftwaffe, and those of the French and British armies and air forces. He, like almost all his advisers, deemed it unthinkable that the Germans could achieve a breakthrough against France's Maginot Line and the combined mass of French, British, Dutch and Belgian forces.

In the days that followed his ascent to Downing Street on May 10, Churchill set about galvanising the British machinery of war and government for a long haul. As war leader, he expected to preside over Britain's part in a massive and protracted clash on the Continent. His foremost hope was that this would entail no such slaughter as that which characterised the 1914–18 conflict. If he cherished no expectation of swift victory, he harboured no fear of decisive defeat. On May 13, headlines in the *Times* asserted confidently: BRITISH FORCES MOVING ACROSS BELGIUM—SUCCESSFUL ENCOUNTERS WITH ENEMY—RAF STRIKES AGAIN.

Addressing the Commons that day, the prime minister apologised for his brevity: "I hope that . . . my friends . . . will make allowance, all allowance, for any lack of ceremony with which it has been necessary to act . . . We have before us an ordeal of the most grievous kind. We have before us many, many long months of struggle and of suffering . . . But I take up my task with buoyancy and hope. I feel sure that our cause will not be suffered to fail among men. At this time I feel entitled to claim the aid of all, and I say: 'Come then, let us go forward together with our united strength.' "

Churchill's war speeches are usually quoted in isolation. This obscures the bathos of remarks by backbench MPs which followed those of the prime minister. On May 13, Maj. Sir Philip Colfox, West Dorset, said that although the country must now pursue national unity, he himself much regretted that Neville Chamberlain had been removed from the premiership. Sir Irving Albery, Gravesend, recalled the new prime minister's assertion: "My policy is a policy of war." Albery said he thought it right to praise his predecessor's commitment to the cause of peace. Col. John Gretton, Burton, injected a rare note of realism by urging the House not to waste words, when "the enemy is almost battering at our gates." The bleakest indication of the Conservative Party's temper came from the fact that while Neville Chamberlain was cheered as he entered the chamber that day, Churchill's appearance was greeted with resentful Tory silence.

This, his first important statement, received more applause from abroad than it did from some MPs. The *Philadelphia Inquirer* editorialised: "He proved in this one short speech that he was not afraid to face the truth and tell it. He proved himself an honest man as well as a man of action. Britain has reason to be enheartened by his brevity, his bluntness and his courage." *Time* magazine wrote: "That smart, tough, dumpy little man, Prime Minister Winston Churchill, knows how to face facts . . . Great Britain's tireless old firebrand has changed the character of Allied warmongering."

That day, May 13, the threat of German air attack on Britain caused Churchill to make his first significant military decision: he rejected a proposal for further fighter squadrons to be sent to France, to reinforce the ten already committed. But, while the news from the Continent was obviously bleak, he asserted that he was "by no means sure that the great battle was developing." He still cherished hopes of turning the tide in Norway, signalling to Admiral Lord Cork and Orrery on May 14: "I hope you will get Narvik cleaned up as soon as possible, and then work southward with increasing force."

Yet the Germans were already bridging the Meuse at Sedan and Dinant, south of Brussels, for their armoured columns emerging from the Ardennes's forests. A huge gap was opening between the French Ninth Army, which was collapsing, and the Second, on its left. Though the BEF, in Belgium, was still not seriously engaged, its C-in-C, Lord Gort, appealed for air reinforcements. Gort commanded limited confidence. Like all British generals, he lacked training and instincts for the handling of large forces. One of the army's cleverest staff officers, Col. Ian Jacob of the War Cabinet Secretariat, wrote: "We have for twenty years thought little about how to win big campaigns on land; we have been immersed in our day-to-day imperial police activities."

This deficiency, of plausible "big battlefield" commanders, would dog British arms throughout the war. Gort was a famously brave officer who had won a Victoria Cross in World War I, and he still carried himself with a boyish enthusiasm. Maj. Gen. John Kennedy, soon to become director of military operations at the War Office, described the BEF's C-in-C as "a fine fighting soldier"—a useful testimonial for a platoon commander. In blunter words, the general lacked brains, as do most men possessed of the suicidal courage necessary to gain a Victoria Cross or Medal of Honor. A shrewd American categorized both Gort and the chief of the Imperial General Staff, Sir William Edmund Ironside, as "purely physical soldiers who had no business in such high places." Yet Sir Alan Brooke or Sir Bernard Montgomery would have been no more capable of averting disaster in 1940, with the small forces available to the BEF. Unlike most of continental Europe, Britain had no peacetime conscription for military service until 1939, and thus no large potential reserves for mobilisation. The army Gort commanded was, in spirit, the imperial constabulary of the interwar years, starved of resources for a generation.

On May 14, for the first time Churchill glimpsed the immensity of the Allies' peril. Paul Reynaud, France's prime minister, telephoned from Paris, reporting the German breakthrough and asking for the immediate dispatch of a further ten RAF fighter squadrons. The Chiefs of Staff Committee and the War Cabinet, which met successively at six and seven o'clock, agreed that Britain's home defences should not be thus weakened. At seven the next morning, May 15, Reynaud telephoned personally to Churchill. The Frenchman spoke emotionally, asserting in English: "the battle is lost." Churchill urged him to steady himself, pointing out that only a small part of the French army was engaged, while the German spearheads were now far extended and thus should be vulnerable to flank attack.

When Churchill reported the conversation to his political and military chiefs, the question of further air support was raised once more. Churchill was briefly minded to accede to Reynaud's pleas. But Chamberlain sided with Air Chief Marshal Sir Hugh Dowding, C-in-C of Fighter Command, who passionately demurred. No further fighters were committed. That day Jock Colville, the prime minister's twenty-five-year-old junior private secretary and an aspiring Pepys, noted in his diary the understated concerns of Maj. Gen. Hastings "Pug" Ismay, chief of staff to Churchill in his capacity as minister of defence. Ismay was "not too happy about the military situation. He says the French are not fighting properly: they are, he points out, a volatile race and it may take them some time to get into a warlike mood."

Sluggish perception lagged behind dreadful reality. Churchill cabled to President Franklin Roosevelt: "I think myself that the battle on land has only just begun, and I should like to see the masses engage. Up to the present, Hitler is working with specialized units in tanks and air." He appealed for American aid, and for the first time begged the loan of fifty old destroyers. Washington had already vetoed a request that a British aircraft carrier should dock at an American port to embark fully assembled, battle-ready fighters. This would breach the U.S. Neutrality Act, said the president. So, too, he decided, would the dispatch of destroyers.

In France on May 15, the RAF's inadequate Battle and Blenheim bombers suffered devastating losses while attempting to break the Germans' Meuse pontoon bridges. A watching panzer officer wrote: "The summer landscape with the quietly flowing river, the light green of the meadows bordered by the darker summits of the more distant heights, spanned by a brilliantly blue sky, is filled with the racket of war . . . Again and again an enemy aircraft crashes out of the sky, dragging a long black plume of smoke behind it . . . Occasionally from the falling machines one or two white parachutes release themselves and float slowly to earth." The RAF's sacrifice was anyway too late. Much of the German armour was already across the Meuse, and racing westward.

On the morning of the sixteenth, it was learned in London that the Germans had breached the Maginot Line. The War Cabinet agreed to deploy four further fighter squadrons to operate over the battlefield. At three o'clock that afternoon, the prime minister flew to Paris, accompanied by Ismay and Gen. Sir John Dill, Ironside's vice chief of the Imperial General Staff (CIGS). Landing at Le Bourget, for the first time they perceived the desperation of their ally. France's generals and politicians were waiting upon defeat. As the leaders of the two nations conferred at the Quai d'Orsay, officials burned files in the garden. When Churchill asked about French reserves for a counterattack, he was told that these had already been committed piecemeal. Reynaud's colleagues did not conceal their bitterness at Britain's refusal to dispatch further fighters. At every turn of the debate, French shoulders shrugged. From the British embassy that evening, Churchill cabled the War Cabinet, urging the dispatch of six more squadrons. "I . . . emphasise the mortal gravity of the hour," he wrote. The chief of the Air Staff, Sir Cyril Newall, proposed a compromise: six further squadrons should operate over France from their British airfields. At two a.m., Churchill drove to Reynaud's flat to communicate the news. The prime minister thereafter returned to the embassy, slept soundly despite occasional distant gunfire, then flew home via Hendon, where he landed before nine a.m. on May 17.

He wore a mask of good cheer, but was no longer in doubt about the catastrophe threatening the Allies. He understood that it had become essential for the BEF to withdraw from its outflanked positions in Belgium. Back in Downing Street, after reporting to the War Cabinet, he set about filling further minor posts in his government, telephoning briskly to prospective appointees, twelve that day in all. Harold Nicolson recorded a typical conversation:

"Harold, I think it would be wise if you joined the Government and helped Duff [Cooper] at the Ministry of Information."

"There is nothing I should like better."

"Well, fall in tomorrow. The list will be out tonight. That all right?"

"Very much all right."

"OK."

Sir Edward Bridges and other Whitehall officials were impressed by Churchill's "superb confidence," the "unhurried calm with which he set about forming his government." At the outset, this reflected failure to perceive the immediacy of disaster. Within days, however, there was instead a majestic determination that his own conduct should be seen to match the magnitude of the challenge he and his nation faced. From the moment Churchill gained the premiership, he displayed a self-discipline which had been conspicuously absent from most of his career. In small things as in great, he won the hearts of those who became his intimates at Downing Street. "What a beautiful handwriting," he told Jock Colville when the private secretary showed him a dictated telegram, "but, my dear boy, when I say stop you must write stop and not just put a blob." Embracing his staff as an extension of his family, it never occurred to him to warn them against repeating his confidences. He took it for granted that they would not do so—and was rewarded accordingly.

Churchill lunched on May 17 at the Japanese embassy. Even in such circumstances, diplomatic imperatives pressed. Japan's militarist expansionism was manifest. Everything possible had to be done to promote its quiescence. That afternoon, he dispatched into exile former foreign secretary Sir Samuel Hoare, most detested of the old appeasers, to become ambassador to Spain. He also established economic committees to address trade, food and transport. A series of telegrams arrived from France, reporting further German advances. Churchill asked Chamberlain, as lord president, to assess the implications of the fall of Paris—and of the BEF's possible withdrawal from the continent through the Channel ports. His day, which had begun in Paris, ended with dinner at Admiralty House in the company of Lord Beaverbrook and Brendan Bracken.

Posterity owes little to Churchill's wayward son, Randolph, but a debt is due for his account of a visit to Admiralty House on the morning of May 18:

I went up to my father's bedroom. He was standing in front of his basin and shaving with his old-fashioned Valet razor . . .

"Sit down, dear boy, and read the papers while I finish shaving." I did as told. After two or three minutes of hacking away, he half turned and said: "I think I see my way through." He resumed his shaving. I was astounded, and said: "Do you mean that we can avoid defeat?" (which seemed credible) "or beat the bastards?" (which seemed incredible).

He flung his Valet razor into the basin, swung around and said:—
"Of course I mean we can beat them."

Me: "Well, I'm all for it, but I don't see how you can do it."

By this time he had dried and sponged his face and turning round to me, said with great intensity: "I shall drag the United States in."

Here was a characteristic Churchillian flash of revelation. The prospect of American belligerence was remote. For years, Neville Chamberlain had repeatedly and indeed rudely rebuffed advances from Franklin Roosevelt. Yet already the new prime minister recognised that U.S. aid alone might make Allied victory possible. He was obliged to acknowledge the probability—though, unlike France's generals, he refused to bow to its inevitability—of German victory on the Continent. Reports from the battlefield grew steadily graver. Churchill urged the Chiefs of Staff to consider bringing large reinforcements from India and Palestine, and holding back some tank units then in transit from Britain to the BEF. The threat of a sudden German descent on England, spearheaded by paratroops, seized his imagination, unrealistic though it was.

A Home Intelligence report suggested to the government that national morale was badly shaken: "It must be remembered that the defence of the Low Countries had been continually built up in the press . . . Not one person in a thousand could visualise the Germans breaking through into France . . . A relieved acceptance of Mr. Churchill as prime minister allowed people to believe that a change of leadership would, in itself, solve the consequences of Mr. Chamberlain. Reports sent in yesterday and this morning show that disquiet and personal fear have returned."

On the evening of May 18, the War Cabinet agreed that Churchill should broadcast to the nation, making plain the gravity of the emergency. Ministers were told that Mussolini had rejected Britain's proposal for an Italian declaration of neutrality. This prompted Navy Minister A. V. Alexander to urge the immediate occupation of Crete, as a base for operations against Italy in the Mediterranean. Churchill dismissed the idea out of hand, saying that Britain was much too committed elsewhere to embark upon gratuitous adventures.

On the morning of Sunday, May 19, it was learned that the BEF had evacuated Arras, increasing the peril of its isolation from the main French forces. Emerging together from a meeting, Ironside said to Eden: "This is the end of the British Empire." The secretary for war noted: "Militarily, I did not see how he could be gainsaid." Yet it was hard for colleagues to succumb to despair, when their leader marvellously sustained his wit. That same bleak Sunday, the prime minister said to Eden: "About time number 17 turned up, isn't it?" The two of them, at a Cannes casino's roulette wheel in 1938, had backed the number and won twice.

At noon, Churchill was driven across Kent to Chartwell, his beloved old home, shuttered for the duration. He sought an interlude of tranquillity in which to prepare his broadcast to the nation. But he had been feeding his goldfish for only a few minutes when he was interrupted by a telephone call. Gort, in France, was seeking sanction to fall back on the sea at Dunkirk if his predicament worsened. The C-in-C was told instead to seek to reestablish contact with the French army, on his right; German spearheads were in between. The French, in their turn, would be urged to counterattack towards him. The Belgians were pleading for the BEF to hold a more northerly line beside their own troops. The War Cabinet determined, however, that the vital priority was to reestablish a common front with the main French armies. The Belgians must be left to their fate, while British forces redeployed southwestwards towards Arras and Amiens.

Broadcasting to the British people that night, Churchill asserted a confidence which he did not feel, saying that the line in France would be stabilised, but he also warned of the peril the nation faced. "This is one of the most awe-striking periods in the long history of France and Britain. It is also beyond doubt the most sublime. Centuries ago words were written to be a call and a spur to the faithful servants of Truth and Justice: 'Arm yourselves, and be ye men of valour . . . for it is better for us to perish in battle than to look upon the outrage of our nation and our altar. As the will of God is in Heaven, even so let it be.' "

This was the first of his great clarion calls to the nation. It is impossible to overstate its impact upon the British people, and indeed upon the listening world. He asserted his resolve, and his listeners responded. That night, he dispatched a minute to Ismay reasserting his refusal to send further RAF squadrons to France. Every fighter would be needed "if it becomes necessary to evacuate the BEF." It was obvious that this decision would be received badly by the French, and not all his subordinates supported it. His personal scientific and economic adviser, Frederick Lindemann—"the Prof"—penned a note of protest.

Britain's forces could exert only a marginal influence on the outcome of the battle for France. Even if every aircraft the RAF possessed had been dispatched to the Continent, such a commitment would not have averted Allied defeat. It would merely have sacrificed the squadrons that later won the Battle of Britain. In May 1940, however, such things were much less plain. As France tottered on the brink of collapse, with eight million terrified refugees clogging roads in a fevered exodus southwards, the bitterness of her politicians and generals mounted against an ally that matched extravagant rhetoric with refusal to provide the only important aid in its gift. France's leaders certainly responded feebly to Hitler's blitzkrieg. But their rancour towards Britain merits understanding. Churchill's perception of British self-interest has been vindicated by history, but scarcely deserved the gratitude of Frenchmen.

He sent an unashamedly desperate message to Roosevelt, regretting America's refusal to lend destroyers. More, he warned that while his own government would never surrender, a successor administration might parley with Germany, using the Royal Navy as its "sole remaining bargaining counter . . . If this country was left by the United States to its fate, no one would have the right to blame those men responsible if they made the best terms they could for the surviving inhabitants. Excuse me, Mr. President, putting this nightmare bluntly." In Hitler's hands, Britain's fleet would pose a grave threat to the United States.

If this was a brutal prospect to lay before Roosevelt, it was by no means a bluff. At that moment, Churchill could not know that Parliament and the British people would stick with him to the end. Chamberlain remained leader of the Conservative Party. Even before the crisis in France, a significant part of Britain's ruling class was susceptible to a compromise peace. Following military catastrophe, it was entirely plausible that Churchill's government would fall, just as Chamberlain's had done, to be replaced by an administration which sought terms from Hitler. Only in the months which followed would the world, and Churchill himself, gradually come to perceive that the people of Britain were willing to risk everything under his leadership.

On May 20, he told the Chiefs of Staff that the time had come to consider whether residual Norwegian operations around Narvik should be sustained, when troops and ships were urgently needed elsewhere. On the Continent, the Germans were driving south and west so fast that it seemed doubtful whether the BEF could regain touch with the main French armies. Gort was still striving to pull back forces from the Scheldt.

That night, German units passed Amiens on the hot, dusty road to Abbeville, cutting off the BEF from its supply bases. Still Churchill declined to despair. He told the War Cabinet late on the morning of the twenty-first that "the situation was more favourable than certain of the more obvious symptoms would indicate." In the north, the British still had local superiority of numbers. Fears focused on the perceived pusillanimity of the French, both politicians and soldiers. That day, a British armoured thrust south from Arras failed to break through. The BEF was isolated, along with elements of the French First Army. Calais and Boulogne remained in British hands, but inaccessible by land.

The House of Commons on May 20, with the kind of inspired madness that contributed to the legend of 1940, debated a Colonial Welfare Bill. Many people in Britain lacked understanding of the full horror of the Allies' predicament. Newspaper readers continued to receive encouraging tidings. The *Evening News* headlined on May 17: BRITISH TROOPS SUCCESS. On the nineteenth, the *Sunday Dispatch* headline read: ATTACKS LESS POWERFUL. Even two days later, the *Evening News* front page proclaimed: ENEMY ATTACKS BEATEN OFF. An editorial in the *New Statesman* urged that "the government should at once grapple with the minor, but important problem of Anglo-Mexican relations."

Gort's chief of staff, Lt. Gen. Henry Pownall, complained bitterly on May 20 about the absence of clear instructions from London: "Nobody minds going down fighting, but the long and many days of indigence and recently the entire lack of higher direction . . . have been terribly wearing on the nerves of all of us." But when orders did come from the prime minister three days later—for a counterattack southeastwards by the entire BEF—Pownall was even angrier: "Can nobody prevent him trying to conduct operations himself as a super Commander-in-Chief? How does he think we are to collect eight divisions and attack as he suggests? Have we no front to hold? He can have no conception of our situation and condition . . . The man's mad."

Only the port of Dunkirk still offered an avenue of escape from the Continent, and escape now seemed the BEF's highest credible aspiration. On May 22 and 23, the British awaited tidings of the promised French counteroffensive northeastward towards Gort. Gen. Maxime Weygand, who had supplanted the sacked Gamelin as Allied supreme commander, declared this to be in progress. In the absence of visible movement Churchill remained sceptical. If Weygand's thrust failed, evacuation would become the only British option. Churchill reported as much to the king on the night of May 23, as Boulogne was evacuated. On the night of the twenty-fourth, he fumed to Ismay about Gort's failure to launch a

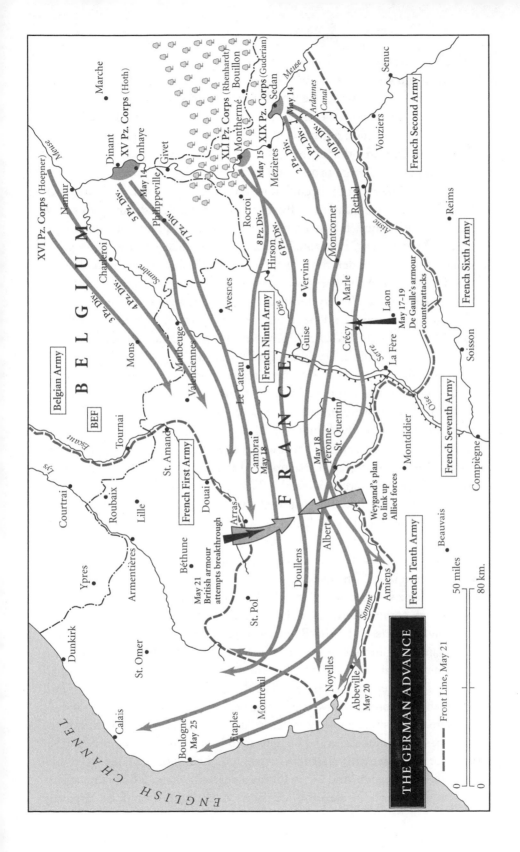

THE GERMAN ADVANCE

ENGLISH CHANNEL

BELGIUM

FRANCE

Front Line, May 21

0   50 miles
0   80 km.

XVI Pz. Corps (Hoepner)

XV Pz. Corps (Hoth)

XLI Pz. Corps (Rhenhardt)

XIX Pz. Corps (Guderian)

French Second Army

French Sixth Army

French Seventh Army

French Ninth Army

French First Army

French Tenth Army

Belgian Army

BEF

5 Pz. Div.
7 Pz. Div.
3 Pz. Div.
4 Pz. Div.
8 Pz. Div.
6 Pz. Div.
2 Pz. Div.
1 Pz. Div.
10 Pz. Div.

Marche
Dinant
Onhaye
May 14
Namur
Givet
Philippeville
Charleroi
Mons
Maubeuge
Valenciennes
Avesnes
Le Cateau
Cambrai
May 18
Rocroi
Hirson
Vervins
Guise
St. Quentin
Péronne
May 18
Monthermé
Bouillon
Mézières
May 15
Sedan
May 14
Vouziers
Senuc
Reims
Rethel
Montcornet
Marle
Crécy
La Fère
Laon
May 17-19
De Gaulle's armour
counterattacks
Soisson
Compiègne
Montdidier
Beauvais
Amiens
Weygand's plan
to link up
Allied forces
Albert
Doullens
St. Pol
Arras
May 21
British armour
attempts breakthrough
Douai
Béthune
Lille
Roubaix
Courtrai
Armentières
Ypres
St. Omer
Dunkirk
Calais
Boulogne
May 25
Étaples
Montreuil
Abbeville
May 20
Noyelles
St. Amand
Tournai

Meuse
Sambre
Oise
Aisne
Serre
Oise
Somme
Lys
Escaut

Ardennes
Canal

May 14
May 15
May 18

force towards Calais, to link up with its garrison. He demanded to know how men and guns could be better used. He concluded, in the first overtly bitter and histrionic words he had deployed against Britain's soldiers since the campaign began: "Of course, if one side fights and the other does not, the war is apt to become somewhat unequal." Ironside, the CIGS, told the Defence Committee that evening that if the BEF was indeed evacuated by sea from France, a large proportion of its men might be lost.

Churchill was now preoccupied with three issues: rescue of Gort's men from Dunkirk; deployment of further units of the British Army to renew the battle in France, following the BEF's withdrawal; and defence of the home island against invasion. Reynaud dispatched a bitter message to London on May 24, denouncing the British retreat to the sea and blaming this for the failure of Weygand's counteroffensive—which in truth had never taken place. "Everything is complete confusion," Sir Alexander Cadogan, permanent under-secretary at the Foreign Office, noted in his diary on the twenty-fifth, "no communications and no one knows what's going on, except that everything's black as black."

Churchill cabled to the dominion prime ministers, warning that an invasion of Britain might be imminent. He rejoiced that reinforcements from the Empire were on their way, and asserted his confidence that the Royal Navy and RAF should be able to frustrate an assault, following which "our land defence will deal with any sea-borne survivors after some rough work." He rejected the notion of a public appeal to the United States. He feared, surely correctly, that such a message would have scant appeal to a nation already disposed to dismiss aid to Britain as wasted motion. In this, as in his judgement of shifting American moods through the months that followed, he displayed deep wisdom. A Gallup poll showed Americans still overwhelmingly opposed, by thirteen to one, to participation in the European conflict.

On May 25, Churchill dispatched a personal message to Brig. Claude Nicholson, commanding the British force in Calais, ordering that his men must fight to the end. The Belgians were collapsing. Gort cancelled his last planned counterattack southwards, instead sending north the two divisions earmarked for it to plug the gap between British and Belgian forces. That evening, at a meeting of the Defence Committee, Churchill accepted the conclusion which Gort, now out of contact with London, had already reached and begun to act upon. The BEF must withdraw to the coast for evacuation. The commander-in-chief's order, issued in advance of consent from Britain, represented his most notable contribution to the campaign, and by no means a negligible one. The prime minister ordered that six skeleton divisions in Britain should be urgently prepared for active service, though scant means existed to accomplish this. Artillery, antitank weapons, transport, even small arms were lacking. He acknowledged that France's leaders, resigned to defeat, would probably depose Reynaud and make terms with Hitler. Henceforward, the future of the French fleet was much in his mind. In German hands, these warships might drastically improve the odds favouring a successful invasion of Britain. That night, Ironside resigned as CIGS, to become commander-in-chief Home Forces. The general had never commanded Churchill's confidence, while Sir John Dill, Ironside's vice chief, did. Next day Dill, fifty-nine years old, clever and sensitive though seldom in good health, became head of the British Army.

At nine o'clock on the morning of May 26, Churchill told the War Cabinet that there was a good chance of "getting off a considerable proportion of the British Expeditionary Force." Paul Reynaud arrived in London. He warned the prime minister over lunch that if Germany occupied a large part of France, the nation's old hero Marshal Philippe Pétain would probably call for an armistice. Reynaud dismissed British fears that the Germans were bent on an immediate invasion of their island. Hitler would strike for Paris, he said, and of course he was right. Churchill told Reynaud that Britain would fight on, whatever transpired. Following a break while Churchill met the War Cabinet, the two leaders resumed their talks. Churchill pressed for Weygand to issue an order for the BEF to fall back on the coast. This was designed to frustrate charges of British betrayal. Reynaud duly requested such a message, to endorse the reality of what was already taking place.

At a four-hour Cabinet meeting that afternoon, following Reynaud's departure, the merits of seeking a settlement with Hitler were discussed. Churchill hoped that France might receive terms that precluded her occupation by the Germans. Halifax, the foreign secretary, expressed his desire to seek Italian mediation with Hitler to secure terms for Britain. He had held preliminary talks with Mussolini's ambassador in London about such a course. Churchill was sceptical, saying this presupposed that a deal might be made merely by returning Germany's old colonies and making concessions in the Mediterranean. "No such option was open to us," said the prime minister.

Six Alexander Cadogan, who joined the meeting after half an hour, found Churchill "too rambling and romantic and sentimental and temperamental." This was harsh. The prime minister bore vast burdens. It behoved him to be circumspect in all dealings with the old appeasers among his colleagues. There were those in Whitehall who, rather than being stirred by Churchill's appeals to recognise a great historic moment, curled their lips. Chamberlain's private secretary, Arthur Rucker, responded contemptuously to the ringing phrases in one of the prime minister's missives: "He is still thinking of his books." Eric Seal, the only one of Churchill's private secretaries who established no close rapport with him, muttered about "blasted rhetoric."

A substantial part of the British ruling class, MPs and peers alike, had since September 1939 lacked faith in the possibility of military victory. Although Churchill was himself an aristocrat, he was widely mistrusted by his own kind. Since the 1917 Russian Revolution, many British grandees, including such dukes as Westminster, Wellington and Buccleuch and such lesser peers as Lord Phillimore, had shown themselves much more hostile to Soviet Communism than to European Fascism. Their patriotism was never in doubt. However, their enthusiasm for a fight to the finish with Hitler, which they feared would end in rubble and ruin, was less assured. Lord Hankey observed acidly before making a speech to the House of Lords early in May that he "would be addressing most of the members of the Fifth Column."

Lord Tavistock, soon to become Duke of Bedford, a pacifist and plausible Nazi collaborator, wrote to former prime minister David Lloyd George that Hitler's strength was "so great . . . it is madness to suppose we can beat him by war on the continent." On May 15, Tavistock urged Lloyd George that peace should be made "now rather than later . . . if the Germans received fair peace terms a dozen Hitlers could never start another war on an inadequate . . . pretext." Harold Nicolson wrote: "It is not the descendants of the old governing classes who display the greatest enthusiasm for their leader." Likewise, some financial magnates were sceptical of any possibility of British victory, and thus of the new prime minister: "Mr. Chamberlain is the idol of the business men . . . They do not have the same personal feelings for Mr. Churchill . . . There are awful moments when they feel that Mr. Churchill does not find them interesting."

There were also defeatists lower down the social scale. Muriel Green, who worked at her family's garage in Norfolk, recorded a conversation at a local tennis match with a grocer's roundsman and a schoolmaster on May 23. "I think they're going to beat us, don't you," said the roundsman. "Yes," said the schoolmaster. He added that, as the Nazis were very keen on sport, he expected "we'd still be able to play tennis if they did win." Muriel Green wrote: "J said Mr. M. was saying we should paint a swastika under the door knocker [sic] ready. We all agreed we shouldn't know what to do if they invade. After that we played tennis, very hard exciting play for 2 hrs, and forgot all about the war."

In those last days of May, the prime minister must have perceived a real possibility, even a likelihood, that if he himself appeared irrationally intransigent, the old Conservative grandees would reassert themselves. Amid the collapse of all the hopes on which Britain's military struggle against Hitler were founded, it was not fanciful to suppose that a peace party might gain control in Britain. Some historians have made much of the fact that at this War Cabinet meeting, Churchill failed to dismiss out of hand an approach to Mussolini. He did not flatly contradict Halifax when the foreign secretary said that if the Duce offered terms for a general settlement "which did not postulate the destruction of our independence . . . we should be foolish if we did not accept them." Churchill conceded that "if we could get out of this jam by giving up Malta and Gibraltar and some African colonies, he would jump at it." At the following day's War Cabinet meeting, he indicated that if Hitler was prepared to offer peace in exchange for the restoration of his old colonies and the overlordship of central Europe, a negotiation could be possible.

It seems essential to consider Churchill's words in context. First, they were made in the midst of long, weary discussions, during which he was taking elaborate pains to appear reasonable. Halifax spoke with the voice of logic. Amid shattering military defeat, even Churchill dared not offer his colleagues a vision of British victory. In those Dunkirk days, the director of military intelligence told a BBC correspondent: "We're finished. We've lost the army and we'll never have time or strength to build another." Churchill did not challenge the view of those who assumed that the war would end, sooner or later, with a negotiated settlement rather than with a British army marching into Berlin. He pitched his case low, because there was no alternative. A display of exaggerated confidence would have invited ridicule. He relied solely upon the argument that there was no more to lose by fighting on, than by throwing in the hand.

How would his colleagues, or even posterity, have assessed his judgement had he sought, at those meetings, to offer the prospect of military triumph? To understand what happened in Britain in the summer of 1940, it is essential to acknowledge the logic of impending defeat. This was what created tensions between the hearts and minds even of staunch and patriotic British people. The best aspiration they and their prime minister could entertain was a manly determination to survive today, and pray for a better tomorrow. The War Cabinet discussions between May 26 and 28 took place while it was still doubtful that any significant portion of the BEF could be saved from France.

At the meeting of May 26, with the support of Attlee, Greenwood and eventually Chamberlain, Churchill summed up for the view that there was nothing to be lost by fighting on, because no terms which Hitler might offer in the future were likely to be worse than those now available. Having discussed the case for a parley, he dismissed it, even if Halifax refused to do so. At seven o'clock that evening, an hour after the War Cabinet meeting ended, the Admiralty signalled the flag officer Dover, Vice Adm. Bertram Ramsay: "Operation Dynamo is to commence." Destroyers of the Royal Navy, aided by a fleet of small craft, began to evacuate the BEF from Dunkirk.

That night yet another painful order was forced upon Churchill. The small British force at Calais, drawn from the Rifle Brigade, possessed only nuisance value. But everything possible had to be done to distract German forces from the Dunkirk perimeter. The Rifles must resist to the last. Ismay wrote: "The decision affected us all very deeply, especially perhaps Churchill. He was unusually silent during dinner that evening, and ate and drank with evident distaste." He asked a private secretary, John Martin, to find for him a passage in George Borrow's 1843 prayer for England. Martin identified the lines next day: "Fear not the result, for either thy end be a majestic and an enviable one, or God shall perpetuate thy reign upon the waters."

On the morning of May 27, even as British troops were beginning to embark at Dunkirk, Churchill asked the leaders of the armed forces to prepare a memorandum, setting out the nation's prospects for resisting invasion if France fell. Within a couple of hours, the Chiefs of Staff submitted an eleven-paragraph response, which identified the key issues with notable insight. As long as the RAF was "in being," they wrote, its aircraft together with the warships of the Royal Navy should be able to prevent an invasion. If air superiority was lost, however, the navy could not indefinitely hold the Channel. Should the Germans secure a beachhead in southeast England, British home forces would be incapable of evicting them. The Chiefs pinpointed the air battle, Britain's ability to defend its key installations and especially aircraft factories, as the decisive factor in determining the future course of the war. They concluded with heartening words: "the real test is whether the morale of our fighting personnel and civil population will counter-balance the numerical and material advantages which Germany enjoys. We believe it will."

The War Cabinet debated at length, and finally accepted, the Chiefs' report. It was agreed that further efforts should be made to induce the Americans to provide substantial aid. An important message arrived from Lord Lothian, British ambassador in Washington, suggesting that Britain should invite the United States to lease basing facilities in Trinidad, Newfoundland and Bermuda. Churchill opposed any such unilateral offer. America had "given us practically no help in the war," he said. "Now that

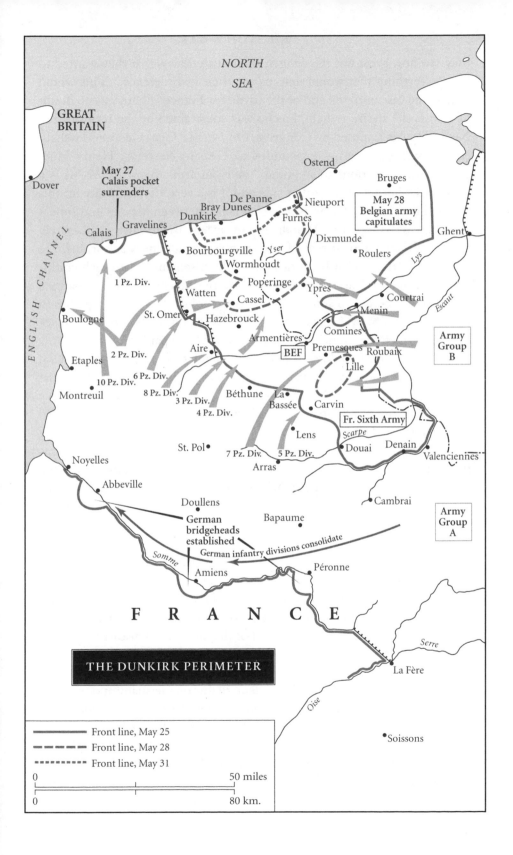

NORTH
SEA

GREAT
BRITAIN

Dover

ENGLISH CHANNEL

May 27
Calais pocket
surrenders

Ostend

Bruges

De Panne
Bray Dunes   Nieuport
Dunkirk   Furnes
Calais   Gravelines   May 28
                                                 Belgian army
                         Dixmunde   capitulates
                                                              Ghent
Bourbourgville Yser
        Wormhoudt   Roulers
1 Pz. Div.   Poperinge   Lys
        Watten   Ypres
                 Cassel   Courtrai
Boulogne   Menin   Escaut
        St. Omer Hazebrouck
                         Comines   Army
Etaples   Aire   Armentières   Group
2 Pz. Div.   BEF   Premesques Roubaix B
10 Pz. Div. 6 Pz. Div.   Lille
Montreuil   8 Pz. Div. Béthune La
             3 Pz. Div.   Bassée Carvin
             4 Pz. Div.   Fr. Sixth Army
                                 Lens   Scarpe
St. Pol   Douai   Denain
         7 Pz. Div. 5 Pz. Div.   Valenciennes
Noyelles   Arras

Abbeville
        Doullens
German   Bapaume   Cambrai   Army
bridgeheads   Group
established German infantry divisions consolidate A
        Somme
        Amiens   Péronne

F R A N C E

Serre

THE DUNKIRK PERIMETER   La Fère

Oise   Soissons

——————— Front line, May 25
– – – – – Front line, May 28
· · · · · · Front line, May 31

0   50 miles

0   80 km.

they saw how great was the danger, their attitude was that they wanted to keep everything that would help us for their own defence." This would remain the case until the end of the battle for France. There was no doubt of Roosevelt's desire to help, but he was constrained by the terms of the Neutrality Act imposed by Congress. On May 17 Gen. George Marshall, chief of staff of the army, expounded to Treasury Secretary Henry Morgenthau his objections to shipping American arms to the Allies: "It is a drop in the bucket on the other side and it is a very vital necessity on this side and that is that. Tragic as it is, that is it." Between May 23 and June 3 Secretary of War Harry Woodring, an ardent isolationist, deliberately delayed shipment to Britain of war matériel condemned as surplus. He insisted that there must be prior public advertisement before such equipment was sold to the Allies. On June 5, the Senate Foreign Relations Committee rejected an administration proposal to sell ships and planes to Britain. The U.S. War Department declined to supply bombs to fit dive-bombers which the French had already bought and paid for.

In the last days of May, a deal for Britain to purchase twenty U.S. patrol torpedo boats was scuttled when news of it leaked to isolationist Senator David Walsh of Massachusetts. As chairman of the Senate's Navy Affairs Committee, Walsh referred the plan to the attorney general—who declared it illegal. In mid-June, the U.S. chiefs of staff recommended that no further war matériel should be sent to Britain, and that no private contractor should be allowed to accept an order which might compromise the needs of the U.S. armed forces. None of this directly influenced the campaign in France. But it spoke volumes, all unwelcome in London and Paris, about the prevailing American mood towards Europe's war.

It was a small consolation that other powerful voices across the Atlantic were urging Britain's cause. The *New York Times* attacked Col. Charles Lindbergh, America's arch-isolationist flying hero, and asserted the mutuality of Anglo-American interests. Lindbergh, said the *Times*, was "an ignorant young man if he trusts his own premise that it makes no difference to us whether we are deprived of the historic defense of British sea power in the Atlantic Ocean." The Republican *New York Herald Tribune* astonished many Americans by declaring boldly, "The least costly solution in both life and welfare would be to declare war on Germany at once." Yet even if President Roosevelt had wished to heed the urgings of such interventionists and offer assistance to the Allies, he had before him the example of Woodrow Wilson, in whose administration he had served. Wilson was renounced by his own legislature in 1919 for making commitments abroad—in the Versailles Treaty—which outreached the will of the American people. Roosevelt had no intention of emulating him.

Chamberlain reported on May 27 that he had spoken the previous evening to Stanley Bruce, Australian high commissioner in London, who argued that Britain's position would be bleak if France surrendered. Bruce, a shrewd and respected spokesman for his dominion, urged seeking American or Italian mediation with Hitler. Australia's prime minister, Robert Menzies, was fortunately made of sterner stuff. From Canberra, Menzies merely enquired what assistance his country's troops could provide. By autumn, three Australian divisions were deployed in the Middle East. Churchill told Chamberlain to make plain to Bruce that France's surrender would not influence Britain's determination to fight on. He urged ministers—and emphasised the message in writing a few days later—to present bold faces to the world. Likewise, a little later, he instructed Britain's missions abroad to entertain lavishly, prompting embassy parties in Madrid and Berne. In Churchill's house, even amid disaster there was no place for glum countenances.

At a further War Cabinet meeting that afternoon, Halifax found himself unsupported when he returned to his theme of the previous day, seeking agreement that Britain should solicit Mussolini's help in exploring terms from Hitler. Churchill said that, at that moment, British prestige in Europe was very low. It could be revived only by defiance. "If, after two or three months, we could show that we were still unbeaten, we should be no worse off than we should be if we were now to abandon the struggle. Let us therefore avoid being dragged down the slippery slope with France." If terms were offered, he would be prepared to consider them. But if the British were invited to send a delegate to Paris to join with the French in suing for peace with Germany, the answer must be no. The War Cabinet agreed.

Halifax wrote in his diary: "I thought Winston talked the most frightful rot. I said exactly what I thought of [the foreign secretary's opponents in the War Cabinet], adding that if that was really their view, our ways must part." In the garden afterwards, when he repeated his threat of resignation, Churchill soothed him with soft words. Halifax concluded in his diary record: "It does drive one to despair when he works himself up into a passion of emotion when he ought to make his brain think and reason." He and Chamberlain recoiled from Churchill's "theatricality," as Cadogan described it. Cold men both, they failed to perceive in such circumstances the necessity for at least a semblance of boldness. But Chamberlain's eventual support for Churchill's stance was critically important in deflecting the foreign secretary's proposals.

Whichever narratives of these exchanges are consulted, the facts seem plain. Halifax believed that Britain should explore terms. Churchill must have been deeply alarmed by the prospect of the foreign secretary, the man whom only three weeks earlier most of the Conservative Party wanted as prime minister, quitting his government. It was vital, at this moment of supreme crisis, that Britain should present a united face to the world. Churchill could never thereafter have had private confidence in Halifax. He continued to endure him as a colleague, however, because he needed to sustain the support of the Tories. It was a measure of Churchill's apprehension about the resolve of Britain's ruling class that it would be another seven months before he felt strong enough to consign "the Holy Fox" to exile.

The legend of Britain in the summer of 1940 as a nation united in defiance of Hitler is rooted in reality. It is not diminished by asserting that if another man had been prime minister, the political faction resigned to seeking a negotiated peace would probably have prevailed. What Churchill grasped, and Halifax and others did not, was that the mere gesture of exploring peace terms would have impacted disastrously upon Britain's position. Even if Hitler's response proved unacceptable to a British government, the clear, simple Churchillian posture of rejecting any parley with the forces of evil would be irretrievably compromised.

It is impossible to declare with confidence at what moment during the summer of 1940 Churchill's grip upon power, as well as his hold upon the loyalties of the British people, became secure. What is plain is that, in the last days of May, he did not perceive himself proof against domestic foes. He survived in office not because he overcame the private doubts of ministerial and military sceptics, which he did not, but by the face of courage and defiance that he presented to the nation. He appealed over the heads of those who knew too much, to those who were willing to sustain a visceral stubbornness. "His world is built upon the primacy of public over private relationships," wrote the philosopher Isaiah Berlin in a fine essay on Churchill, "upon the supreme value of action, of the battle between simple good and simple evil, between life and death; but above all battle. He has always fought." The simplicity of Churchill's commitment, matched by the grandeur of the language in which he expressed this, seized popular imagination. In the press, in the pubs and everywhere that Churchill himself appeared on his travels across the country, the British people passionately applauded his defiance. Conservative seekers after truce were left beached and isolated; sullenly resentful, but impotent.

Evelyn Waugh's fictional Halberdier officer, the fastidious Guy Crouchback, was among many members of the British upper classes who were slow to abandon their disdain for the prime minister, displaying an attitude common among real-life counterparts such as Waugh himself:

Some of Mr. Churchill's broadcasts had been played on the mess wireless-set. Guy had found them painfully boastful and they had, most of them, been immediately followed by the news of some disaster . . . Guy knew of Mr. Churchill only as a professional politician, a master of sham-Augustan prose, an advocate of the Popular Front in Europe, an associate of the press-lords and Lloyd George. He was asked: "Uncle, what sort of fellow is this Winston Churchill?" "Like Hore-Belisha [a sacked secretary for war, widely considered a charlatan], except that for some reason his hats are thought to be funny" . . . Here Major Erskine leant across the table. "Churchill is about the only man who may save us from losing this war," he said. It was the first time that Guy had heard a Halberdier suggest that any result, other than complete victory, was possible.

Some years before the war, the diplomat Lord D'Abernon observed with patrician complacency that "an Englishman's mind works best when it is almost too late." In May 1940, he might have perceived Churchill as an exemplar.

TWO

The Two Dunkirks

ON MAY 28, Churchill learned that the Belgians had surrendered at dawn. He observed that it was not for him to pass judgement on King Leopold's decision. He repressed until much later his private bitterness, though this was unjustified when Belgium had no rational prospect of sustaining the fight. Overnight a few thousand British troops had been retrieved from Dunkirk, but Gort was pessimistic about the fate of more than 200,000 who remained, in the face of overwhelming German airpower. "And so here we are back on the shores of France on which we landed with such high hearts over eight months ago," Pownall, Gort's chief of staff, wrote that day. "I think we were a gallant band who little deserve this ignominious end to our efforts . . . If our skill be not so great, our courage and endurance are certainly greater than that of the Germans." The stab of self-knowledge reflected in Pownall's phrase about the inferior professionalism of the British Army lingered in the hearts of its intelligent soldiers until 1945.

That afternoon at a War Cabinet meeting in Churchill's room at the Commons, the prime minister again—and for the last time—rejected Halifax's urgings that the government could obtain better peace terms before France surrendered and British aircraft factories were destroyed. Chamberlain, as ever a waverer, now supported the foreign secretary in urging that Britain should consider "decent terms if such were offered to us." Churchill said that the odds were a thousand to one against any such Hitlerian generosity, and warned that "nations which went down fighting rose again, but those which surrendered tamely were finished." Attlee and Greenwood, the Labour members, endorsed Churchill's view. This was the last stand of the old appeasers. Privately, they adhered to the view, shared by former prime minister Lloyd George, that sooner or later negotiation with Germany would be essential. As late as June 17, the Swedish ambassador reported Halifax and his junior minister R. A. Butler declaring that no "diehards" would be allowed to stand in the way of peace "on reasonable conditions." It remains extraordinary that some historians have sought to qualify verdicts on the foreign secretary's behaviour through the summer of 1940. It was not dishonourable—the lofty eminence could never have been that. But it was craven.

Immediately following the May 28 meeting, some twenty-five other ministers—all those who were not members of the War Cabinet—filed into the room, to be briefed by the prime minister. He described the situation at Dunkirk, anticipated the French collapse and expressed his conviction that Britain must fight on. "He was quite magnificent," wrote Hugh Dalton, the minister of economic warfare, "the man, and the only man we have, for this hour . . . He was determined to prepare public opinion for bad tidings . . . Attempts to invade us would no doubt be made." Churchill told the ministers that he had considered the case for negotiating with "that man"—and rejected it. Britain's position, with its fleet and air force, remained strong. He concluded with a magnificent peroration: "I am convinced that every man of you would rise up and tear me down from my place if I were for one moment to contemplate parley or surrender. If this long island story of ours is to end at last, let it end only when each one of us lies choking in his own blood upon the ground."

He was greeted with acclamation extraordinary at any assembly of ministers. No word of dissent was uttered. The meeting represented an absolute personal triumph. He reported its outcome to the War Cabinet. That night, the British government informed Reynaud in Paris of its refusal of Italian mediation for peace terms. A further suggestion by Halifax of a direct call upon the United States was dismissed. A bold stand against Germany, Churchill reiterated, would carry vastly more weight than "a grovelling appeal" at such a moment. At the following day's War Cabinet meeting, new instructions to Gort were discussed. Halifax favoured giving the C-in-C discretion to capitulate. Churchill would hear of no such thing. Gort was told to fight on at least until further evacuation from Dunkirk became impossible. Mindful of Allied reproaches, he told the War Office that French troops in the perimeter must be allowed access to British ships. He informed Reynaud of his determination to create a new British Expeditionary Force, based on the Atlantic port of St.-Nazaire, to fight alongside the French army in the west.

All through those days, the evacuation from the port and beaches continued, much hampered by lack of small craft to ferry troops out to the larger ships, a deficiency which the Admiralty strove to make good by a public appeal for suitable vessels. History has invested the saga of Dunkirk with a dignity less conspicuous to those present. John Horsfall, a company commander of the Royal Irish Fusiliers, told a young fellow officer: "I hope you realise your distinction. You are now taking part in the greatest military shambles ever achieved by the British Army." Many rank-and-file soldiers returned from France nursing a lasting resentment towards the military hierarchy that had exposed them to such a predicament. Horsfall noticed that in the last phase of the march to the beaches, his men fell unnaturally silent: "There was a limit to what any of us could absorb, with those red fireballs flaming skywards every few minutes, and I suppose we just reached the point where there was little left to say." They were joined by a horse artillery major, superb in Savile Row riding breeches and scarlet-and-gold forage cap, who said, "I'm a double blue at this, old boy—I was at Mons [in 1914]." A young Grenadier Guards officer, Edward Ford, passed the long hours of waiting for a ship reading a copy of Chapman's *Homer* which he found in the sands. For the rest of his days, Ford was nagged by unsatisfied curiosity about who had abandoned his Chapman amid the detritus of the beaches.

Though the Royal Navy's achievement at Dunkirk embraced its highest traditions, many men noted only the chaos. "It does seem to me incredible that the organisation of the beach work should have been so bad," wrote Lt. Robert Hichens of the minesweeper *Niger*, though he admired the absence of panic among embarking soldiers.

We were told that there would be lots of boats and that the embarkation of the troops would all be organised . . . That was what all the little shore boats were being brought over from England for . . . One can only come to the conclusion that the civilians and small boats packed up and went home with a few chaps instead of staying there to ferry to the big ships which was their proper job. As for the shore organisation, it simply did not exist . . . It makes one a bit sick when one hears the organisers of the beach show being cracked up to the skies on the wireless and having DSOs showered upon them, because a more disgraceful muddle and lack of organisation I have never seen . . . If a few officers had been put ashore with a couple of hundred sailors . . . the beach evacuation would have been a different thing . . . When the boats were finally hoisted I found that I was very tired and very hoarse as well as soaking wet. So I had a drink and then changed. I had an artillery officer in my cabin who was very interesting. They all seem to have been very impressed by the dive bombers and the vast number of them, and by the general efficiency of the German forces. The soldiers are not very encouraging, but they were very tired which always makes one pessimistic, and they had been out of touch for a long time. This officer did not even know that Churchill had replaced Chamberlain as Premier.

Pownall arrived in London from France to describe to the Defence Committee on May 30 Gort's plans for holding the Dunkirk perimeter. "No one in the room," wrote Ian Jacob of the War Cabinet Secretariat, "imagined that they could be successful if the German armoured divisions supported by the Luftwaffe pressed their attack." It was, of course, a decisive mercy that no such attack was "pressed." In the course of the Second World War, victorious German armies displayed a far more consistent commitment to completing the destruction of their enemies when opportunity offered than did the Allies in similarly advantageous circumstances. Dunkirk was an exception. Most of the BEF escaped not as a consequence of Hitler's forbearance, but through a miscellany of fortuities and misjudgements. Success beyond German imagination created huge problems of its own. Commanders' attention was fixed upon completing the defeat of Weygand's forces, of which large elements remained intact. The broken country around Dunkirk was well-suited to defence. The French First Army, south of the port, engaged important German forces through the critical period for the BEF's escape, a stand which received less credit from the British than it deserved.

On May 24 Karl Rudolf Gerd von Rundstedt, commanding Army Group A, ordered his panzers, badly in need of a logistical pause, not to cross the Aa Canal and entangle themselves with British "remnants," as Gort's army was now perceived. Hitler supported his decision. He was amenable to Hermann Göring's eagerness to show that his aircraft could complete the destruction of the BEF. Yet, in the words of the most authoritative German history, "the Luftwaffe, badly weakened by earlier operations, was unable to meet the demands made on it." In the course of May, Göring's force lost 1,044 aircraft, a quarter of them fighters. Thanks to the efforts of the RAF's Fighter Command over Dunkirk, the German Fourth Army's war diary recorded on May 25: "The enemy has had air superiority. This is something new for us in this campaign." On June 3, the German air effort was diverted from Dunkirk to increase pressure on the French by bombing targets around Paris.

Almost the entire RAF Air Striking Force was reduced to charred wreckage, strewn the length of northern France. It scarcely seemed to the Germans to matter if a few thousand British troops escaped in salt-stained battle dress, when they left behind every tool of a modern army—tanks, guns, trucks, machine guns and equipment. Hitler's failure to complete the demolition of the BEF represented a historic blunder, but an unsurprising one amid the magnitude of German triumphs and dilemmas in the last days of May 1940. The Allies, with much greater superiority, indulged far more culpable strategic omissions when they returned to the Continent for the campaigns of 1943–45.

Ian Jacob was among those impressed by the calm with which Churchill received Pownall's Dunkirk situation report of May 30. Thereafter, the War Cabinet addressed another budget of French requests: for troops to support them on the Somme front; more aircraft; concessions to Italy; and a joint appeal to Washington. Churchill interpreted these demands as establishing a context for French surrender, once Britain had refused them. The decision was taken to withdraw residual British forces from northern Norway. The prime minister determined to fly again to Paris to press France to stay in the war, and to make plain that Britain would dissociate itself from any parley with Germany mediated by the Italians. The next morning, as Churchill's Flamingo took off from Northolt, he knew that 133,878 British and 11,666 Allied troops had been evacuated from Dunkirk.

The prime minister's old friend Sir Edward Spears was serving as a British liaison officer with the French, a role he had also filled in World War I. Spears, waiting at Villacoublay airfield to meet the party, was impressed by the prime minister's imposture of gaiety. Churchill poked the British officer playfully in the stomach with his stick, and as ever appeared stimulated by finding himself upon the scene of great events. He beamed upon the pilots of the escorting Hurricanes which had landed behind him, was driven into Paris for lunch at the British embassy, then went to see Reynaud at the Ministry of War.

Amid the gloom that beset all of France's leaders, gathered with her prime minister, Pétain and Admiral Jean-François Darlan showed themselves foremost in despair. As Ismay described it: "A dejected-looking old man in plain clothes shuffled towards me, stretched out his hand and said: 'Pétain.' It was hard to believe that this was the great Marshal of France." The rationalists, as they saw themselves, listened unmoved to Churchill's outpouring of rhetoric. He spoke of the two British divisions already in northwestern France, which he hoped could be further reinforced to assist in the defence of Paris. He described in dramatic terms the events at Dunkirk. He declared in his extraordinary franglais, reinforced by gestures, that French and British soldiers would leave arm in arm— "*partage—bras dessus, bras dessous.*" On Cabinet orders, Gort was to quit Dunkirk that night. If, as expected, Italy entered the war, British bomber squadrons would at once strike at her industries. Churchill beamed once more. If only France could hold out through the summer, he said, all manner of possibilities would open. In a final surge of emotion, he declared his conviction that American help would come. Thus this thirteenth meeting of the Allied Supreme War Council concluded its agenda.

Reynaud and two other ministers were guests for dinner that night at the palatial British embassy, in the Rue St.-Honoré. Churchill waxed lyrical about the possibility of launching striking forces against German tank columns. He left Paris the next morning knowing he had done all that force of personality could achieve to breathe inspiration into the hearts of the men charged with saving France. Yet few believed a word of it. The Allies' military predicament was irretrievably dire. It was impossible to conceive any plausible scenario in which Hitler's armies might be thrown back, given the collapse of French national will.

Paul Reynaud was among a handful of Frenchmen who, momentarily at least, remained susceptible to Churchill's verbiage. To logical minds, there was an absurdity about almost everything the Englishman said to ministers and commanders in Paris. Britain's prime minister paraded before his ally his own extravagant sense of honour. He promised military gestures which might further weaken his own country, but could not conceivably save France. He made wildly fanciful pledges of further military aid, though its impact would have been insignificant. Britain's two divisions in the northwest were irrelevant to the outcome of the battle, and were desperately needed to defend the home island. But Churchill told the War Cabinet in London on June 1 that more troops must be dispatched across the Channel, with a suitable air component. Even as the miracle of Dunkirk unfolded, he continued to waver about dispatching further fighters to the Continent. He trumpeted the success of the RAF in preventing the Luftwaffe from frustrating the evacuation, which he declared a splendid omen for the future.

Chamberlain and Halifax urged against sending more men to France, but Churchill dissented. He felt obliged to respond to fresh appeals from Reynaud. He envisaged a British enclave in Brittany, a base from which the French might be inspired and supported to maintain "a gigantic guerrilla . . . The B.E.F. in France must immediately be reconstituted, otherwise the French will not continue in the war." Amid the dire shortage of troops, he committed to France the 1st Canadian Division, which had arrived in Britain virtually untrained and unequipped. The prime minister told one of the British generals who would be responsible for sustaining the defence of northwest France that "he could count on no artillery." An impromptu new "division" was created around Rouen from lines-of-communications personnel equipped with a few Bren and antitank guns which they had never fired, and a single battery of field artillery that lacked dial sights for its guns. Until Lt. Gen. Alan Brooke, recently landed from Dunkirk, returned to France on June 12, British forces there remained under French command, with no national C-in-C on the spot.

By insisting upon resumption of an utterly doomed campaign, Churchill made his worst mistake of 1940. It is unsurprising that his critics in the inner circle of power were dismayed. The strength of Churchill's emotions was wonderful to behold. But when sentiment drove him to make deployments with no possibility of success, he appalled his generals, as well as the old Chamberlainite umbrella men. Almost every senior civilian and uniformed figure in Whitehall recognised that the Battle of France was lost. Further British commitments threatened to negate the extraordinary deliverance of Dunkirk. The Air Staff closed ranks with Halifax, Chamberlain and others to resist Churchill's demands that more fighters should be sent to France, in addition to the three British squadrons still operating there. On the air issue, Churchill himself havered, then reluctantly gave way. This was the first of many occasions on which he mercifully subordinated his instincts to the advice of service chiefs and colleagues. Chamberlain and Halifax were not wrong about everything. The moral grandeur of Churchill's gestures towards his ally in the first days of June was entirely subsumed by the magnitude of France's tragedy and Britain's peril.

The Dunkirk evacuation approached a conclusion on June 4, by which time 224,328 British troops had been evacuated, along with 111,172 Allied troops, most of whom subsequently elected to be repatriated to France rather than fight on in exile. For thirty-five minutes that afternoon, Churchill described the operation to the Commons, concluding with some of his greatest phrases: "We shall fight on the beaches, we shall fight on the landing grounds, we shall fight in the fields and in the streets, we shall fight in the hills, we shall never surrender."

That evening he found time to dispatch brief notes, thanking the king for withdrawing his character objections to Brendan Bracken's membership of the Privy Council and expressing appreciation to former prime minister Stanley Baldwin for a letter offering good wishes. Churchill apologised for having taken a fortnight to respond. "We are going through v[er]y hard times & I expect worse to come," he wrote; "but I feel quite sure better days will come; though whether we shall live to see them is more doubtful. I do not feel the burden weigh too heavily, but I cannot say that I have enjoyed being Prime Minister v[er]y much so far."

The German drive on Paris began on June 5. Anglo-French exchanges in the days that followed were dominated by increasingly passionate appeals from Reynaud for fighters. Five RAF squadrons were still based in France, while four more were operating over France from British bases. The War Cabinet and Chiefs of Staff were united in their determination to weaken Britain's home defence no further. On June 9, Churchill cabled to South African premier Jan Smuts, who had urged the dispatch of more aircraft, saying: "I see only one sure way through now, to wit, that Hitler should attack this country, and in so doing break his air weapon. If this happens he will be left to face the winter with Europe writhing under his heel, and probably with the United States against him after the Presidential election is over." The Royal Navy was preoccupied with fears about the future of the French fleet. Admiral Sir Dudley Pound, the first sea lord, declared that only its sinking could ensure that it would not be used by the Germans.

Yet perversely and indeed indefensibly, Churchill continued to dispatch more troops to France. The draft operation order for the 1st Canadian Division, drawn up as it embarked on June 11, said: "The political object of the re-constituted BEF is to give moral support to the French Government by showing the determination of the British Empire to assist her ally with all available forces ... It is the intention ... to concentrate ... in the area North and South of Rennes ... A division may have to hold 50 miles of front." At a meeting of ministers in London that day, Dill was informed that a study was being undertaken for the maintenance of a bridgehead in Brittany, "the Breton redoubt." As late as June 13, Royal Engineers were preparing reception points and transit camps on the Brittany coast, to receive further reinforcements from Britain.

Churchill recognised the overwhelming likelihood of French surrender, yet still cherished hopes of maintaining a foothold across the Channel. It seemed to him preferable to face the difficulties of clinging on in France, rather than those of mounting from Britain a return to a German-defended coast. He sought to sustain French faith in the alliance by the deployment of a mere three British divisions. He seemed unmoved by Mussolini's long-expected declaration of war on June 10, merely remarking to Jock Colville: "People who go to Italy to look at ruins won't have to go as far as Naples and Pompeii again." The private secretary noted his master's bitter mood that day. On the afternoon of June 11, Churchill flew with Eden, Dill, Ismay and Spears to the new French army headquarters at Briare, on the Loire, seventy miles from Paris, to meet the French government once again. The colonel who met their plane, wrote Spears, might have been greeting poor relations at a funeral. At their destination, the Château du Muguet, there was no sense of welcome. At that evening's meeting of the Supreme War Council, after the French had unfolded a chronicle of doom, Churchill summoned all his powers. He spoke with passion and eloquence about the forces which Britain could deploy in France in 1941—twenty, even twenty-five divisions. Weygand said dismissively that the outcome of the war would be determined in hours, not days or weeks. Dill, pathetically, invited the supreme commander to use the makeshift British forces now in France wherever and however he saw fit.

The French, with the Germans at the gates of Paris, could scarcely be blamed for thinking themselves mocked. Eden wrote: "Reynaud was inscrutable and Weygand polite, concealing with difficulty his scepticism. Marshal Pétain was overtly incredulous. Though he said nothing, his attitude was obviously *c'est de la blague*"—"it's a joke." The harshest confrontation came when Weygand asserted that the decisive point had been reached, that the British should commit every fighter they had to the battle. Churchill replied: "This is not the decisive point. This is not the decisive moment. The decisive moment will come when Hitler hurls his Luftwaffe against Britain. If we can keep command of the air over our own island—that is all I ask—we will win it all back for you." Britain would fight on "for ever and ever and ever."

Reynaud seemed moved. The newly appointed army minister, Brig. Gen. Charles de Gaulle, was much more impressed by the prime minister's representation of himself as an Englishman than as an ally: "Mr. Churchill appeared imperturbable, full of buoyancy. Yet he seemed to be confining himself to a cordial reserve towards the French at bay, being already seized—not, perhaps, without an obscure satisfaction—with the terrible and magnificent prospect of an England left alone in her island, with himself to lead her struggle towards salvation." The other Frenchmen present made nothing of the prime minister's words. Though courtesies were sustained through a difficult dinner that night, Reynaud told Britain's leader over brandy that Pétain considered it essential to seek an armistice.

To his staff, Churchill fumed at the influence upon Reynaud of his mistress, the Comtesse de Portes, an impassioned advocate of surrender: "That woman . . . will undo everything during the night that I do during the day. But of course she can furnish him with facilities that I cannot afford him. I can reason with him, but I cannot sleep with him." For all the hopes which Churchill reposed in Reynaud, even at his best the French prime minister never shared the Englishman's zest for war *à l'outrance*. The American undersecretary of state, Sumner Welles, reported a conversation with France's leader earlier that summer: "M. Reynaud felt that while Mr. C[hurchill] was a brilliant and most entertaining man with a great capacity for organization, his kind has lost elasticity. He felt that Mr. C could conceive of no possibility other than war to the finish—whether that resulted in utter chaos and destruction or not. That, he felt sure, was not true statesmanship." This seems a convincing representation of Reynaud's view in June 1940. Like a significant number of British politicians in respect of their own society, the French prime minister perceived, as Churchill did not, a limit to the injury to the fabric and people of France which might be acceptable in the cause of sustaining the struggle against Nazism.

The next morning, June 12, Churchill told Spears to stay with the French, and to do everything possible to sustain them: "We will carry those who will let themselves be carried." Yet Britain had no power to "carry" France. Pétain absented himself from the ensuing meeting of the Supreme War Council. His own decision was reached. Churchill raged at news that a planned RAF bombing mission to Italy the previous night had been frustrated by farm carts pushed across the runway by French airmen. Reynaud said that any further such missions must be launched from England. At the Briare airfield, Ismay observed encouragingly that with no more allies to worry about, "we'll win the Battle of Britain." Churchill stared hard at him and said: "You and I will be dead in three months' time." There is no reason to doubt this exchange. Churchill claimed later that he had always believed Britain would come through. He certainly had a mystical faith in destiny, however vague his attachment to a deity. But it is plain that in the summer of 1940 he suffered cruel moments of rationality, when defeat seemed far more plausible than victory, when the huge effort of will necessary to sustain the fight was almost too much for him. Six months later, Eden confessed to the prime minister that during the summer he and Pound, the first sea lord, had privately acknowledged despair to each other. Churchill said: "Normally I wake up buoyant to face the new day. Then, I awoke with dread in my heart."

When so many others were dying, he could scarcely take for granted his own survival. A German bomb, a paratroop landing in Whitehall, an accident by land, sea or air—such as befell many other prominent wartime figures—could extinguish him at any time. His courage, and that of those who followed and served him, lay in defying probability, sweeping aside all thought of the most plausible outcome of the struggle, and addressing each day's battles with a spirit undaunted by the misfortunes of the last. That Wednesday morning of June 12, his Flamingo hedgehopped home over the lovely countryside of Brittany. Near the smoking docks of Le Havre, the pilot dived suddenly to avoid the attentions of two German planes which were strafing fishing boats. The Flamingo escaped unseen, landing safely at Hendon, but this was one of Churchill's closest. Later in the afternoon, he told the War Cabinet that it was obvious French resistance was approaching an end. He spoke admiringly of de Gaulle, whose resolution had made a strong impression on him.

Churchill had been back in London less than thirty-six hours when Reynaud telephoned, soon after midnight, demanding a new and urgent meeting at Tours, to which he had now retreated. The prime minister left the next morning, accompanied by Halifax and Beaverbrook, driving through the incongruous London summer shopping crowds. He was greeted at Hendon with news that bad weather required a takeoff postponement. "To hell with that," he growled. "I'm going, whatever happens. This is too serious a situation to bother about the weather!" They landed at Tours amid a thunderstorm, on an airfield which had been heavily bombed the previous night, and solicited transport from a jaded rabble of French airmen. Churchill, Beaverbrook and Halifax crowded with difficulty into a small car which took them to the local prefecture, where they wandered unrecognised through the corridors. At last a staff officer escorted them to a nearby restaurant for cold chicken and cheese. This was black comedy. It is not difficult to imagine Halifax's disdain for the ordeal to which Churchill had exposed him.

Back at the prefecture, the British waited impatiently for Reynaud. It was essential that they take off again in daylight, because the bomb-cratered and unlit runway was unfit for night operations. At last the French prime minister arrived, with Spears. He told the English party that, while Weygand was ready to surrender, it was still possible that he could persuade his colleagues to fight on—if he received a firm assurance that the Americans would enter the war. Otherwise, would Britain concede that it was now impossible for France to continue the war? Churchill responded with expressions of sympathy for France's agony. He concluded simply, however, that Britain would fight on: no terms, no surrender. Reynaud said that the prime minister had not answered his question. Churchill said he could not accede to a French capitulation. He urged that Reynaud's government should make a direct appeal to President Roosevelt before taking any other action. Some of the British party were dismayed that nothing was said about continuing the fight from France's North African empire. They were fearful that Reynaud's nation would not only cease to be their ally, but might join Germany as their foe. They were acutely aware that, even though the French leader still had some heart, his generals, excepting only de Gaulle, had none.

In the courtyard below, a throng of French politicians and officials, emotional and despairing, milled around Churchill as he left. Hands were wrung, tears shed. The prime minister murmured to de Gaulle: "*L'homme du destin.*" He ignored an impassioned intervention by the Comtesse de Portes, who pushed forward crying out that her country was bleeding to death, and that she must be heard. French officials told the assembled politicians that Churchill at this last meeting of the Supreme War Council had shown full understanding of France's position, and was resigned to her capitulation. Reynaud did not invite Churchill to meet his ministers, as they themselves wished. They felt snubbed in consequence, though the omission changed nothing.

Churchill landed back at Hendon after a two-and-a-half-hour flight. At Downing Street, he learned that President Roosevelt had responded to an earlier French appeal with private promises of more matériel aid, and declared himself impressed that Reynaud was committed to fight on. Churchill told the War Cabinet that such a message came as close to an American declaration of war as was possible without Congress. This was, of course, wildly wishful thinking. Roosevelt, on Secretary of State Cordell Hull's advice, rejected Churchill's plea that he should allow his cable to be published.

On June 12, the 51st Highland Division at St.-Valéry-en-Caux was forced to join a local capitulation by troops of the French Tenth Army, to which the British formation was attached. Had an order been given a few days earlier, it is plausible that the troops could have been evacuated to Britain through Le Havre. Instead, they became a sacrifice to Churchill's commitment to be seen to sustain the campaign. That same day, Gen. Sir Alan Brooke arrived with orders to lead British forces to the aid of the French. Reinforcements were still landing at the Brittany ports on the thirteenth.

When Ismay suggested that British units moving to France should hasten slowly, Churchill said: "Certainly not. It would look very bad in history if we were to do any such thing." This was of a piece with his response to Chancellor of the Exchequer Kingsley Wood's suggestion a few weeks later, that since Britain was financially supporting the Dutch administration in exile, in return the government should demand an increased stake in the Royal Dutch Shell oil company. "Churchill, who objected to taking advantage of another country's misfortunes, said that he never again wished to hear such a suggestion." At every turn, he perceived his own words and actions through the prism of posterity. He was determined that historians should say: "He nothing common did or mean upon that memorable scene." Indeed, in those days Andrew Marvell's lines on King Charles I's execution were much in his mind. He recited them repeatedly to his staff, and then to the House of Commons. Seldom has a great actor on the stage of human affairs been so mindful of the verdict of future ages, even as he played out his own part and delivered his lines.

On June 14, the Germans entered Paris unopposed. Yet illusions persisted in London that a British foothold on the Continent might even now be maintained. Jock Colville wrote from Downing Street that day: "If the French will go on fighting, we must now fall back on the Atlantic, creating new lines of Torres Vedras behind which British divisions and American supplies can be concentrated. Paris is not France, and . . . there is no reason to suppose the Germans will be able to subdue the whole country." Colville himself was a very junior civil servant, but his fantasies were fed by more important people. That evening, Churchill spoke by telephone to Brooke in France. The prime minister deplored the fact that the remaining British formations were in retreat. He wanted to make the French feel that they were being supported. Brooke, with an Ulster bluntness of which Churchill would gain much more experience in the course of the war, retorted that "it was impossible to make a corpse feel." After what seemed to the soldier an interminable and absurd wrangle, Churchill said: "All right, I agree with you."

In that conversation, Brooke saved almost 200,000 men from death or captivity. By sheer force of personality, not much in evidence among British generals, he persuaded Churchill to allow his forces to be removed from French command and evacuated. On June 15, orders were rushed to the Canadians en route by rail from the Normandy coast to what passed for the battlefront. Locomotives were shunted from the front to the rear of their trains, which then set off once more for the ports. At Brest, embarking troops were ordered to destroy all vehicles and equipment. However, some determined and imaginative officers laboured defiantly and successfully to evacuate precious artillery. For the French, Weygand was further embittered by tidings of another British withdrawal. It seems astonishing that his compatriots did nothing to impede the operation, and even something to assist it.

Much has been written about Churchill's prudence in declining to reinforce defeat by dispatching further fighter squadrons to France in 1940. The contrary misjudgement is often passed over. Alan Brooke understood the prime minister's motive—to demonstrate to the French that the British Army was still committed to the fight. But he rightly deplored its futility. If Dunkirk represented a miracle, it was scarcely a lesser one that two weeks later it proved possible to evacuate almost all of Brooke's force to Britain through the northwestern French ports. There were, in effect, two Dunkirks, though the latter is much less noticed by history. Churchill was able to escape the potentially brutal consequences of his last rash ges-

ture to Reynaud, because of Brooke's resolution and the Germans' preoccupation with completing the destruction of the French army. Had not
providence been merciful, all Brooke's men might have been lost, a shattering blow to the British Army's prospects of reconstitution.

On June 15, at Churchill's behest Dill telephoned Brooke on a weak,
crackling line, and told him to delay evacuation of the 52nd Division from
Cherbourg. In London, there were renewed hopes of clinging to a
foothold in France, though these had no visible foundation in reality. The
French anyway discounted all such British aspirations. Brooke was exasperated. He told the CIGS: "It is a desperate job being faced with over
150,000 men and a mass of material, ammunition, petrol, supplies etc, to
try to evacuate or dispose of, and nothing to cover this operation except
the crumbling French army . . . We are wasting shipping and precious
hours." The next day, London grudgingly agreed that the 52nd Division
could continue returning to Britain. Yet administrative confusion persisted. Some troops were embarked at Le Havre for Portsmouth, only to
be off-loaded at Cherbourg and entrained for Rennes. A ship arrived at
Brest on the morning of June 18, bearing artillery and ammunition from
England. At a dozen northwest French ports, tens of thousands of British
troops milled in chaos, many of them lacking orders and officers.

German preoccupation with the French army alone made it possible to
get the men and a few heavy weapons away, amid chaos and mismanage-
ment. There were skirmishes between British and enemy forces, but no
fatal clash. Between June 14 and 25, from Brest, St.-Nazaire, Cherbourg
and lesser western French ports, 144,171 British troops were successfully
rescued and brought home, along with 24,352 Poles and 42,000 other
Allied soldiers. There were losses, notably the sinking of the liner *Lancas-
tria* at a cost of at least 3,000 lives; but these were negligible in proportion
to the forces at risk, which amounted to two-thirds of the numbers
brought back from Dunkirk.

It is hard to overstate the chaos of British command arrangements in
France during the last three weeks of the campaign, even in areas where
formations were not much threatened by the Germans. Two trainloads of
invaluable and undamaged British tanks were gratuitously abandoned in
Normandy. "Much equipment had been unnecessarily destroyed," in the
angry words of Maj. Gen. Andrew McNaughton, commanding the 1st
Canadian Division. Though the war had been in progress for almost nine
months, Lt. Gen. Sir Henry Karslake, commanding at Le Mans until
Brooke's arrival, wrote in a report: "The lack of previous training for our
formations showed itself in many ways." Men of the 52nd Division arrived
in France in June with equipment issued two days earlier, never having

fired their antitank guns or indeed seen a tank. Karslake was appalled by the perceived indiscipline of some regular units, even before they were engaged: "Their behaviour was terrible!" Far more vehicles, stores and equipment could have been evacuated but for administrative disorder prevailing at the ports, where some ships from England were still being unloaded, while, at nearby quays, units embarked for home. The commitment to northwest France represented a serious misjudgement by Churchill, which won no gratitude from the French, and could have cost the Allies as many soldiers as the later disasters in Greece, Crete, Singapore and Tobruk put together.

While the horror of Britain's predicament was now apparent to all those in high places and to many in low, Churchill was visibly exalted by it. At Chequers on the warm summer night of June 15, Jock Colville described how tidings of gloom were constantly telephoned through, while sentries with steel helmets and fixed bayonets encircled the house. The prime minister, however, displayed the highest spirits, "repeating poetry, dilating on the drama of the present situation . . . offering everybody cigars, and spasmodically murmuring: 'Bang, bang, bang, goes the farmer's gun, run rabbit, run rabbit, run, run, run.' " In the early hours of the morning, when U.S. ambassador Joseph Kennedy telephoned, the prime minister unleashed upon him a torrent of rhetoric about America's opportunity to save civilisation. Then he held forth to his staff about Britain's growing fighter strength, "told one or two dirty stories," and departed for bed at 1:30, saying, "Goodnight, my children." At least some part of this must have been masquerade. But it was a masquerade of awesome nobility. Churchill's private secretary Eric Seal thought him much changed since May 10, more sober, "less violent, less wild, less impetuous." If this was overstated, there had certainly been an extraordinary accession of self-control.

On June 16, the War Cabinet dispatched a message to Reynaud, now in Bordeaux, offering to release France from its obligation as an ally to forswear negotiations with Germany, on the sole condition that the French fleet should be sailed to British harbours. De Gaulle, having arrived in London, was invited to lunch with Churchill and Eden at the Carlton Club. He told the prime minister that only the most dramatic British initiative might stave off French surrender. He urged formalising a proposal for political union between France and Britain, over which the Cabinet had been dallying for days. Amid crisis, these desperate men briefly embraced this fanciful idea. An appropriate message, setting forth the offer in momentous terms, was dispatched to Reynaud. Churchill prepared to set forth once more for France, this time by sea, to discuss a draft "Proclamation of Union." He was already aboard a train at Waterloo Station with Clement Attlee, Archibald Sinclair and the Chiefs of Staff, bound for embarkation on a destroyer, when word was brought that Reynaud could not receive them. With a heavy heart, the prime minister returned to Downing Street. It was for the best. The proposal for union was wholly unrealistic, and could have changed nothing. France's battle was over. Reynaud's government performed one last service to its ally: that day in Washington, all the French nation's American arms contracts were formally transferred to Britain.

During the night, it was learned at Downing Street that Reynaud had resigned as prime minister and been replaced by Marshal Pétain, who was seeking an armistice. Pétain's prestige among the French people rested, first, upon his defence of Verdun in 1916, and, second, upon an ill-founded belief that he possessed a humanity unique among generals, manifested in his merciful handling of the French army during its 1917 mutinies. In June 1940, there is little doubt that Pétain's commitment to peace at any price reflected the wishes of most French people. Reynaud, however, probably committed a historic blunder by agreeing to forsake his office. Had he and his ministerial colleagues chosen instead to accept exile, as did the Norwegian, Polish, Belgian and Dutch governments, he could have prevented his nation's surrender of democratic legitimacy and established French resistance to tyranny on strong foundations in London. As it was, he allowed himself to be overborne by the military defeatists, led by Pétain and Weygand, and denied himself a famous political martyrdom.

De Gaulle, Reynaud's army minister, almost alone among prominent Frenchmen, chose to pitch camp in London, and secured the evacuation of his wife. The War Cabinet opposed his request that he should be permitted to broadcast to his people on the BBC. Churchill, however, urged on by Spears, insisted that the renegade—for so de Gaulle was perceived by many of his own people—should be given access to a microphone. De Gaulle's legal adviser, Professor Cassin, enquired of his new chief what the status was of his embryo movement in Britain. De Gaulle answered magnificently: "We are France! . . . The defeated are those who accept defeat." The general had an answer, too, to the problem of establishing his own stature: "Churchill will launch me like a new brand of soap." The British government indeed hired an advertising agency, Richmond Temple, to promote Free France. De Gaulle would need all the help he could get. Few Frenchmen, even those evacuated to Britain from the battlefield, were willing to fight on if their government quit. While travelling as a passenger on the French destroyer *Milan*, de Gaulle asked its captain if he would serve under British colours. The naval officer answered that he would not. Most of his compatriots proved like-minded. "Mr. Churchill finds that there are not enough French and German bodies to satisfy him," declared a sulphurous front-page editorial in the Paris paper *Le Matin*, in one of its first issues after the surrender. "We ask if the British prime minister has lost his head. If so, what a pity that our ministers did not perceive it sooner." The paper went on to denounce de Gaulle, and to accuse the British of fomenting revolt in France's overseas empire.

In 1941 and 1942, the prime minister would be obliged to preside over many British defeats and, indeed, humiliations. Yet no trauma was as profound, no shock as far-reaching, as that which befell him in his first weeks of office, when the German army destroyed France as a military power and swept the British from the Continent. Henceforward, the character of the war became fundamentally different from that of 1914–18. All assumptions were set at naught upon which Allied war policy, and Churchill's personal defiance of Hitler, had been founded. Whatever Britain's continuing capabilities at sea and in the air, since September 1939 it had been taken for granted that the British Army would confront the Nazi legions alongside the French, in the frankly subordinate role demanded by its inferiority of numbers—just ten divisions to ninety-four French on the Western Front. The British Army could never alone aspire to dispute a battlefield with the Wehrmacht, and this knowledge dominated British strategy.

It was hard for many people, even the highest in the land, to absorb the scale of the disaster which had befallen Allied arms, and which now threatened to overwhelm Britain. Alan Brooke was struck by a Churchillian observation about human nature. The prime minister said that the receptive capacity of a man's mind was like a three-inch pipe running under a culvert. "When a flood comes the water flows over the culvert whilst the pipe goes on handling its 3 inches. Similarly the human brain will register emotions up to its '3 inch limit' and subsequent additional emotions flow past unregistered." So it now seemed to Brooke himself, and to a host of others. They perceived that a catastrophe was unfolding, but their hearts could not keep pace with the signals from their brains about its significance. Harold Nicolson wrote in his diary on June 15: "My reason tells me that it will now be almost impossible to beat the Germans, and that the probability is that France will surrender and that we shall be bombed and invaded . . . Yet these probabilities do not fill me with despair. I seem to be impervious both to pleasure and pain. For the moment we are all anaesthetised."

Another eyewitness, the writer Peter Fleming, then serving as an army staff officer, identified the same emotional confusion: "This period was one of carefree improvisation as far as most civilians were concerned. It was as though the whole country had been invited to a fancy-dress ball and everybody was asking everybody else 'What are you going as?' A latent incredulity, and the fact that almost everybody had more than enough to do already, combined to give problems connected with invasion the status of engrossing digressions from the main business of life . . . The British, when their ally was pole-axed on their doorstep, became both gayer and more serene than they had been at any time since the overture to Munich struck up in 1937."

British casualties in France were large in relation to the size of the BEF, but trifling by comparison with those of the French, and with the infinitely more intense struggles that would take place later in the war. The army lost just 11,000 killed and missing, against more than 50,000 French dead. In addition, 14,070 British wounded were evacuated, and 41,030 BEF prisoners fell into German hands. The loss of tanks, artillery and weapons of all kinds was, of course, calamitous. It is a familiar and ill-founded cliché that the 1940 British Expeditionary Force was ill-equipped. In reality, it was much better supplied with vehicles than the Germans, and the quality of its tanks was good enough, had they been imaginatively employed. When Hitler's Field Marshal Fedor von Bock saw the wreckage at Dunkirk, he wrote in astonishment: "Here lies the material of a whole army, so incredibly well-equipped that we poor devils can only look on with envy and amazement." The BEF was driven from Dunkirk after relatively light fighting and very heavy retreating because it lacked enough mass to change the outcome of the campaign once the French front was broken, and was outfought by German formations with better leadership, motivation, and air support. The British Army was now, for all practical purposes, disarmed. Almost a thousand RAF aircraft were gone, half of these fighters.

But Britain had human material to forge a new army—though not one that alone could ever be large enough to face the Germans in a continental war—if only time was granted before it must fight again. An American correspondent reported home that Londoners received news of the French surrender in grim silence rather than with jokes or protestations of defiance. The Battle of France was over, Churchill told the British people on the following night. The Battle of Britain was about to begin. The position of Churchill's nation on June 17 was scarcely enviable. But it was vastly better than had seemed possible a month earlier, when the BEF had faced annihilation.

THREE

Invasion Fever

IN THE MONTHS after September 1939, Britain found itself in the bleak—indeed, in some eyes absurd—position of having declared war on Germany while lacking means to undertake any substantial military initiative, least of all to save Poland. The passivity of the "Phoney War" ate deeply into the morale of the British people. By contrast, the events of May and June 1940 had at least the merit, brilliantly exploited by Churchill, that they thrust before the nation a clear and readily comprehended purpose: to defend itself against assault by an overwhelmingly powerful foe. The Royal Irish Fusiliers, back from Dunkirk, staged a mess party to celebrate news that the French had surrendered. "Thank heavens they have," said an officer gaily. "Now at last we can get on with the war." A middle-aged court reporter named George King, living in Surrey, wrote in a diary letter intended for his gunner son, left behind in France and on his way to captivity in Germany: "Winston Churchill has told us just exactly where we stand. We are on our own, and have got to see this thing through; and we can do it, properly led. Goodness knows what the swines will try, but somehow we've got to stick it."

Naval officer Robert Hichens wrote on June 17: "Now we know that we have got to look to ourselves only, I have an idea that England will respond wonderfully to this setback. She is always greatest in taking reverses." After Churchill addressed the Commons on the eighteenth, a Labour backbencher, Dr. Hastings Lees-Smith of Keighley, stood up: "My hon. friends on these benches have asked me on their behalf to say one or two sentences. They wish to say to the PM that in their experience among the broad masses of the people of this country never in their lives has the country been more united than it is today in its support of the PM's assertion that we shall carry on right to the end. One sentence can summarise what we feel. Whatever the country is asked for in the months and, if necessary, in the years to come, the PM may be confident that the people will rise to their responsibilities."

Yet, while the grit displayed by King, Hichens and Lees-Smith was real enough, it would be mistaken to suppose that it was universal. Not all sceptics about Britain's chances of survival were elderly politicians or businessmen. An RAF Hurricane pilot, Paul Mayhew, wrote in a family newsletter:

> Now I suppose it's our turn and though my morale is now pretty good . . . I can't believe that there's much hope for us, at any rate in Europe. Against a ferocious and relentless attack, the Channel's not much of an obstacle and with the army presumably un-equipped, I don't give much for our chances. Personally I have only two hopes; first that Churchill is more reliable than Reynaud and that we will go on fighting if England is conquered, and secondly that Russia, in spite of our blunders, will now be sufficiently scared to stage a distraction in the East. In America I have little faith; I suppose in God's own time God's own country will fight. But at present their army is smaller than the Swiss, their Air Force is puny and rather "playboy," and I doubt whether we need their Navy.

A week later, Mayhew apologised to his family for being "ludicrously defeatist." But here was a young airman voicing fears widely shared among his elders.

The summer and autumn of 1940 were poor seasons for truth-telling in Britain. That is to say, it was hard for even good, brave and honourable men to know whether they better served their country by voicing their private thoughts, allowing their brains to function, or by keeping silent. Logic decreed that Britain had not the smallest chance of winning the war in the absence of American participation, which remained implausible. Churchill knew this as well as anyone. Yet he and his supporters believed that the cause of freedom, the defiance of tyranny, made it essential that the British people should fight on regardless, sweeping aside all calculations of relative strengths and strategic disabilities. Posterity has heaped admiration upon the grandeur of this commitment. Yet, at the time, it demanded from intelligent men and women a suspension of reason which some rejected.

For instance, Captain Ralph Edwards, director of naval operations at the Admiralty, was an almost unwavering sceptic. On June 17, he noted in his diary: "[Captain] Bill Tennant came in to say that he'd told Sir Walter Monckton of all our misgivings about the higher direction of the war."

And again on the twenty-third: "Our cabinet with that idiot Winston in charge changes its mind every 24 hours . . . I'm rapidly coming to the conclusion that we're so inept we don't deserve to win & indeed are almost certain to be defeated. We never do anything right." Through the lonely eighteen months ahead, Churchill was galled that such scourges as Aneurin Bevan, MP, taxed him in the Commons with unwelcome facts of which he was thoroughly aware, painful realities such as he confronted every hour. From the outset, while he always insisted that victory would come, his personal prestige rested upon the honesty with which he acknowledged to the British people the gravity of the ordeal they faced.

Churchill told the MPs on June 4: "Our thankfulness at the escape of our Army and so many men, whose loved ones have passed through an agonising week, must not blind us to the fact that what has happened in France and Belgium is a colossal military disaster. I have myself full confidence that if all do their duty, if nothing is neglected, and if the best arrangements are made, as they are being made, we shall prove ourselves once again able to defend our island home, to ride out the storm of war, and to outlive the menace of tyranny, if necessary for years, if necessary alone. That is the resolve of His Majesty's Government."

Churchill's conduct after the fall of France exasperated some sceptics who perceived themselves as clear thinkers. His supreme achievement in 1940 was to mobilise Britain's warriors, to shame into silence its doubters, and to stir the passions of the nation, so that for a season the British people faced the world united and exalted. The "Dunkirk spirit" was not spontaneous. It was created by the rhetoric and bearing of one man, displaying powers that will define political leadership for the rest of time. Under a different prime minister, the British people in their shock and bewilderment could as readily have been led in another direction. Nor was the mood long-lived. It persisted only until winter, when it was replaced by a more dogged, doubtful and less exuberant national spirit. But that first period was decisive: "If we can get through the next three months, we can get through the next three years," Churchill told the Commons on June 20.

Kingsley Martin argued in that week's *New Statesman* that Churchill's June 18 "finest hour" broadcast to the nation was too simplistic: "He misunderstood [the British people's] feelings when he talked of this as the finest moment of their history. Our feelings are more complex than that. To talk to common people in or out of uniform is to discover that determination to defend this island is coupled with a deep and almost universal bitterness that we have been reduced to such a pass." Yet the prime minister judged the predominant mood much more shrewdly than the veteran socialist. In 1938, the British had not been what Churchill wanted them to be. In 1941 and thereafter, they would often disappoint his hopes. But in 1940, to an extraordinary degree, he was able to shape and elevate the nation to fulfil his aspirations.

Mollie Panter-Downes wrote in the *New Yorker* of June 29:

> It would be difficult for an impartial observer to decide today whether the British are the bravest or merely the most stupid people in the world. The way they are acting in the present situation could be used to support either claim. The individual Englishman seems to be singularly unimpressed by the fact that there is now nothing between him and the undivided attention of a war machine such as the world has never seen before. Possibly it's lack of imagination; possibly again it's the same species of dogged resolution which occasionally produces an epic like Dunkirk. Millions of British families, sitting at their well-stocked breakfast tables eating excellent British eggs and bacon, can still talk calmly of the horrors across the Channel, perhaps without fully comprehending even now that anything like that could ever happen in England's green and pleasant land.

Many Americans, by contrast, thought it unlikely that Britain would survive. In New York, "one thing that strikes me is the amount of defeatist talk," wrote U.S. general Raymond Lee, "the almost pathological assumption that it is all over bar the shouting . . . that it is too late for the United States to do anything." Key Pittman, chairman of the Senate Foreign Relations Committee, called on Churchill to send the British fleet to the New World: "It is no secret that Great Britain is totally unprepared for defense and that nothing the US has to give can do more than delay the result . . . It is to be hoped that this plan will not be too delayed by futile encouragement to fight on. It is conclusively evident that Congress will not authorize intervention in the European war." *Time* magazine reported on July 1: "So scared was many a US citizen last week that he wanted to shut off aid to Britain for fear that the US would weaken its own defenses, wanted to have the US wash its hands of help for Britain, for fear of getting involved on the losing side."

A *Fortune* opinion survey showed that, even before France collapsed, most Americans believed that Germany would win the war. Only 30.3 percent saw any hope for the Allies. A correspondent named Herbert Jones wrote a letter to the *Philadelphia Inquirer* which reflected widespread sentiment: "The great majority of Americans are not pacifists or isolationists, but, after the experience of the last war and Versailles, have no desire to pull Britain's chestnuts out of the fire for her, under the slogan of 'Save the World for Democracy.' They rightly feel that little is to be gained by pouring out our money and the lives of our young men for the cause of either the oppressor of the Jews and Czechs or the oppressor of the Irish and of India . . ." Richard E. Taylor of Apponaugh, Rhode Island, wrote to a friend in England, urging him to draw the attention of the authorities to the danger that the Germans might tunnel under the Channel.

Yet some Americans did not despair. An "aid to Britain" committee gathered three million signatures on petitions to the White House. The organisation spawned a Historians' Committee, under Charles Seymour of Yale; a Scientists' Committee, under Nobel Prize winner Harold Urey; a Theatre Committee, under playwright and Roosevelt speechwriter Robert Sherwood. Americans were invited to set aside their caricatured view of Britain as a nation of stuffed-shirt sleepyheads, and to perceive instead battling champions of freedom. Novelist Somerset Maugham, arriving in New York, predicted a vastly different postwar Britain, and hinted at the beginnings of one more sympathetic to an American social vision: "I have a feeling . . . that in the England of the future evening dress will be less important than it has been in the past." America was still far, far from belligerence, but forces favouring intervention were stirring.

In 1941, Churchill devoted immense energy to wooing the United States. But in 1940, once his June appeals to Roosevelt had failed, for several weeks he did not write to the president at all, and dismissed suggestions for a British propaganda offensive. "Propaganda is all very well," he said, "but it is events that make the world. If we smash the Huns here, we shall need no propaganda in the United States . . . Now we must live. Next year we shall be winning. The year after that we shall triumph. But if we can hold the Germans in this coming month of July . . . our position will be quite different from today."

Yet how to "hold them"? U.S. general Raymond Lee, military attaché at the London embassy, wrote: "One queer thing about the present situation is that it is one which has never been studied at the Staff College. For years [British officers] had studied our [U.S. Civil War] Valley campaign, operations in India, Afghanistan, Egypt and Europe, had done landings on a hostile shore, but it had never occurred to them that some day they might have to defend the non-combatants of a country at war." An MP recounted Churchill saying at this time: "I don't know what we'll fight them with—we shall have to slosh them on the head with bottles—empty ones, of course." This joke was almost certainly apocryphal, but as the prime minister himself observed of the manner in which spurious Churchilliana accrued, he became "a magnet for iron filings."

On June 8, Britain's Home Forces boasted an inventory of just 54 2-pounder antitank guns; 420 field guns, with 200 rounds of ammunition apiece; 613 medium and heavy guns, with 150 rounds for each; and 105 medium and heavy tanks and 395 light tanks. There were only 2,300 Bren light machine guns and 70,000 rifles. Visiting beach defences at St. Margaret's Bay, in Kent, on June 26, Churchill was told by the local brigadier that he had three antitank guns, with six rounds of ammunition apiece. Not one shot must be wasted on practise, said the prime minister. He dismissed a suggestion that London might, like Paris, be declared an open city. The British capital's dense streets, he said, offered peerless opportunities for local defence. So dire was the shortage of small arms that, when a consignment of World War I–vintage rifles arrived from the United States on July 10, Churchill decreed that they must be distributed within forty-eight hours. He rejected a proposal that Britain should try to deter Spain from entering the war by promising talks about the disputed sovereignty of Gibraltar as soon as peace returned. The Spanish, he said, would know full well that if Britain won, there would be no deal.

His wit never faltered. When he heard that six people had suffered heart failure following an air-raid warning, he observed that he himself was more likely to die of overeating. Yet he did not want to perish quite yet, "when so many interesting things were happening." Told that the Luftwaffe had bombed ironworks owned by the family of Stanley Baldwin, the archappeasing thirties prime minister, he muttered, "very ungrateful of them." When his wife, Clementine, described how she had marched disgusted out of a service at St. Martin-in-the-Field after hearing its preacher deliver a pacifist sermon, Churchill said, "You ought to have cried 'Shame,' desecrating the House of God with lies." He turned to Jock Colville and said, "Tell the Minister of Information with a view to having the man pilloried." General Sir Bernard Paget exclaimed to Colville: "What a wonderful tonic he is!"

Between June and September 1940, and to a lessening degree for eighteen months thereafter, the minds of the British government and people were fixed upon the threat that Hitler would dispatch an army to invade their island. It is a perennially fascinating question, how far such a peril was ever realistic—or perceived as such by Winston Churchill. The collapse of France and expulsion of the British Army from the Continent represented the destruction of the strategic foundations upon which British policy was founded. Yet if the German victory in France had been less swift, if the Allies had become engaged in more protracted fighting, the cost in British and French blood would have been vastly greater, while it is hard to imagine any different outcome. John Kennedy was among the senior British soldiers who perceived this: "We should have had an enormous army in France if we had been allowed to go on long enough, and it would have lost its equip[men]t all the same." Sir Hugh Dowding, C-in-C of Fighter Command, claimed that on news of the French surrender "I went on my knees and thanked God," because no further British fighters need be vainly destroyed on the Continent. Only German perceptions of the BEF's marginal role permitted so many of Britain's soldiers to escape from the battlefield by sea not once, but twice, in June 1940. No staff college war game would have allowed so indulgent an outcome. Though it was hard to see matters in such terms at the time, if French defeat had been inevitable, Britain escaped from its consequences astonishingly lightly.

The British in June 1940 believed that they were threatened by imminent invasion followed by likely annihilation. Unsurprisingly, they thought themselves the focus of Hitler's ambitions. Few comprehended his obsession with the east. They could not know that Germany was neither militarily prepared nor psychologically committed to launch a massive amphibious operation across the Channel. The Wehrmacht needed months to digest the conquest of France and the Low Countries. The Nazis' perception of Britain and its ruling class was distorted by prewar acquaintance with so many aristocratic appeasers. Now, they confidently awaited the displacement of Churchill's government by one which acknowledged realities. "Are the English giving in? No sure signs visible yet," Goebbels wrote in his diary on June 26. "Churchill still talks big. But then he is not England." Some historians have expressed surprise that Hitler prevaricated about invasion. Yet his equivocation was matched by the Allies later in the war. For all the aggressive rhetoric of Churchill, the British for years nursed hopes that Germany would collapse without an Allied landing in France. The Americans were much relieved that Japan surrendered without being invaded. No belligerent nation risks a massive amphibious operation on a hostile shore until all other options have been exhausted. Germany in 1940 proved no exception.

Churchill's people might have slept a little easier through that summer had they perceived that they were more happily placed to withstand the siege and bombardment of their island than any other conceivable strategic scenario. Their army had been delivered from the need to face the Wehrmacht on the battlefield, and indeed would not conduct major operations on the Continent for more than three years. The Royal Navy, despite its Norwegian and Dunkirk losses, remained an immensely powerful force. A German fleet of towed barges moving across the Channel at a speed of only three or four knots would have remained within range of warship guns for many hours. On July 1, the German navy had only one heavy and two light cruisers, together with four destroyers and some E-boats, available for duty as escorts. The Royal Air Force was better organised and equipped to defend Britain against bomber attack than for any other operation of war. If a German army secured a beachhead, Churchill's land forces were unfit to expel it. But in the summer of 1940 England's moat, those twenty-one miles of choppy sea between rival chalk cliffs, represented a formidable, probably decisive obstacle to Hitler's landlubbing army.

Among the government's first concerns was that of ensuring that the Vichy French fleet did not become available to Hitler. During days of Cabinet argument on this issue, Churchill at one moment raised the possibility that the Americans might be persuaded to purchase the warships. In the event, however, a more direct and brutal option was adopted. Horace Walpole wrote two centuries earlier: "No great country was ever saved by good men, because good men will not go to the lengths that may be necessary." At Mers el-Kébir, Oran, on July 3, French commanders rejected an ultimatum from Admiral Sir James Somerville, commanding the Royal Navy's Force H offshore, either to scuttle their fleet or sail to join the British. The subsequent bombardment and destruction of France's warships was one of the most ruthless acts by a democracy in the annals of war. It resulted from a decision such as only Churchill would plausibly have taken. Yet it commands the respect of posterity, as it did of Franklin Roosevelt, as an earnest of Britain's iron determination to sustain the struggle. Churchill told the House of Commons the next day, "We had hoped until the afternoon that our terms would be accepted without bloodshed." As to passing judgement on the action, he left this "with confidence to Parliament. I leave it also to the nation, and I leave it to the United States. I leave it to the world and to history."

As MPs cheered and waved their order papers in a curiously tasteless display of enthusiasm for an action which, however necessary, had cost 1,250 French lives, Churchill resumed his seat with tears pouring down his face. He, the Francophile, perceived the bitter fruits that had been plucked at Oran. He confided later: "It was a terrible decision, like taking the life of one's own child to save the State." He feared that the immediate consequence would be to drive Vichy to join Germany in arms against Britain. But, at a moment when the Joint Intelligence Committee was warning that invasion seemed imminent, he absolutely declined to acquiesce in the risk that French capital ships might screen a German armada.

Pétain's regime did not declare war, though French bitterness about

Oran persisted for years to come. The bombardment was less decisive in its strategic achievement than Churchill claimed, because one French battle cruiser escaped, and a powerful fleet still lay at Toulon under Vichy orders. But actions sometimes have consequences which remain unperceived for long afterwards. This was the case with the attack on Mers el-Kébir, followed by the failure two months later of a Free French attempt to take over Dakar, capital of France's African colony Senegal. When Gen. Francisco Franco, Spain's dictator, submitted to Hitler his shopping list for joining the Axis, it was headed by a demand that Hitler should transfer to Spain French colonies in Africa. Yet Vichy France's rejection of both British diplomatic advances and military threats, together with the refusal of most of France's African colonies to "rally" to de Gaulle, persuaded Hitler to hope that Pétain's nation would soon become his fighting ally. He therefore refused to satisfy Franco at French expense. The attack on Oran, a painful necessity, and Dakar, an apparent fiasco, contributed significantly to keeping Spain out of the war.

One part of the British Commonwealth offered no succour to the "mother country": the Irish Free State, bitterly hostile to Britain since it gained independence in 1922, sustained nominal allegiance by a constitutional quirk, under the terms of the island's partition treaty. Churchill had heaped scorn upon Neville Chamberlain's 1938 cession of Britain's Irish "treaty ports" to the Dublin government. As first lord of the Admiralty, in 1939, he contemplated military action against Eire, as the southern Irish dominion was known. Amid the desperate circumstances of June 1940, however, he responded cautiously to a suggestion by Chamberlain—of all people—that Ireland should be obliged by force to yield up its harbours, which might play a critical role in keeping open Britain's Atlantic lifeline. Churchill opposed this, fearing a hostile reaction in the United States. Instead, the British government urged Lord Craigavon, prime minister of the Protestant north, which remained part of the United Kingdom, to seek a meeting with Irish prime minister Eamon de Valera to discuss the defence of their common island. Craigavon, like most of his fellow Ulstermen, loathed the Catholic southerners. He dismissed this notion out of hand.

Yet in late June, London presented a remarkable and radical secret proposal to Dublin: Britain would make a principled commitment to a postwar united Ireland, in return for immediate access to Irish ports and bases. Britain's ambassador in Dublin reported de Valera's stony response. The *taoiseach* would commit himself only to the neutrality of a united Ireland, though he said unconvincingly that he "might" enter the war after the British government made a public declaration of commitment to union.

The British government nonetheless urged Dublin to conduct talks with the Belfast regime about a prospective union endorsed by Britain, in return for Eire's belligerence. Chamberlain told the Cabinet, "I do not believe that the Ulster government would refuse to play their part to bring about so favourable a development." De Valera again declined to accept deferred payment. MacDonald cabled London, urging Churchill to offer personal assurances. The prime minister wrote in the margin of this message: "But all contingent upon Ulster agreeing & S. Ireland coming into the war."

On June 26, Chamberlain belatedly reported these exchanges to Craigavon, saying: "You will observe that the document takes the form of an enquiry only, because we have not felt it right to approach you officially with a request for your assent unless we had first a binding assurance from Eire that they would, if the assent were given, come into the war . . . If therefore they refuse the plan you are in no way committed, and if they accept you are still free to make your own comments or objections as may think fit." The Ulsterman cabled back: "Am profoundly shocked and disgusted by your letter making suggestions so far-reaching behind my back and without any pre-consultation with me. To such treachery to loyal Ulster I will never be a party." Chamberlain, in turn, responded equally angrily to what he perceived as Craigavon's insufferable parochialism. He concluded, "Please remember the serious nature of the situation which requires that every effort be made to meet it."

The War Cabinet, evidently unimpressed by Craigavon's anger, now strengthened its proposal to Dublin: "This declaration would take the form of a solemn undertaking that the Union is to become at an early date an accomplished fact from which there shall be no turning back." When Craigavon was informed, he responded: "Your telegram only confirms my confidential information and conviction de Valera is under German dictation and far past reasoning with. He may purposely protract negotiations till enemy has landed. Strongly advocate immediate naval occupation of harbours and military advance south."

Craigavon asserted in a personal letter to Churchill that Ulster would only participate in an All-Ireland Defence Force "if British martial law is imposed throughout the island." The two men met in London on July 7. There is no record of their conversation. It is reasonable to assume that it was frosty, but by then Churchill could assuage the Ulsterman's fears. Two days earlier, de Valera had finally rejected the British plan. He, like many

Irishmen, was convinced that Britain was doomed to lose the war. He doubted Churchill's real willingness to coerce Craigavon. If he ever seriously contemplated accepting London's terms, he also probably feared that once committed to belligerence, Ireland would become a British puppet.

Churchill makes no mention of the Irish negotiation in his war memoirs. Since the British offer to Dublin was sensational, this suggests that recollection of it brought no pleasure to the prime minister. Given de Valera's implacable hostility, the Irish snub was inevitable. But it represented a massive miscalculation by the Irish leader. Ernest Bevin wrote in confidence to an academic friend who was urging a deal on a united Ireland: "There are difficulties which appear at the moment almost insurmountable. You see, de Valera's policy is, even if we get a united Ireland, he would still remain neutral. On that, he is immovable. Were it not for this attitude, I believe a solution would be easy . . . You may rest assured that we are watching every possible chance." If Ireland had entered the war on the Allied side at any time, even after the United States became a belligerent in December 1941 and Allied victory was assured, American cash would have flooded into the country, perhaps advancing Ireland's economic takeoff by two generations.

The exchanges of July were not quite the end of the story. In December 1940, Churchill suggested in a letter to President Roosevelt that, "if the Government of Eire would show its solidarity with the democracies of the English-speaking world . . . a Council of Defence of all Ireland could be set up out of which the unity of the island would probably in some form or other emerge after the war." Here was a suggestion much less explicit than that of the summer, obviously modified by the diminution of British peril. It is impossible to know whether, if de Valera had acceded to the British proposal of June 1940, Churchill would indeed have obliged the recalcitrant Ulster Protestants to accept union with the south. Given his high-handed treatment of other dominions and colonies in the course of the war—not least the surrender of British overseas bases to the United States—it seems by no means impossible. So dire was Britain's predicament, of such vital significance in the U-boat war were Irish ports and airfields, that it seemed worth almost any price to secure them. But the gambit failed, leaving Britain and Ireland alike losers.

Churchill threw himself into the struggle to prepare his island to resist invasion. He decreed that if the Germans landed, all measures including poison gas were to be employed against them. On July 6, he inspected an exercise in Kent. "Winston was in great form," Ironside wrote in his diary, "and gave us lunch at Chartwell in his cottage. Very wet but nobody minded at all." A consignment of 250,000 rifles and 300 old 75mm field guns arrived from America—poor weapons, but desperately welcome. Ironside expected the German invasion on July 9, and was surprised when it did not come. On July 10, instead, the Luftwaffe launched its first big raid on Britain, by seventy aircraft against southern Wales dockyards. Churchill knew this was the foretaste of a heavy and protracted air assault. Two days later, he visited RAF Hurricane squadrons at Kenley. Straining to harness every aid to public morale, he demanded that military bands should play in the streets. He urged attention to gas masks, because he feared that Hitler would unleash chemical weapons. He resisted the evacuation of children from cities, and deplored the shipment of the offspring of the rich to sanctuary in the United States. He argued vigorously against overstringent rationing, and deplored pessimism wherever it was encountered. Dill, less than two months head of the army, was already provoking his mistrust: the CIGS "strikes me as tired, disheartened and overimpressed with the might of Germany," wrote the prime minister to Eden. In Churchill's eyes, all through the long months which followed, defeatism was the only crime beyond forgiveness.

On July 19, Ironside was dismissed as C-in-C Home Forces, and replaced by Sir Alan Brooke. Ironside wanted to meet an invasion with a thin crust of coastal defences, and to rely chiefly upon creating strong lines inland. Brooke, by contrast, proposed swift counterattacks with mobile forces. Brooke and Churchill were surely correct in perceiving that if the Germans secured a lodgement and airfields in southeast England, the battle for Britain would be irretrievably lost. Inland defences were worthless, save for sustaining a sense of purpose among those responsible for building them.

Peter Fleming argued in his later history of the period that although the British went through the motions of anticipating invasion, they did not in their hearts believe in such an eventuality, because they had no historical experience of it: "They paid lip-service to reality. They took the precautions which the Government advised, made the sacrifices which it required of them and worked like men possessed . . . But . . . they found it impossible, however steadfastly they gazed into the future, to fix in a satisfactory focus the terrible contingencies which invasion was expected to bring forth." Fleming added a perceptive observation: "The menace of invasion was at once a tonic and a drug . . . The extreme and disheartening bleakness of their long-term prospects was obscured by the melodramatic nature of the predicament in which . . . the fortunes of war had placed them."

Churchill understood the need to mobilise the British people to action for its own sake, rather than allowing them time to brood, to contemplate dark realities. He himself thought furiously about the middle distance. "When I look around to see how we can win the war," he wrote to Beaverbrook on July 10, "I see only one sure path. We have no continental army which can defeat the German military power. The blockade is broken and Hitler has Asia and probably Africa to draw upon. Should he be repulsed here or not try invasion, he will recoil eastward and we have nothing to stop him. But there is one thing that will bring him back and bring him down, and that is an absolutely devastating, exterminating attack by very heavy bombers from this country upon the Nazi homeland." Likewise, at Chequers on July 14: "Hitler must invade or fail. If he fails he is bound to go east, and fail he will." Churchill had no evidential basis in intelligence for his assertion that the Germans might lunge towards Russia. At this time, only a remarkable instinct guided him, shared by few others. Not until March 1941, three months before the event, did British intelligence decide that a German invasion of the Soviet Union was likely.

As for aircraft production, while fighters were the immediate need, the prime minister urged the creation of the largest possible bomber force. This, a desperate policy born out of desperate circumstances and the absolute lack of any plausible alternative, would achieve destructive maturity only years later, when victory was assured by other means. Churchill appointed Admiral Sir Roger Keyes, the brainless old hero of the 1918 Zeebrugge raid, to become director of combined operations with a brief to prepare to launch raids on the continent of Europe. He wanted no pin-prick fiascos, he said, but instead attacks by five to ten thousand men. He ordered the establishment of the Special Operations Executive (SOE), under the direction of Hugh Dalton as minister of economic warfare, with a mandate to "set Europe ablaze." He endorsed de Gaulle as the voice and leader of Free France. Brooke, at Gosport with Churchill on July 17, found him "in wonderful spirits and full of offensive plans for next summer." Most of the commitments made in those days remained ineffectually implemented for years to come. Yet they represented earnests for the future that inspired Churchill's colleagues, which was, of course, exactly as he intended.

And above all, in those days, there were his words. "Faith is given to us to help and comfort us when we stand in awe before the unfurling scroll of human destiny," he told the British people in a broadcast on July 14, Bastille Day, in which he recalled attending a magnificent military parade in Paris just a year before. "And I proclaim my faith that some of us will live to see a Fourteenth of July when a liberated France will once again rejoice in her greatness and her glory." He continued:

> Here in this strong City of Refuge which enshrines the title-deeds of human progress and is of deep consequence to Christian civilization; here, girt about by the seas and oceans where the Navy reigns; shielded from above by the prowess and devotion of our airmen—we await undismayed the impending assault. Perhaps it will come tonight. Perhaps it will come next week. Perhaps it will never come. We must show ourselves equally capable of meeting a sudden violent shock or—what is perhaps a harder test—a prolonged vigil. But be the ordeal sharp or long, or both, we shall seek no terms, we shall tolerate no parley; we may show mercy—we shall ask for none.

One of the prime minister's listeners wrote: "Radio sets were not then very powerful, and there was always static. Families had to sit near the set, with someone always fiddling with the knobs. It was like sitting round a hearth, with someone poking the fire; and to that hearth came the crackling voice of Winston Churchill." Vere Hodgson, a thirty-nine-year-old London woman, wrote: "Gradually we came under the spell of that wonderful voice and inspiration. His stature grew larger and larger, until it filled our sky." Vita Sackville-West wrote to her husband, Harold Nicolson, saying that one of Churchill's speeches "sent shivers (not of fear) down my spine. I think that one of the reasons why one is stirred by his Elizabethan phrases is that one feels the whole massive backing of power and resolve behind them, like a great fortress: they are never words for words' sake." Mollie Panter-Downes told readers of the *New Yorker*: "Mr. Churchill is the only man in England today who consistently interprets the quiet but completely resolute national mood."

Isaiah Berlin wrote: "Like a great actor—perhaps the last of his kind—upon the stage of history, he speaks his memorable lines with a large, unhurried, and stately utterance in a blaze of light, as is appropriate to a man who knows that his work and his person will remain the objects of scrutiny and judgement to many generations." Tory MP Cuthbert Headlam wrote on July 16: "It is certainly his hour—and the confidence in him is growing on all sides." Churchill's sublime achievement was to rouse the most ordinary people to extraordinary perceptions of their own destiny. Eleanor Silsby, an elderly psychology lecturer living in south London, wrote to a friend in America on July 23, 1940: "I won't go on about the war. But I just want to say that we are proud to have the honour of fighting alone for the things that matter much more than life and death. It makes me hold my chin high to think, not just of being English, but of having been chosen to come at this hour for this express purpose of saving the world . . . I should never have thought that I could approve of war . . . There is surprisingly little anger or hate in this business—it is just a job that has to be done . . . This is Armageddon." Churchill was much moved by receiving through the post a box of cigars from a working girl, who said that she had saved her wages to buy them for him. One morning at Downing Street, John Martin found himself greeting a woman who had called to offer a £60,000 pearl necklace to the service of the state. Told of this, Churchill quoted Macaulay:

> *"Romans in Rome's quarrel,*
> *Spared neither land nor gold"*

On July 19, Hitler addressed the Reichstag and the world, publicly offering Britain a choice between peace and "unending suffering and misery." Churchill responded, "I don't propose to say anything in reply to Herr Hitler's speech, not being on speaking terms with him." He urged Lord Lothian, Britain's ambassador in Washington, to press the Americans to fulfil Britain's earlier request for the "loan" of old destroyers. On August 1, he delivered a magisterial rebuke to the Foreign Office for the elaborate phrasing of its proposed response to a message from the king of Sweden, who was offering to mediate between Britain and Germany. "The draft errs," he wrote, "in trying to be too clever, and to enter into refinements of policy unsuited to the tragic simplicity and grandeur of the times and the issues at stake." That day, Hitler issued his Directive No. 17, unleashing the Luftwaffe's massive air campaign against Britain.

FOUR

The Battle of Britain

THUS BEGAN THE events that will define for eternity the image of Britain in the summer of 1940. Massed formations of German bombers with their accompanying fighter escorts droned across blue skies towards Kent and Sussex, to be met by intercepting Hurricanes and Spitfires, tracing white condensation trails through the thin air. The most aesthetically beautiful aircraft the world has ever seen, their grace enhanced in the eyes of posterity by their role as the saviours of freedom, pierced the bomber formations, diving, twisting, banking, hammering fire. Onlookers craned their heads upwards, mesmerised by the spectacle. Shopworkers and housewives, bank clerks and schoolchildren heard the clatter of machine guns and found aircraft fragments and empty cartridge cases tinkling onto their streets and littering suburban gardens; they sometimes even met fallen aircrew of both sides, stumbling to their front doors.

Stricken planes spewing smoke plunged to the ground in cascades of churned-up earth, if their occupants were fortunate enough to crash-land, or exploded into fiery fragments. This was a contest like no other in human experience, witnessed by millions of people continuing humdrum daily lives, bemused by the fact that kettles boiled in kitchens, flowers bloomed in garden borders, newspapers were delivered and honey was served for tea a few thousand feet beneath one of the decisive battlefields of history. Pilots who faced oblivion all day sang in their "locals" that night, if they lived. Their schoolboy slang—"wizard prang" and "gone for a burton"—passed into the language, fulfilling the observation of a French writer quoted by Dr. Johnson: "*Il y a beaucoup de puérilités dans la guerre.*"

Once bombs began to fall on Britain's cities in August, their blasts caused a layer of dust to settle upon every surface, casting over the urban fabric of the country a drab greyness which persisted throughout the blitz. Yet islands of seasonal beauty survived. John Colville was struck by the tortoiseshell butterflies fluttering gaily over the lawn behind Downing

Street: "I shall always associate that garden in summer, the corner of the Treasury outlined against a china-blue sky, with 1940." Churchill, intensely vulnerable to sentiment, witnessed many scenes which caused him to succumb. While driving to Chequers one day, he glimpsed a line of people. Motioning the driver to stop, he asked his detective to enquire what they were queuing for. Told that they hoped to buy birdseed, Churchill's private secretary John Martin noted: "Winston wept."

July 10 was later officially designated as the first day of the Battle of Britain, though to the aircrew of both sides it seemed little different from those which preceded and followed it. The next month was characterised by skirmishes over the Channel and south coast, in which the Luftwaffe never lost more than 16 aircraft in a day's combat—on July 25—and Fighter Command not more than 15. Churchill insisted that coastal convoys should continue to sail the Narrows, partly to assert British rights of navigation, partly to provoke the Luftwaffe into action on what were deemed favourable terms for the RAF. On August 11, attrition sharply increased: 30 British aircraft were shot down for 35 German. In the month thereafter, Göring launched his major assault on Fighter Command, its airfields, control centres and radar stations. Between August 12 and 23, the RAF lost 133 fighters in action and a further 44 to mishaps, while the Luftwaffe lost 299 aircraft to all causes.

By early autumn, British casualties and damage to installations had reached critical proportions. Among Dowding's squadron commanders, 11 out of 46 were killed or wounded in July and August, along with 39 of 97 flight commanders. One Fighter Command pilot, twenty-one-year-old George Barclay of 249 Squadron, a Norfolk parson's son, wrote after the bitter battles of September 7: "The odds today have been unbelievable (and we are all really very shaken!) . . . There are bombs and things falling around tonight and a terrific gun barrage. Has a blitz begun? The wing-commander's coolness is amazing and he does a lot to keep up our morale—very necessary tonight." As in every battle, not all participants showed the stuff of heroes. After repeated German bombings of Manston, one of the RAF's forward airfields, ground crews huddled in its air-raid shelters and rejected pleas to emerge and service Hurricanes. The work was done by off-duty Blenheim night-fighter crews.

The prime minister intently followed the progress of each day's clashes. The Secret Intelligence Service warned that a German landing in Britain was imminent. Yet it was not easy to maintain the British people at the highest pitch of expectancy. On August 3, Churchill felt obliged to issue this statement: "The Prime Minister wishes it to be known that the possibility of German attempts at invasion has by no means passed away."

He carried this spirit into his own household. Downing Street and the underground Central War Rooms were protected by Royal Marine pensioners, Chequers by a Guards company. The prime minister took personal charge of several practise alerts, against the possibility of German paratroop landings in St. James's Park. "This sounds very peculiar today, but was taken quite seriously by us all in the summer of 1940," a War Cabinet Secretariat officer recalled.

Churchill practised with a revolver and with his own Mannlicher on a rifle range at Chequers, entirely in earnest and not without pleasurable anticipation. It was odd that the Germans, having used special forces effectively in the May blitzkrieg on the Continent, never thereafter showed much interest in their possibilities. A direct assault on Churchill in 1940, most plausibly by a paratroop landing at Chequers, could have paid handsome dividends. Britain was fortunate that such piratical ventures loomed far less prominently in Hitler's mind, and in Wehrmacht doctrine, than in Churchill's imagination. In the summer of 1940, the Germans had yet to understand how pivotal to Britain's war effort was the person of the prime minister.

The supply of aircraft to Fighter Command was a critical factor. While propaganda lauded the achievements of the Ministry of Aircraft Production, the conduct of its leader, Lord Beaverbrook, provoked bitter criticism in Whitehall. For some weeks, he ran the department from his private residence, Stornoway House, in Arlington Street, behind the Ritz Hotel. It is easy to perceive why many people, Clementine Churchill prominent among them, deplored the press baron, then sixty-one. He was a former appeaser who had secretly subsidised the prewar political career of Sir Samuel Hoare, most egregious of Chamberlain's ministers. In January 1940, Beaverbrook addressed the Duke of Windsor—the former King Edward VIII—about a possible peace offer to Germany. On May 6, he asserted in his own *Daily Express* that London would not be bombed, and that the Germans would not attack the Maginot Line. Deputy Führer Rudolf Hess later told the press baron: "Hitler likes you very much." It was once said of Beaverbrook's newspapers that they never espoused a cause which was both honourable and successful. The king opposed his inclusion in the Cabinet, but among all men Churchill chose this old colleague from the 1917–18 Lloyd George government as his luncheon companion on May 10, 1940.

Beaverbrook cast a spell over Churchill which remained unbroken by his old friend's petulance, disloyalty and outrageous mischief-making. The Canadian-born magnate's command of wealth, such as the prime minister himself had always craved, impressed him almost mystically.

Churchill recognised in "dear Max" a fellow original, full of impish fun which was scantily available in Downing Street that summer. It is often remarked that Churchill had acolytes, but few intimates. More than any other person save his wife, Beaverbrook eased the loneliness of the prime minister's predicament and responsibilities. Churchill's belief in his old comrade's fitness for government was excessive. But who among Beaverbrook's Cabinet colleagues was more blessed with dynamism and decision, such as seemed vital to meet the challenges of 1940?

Daily pressures upon the prime minister were unrelenting. The War Cabinet met 108 times in the ninety-two days between May 10 and July 31. His black dispatch box contained a pile of papers which seemed never to diminish, "a farrago of operational, civil, political and scientific matters." Overriding War Office objections, he promoted Maj. Millis Jefferis, a clever soldier engaged in weapons experimental work, and ordered that he should report directly to Lindemann at the Cabinet Office. He insisted that the maverick armoured enthusiast Maj. Gen. Percy Hobart should be given suitable employment, overruling Dill's objections with the assertion that he should remember that not only good boys help to win wars: "It is the sneaks and stinkers as well." He harassed the service chiefs in support of one of "the Prof's" most foolish personal initiatives, aerial rocket deployments against enemy aircraft. Sir Hugh Dowding of Fighter Command wanted his pilots to kill German aircrew who took to their parachutes. Churchill, recoiling from what he perceived as dishonourable conduct, would have none of this. Travelling with Roger Keyes at the end of July, he told the admiral that he had "many detractors" as chief of combined operations. Keyes responded tartly, "So had you, but you are now there in spite of it." Churchill said, "There are no competitors for my job now—I didn't get it until they had got into a mess."

Beyond pressing the urgency of fighter production, Churchill made few tactical interventions in the Battle of Britain, but one of the most justly celebrated took place in the Downing Street Cabinet Room on June 21. There was fierce controversy between Lindemann and Sir Henry Tizard, chairman of the Aeronautical Research Committee, about a suggestion from air intelligence that the Luftwaffe intended to use electronic beams to guide its night raiders to British targets. Tizard dismissed the feasibility of such a technique. Churchill summoned him, together with Lindemann and senior airmen, to a meeting attended by the twenty-eight-year-old scientific intelligence officer R. V. Jones. It soon became obvious that Jones alone understood the issue. Though awed by finding himself in such company, he said to the prime minister, "Would it help, sir, if I told you the story right from the start?" Churchill was initially taken aback, then said, "Well, yes, it would!" Jones spent twenty minutes explaining how his own researches, aided by "Ultra"—German signals decrypted by the code breakers at Bletchley Park, which were still fragmentary at this stage of the war—had led him to an understanding of the Luftwaffe's navigational aids. Churchill, characteristically, found himself paraphrasing in his mind lines from *The Ingoldsby Legends:* "But now one Mr. Jones / Comes forth and depones / That fifteen years since, he had heard certain groans."

When Jones finished, Tizard expressed renewed scepticism. Churchill overruled him. He ordered that the scientist should be given facilities to explore the German beams. Initially much dismayed by Jones's revelations, he exulted when the young man told him that, once wavelengths were identified, the transmissions could be jammed. The "boffin" himself, of course, was enchanted by the prime minister's receptiveness: "Here was strength, resolution, humour, readiness to listen, to ask the searching question and, when convinced, to act." The beams were indeed jammed. Jones became one of the outstanding British intelligence officers of the war. The episode showed Churchill at his best: accessible, imaginative, penetrating, decisive and always suggestible about technological innovation.

From the summer of 1940 onwards, decrypts of German signals assumed a steadily rising importance to the British war effort. Selected samples code-named Boniface were delivered to Churchill daily, in a special box to which even the private secretaries were denied a key. The Chiefs of Staff deplored his direct access to Ultra, arguing that he often derived false impressions from raw intelligence, and misjudged the significance of enemy exchanges. Yet Ultra armed the prime minister for the direction of the war in a fashion unknown to any other national leader in history. It played a critical role in guiding Churchill's own perceptions of strategy, both for good and ill, and fortified his confidence in overruling commanders.

The Bletchley Park code-breaking operation, still in its infancy in 1940, was the greatest British achievement of the war, and from 1941 became the cornerstone of the nation's intelligence operations. The Secret Intelligence Service was directed by Brig. Sir Stewart Menzies, "C," a quintessential officer and gentleman, former president of "Pop" and captain of the cricket team at Eton, Life Guardsman and member of White's club. Menzies owed his appointment to Halifax. His record was more impressive as a Whitehall intriguer than as a spymaster. SIS never gained significant "humint"—agent intelligence—about the Axis high command. Before Ultra hit its stride, most of Menzies's assessments of—

for instance—German intentions in 1940–41 were wildly mistaken. He had little to do with the prewar development of Bletchley Park, but by a skilful coup gained administrative control of its operations. He made it his business to deliver personally to the prime minister the most delectable code breakers' delicacies, and in consequence was always a welcome visitor at Downing Street. All national leaders gain a frisson of excitement from access to secret intelligence. This was especially and understandably so of Churchill. Menzies, purveyor of Bletchley's golden eggs, gained exaggerated credit and influence as owner of the goose.

Amid the great issues of national defence, there were constitutional responsibilities, including regular meetings with the monarch. The king and queen were "a little ruffled," Jock Colville learned, "by the offhand way he treated them—says he will come at six, puts it off until 6.30 by telephone, then comes at seven." Only a king would dare to resent his prime minister's tardiness at a time when Churchill had to supervise the creation of the Takoradi aircraft ferry route across Africa to Egypt, visit blitzed airfields, bully the Treasury into paying compensation for private homes destroyed by bombs, and write at length in his own hand to Neville Chamberlain, now stricken with the cancer that would kill him within three months. There were certainly difficulties, the prime minister acknowledged to his predecessor in a letter of August 31: "however when all is said and done I must say I feel pretty good about this war."

But Churchill was exasperated on August 10 when Sir Stafford Cripps, the Moscow ambassador, submitted to him a paper detailing proposals on postwar reconstruction. There would come a time for such things, but it was not the summer of 1940. Only a fool could have thought otherwise. Meanwhile, Britain was running out of money. The war was costing £55 million a week, and Washington was implacable in its demands for immediate cash payment for every ton of weapons and supplies shipped across the Atlantic. Kingsley Wood, the chancellor, suggested melting down the nation's gold wedding rings, which would raise £20 million. The prime minister said that the Treasury should hold back from such a drastic measure, unless it became necessary to make a parade of it, to shame the United States. On August 16, he visited Fighter Command's 11 Group operations room, and intently watched progress of the day's fighting on the huge plotting board. On the way back to Chequers in his car, "Pug" Ismay, his chief of staff, made some remark. Churchill said: "Don't speak to me. I have never been so moved." After a few minutes' silence, he leaned forward and said, "Never in the field of human conflict has so much been owed by so many to so few." Ismay wrote, "The words burned into my brain." That day, the Combined Intelligence Centre reported its belief that Hitler would make no decision about invasion until the outcome of the air battle became clear. On August 24, the first German bombs fell on outer London, and Fighter Command's airfields were again badly hit.

Sunday, September 1, yet another day when intelligence suggested that invasion might come, passed without incident. On the third, for the second time the War Cabinet met in the new underground Central War Rooms. Churchill declared it to be "lamentable" that only 500,000 rifles were scheduled to be produced by British manufacturers before the end of 1941. On September 5, he used the same adjective to deplore the "passivity" to which the Royal Navy seemed reduced when it declined to bombard new German batteries at Cape Gris-Nez, only twenty miles from the English south coast. He told Cunningham, Mediterranean C-in-C, that the supposed vulnerability of his fleet to Italian aircraft was "exaggerated." He urged the swift construction of landing craft, to facilitate the raids on enemy shores which he was so impatient to launch.

A wag in the War Office discovered in the book of Job a description of a warhorse which the generals thought entirely fitting to their political master: "He paweth in the valley, and rejoiceth in his strength; he goeth on to meet the armed men. He mocketh at fear, and is not affrighted; neither turneth he back from the sword. The quiver rattleth against him, the glittering spear and the shield. He swalloweth the ground with fierceness and rage . . . He saith among the trumpets, Ha, ha; and he smelleth the battle afar off, the thunder of the captains, and the shouting." Yet while Churchill never disdained the gestures and symbols of warriorhood, he strove also for substance. Each night, he told Colville, "I try myself by court martial to see if I have done anything effective during the day. I don't mean just pawing the ground—anyone can go through the motions—but something really effective."

It is hard for a historian, as it was for Churchill's contemporaries, to conceive what it was like for a man to bear sole responsibility for preserving European civilisation. Harold Nicolson wrote of the prime minister's remoteness from ordinary mortals. His eyes were "glaucous, vigilant, angry, combative, visionary and tragic . . . the eyes of a man who is much preoccupied and is unable to rivet his attention on minor things . . . But in another sense they are the eyes of a man faced by an ordeal or tragedy, and combining vision, truculence, resolution and great unhappiness." Throughout the war, there were moments when Churchill was oppressed by loneliness, which only Beaverbrook's company seemed able to assuage.

It was by his personal choice, indeed unflagging insistence, that he delegated to others few of the responsibilities of supreme command. But the thrill and exaltation of playing out his role gave way, at times, to a despondency which required all his powers to overcome. In 1940, he sustained his spirit wonderfully well, but in the later war years he became prone to outbursts of self-pity, often accompanied by tears.

His personal staff's awareness of the prime minister's burden caused them to forgive his outbursts of discourtesy and intemperance. Ministers and commanders were less sympathetic. Their criticisms of Churchill's behaviour were human enough, and objectively just. But they reflected lapses of imagination. Few men in human history had borne such a load, which was ever at the forefront of his consciousness, and even subconsciousness. Dreams drifted through his sleeps, though he seldom revealed their nature to others. What is astonishing is that, in his waking hours, he preserved such gaiety. Although an intensely serious man, he displayed a capacity for fun as remarkable as his powers of concentration and memory, and his unremitting commitment to hard labour. Seldom, if ever, has a great national leader displayed such power to entertain his people, stirring them to laughter even amid the tears of war.

Churchill never doubted his own genius (subordinates often wished that he would). But there were many moments when his confidence in a happy outcome faltered, amid bad tidings from the battlefield. He believed that destiny had marked him to enter history as the saviour of Western civilisation, and this conviction coloured his smallest words and deeds. When a Dover workman said to his mate, as Churchill passed, "There goes the bloody British Empire," the prime minister was enchanted. "*Very* nice," he lisped to Jock Colville, his face wreathed in smiles. But, in profound contrast to Hitler and Mussolini, he preserved a humanity, an awareness of himself as mortal clay, which seldom lost its power to touch the hearts of those who served him, just as the brilliance of his conversation won their veneration.

He was fearless about everything save the possibility of defeat. Hurrying from Downing Street to the Annexe with Colville one day, in his customary uniform of short black coat, striped trousers and white-spotted blue bow tie, they heard the whistle of descending bombs. The young official took cover as two explosions resounded nearby. He rose to observe the prime minister still striding up King Charles Street, gold-headed walking stick in hand.

Disraeli said: "Men should always be difficult. I can't bear men who come and dine with you when you want them." When taking dictation, Churchill, with his tempestuous moods and unsocial hours, certainly fulfilled this requirement. The prime minister's typists were expected instantly to comprehend the meaning of some mumbled injunction, such as "Gimme 'Pug'!" They were required to respect every nuance of his precision of language. Alan Brooke was once outraged when Churchill shouted down the telephone to him, "Get off, you fool!" It required intercession by the staff to soothe the general's ruffled feathers with the explanation that the prime minister, who was in bed when he called Brooke, had been telling Smokey the black cat to stop biting his toes. Jock Colville and the king's assistant private secretary Tommy Lascelles, lunching together one day, debated "whether very great men usually had a touch of charlatanism in them," and of course they were thinking of the prime minister. Some fastidious souls recoiled from Churchill's perceived ruthlessness, though U.S. military attaché Raymond Lee applauded him as "an unscrupulously rough-and-tumble fighter . . . perfectly at home in his dealings with Hitler and Mussolini."

Churchill was self-obsessed, yet displayed spasms of concern for his intimates just often enough to prevent them from becoming disgusted by his selfishness. After one outburst, he suddenly put his hand on private secretary John Martin's shoulder and said, "You know, I may seem to be very fierce, but I am fierce only with one man—Hitler." He expressed regret that he had lacked leisure to get to know Martin at the start of their relationship, back in May.

He was always happy to reminisce about himself, but had no small talk, in the sense of being willing to display a polite interest in the affairs of others, save those important to the state. He was reluctant even to pretend to pay attention to people who failed to capture his interest. Leo Amery contrasted him with Britain's First World War leader: "Ll[oyd] G[eorge] was purely external and receptive, the result of intercourse with his fellow men, and non-existent in their absence, while Winston is literary and expressive of himself with hardly any contact with other minds." "Pug" Ismay shook his head in dismay when the prime minister once wantonly kept an entire ship's crew waiting half an hour to be addressed by him: "It's very naughty of the PM. It's this unbridled power."

Churchill's doctor Sir Charles Wilson wrote of "the formidable ramparts of indifference which he presents to women," and which only his wife, Clementine, and their daughters were sometimes capable of scaling. Clementine—highly strung, intensely moral, sensitive to vulgarity—was often ignored, mauled, taken for granted. Yet beyond her fierce loyalty to her husband, she marvellously sustained her commitment to rebuke his excesses, to repair the fractured china of his relationships. On June 27, she wrote a letter which has become justly famous:

Darling Winston, One of the men in your entourage (a devoted friend) has been to me & told me that there is a danger of your being generally disliked by your colleagues and subordinates because of your rough sarcastic & overbearing manner . . . My darling Winston—I must confess that I have noticed a deterioration in your manner; & you are not so kind as you used to be. It is for you to give the Orders & if they are bungled—except for the King, the Archbishop of Canterbury & the Speaker—you can sack anyone & everyone. Therefore with this terrific power you must combine urbanity, kindness & if possible Olympic [*sic*] calm . . . I cannot bear that those who serve the country & your self should not love you as well as admire and respect you. Besides you won't get the best results by irascibility & rudeness. They will breed either dislike or a slave mentality—"Rebellion in War Time being out of the question!" Please forgive your loving devoted & watchful Clemmie.

This note, of which the signature was decorated with a cat drawing, she tore up. But four days later, she pieced it together and gave it to her husband—the only letter she is known to have written to him in 1940. The country, as much as the recipient, owed a debt to such a wife. More than any other human being, Clementine preserved Churchill from succumbing to the corruption of wielding almost absolute authority over his nation.

Churchill seldom found a moment to read a book in 1940, but he addressed with close attention each day's newspapers, windows upon the minds of the British people. His hunger for information was insatiable. Not infrequently, he telephoned personally to the *Daily Telegraph* or *Daily Express* at midnight, to enquire what their front page "splash" for the next day would be. One night at Chequers, he caused Colville to ring the Admiralty three times in quest of news. On the third occasion, the exasperated duty captain at the other end gave way to invective. The prime minister, overhearing the babble of speech from the other end, assumed that at least a cruiser must have been sunk. He seized the receiver from Colville's hand, "to find himself subjected to a flow of uncomplimentary expletives which clearly fascinated him. After listening for a minute or two he explained with great humility that he was only the Prime Minister and that he had been wondering whether there was any naval news."

He detested wanton as distinct from purposeful physical activity, and enjoyed relaxing with bezique or backgammon, which could be indulged without abandoning conversation. His companions remarked on his lack of manual dexterity, evident when his pudgy fingers shuffled a pack of cards. "He has more wit than humour," suggested Charles Wilson. Colville noticed that, while Churchill often smiled and chuckled, he never laughed outright, perhaps perceiving this as a vulgarity. The devotion he inspired in most of those who served him derived from a deportment which was at once magnificent and devoid of pomposity. In the early hours of a Sunday morning in his bedroom at Chequers, Colville recorded that Churchill "collapsed between the chair and the stool, ending in a most absurd position on the floor with his feet in the air. Having no false dignity, he treated it as a complete joke and repeated several times, 'a real Charlie Chaplin!' " He displayed a lack of embarrassment about his own nakedness characteristic of English public schoolboys, soldiers and patricians accustomed to regard servants as mere extensions of the furniture.

He inspired more equivocal sentiments in his ministers and service chiefs. They were obliged to endure his monologues and sometimes rambling reminiscences, when it would have been more useful for him to heed their reports and—so they thought—their opinions. "Winston feasts on the sound of his adjectives," wrote Charles Wilson, "he likes to use four or five words all with the same meaning as an old man shows you his orchids; not to show them off, but just because he loves them. The people in his stories do not come to life; they are interred in a great sepulchre of words . . . So it happens that his audience, tired by the long day, only wait for the chance to slip off to bed, leaving Winston still talking to those who have hesitated to get up and go."

His changeability, sometimes on matters of the utmost gravity, exasperated those who themselves bore large responsibilities. Ian Jacob observed: "No one could predict what his mind would be on any problem." It was galling for an exhausted general or administrator, denied the prime minister's powers of choosing his hours, to hear that Churchill could not discuss vital matters in the afternoon, because a note bearing the sacrosanct word "Resting" was pinned to his bedroom door. Then the hapless officer or minister found himself summoned to do business at midnight or later.

The most damaging criticism of Churchill made by important people was that he was intolerant of evidence unless it conformed to his own instinct, and was sometimes wilfully irrational. Displays of supreme wisdom were interspersed with outbursts of childish petulance. Yet when the arguments were over, the shouting done, on important matters he usually deferred to reason. In much the same way, subordinates exasperated by his excesses in "normal" times—insofar as war admitted any—marvelled at the manner in which the prime minister rose to crisis. Bad news brought out the best in him. Disasters inspired responses which compelled recognition of his greatness. Few colleagues doubted his genius, and all admired his unswerving commitment to waging war. John Martin wrote of "the ferment of ideas, the persistence in flogging proposals, the goading of commanders to attack—these were all expressions of that blazing, explosive energy without which the vast machine, civilian as well as military, could not have been moved forward so steadily or steered through so many setbacks and difficulties." Churchill conducted the affairs of his nation with a self-belief that was sometimes misplaced, but which offered an elixir of hope to those chronically troubled by rational fears. Amid Britain's sea of troubles, he represented a beacon of warmth and humanity, as well as of will and supreme courage, for which even the most exalted and sceptical of his fellow countrymen acknowledged gratitude.

A widespread illusion persists, that in 1940 Churchill broadcast constantly. In reality, he delivered only seven speeches over the BBC between May and December, roughly one a month. But the impact of these was enormous, upon a nation which in those days clung to its radio receivers as storm-bound sailors once lashed themselves to the masts of their ships. There were no advancing British armies to follow on the map, no fleets reporting victories. Instead the prime minister's rolling periods, his invincible certainties in a world of raving tyrants, anchored his people and their island.

Few interventions of his own that summer were more significant than that which he made on August 23, at the height of the perceived peril of German invasion. Britain's threadbare defences were further denuded by the dispatch to Gen. Sir Archibald Wavell's Middle East Command of 154 priceless tanks, to resist the anticipated Italian assault on Egypt. This was one of Churchill's most difficult decisions of the war. Eden and Dill deserve credit for urging it, at first in the face of the prime minister's doubts. It is impossible that they could have made such a commitment without a profound, almost perverse, belief that Hitler would not risk invasion—and perhaps also a recognition that Britain's defence rested overwhelmingly on the Royal Navy and RAF rather than the army.

It is not surprising that an ignorant civilian such as "Chips" Channon should have written on September 16 of expecting "almost certain invasion." It is more remarkable that Britain's military commanders and intelligence chiefs shared this fear, supposing that a massive German descent might take place without warning. Amphibious operations, opposed landings where port facilities are unavailable, do not require mere mechanical transfers of troops from sea to shore. They rank among the most difficult and complex of all operations of war. Two years of planning and prepara-

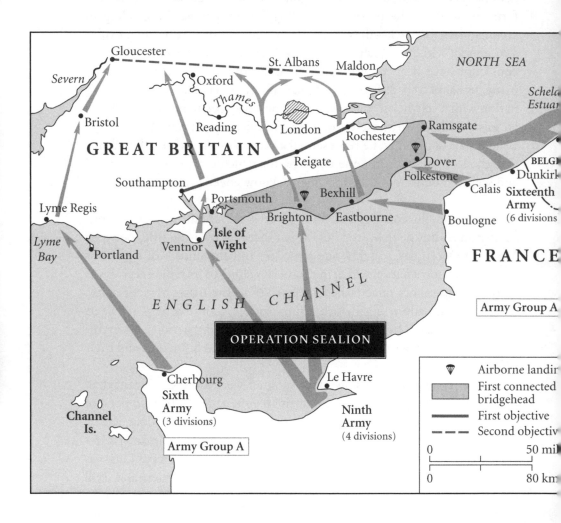

OPERATION SEALION

NORTH SEA

Schelda Estuary

GREAT BRITAIN

FRANCE

ENGLISH CHANNEL

Lyme Bay

Channel Is.

Gloucester
St. Albans
Maldon
Oxford
Thames
Severn
Bristol
Reading
London
Ramsgate
Reigate
Rochester
Dover
Folkestone
BELGI
Dunkirk
Calais
Sixteenth
Army
(6 divisions)
Southampton
Portsmouth
Bexhill
Isle of
Wight
Brighton
Eastbourne
Boulogne
Lyme Regis
Ventnor
Portland

Cherbourg
Le Havre
Sixth
Army
(3 divisions)
Ninth
Army
(4 divisions)

Army Group A

Army Group A

Airborne landir

First connected
bridgehead

First objective

Second objectiv

0   50 mi

0   80 km

tion were needed in advance of the return to France of Allied armies in June 1944. It is true that, in the summer of 1940, Britain lay almost naked, while four years later Hitler's Atlantic Wall was formidably fortified and garrisoned. In 1940, Britain lacked the deep penetration of German wireless traffic which was attained later in the war, so that the Chiefs of Staff had only the patchiest picture of the Wehrmacht's movements on the Continent.

Nonetheless it remains extraordinary that, at every suitable tide until late autumn, Britain's commanders feared that a German army might arrive on the southern or eastern coast. The navy warned—though the prime minister disbelieved them—that the Germans might achieve a surprise landing of 100,000 men. The most significant enemy preparation for invasion was the assembly of 1,918 barges on the Dutch coast. Hitler's military planners envisaged putting ashore a first wave of three airborne regiments, nine divisions—and 125,000 horses—between Ramsgate and Lyme Bay, a commitment for which available shipping was wholly inadequate. Another serious problem, never resolved, was that the Wehrmacht's desired initial dawn landing required an overnight Channel passage. It would be almost impossible to embark troops and concentrate barges without attracting British notice. The defenders would be granted at least six hours of darkness in which to engage German invasion convoys, free from Luftwaffe intervention. The Royal Navy deployed around twenty destroyers at Harwich, and a similar force at Portsmouth, together with powerful cruiser elements. Channel invasion convoys would have suffered shocking, probably fatal losses. Once daylight came, German pilots had shown themselves much more skilful than those of the RAF and Fleet Air Arm in delivering attacks on shipping. The defending warships would have been badly battered. But for a German amphibious armada, the risk of destruction was enormous. It was less the RAF than the Royal Navy, outnumbering the German fleet ten to one, that provided the decisive deterrent against invasion.

The British, however, with the almost sole exception of the prime minister, perceived all the perils on their own side. Dill, the CIGS, seemed "like all the other soldiers . . . very worried and anxious about the invasion, feeling that the troops are not trained and may not be steady." Brooke, as C-in-C Home Forces, wrote on July 2 of "the nakedness of our defences." The Royal Navy was apprehensive that, if German landings began, it might not receive adequate support from the RAF. Adm. Sir Reginald Ernle-Drax, C-in-C Nore, expressed himself "not satisfied that . . . the co-operation of our fighters was assured."

The service chiefs were justified in fearing the outcome, if German forces secured a beachhead. Brooke believed, probably rightly, that if invaders got ashore, Churchill would seek to take personal command of the ground battle—with disastrous consequences. In the absence of a landing, of course, the prime minister was able to perform his extraordinary moral function. The British generals' fears of an unheralded assault reflected the trauma which defeat in France had inflicted upon them. It distorted their judgement about the limits of the possible, even for Hitler's Wehrmacht. Churchill, by contrast, was always doubtful about whether the enemy would come. He grasped the key issue: that invasion would represent a far greater gamble than Germany's May 10 attack in the west. Operation Sealion could not partially succeed. It must either achieve fulfilment or fail absolutely. Given Hitler's mastery of the Continent, and the impotence of the British Army, he had no need to stake everything upon such a throw.

But in the summer and autumn of 1940, preparing a defence against invasion was not merely essential—it represented almost the only military activity of which Britain was capable. It was vital to incite the British people. If they were allowed to lapse into passivity, staring fearfully at the array of German might, all-conquering beyond the Channel, who could say whether their will for defiance would persist? One of Churchill's great achievements, in those months, was to convince every man and woman in the country that they had roles to play in the greatest drama in their history, even if the practical utility of their actions and preparations was often pathetically small. Young Lt. Robert Hichens of the Royal Navy wrote: "I feel an immense joy at being British, the only people who have stood up to the air war blackmail."

Between August 24 and September 6, the Luftwaffe launched six hundred sorties a day. British civilians were now dying by the hundreds. Devastation mounted remorselessly. Yet September 7 marked the turning point of the Battle of Britain. Göring switched his attacks from the RAF's airfields to the city of London. A sterile debate persists, about whether Britain or Germany first provoked attacks on each other's cities. On August 25, following civilian casualties caused by Luftwaffe bombs falling on Croydon, Churchill personally ordered that the RAF's Bomber Command should retaliate against Berlin. Some senior RAF officers resisted, on the grounds that such an attack, by the forces available, could make little impact and would probably incite the Germans to much more damaging action against British urban areas. Churchill overruled them, saying: "They had bombed London, whether on purpose or not, and the British people and London especially should know that we could hit back. It would be good for the morale of us all." Some fifty British aircraft were dispatched to Berlin, and a few bombs fell on the city. Though the material damage was negligible, the Nazi leadership was indeed moved to urge a devastating response against London, though this would assuredly have come anyway.

On the night of September 7, two hundred Luftwaffe aircraft raided the capital. Air Vice Marshal Keith Park, commanding 11 Group, wrote on September 8: "It was burning all down the river. It was a horrid sight. But I looked down and said: 'Thank God for that.'" The next day, Churchill visited the capital's stricken East End. He saw misery and destruction, but knew how vastly these were to be preferred in Bethnal Green and Hackney than at Biggin Hill airfield or the south coast radar sites. The Germans had made a decisive strategic error. Thereafter, the urban centres of Britain paid a heavy price for the Luftwaffe's raids, first by day and then by night. Daylight fighting continued over southern England until the end of October. But never again was Fighter Command's survival in doubt. In a broadcast on September 11, Churchill told the British people that the German air force had "failed conspicuously" to gain air mastery over southern England. As for invasion, "we cannot be sure that they will try at all." But the danger persisted, and every precaution must be taken.

On September 12, when the prime minister visited Dungeness and North Foreland, on the Kent coast, with the C-in-C Home Forces, Alan Brooke wrote: "His popularity is astounding, everywhere crowds rush up and cheer him wildly." U.S. general Raymond Lee perceived an improvement of temper even among the governing class, formerly so sceptical of Britain's prospects. He wrote in his diary on September 15: "Thank God . . . the defeatist opinions expressed after Dunkirk are now no longer prevalent." On September 17, Churchill told the Commons that in future its sessions should not be advertised beforehand: "We ought not to flatter ourselves by imagining that we are irreplaceable," he said, addressing his fellow MPs in masterly language which suggested that he was confiding in a band of brothers, "but at the same time it cannot be denied that two or three hundred by-elections would be a quite needless complication of our affairs at this particular juncture."

Once more, he asserted serene confidence: "I feel as sure as the sun will rise tomorrow that we shall be victorious." He harangued Dalton, minister of economic warfare, with what that assiduous diarist described as his "usual vigorous rhetorical good sense," pacing up and down his room all the while: "This is a workman's war . . . The public will stand everything except optimism . . . The nation is finding the war not so unpleasant as it expected . . . The air attacks are doing much less damage than was expected before the war began . . . Don't .be like the knight in the story who was so slow in buckling on his armour that the tourney was over before he rode into the ring."

The bombs that were now falling upon city streets, as well as upon aircraft factories and dockyards, at first caused some government alarm. Cheering cockneys cried "Stick it, Winnie!" and "We can take it!" as the prime minister toured blitz-stricken areas. But was this true? Tens of thousands of fugitives from cities became "trekkers," plodding out into the countryside at dusk to escape the night raiders. There was evidence of near social breakdown in some bombed areas. Fighter Command, with its primitive air interception radar, had no effective counter to Luftwaffe assaults in darkness. Industrial production suffered severely. The destruction of homes and property, the incessant fear of bombardment, ate deep into many people's spirits.

But as the blitz continued, the nation learned to live and work with its terrors and inconveniences. Ministers' fears about morale subsided. Churchill rang Fighter Command one September night, to complain irritably to its duty officer: "I am on top of the Cabinet Office in Whitehall and can neither see nor hear a raider. Why don't you clear London of the Red warning? We have all been down too long." The RAF's daily reports of losses inflicted on the enemy cheered Churchill and his people, though they were heavily exaggerated. On August 12, for instance, Churchill was told that 62 German aircraft had been shot down for 25 British. In reality, the Luftwaffe had lost only 27 planes. Likewise, two days later, Fighter Command claimed 78 for 3 British losses, whereas Göring had lost 34 for 13 RAF fighters shot down. The Duxford wing once alleged that it had destroyed 57 Luftwaffe aircraft. The real figure proved to be 8.

This chasm between claim and actuality persisted through the battle, and indeed the war. It attained a climax after the clashes of September 11, when the RAF suggested that 89 enemy aircraft had been lost for 28 of its own. In fact, 22 German planes had been shot down for 31 British. Yet the inflated figures were very serviceable to British spirits, and a towering reality persisted: Göring's air groups were suffering unsustainable losses, two-to-one against those of Dowding's squadrons. This was partly because almost all shot-down German aircrew became prisoners, while parachuting RAF pilots could fight again. More important still, British aircraft factories were outproducing those of Germany. In 1940, the Luftwaffe received a total of 3,382 new single- and twin-engined aircraft, while 4,283 single-engined machines were delivered to the RAF. The wartime direction of British industry was flawed by many misjudgements and failures. Here, however, was a brilliant and decisive achievement.

Air Chief Marshal Sir Hugh Dowding, C-in-C of Fighter Command, was a difficult man, not for nothing nicknamed "Stuffy." He made his share of mistakes in the Battle of Britain, for instance in being slow to reinforce 11 Group when it became plain that the German effort was overwhelmingly directed against southeast England. Most of Fighter Command's tactical doctrine proved mistaken. But Dowding was more farsighted than the Air Ministry; for instance, early in the war he urged the need for radar-equipped night fighters and long-range escorts. He displayed notable tenacity of purpose and made fewer blunders than the other side, which is how all battles are won.

His most significant contribution derived from understanding that his purpose must be to sustain Fighter Command in being, rather than to hazard everything upon the destruction of enemy aircraft. Each day, he husbanded reserves for the next. Churchill never acknowledged this refinement. Dowding's policy offended the prime minister's instinct to hurl every weapon against the foe. The airman, an austere spiritualist, could not offer Churchill congenial comradeship. Dowding's remoteness rendered him unpopular with some of his officers. It was probably right to enforce his scheduled but delayed retirement when the battle was won. Nonetheless, the brutally abrupt manner in which this was done was a disgrace to the leaders of the RAF. Dowding's cautious management of his squadrons contributed importantly to British victory.

Some historians today assert that Hitler was never serious about invading Britain. This view seems quite mistaken. It is true that the German armed forces' preparations were unconvincing. British fears of imminent assault were unfounded, and reflected poorly upon the country's intelligence and defence chiefs. But Hitler the opportunist would assuredly have launched an armada, if the Luftwaffe had gained control of the airspace over the Channel and southern England. Mediterranean experience soon showed that, in a hostile air environment, the Royal Navy would have found itself in deep trouble.

The Luftwaffe failed first because Fighter Command and its associated control facilities and radar stations were superbly organised. Second, the RAF had barely sufficient Hurricanes and Spitfires, and just enough skilled pilots, to engage superior numbers of enemy aircraft—though not as much superior as contemporary legend suggested. The Luftwaffe started its campaign with 760 serviceable Messerschmitt Bf-109 fighters, its most important aircraft, against some 700 RAF Hurricanes and Spitfires. Almost as important, the Bf-109 carried only sufficient fuel to overfly southern Britain for a maximum of thirty minutes. The Luftwaffe had the technology to fit its planes with disposable fuel tanks, but did not use it. If the Bf-109s had indeed possessed greater endurance, Fighter Command's predicament would have been much worse. As it was, the Germans could not sustain decisively superior forces over the battlefield, and were handicapped by failures of strategy and intelligence. In the early stages of the battle, Luftwaffe fighter tactics were markedly superior to those mandated by Fighter Command. But Dowding's pilots learned fast, and by September matched the skills of their opponents.

The Royal Air Force, youngest and brashest of the three services, was the only one which thoroughly recognised the value of publicity. The Battle of Britain caused the prestige of the nation's airmen to ascend to lofty heights, where it remained through the ensuing five years of the war. The RAF gained a glamour and public esteem which never faded. As Churchill always recognised, modern war is waged partly on battlefields, and partly also on airwaves, front pages and in the hearts of men and women. When Britain's powers were so small it was vital to create an inspiriting legend for the nation, and for the world. To this in 1940 Britain's airmen contributed mightily, both through their deeds and the recording of them. The RAF was a supremely twentieth-century creation, which gained Churchill's admiration but incomplete understanding. He displayed an enduring emotionalism about the courage and sacrifices of the aircrews. The men of Bomber as well as Fighter Command were never subjected to the accusations of pusillanimity which the prime minister regularly hurled at Britain's soldiers, and sometimes sailors. Like the British people, he never forgot that, until November 1942, the RAF remained responsible for their country's only visible battlefield victory, against the Luftwaffe in 1940.

On October 11 at Chequers, Churchill said: "That man's effort is flagging." Göring's Luftwaffe was by no means a spent force. The months of night blitz that lay ahead inflicted much pain and destruction, which Fighter Command lacked adequate technology to frustrate. When John Martin telephoned the Reform Club from Downing Street one night to enquire how it had been affected by a nearby blast, the porter responded: "The club is burning, sir." But the RAF had denied the Germans daylight control of Britain's airspace, and inflicted an unsustainable rate of loss. The Luftwaffe lacked sufficient mass to inflict decisive damage upon Britain. Hitler, denied the chance of a cheap victory, saw no need to take further risks by continuing the all-out air battle. Churchill's nation and army remained incapable of frustrating his purposes on the Continent, or challenging his dominion over its peoples. German attention, as Churchill suspected, was now shifting eastwards, in anticipation of an assault upon Russia.

The Luftwaffe continued its night blitz on Britain for months into 1941, maintaining pressure upon the obstinate island at minimal cost in aircraft losses. It was long indeed before the British themselves felt secure from invasion. Home defence continued to preoccupy Churchill and his commanders. He suffered spasms of renewed concern, which caused him to telephone the Admiralty and enquire about Channel conditions on nights thought propitious for a German assault. But the coming of autumn weather, and the Luftwaffe's abandonment of daylight attacks, rendered Britain almost certain of safety until spring. Churchill had led his nation through a season which he rightly deemed critical for its survival.

Across the Atlantic, a host of Americans were dazzled by his achievement. Nazi propagandists sought to exploit a famous photo of Churchill wielding a tommy gun to suggest an image of Britain's prime minister as a gangster. But instead the picture projected an entirely positive image to Roosevelt's nation. Over there, what counted was the fact that the weapon was made in the United States. Americans were shown the leader of Britain putting to personal use a gun shipped from their country, and they loved it. By September 30, a Gallup survey showed that 52 percent of Americans favoured giving assistance to Churchill's people, even at risk of war. *Time's* cover story on September 30, 1940, "The Battle of Britain," declared that

> Winston Churchill so aptly and lovingly symbolizes Great Britain's unwillingness to give up when apparently cornered . . . There is an extraordinary fact about English democracy—namely, that at almost any given time some English leader turns out to be a perfect symbol of his people. At the time of Edward VIII's abdication, Stanley Baldwin was the typical Englishman. At the time of the Munich crisis, Neville Chamberlain was pathetically typical. But as of the fourth week of September 1940, Winston Churchill was the essence of his land. The three men are as dissimilar as fog, rain and hail, which are all water. But the country they ruled has changed. This England is different . . . [Churchill] is a Tory, an imperialist, and has been a strike-breaker and Red-baiter; and yet, when he tours the slums of London, old women say: "God bless you, Winnie."

A few weeks later, by American readers' acclamation, Churchill became *Time's* Man of the Year.

One evening at Chequers, in an irresistibly homely metaphor, he compared himself to "a farmer driving pigs along a road, who always had to be prodding them on and preventing them from straying." He professed that he "could not quite see why he was so popular." For all his undoubted vanity, almost everything that he had to tell the British people was bleak. His public confidence masked private uncertainty which goes far to explain his caution about government appointments and dismissals in 1940. For more than a decade, he had been an outcast, clinging precariously to a handhold on the parapet of power. Though from May 1940 he acted the part of prime minister with supreme outward conviction, it was many months before he became assured of his own authority. "For something like a year after he took office, Winston had no idea of his political strength among the voters, which is a mercy," observed his aide Maj. Desmond Morton.

Ivan Maisky, the Soviet ambassador in London, displayed in his reports home an increasing enthusiasm for Churchill: "One can now say confidently," he told Moscow at the end of June,

> that the government's decision to continue the war has gained overwhelming popular support, especially among the working class. The confusion and despondency which I reported in the first days of the war are gone. Churchill's speeches have played a great part in this . . . Although Churchill thus far commands the support of the working class, the ruling classes are clearly split . . . [The faction] headed by Chamberlain is terribly fearful and willing to make peace with Germany on any acceptable terms . . . these elements are the real "Fifth Column" in England . . . The problem is that, for all Churchill's determination to continue the war, he is afraid to split the Conservative Party and rely upon a workers' coalition.

Maisky's view of political divisions in Britain was not entirely fanciful. He was wrong to ascribe leadership of a peace party to Chamberlain, but correct in asserting that some old Chamberlain supporters, as well as a few Labour MPs, remained eager to parley with the Axis. Lord Lothian, Britain's ambassador in Washington, telephoned Halifax in July, begging him to say nothing publicly that would close the door to possible negotiated terms. Harold Nicolson expressed relief that Halifax appeared unmoved by Lothian's "wild" appeal. Raymond Lee wrote after a conversation with a businessman: "[He] was very interesting about the City . . . he . . . confirmed my belief that the City is ready for appeasement at any time and is a little bit irritated because it has no hold at all on Churchill."

Privately, the prime minister expressed concerns about the staunchness of the upper classes. Among some of Britain's ruling caste, admiration for his dazzling oratory did not confirm his fitness for the premiership. At dinner tables in some great houses, traditional arbiters of power muttered into their soup about the perceived vulgarities, follies and egomania of the chubby cuckoo whom fate had so rashly planted in Downing Street, and entrusted with Britain's destinies. Some people in high places—senior officers as well as politicians—resented his popularity with the public. They failed to perceive how desperately the nation needed to suppose itself led by a superman. How else might its survival be secured?

The House of Commons, through the summer, was swept along by the national mood and Churchill's stunning speeches. George Lambert, a Liberal MP since 1891, told the House at a secret session on July 30 that he had not heard such oratory since Gladstone. But old Chamberlainites continued to sulk, withholding trust as well as warmth from the prime minister. More than a few Tories still expected his administration to be short-lived. They hankered to identify a credible replacement for Churchill. "Feeling in the Carlton Club is running high against him," wrote "Chips" Channon on September 26. When Chamberlain died in November, it was deemed unavoidable but regrettable that Churchill should be elected in his place as Tory leader.

Clementine strongly advised him against embracing the inescapably partisan role of Tory leader. He would have enhanced his stature as national warlord by declining. But acceptance fulfilled a lifelong ambition. More important, he knew how fickle was the support of public and Parliament. He was determined to indulge no possible alternative focus of influence, far less power, such as the election of another man as Tory leader—most plausibly Anthony Eden—might create. There remained a small risk, and an intolerable one, that if Churchill refused, the Tories' choice might fall upon Halifax. It seemed to the prime minister essential to ensure control of the largest voting bloc in the Commons. Subsequent experience suggested that he was probably right. Had he placed himself beyond party, in the dog days of 1942 he might have become dangerously vulnerable to a party revolt.

As autumn 1940 turned to winter, the toll of destruction imposed by the Luftwaffe mounted. But so too did government confidence in the spirit of the nation. Some British people seemed to derive an almost masochistic relish from their predicament. Londoner Mrs. Yolande Green wrote to her mother: "I think it's a good thing that we've suffered all the reverses we have this last year for it has shaken us all out of our smug complacency better than any pep talk by our politicians . . . last weekend we had a nice quiet time in spite of six [air-raid] alarms—one gets so used to them they hardly disturb one nowadays." By October Churchill, drawing on a great cigar as he sat at the Chequers dining table in his coverall, was able to observe with equanimity that he thought "this was the sort of war which would suit the English people once they got used to it. They would prefer all to be in the front line taking part in the battle of London than to look on hopelessly at mass slaughters like Passchendaele."

Bombing created mountains of rubble, obliterated Wren churches, killed thousands of people, damaged factories and slowed production. But it became progressively apparent to Churchill and his colleagues that the industrial fabric of Britain stretched too wide to be vulnerable to destruction from the air. The blitz never came close to threatening Britain's ability to continue the war. The aerial bombardment of cities, which a few years earlier had been perceived by many strategists as a potential war-winning weapon, now proved to have been much exaggerated in its effects, unless conducted with a weight of bombs undeliverable by the Luftwaffe—or, for years to come, by the Royal Air Force.

Millions of British people maintained existences compounded in equal parts of normality, inside their own homes, and perils that might at any moment destroy everything around them which they held dear. Almost eighty years earlier, the novelist Anthony Trollope visited the United States during its civil war. He noted the banalities of domestic life amid the struggle, and suggested with droll prescience: "We . . . soon adapt ourselves to the circumstances around us. Though three parts of London were in flames, I should no doubt expect to have my dinner served to me, if I lived in the quarter which was free from fire." In 1940 Lady Cynthia Colville echoed Trollope, observing at breakfast one morning that "if one looked on all this as ordinary civilian life it was indeed hellish, but if one thought of it as a siege then it was certainly one of the most comfortable in history."

Churchill himself was sometimes very weary, especially after striving to arbitrate on a dozen intractable strategic issues and enduring perceived petulance from MPs in the Commons. "Malaya, the Australian government's intransigence and 'nagging' in the House was more than any man could be expected to endure," he grumbled crossly one night to Eden. Yet his generosity of spirit seldom weakened, even towards the enemy. For all his frequent jibes at "the horrible Huns," and at a moment when Britain's very existence was threatened, he displayed no vindictiveness when discussing a postwar vision. "We [have] got to admit that Germany should remain in the European family," he observed. "Germany existed before the Gestapo."

His energy seemed inexhaustible. That same evening at Chequers on which he likened himself to a swineherd, he conferred with two generals about Home Guard tasks in the event of invasion. He then studied aircraft production charts, which prompted him to marvel aloud that Beaverbrook had genius, "and also brutal ruthlessness." He led his guests for a moonlit walk in the garden, then settled down to quiz an officer newly returned from Egypt about tactics in the Western Desert. In both London and Buckinghamshire, he received an endless stream of visitors. There was always time for Americans. Whitelaw Reid, the twenty-eight-year-old London correspondent of the *New York Herald Tribune*, was awed to find himself invited to lunch with the prime minister at Downing Street. Rear Adm. Robert Ghormley of the U.S. Navy, on a mission to London, was presented with inscribed copies of the four volumes of Churchill's biography of Marlborough.

The death of Neville Chamberlain on November 9 roused Churchill to one of his most notable displays of magnanimity. His private view of the former prime minister was contemptuous: "the narrowest, most ignorant, most ungenerous of men." He felt gratitude for Chamberlain's loyal service as his subordinate since May 10, and admiration for the courage with which he faced his mortal illness, but none for his record as prime minister. Now, however, he summoned his utmost powers of statesmanship to draft a tribute. On November 12, he delivered to the House of Commons a eulogy which forfeited nothing of its power and dignity by the fact that it memorialised a man so uncongenial to him:

> In paying a tribute of respect and regard to an eminent man who has been taken from us, no one is obliged to alter the opinions which he has formed or expressed upon issues which have become a part of history; but at the Lychgate we may all pass our own conduct and our own judgements under a searching review. It is not given to human beings—happily for them, for otherwise life would be intolerable—to foresee or to predict to any large extent the unfolding course of events. In one phase men seem to have been right, in another they seem to have been wrong . . . History with its flickering lamp stumbles along the trail of the past, trying to reconstruct its scenes, to revive its echoes, and kindle with pale gleams the passion of former days. What is the worth of all this? The only guide to a man is his conscience; the only shield to his memory is the rectitude and sincerity of his actions. It is very imprudent to walk through life without this shield, because we are so often mocked by the failure of our hopes and the upsetting of our calculations; but with this shield, however the fates may play, we march always in the ranks of honour.

It fell to Neville Chamberlain in one of the supreme crises of the world to be contradicted by events, to be disappointed in his hopes, and to be deceived and cheated by a wicked man. But what were these high hopes in which he was disappointed? What were these wishes in which he was frustrated? What was that faith that was abused? They were surely among the most noble and benevolent instincts of the human heart—the love of peace, the toil for peace, the strife for peace, the pursuit of peace, even at great peril, and certainly to the utter disdain of popularity or clamour.

It was a supreme political act, to exhibit such grace towards the memory of a man who had failed the British people, and whom Churchill himself justly despised. Yet by November 1940, he could afford to display generosity. His mastery of the nation was secure. His successful defiance of Hitler commanded the admiration of much of the world. He had displayed gifts of self-discipline and political management such as had hitherto been absent from his career. His speeches were recognised as among the greatest ever delivered by a statesman, in war or peace. All that now remained was to devise some means of waging war against an enemy whose control of the Continent was unchallengeable, and whose superiority over Britain remained overwhelming. For Winston Churchill, the hardest part began when the achievement of "the few" was already the stuff of legend.

FIVE

Greek Fire

1. Seeking Action

IN THE AUTUMN of 1940, even Churchill's foes at Westminster and in Whitehall conceded that, since taking office, he had revealed a remarkable accession of wisdom. He had not become a different person from his old self, but shed the maverick's mantle. He looked and sounded a king, "ay, every inch a king," albeit one movingly conscious that he was the servant of a democracy. In a few months, he had achieved a personal dominance of the country which rendered his colleagues acolytes, almost invisible in the shadow of his pedestal. Only Eden and Bevin made much impact on the popular imagination.

Among politicians and service chiefs, however, widespread uncertainty persisted, even if it was discreetly expressed. Though the Germans had not invaded Britain, what happened next? What chance of victory did Britain have? The well-known military writer Captain Basil Liddell Hart saw no prospect beyond stalemate, and thus urged a negotiated peace. In September Dalton reported Beaverbrook as "very defeatist," believing that Britain should merely "sit tight and defend ourselves until the USA comes into the war." But would this ever happen? Raymond Lee, U.S. military attaché in London, was among many Americans bemused about what President Roosevelt meant when he promised that their country would aid the British "by all means short of war." Lee sought an answer from senior diplomats at his own embassy: "They say no one knows, that it depends on what R thinks from one day to another. I wonder if it ever occurs to the people in Washington that they have no God-given right to declare war. They may wake up one day to find that war has suddenly been declared upon the United States. That is the way Germany and Japan do business. Or, can it be that this is what Roosevelt is manoeuvring for?"

Once the Battle of Britain was won, the foremost challenge facing Churchill was to find another field upon which to fight. In July 1940, Lee was filled with admiration for Britain's staunchness amid the invasion threat. But he suggested sardonically that if Hitler instead launched his armies eastward, "in a month's time England would go off sound asleep again." Likewise MP Harold Nicolson: "If Hitler were to postpone invasion and fiddle about in Africa and the Mediterranean, our morale might weaken." As long as Britain appeared to face imminent catastrophe, its people displayed notable fortitude. Yet it was a striking feature of British wartime behaviour that the moment peril fractionally receded, many ordinary people allowed themselves to nurse fantasies that their ordeal might soon be over, the spectre of war somehow banished. Soldier Edward Stebbing wrote on November 14: "I have heard a good many members of this unit say that they wished the war would end whether we win or lose . . . almost every day I hear some variations of the same idea, the common reason being that most of us are fed up with the whole business . . . The government is criticised for its lack of aggressiveness."

A correspondent wrote to Ernest Bevin from Portsmouth:

At our weekly meeting last night of delegates representing thousands of workers . . . the members were very disappointed at your not telling the public that the government intended to prosecute the war more vigorously, and take the offensive, instead of always being on the defensive . . . We have retired service officers who tell us that we have no leaders. We have not won a battle since the war started and it is for that reason no country will join us, knowing full well that Germany will attack and swallow them, whilst our own government are debating the issue . . . Our workers' clubs contain Unionists, Liberals and Labour, all united to push the present government out of office at the first chance, and if something don't happen soon, the leaders will not be able to hold the workers.

Yet how could Britain display aggressiveness, a capability to do more than merely withstand Axis onslaughts by bombers and U-boats? Clementine Churchill enquired at lunch one day: "Winston, why don't we land a million men on the continent of Europe? I'm sure the French would rise up and help us." The prime minister answered with unaccustomed forbearance that it would be impossible to land a million men at once, and that the vanguards would be shot to pieces. Back in 1915, as Lt. Col. Winston Churchill prepared to lead a battalion of the Royal Scots Fusiliers into the trenches, he told his officers, "We will go easy at first: a little digging and feeling our way, and then perhaps later on we may *attempt a deed.*" This latter proposition commanded little enthusiasm among his comrades at the time, and even less among his generals a generation later. But, by the winter of 1940, Churchill knew that a "deed" must be attempted in order to sustain an appearance of momentum in Britain's war effort.

At home, there could be no German invasion before spring. The nation's city dwellers must bear the blitz, while the Royal Navy sustained the Atlantic lifeline against U-boats and surface commerce raiders. The navy had already suffered heavily, losing since 1939 one battleship, two aircraft carriers, two cruisers, twenty-two submarines and thirty-seven destroyers. More ships were building, but 1941 losses would be worse. Churchill pinned great hopes on the RAF's offensive against Germany, but as he himself observed on November 1, 1940, "the discharge of bombs is pitifully small." It would remain so for a long time to come. Chief of the Imperial General Staff Sir John Dill instructed his director of military operations, Maj. Gen. John Kennedy, to draft a strategy paper on how the war might be won. Kennedy said the best that he could offer was a plan for averting defeat. To make victory possible, American belligerence was indispensable.

Lt. Gen. Henry Pownall attended an army conference addressed by the prime minister in November 1940, and was impressed by his robust good sense: "No more than anyone else did he see clearly how the war was going to be won, and he reminded us that for four years in 1914–18 nobody could foretell the final collapse of Germany, which came so unexpectedly . . . All we could do for the present, as during the Great War, was to get on with it and see what happened . . . He talked as well as ever, and I was much impressed by the very broad and patient view that he took of the war as a whole." Churchill expressed the same sentiments to senior RAF officers conferring at Downing Street: "As the PM said goodnight to the Air Marshals, he told them he was sure we were going to win the war, but confessed he did not see clearly how it was to be achieved."

A Chiefs of Staff paper on future strategy, dated September 4, 1940, suggested that Britain should aim "to pass to the general offensive in all spheres and in all theatres with the utmost possible strength in the Spring of 1942." If even this remote prospect was fanciful, what meanwhile was the army to do? Churchill, with his brilliant intuitive understanding of the British people, recognised the importance of military theatre, as his service chiefs often did not. The soldiers' caution might be prudent, but much of the public, like unheroic Edward Stebbing and his comrades, craved action, an outcome, some prospect beyond victimhood. There was a rueful War Office joke at this time, prompted by the blitz, that Britain's soldiers were being put to work knitting socks for the civilians in the trenches.

Here was one of the foremost principles of wartime leadership which Churchill got profoundly right, yet he often erred in implementation. He perceived that there must be action, even if not always useful; there must be successes, even if overstated or imagined; there must be glory, even if undeserved. Attlee said later, very shrewdly: "He was always, in effect, asking himself . . . 'What must Britain do now so that the verdict of history will be favourable?' . . . He was always looking around for 'finest hours,' and if one was not immediately available, his impulse was to manufacture one."

Churchill addressed the conduct of strategy with a confidence that dismayed many of his commanders, but which had evolved over a lifetime. As early as 1909, he wrote to Clementine about Britain's generals: "These military men v[er]y often fail altogether to see the simple truths underlying the relationship of all armed forces . . . Do you know I would greatly like to have some practice in the handling of large forces. I have much confidence in my judgement on things, when I see clearly, but on nothing do I seem to feel the truth more than in tactical combinations." While he was travelling to America in 1932, Clementine read G. F. R. Henderson's celebrated biography of Stonewall Jackson. She wrote to her husband: "The book is full of abuse of politicians who try to interfere with Generals in the field—(Ahem!)." Her exclamation was prompted, of course, by memories of his battles with the service chiefs during the First World War.

Churchill believed himself exceptionally fitted for the direction of armies, navies and air forces. He perceived no barrier to such a role in the fact that he possessed neither military staff training nor experience of higher field command. He wrote in his own history of the First World War:

> A series of absurd conventions became established, perhaps inevitably, in the public mind. The first and most monstrous of these was that the Generals and Admirals were more competent to deal with the broad issues of the war than abler men in other spheres of life. The general no doubt was an expert on how to move his troops, and the admiral upon how to fight his ships . . . But outside this technical aspect they were helpless and misleading arbiters in problems in whose solution the aid of the statesman, the financier, the manufacturer, the inventor, the psychologist, was equally required . . . Clear leadership, violent action, rigid decision one way or the other, form the only path not only of victory, but of safety and even of mercy. The State cannot afford division or hesitation at the executive centre.

Tensions between his instincts and the judgements of Britain's professional commanders would characterise Churchill's leadership. A Polish
officer, attending a lecture at the British staff college on principles of war,
rose at its conclusion to suggest that the speaker had omitted the most
important: "Be stronger." Yet where might Britain achieve this? As minister of defence, Churchill issued an important directive. Limitations of
numbers, he said, "make it impossible for the Army, except in resisting
invasion, to play a primary role in the defeat of the enemy. That task can
only be done by the staying power of the Navy and above all by the effect
of Air predominance. Very valuable and important services may be rendered Overseas by the Army in operations of a secondary order, and it is
for these special operations that its organization and character should be
adapted." After a British commando raid on the Lofoten Islands, Churchill
wrote to the C-in-C Home Fleet: "I am so glad you were able to find the
means of executing '*Claymore*.' This admirable raid has done serious injury
to the enemy and has given an immense amount of innocent pleasure at
home." The latter proposition was more plausible than the former.

Churchill and his military chiefs renounced any prospect of engaging
Hitler's main army. They committed themselves to a strategy based on
minor operations which persisted, in substantial measure, until 1944. Pantelleria, the tiny Italian island between Tunisia and Sicily, exercised a baleful fascination upon the War Cabinet. After a dinner at Chequers in
November 1940, Churchill fantasised about an assault "by 300 determined men, with blackened faces, knives between their teeth and
revolvers under their tails." Eden in 1940–41 cherished absurd notions of
seizing Sicily: "The Sicilians have always been anti-fascist," he enthused.
A War Office plan dated December 28 called for a descent on the island by
two infantry brigades. There was talk of Sardinia, and of the Italian-held
Dodecanese Islands. The Chiefs of Staff learned to dread mention of
northern Norway in the prime minister's flights of fancy.

None of these schemes was executed, save a brief and embarrassingly
unsuccessful foray into the Dodecanese, because the practical objections
were overwhelming. Even the most modest raid required scarce shipping,
which could not sensibly be hazarded within range of the Luftwaffe unless
air cover was available, as it usually was not. It was hard to identify credible objectives for "butcher and bolt" strikes, and to gather sufficient intelligence to give them a reasonable chance of success. However strongly the
prime minister pressed for British forces to display initiative and aggression, the Chiefs of Staff resolutely opposed operations which risked substantial losses in exchange for mere passing propaganda headlines.

. . .

In the autumn of 1940, Africa offered the only realistic opportunities for British land engagement. Libya had been an Italian colony since 1911, Abyssinia since 1936. Churchill owed a perverse debt of gratitude to Mussolini. If Italy had remained neutral, if her dictator had not chosen to seek battle, how else might the British Army have occupied itself after its expulsion from France? As it was, Britain was able to launch spectacular African campaigns against one of the few major armies in the world which it was capable of defeating. Not all Italian generals were incompetents, not all Italian formations fought feebly. But never for a moment were Mussolini's warriors in the same class as those of Hitler. North Africa, and the Duce's pigeon-chested posturing as an Axis warlord, offered Britain's soldiers an opportunity to show their mettle. If the British Army was incapable of playing in a great stadium against top-class opposition, it could nonetheless hearten the nation and impress the world by a demonstration in a lesser league.

Britain's Chiefs of Staff, however, remained sceptical about the strategic value of any big commitment in the Middle East, win or lose. The Suez Canal route to the east was anyway unusable, because the Mediterranean was too perilous for merchant shipping, and remained so until 1943. The Persian oil fields fuelled British military operations in the theatre of Middle East C-in-C Sir Archibald Wavell, but lay too far from home by the Cape route to provide petrol for Britain, which instead relied upon American supplies. It is often forgotten that, in those days, the United States was overwhelmingly the greatest oil producer in the world. Dill advocated reinforcing the Far East against likely Japanese aggression, and remained in his heart an opponent of the Middle East commitment throughout his tenure as head of the army. The CIGS understood the political imperatives facing Churchill, but foremost in his mind was a fear that acceptance of unnecessary new risk might precipitate further gratuitous disaster. The prime minister overruled him. He believed that the embarrassment of inertia in the Middle East much outweighed the perils of seizing the initiative. In the midst of a war, what would the world say about a nation that dispatched large forces to garrison its possessions on the far side of the world against a possible future enemy, rather than engage an actual one much nearer to hand?

In September 1940, an Italian army led by Marshal Rodolfo Graziani, 200,000 strong and thus outnumbering local British forces by four to one, crossed the eastern Libyan frontier and drove fifty miles eastward into

Egypt before being checked. Meanwhile, in East Africa, Mussolini's troops seized the little colony of British Somaliland and advanced into Kenya and Sudan from their bases in Abyssinia. Wavell ordered Somaliland evacuated after only brief resistance. He remained impenitent in the face of Churchill's anger about another retreat.

This first of Britain's "desert generals" was much beloved in the army. In World War I, Wavell won an MC and lost an eye at Ypres, then spent 1917–18 as a staff officer in Palestine under Gen. Edmund Allenby, whose biography he later wrote. A reader of poetry and prone to introspection, among soldiers Wavell passed as an intellectual. His most conspicuous limitation was taciturnity, which crippled his relationship with Churchill. Many who met him, perhaps overimpressed by his enigmatic persona, perceived themselves in the presence of greatness. But uncertainty persisted about whether this extended to mastery of battlefields, where a commander's strength of will is of greater importance than his cultural accomplishments.

On October 28, 1940, the Italians invaded northwestern Greece. Contrary to expectations, after fierce fighting they were evicted by the Greek army and thrown back into Albania, where the rival forces languished in considerable discomfort through the five months that followed. British strategy during this period became dominated by Mediterranean dilemmas, among which aid to Greece and offensive action in Libya stood foremost. Churchill constantly incited his C-in-C to take the offensive against the Italians in the Western Desert, using the tanks shipped to him at such hazard during the summer. Wavell insisted that he needed more time. Now, however, overlaid upon this issue was that of Greece, about which Churchill repeatedly changed his mind. On October 27, the day before Italy invaded, he dealt brusquely with a proposal from Leo Amery and Lord Lloyd, respectively the India and colonial secretaries, that more aid should be dispatched: "I do not agree with your suggestions that at the present time we should make any further promises to Greece and Turkey. It is very easy to write in a sweeping manner when one does not have to take account of resources, transport, time and distance."

Yet as soon as Italy attacked Greece, the prime minister told Dill that "maximum possible" aid must be sent. Neville Chamberlain in March 1939 had assured the Greeks of British support against aggression. Now, Churchill perceived that failure to act would make the worst possible impression upon the United States, where many people doubted Britain's ability to wage war effectively. At the outset, he proposed sending planes and weapons to Greece, rather than British troops. Dill, Wavell and

Eden—then visiting Cairo—questioned even this. Churchill sent Eden a sharp signal urging boldness, dictated to his typist under the eye of Jock Colville.

> He lay there in his four-post bed with its flowery chintz hangings, his bed-table by his side. Mrs. Hill [his secretary] sat patiently opposite while he chewed his cigar, drank frequent sips of iced soda-water, fidgeted his toes beneath the bedclothes and muttered stertorously under his breath what he contemplated saying. To watch him compose some telegram or minute for dictation is to make one feel that one is present at the birth of a child, so tense is his expression, so restless his turnings from side to side, so curious the noises he emits under his breath. Then out comes some masterly sentence and finally with a "Gimme" he takes the sheet of typewritten paper and initials it, or alters it with his fountain-pen, which he holds most awkwardly half way up the holder.

On November 5, Churchill addressed the Commons, reporting grave shipping losses in the Atlantic, and describing a conversation he had held on his way into the Commons with the armed and helmeted guards at its doors. One soldier offered a timeless British cliché to the prime minister: "It's a great life if you don't weaken." This, Churchill told the MPs, was Britain's watchword for the winter of 1940: "We will think of something better by the winter of 1941." Then he adjourned to the smoking room, where he devoted himself to an intent study of the *Evening News*, "as if it were the only source of information available to him." Forget for a moment the art of his performance in the chamber. What more brilliant stagecraft could the leader of a democracy display than to read a newspaper in the common room of MPs of all parties, in the midst of a war and a blitz? " 'How are you?' he calls gaily to the most obscure Member . . . His very presence gives us all gaiety and courage," wrote an MP. "People gather round his table completely unawed."

Despite Wavell's protests, Churchill insisted upon sending a British force to replace Greek troops garrisoning the island of Crete, who could thus be freed to fight on the mainland. The first consignment of matériel dispatched to Greece consisted of 8 antitank guns, 12 Bofors antiaircraft guns, and 20,000 American rifles. To these were added, following renewed prime ministerial urgings, 24 field guns, 20 antitank rifles and 10 light tanks. This poor stuff reflected the desperate shortage of arms available for Britain's soldiers, never mind those of other nations. Some Gladiator fighters, biplanes capable of fighting the Italian air force but emphatically not the Luftwaffe, were also committed. Churchill was enraged by a cable from Sir Miles Lampson, British ambassador in Egypt, dismissing aid to Greece as "completely crazy." The prime minister told the Foreign Office: "I expect to be protected from this kind of insolence." He dispatched a stinging rebuke to Lampson: "You should not telegraph at Government expense such an expression as 'completely crazy' when applied by you to grave decisions of policy taken by the Defence Committee and the War Cabinet after considering an altogether wider range of requirements and assets than you can possibly be aware of."

On the evening of November 8, however, the prospect changed again. Eden returned from Cairo to confide to the prime minister first tidings of an offensive Wavell proposed to launch in the Western Desert the following month. This was news Churchill craved: "I purred like six cats." Ismay found him "rapturously happy." The prime minister exulted: "At long last we are going to throw off the intolerable shackles of the defensive. Wars are won by superior will-power. Now we will wrest the initiative from the enemy and impose our will on him." Three days later, he cabled Wavell, "You may . . . be assured that you will have my full support at all times in any offensive action you may be able to take against the enemy." That same night of November 11, twenty-one Swordfish biplane torpedo bombers, launched from the carrier *Illustrious*, delivered a brilliant attack on the Italian fleet at Taranto, and sank or crippled three battleships. Britain was striking out at the enemy.

Churchill accepted that the North African offensive must now assume priority over all else, that no troops could be spared for Greece. A victory in the desert might persuade Turkey to come into the war. His foremost concern was that Wavell, whose terse words and understated delivery failed to generate prime ministerial confidence, should go for broke. Dismayed to hear that Operation Compass was planned as a limited "raid," Churchill wrote to Dill on December 7: "If, with the situation as it is, General Wavell is only playing small, and is not hurling in his whole available forces with furious energy, he will have failed to rise to the height of circumstances . . . I never 'worry' about action, but only about inaction."

On December 9, at last came the moment for the "Army of the Nile," as Churchill had christened it, to launch its assault. Wavell's 4th Indian and 7th Armoured divisions, led by Lt. Gen. Sir Richard O'Connor, attacked the Italians in the Western Desert. Operation Compass achieved brilliant success. Mussolini's generals showed themselves epic bunglers. Some 38,000 prisoners were taken in the first three days, at a cost of just 624 Indian and British casualties. "It all seems too good to be true," wrote Eden on December 11. Wavell decided to exploit this success, and gave O'Connor his head. The little British army, by now reinforced by the 6th

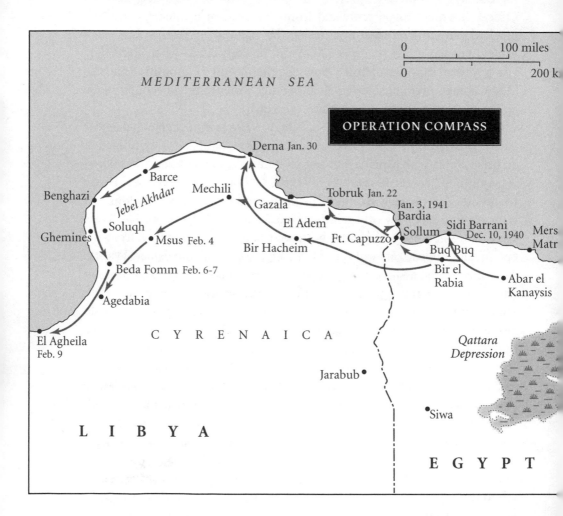

MEDITERRANEAN SEA

0   100 miles
0   200 k

OPERATION COMPASS

Derna Jan. 30

Barce

Benghazi

Jebel Akhdar

Mechili

Gazala

Tobruk Jan. 22

Jan. 3, 1941
Bardia

Soluqh

El Adem

Sollum

Sidi Barrani
Dec. 10, 1940

Mers
Matr

Ghemines

Msus Feb. 4

Ft. Capuzzo

Bir Hacheim

Buq Buq

Beda Fomm Feb. 6-7

Bir el
Rabia

Abar el
Kanaysis

Agedabia

C Y R E N A I C A

Qattara
Depression

El Agheila
Feb. 9

Jarabub

L I B Y A

Siwa

E G Y P T

Australian Division, stormed along the coast into Libya, taking Bardia on January 5. At 5:40 a.m. on January 21, 1941, red Very lights arched into the sky to signal the start of O'Connor's attack on the port of Tobruk. Bangalore torpedoes blew gaps in the Italian wire. An Australian voice shouted: "Go on, you bastards!"

At 6:45, British tanks lumbered forward. The Italians resisted fiercely, but by dawn the next day the sky was lit by the flames of their blazing supply dumps, prisoners in the thousands were streaming into British cages, and the defenders were ready to surrender. O'Connor dispatched his tanks on a dash across the desert to cut off the retreating Italians. The desert army was in a mood of wild excitement. "Off we went across the unknown country in full cry," wrote Michael Creagh, one of O'Connor's division commanders. In a rare exhibition of emotion, O'Connor asked his chief of staff: "My God, do you think it's going to be all right?" It was indeed "all right." The British reached Beda Fomm ahead of the Italians, who surrendered. In two months, the desert army had advanced four hundred miles and taken 130,000 prisoners. On February 11, another of Wavell's contingents advanced from Kenya into Abyssinia and Somaliland. After hard fighting—much tougher than in Libya—here, too, the Italians were driven inexorably towards eventual surrender.

For a brief season, Wavell became a national hero. For the British people in the late winter and early spring of 1940–41, battered nightly by the Luftwaffe's bombardment, still fearful of invasion, conscious of the frailty of the Atlantic lifeline, success in Africa was precious. It was Churchill's delicate task to balance exultation about a victory with caution about future prospects. Again and again, in his broadcasts and speeches, he emphasised the long duration of the ordeal that must lie ahead, the need for unremitting exertion. To this purpose he continued to stress the danger of a German landing in Britain: in February 1941, he demanded a new evacuation of civilian residents from coastal areas in the danger zone.

Churchill knew how readily the nation could lapse into inertia. The army's Home Forces devoted much energy to anti-invasion exercises, such as Operation Victor in March 1941. Victor assumed that five German divisions, including two armoured and one motorised, had landed on the coast of East Anglia. On March 30, presented with a report on the exercise, Churchill minuted mischievously, but with serious intent: "All this data would be most valuable for our future offensive operations. I should be very glad if the same officers would work out a scheme for our landing an exactly similar force on the French coast." Even if no descent on France was remotely practicable, Churchill was at his best in pressing Britain's generals to forswear a fortress mentality.

But public fear and impatience remained constants. "For the first time the possibility that we may be defeated has come to many people—me among them," wrote Oliver Harvey, Eden's private secretary, on February 22, 1941. "Mr.Churchill's speech has rather sobered me," wrote London charity worker Vere Hodgson after a prime ministerial broadcast that month. "I was beginning to be a little optimistic. I even began to think there might be no Invasion . . . but he thinks there will, it seems. Also I had a feeling the end might soon be in sight; he seems to be looking a few years ahead! So I don't know what is going to happen to us. We seem to be waiting—waiting, for we know not what."

Churchill had answers to Miss Hodgson's question. "Here is the hand that is going to win the war," he told guests at Chequers, who included Duff Cooper and General Wladyslaw Sikorski, one evening in February. He extended his fingers as if displaying a poker hand: "a Royal Flush—Great Britain, the Sea, the Air, the Middle East, American aid." Yet this was flummery. British successes in Africa promoted illusions that were swiftly shattered. Italian weakness and incompetence, rather than British strength and genius, had borne O'Connor's little force to Tobruk and beyond. Thereafter, Wavell's forces found themselves once more confronted with their own limitations in the face of energetic German intervention.

In the autumn of 1940, Hitler had declared that "not one man and not one pfennig" would he expend in Africa. His strategic attention was focused upon the east. Mussolini, with his ambition to make the Mediterranean "an Italian lake," was anyway eager to achieve his own conquests without German aid. But when the Italians suffered humiliation, Hitler was quite unwilling to see his ally defeated, and to risk losing Axis control of the Balkans. In April, he launched the Wehrmacht into Yugoslavia and Greece. An Afrika Korps of two divisions under Gen. Erwin Rommel was dispatched to Libya. A new chapter of British misfortunes opened.

Churchill's decision to dispatch a British army to Greece in the spring of 1941 remains one of the most controversial of his wartime premiership. When the commitment was first mooted back in October, almost all the soldiers opposed it. On November 1, Eden, the secretary for war, cabled from Cairo: "We cannot, from Middle East resources, send sufficient air or land reinforcements to have any decisive influence upon course of fighting . . . To send such forces there . . . would imperil our whole position in the Middle East and jeopardize plans for offensive operations." These remarks prompted a tirade from the prime minister, and caused Eden to write in his diary two days later: "The weakness of our policy is that we never adhere to the plans we make."

Germany triumphs in both west and east. (*above*) Blazing shore facilities on Crete in May 1941, and (*right*) one of some three million Russian soldiers who surrendered to the Wehrmacht during the first year of Operation Barbarossa

Friendship of state. (*above*) Harry Hopkins and his host pose outside Downing Street on January 10, 1941, with Brendan Bracken behind; (*left*) FDR and Churchill at Placentia Bay on August 10, the president leaning on the arm of his unlovable son Elliot

War in the desert. (*right*) British troops advance through a minefield. (*below*) Some of the tens of thousands of Italian prisoners who fell into British hands during Wavell's Operation Compass

Civilian chroniclers of the
wartime experience: Vere
Hodgson (*top left*) and
George King (*top right*) in
Home Guard battle dress

Whitehall diarists:
(*below left*) Sir John Kennedy;
(*below center*) Sir Alexander Cadogan;
(*below right*) Harold Nicolson

Clockwise from top left: Charles Wilson, Lord Moran; Hugh Dalton; Leo Amery; Cuthbert Headlam; Oliver Harvey; Lt. Gen. Sir Henry Pownall

Working on his train, with a secretary's "silent" typewriter at hand to take dictation

Viewing new aircraft with (*left to right*) Lindemann, Portal and Pound

Jock Colville's September 1941 farewell to Downing Street gathering, on the steps to the garden. *Front row, left to right:* Colville, Churchill, John Martin, Tony Bevir; (*back row, left to right*) Leslie Rowan, "Master" John Peck, Miss Watson, Commander "Tommy" Thompson, Charles Barker

Return from Arcadia: Churchill briefly at the controls of the British plane that brought him home from Washington in January 1942

One of the many impassioned Second Front rallies held in Britain's cities in 1942–43

It seemed extraordinarily unlikely that a mere four divisions—all that could be spared from Wavell's resources—would make the difference between Greek victory and defeat. Aircraft especially were lacking. With German intervention looming in North Africa, such a diversion of forces threatened Britain's desert campaign. Kennedy told Dill on January 26 that he would have liked to see the Chiefs of Staff adopt much firmer resistance to the Greek proposal—"We were near the edge of the precipice . . . CIGS said to me that he did not dissent, and considered the limitation placed upon the first reinforcements to be offered to the Greeks to be a sufficient safeguard. This seemed to me to be frightfully danger-ous . . . If the Germans come down to Salonika the whole thing is bound to collapse, and nothing short of 20 divisions and a big air force, main-tained by shipping we cannot afford, would be of any use . . . What we should do is keep the water in front of us. Anything we send to Greece will be lost if the Germans come down." As so often with the counsels of Churchill's generals, this view represented prudence. Yet what would the British people, never mind Goebbels, say if the British lion skulked timo-rous beside the Nile?

Probably the most significant indication of Churchill's innermost belief derives from his remarks to Roosevelt's envoy Harry Hopkins early in January. Hopkins reported to Washington on the tenth: "He thinks Greece is lost—although he is now reinforcing the Greeks and weakening his African army." Just as the prime minister's heart had moved him to dis-patch more troops to France in June 1940 against military logic, so now it inspired him to believe that the Greeks could not be abandoned to their fate. An overriding moral imperative, his familiar determination to do nothing common or mean, drove the British debate in the early months of 1941. He nursed a thin hope that, following the success of Operation Compass, Turkey might join the Allies if Britain displayed staunchness in the Balkans.

It is likely that Churchill would have followed his instinct to be seen to aid Greece, even if Wavell, in the Middle East, had sustained opposition. As it was, however, the C-in-C provoked amazement among senior sol-diers by changing his mind. When Dill and Eden arrived in Cairo in mid-February on a second visit, they found Wavell ready to support a Greek commitment. On the nineteenth, the general said: "We have a difficult choice, but I think we are more likely to be playing the enemy's game by remaining inactive than by taking action in the Balkans." Now, it was Churchill's turn to wobble. "Do not consider yourself obligated to a Greek enterprise if in your hearts you feel it will only be another Norwe-gian fiasco," he signalled Eden on February 20. Dill, however, said that they believed there was "a reasonable chance of resisting a German advance." Eden said to Wavell: "It is a soldier's business. It is for you to say." Wavell responded: "War is an option of difficulties. We go." On the twenty-fourth, Churchill told his men in Cairo: "While being under no illusions, we all send you the order 'Full Steam Ahead.' "

The Greek commitment represented one of Anthony Eden's first tests as foreign secretary, the role to which he had been translated in December, on the departure of Lord Halifax to become British ambassador in Washington. In the eyes of many of his contemporaries, Eden—still only forty-four in 1941—displayed a highly strung temperament, petulance and lack of steel, which inspired scant confidence. An infantry officer in the First World War, endowed with famous charm and physical glamour, he established his credentials as an antiappeaser by resigning from Chamberlain's government in 1938. Throughout the war, as afterwards, he cherished a passionate ambition to succeed Churchill in office, which the prime minister himself encouraged. Churchill valued Eden's intelligence and loyalty, but the soldiers thought him incorrigibly "wet," with affectations of manner which they identified with those of homosexuals. Sir James Grigg, permanent under-secretary at the War Office, and later secretary for war, dismissed Eden as "a poor feeble little pansy," though it should be noted that Grigg seldom thought well of anyone. In a world in which talent is rarely, if ever, sufficient to meet the challenges of government, it remains hard to identify a better candidate for the wartime foreign secretaryship. Eden often stood up to Churchill in a fashion which deserves respect. But his reports to Downing Street from the Mediterranean in 1940–41 reflected erratic judgement and a tendency towards vacillation.

Dill, head of the army, remained deeply unhappy about sending troops to Greece. But in the Middle East theatre, Wavell's was the decisive voice. Many historians have expressed bewilderment that this intelligent soldier should have committed himself to a policy which promised disaster. Yet it does not seem hard to explain Wavell's behaviour. For months, the Middle East C-in-C had been harassed and pricked by the prime minister, who deplored his alleged pusillanimity. As early as August 1940, when Wavell visited London, Eden described the general's dismay at Churchill's impatience with him: "Found Wavell waiting for me at 9am. He was clearly upset at last night's proceedings and said he thought he should have made it plain that if the Prime Minister could not approve his dispositions and had not confidence in him he should appoint someone else." Though this early spat was patched up, the two men never established a rapport. All through the autumn of 1940, bad-tempered signals flew to and fro between Downing Street and Cairo, provoked by the prime minister's impatience with Wavell's caution, and his C-in-C's exasperation with Churchill's indifference to military realities, as he himself perceived them.

Again and again Churchill pressed Wavell, and indeed all his generals, to overcome their fears of the enemy, to display the fighting spirit which he prized above all things, and which alone, he believed, would enable Britain to survive. Even after the Libyan battlefield successes of recent months, the C-in-C in Cairo would have been less than human had he not been galled by Churchill's goading. In 1939 Poland had been left to face defeat alone, for it lay beyond the reach of a British or French army. In 1940 many Frenchmen and Belgians believed themselves betrayed by their Anglo-Saxon ally. In 1941, Britain's prime minister almost daily urged the peoples of the free world to join hands to contest mastery with the Nazis. Was a British army now to stand ingloriously idle, and watch Greece succumb?

At a War Cabinet meeting in London on March 7, attended by Australian prime minister Robert Menzies, Churchill's enthusiasm for the Greek commitment caused him, as so often, to talk roughshod over inconvenient material realities. He asserted, for instance: "We should soon have strong air forces in Greece." On the contrary, the RAF's feeble contingent—barely a hundred aircraft strong—was drastically outnumbered by the 1,350 planes of the Axis. Tokenism dominated the subsequent campaign. The British bombed Sofia's rail yards, in an attempt to hamper German supply movements to Yugoslavia. Yet this night attack was carried out by just six Wellingtons, a force insufficient to convincingly disrupt an exercise on the Aldershot ranges. The nine squadrons committed by the RAF chiefly comprised obsolete and discredited aircraft, Gladiator biplane fighters and Blenheim light bombers. After achieving some early successes against the Italians, faced with modern German fighters such types could contribute nothing. Their destruction also entailed the loss of precious pilots. From January onwards, as the Luftwaffe ranged increasingly assertively over the Mediterranean, the Royal Navy was obliged to operate almost without air cover—and paid the price. By April 14, the RAF in Greece had just forty-six serviceable planes.

There is no objective test by which the moral benefits of attempting to aid Greece can be measured against the cost of subjecting yet another British army to defeat. The official historians of wartime intelligence have highlighted one misjudgement in the spring of 1941: Churchill and his generals failed to perceive, because Ultra signal intercepts did not tell them, that Hitler's fundamental purpose in the Balkans was not offensive, but defensive. He sought to protect the Romanian oil fields and secure his southern flank before attacking Russia. It is unlikely, however, even had this been recognised in London, that it would have caused Churchill to opt for inaction. Throughout its history, Britain has repeatedly sought to ignore the importance of mass on the battlefield, dispatching inadequate forces to assert moral or strategic principles. This was the course which Churchill adopted in March 1941. It has been suggested that Wavell should have resigned, rather than send troops to Greece. But field commanders have no business to make such gestures. Wavell did his utmost to support his nation's purposes, though he knew that, as commander-in-chief, he would bear responsibility for what must follow. On April 7, when he bade farewell to Dill as the CIGS left Cairo for London with Eden, he said, "I hope, Jack, you will preside at my court martial."

The outcome was as swift as it was inevitable. The Germans crushed Yugoslav resistance during two days' fighting in Macedonia on April 6–7, then embarked upon a series of dramatic outflanking operations against the Greeks. The Greek army was exhausted and demoralised, following its winter campaign against the Italians. Its initial achievement in pushing forward into Albania, which had so impressed the British, represented the only effort of which it was capable. Within days, sixty-two thousand British, Australian and New Zealand troops in Greece found themselves retreating southwards in disarray, harried at every turn by the Luftwaffe. An April 6 air raid on Piraeus blew up a British ammunition ship, wrecking the port. The RAF's little fighter force was ruthlessly destroyed.

Worse, even before the Germans occupied Greece, the Afrika Korps attacked in Libya. On April 3, the British evacuated Benghazi, then found themselves retreating eastwards pell-mell back down the coast road, along which they had advanced in triumph two months earlier. By April 11, when Rommel reached the limit of his supply chain, he had driven the British back almost to the start line of their Compass offensive. It was fortunate that Hitler had dispatched to Libya too small a force and inadequate logistical support to convert British withdrawal into outright disaster. So much was wrong with the leadership, training, weapons and tactics of Wavell's desert army that it is questionable whether it could have repulsed the Afrika Korps even in the absence of the Greek diversion. Inevitably, however, Greece was deemed responsible for defeat in Libya.

The desert fiasco brought out both the worst and best in Churchill. He offered absurd tactical suggestions. He chafed at the navy's failure to bombard Tripoli, Rommel's supply base—an intolerable risk beneath the German air threat. On land, he urged foolishly: "General Wavell should regain unit ascendancy over the enemy and destroy his small raiding parties, instead of our own being harassed and hunted by them. Enemy patrols must be attacked on every occasion, and our own patrols should be used with audacity. Small British parties in armoured cars, or mounted on motor-cycles, or, if occasion offers, infantry, should not hesitate to attack individual tanks with bombs and bombards, as is planned for the defence of Britain." By contrast, the prime minister was at his best in overruling objections from the Chiefs of Staff, and accepting the huge risk of dispatching a convoy, code-named Operation Tiger, direct through the Mediterranean to Egypt, instead of by the much safer but longer Cape route, with reinforcements of tanks.

Dill returned from Cairo steeped in gloom. John Kennedy, the director of military operations (DMO), sought to revive his spirits, but the CIGS dismissed reassuring words about the outlook. "I think it is desperate. I am terribly tired." The next day Kennedy noted, "CIGS is miserable & feels he has wrecked the Empire." That evening, Kennedy, at dinner with a friend, discussed possible evacuation of the entire Middle East. "On balance it was doubtful if we gained more than we lost by staying there. Prestige and effect on Americans perhaps the biggest arguments for staying." Like most senior soldiers, Kennedy was appalled by events in Greece, and by Britain's role in the debacle: "Chiefs of staff overawed & influenced enormously by Winston's overpowering personality . . . I hate my title now, for I suppose outsiders think I really 'direct' oper[atio]ns & am partly responsible for the foolish & disastrous strategy which our armies are following." The self-confidence of Britain's senior soldiers was drained by successive battlefield defeats. They felt themselves incapable of opposing Churchill, but likewise unable to support many of his decisions with conviction. They saw themselves bearing responsibility for losing the war, while offering no alternative proposals for winning it. Left to their own devices, the generals would have accepted battle only on the most favourable terms. The prime minister, however, believed that operational passivity must spell doom for his hopes both of preventing the British people from succumbing to inertia and persuading the Americans to belligerence.

Following the suicide of the Greek prime minister, Alexander Korizis, on April 18, the will of his nation's leadership collapsed. In London, Robert Menzies wrote after a War Cabinet on April 24, 1941: "I am afraid of a disaster, and understand less than ever why Dill and Wavell advised that the Greek adventure had military merits. Of the moral merits I have no doubt. Better Dunkirk than Poland or Czechoslovakia." Menzies added two days later: "War cabinet. Winston says 'We will lose only 5000 men in Greece.' We will in fact lose at least 15000. W is a great man, but he is more addicted to wishful thinking every day."

Towards the end of April, a young soldier on leave in Lancashire who was visiting housewife Nella Last got up and left the living room as the family tuned to a broadcast by the prime minister. Mrs. Last said: "Aren't you going to listen to Winston Churchill?" Her guest demurred, as she recorded in her diary: "An ugly twist came to his mouth and he said 'No, I'll leave that for all those who like dope.' I said, 'Jack, you're liverish, pull yourself together. We believe in Churchill—one must believe in someone.' He said darkly, 'Well, everyone is not so struck.' " Mrs. Last, like the overwhelming majority of British people, yearned to sustain her faith in the prime minister. Yet it seemed hard to do so, on such an evening as this: "Did I sense a weariness and . . . foggy bewilderment as to the future in Winston's speech—or was it all in my tired head, I wonder? Anyway, I got no inspiration—no little banner to carry. Instead I felt I got a glimpse of a horror and carnage that we have not yet thought of . . . More and more do I think it is the 'end of the world'—of the old world, anyway." The poor woman acknowledged that she was unhappy and frightened. "Its funny how sick one can get, and not able to eat—just through . . . fear." Harold Nicolson, parliamentary under-secretary at the Ministry of Information, wrote: "All that the country really wants is some assurance of how victory is to be achieved. They are bored by talks about the righteousness of our cause and our eventual triumph. What they want are facts indicating how we are to beat the Germans. I have no idea at all how we are to give them those facts."

In Greece, the retreating army was much moved by the manner of its parting from the stricken people: "We were nearly the last British troops they would see and the Germans might be at our heels," wrote Lt. Col. R. P. Waller of his artillery unit's withdrawal through Athens, "yet cheering, clapping crowds lined the streets and pressed about our cars . . . Girls and men leapt on the running boards to kiss or shake hands with the grimy, weary gunners. They threw flowers to us and ran beside us crying 'Come back—You must come back again—Goodbye—Good luck.' " The Germans took the Greek capital on April 27. They had secured the country with a mere 5,000 casualties. The British lost 12,000 men, 9,000 of these becoming prisoners. The rest of Wavell's expeditionary force was fortunate to escape to Crete from the ports of the Peloponnese.

Dill broadcast his gloom beyond the War Office. "He himself took a depressed view of our prospect in Libya, Syria and even Ira[q]," Lord Hankey recorded after a conversation with the CIGS, "and said that the German armoured forces are superior to ours both in numbers and efficiency—even in the actual Tanks. He was evidently very anxious about invasion, and seemed to fear that Winston would insist on denuding this country of essential defensive forces. He asked what a CIGS could do if he thought the PM was endangering the safety of the country." In such a case he should resign, said Hankey, an increasingly malevolent critic of the prime minister. Dill mused aloud: "But can one resign in war?" It is extraordinary that the head of Britain's army allowed himself to voice such defeatist sentiments at such a moment in the nation's fortunes, even to a member of the government, such as Hankey was. Yet it would be another six months before Churchill ventured to sack Dill. The general's limitations reflected a chronic shortage of plausible warrior chieftains at the summit of Britain's forces. It was not that Dill was a stupid man—far from it. Rather, he displayed an excess of rationality, allied to an absence of fire, which deeply irked the prime minister.

On May 20, three weeks after Greece was occupied, Gen. Kurt Student's Luftwaffe paratroops began landing on Crete—to face slaughter at the hands of forty thousand British defenders commanded by Maj. Gen. Bernard Freyberg. Thanks to Ultra, the entire German plan, and even its timings, was known to the British. On the first day, the battle appeared a disaster for the Germans. New Zealand infantrymen, perhaps the finest Allied fighting soldiers of the Second World War, dominated the struggle to hold the island's key airfields. But that evening, a fatal mistake was made. Defenders withdrew from Máleme airfield to reorganise for a counterattack the next day. On the afternoon of May 21, a fresh battalion of German mountain troops crash-landed at Máleme in Junkers transports. Once they secured the airfield, reinforcements poured in. Freyberg's force began to withdraw eastwards. The Royal Navy inflicted heavy loss on the German amphibious landings, but itself suffered gravely. "We hold our breath over Crete," wrote Vere Hodgson on May 25. "I feel Churchill is doing the same. He did not seem to mind evacuation of Greece, but he will take the loss of Crete very hard."

As the Germans strengthened their grip on the island and Freyberg received Wavell's consent to evacuate, the Luftwaffe pounded the British fleet. Two battleships, an aircraft carrier and many lesser vessels were damaged, four cruisers and six destroyers sunk. Crete became the costliest single British naval campaign of the Second World War. On shore, the defenders lost 2,000 men killed and 12,000 taken prisoner. Some 18,000 were rescued and carried to Egypt by the navy. Freyberg persuaded Churchill to assert in his postwar memoirs that the campaign had cost the Germans 15,000 casualties. The true figure, well known by that time, was 6,000, including 2,000 dead. Some 17,500 German invaders had defeated a British force more than twice as numerous. By June 1, it was all over.

Strategically, the fall of Crete was a much less serious matter for the

British than would have been the loss of Malta. Admiral Cunningham believed that, if the island had been held, the British would have paid a heavy price for continuing to supply it, in the face of overwhelming German air superiority. It was Hitler's mistake to allow Student to deploy his parachute division against Freyberg's garrison, rather than commit the *Fallschirmjäger* against Malta, Britain's key Mediterranean island, which the Germans could probably have taken. But Churchill had promised the British people, and the world, that Crete would be staunchly defended. Its loss was a heavy blow to his authority, and even more to his faith in the fighting power of the British Army. Thoughtful civilians, too, perceived the limitations of their own forces. "The difference between the capability of the B[ritish] Army when dealing with the Italians and with the Germans is surely too plain to be missed," Elizabeth Belsey, a Communist living in Huntingdonshire who was deeply cynical about her nation's rulers, wrote to her army officer husband. "One can detect here and there, especially in Churchill's speeches, hints that Britain realises the stickiness of her position."

The prime minister was driven to offer threadbare explanations for the Mediterranean disaster, telling the House of Commons on June 10, "A very great number of the guns which might have usefully been employed in Crete have been, and are being, mounted in merchant vessels to beat off the attacks of the Focke Wulf and Heinkel aircraft, whose depredations have been notably lessened thereby." But then he tired of his own equivocations, saying: "Defeat is bitter. There is no use in trying to explain defeat. People do not like defeat, and they do not like the explanations, however elaborate or plausible, which are given to them. For defeat there is only one answer. The only answer to defeat is victory. If a government in time of war gives the impression that it cannot in the long run procure victory, who cares for explanations? It ought to go."

Churchill believed, surely rightly, that Crete could have been held. Yet Freyberg had been his personal choice to lead its defence. The New Zealander, like Gort awarded a World War I Victoria Cross, was the sort of hero he loved. Freyberg was a fine and brave man, but on Crete he showed himself unfit for command responsibility. Many of his troops were fugitives from Greece. The British Army never had the skill, which the Germans later displayed, for welding "odds and sods" into effective impromptu battle groups. In April 1940, for instance, the survivors of German navy destroyers sunk at Narvik were immediately conscripted to join Wehrmacht troops contesting possession of the port with the British. Compare and contrast the attitude of RAF ground personnel in Greece in 1941 and later on other battlefields: they flatly rejected suggestions that they should take up rifles and join the struggle, saying that this was not their job. Almost all chose to accept captivity rather than undertake unfamiliar duties as warriors.

A shortage of wireless sets crippled British communications, and Freyberg's understanding of the battle. There was little transport to move troops, and the Luftwaffe wrought havoc on such roads as existed. All these factors contributed to defeat, but the ultimate verdict remained inescapable: once again, a British army had been outfought, in a battle conducted on terms which should have favoured it. The New Zealanders' contribution was outstanding, but other units performed poorly. During the evacuation, much of Freyberg's force degenerated into a rabble.

Churchill, a few months later, claimed to regret the Greek commitment, which he described to Colville as the only error of judgement his government had made. Wavell should have garrisoned Crete, he said, and advised the Athens government to make the best terms with Germany that it could. But this was a view expressed while Britain was still struggling for survival. In the longer run of history, the nobility of his purpose in Greece commands respect. As Robert Menzies and others perceived, British passivity in the face of the destruction of Greek freedom would have created a sorry impression upon the world, and especially the United States. Nonetheless, events in the Mediterranean dismayed every enemy of Nazism. A Bucharest Jew, Mikhail Sebastian, wrote: "Once more Germany gives the impression of an invincible, demonic, overwhelming force. The general feeling is one of bewilderment and impotence."

A German war correspondent, Kurt Pauli, approached some British prisoners near Corinth and struck a posture of chivalrous condescension. "You've lost the game," he said. Not so, the POWs replied defiantly: "We've still got Winston Churchill." Was this enough, however? Alan Brooke wrote later of "the utter darkness of those early days of calamities when no single ray of hope could pierce the depth of gloom." It was astonishing that the prime minister maintained his exuberance. Robert Menzies wrote: "The PM in conversation will steep himself (and you) in gloom on some grim aspect of the war . . . only to proceed to fight his way out while he is pacing the floor with the light of battle in his eyes. In every conversation he inevitably reaches a point where he positively enjoys the war: 'Bliss in that age was it to be alive.' (He says) 'Why do people regard a period like this as years lost out of our lives when beyond question it is the most interesting period of them? Why do we regard history as of the past and forget we are making it?' "

The near Middle East was only one among many theatres from which bad tidings crowded in upon Britain's prime minister. On April 30, Iraqi troops attacked the RAF's Habbaniya air base, outside Baghdad, prompting Churchill and Eden to conclude that they must seize Iraq to preempt a German takeover. The Luftwaffe's blitz on Britain continued relentlessly, and had by now killed more than thirty thousand civilians. On May 10, the demented deputy führer, Rudolf Hess, parachuted into Scotland on a personal peace mission, which perversely served Nazi propaganda interests better than British. Bewildered people, especially in Moscow and Washington, supposed that some parley between Britain and Germany must indeed be imminent. Fears persisted that Spain would join the Axis. Although foreign exchange was desperately short, the government somehow found the huge sum of $10 million to bribe Spanish generals to keep their country out of the war. The payments, arranged through Franco's banker Juan March, were made into Swiss accounts. There is no evidence that this largesse influenced Spanish policy, but it represented an earnest of British anxiety about Franco's neutrality.

On May 20, Germans began to appear in Vichy French Syria, causing Churchill to decree, once more against Wavell's opposition: "We must go in." British, Australian and Free French troops were soon fighting a bitter little campaign against the Vichyites, who resisted. Churchill observed crossly that it was a pity they had not displayed the same determination against the Germans in 1940. Pétain's troops were finally overcome. Britain's seizure of Iraq and Syria attracted little popular enthusiasm at the time, and has not attracted much interest or applause from historians since. Yet these two initiatives reflected Churchill's boldness at its best. British action removed dangerous instability on Wavell's eastern flank. The diversion of troops caused much hand-wringing in Cairo, but represented strategic wisdom. If the Germans had been successful in their tentative efforts to rouse the Arab world against Britain, its predicament in the Middle East would have worsened dramatically. The most authoritative modern German historians of the war, the authors of the monumental Potsdam Institute series, consider British successes in Syria, Iraq and Abyssinia more important to the 1941 strategic pattern than defeat on Crete. Churchill, they say, "was right when he asserted that on the whole, the situation in the Mediterranean and the Middle East was far more favourable to Britain than it had been a year earlier." Yet it did not seem so at the time, to the sorely tried British people.

On May 23, a Friday, the battle cruiser *Hood* blew up during a brief engagement with the *Bismarck* west of Iceland. The days that followed, with the German battleship loose in the North Atlantic, were terrible ones for the prime minister. His despondency lifted only on the twenty-seventh, when, as he addressed the House of Commons, he received news that the *Bismarck* had been sunk. But convoy losses remained appalling. American assistance fell far short of British hopes, and Churchill not infrequently vented his bitterness at the ruthlessness of the financial terms extracted by Washington for supplies. "As far as I can make out," he wrote to Chancellor Kingsley Wood, "we are not only to be skinned, but flayed to the bone."

The Middle East remained Britain's chief battleground. Despite success in securing the eastern flank in Syria and seizing control of Iraq, Churchill's confidence in his C-in-C, never high, was ebbing fast. "He said some very harsh things about Wavell, whose excessive caution and inclination to pessimism he finds very antipathetic." For a few weeks, confidence flickered about a fresh offensive, Battleaxe. Admiral Cunningham was told that if this succeeded, and Wavell's forces reached Tripoli, the next step would be a landing in Sicily. Such fantasies were swiftly crushed. On June 17, it was learned in London that Battleaxe had failed with the loss of a hundred priceless tanks. Churchill was exasperated to hear that Wavell wanted to evacuate Tobruk. This was militarily rational, for the port's logistic value was small, yet seemed politically intolerable. In April Churchill had described Wavell in a broadcast as "that fine commander whom we cheered in good days and will back through bad." Now, on June 20, he sacked the Middle East C-in-C, exchanging him with Sir Claude Auchinleck, C-in-C India, whose seizure of Iraq had been executed with impressive efficiency. Wavell was given the Delhi command only because Churchill feared that to consign him to oblivion would play poorly with the public, to whom the general had been represented as a hero.

Clementine Churchill once wrote contemptuously to her husband about the deposed Middle East C-in-C: "I understand he has a great deal of personal charm. This is pleasant in civilized times but not much use in total War . . . " Too many of the British Army's senior officers were agreeable men who lacked the killer instinct indispensable to victory. Wavell's best biographer, Ronald Lewin, has observed that he seemed destined for greatness in any field save that of high command in battle. It might more brutally be suggested that there was less to Wavell than his enigmatic persona led admirers to suppose. He once said to Pownall, "My trouble is that I am not really interested in war." This was a surprisingly common limitation among Britain's senior soldiers. It goes far to explain why Winston Churchill was much better suited to his own role than were some of his generals to theirs.

2. The War Machine

IT IS SOMETIMES suggested that in the Second World War there was none of the mistrust and indeed hostility between generals and politicians, "brass" and "frocks," which characterised the British high command in the 1914–18 conflict. This is untrue. Ironside, when he was CIGS in 1939, remarked contemptuously to a staff officer as he set out for a War Cabinet meeting, "Now I'm going to waste a morning educating these old gentlemen on their job." Though Churchill was not then prime minister, he was categorised among the despised "old gentlemen."

Lt. Gen. Henry Pownall wrote of Churchill's Cabinet, "They are a pretty fair lot of gangsters some of them—Bevin, Morrison and above all Beaverbrook who has got one of the nastiest faces I ever saw on any man." John Kennedy wrote later in the war: "It is a bad feature of the present situation, that there is such a rift between the politicians and the services. Winston certainly does not keep his team pulling happily in harness together. It is very wrong of him to keep abusing the services—the cry is taken up by other politicians & it is bad for the Service advisers to be made to feel ashamed of their uniforms."

Yet the evidence of events suggests that the prime minister's criticisms of his soldiers were well merited. The shortcomings of the wartime British Army will be addressed below. Here, it will only be remarked that Churchill's machinery for directing the war effort was much more impressive than the means for implementing its decisions on the battlefield. The War Cabinet was Britain's principal policy-making body, regularly attended by the Chiefs of Staff as well as by its own eight members—in 1941 Churchill, Attlee, Eden, Bevin, Wood, Beaverbrook, Greenwood and Sir John Anderson. Some four hundred committees and subcommittees, of varying membership and importance, devolved from it. Service business was addressed by the Chiefs at their own gatherings, usually in Churchill's absence. Of 391 Chiefs of Staff meetings in 1941, Churchill presided at only 23, whereas he chaired 97 of 111 meetings of the War Cabinet. He also conducted 60 out of 69 meetings of its Defence Committee's operational group, and 12 out of 13 meetings of its supply group.

Formalities were always maintained, with the prime minister addressing ministers and commanders by their titles rather than names. On Churchill's bad days, his subordinates were appalled by his intemperance and irrationality. But on his good ones—and what an astonishing number of these there were!—his deportment went far to render a war of national survival endurable for those conducting it. "When he is in the right mood, no entertainment can surpass a meeting with him," wrote a general. "The other day he presided over a meeting on supply of equipment to allies and possible allies. He bustled in and said 'well, I suppose it is the old story— too many little pigs and not enough teats on the old sow.' "

The Chiefs of Staff met every day save Sunday at 10:30 a.m., in a room beneath the Home Office connected to the Cabinet War Rooms. Sessions customarily continued until one p.m. In the afternoons, the Chiefs worked in their own offices, to which they returned after dinner unless a further evening meeting had been summoned, as happened at moments of crisis, of which there were many. Every Monday evening, the Chiefs attended War Cabinet meetings. The 1914–18 conflict precipitated the beginnings of a historic shift in the balance of decision making from commanders in the field towards the prime minister and his service chiefs in London. In the Second World War, this became much more pronounced. Generals at the head of armies, and admirals at sea, remained responsible for winning battles. But modern communications empowered those at the summit of national affairs to influence the conduct of operations in remote theatres, for good or ill, in a fashion impossible in earlier ages. Alan Brooke wrote later: "It is a strange thing what a vast part the COS [committee] takes in the running of the war and how little it is known or its functions appreciated! The average man in the street has never heard of it."

For any minister or service chief successfully to influence the prime minister, it was essential that he should be capable of sustaining himself in argument. Churchill considered that unless commanders had the stomach to fight him, they were unlikely to fight the enemy. Few found it easy to do this. Adm. Sir Dudley Pound, the first sea lord, was one of many senior officers who cherished ambivalent attitudes towards Churchill: "At times you could kiss his feet, at others you feel you could kill him." Pound was a capable organiser whose tenure as chairman of the Chiefs of Staff until March 1942 was crippled, first by a reluctance to assert his own will against that of the prime minister and, later, by worsening health. Capt. Stephen Roskill, the official historian of the wartime Royal Navy, believed that Pound was never a big enough man for his role. The admiral had doubts about his own capacities, and once asked Cunningham whether he should resign his post. Churchill bears substantial blame for allowing Pound to keep his job when his failing body, as well as inadequate strength of character, had become plain. It was fortunate for the Royal Navy that the admiral had some able and energetic subordinates.

Adm. Sir Andrew Cunningham, the Mediterranean C-in-C who succeeded Pound when he became mortally stricken, was frustrated by his own inarticulacy: "I . . . have to confess to an inherent difficulty in expressing myself in verbal discussion, which I have never got over except on certain occasions when I am really roused . . . I felt rather like a spider sitting in the middle of a web vibrating with activity." Soon after Cunningham took up his post at the Admiralty, one Saturday afternoon the telephone rang at his Hampshire home. The prime minister wanted to talk on the scrambler. Cunningham explained that he possessed no scrambler. Churchill said impatiently that a device would be installed immediately. The admiral and his wife were kept awake until engineers finished their task at one a.m., when a call was duly put through to Downing Street. The prime minister was by then asleep. Cunningham, considerably cross, was told that the emergency had passed.

Air Chief Marshal Sir Charles Portal, who assumed direction of the RAF in October 1940, was widely considered the cleverest of the Chiefs of Staff. "Peter" Portal displayed notable diplomatic gifts, especially later, in dealing with the Americans. Like many senior airmen, his principal preoccupation was with the interests of his own service, and above all its bomber offensive. His personality lacked the bright colours, his conduct the anecdotage which enabled a man to shine at dinner tables or in the historiography of the war, but Ismay's key subordinate Brig. Leslie Hollis paid tribute to Portal's incisive mind and infectious calm: "I never saw him ruffled," said Hollis, "even under vicious and uninformed attacks on the Air Force. He would sit surveying the critic coldly from beneath his heavy-lidded eyes, never raising his voice or losing his temper, but replying to rhetoric with facts." The army was envious of the skill with which Portal exercised his influence upon the prime minister, often more successfully than the CIGS. Gen. Sir John Dill was liked and respected by his colleagues, but by the summer of 1941 he was deeply scarred by the failures of his service. His fires were flickering, his self-confidence had ebbed. Chiefs of Staff's meetings throughout 1941–42 were pervaded by consciousness of the army's inability to deliver victories, and of the prime minister's consequent disaffection towards its leaders.

Maj. Gen. Hastings "Pug" Ismay, throughout Churchill's premiership his chief of staff as minister of defence and personal representative on the Chiefs of Staff Committee, was sometimes criticised as a courtier, too acquiescent to his master's whims. John Kennedy, for instance, disliked Ismay: "I am thankful I have so little to do with him," he said. On another occasion he noted, "Ismay is such a devotee of PM's that he is a danger. He said the other evening in the club 'if the PM came in & said he'd like to wipe his boots on me, I'd lie down & let him do it. He is such a great man everything should be done for him.' This is a dangerous attribute for a man who has such an influence on military advice."

Yet this was a minority view. Most people—ministers, commanders and officials alike—respected Ismay's tact and discretion. He perceived his role as that of representing the prime minister's wishes to the service chiefs, and vice versa, rather than himself acting as a prime mover. He never offered strategic advice, because he believed, surely rightly, that this would usurp the Chiefs' functions. He was a superb diplomat, who presided over a small staff of which the principal members were Hollis, who had served as a Royal Marine officer aboard a cruiser at the 1916 Battle of Jutland, and the brilliant, austere, bespectacled Col. Ian Jacob, a field marshal's son. Whatever mistakes were made by the British high command, however acute became the personal tensions between the prime minister and his generals, admirals and air marshals, throughout Churchill's war premiership the highest standards of coordination, staff discipline and exchange of information prevailed between Downing Street and the service ministries.

On the civil side, the prime minister was served by a remarkable group of officials. Cabinet Secretary Sir Edward Bridges preserved an enthusiasm for cerebral diversions, even amid the blitz. He presided over self-consciously intellectual debates in the Downing Street staff mess at supper, such as one in pursuance of the theme "Is there any evil except in intent?" Bridges had the additional merit of being as passionately committed as the prime minister was to victory at any cost, and in June 1940 he rejected out of hand proposals to establish skeleton Whitehall departments in Canada, against the eventuality of German occupation of Britain.

The Downing Street staff understood, as some outsiders did not, that while the prime minister's regime might be unusual, it was remarkably disciplined. Minutes were typed and circulated within an hour or two of meetings taking place, even after midnight. The private secretaries—for most of the war Leslie Rowan, John Martin, Tony Bevir and John Colville—worked in shifts through the day and much of the night. "The chief difficulty is understanding what he says," wrote Martin in his early days of service, "and great skill is required in interpreting inarticulate grunts or single words thrown out without explanation. I think he is consciously odd in these ways." Colville, as a young patrician—he was the grandson of Lord Crewe—who had also attended Harrow, Churchill's old school, basked in paternalistic indulgence from his master. His social self-assurance, indeed conceit, enabled him to gossip among potentates at the prime minister's dinner table without awe, though his role was only that of a humble official. As a diarist, Colville fulfilled a priceless historical function as chronicler of the prime minister's domestic routine.

Churchill's personal followers inspired mistrust outside the "secret circle," and sometimes inside it also. There was frequent criticism of his willingness to indulge old friends and family connections in significant posts. Later in the war, his son-in-law Duncan Sandys made himself deeply unpopular as a junior army minister. Alan Brooke swore that he would resign if, as was rumoured likely though it never became a reality, Sandys was promoted to become secretary for war. It was often asserted that Beaverbrook, Cherwell and Brendan Bracken were unsuitable intimates for the prime minister, just as important Americans resented Harry Hopkins's relationship with Roosevelt. Yet in judging Churchill's chosen associates, the only relevant issue is whether acolytes—the so-called cronies—improperly influenced his decisions.

Beaverbrook was the most wilful and intrusive. Whether in or out of office, he occupied an astonishing amount of the prime minister's time and attention. Churchill never appeared to notice Beaverbrook's physical cowardice, unusual in any member of his circle, and widely remarked by colleagues during the blitz, when as often as possible he retired to the country, and on long wartime journeys abroad. The press baron exercised notable power as minister of aircraft production in 1940, then as minister of supply in 1941. He remained thereafter one of the few civilians to whose views Churchill listened. Beaverbrook made much mischief about personalities. His contempt embraced the entire wartime Commons. "In truth it is only a sham of a parliament," he wrote to Hoare in Madrid in May 1941. "The Front Bench is part of the sham. There Attlee and Greenwood, a sparrow and a jackdaw, are perched on either side of the glittering bird of paradise." It is easy to identify issues on which Beaverbrook urged the prime minister to do the wrong thing, of which more will be said later. It is much harder to discover a case in which his imprecations were successful.

Brendan Bracken, Churchill's familiar for a decade before the war, enjoyed ready access, much resented by rivals. But his influence was deemed greater than it was, because the garrulous Bracken boasted so much about it. Fellow ministers and officials were sometimes shocked by the familiarity with which he addressed the prime minister as "Winston." He and Beaverbrook were dubbed the "knights of the bath" in recognition of the implausible rendezvous they sometimes shared with Churchill. Nonetheless, this clever, elusive Irishman, his bespectacled features surmounted by what looked like a wig of red steel wool, provided Churchill with a useful source of intelligence and gossip about domestic affairs and served as a successful minister of information from July 1941 to 1945. Forty in 1941, Bracken had high intelligence and a remarkable capacity for private kindness. As a pocket press baron himself, owner of the *Econo-*

mist and chairman of the *Financial News*, he thoroughly understood the demands of the media. He frequently intervened to improve journalists' access to the services, and to curb the prime minister's rage when newspapers were deemed to have exceeded the bounds of reasonable criticism. He exercised no influence on strategy, and was seldom present when it was discussed.

Professor Frederick Lindemann, the prime minister's personal scientific adviser who became Lord Cherwell in June 1941, was the most widely disliked of Churchill's intimates. His cleverness was not in doubt, but his intellectual arrogance and taste for vendettas bred many enemies. Fifty-five in 1941, Cherwell had inherited a fortune gained from waterworks in Germany. He enjoyed flaunting his wealth before less fortunate scientific colleagues, often arriving for Oxford meetings in a chauffeur-driven Rolls-Royce. His habit of crossing roads looking straight ahead, indifferent to oncoming traffic, reflected his approach to issues of state and war. A bachelor and vegetarian, of strongly right-wing and indeed racist convictions, he was an unself-conscious eccentric. When three of his Cabinet Office staff insisted on being transferred to the merchant navy to play a more active part in the war, he was alarmed by the secrets which they would take with them to sea. He told them: "If you see that you are about to be captured, you must kill yourselves immediately!"

When the scientist's judgement was mistaken, his obstinacy did considerable harm. He campaigned obsessively for aerial mines as a defence against air attack, wasting significant design and production effort. His advocacy of "area bombing" was founded on a misreading of data, and caused him to injure the Royal Navy's cause in the Battle of the Atlantic. Because Churchill trusted Cherwell, "the Prof's" errors were disproportionately damaging. The prime minister sometimes abused Cherwell's statistics to advance rash theses of his own. Ian Jacob described him as a "licensed gadfly." On balance, however, Cherwell's contribution to Churchill's governance was positive. It enabled him to support with evidence arguments on a vast range of issues.

Among lesser figures, the booming Maj. Desmond Morton was an able intelligence officer who provided important information to Churchill in his prewar wilderness years, and exercised considerable influence at Downing Street in 1940. Thereafter, however, Morton became marginalised, with a significant voice only on French matters. Charles Wilson, the prime minister's physician who became Lord Moran in 1943, inspired the postwar anger of Churchill's staff by publishing intimate diaries of his experiences. Jock Colville wrote contemptuously of the self-regarding doctor: "Moran was seldom, if ever, present when history was made; but he was quite often invited to dinner afterwards." This was to address a gerbil with an elephant gun. Moran was never a policy maker, nor did he even wield influence. It seems enough that he served Churchill well in his medical capacity, and proved an acceptable companion on the prime minister's historic journeys.

The "cronies" were viewed by Churchill's critics as charlatans. Yet each had real merits, above all brains. There were no fools in the prime minister's entourage, though steadiness of judgement was less assured. None of his chosen associates was a conformist. All were loners who walked by themselves, however readily they embraced social intercourse as a tool of influence. In Whitehall and at Westminster, less gifted men, both in and out of uniform, denounced the false prophets who supposedly led the prime minister astray. Yet most of Churchill's wilder schemes derived from his own supremely fertile imagination, not from mischief-makers in his inner circle. "He always retained unswerving independence of thought," wrote Jock Colville. "He approached a problem as he himself saw it and of all the men I have ever known he was the least liable to be swayed by the views of even his most intimate counsellors." In the same fashion, Churchill formed his own judgements of men, favourable or otherwise, and was deeply resistant to the influence of others in adjusting them.

Many misunderstandings of Churchill's conduct of governance by his contemporaries, including some close to the seat of power, derived from the promiscuity of his conversation. Every day, whether in the company of generals, ministers, visitors or personal staff, he gave vent to impulsive and intemperate judgements on people and plans. These sometimes amused, but often alarmed and appalled, even those with long experience of him. Yet his intimates, above all the officers of the War Cabinet Secretariat, knew that nothing Churchill said was intended as a basis for action, unless subsequently confirmed in writing. They knew that he often spoke merely as a means of helping himself to formulate ideas. It has been remarked that he had an undisciplined mind, the source of a cornucopia of ideas, some brilliant, others absurd. Ismay called him "a child of nature." Yet the most notable aspect of the machine for the direction of Britain's war was that it was better ordered than that of any other belligerent, notably including those of Germany and later the United States. A cynic might suggest that Churchill created a system to protect himself from his own excesses. In remarkable degree, this was successful.

The late spring of 1941 found the British no nearer than they had been six months earlier to perceiving a path to victory. When Gen. Raymond Lee returned to London after a trip to Washington in April, he wrote, "The people strike me . . . as being much more solemn than they were in January." Churchill's enthusiasm for special forces and raiding operations derived from his awareness of the need to strive constantly to sustain a semblance of momentum. A story was told to a general by his brother which achieved wide circulation in the War Office. As a boy, the narrator had been a guest at a game shoot at Blenheim Palace, where Churchill attempted an absurdly long shot at a hare. The boy asked him why he had wasted a cartridge. "Young man," replied Churchill blithely, "I wished that hare to understand it was taking part in these proceedings." The same spirit, addressed to matters of vastly greater import, impelled Churchill in the spring and summer of 1941. The War Office deemed it futile to hold Tobruk after Rommel had bypassed it in April. Only Churchill's insistence prompted deployment there of an Australian garrison, which was soon more numerous than the German force encircling it. But in that season of defeats, the saga of Australia's infantrymen—the "diggers"—withstanding the "siege of Tobruk" was elevated by British propaganda into a serviceable legend.

Military theatre had its limitations, however. Churchill had a grossly exaggerated belief in the power of boldness alone to overcome material and numerical deficiencies. "War," he wrote, "consists of fighting, gnawing and tearing, and . . . the weaker or more frail gets life clawed out of him by this method. Manoeuvre is a mere embellishment, very agreeable when it comes off . . . Fighting is the key to victory." Yet the events of 1940–41 showed, and subsequent experience confirmed, that British forces could defeat those of the Wehrmacht only when they were substantially stronger. If Hitler had dispatched to North Africa even a further two or three divisions from his vast order of battle, it is likely that Britain would have been driven from Egypt in 1941. Many senior soldiers thought this outcome likely, though they underrated Rommel's logistics problems. "I suppose you realise that we shall lose the Middle East," Dill said to Kennedy on June 21. Kennedy, in his turn, incurred Churchill's ire merely by mentioning that contingency in his presence. The British were spared from disaster in the Mediterranean in 1941 because Hitler's strategic priorities lay elsewhere. On June 22, Germany invaded Russia.

SIX

Comrades

THE GERMAN INVASION of Russia on June 22, 1941, transformed the
Second World War. The British, through Ultra intercepts, had long been
aware of Hitler's impending onslaught. They persuaded themselves that
their intervention in Greece had imposed a delay upon Operation Barbarossa. In reality, a late thaw and German equipment shortages were the
decisive factors in causing the assault to take place later than Hitler had
wished. The British and American peoples to this day perceive their contribution to the eastern war in terms of convoys heroically fought across
the Arctic to Murmansk, bearing massive Western aid. Reality was less
simple. In 1941–42, both Britain and the United States were desperately
short of war matériel for their own armed forces, and had little to spare for
Stalin's people. For eighteen months after Russia was invaded, the period
during which its survival hung in the balance, Western aid was much more
marginal than the rhetoric of Winston Churchill and Franklin Roosevelt
suggested and ordinary citizens in the West were encouraged to suppose.

In June 1941, the immediate impact of Barbarossa in Britain was surprisingly muted. The shocks of the previous year had imposed an anaes-
thetizing effect. Largely due to people's gratitude at finding themselves
still unscathed at their breakfast tables each morning, their island spared
from Nazi pillage, many received tidings of this epochal event with surprising insouciance. Edward Stebbing, a twenty-one-year-old soldier
whose impatience with the struggle was cited earlier, felt bewildered:
"There is nothing straightforward about this war. In the maze of lies and
treachery it is almost impossible to find the truth." The *Financial Times*
columnist Lex wrote on June 23: "Markets spent the morning trying to
make up their minds whether the German aggression against Russia was a
bull or a bear . . . The majority concluded that whatever happened we
could hardly be worse off as a result of Hitler's latest somersault." Here
was another manifestation of Churchill's "three-inch pipe" theory about

human emotions. Amid a surfeit of drama and peril, many people took refuge in the sufficient cares of their own daily lives, and allowed a torrent of world news, good and ill, to flow past them to the sea.

Most of Britain's ruling class, from the prime minister downwards, regarded the Soviet Union with abhorrence. The Russians had rebuffed all British diplomatic advances since the outbreak of war, and likewise London's warnings of Nazi intentions. Until the day of the German assault, under the terms of the 1939 Nazi-Soviet Pact Stalin provided Hitler with huge and material assistance. Only a few months earlier Vyacheslav Molotov, Stalin's foreign minister, bargained with the Nazis, albeit unsuccessfully, for a share of the spoils of British defeat. The extravagance of Soviet demands provided Hitler with a final pretext for launching Barbarossa.

In addressing the history of the Second World War, it is necessary to recognise the huge moral compromises forced upon the nations fighting under the banner of democracy and freedom. Britain, and subsequently America, strove for the triumph of these admirable principles wherever they could be secured—with the sometimes embarrassing exceptions of the European overseas empires. But again and again, hard things had to be done which breached faith with any definition of absolute good. If this is true of politics at all times, it was especially so between 1939 and 1945. Whether in dealing with France, Greece, Iraq, Persia, Yugoslavia or other nations, attitudes were struck and courses adopted by the Allies which no moral philosopher could think impeccable. British wartime treatment of its colonies, of Egypt and, above all, India, was unenlightened. But, if Churchill's fundamental nobility of purpose is acknowledged, most of his decisions deserve sympathy.

He governed on the basis that all other interests and considerations must be subordinated to the overarching objective of defeating the Axis. Those who, to this day, argue that Churchill "might have saved the British Empire" by making a bargain with Hitler, leaving Russia and Germany to destroy each other, ignore the practical difficulty of reaching a sustainable deal with the Nazi regime, and also adopt a supremely cynical insouciance towards its turpitude. The moral and material price of destroying Hitler was high, but most of mankind has since acknowledged that it had to be paid. In the course of the war, the prime minister was repeatedly called upon to decide not which party, nation or policy represented virtue but which must be tolerated or supported as the least base option. This imperative was never more conspicuous than in Britain's dealings with the Soviet Union.

Between 1917 and 1938, Churchill sustained a reputation as an implacable foe of Bolshevism. Yet in the last years before attaining the premiership, he changed key, displaying a surprising willingness to reach out to the Russians. In October 1938, against Chamberlain's strong views, he urged an alliance with Moscow, and counselled the Poles to seek an accommodation with Stalin. This line did as much to raise his standing with British Labour MPs as it did to lower it among Tories. In September 1939, he urged Chamberlain to perceive the Soviet advance into Poland as a favourable development: "None of this conflicts with our main interest, which is to arrest the German movement towards the East and South-East of Europe." In a broadcast a fortnight later, he said: "That the Russian armies should stand on this line [in Poland] was clearly necessary for the safety of Russia against the Nazi menace." In January 1940, it is true, he became an enthusiastic supporter of Finland, then beset by the Russians. He once enquired about the possibility of bombing Soviet oil fields at Baku, in the Caucasus, to stem fuel deliveries to Germany. Excepting this interruption, however, Churchill showed himself willing to make common cause with the Russians, if they would share the burden of defeating Hitler. This was probably because, even in 1939–40 before France fell, he could not see how else victory was to be accomplished.

He was at Chequers on that June Sunday morning when news came of Barbarossa. He immediately told Eden, a house guest, of his determination to welcome the Soviet Union as a partner in the struggle, then spent the rest of the day roaming restlessly under hot sunshine, refining themes and phrases for a broadcast. He communed with Beaverbrook and Sir Stafford Cripps, the Moscow ambassador who chanced to be in Britain, but did not trouble to summon the Cabinet. When at last he sat before the BBC microphone that evening, he began by acknowledging his own past hostility towards the Soviets: "The Nazi regime is indistinguishable from the worst features of Communism. It is devoid of all theme and principle except appetite and racial domination. No one has been a more consistent opponent of Communism than I have for the last twenty-five years. I will unsay no word that I have spoken about it." But then he asserted, in bold and brilliant terms, Britain's commitment to fight alongside Stalin's Russia:

> The past, with its crimes, its follies, and its tragedies flashes away. I see the Russian soldiers standing on the threshold of their native land, guarding the fields which their fathers tilled from time immemorial. I see them guarding their homes where mothers and wives pray—ah, yes, for there are times when all pray—for the safety of their loved ones, the return of the bread-winner, of their champion, of their pro-tector. I see the ten thousand villages of Russia where the means of

existence is wrung so hardly from the soil, but where there are still primordial human joys, where maidens laugh and children play.

I see advancing upon all this in hideous onslaught the Nazi war machine, with its clanking, heel-clicking Prussian officers, its crafty agents expert from the cowing and tying down of a dozen countries. I see also the dull, drilled, docile, brutish masses of the Hun soldiery plodding on like a swarm of crawling locusts. I see the German bombers and fighters in the sky, still smarting from many a British whipping, delighted to find what they believe is an easier and a safer prey.

I have to declare the decision of His Majesty's Government . . . Any man or state who fights on against Nazi-dom will have our aid . . . We shall give whatever aid we can to Russia and the Russian people . . . The Russian danger is therefore our danger, and the danger of the United States, just as the cause of any Russian fighting for his hearth and home is the cause of free men and free people in every quarter of the globe.

Not for the first time in the war, Churchill's words received the acclaim of most British people, while inspiring doubts among some Tory MPs and senior officers. Repugnance towards the bloodstained Soviets ran deep through the upper echelons of British society. Leo Amery, the India secretary, recoiled from making common cause with Communists. Col. John Moore-Brabazon, minister of aircraft production, was rash enough to publicly assert a desire to see the Germans and Russians exterminate each other. Jock Colville described this as "a sentiment widely felt." Lieutenant General Pownall complained about the limp-wristed attitude which he perceived in approaches towards the Russians by Foreign Secretary Anthony Eden and the diplomats of his department. "They think they are dealing with normal people. They are not. Russians are orientals and need treating quite differently and far more roughly. They are not Old Etonians . . ." Tory MP Cuthbert Headlam observed with curious detachment: "I don't suppose that the 'conquest' of Russia will take very long. And what then—presumably either Hitler will make some kind of peace offer based upon our acceptance of the 'New Order,' " or he will try his hand at an invasion here or push on in the [Middle] Eastern theatre." Headlam thought Churchill's posture tactically sensible, but like many other people found himself unable to anticipate a happy ending without the Americans. He fell back upon hopes of loftier assistance: "One feels that God is on our side—that's the great thing."

Among the British left, however, and the public at large, enthusiasm for Churchill's declaration of support for Russia was overwhelming. Independent Labour MP Aneurin Bevan, an almost unflagging critic of Churchill's leadership, nonetheless congratulated him on his welcome to the Russians as comrades in arms: "It was an exceedingly clever statement, a very difficult one to make, but made with great wisdom and strength." Surrey court reporter George King wrote: "I glory in all this. I have always had a soft spot for the Russians, and never blamed them for their dislike of us. We gave them good cause in the years after the last war ... Thank God for Russia. They have saved us from invasion this year." Londoner Vere Hodgson wrote on June 22: "The Russians have not been too nice to us in the past, but now we have to be friends and help one another ... So we have got one fighting ally left in Europe. I felt my morale rising." She added in the following month, with notable sagacity: "Somehow I think Stalin is more a match for Hitler than any of us ... he looks such an unpleasant kind of individual." It was never plausible that, in order to defeat Hitler, British people would have been willing to eat one another, but the Russians did so during the siege of Leningrad. Indeed, they endured incomparable horrors between 1941 and 1945, which spared the Western Allies from sacrifices such as Britain's prime minister might not flinch from, but his people certainly would have.

British Communists, many of whom had hitherto been indifferent to the war, now changed tune dramatically. Some, like Mrs. Elizabeth Belsey, henceforward matched impassioned admiration for Mother Russia's struggle with unremitting scorn for Britain's leaders. She wrote to her soldier husband:

> I was agreeably surprised ... that Churchill received Russia so promptly into the circle of our gallant allies. I had thought he might either continue his own war, ignoring Russia's, or clear out & let Russia hold the baby. On mature reflection, I realise that the course he took was for him the only realistic one. His speech disgusted me ... The damnably sloppy picture he drew of the Russians "defending their soil," and the even-atheists-pray-sometimes attitude towards Soviet women! And the way in which every single speaker on the subject makes it quite frankly clear that whereas we supported Greece for the Greeks, Norway for the Norwegians, Abyssinia for the Abyssinians and so on, we are now supporting Russia solely for ourselves ... And as for Churchill's personal record! Who's going to remind him of his statement that if he had to choose between communism & fascism he wasn't sure he'd choose communism?

Churchill derived Micawberish satisfaction from the fact that Hitler's lunge eastward signified that "something had turned up." But he shared with his generals a deep scepticism about Russia's ability to withstand the Wehrmacht. A year earlier, tiny Finland had humiliated the Red Army. British national pride argued that it was wildly implausible for Russia to repulse Hitler's legions, where the combined might of the French and British armies had failed to do so in 1940. Pownall wrote on June 29: "It's impossible to say how long Russian resistance will last—three weeks or three months?" The best that Britain's service chiefs sought from the new Eastern Front, following the launching of Barbarossa, was that the Russians might hold out until winter. British troops continued making preparations against a German descent on the home shore, partly because there was no other credible occupation for them. Pownall expressed scepticism: "I don't believe Winston is at heart a believer in invasion of this country. Of course he can't say that, because everyone would then immediately slacken off."

Much of the British Army—a substantially larger part than that deployed in the Middle East—stayed in Britain, where it would remain for three more years, to the chagrin of the Russians and later also of the Americans. Of some twenty-five infantry and four armoured divisions at home, only perhaps ten were battleworthy. There was no purpose in shipping formations to the Middle East, or for that matter to Britain's eastern empire, any faster than they could be equipped with tanks, antitank guns, automatic weapons and artillery. All these things remained in short supply. It was considered necessary to sustain production of weapons and aircraft known to be obsolete, because introduction of new designs imposed delays that seemed unacceptable. A host of ill-equipped, half-trained, profoundly bored British soldiers lingered in their own country month after month, and eventually year after year, while much smaller numbers of their comrades fought abroad. Alan Brooke, C-in-C Home Forces, complained how difficult it was to hone units to fighting pitch when they lacked the stimulus of action.

Moreover, the overwhelming bulk of the RAF's fighter strength continued to be deployed in southern England, conducting "sweeps" over northern France which were deemed morally important, but cost the RAF far greater losses than the Luftwaffe—411 pilots between June and September, for 103 Luftwaffe aircraft shot down (though the RAF claimed 731). Generals and admirals fumed at this use of air resources. Fighters were of priceless value in the Middle East and over the Mediterranean. When Admiral Cunningham was told that he was to become a Knight Grand Cross of the Bath, he responded tartly that he would rather be given three squadrons of Hurricanes. "Why the authorities at home apparently could not see the danger of our situation in the Mediterranean without adequate air support passed my comprehension," he wrote. There was a further difficulty, which would handicap the RAF for the rest of the war: the Spitfire and Hurricane were superb interceptors, ideal for home defence, but had very limited fuel endurance. The farther afield the war extended, the more severely Britain suffered from lack of long-range fighters. The Royal Navy lacked good carrier aircraft until American types became available in 1944–45. The large home deployment of fighters was justified by the Chiefs of Staff on the grounds that if Hitler launched an invasion, the RAF would play the critical role in national defence. It nonetheless seems an important strategic mistake that Britain retained extravagantly large air forces on domestic airfields—seventy-five squadrons of day fighters against thirty-four in the whole of the Middle and Far East in late 1941—even after most of the Luftwaffe had departed for the Eastern Front. Britain remained heavily overinsured against invasion well into 1942, at important cost to its overseas battlefield forces.

If Hitler, rather than turn east, had instead chosen to increase pressure on Britain, and even if he still flinched from invasion, he might have intensified the night blitz, seized Gibraltar and Malta, reinforced Rommel, and expelled the Royal Navy from the Mediterranean. Had these things come to pass, it is by no means assured that Churchill could have retained the premiership. As it was, providence lifted the spectre of immediate catastrophe in the west—if only the Atlantic convoy routes could be kept open. Here, in mid-1941, Ultra's role became critical. More and more German naval signals, above all orders to U-boats at sea, were being broken at Bletchley Park in "real time." From July, some convoys were successfully diverted away from known submarine concentrations, substantially reducing losses.

The critical choice for Britain, after June 22, 1941, was how far to deplete its own inadequate armoury to aid the Russians. The Cretan experience intensified British paranoia about paratroops. It was feared that German night airborne landings in southern England might negate all calculations about the Royal Navy's and the RAF's ability to frustrate an amphibious armada. On June 29, Churchill offered the War Office one of his more fanciful projections: "We have to contemplate the descent from the air of perhaps a quarter of a million parachutists, glider-borne or crash-landed aeroplane troops. Everyone in uniform, and anyone else who likes, must fall upon these wherever they find them and attack them with the utmost alacrity—'Let every one / Kill a Hun.' "

Against this background, the service ministers and Chiefs of Staff strongly opposed sending planes and tanks to Russia. Here was a mirror image of the debate in Washington about Britain. Churchill's soldiers, sailors and airmen displayed as much reluctance as their American brethren had done a year earlier to dispatch precious weapons to a nation that might be defeated before they could be put to use.

The Russians scarcely assisted their own cause. On the one hand, they made fantastic demands upon Churchill's government: for twenty-five British divisions to be shipped to Russia; for an army to stage an immediate landing on the Continent, to force the Germans to fight on a "second front"—a phrase of which much more would be heard. On the other hand, they confronted British diplomats and soldiers in Russia with a wall of silence about their own struggle. An American guest at a London lunch party dominated by political grandees wrote afterwards: "It was quite evident that all of the Britishers were deeply distrustful of the Russians. Nobody really knew much about what was happening."

Until the end of the war, the British learned more about the Eastern Front from Ultra intercepts of enemy signals than from their supposed allies in Moscow. Many German operational reports were swiftly available in London. Rigorous security sought to conceal from the enemy the fact that Bletchley Park was breaking their codes. Churchill was much alarmed by a report which appeared in the *Daily Mirror* headed SPIES TRAP NAZI CODE. The story began: "Britain's radio spies are at work every night . . . taking down the Morse code messages which fill the air . . . In the hands of experts they might produce a message of vital importance to our Intelligence Service." The *Mirror* piece was published in absolute ignorance of Ultra, and merely described the activities of British amateur radio "hams." But Churchill wrote to Duff Cooper, then still information minister, deploring such reporting. He was morbidly sensitive to the peril of drawing the slightest German attention to their radio security.

Yet there were dangerous indiscretions, including one by the prime minister himself in a BBC broadcast on August 24. He drew upon Ultra intercepts to highlight the numbers of civilians being murdered by the SS in Russia. The Germans noticed. Hitler's top police general, SS-Obergruppenführer Kurt Daluege, signalled all his units on September 13: "The danger of enemy decryption of wireless messages is great. For this reason only non-sensitive information should be transmitted." It was fortunate that the German high command failed to draw more far-reaching conclusions from Churchill's words.

In the first weeks after the panzers swept across the Soviet frontier, intelligence revealed that the Russians were suffering colossal losses of men, tanks, planes and territory. Everything the War Office could learn confirmed the generals' predisposition to assume that Stalin would be beaten. Only two important powers in Britain pressed the case for aid to Russia. The first was public opinion. Beyond the orbit of senior officers, aristocrats and businessmen who disliked the Soviets, Barbarossa unleashed a surge of British sentiment, indeed sentimentality, in favour of the Russian people, which persisted until 1945. Factories and shipyards, where Communist trade unionists had hitherto shown lukewarm support for a "bosses' war," were suddenly swept by enthusiasm for Russia. Communist Party membership in Britain rose—not least because frank discussion of the Soviet regime's barbarity was suspended for the duration. The British people nursed a shame about their own defeats, a guilt that their nation was accomplishing so little towards the defeat of Hitler, which would be ever more stridently articulated in the years ahead.

Then there was the prime minister. In the matter of Russia, as in his defiance of Hitler a year earlier, he embraced a policy which entirely accorded with the public mood: all aid to Britain's new comrades-in-arms. American military attaché Raymond Lee found it droll to see the Soviet ambassador, Ivan Maisky, "almost a pariah in London for so many years," now communing constantly with Churchill, Eden and U.S. ambassador John "Gil" Winant. Churchill's bigness on this issue emphasised the smallness of most of his colleagues. He perceived that whatever the difficulties, however slight the prospect of success, it must not be said that Russia suffered defeat because Britain failed to do what it could to assist her. At first, following Barbarossa, he pressed the Chiefs of Staff for a landing in northern Norway, to open a direct link to the Red Army. When this notion was quashed, in large part because Norway lay beyond range of land-based air cover, he ordered that every possible tank and aircraft, including some bought by Britain from the Americans, should be shipped to Stalin. There persisted, however, a very long day's march—much longer than most historians have allowed—between intent and effective implementation. Through the summer of 1941, while Russia's survival hung in the balance, pitifully little war matériel was dispatched.

As for the United States, the country was at first uncertain what to make of the new situation. Roosevelt sounded almost flippant in a letter to U.S. ambassador Adm. William Leahy in Vichy on June 26: "Now comes this Russian diversion. If it is more than just that it will mean the liberation of Europe from Nazi domination—and at the same time I do not think we need worry about any possibility of Russian domination." But the isolationist *Chicago Tribune* asked why the United States should ally itself with "an Asiatic butcher and his godless crew." The *New York Times* remained hesitant even in August: "Stalin is on our side today. Where will he be tomorrow?" Senator Bennett Champ Clark of Missouri shrugged, saying, "It's a case of dog eat dog." Archisolationist Senator Burton K. Wheeler of Montana declared his matching contempt for Stalin, Churchill and Roosevelt.

The U.S. Chiefs of Staff were even more reluctant to see weapons shipped to Russia than to Britain. Though the president forcefully expressed his determination to aid Stalin's people, months elapsed before substantial U.S. matériel moved. At the beginning of August, Roosevelt berated the State and War departments for their failure to implement his wishes on aid: "The Russians feel that they have been given the run-around in the United States." By the end of September, only $29 million worth of supplies had been dispatched. There was a sharp contrast between U.S. financial treatment of Britain and Russia. Where Britain in 1940–41 was obliged to sell its entire negotiable assets to pay American bills before receiving Lend-Lease aid, when Washington put a similar proposal to Moscow it was angrily rejected. Roosevelt acquiesced with a docility the British would have welcomed for themselves. American supplies to Russia were provided gratis, under Lend-Lease. But progress towards implementation remained slow. As in Britain, there was a lack of will as well as of immediate means.

The absence of Western aid made it all the more urgent that Britain should be seen to fight in the west, that the desert army should once more take the offensive. Auchinleck, "an obstinate, high-minded man" as Churchill described him in an unpublished draft of his war memoirs, insisted that he could not attack before autumn. Operation Crusader, as the new desert push was code-named, was repeatedly postponed. Churchill chafed and fulminated, even muttering implausibly about replacing Auchinleck with Lord Gort. But he continued to receive the same message from Cairo. The only bright spot in North Africa was the continuing defence of Tobruk by the 7th Australian Division. Churchill was exasperated beyond measure later in the year when the Australian government, in Canberra, by then led by Labor's John Curtin after Robert Menzies's eviction from power, insisted that this formation should be evacuated from the beleaguered port and replaced by British troops. On August 25, British forces entered Persia after the pro-Nazi shah's rejection of an ultimatum from London, demanding the expulsion of several hundred Germans from the country. Churchill and Eden shared an embarrassment about the Persian incursion, intensified when Russian forces moved into the north of the country. Persia became an important supply route for aid to Stalin, but the British were conscious that their seizure of power there echoed Hitler's method of doing business.

At home, Churchill urged the RAF's Bomber Command to intensify its night attacks on German industry. Yet these were not merely ineffectual, they were also shockingly costly. Between August 1 and 18 alone, 107 British bombers were lost over Germany and France. The night blitz on Britain incurred Luftwaffe losses of less than 1 percent for each raid, a substantial proportion of these to accidents. Yet the RAF's wartime bomber losses averaged 4 percent. This was a sobering statistic for young aircrew obliged to carry out thirty sorties to complete a tour of operations. Meanwhile, the Royal Navy's heroic and bloody Mediterranean convoy battles to sustain the defence of Malta commanded much media attention, but did nothing to divert German attention from the east.

As the Russians fell back, whole armies disintegrating before the Nazi juggernaut, Stalin was infuriated when Eden and Lord Moyne, government leader in the House of Lords, made speeches ruling out any prospect of an early Second Front. The ministers' intention was, of course, to quash speculation at home. But in Moscow, their remarks were perceived as crass. They obliged Hitler, by explicitly forswearing any threat to his rear. Stalin cabled Maisky at the end of August: "The British government, by its passive, waiting policy, is helping the Nazis. The Nazis want to knock off their enemies one at a time—today the Russians, tomorrow the British . . . Do the British understand this? I think they do. What do they want out of this? They want us to be weakened. If this suspicion is correct, we must be very severe in our dealings with the British."

British efforts to guard secrets from their new cobelligerent were fatally compromised by the plethora of Communist sympathisers, headed by Donald Maclean and John Cairncross, who had access to privileged information. More British documents, cables, committee minutes and Ultra intercepts were passed to the Soviet Union than Russia's intelligence service had resources to translate. For instance Lavrenty Beria, Stalin's intelligence chief, reported to his leader on August 28, 1941:

We would like to inform you on the contents of a telegram from the Ministry of Foreign Affairs of England dated 18 August this year addressed to the English ambassador to the USA. Contents of this telegram have been obtained by the Intelligence Department of NKVD of the USSR in London using our agents. "In response to Paragraph 3 of your telegram No. 3708 of 8 August. Our attitude towards Russians will be determined entirely on the principle of reciprocity. We must make them open their military installations and other objects of interest to our people in Russia. So far we have shown Russians almost nothing. In the near future they will be shown factories producing standard weapons. They will not, however, be admitted to experimental plants. Chiefs of staff have established the general principle for all institutions, whereby Russians can only be given such information or reports as would be useless to the Germans even if they gained possession of them . . . We hope that American authorities will not exceed the limits to which we adhere.

Such privileged insights into British thinking did nothing to persuade the Russians to lift the obsessive secrecy cloaking their own military and industrial activities.

For all Churchill's professions of enthusiasm about dispatching war matériel from Britain, precious little was happening. Within his own government, the policy commanded wholehearted support only from Eden and Beaverbrook. Lord Hankey was among those who openly opposed aiding Stalin, urging instead a higher priority for the Atlantic battle. Churchill declared in a BBC broadcast on September 9 that "large supplies are on the way" to the Soviet Union. Three weeks later he told the House of Commons: "In order to enable Russia to remain indefinitely in the field as a first-class war-making power, sacrifices of the most serious kind and the most extreme efforts will have to be made by the British people, and enormous new installations or conversions from existing plants will have to be set up in the United States, with all the labour, expense and disturbance of normal life which these entail."

Yet the Chiefs of Staff's objections delayed even a shipment of two hundred U.S.-built Tomahawk fighters and a matching number of Hurricanes promised to Stalin by the prime minister. These planes reached Russia at the end of August. Otherwise, Britain's main contribution by autumn was a consignment of rubber. Churchill's people were as bemused as Moscow was angered by Britain's failure to employ its own forces in some conspicuous emergency action to distract the Germans. Surrey court reporter George King wrote on September 16: "Hitler is throwing all he has got into the Eastern battles. I think we all wish here we could strike him somewhere in the West, but I suppose we are not ready yet." And again a few weeks later: "The marvellous Russians are still holding the enemy."

Late in September, the British government undertook an important initiative. Lord Beaverbrook, now minister of supply, sailed for Russia with a twenty-two-member British delegation including Ismay, Churchill's chief of staff, and accompanied—remarkably, given that the United States was still a nonbelligerent—by eleven Americans led by Averell Harriman, Roosevelt's emissary. "Make sure we are not bled white," Churchill told

Beaverbrook on parting. But Beaverbrook was determined to stretch out a hand to Stalin, to demonstrate a goodwill and generosity beyond anything the British government and Chiefs of Staff had mandated. In three meetings with Stalin, at which the Russian leader displayed insatiable curiosity about Churchill, Beaverbrook deployed all his charm and enthusiasm. He swallowed Stalin's insults—"What is the use of an army if it does not fight? . . . The paucity of your offers shows you want to see the Soviet Union defeated." The press lord sought to amuse as well as encourage the warlord. A civil servant observed cynically that Beaverbrook and Stalin achieved a rapport because they were both racketeers. The British promised tanks, planes and equipment—explicitly 200 aircraft and 250 tanks a month—while Harriman, on behalf of the Americans, offered matching largesse. The British proposal represented between a quarter and a third of 1941–42 domestic production of fighters, and more than a third of tank output. It was as much as any minister could have offered, but the Russians considered it nugatory in the context of the titanic struggle to which they were committed.

Beaverbrook returned to London on October 10 in messianic mood. In public, he praised to the skies Stalin and his nation. To the Defence Committee of the War Cabinet, he wrote: "There is today only one military problem—how to help Russia. Yet on that issue the chiefs of staff content themselves with saying that nothing can be done." So violently did he press the Russian case that Ian Jacob of the War Cabinet Secretariat became persuaded that he aspired to supplant Churchill as prime minister. Beaverbrook urged an immediate landing in Norway, while from Moscow Cripps cabled, proposing that British troops should be sent to reinforce the Red Army. Thenceforward, Beaverbrook became the foremost advocate of an early Second Front, exploiting his own newspapers to press the case. It is sometimes suggested that he made his only important contribution to Britain's war effort during the summer of 1940, as minister of aircraft production. But his intervention in the autumn of 1941, to demand supplies for Russia, was of even greater significance. At a time when many others in London, commanders and ministers alike, were dragging their feet, the press baron's intemperate zeal made a difference to both public and political attitudes.

Beaverbrook's subsequent Second Front campaign, of which more will be said below, was irresponsible and disloyal. He displayed naïveté or worse in his extravagant eulogies of the Soviet Union, ignoring and even denying the bloodstained nature of Stalin's tyranny in a fashion Churchill never stooped to. Alan Brooke was among those who harboured lasting bitterness about the commitments which Beaverbrook made in Moscow, which he considered irresponsibly generous. Yet as minister of supply, Beaverbrook grasped a fundamental point that more fastidious British politicians, generals and officials refused to acknowledge. Whatever the shortcomings of Russia as an ally, the outcome of the struggle in the east must be decisive in determining Britain's fate. The North African campaign might loom large in British perceptions and propaganda, but was of negligible importance alongside Stalin's war. If Hitler overwhelmed Russia, he might become invincible in Europe even if America later entered the war.

Until March 1942, when the Germans awoke to the importance of interdicting Allied supplies and strongly reinforced their air and naval forces in northern Norway, convoys to Russia were almost unmolested, and only two British ships were lost. Churchill appointed Beaverbrook chairman of a new Allied Supplies Executive, to plan and supervise deliveries. Yet even with his support, shipments remained modest. The British dispatched obsolescent Hurricanes, many of which arrived damaged; U.S.-built Tomahawk fighters, which the Russians found unreliable, and for a time grounded; together with tanks and Boyes antitank rifles, which the British Army recognised as inadequate. The second so-called PQ convoy to Russia sailed only on October 18, 1941, the third on November 9. In their desperation, the Russians came as near as ever in the war to displaying gratitude. A Soviet admiral said later: "I can still remember with what close attention we followed the progress of the first convoys in the late autumn of 1941, with what speed and energy they were unloaded in Archangel and Murmansk."

Lord Hankey, however, wrote with malicious satisfaction about the perceived hypocrisy of Beaverbrook's enthusiasm for arming Russia, when as minister of supply he was responsible for the shortcomings of British tank production: "Now I have to bring to light the fact that he is building nothing but dud tanks when he is vociferously appealing to the workers to work all day and all night to produce for Russia innumerable Tanks—all dud Tanks." The Russians valued the Valentine, which coped with the conditions of the Eastern Front much better than the Matilda, which was also shipped in quantity. But they quickly grasped that most of the weapons dispatched from Britain were those its own forces least wanted. They scarcely helped themselves by contemptuously dismissing British offers of technical instruction. The new users' unfamiliarity caused much equipment to be damaged or destroyed. Several Russian pilots killed themselves by attempting to take off without releasing their Tomahawks' brakes.

When large-scale American supplies reached Russia in 1943–44, these exercised a dramatic influence on the feeding and transport of the Red Army. The Russians soon lost interest in tanks and planes, which they preferred to build for themselves, seeking instead American trucks, boots, technical equipment, aluminium and canned meat. It is arguable that food deliveries narrowly averted starvation in Russia in the winter of 1942–43. U.S. shipments eventually totalled £2.5 billion, against Britain's £45.6 million. Allied aid is thought to have contributed 10 percent to the Soviet war effort in 1943–44—but only 5 percent in 1942, and a negligible proportion in 1941. Chris Bellamy, among the best-informed Western historians of the Soviet Union's war, suggests that while such a contribution seems marginal, when the Soviet Union hung close to defeat it may have been decisive.

In 1941–42 the British and Americans cannot realistically be blamed for dispatching so little to Russia, because both weapons production and shipping were inadequate to meet their own needs. The relevant point is merely that there was a chasm between Anglo-American rhetoric and the real Western contribution. In the first year after Barbarossa was launched, of 2,443 tanks promised by the Western powers only 1,442 arrived on time, together with 1,323 of 1,800 aircraft. During this period, the Russians were themselves producing two thousand tanks a month—most of notably higher quality than those shipped to Murmansk and Archangel. The Red Army sometimes lost a thousand tanks a week on the battlefield.

By the autumn of 1941, the tension between popular enthusiasm in Britain for Stalin's people and contempt for the Russians in some parts of the war machine was imposing intense pressure on the prime minister. An *Observer* columnist suggested that Russia's entry into the war fed Britain's instinctive complacency: "The effect upon us psychologically is unhealthy. We have found a short cut to victory . . . We settle back to read with satisfaction how our air offensive against Germany is helping our great Soviet ally. With Russia and U.S.A. on our side, now surely all will be well." Edward Stebbing, discharged from the army and working as a laboratory technician, wrote in October: "My main feeling is one of bitter, flaming anger at the inertia of our government . . . our help to Russia has been almost negligible."

Even as Stebbing was penning his angry reflections, the prime minister warned Middle East Command of "the rising temper of the British people against what they consider our inactivity." To his son, Randolph, in the Middle East, he described on October 31 the sniping of his critics in Parliament and Beaverbrook's frequent threats of resignation: "Things are pretty hard here . . . The Communists are posing as the only patriots in the country. The Admirals, Generals and Air Marshals chant their stately hymn of 'Safety First.' . . . In the midst of this I have to restrain my natural pugnacity by sitting on my own head. How bloody!" Gen. John Kennedy wrote in his diary in September: "The fundamental difficulty is that altho we want the Germans to be knocked out above all, most of us feel . . . that it would not be a bad thing if the Russians were to be finished as a military power too . . . The CIGS constantly expresses his dislike of the Russians . . . The Russians on their side doubtless feel the same about us."

Pownall, Dill's vice chief, wrote in October: "Would that the two loathsome monsters, Germany and Russia, drown together in a death grip in the winter mud." Oliver Harvey, at the Foreign Office, was astonished by the strength of ill will towards Moscow within the government: "The Labour ministers . . . are as prejudiced as the P.M. against the Soviets because of their hatred and fear of the Communists at home." Churchill himself, according to the diplomat, was prone to spasms of doubt about how far aid to Russia was cost-effective: "After his first enthusiasm, he is now getting bitter as the Russians become a liability and he says we cannot afford the luxury of helping them with men, only with material."

Yet Churchill recognised how fortunate his nation had been thus far to wage war at relatively small cost in lives compared to those lost by Poland and France, not to mention Russia. He marvelled: "In two years struggle with the greatest military Power, armed with the most deadly weapons, barely 100,000 of our people have been killed, of which nearly half are civilians." Such a cool assessment of what would, in other times, have been deemed a shocking "butcher's bill," helps to explain his fitness for the nation's leadership. Robert Menzies, when still Australian prime minister, noted this: "Winston's attitude to war is much more realistic than mine. I constantly find myself looking at 'minor losses' and saying 'there are some darkened homes.' But he is wise. War is terrible and it cannot be won except by lost lives. That being so, don't think of them."

Churchill, once more desperate for military theatre, urged the War Office to accelerate plans for raids on the Continent. "The Army must do something—the people want it," he told John Kennedy and the director of military intelligence during a lunch at Downing Street. "Surely this [is] within our powers—The effects might be enormous—The Germans engaged in Russia—now [is] the time." Kennedy wrote: "Winston is in a difficult position. He is hard pressed politically to take action while Russia is struggling so desperately. He keeps saying 'I cannot hold the position.' The difficulty is that with a disaster the position may be harder to hold." News from the Eastern Front was unremittingly grim. The Red Army's losses were appalling. A great swath of Stalin's empire had already fallen to Hitler. Churchill, after a meeting with his generals on October 11, bade them farewell with a mournful headshake: "Yes, I am afraid Moscow is a gone coon," he said, padding off along the Downing Street passage towards his afternoon nap.

The Soviet Union had not the smallest moral claim upon Britain. Even if Churchill had stripped his own nation's armed forces and dispatched heavier shipments to Murmansk after Barbarossa was launched, the impact on the early Eastern Front campaigns would have been small. As it was, the Chiefs of Staff were dismayed by the impact of aid to Russia upon British tank and aircraft strengths in the Middle and Far East, which were anyway grievously inadequate. Worse, American deliveries to Britain were significantly cut so that Roosevelt could meet his own commitments to Stalin. Given the weakness of British arms in 1941, it was unrealistic to suppose that Churchill could have done much more. In 1942, however, a yawning gap opened between British and American undertakings, and quantities of matériel delivered. It was ironic, of course, that the boundlessly duplicitous Soviets should thereupon have proclaimed, and even sincerely harboured, moral indignation towards Britain and the United States. But the principal reality of subsequent military operations would be that Russians did most of the dying necessary to undo Nazism, while the Western powers advanced at their own measured pace towards a long-delayed confrontation with the Wehrmacht.

For many years after 1945, the democracies found it gratifying to perceive the Second World War in Europe as a struggle for survival between themselves and Nazi tyranny. Yet the military outcome of the contest was overwhelmingly decided by the forces of Soviet tyranny, rather than by Anglo-American armies. Perversely, this reality was better understood by contemporary Americans and British than it has been by many of their descendants.

SEVEN

The Battle of America

1. Strictly Cash

THROUGHOUT 1941, even after torrents of blood began to flow across the plains of Russia, Churchill's foremost priority remained the enlistment of the United States as a fighting ally. As he followed the fortunes of Britain's desert battles, the pursuit of the *Bismarck*, the Atlantic convoy struggle, the campaign in Greece and the faltering bomber offensive, his American vision dominated the far horizon. Unless or until the United States joined the war, Britain might avert defeat, but could not aspire to victory. Among Churchill's priceless contributions to Britain's salvation was his wooing of the United States, when many of his compatriots were rash enough to indulge rancour towards what they perceived as the fat, complacent nation across the Atlantic. "I wonder if the Americans realise how late they are leaving their intervention," wrote John Kennedy in May 1941, "that if they wait much longer we may be at the last gasp." In a notable slip of the tongue, a BBC announcer once referred to the threat of "American" rather than "enemy" parachutists descending on Britain.

It would be hard to overstate the bitterness among many British people, high and low, about the United States' abstention from the struggle. The rhetoric of Roosevelt and Churchill created an enduring myth of U.S. generosity in 1940–41. Cordell Hull, the secretary of state, wrote of "rushing vast quantities of weapons to Britain in the summer of 1940." In truth, however great the symbolic importance of early U.S. consignments, their practical value was small. American-supplied artillery and small arms were obsolete, and made a negligible contribution to Britain's fighting power. Aircraft deliveries in 1941 were moderate both in quantity and quality. The fifty old destroyers loaned by the United States in exchange for British colonial basing rights were scarcely seaworthy: just nine were operational at the end of 1940, and the rest required long refits. Only from 1942 onwards, when Britain received Grant and Sherman tanks,

105mm self-propelled guns, Liberator bombers and much else, did U.S. war matériel dramatically enhance the capabilities of Churchill's forces.

Moreover, the guns, tanks and planes shipped across the Atlantic didn't represent American largesse, because until the end of 1941 these were cash purchases. Under the terms of the Neutrality Act imposed by Congress, no belligerent could be granted credit. For the first two years of the war the United States reaped huge profits from arms sales. "The United States Administration is pursuing an almost entirely American policy, rather than one of all possible aid to Britain," Eden wrote to Churchill on November 30, 1940. Roosevelt anticipated British bankruptcy and adopted the notion of "loaning" supplies, which originated with New York's Century Association, before Churchill asked him to do so. But the president was furious when Lord Lothian, in October 1940 still British ambassador in Washington, told American journalists: "Well, boys, Britain's broke. It's your money we want." There is doubt whether the ambassador used these exact words, but the thrust of his remarks was undisputed.

Roosevelt told Lothian there could be no suggestion of American subsidy until Britain had exhausted her ability to pay cash, for Congress would never hear of it. He might have added that the British adopted the same attitude to Finland, when that country was fighting the Soviets in 1940. London insisted on cash terms for such scanty war supplies as Britain dispatched. Now, on America's part, there was a widespread belief in British opulence, quite at odds with reality. Amid the Battle of Britain, the U.S. administration questioned whether Churchill's government had honestly revealed its remaining assets. Washington insisted upon an audited account, a demand British ministers found humiliating. Churchill wrote to Roosevelt on December 7, 1940, saying that if Britain's cash drain to the United States continued, the nation would find itself in a position in which "after the victory was won with our blood and sweat, and civilization saved and the time gained for the United States to be fully armed against all eventualities, we should stand stripped to the bone. Such a course would not be in the moral or economic interests of either of our countries."

In responding to Churchill, Roosevelt never addressed this point, and his evasion was significant. He acknowledged a strong U.S. national interest in Britain's continued resistance, displaying extraordinary energy and imagination in moving public and congressional opinion, but not in its postwar solvency. American policy throughout the war emphasised the importance of strengthening its competitive trading position vis-à-vis Britain, by ending "imperial preference." The embattled British began to receive direct aid, through Lend-Lease, only when the last of their gold and foreign assets had been surrendered. Many British businesses in America were sold at firesale prices. The Viscose rayon-manufacturing company, the jewel in the overseas crown of the Courtaulds company and possessing assets worth $120 million, was knocked down for a mere $54 million, because Treasury Secretary Henry Morgenthau insisted that the cash should be realised at a week's notice. New York bankers pocketed $4 million of this sum in commission on a riskless transaction. Shell, Lever Brothers, Dunlop Tire and British insurance interests were alike compelled to sell off their U.S. holdings for whatever American rivals chose to pay. The governor of the Bank of England, Montagu Norman, wrote in March 1941: "I have never realised so strongly as now how entirely we are in the hands of American 'friends' over direct investments, and how much it looks as if, with kind words and feelings, they were going to extract these one after another."

The British government exhausted every expedient to meet U.S. invoices. The Belgian government in exile lent £60 million worth of gold which had been brought out of Brussels, although their Dutch and Norwegian counterparts refused to sell gold for sterling. An American cruiser collected from Cape Town Britain's last £50 million in bullion. Lend-Lease came with ruthless conditions constraining British overseas trade, so stringent that London had to plead with Washington for minimal concessions enabling them to pay for Argentine meat, vital to feeding Britain's people. Postwar British commercial aviation was hamstrung by the Lend-Lease terms. If Roosevelt's behaviour was founded upon a pragmatic assessment of political realities and protection of U.S. national interests, only the imperatives of the moment could have obliged Churchill publicly to assert its "unselfishness." Whatever U.S. policy towards Britain represented between 1939 and 1945, it was never that. "Our desperate straits alone could justify its terms," wrote Eden about the first round of Lend-Lease.

Most of the British anyway did not care for their transatlantic cousins. Anti-Americanism was pronounced among the aristocracy. Halifax, whom Churchill dispatched to Britain's Washington embassy in December 1940, told Stanley Baldwin: "I have never liked Americans, except odd ones. In the mass I have always found them dreadful." Lord Linlithgow, a fellow grandee who was viceroy of India, wrote to commiserate with Halifax on his posting: "The heavy labour of toadying to your pack of pole-squatting parvenus! What a country, and what savages those who inhabit it!" Halifax told Eden that he had proposed him as an alternative candidate for the ambassadorship: "I only said that I thought you might hate it a little less than myself!"

Installed at the embassy, the former foreign secretary endured much suffering in the service of Britain, not least during a visit to a Chicago White Sox game in May 1941, at which he found himself invited to eat a hot dog. This was too much for the fastidious ambassador, who declined. During a trip to Detroit, he was pelted with eggs and tomatoes by a group calling itself "The Mothers of America." Oliver Harvey, Eden's private secretary, described the aloof Halifax's performance in his role as "pretty hopeless—the old trouble of being unable to make real personal contacts . . . All business in the U.S.A. is now transacted by telephoning and 'popping-in,' both of which H can't abide. He only goes to see the President on business—and naturally usually to ask for things—he has never got onto a more intimate chat basis with him." Dalton related a mischievous story that Halifax broke down and wept soon after his arrival in Washington, "because he couldn't get on with these Americans."

Many Tory MPs, Eden among them, shared the grandees' distaste for the United States. Cuthbert Headlam, admittedly something of an old woman, wrote of Americans with condescension: "They really are a strange and unpleasing people: it is a nuisance that we are so dependent on them." A Home Intelligence report found "no great enthusiasm for the US or for US institutions among any class of the British people . . . There was an underlying irritation largely due to American 'apathy.' " Fantastically, some British officers questioned whether it would be in Britain's interests for America to become a belligerent. Air Marshal Sir John Slessor, with the British mission in Washington in April 1941, noted that some of his colleagues believed that "it wouldn't really pay us for the US to be actively engaged in the war." Air Marshal Sir Arthur Harris, later C-in-C of Bomber Command, wrote with characteristic intemperance about the difficulties of representing the RAF in Washington in 1941. It was hard to make progress, he said bitterly,

> when one is dealing with a people so arrogant as to their own ability and infallibility as to be comparable only to the Jews and the Roman Catholics in their unshakeable conviction that they alone possess truth. As to production generally out here. This country is now at a crossroads. Up to date they have had a damn fine war. On British dollars. Every last one of them. The result has been a magnificent boom after long years of black depression and despair . . . They lose no opportunity of impressing upon us individually how magnificently they are fighting [sic] and how inept, inefficient and idiotic and cowardly is our conduct of those few miserable efforts we ourselves are making in battle and in industry . . . Such production of war materials as has been

achieved up to date has therefore been all to their profit and in no way to their inconvenience . . . They will come in when they think that we have won it. Not before. Just like they did last time. They will then tell the world how they did it. Just like they did last time.

If Harris's tone was absurdly splenetic, it was a matter of fact that Britain and France provided the surge of investment that launched America's wartime boom. In 1939, U.S. gross national output was still below its 1929 level. Anglo-French weapons orders and cash thereafter galvanised U.S. industry, even before Roosevelt's huge domestic arms programme took effect. Between 1938 and the end of 1942 average income per family in Boston rose from $2,418 to $3,618 and in Los Angeles from $2,031 to $3,469, figures admittedly boosted by inflation and longer working hours. It could be argued—and indeed was, by the likes of Harris—that Britain exhausted its gold and foreign currency reserves to fund America's resurrection from the Depression.

In London, ministers and generals found it irksome to be required to lavish extravagant courtesies upon transatlantic visitors. Hugh Dalton grumbled about attending a party given at the Savoy by the *Sunday Express* for American broadcaster Raymond Gram Swing: "It is just a little humiliating, though we shall soon get more and more used to this sort of thing, that the majority of the Ministers of the Crown plus foreign diplomats, British generals and every kind of notability in the press world have to be collected to help to boost this, I am sure, quite admirable and well-disposed American broadcaster." Dalton was disgusted when the guest of honour asked him blithely whether there were factions in Britain willing to make peace with Germany. Nor was such impatience confined to ministers. Kenneth Clark of the Ministry of Information suggested the need for a campaign against "the average man's . . . unfavourable view of the United States as being a country of luxury, lawlessness, unbridled capitalism, strikes and delays."

The British were exasperated by American visitors who told them how to run their war, while themselves remaining unwilling to fight. A British officer wrote of Roosevelt's friend the flamboyant Col. William "Wild Bill" Donovan: "Donovan . . . is extremely friendly to us & a shrewd and pleasant fellow and good talker. But I could not but feel that this fat & prosperous lawyer, a citizen of a country not in the war, & which has failed to come up to scratch even in its accepted programme of assistance, possessed very great assurance to be able to lay down the law so glibly about what we and other threatened nations should & sh[ou]ld not do."

It is against this background of British resentment and indeed hostility towards the United States that Churchill's courtship of Roosevelt must be perceived. The challenge he faced was to identify what D. C. Watt has called "a possible America," able and willing to deliver. This could only be sought through the good offices of its president. Churchill, least patient of men, displayed almost unfailing public forbearance towards the United States, flattering its president and people, addressing with supreme skill both American principles and self-interest. He was much more understanding than most of his countrymen of American utopianism. On the way to Chequers one Friday night late in 1940, he told Colville that "he quite understood the exasperation which so many English people feel with the American attitude of criticism combined with ineffective assistance; but we must be patient and we must conceal our irritation. (All this was punctuated with bursts of 'Under the Spreading Chestnut Tree'.)"

Churchill himself knew the United States much better than most of his compatriots, having spent a total of five months there on visits in 1895, 1900, 1929 and 1931. "This is a very great country, my dear Jack," he wrote enthusiastically to his brother back in 1895, when he stopped by en route to the Spanish war in Cuba. "What an extraordinary people the Americans are!" He was shocked by the spartan environment of the West Point Military Academy, but much flattered by his own reception there: "I was . . . only a Second Lieutenant, but I was . . . treated as if I had been a General." During his December 1900 lecture tour, he was introduced in New York by Mark Twain, and told an audience in Boston: "There is no one in this room who has a greater respect for that flag than the humble individual to whom you, of the city which gave birth to the idea of a 'tea party,' have so kindly listened. I am proud that I am the natural product of an Anglo-American alliance; not political, but stronger and more sacred, an alliance of heart to heart."

He had met Presidents Theodore Roosevelt, Woodrow Wilson and Herbert Hoover, along with Vanderbilts and Rockefellers, Hollywood stars, Henry Morgenthau, William Randolph Hearst and Bernard Baruch. He had lectured to American audiences in 1931–32 about the perceived shared destiny of the English-speaking peoples. Many of his British contemporaries saw in Churchill American behavioural traits, above all a taste for showmanship, that his own class disliked, but which were now of incomparable value. Humble London spinster Vere Hodgson perceived this, writing in her diary: "Had he been pure English aristocracy he would not have been able to lead in the way he has. The American side gives him a superiority complex—in a way that Lord Halifax would not think in good taste—but we need more than good taste to save Britain at this particular moment."

In 1940–41, Churchill sometimes displayed private impatience towards perceived American pusillanimity. "Here's a telegram for those bloody Yankees," he said to Jock Colville as he handed the private secretary a cable in the desperate days of May 1940. In dispatches to Washington, the malignant U.S. ambassador Joseph Kennedy made the worst of every such remark which he intercepted. He translated Churchill's well-merited dislike of himself into allegations that the prime minister was anti-American. Kennedy's dispatches inflicted some injury upon Britain's cause in Washington, cauterised only when Roosevelt changed ambassadors in 1941, replacing Kennedy with John "Gil" Winant, and Churchill embarked upon personal relationships with the president, Harry Hopkins and Averell Harriman. Churchill's broadcasts, however, already commanded large American audiences, and imposed his personality upon Roosevelt's nation in 1940–41 almost as effectively as upon his own people. By late 1941, Churchill ran second only to the president in a national poll of U.S. radio shows' "favourite personality." "Did you hear Mr. Churchill Sunday?" Roscoe Conkling Simmons asked his readers in the *Chicago Defender* on May 3, 1941. "You may be against England, but hardly against England as Mr. Churchill paints her . . . Did you note how he laid on the friendship of Uncle Sam?" Churchill's great phrases were repeated again and again in the U.S. press, "blood, toil, tears and sweat" notable among them.

If Churchill had not occupied Britain's premiership, who among his peers could have courted the United States with a hundredth part of his warmth and conviction? There was little deference in his makeup—none, indeed, towards any of his own fellow countrymen save the king and the head of his own family, the Duke of Marlborough. Yet in 1940–41, he displayed this quality in all his dealings with Americans, and, above all, with their president. When the stakes were so high he was without self-consciousness, far less embarrassment. To a degree that few of his fellow countrymen proved able to match between 1939 and 1945, he subordinated pride to need, endured slights without visible resentment, and greeted every American visitor as if his presence did Britain honour.

By far the most important of these was, of course, Harry Hopkins, who arrived on January 8, 1941, as the president's personal emissary, bearing a letter to King George VI from his fellow head of state, saying that "Mr. Hopkins is a very good friend of mine, in whom I repose the utmost confidence." Hopkins was a fifty-year-old Iowan, a harness maker's son who had been a lifelong crusader for social reform. He met Roosevelt in 1928, and the two men formed an intimacy. Hopkins, the archetypal New

Dealer, in 1932 federal relief administrator, and one of the strongest influences on the administration. Roosevelt liked him in part because he never asked for anything. It was the heady scent of power that Hopkins savoured, not position or wealth, though he had a gauche enthusiasm for nightclubs and racetracks, and was oddly flattered by press denunciations of himself as a playboy. He cherished contrasting passions for fungi and the poetry of Keats. The high spot of his only prewar visit to London, in 1927, was a glimpse of Keats's house. A lonely figure after the death of his second wife from cancer in 1937, he was invited by FDR to live at the White House. Hopkins had pitched camp there ever since, with the title of secretary of commerce and the undeclared role of chief of staff to the president, until he was given responsibility for making Lend-Lease work.

Hopkins's influence with the president was resented by many Americans, not all of them Republicans. He was widely unpopular, being described by critics as "FDR's Rasputin," and an "extreme New Dealer." At the outset of World War II, he had been an instinctive isolationist, writing to his brother: "I believe that we really can keep out . . . Fortunately there is no great sentiment in this country for getting into it, although I think almost everyone wants to see England and France win." Physically, he cut an unimpressively dishevelled figure, his long neck and gaunt features ravaged by the stomach cancer that had almost killed him. Many people who met Hopkins perceived, through the haze from the cigarettes he chain-smoked, "a walking corpse." A *Time* photograph of him carried the caption: "He can work only seven hours a day." Brendan Bracken, sent to greet Hopkins when his flying boat landed at Poole Harbour, was appalled to find this vital visitor slumped apparently moribund in his seat, unable even to unfasten his seatbelt. The relationship with the British upon which the envoy now embarked became the last important mission of his life.

On January 10, 1941, Churchill welcomed Hopkins for the first time in the little basement dining room of Downing Street—the house was somewhat battered by bomb blast—for a tête-à-tête lunch which lasted three hours. The guest opened their conversation with the forthrightness which characterised Hopkins's behaviour: "I told him there was a feeling in some quarters that he, Churchill, did not like America, Americans or Roosevelt." This was Joseph Kennedy's doing, expostulated the prime minister, and a travesty. He promised absolute frankness. He said that he hoped Hopkins would not go home until he was satisfied "of the exact state of England's need and the urgent necessity of the exact material assistance Britain requires to win the war." He then deployed all his powers to charm his guest, with unqualified success.

Hopkins's intelligence and warmth immediately endeared him to Churchill. Throughout his political life, the president's man had decided upon courses of action, then pursued them with unstinting energy. If he arrived in Britain with a relatively open mind, within days he embraced the nation, its leader, and its cause with a conviction that persisted for many months, and did incalculable service. That first Friday evening, the American drove to join the prime minister and his entourage at Ditchley, in Oxfordshire, Churchill's weekend residence on moonlit nights during the blitz, when Chequers was perceived to be vulnerable to the Luftwaffe. The text of the Lend-Lease bill, now beginning its hazardous passage through Congress, had just been published. Britain's dependence on the outcome was absolute. However, Churchill warned the chancellor, Kingsley Wood, that he himself would say nothing to Washington about looming British defaults on payments for arms should Lend-Lease fail to pass the U.S. legislature: "We must trust ourselves to [the president]."

Hopkins was extraordinarily forthcoming to his hosts, who welcomed his enthusiasm after the cold scepticism of Joseph Kennedy. That first weekend, on the way to see Churchill's birthplace at Blenheim Palace, the envoy told Brendan Bracken that Roosevelt was "resolved that we should have the means of survival and of victory." Hopkins mused to the great CBS broadcast correspondent Ed Murrow, then reporting from London, "I suppose you could say—but not out loud—that I've come to try to find a way to be a catalytic agent between two prima donnas." Churchill, for his part, diverted his guest during the month of his visit with a succession of monologues, strewing phrases like rose petals in the path of this most important and receptive of visitors. At dinner at Ditchley, the prime minister declared:

> We seek no treasure, we seek no territorial gain, we seek only the right of man to be free; we seek his rights to worship his God, to lead his life in his own way, secure from persecution. As the humble labourer returns from his work when the day is done, and sees the smoke curling upwards from his cottage home in the serene evening sky, we wish him to know that no rat-a-tat-tat [here he rapped on the table] of the secret police upon his door will disturb his leisure or interrupt his rest. We seek government with the consent of the people, man's freedom to say what he will, and when he thinks himself injured, to find himself equal in the eyes of the law. But war aims other than these we have none.

Churchill's old colleagues—the likes of Balfour, Lloyd George, Chamberlain, Baldwin, Halifax—had for years rolled their eyes impatiently in the face of such outpourings. Familiarity with Winston's extravagant rhetoric rendered them readily bored by it, especially when it had been deployed in support of so many unworthy and unsuccessful causes in the past. Yet now, at last, Churchill's words and the mood of the times seemed perfectly conjoined. His sonorous style had an exceptional appeal for Americans. Hopkins had never before witnessed such effortless, magnificent dinner-table statesmanship. He was entranced by his host: "Jesus Christ! What a man!" He was impressed by the calm with which the prime minister received news, often bad. One night during the usual evening film at Ditchley, word came that the cruiser *Southampton* had been sunk in the Mediterranean. The show went on.

During the weeks that followed, Hopkins spent twelve evenings with Churchill, travelled with him to visit naval bases in Scotland and blitzed south coast towns. He marvelled at his host's popularity and absolute mastery of Britain's governance, though he was less impressed by the calibre of Churchill's subordinates: "Some of the ministers and underlings are a bit trying," he told Roosevelt. Eden, for instance, he thought talked too much. Hopkins attained a quick, shrewd grasp of the private distaste towards the prime minister that persisted among Britain's ruling caste: "The politicians and upper crust pretend to like him." He was in no doubt, however, about the fortitude of the British people. "Hopkins was, I think, very impressed by the cheerfulness and optimism he found everywhere," wrote Churchill's private secretary Eric Seal. "I must confess that I am surprised at it myself . . . PM . . . gets on like a house afire with Hopkins, who is a dear, & is universally liked." Roosevelt's envoy told Raymond Lee, "I have never had such an enjoyable time as I had with Mr. Churchill."

Back in Washington, the president was much tickled by reports of Hopkins's popularity in Britain, as Interior Secretary Harold Ickes noted: "Apparently the first thing that Churchill asks for when he gets awake in the morning is Harry Hopkins, and Harry is the last one he sees at night." Maybe so, growled the cynical Ickes, but even if the president had sent a bubonic plague carrier, Britain's prime minister would have found it expedient to see plenty of him. Among the envoy's most important functions was to brief Churchill about how best to address the American people and assist Roosevelt's efforts to assist Britain. Above all, the prime minister was told, he should not suggest that any commitment of U.S. ground troops was either desirable or likely. Hopkins concluded his report to the president: "People here are amazing from Churchill down," he wrote, "and if courage alone can win—the result will be inevitable. But they need our help desperately."

When the envoy landed back at New York's LaGuardia Airport in February 1941, the new ambassador-designate to Britain, "Gil" Winant, called out to him as he descended from his plane, "Are they going to hold out?" Hopkins shouted back, "Of course they are." This was a self-consciously theatrical exchange for the benefit of the assembled throng of reporters, but nonetheless sincere. Thereafter, Hopkins's considerable influence upon the president was exercised towards gaining maximum U.S. support for Britain. Londoner Vere Hodgson was among those who thrilled to a BBC broadcast by Roosevelt's envoy: "He finished with really glorious words of comfort: 'People of Britain, people of the British Commonwealth of Nations, you are not fighting alone.' I felt after this the War was won."

Yet, however successful was the Hopkins visit from a British perspective, it did not alter fundamentals. "Winston is completely certain of America's full help," the Australian prime minister, Robert Menzies, wrote doubtingly during a visit to Chequers at the end of February 1941. "Is he right? I cannot say." Franklin Roosevelt was conducting his nation's policy in accordance with a belief that he could not move faster than public opinion would allow. Such opinion was moving Britain's way. To the boundless relief of the prime minister, on February 8 the Lend-Lease bill passed the House by 260 votes to 165, and on March 8 was endorsed by the Senate, 60 votes to 13. For months thereafter, the last of Britain's foreign exchange continued to be drained to pay for supplies—only 1 percent of war matériel used by Britain in 1941 represented fruits of Lend-Lease. But the new measure ensured that, even when Britain's cash was exhausted, shipments kept coming. Importantly, 1940 Republican presidential candidate Wendell Willkie supported it—and Britain.

The president extracted for the British through Lend-Lease the most generous terms a U.S. legislature would swallow, much preferable to the straight loans of World War I, which Britain alienated U.S. opinion by failing to repay. A substantial minority of Americans, including many at the summits of industry and commerce, not merely opposed Roosevelt's policies, but hated the man. He perceived his own power as circumscribed, in a fashion which the prime minister underestimated. Unlike Churchill, Roosevelt never led a coalition government, though he included some prominent Republicans such as Henry Stimson in his Cabinet. He always faced substantial opposition in Congress—sometimes only on lesser matters, but sometimes also on great ones. There was no doubt of his sincerity in desiring British victory. Having overcome his initial reservations about Churchill, partly thanks to Hopkins, by March 1941 he could declare to the American people: "In this historic crisis,

Britain is blessed with a brilliant and great leader." But Roosevelt considered himself lacking any mandate to dispatch American soldiers to fight in Europe. Until December 1941, while he provided increasing aid to Britain—"we must become the great arsenal of democracy," a phrase borrowed from French economist Jean Monnet by way of Felix Frankfurter— he remained unwilling to lead a charge towards war. In this, he was assuredly wise. If the United States had plunged into belligerence with Germany before Pearl Harbor, and even in the unlikely event that Roosevelt could have pushed a declaration of war through Congress, he would thereafter have led a divided country.

The historian Michael Howard, in 1941 a student at Oxford awaiting a summons to the army, has written: "It is never very easy for the British to understand that a very large number of Americans, if they think about us at all, do so with various degrees of dislike and contempt . . . In the 1940s the Americans had some reason to regard the British as a lot of toffee-nosed bastards who oppressed half the world and had a sinister talent for getting other people to do their fighting for them." Melville Troy was an American cigar importer living in London. Though he admired the fortitude of the British amid the blitz, he was deeply anxious to see his own country spared from its horrors: "Personally I am very sorry to see America turning her pruning hooks and ploughshares into implements of war, and wish we had a Woodrow Wilson to keep us out of it." Many of Troy's fellow countrymen thought likewise.

There was much, much more British wooing to be done. The extravagant courtesies shown by the government to Harry Hopkins were outdone when Winant arrived as ambassador. He was met at Bristol by Brendan Bracken and the Duke of Kent. A special train took him to Windsor, where King George VI was waiting at the station. The monarch then drove Winant in his own car to the castle. Never in history had a foreign envoy been received with such ceremony. Meanwhile, implementation of the Lend-Lease programme enlisted another key American player in Britain's cause. Averell Harriman, fifty-year-old son of a railroad millionaire, was a supremely gilded product of Groton and Yale, a polo player and skier, international banker and collector of Impressionist paintings, a cosmopolitan of considerable gifts. Roosevelt explained Harriman's new mission to reporters at the White House: "As soon as the Lend-Spend, Lend-Lease—whatever you call it—bill is perfected, more or less, he will go over and— Oh, I suppose you will ask all about his title, so I thought I would invent one . . . we decided it was a pretty good idea to call him an 'Expediter.' That's a new one for you. I believe it is not in the diplomatic list or any other list. So he will go over as 'Defense Expediter.' "

In the spring of 1941 Harriman became an important American advocate of aid to Britain. Nonetheless, in Washington Hopkins and Henry Stimson, the secretary of war, remained the only prominent members of the administration wholeheartedly committed to such a policy. Other leading Americans remained sceptical. In the War Department, U.S. generals cloaked dogged resistance to shipping abroad arms that were needed at home in a mantle of complaints about allegedly amateurish British purchasing policy. One officer, contemptuous of the informality of the Hopkins mission, told Harriman: "We can't take seriously requests that come late in the evening over a bottle of port."

Among Chief of Staff of the U.S. Army George Marshall's key subordinates, there were deep divisions about the merits of participation in the war, and of the British as prospective allies. Some senior officers unashamedly reserved their admiration for the Germans. Maj. Gen. Stanley Embick was a former chief of the War Plans Division who had become sceptical about Churchill and his people during service in France in World War I. Now he believed that Britain's war effort would fare better if the country changed prime ministers. He thought that U.S. aid should stop far short of belligerency. Like his son-in-law, Maj. Albert Wedemeyer of the War Plans Division, Embick addressed every Anglo-American issue with a determination that his country should not be duped into pulling British chestnuts out of the fire. Maj. Gen. Charles "Bull" Wesson hated the British, because he had once been dispatched from Washington to London with a message for the Chiefs of Staff, and was kept waiting to deliver it. Raymond Lee wrote: "He resented this so much that it led to a wrangle and almost hatred on his part for the British, which he exploits at every opportunity. So small an act of discourtesy, either real or imagined, which took place many years ago, is having ill effects in the relations between the two countries today."

By contrast Col.—soon to be lieutenant general and a key figure in Marshall's team—Joseph McNarney, who had visited Britain, believed it was vital to American national security that Churchill's island should not fall. Marshall himself was less implacably hostile to the British than Embick, but in the summer of 1941, in the words of a biographer, "if rather than when continued to dominate his thinking about American involvement." Nor was such caution confined to senior officers. *Time* and *Life* magazines interviewed U.S. Army draftees, and reported their morale to be low. At a camp movie night in Mississippi, men booed when FDR and Marshall appeared on a newsreel.

Averell Harriman was in no doubt that America should fight. But he departed for London on March 15, 1941, fearful that Roosevelt was still unwilling to lead the United States anywhere near as far or fast as was necessary to avert a Nazi triumph: "I was deeply worried the president did not have a policy and had not decided how far he could go . . . The President obviously hoped that he would not have to face an unpleasant decision. He seemed unwilling to lead public opinion or to force the issue but [he] hoped . . . that our material aid would let the British do the job." Few doubted that Roosevelt already stood among America's greatest presidents. But he was sometimes also a notably cautious one.

Harriman noted in a memorandum of March 11: "I must attempt to convince the Prime Minister that I, or someone, must convey to our people his war strategy or else he cannot expect to get maximum aid." Like Hopkins, he was received in Britain on the reddest of carpets. He was met at Bristol by Commander "Tommy" Thompson, Churchill's administrative aide, who led him aboard a plane which took them straight to Chequers. Harriman's guest gift to Clementine Churchill was a box of tangerines, which she received with unfeigned gratitude. The envoy was enfolded in a warm prime ministerial embrace. Kathleen Harriman, who accompanied her father's mission, wrote to her sister: "The PM is much smaller than I expected and a lot less fat . . . and looks rather like a kindly teddy bear . . . I'd expected an overpowering, rather terrifying man. He's quite the opposite: very gracious, has a wonderful smile and isn't at all hard to talk to. He's got the kind of eyes that look right through you. Mother [Clementine] is a very sweet lady. She's given up her whole life to her husband and takes a back seat graciously. Everyone in the family looks upon him as God and she's rather left out."

In London, Harriman established himself on the second floor of a Grosvenor Square building adjoining the U.S. Embassy, and was also given his own office at the Admiralty. Churchill invited him to attend the weekly meetings of the Cabinet's Atlantic Committee. Of Harriman's first eight weekends in Britain, he spent seven at Chequers, though like most American guests he found his sense of privilege tempered by dismay at the coldness of the house. Churchill convoyed him, like Hopkins, as a prize exhibit on his own travels around the country. Here, he told the British people, was a living earnest of America's commitment—the president's personal representative.

In private to Harriman, "the PM bluntly stated that he could see no prospect of victory until the United States came into the war." If Japan attacked, said Churchill, the British naval base of Singapore would be at risk. At every turn, the prime minister sought to balance his desire to convince Roosevelt that Britain was a prospective winner against the need to exert pressure by emphasising the threat of disaster if America held back.

Harriman urged Churchill to bolster Britain's case by publishing details of its appalling shipping losses. Between February and April 1941, 142 ships totalling 818,000 tons had gone to the bottom, more than double the rate of sinkings in the early months of the war. At a Defence Committee meeting in May, Eden and Beaverbrook suggested that at least meat-ship losses might be disclosed, to emphasise the gravity of the food situation. Churchill, with the support of several other ministers, opposed this, "believing that we shall get the Americans in by showing courage and boldness and prospects of success and not by running ourselves down." Moreover, figures which privately frightened the British government would deal a shocking blow to domestic morale if they were revealed, and would have provided a propaganda gift to Hitler.

Some Americans displayed a condescension which irked the recipients of their aid. Kathleen Harriman described British reluctance to enthuse about American Spam and cheese: "The great difficulty is re-educating the people," she wrote to her sister. "They prefer to go hungry rather than change their feeding habits." A Tory MP wrote: "The idea of being our armoury and supply furnishers seems to appeal to the Yanks as their share in the war for democracy . . . They are a quaint lot—they are told that if we lose the war they will be next on Hitler's list . . . and yet they seem quite content to leave the actual fighting to us; they will do anything except fight." Duff Cooper, as minister of information, told newspaper editors on March 21, 1941: "The great thing is not to antagonise the United States . . . When we offered the bases against the [fifty loaned] destroyers we imagined, in Winston's words, that we were exchanging 'a bunch of flowers for a sugar cake.' But not at all. The Americans have done a hard business deal." After Lend-Lease was passed, Franks, the British driver for U.S. military attaché Raymond Lee, told his master that he noticed more goodwill towards Americans. "Well, yes," agreed Lee sardonically. "Perhaps you might describe it that way, but it is only natural, don't you think, that for seven thousand million dollars—that's nearly a billion pounds—we ought to be entitled to a little bonhomie!" "Oh yes, sir, yes, sir, quite. That's just what I mean, sir. I should say there is quite a bit more bonhomie in the air, sir." This was only half true. Most British people considered that the United States was providing them with minimal means to do dirty work that Americans ought to be sharing themselves.

The threat of Japanese aggression against the British Empire in the Far East dogged Churchill that summer of 1941. Germany was fully committed in Russia. Britain's land forces in North Africa seemed to have a real prospect of victory against the Italians and such German troops as Hitler was willing to spare from the Eastern Front. But if Japan attacked, the

strategic balance would once more be overturned. Cadogan, at the Foreign Office, wrote in July that Churchill was "frightened of nothing but
Japan." The prime minister expressed confidence that, if Tokyo moved
against the British Empire, the Americans would intervene. His ministers,
generals and officials were much less convinced. It was a nightmare
prospect: that Britain might find itself at war in the east while America
remained neutral. Some thought it likely that Japan would join Germany's
attack on Russia, rather than strike at Malaya. Eden asked Churchill what
he would do in such an eventuality. The prime minister replied firmly that
Britain would never herself initiate hostilities with Japan, unless the
United States did so. Month after month in 1941, he sought to promote
the illusion that Britain's war effort was viable and purposeful. In private,
however, he recognised its ultimate futility unless Roosevelt's nation came
in with both feet.

2. Walking Out

THAT SUMMER, countless hours were expended by British diplomats,
staff officers and the prime minister himself, weighing and debating every
subtlety of U.S. behaviour and opinion. Few lovers expended as much ink
and thought upon wartime correspondence as did the prime minister on
his long letters to Roosevelt, sometimes dispatched twice or thrice weekly,
in which he described the progress of Britain's war. He adopted a confiding tone, taking it for granted that the president shared his own, and his
country's, purposes. He extended his courtship to the president's people.
On June 16, the award in absentia of an honorary doctorate from the University of Rochester, New York, inspired one of his finest radio broadcasts
to Americans:

> A wonderful story is unfolding before our eyes. How it will end we are
> not allowed to know. But on both sides of the Atlantic we all feel—I
> repeat, all—that we are a part of it, that our future and that of many
> generations is at stake. We are sure that the character of human society
> will be shaped by the resolves we take and the deeds we do. We need
> not bewail the fact that we have been called upon to face such solemn
> responsibilities. We may be proud, and even rejoice amid our tribula-
> tions, that we have been born at this cardinal time for so great an age
> and so splendid an opportunity of service here below. Wickedness—
> enormous, panoplied, embattled, seemingly triumphant—casts its
> shadow over Europe and Asia. Laws, customs, and traditions are bro-
> ken up. Justice is cast from her seat. The rights of the weak are tram-

pled down. The grand freedoms of which the President of the United States has spoken so movingly are spurned and chained. The whole stature of man, his genius, his initiative, and his nobility, is ground down under systems of mechanical barbarism and of organized and scheduled terror.

Churchill's words moved many people in his audience. Yet in Washington, Halifax observed wearily that trying to pin down the Americans was like "a disorderly day's rabbit-shooting." Roosevelt offered much to Britain—aircrew training, warship repair facilities, the loan of transports, an American garrison to replace British troops in Iceland, secret military staff talks throughout February and March, growing assistance to Atlantic convoy escorts. But still the United States stood well short of belligerence. In July, Roosevelt's Draft Renewal Bill passed the House of Representatives by only one vote. Churchill hankered desperately for a meeting with the president. More than that, he persuaded himself that if such an encounter took place, it would presage a decisive change in the Anglo-American relationship.

When, at last, Roosevelt fixed an August rendezvous at Placentia Bay, off Newfoundland, the prime minister's hopes were unbounded. He wrote to the queen before his departure on the fourth: "I must say I do not think our friend would have asked me to go so far for what must be a meeting of world-wide notice, unless he had in mind some further forward step." He was in tearing spirits on the rail journey north, as was his entourage on discovering the lavish scale of catering provided. From Scapa Flow he cabled the president, using language that assumed a community of purpose far closer than that which Roosevelt acknowledged: "We are just off. It is 27 years ago to-day that Huns began their last war. We must make a good job of it this time. Twice ought to be enough." Then, in Colville's words "with a retinue which Cardinal Wolsey might have envied," Churchill set sail aboard the great battleship *Prince of Wales* for Newfoundland. Harry Hopkins, newly returned from Moscow and once more in a state of collapse, joined them for the passage. That marvellously brave man had travelled most of the way from Russia in the gun blister of a Catalina flying boat.

One of the few useful purposes fulfilled by British battleships in the Second World War was to convey Churchill on his wartime journeys in a style befitting the arbiter of an embattled empire. There was an irony about his presence aboard *Prince of Wales*. Only a few weeks earlier, he had demanded courts-martial of officers deemed to have lacked resolution in the navy's contest with the *Bismarck*. He was furious that *Prince of Wales* had broken off action after *Hood*'s sinking, even though the British battle-ship was damaged. The court-martial proposal was dropped only when Adm. Sir John Tovey, C-in-C Home Fleet, said that if any such retribution was attempted, he himself would resign his post and serve as "prisoner's friend."

En route to the Atlantic rendezvous, much less work was done than became usual on later voyages. There was no agenda to prepare, because the British delegation had no notion how the meeting might evolve. They seized the opportunity for rest. Churchill read with relish three of C. S. Forester's Hornblower novels, tales of derring-do about the Royal Navy in the Napoleonic Wars. He fantasised enthusiastically about a possible sortie from northern Norway by the *Tirpitz*, sister ship of the *Bismarck*, which might enable him to participate in a great naval engagement. Mothersill's pills were much in demand as specifics against seasickness.

Humble members of the British delegation, such as a cluster of clerks, were amazed by manifestations of the prime minister's informality. "Working in H[arry] H[opkins]'s cabin this morning," Corporal Geoffrey Green wrote in his diary, "& WSC came in wearing only pyjama coat & cigar—no pants—grinned at us and said 'good morning'—too amazed to reply properly!" The ship's storerooms were packed with delicacies from Fortnum & Mason, together with ninety grouse, killed ahead of the usual shooting season to provide a treat for the prime minister's exalted guests. On the American side, Hopkins cabled Washington suggesting that hams, wine and fruit, especially lemons, would be acceptable to the British party.

Placentia Bay is a rocky inlet on the south coast of Newfoundland, where some five hundred inhabitants occupied a fishing settlement ashore. The British discerned a resemblance to a Hebridean sea loch. Early on the morning of August 9, *Prince of Wales* began to stand in. Then her officers realised that the ship's clocks were set ahead of the Newfoundland Time Zone. The ship turned and ploughed a lazy course offshore for ninety minutes, before once more heading into the anchorage. At nine a.m., her anchors rattled down a few hundred yards from the U.S. cruiser *Augusta*, which bore the president. The British remarked the contrast between the zigzag camouflage of their own vessel, dressed for battle, and the pale peacetime shading of the American warship's paintwork.

No one knows exactly what was said at the encounters aboard *Augusta* between Churchill and Roosevelt. But Hopkins, who was present, described the mood. The president adopted his almost unfailing geniality, matched by the opacity which characterised his conversation on every issue of delicacy. As for his companion, no intending suitor for marriage could have matched the charm and enthusiasm with which the prime minister of Great Britain addressed the president of the United States.

Churchill and Roosevelt were the most fluent conversationalists of their age. Even when substance was lacking in their exchanges, there was no danger of silences. They had in common social background, intense literacy, love of all things naval, addiction to power and supreme gifts as communicators. Both were stars on the world stage. In the twenty-first century, when physical fitness is a preoccupation of many national leaders, it may also be remarked that neither of the two greatest statesmen on earth seemed much reduced by the fact that one was a fifty-nine-year-old cripple and the other a man of sixty-six famous for his overindulgence in alcohol and cigars.

One of Roosevelt's intimates, Marguerite "Missy" LeHand, declared him "really incapable of a personal friendship with anyone." Yet for all his essential solitariness, the president had a gift for treating every new acquaintance as if the two had known each other all their lives, a capacity for forging a semblance of intimacy which he exploited ruthlessly. Churchill, by contrast, had scant social interest in others. After the untimely death of his close friend F. E. Smith, Lord Birkenhead, in 1930, he was unwilling to interest himself in any other human being save possibly Beaverbrook and Jan Smuts for long enough to establish a social, as distinct from political, communion. Indeed, at Placentia he pricked the president's vanity by forgetting that the two had met earlier—in London in 1918.

Churchill loved only himself and Clementine, while to Roosevelt's mistresses it was rumoured—almost certainly mistakenly—that he had recently added the exiled Crown Princess Marthe of Norway. While Roosevelt sometimes uttered great truths, he was a natural dissembler. Henry Morgenthau claimed to be baffled by the president's contradictions: "weary as well as buoyant, frivolous as well as grave, evasive as well as frank . . . a man of bewildering complexity of moods and motives." Roosevelt was much more politically imaginative than Churchill. He told Wendell Willkie in the spring of 1941 that he thought Britain would experience a social revolution when the war was over, and he was right. Churchill, meanwhile, gave scarcely a moment's thought to anything that might follow Britain's desperate struggle for survival against the Axis, and was implacably hostile to socialism. Roosevelt, like his people, regarded the future without fear. Optimism lay at the heart of his genius as U.S. national leader through the Depression. Churchill, by contrast, was full of apprehension about the threats a new world posed to Britain's greatness.

At Placentia Bay the prime minister strove to please the president, and Roosevelt, fascinated by the prime minister's personality, was perfectly willing to be pleased. However, the shipboard meetings between British and U.S. service chiefs were tense and stilted. The Americans—generals George Marshall and Henry "Hap" Arnold, Admirals Harold Stark and Ernest King—were wary. On security grounds, Roosevelt had given them no warning of the intended meeting until they boarded *Augusta*. They had thus prepared nothing, and were determined to say nothing, which committed their nation an inch further than existing policy avowed. The British—CIGS Sir John Dill, First Sea Lord Sir Dudley Pound and Vice Chief of the Air Staff Sir Wilfrid Freeman—were bemused by the fact that the U.S. Army and Navy chose to conduct briefings separately, and outlined entirely different strategic viewpoints.

When Marshall spoke of creating an army of four million men, the British expressed amazement. There seemed no prospect, they said, that land fighting would take place in the continental United States. Shipping did not exist to transport and supply a large army overseas. What need could there be for such a mobilization? Churchill himself was at pains to assure the mothers of America that, even if their nation entered the war, their sons would not be required to shed blood on the battlefields of Europe. A month before Placentia, he rebuked Auchinleck for telling journalists that U.S. troops were needed. Such remarks, said the prime minister, strengthened the hand of American isolationists, and ran "contrary to what I have said about our not needing the American Army this year, or next year, or any year that I could foresee." British strategic calculations denied a requirement for British or U.S. land forces capable of engaging the Wehrmacht on the Continent, because Dill and his colleagues did not perceive this as a viable objective.

At Placentia, Arnold said little on behalf of the U.S. Army Air Forces, while Marshall talked more about equipment than strategy. The Americans said they found it hard to satisfy British demands for weapons. They claimed that requests were submitted in muddled profusion, through a variety of channels. The British felt a chasm between their own mind-set, formed and roughened by the experience of war, and that of their American counterparts, still imbued with the inhibitions of peace. It was not easy for men with lesser gifts of statesmanship than the prime minister to subdue their consciousness that the leaders of America's armed forces resented shipping to Britain arms which they wanted for themselves. It was hard for Dill and his colleagues not to be irked by the caution of these rich, safe Americans, when they themselves were battered by the responsibility of conducting Western civilisation's struggle for survival. The Royal

Navy's officers noted the lack of curiosity displayed by the Americans, notably Admiral King, about their experiences of battle, for instance against the *Bismarck*. Privately, U.S. sailors mocked Dudley Pound, "the old whale," as British soldiers called him. Dill got on well with Marshall, but Ian Jacob wrote bleakly in his diary: "Not a single American officer has shown the slightest keenness to be in the war on our side. They are a charming lot of individuals, but they appear to be living in a different world from ourselves."

Roosevelt was irritated to learn that the prime minister had brought with him two well-known journalists, H. V. Morton and Howard Spring. Though they were barred from filing dispatches until back on British soil, this was a reminder that Churchill sought to extract from the meeting every ounce of propaganda capital. Roosevelt, meanwhile, was determined to keep open every option, to proceed with utmost caution. The reporters were denied access to U.S. ships.

It is important to recognise that both the British and Americans still expected Russia to suffer defeat, leaving Britain alone once more to face the Nazi empire—and soon also, perhaps, the Japanese. Churchill urged Roosevelt to offer the strongest possible warnings to Tokyo against additional aggression. It has been suggested that he went further, pleading for preemptive U.S. military action in the Far East, but this seems implausible. Several times during the conference, Churchill asked Averell Harriman if the president liked him. Here was an admission of the prime minister's vast anxiety, and vulnerability.

"It would be an exaggeration to say that Roosevelt and Churchill became chums at this conference, or at any subsequent time," wrote Robert Sherwood, White House familiar and later biographer of Harry Hopkins. "They established an easy intimacy, a joking informality and a moratorium on pomposity and cant—and also a degree of frankness in intercourse which, if not quite complete, was remarkably close to it. But neither of them ever forgot for one instant what he was and represented or what the other was and represented . . . They were two men in the same line of business—politico-military leadership on a global scale . . . They appraised each other through the practiced eyes of professionals, and from this appraisal resulted a degree of admiration and sympathetic understanding of each other's professional problems that lesser craftsmen could not have achieved." While the prime minister eagerly succumbed to sentiment in forming a view of his fellow potentate, the president did not reciprocate. The American and British peoples felt that they understood their respective leaders, but the British had better reason to make the claim. Churchill was what he seemed. Roosevelt was not.

The prime minister brilliantly stage-managed his part in the Placentia meeting, himself choosing hymns for the Sunday church service beneath the huge guns of *Prince of Wales*, before a pulpit draped with the flags of the two nations: "Onward Christian Soldiers," "O God Our Help in Ages Past" and "Eternal Father Strong to Save." Scarcely a man present went unmoved. "My God, this is history!" muttered a fellow clerk "in a hushed, awed voice" to Corporal Geoffrey Green. As excited photographers clicked shutters from vantage points on the turrets and superstructure, a colleague said to Ian Jacob that the occasion must fulfil the fantasies of "a pressman high on hashish."

That afternoon, Churchill took a launch on a brief visit to the shore, wandering awhile with Cadogan, the Prof and his secretaries, and somewhat unexpectedly picking wildflowers. Senior officers of the two nations continued to shuttle to and fro between their ships, each arrival and departure being greeted with full ceremony by bands and honour guards, which ensured that the anchorage was never tranquil. The next day, there were further talks, desultory as before, between the service chiefs. Roosevelt marginally raised the stakes in the Atlantic war, by agreeing that U.S. warships should escort convoys as far east as Iceland. He justified this measure back in Washington by asserting that there was little purpose in providing American supplies to Britain without seeking to ensure that they reached their destination.

The most substantial outcome of the president and prime minister's encounter was the Atlantic Charter, a strange document. It had its origin in a suggestion by Roosevelt that the two leaders should issue a statement of common principles. As published, it represented a characteristically American expression of lofty intentions. Yet it was drafted by Sir Alexander Cadogan, the attendant Foreign Office mandarin. The charter was signalled to London for approval by the War Cabinet, whose members were dragged out of bed for the purpose. In the small hours of the next morning—another drizzly affair, like most in Newfoundland—an officer reported to Churchill just as he was going to bed that London's reply had arrived. "Am I going to like it?" the prime minister demanded—in Jacob's words "like a small boy about to take medicine." Yes, he was told, all was well. His ministers had endorsed the Anglo-American statement. When published, its noble phrases in support of a common commitment to freedom rang around the world, and gave hope to colonial subjects in a fashion that Churchill certainly did not intend. Back in the United States, however, the charter roused little popular enthusiasm. It was never signed, because this would have made it necessary to present the document to the Senate for ratification as a treaty.

Before they parted, the president offered the prime minister warm words of goodwill and a further 150,000 old rifles. But there was nothing that promised America's early belligerence. This was what Churchill had come for, and he did not get it. By 2:50 p.m. on August 12 it was all over. Low cloud cut off the ships' view of the shore. *Augusta* slid away into a fog, as sailors lined the side of *Prince of Wales* to salute the departing president. Then the British set their own course for home. "It was hard to tell whether Churchill returned from Newfoundland entirely satisfied with his conference with Roosevelt," wrote Ian Jacob. The prime minister told his son, Randolph, that he had enjoyed "a very interesting and by no means unfruitful meeting with the president . . . and in the three days when we were continually together, I feel we made a deep and intimate contact of friendship. At the same time one is deeply perplexed to know how the deadlock is to be broken and the United States brought boldly and honourably into the war."

Churchill revealed nothing of his private disappointment in the exuberant rhetoric with which he addressed his colleagues and the nation on returning to Britain. He felt obliged to satisfy their craving for good news, and told the War Cabinet that American naval commanders were bursting with impatience to join the struggle, though others at Placentia detected nothing of the kind. His report of Roosevelt's private remarks appears wilfully to have exaggerated the president's carefully equivocal expressions of support. Pownall, now Dill's vice CIGS, wrote in his diary: "Roosevelt is all for coming into the war, and as soon as possible . . . But he said that he would never declare war, he wishes to provoke it." Uncertainty persists about whether the president really used these words, or whether Churchill put them into his mouth. Even such sentiments fell short of British hopes. For all the president's social warmth, he never indulged romantic lunges of the kind to which Churchill was prone. If not quite an Anglophobe, Roosevelt never revealed much private warmth towards Britain. He left Placentia with the same mind-set he had taken there. He was bent upon assisting the British by all possible means to avert defeat. But he had no intention of outpacing congressional and popular sentiment by leading a dash towards U.S. belligerence. American public opinion was vastly more supportive of its government's oil embargo against Japan, in response to Tokyo's descent on Indochina, than it was of Roosevelt's increasing naval support for Britain in the Battle of the Atlantic; this, ironically, though the embargo provoked the Japanese to bomb America into the war.

Churchill, at an off-the-record British newspaper editors' briefing on August 22, predicted that Japan would not attack in the east, and observed that the Battle of the Atlantic was going better. Suggesting that German

U-boats would be reluctant to risk tangling with American warships, which were now operating actively in the western Atlantic, he said: "I assume that Hitler does not want to risk a clash with Roosevelt until the Russians are out of the way." The flush of British excitement faded. The prime minister's lofty rhetoric could not overcome a sense of anticlimax, which extended across the nation. A War Office clerk seemed to a British general to judge Placentia rightly when he dismissed Churchill's broadcast, describing the meeting as "nothing dressed up very nicely."

Vere Hodgson, the Notting Hill charity worker, heard the BBC promise "an important government announcement" on the afternoon of August 14, and expected a declaration of Anglo-American union. When, instead, radio listeners heard the words of the Atlantic Charter, she wrote in disappointment: "There was a statement of War Aims. All very laudable in themselves—the only difficulty will be in carrying them out." Churchill cabled Hopkins, revealing unusually explicit impatience: "I ought to tell you that there has been a wave of depression through cabinet and other informed circles here about President's many assurances about no commitments and no closer to war, etc . . . If 1942 opens with Russia knocked out and Britain left again alone, all kinds of dangers may arise. I do not think Hitler will help in any way . . . You know best whether anything more can be done . . . Should be grateful if you could give me any sort of hope."

At Downing Street, Churchill observed irritably that Americans had committed themselves to suffer all the inconveniences of war, "without its commanding stimuli." Over dinner with John Winant, the U.S. ambassador, on August 29, he again appealed explicitly for American belligerence. Colville recorded: "The PM said that after the joint declaration [the Atlantic Charter], America could not honourably stay out . . . If R declared war now . . . they might see victory as early as 1943; but if she did not, the war might drag on for years, leaving Britain undefeated but civilization in ruins." Influential American visitors continued to be courted with unflagging zeal. The journalist John Gunther was entertained at Chequers. A tedious Pennsylvania Democrat, Congressman J. Buell Snyder, chairman of the House military appropriations subcommittee, was warmly received at Downing Street. Yet at the end of August Charles Peake, minister at Britain's Washington embassy, expressed profound gloom about the prospect of the United States entering the war soon, perhaps at all. He even questioned—as did some members of the U.S. administration—whether Roosevelt desired such an outcome. Although America could no longer be deemed neutral, it seemed plausible that it might cling indefinitely to nonbelligerent status. There was, and remains, no evidence that Roosevelt was willing to risk a potentially disastrous clash with Congress. Unless America became a fighting ally, Lend-Lease would merely suffice to stave off British defeat.

The autumn of 1941 was one of many wartime seasons which must be viewed without the benefit of hindsight about what followed. British prospects everywhere seemed bleak. An American diplomat who spent ten days in Scotland returned to report to his embassy: "The attitude of the people he had been with, most of them big industrialists and realists in their points of view, is that the British are now losing the war, and that it is ridiculous to talk about subduing the German Army by bombing cities inside Germany . . . The German Army . . . must be beaten somehow or other on the ground, or the war is lost." Churchill agreed. "It will not be possible for the whole British Army (other than those in the Middle East) to remain indefinitely inert and passive as a garrison of this island against invasion," Churchill wrote to Ismay on September 12. "Such a course, apart altogether from military considerations, would bring the Army into disrepute. I do not need to elaborate this."

Moscow regarded the meeting of Churchill and Roosevelt with its accustomed paranoia. A Soviet biographer of Churchill, writing more than thirty years later, asserted that at Placentia Bay, "plans were worked out to establish Anglo-American domination of the post-war world. The leaders of Britain and the USA were drawing up these plans while the USSR was bearing the brunt of the war and America had not yet entered it." Stalin, in desperate straits, wanted thirty thousand tons of aluminium, together with four hundred planes and five hundred tanks a month from Britain. Churchill told Ambassador Maisky that Moscow would have to be content with half these quantities, and look to the Americans for the rest. On September 15, Stalin demanded that twenty-five British divisions should be sent to the Russian front via Iran or Archangel. He had already asked Harry Hopkins to solicit Roosevelt to dispatch an American army to Russia. Hopkins, suitably amazed, said that even if the United States entered the war, it was unlikely that she would send soldiers to fight in the Caucasus.

It was a measure of Churchill's anxiety to appease Moscow that he agreed in principle to send British troops to Russia. He speculated wildly that Wavell, a Russian speaker, might command such a force. To try to assist the Russians and fail, he declared, was better than to make no attempt. He was flailing. On October 23, the notion was formally abandoned. Stalin complained that badly crated British aircraft were arriving "broken" at Archangel. The British hoped against hope that dire Russian threats to seek a separate peace were as much bluff as their own mutterings about launching a Second Front.

As Britain's merchant fleet suffered relentless attrition in the Atlantic, Food Minister Lord Woolton briefed the Cabinet on the necessity to ration canned goods. Churchill murmured in sorrowful jest: "I shall never see another sardine!" In reality, of course, he suffered less than any other British citizen from the exigencies of war, and occasionally professed embarrassment that he had never lived so luxuriously in his life. If his energy was somewhat diminished by age, he had less need than ever before to trouble himself about personal wants, which were met by his large staff of domestics and officials. No ministerial colleague enjoyed his privileges in matters of diet, comfort and domestic and travel arrangements. Eden, as foreign secretary, waxed lyrical about being offered a slice of cold ham at a Buckingham Palace luncheon, and oranges at the Brazilian embassy. Every wartime British government diarist fortunate enough to travel, including the most exalted ministers and generals, devoted much space to applauding the food they enjoyed abroad, because the fare at home was so dismal.

The prime minister seldom ate in other people's houses, but enjoyed an occasional meal at Buck's Club. He sometimes attended gatherings at the Savoy of the Other Club, the dining group he and F. E. Smith had founded in 1910. There, more often than not, he sat beside Lord Camrose, proprietor of the *Daily Telegraph*, a friend who vainly coveted a government job. One night in the autumn of 1941, he slipped out of Downing Street with Eden and Beaverbrook to dine at the Ritz. Reminiscing, he said he would like to have his old First World War colleagues Balfour and Smith with him now. Beaverbrook suggested that, if Churchill had played his cards better, he might have become prime minister in 1916. Churchill said that the worst moment of his life came when Lloyd George told him that there was no place for him in the new Cabinet.

The housekeepers at both Downing Street and Chequers were issued with unlimited supplies of Diplomatic Food Coupons for official entertaining. These enabled Churchill and his guests to indulge a style unknown to ordinary citizens. The costs of Chequers rose dramatically in the Churchill years from those of Neville Chamberlain, matching the expansiveness of the hospitality. The Chequer Trust's solicitor agreed with Kathleen Hill, Churchill's secretary, in January 1942 that "the Food Account was very high." The family made a modest cash contribution to compensate the trustees for the Churchills' private share of the house's cost, including paying a quarter of the bill for a little Ford car used by Clementine.

Privileged though the family's domestic circumstances might be, the prime minister's wife often found it no easier than her humbler compatriots to purchase acceptable food. This caused dismay to insensitive visitors. Once in the following year, when Eleanor Roosevelt and other Washingtonians were guests in the No. 10 Annexe, Mrs. Churchill apologised for the fare: "I'm sorry dear, I could not buy any fish. You will have to eat macaroni." Henry Morgenthau noted without enthusiasm: "Then they gave us little left-over bits made into meat loaf." By contrast, some of Churchill's guests recoiled from his self-indulgence at a time when the rest of the country was enduring whale steaks. One night when Churchill took a party to the Savoy, Canadian premier Mackenzie King was disgusted that his host insisted on ordering both fish and meat, in defiance of rationing regulations. The ascetic King found it "disgraceful that Winston should behave like this."

Churchill's wit served better than his hospitality or the war news to sustain the spirit of his colleagues. At a vexed Defence Committee meeting to discuss supplies for Russia, he issued Cuban cigars, recently arrived as a gift from Havana. "It may well be that these each contain some deadly poison," he observed complacently, as those so inclined struck matches. "It may well be that within days I shall follow sadly the long line of your coffins up the aisle of Westminster Abbey—reviled by the populace as the man who has out-borgiaed Borgia!" Eden, arriving for a Chequers weekend, was shown upstairs by Churchill, who himself lit his guest's bedroom fire. The foreign secretary wrote a trifle cattily: "I know no-one with such perfect manners as a host—especially when he feels like it."

While great men discussed affairs of state at Downing Street or Chequers, below stairs the staff gossiped about the Master in the fashion of every patrician household. "Oh, Miss, you'll never guess what he did next . . . ," Nellie the Downing Street parlour maid would say to Elizabeth Layton, one of the prime minister's three typists. Mrs. Landemore the cook was a fount of tittle-tattle about the British aristocracy, while Sawyers, the prime minister's valet, dispensed among the staff glasses of wine diverted from the dining room. Every Friday afternoon, or sometimes on Saturday morning, a column of three big black cars stood waiting by the garden gate of Downing Street to waft the prime minister to Chequers at breakneck speed, his journey hastened by police outriders and sirens. Unless he took with him in the car some visitor with whom he wished to converse, he customarily dictated to a typist all the way. Arrived at his destination one day, he said to Elizabeth Layton: "Now run inside and type like HELL." The staff late shift were seldom released to their beds before three a.m.

Churchill was exultant when, on September 8, Roosevelt issued a "shoot first" order to U.S. warships in the Atlantic, dramatically raising his nation's stakes against Germany's U-boats. But two weeks later, when Eden dined with the Churchills and Oliver Lyttelton, the Middle East minister of state just back from Cairo, Eden noted: "Winston was depressed at outset, said he felt that we had harsh times ahead." The prime minister knew from intercepted Japanese diplomatic traffic that Tokyo was winding down its foreign missions and evacuating nationals from British territory. Sir Stewart Menzies, "C," showed him a cable from Berlin to Tokyo, in which Hitler's staff assured the Japanese that "in the event of a collision between Japan and the United States, Germany would at once open hostilities with America." After Churchill was glimpsed by Bletchley code beakers one Saturday, visiting their dank, hutted encampment, four of the most senior staff wrote to him personally, appealing for more resources. This prompted an "Action This Day" note to "C": "Make sure they have all they want on extreme priority."

On October 20 Churchill told the Defence Committee that "he did not believe that the Japanese would go to war with the United States and ourselves." After many months in which he had wilfully exaggerated the prospect of America entering the war, the chances of such a development were now greater than he avowed. It may be that, following so many disappointments, he did not dare to hope too much. The terrible, nagging fear persisted that Tokyo might launch a strike only against British possessions, without provoking the United States to fight. The views of the British and American governments were distorted by logic. Both possessed strong intelligence evidence of an impending Japanese assault. Yet it remained hard to believe that the Tokyo regime would start a war with the United States that it could not rationally hope to win.

The dispatch of a naval battle squadron to the Far East, supposedly to deter Japanese aggression, was the prime minister's personal decision, and reflected his anachronistic faith in capital ships. Likewise, the squadron's commander, Adm. Tom Phillips—ironically, one of Churchill's severest critics in the Admiralty—was his own choice, and a poor one, because Phillips's entire war experience had been spent in shore-based staff appointments. Churchill likened the prospective impact of British battleships in the Far East to that achieved by the presence of Hitler's *Tirpitz* in Arctic waters, "a threat in being." Just as the Americans absurdly overrated the deterrent power of deploying a mere thirty-six U.S. Army Air Forces (USAAF) B-17 bombers in the Philippines, so the prime minister failed to grasp the fact that, with or without Admiral Phillips's squadron, British forces in the Far East were woefully deficient in strength and leadership.

The British director of naval operations, Capt. Ralph Edwards, wrote in his diary when the battleship commitment was made:

> Another Prayer from the prime minister, who wishes us to form a squadron of "fast, powerful modern ships—only the best to be used" in the Indian Ocean. This, he avers, will have a paralysing effect on the Japanese—why it should, the Lord alone knows . . . This, mind you, at the same time as he wishes to form a force at Malta, reinforce the Mediterranean, help Russia and be ready to meet a break-out by the *Tirpitz*. The amount of unnecessary work which that man throws on the Naval Staff would, if removed, get us all a month's leave . . . If only the honourable gentleman were to confine himself to statesmanship and politics and leave naval strategy to those properly concerned, the chances of winning the war would be greatly enhanced. He is without doubt one of history's worst strategists.

Churchill wrote to Roosevelt, reporting dispatch of *Prince of Wales*, *Repulse* and the carrier *Indomitable*: "There is nothing like having something that can catch and kill anything." This was a bizarre assertion, after two years of war had demonstrated both the vulnerability of capital ships and the shortcomings of the Fleet Air Arm.

In almost all respects, during the Second World War the Royal Navy showed itself the finest of Britain's three fighting services, just as the U.S. Navy was the best of America's. Axis submarines and air attack inflicted heavy losses, but British seamen displayed consistently high courage and professionalism. The navy's institutional culture proved more impressive than that of the army, perhaps also of the RAF. The Battle of the Atlantic was less visible and glamorous than the Battle of Britain, but preservation of the convoy routes was an equally decisive achievement. The sea service's chronic weaknesses, however, were air support and antiaircraft defence. From the beginning to the end of the war, the Fleet Air Arm's performance lagged far behind that of the U.S. Navy's air squadrons, partly because of inadequate aircraft, partly because the British did not handle them so well, and partly because there were never enough carriers. Churchill served the navy's interests poorly by failing to insist that the RAF divert more long-range aircraft to maritime support operations, and especially to help protect the Atlantic convoys.

As autumn turned to winter, there seemed little cause for optimism at sea, in the air, or on land. Shrewd old Field Marshal Smuts cabled Churchill from South Africa in considerable dismay on November 4: "I am struck by the growth of the impression here and elsewhere that the war is going to end in stalemate and thus fatally for us." Many Americans perceived the British sitting idle behind their Channel moat, waiting for the United States to ride to their rescue. Averell Harriman wrote a personal letter to Churchill from Washington: "People are wondering why you don't do something offensively. In my opinion it is important that more should be said about what you are doing." The diplomat urged energetic media promotion of the RAF's bomber offensive, and of the Royal Navy's convoys to Russia.

Smuts, meanwhile, believed that Russia was being beaten, and that the United States was still determined to avoid belligerence. This view was widely shared in London. Britain's army vice chief of staff remained fearful of a German invasion of Britain, and baffled about how his own side might win the war: "Whatever may happen on the Russian front, it is only by successful invasion of these islands that Hitler can definitely win the war . . . I wish we had so clear an idea of how we could win. At present we cling rather vaguely to a combination of dissatisfied populations, lowering of morale amongst Germans and German troops, blockade and somewhat inaccurate bombing at night . . . America . . . seems further removed now from coming into the war than she was last April."

Yet there is evidence that Churchill's personal view was shifting towards an expectation of U.S. belligerence. He asserted to Lord Camrose at the Other Club on November 14 that he was confident the Americans would soon be in the war. Camrose was sufficiently impressed to write to his son, repeating the prime minister's words. On the nineteenth, Churchill told guests during a lunch at Downing Street that he expected to land the second of four possible "prizes." The first would be U.S. entry into the war without involving Japan; the second would be America's accession as an ally, matched by that of Japan as an enemy; the third would be that neither country entered the war; and the fourth, that Japan became an enemy, while the United States remained neutral. Yet to others, even those privy to secret intelligence of Japanese movements, the prime minister's hopes seemed ill-founded.

Churchill strove to provide cause for Americans to modify their impression of British passivity. Briefing Commodore Lord Louis Mountbatten on his new role as "chief adviser" to Combined Operations, which soon became translated into overall command, the prime minister said: "Your whole attention is to be concentrated on the offensive." This was another of the periods when he enthused about a possible descent on Norway, heedless of the intractable reality that its coastline was beyond British fighter range. Eden expressed dismay about this plan to his private secretary: "A.E. is much perplexed—he feels as I do so many of W.'s gorgeous schemes have ended in failure . . . a false step—a faulty short-cut—would set us back years."

The prime minister often felt oppressed by the perceived pettiness and petulance of Parliament. In the House on November 11, 1941, he faced a barrage of questions and supplementaries: first about alleged Italian atrocities in Montenegro, then about the government's apparent unwillingness to allow the RAF to bomb Rome. When he answered evasively, Sir Thomas Moore, MP for Ayr, demanded: "Does my right hon. friend really think it wise to provide a hide-out for this rat Mussolini?" The prime minister responded: "I think it would be as well to have confidence in the decisions of the Government, whose sole desire is to inflict the maximum of injury upon the enemy." Another MP drew attention to shortages of equipment, described in Lord Gort's recently published dispatch on the 1940 campaign in France. Churchill brusquely rejected calls for an enquiry. He might have suggested that such matters came under the heading of archaeology, rather than conduct of the war.

Another member demanded information about the precise composition of the prime minister's party at the Placentia Bay meeting, and asked, "whether in view of the fact that we are fighting for our existence, he will consider removing from Government service all persons of German education and of German origin." Churchill invited the questioner to be explicit. This the MP declined to do, but the House readily comprehended the enquiry as an attack upon Lord Cherwell. Other MPs then raised questions in which Cherwell was named. "The Prof" was widely perceived as a pernicious influence upon the prime minister. MPs who did not dare to attack Churchill himself instead vented their frustrations upon his associates. The prime minister defended Cherwell, but he bitterly resented being obliged to do so.

Such exchanges filled twelve columns of Hansard, and caused Churchill to return to Downing Street in dudgeon. Who could blame him? How pettifogging seemed the issues raised by MPs, how small-minded the pinpricks of their criticisms, alongside the great issues with which he wrestled daily. If self-pity about the intrusions of democracy is in some measure common to all national leaders in war or peace, such carping became infinitely irksome to the leader of a nation struggling for survival against overwhelming odds.

The best news in November was of Auchinleck's long-delayed offensive in the desert, Operation Crusader, which began on November 18. Churchill trumpeted its progress: "For the first time, the Germans are getting a taste of their own bitter medicine." On the twentieth, before the House of Commons, he described the North African assault in the most dramatic terms: "One thing is certain—that all ranks of the British Empire troops involved are animated by a long-pent-up and ardent desire to engage the enemy . . . This is the first time that we have met the Germans at least equally well-armed and equipped." Churchill knew from Ultra that Auchinleck had launched 658 tanks against Rommel's 168, that the RAF deployed 660 aircraft against 642 of the Luftwaffe's. Yet, in Crusader's first days, the British suffered much heavier losses than the Germans. The prime minister continued to cherish hopes for the tangled, messy desert fighting, but there was no sign of a breakthrough. On November 23 Auchinleck sacked Alan Cunningham, commander of the newly christened Eighth Army, and replaced him with his own chief of staff, Neil Ritchie. Rommel had destroyed the career of yet another British general. The Germans were once again fighting harder, faster and more effectively than the British.

It was at this time that Churchill's patience with his senior soldier, Sir John Dill, chief of the imperial general staff since May 1940, at last expired. Dill's difficulty was that, like his predecessor, Sir Edmund "Tiny" Ironside, he suffered from a surfeit of realism. This inspired in both men successively a gloom about their own nation's prospects which grated intolerably upon the prime minister. Dill was exhausted by Churchill's insistence upon deciding every issue of strategy through trial by combat, testing arguments to destruction at interminable Downing Street meetings. "Winston's methods were frequently repulsive to him," wrote Alan Brooke. He recoiled from the need to work with the Russians, whom he abhorred. He believed that whenever Hitler chose to reinforce Rommel, the Middle East would be lost, and feared that neglect of Britain's Far East defences would precipitate disaster if the Japanese attacked. Dill never doubted Churchill's greatness as national leader. But he considered him wholly unfit to direct strategy.

Churchill, in his turn, had told John Kennedy many months earlier that he found Dill "too much impressed by the enemy's will." The CIGS was an intelligent man, possessed of famous charm. But, like many other British officers, he lacked steel to bear the highest responsibilities in a war of national survival. On November 16, 1941, Churchill told Dill he must go, designating as his replacement Sir Alan Brooke, C-in-C Home Forces. The change provoked dismay in high places. Dill's colleagues and friends indulged that fatal British sympathy for agreeable gentlemen, however inadequate to their appointed tasks. He was perceived as a victim of Churchill's determination to bar dissent from his own conduct of the war. There is no doubt, however, that his removal was right. Never a driving force, he was now a spent one.

His successor proved the outstanding British command appointment of the Second World War. Brooke—like Dill, Montgomery and Alexander—was a Northern Irishman, fifty-eight years old. He had characteristics often identified with Protestant Ulster: toughness, diligence, intolerance, Christian commitment and a brusqueness that sometimes tipped over into ill-temper. His sharp brain was matched by extraordinary strength of purpose. A passionate bird-watcher, Brooke saved his softer side for his feathered friends, his adored second wife, Benita, and their two young children. A misanthrope, he had a low opinion of his fellow men, fellow soldiers and allies, expressed in his wartime diaries with a heavy dressing of exclamation marks. His booming voice and thick-rimmed spectacles intimidated strangers. Intensely active and indeed restless, Brooke was so little seen in the War Office that it was said of him that he knew his way to only two rooms there—his own and the lavatory.

Though the new CIGS was often charmed by the prime minister's puckish wit, and did not doubt his greatness, he and Churchill never achieved full mutual understanding. Brooke was disgusted by the selfishness of Churchill's working habits, late hours and strategic flights of fancy. Like Dill and Wavell, he loathed war as much as the prime minister relished it. But he displayed a tenacity and resolve in the face of difficulties and Churchillian follies which Dill lacked. David Margesson, the secretary for war, said that Brooke was sustained by "his ability to shake himself like a dog coming out of water after unpleasant interviews with Winston, and . . . his power of debate (& his rasping voice)." The new CIGS was a harsh and ruthless man. These qualities equipped him to fulfil his role far more effectively than the mild-mannered Dill.

Brooke proved a superb planner and organiser. He gained nothing like the public celebrity of Montgomery and Alexander. The CIGS and prime minister could not be described as brothers in arms. But they forged a partnership in the direction of British strategy which, however stormy, served their nation wonderfully well. Churchill, so often accused of surrounding himself with acolytes and yes-men, deserves the utmost credit for appointing and retaining as CIGS an officer who, when their views differed, fought him to the last gasp. The ascent of Brooke, on the eve of another critical turning point in the war, was a great day for British arms.

In the first days of December, a flood of intelligence revealed Japanese forces redeploying in Southeast Asia. The suspense was very great, as the British waited for Tokyo to reveal its objectives. To the end, there was apprehension that a Nipponese whirlwind might bypass the United States and its possessions. On Sunday, December 7, Churchill learned that Roosevelt proposed to announce in three days' time that he would regard an attack on British or Dutch possessions in the Far East as an attack on America. That day at lunch, U.S. ambassador "Gil" Winant was among the guests at Chequers. Churchill asserted vigorously that if the Japanese attacked the United States, Britain would declare war on Japan. Winant said he understood that, for the prime minister had declared it publicly. Then Churchill demanded: "If they declare war on us, will you declare war on them?" Winant responded: "I can't answer that, Prime Minister. Only the Congress has the right to declare war under the United States constitution." Churchill lapsed into silence. That terrible apprehension persisted, of facing the Japanese alone. Then he said, with his utmost charm: "We're late, you know. You get washed and we will go into lunch together."

Harriman, a fellow guest at dinner that night, found Churchill "tired and depressed. He didn't have much to say throughout dinner and was immersed in his thoughts, with his head in his hands part of the time." Then they heard the radio news of Japan's attack on Pearl Harbor, and looked incredulously at one another. Churchill jumped up and started for the door, saying, "We shall declare war on Japan." Within a few minutes, he and Winant were speaking by phone to Roosevelt. Soon afterwards the Admiralty called, reporting Japanese attacks on Malaya.

Churchill could not claim that his long campaign of seduction was responsible for U.S. entry into the war. This had followed only upon Japanese aggression. America's policy of deterrence in the east, fortified by sanctions, had instead provoked Tokyo to fight. Though the "day of infamy" resolved many dilemmas and uncertainties, it is unlikely that Roosevelt viewed Pearl Harbor with the same enthusiasm as the prime minister. Events had produced an outcome which the president, left to himself, would not have willed or accomplished for many months—if ever. What is certain is that Churchill had sown seeds of a fertility such as only he could have nurtured, for a harvest which he now gathered. He possessed a stature and commanded an affection among the American people incomparably greater than any respect won by the faltering performance of Britain's war machine. In the years ahead, his personality would enable him to exercise an influence upon American policies which, for all its limitations, no other British leader could have aspired to.

When Britain's Tokyo ambassador, Sir Robert Craigie, later submitted a valedictory dispatch, he was sharply censured by the prime minister for describing Japan's assault in the east as "a disaster for Britain." On the contrary, said Churchill, it was "a blessing . . . Greater good fortune has never happened to the British Empire." That night of December 7, 1941, Churchill wrote in a draft of his memoirs: "Saturated and satiated with emotion and sensation, I went to bed and slept the sleep of the saved and thankful. One hopes that eternal sleep will be like that."

EIGHT

A Glimpse of Arcadia

DE GAULLE SAID after Pearl Harbor: "Well then, this war is over. Of course, there are more operations, battles and struggles ahead; but . . . the outcome is no longer in doubt. In this industrial war, nothing can resist the power of American industry. From now on, the British will do nothing without Roosevelt's agreement." The U.S. president told Churchill: "Today all of us are in the same boat with you and the people of the Empire, and it is a ship which will not and cannot be sunk." Unlike Churchillian assertions earlier in the war, born of blind faith, Roosevelt's words were rooted in realities of power.

Harold Nicolson wrote on December 11: "We simply can't be beaten with America in. But how strange it is that this great event should be recorded and welcomed here without any jubilation. We should have gone mad with joy if it had happened a year ago . . . Not an American flag flying in the whole of London. How odd we are!" Part of the explanation was given by London charity worker Vere Hodgson. Like many of her compatriots, she felt that Pearl Harbor served the Americans right: "Though I do not wish anyone to be bombed, a little wholesome shaking-up is good for people who contemplate the sufferings of others with equanimity . . . Poor dear people in those islands of bliss, sunshine and fruit drinks. They must have had an unpleasant Sunday afternoon . . . I should think Colonel Lindbergh has retired to a room with dark blinds—not to be heard of for many a long day."

A Home Intelligence report said: "While the public are prepared to make any sacrifices necessary to help Russia . . . they have no such disposition towards America . . . America is 'too damned wealthy' . . . Americans are too mercenary-minded, and . . . the hardship and suffering of war 'will do them a lot of good.' " Few British people felt minded to thank the Americans for belatedly entering the war not from choice or principle, but because they were obliged to. Some were fearful that U.S. belligerence would check the flow of supplies to Britain and Russia. It was left to the prime minister to open his arms to a transatlantic embrace, which many of his compatriots were foolish enough to grudge.

In the days following Pearl Harbor, from everywhere save Malaya the war news reaching Churchill briefly brightened. The Royal Navy was faring better in its struggle with Hitler's U-boats. Auchinleck continued to signal optimistically about the progress of Crusader in the desert. "Consider tide turned," he reported from Cairo on December 9, and two days later: "We are pressing pursuit vigorously." The Russians were still holding Moscow, Leningrad and the Baku oil fields. Churchill told the House of Commons on December 8: "We have at least four-fifths of the population of the globe upon our side. We are responsible for their safety and for their future. In the past we have had a light which flickered, in the present we have a light which flames, and in the future there will be a light which shines over all the land and sea."

On December 10 came ghastly tidings, of the destruction of *Prince of Wales* and *Repulse* by Japanese air attack off Malaya. Churchill was stunned. Their deployment reflected his personal decision, their loss an indictment of his misplaced faith in "castles of steel" amid oceans now dominated by air and submarine power. It is often claimed that the fate of the two capital ships was sealed by the absence of the carrier *Indomitable*, prevented by accidental damage from joining the battle squadron. Given the shortcomings of the Fleet Air Arm and its fighters, it seems more plausible that if *Indomitable* had been at sea off Malaya, as intended by Churchill and the Admiralty, it would have been lost with *Prince of Wales* and *Repulse*.

Yet even this blow was endurable, in the context of American belligerency. On December 11, Germany and Italy removed a vital lingering doubt, by declaring war on the United States. The next day Churchill cabled to Eden, who was en route to Moscow: "The accession of the United States makes amends for all, and with time and patience will give certain victory." There were short-term hazards. Washington would cut overseas weapons shipments, to meet the needs of its own armed forces. Ten RAF squadrons en route to Persia to support Stalin's southern front would have to be diverted to the Far East. But these were mere inconveniences alongside the glittering prospect opened by American might.

The prime minister's first priority was to meet Roosevelt and his military chiefs face to face, to cement the alliance created by events, though never ratified by formal treaty. Henceforward, Anglo-American dealings would be influenced by formal agreements on matériel issues, above all Lend-Lease, but governed chiefly by personal understandings, or lack of them, between the leaders of the two nations and their Chiefs of Staff. When Churchill proposed himself for an immediate descent on Washington, the president demurred. On security grounds, he suggested a rendezvous in Bermuda, which he said that he could not himself attend before January 7. In reality, Roosevelt was hesitant about making space at the White House for the overpowering personality of Britain's prime minister and the torrent of rhetoric with which he would assuredly favour the American people. Nonetheless, in the face of Churchill's chafing, the president agreed that he should come to Washington before Christmas.

As the prime minister prepared to sail, there was a flurry of last-minute business. He cabled Eden that while it might be desirable for Russia to declare war on Japan, Stalin should not be pressed too hard on this issue, "considering how little we have been able to contribute" to the Soviet war effort. The foreign secretary was told, however, that on no account should he appear willing to satisfy Moscow's demands for recognition of the frontiers which the Russians had established for themselves by agreement with Hitler, absorbing eastern Poland and the Baltic states. Not only would such action be unprincipled, it would discomfit the Americans, who were at that time even more hostile than the British to Stalin's territorial ambitions. Meanwhile, Attlee was urged not to implement a threatened cut in the British people's rations: "We are all in it together and [the Americans] are eating better meals than we are." Reducing supplies would savour of panic, said the prime minister. From Gourock, on the Clyde, on the morning of December 13, he telephoned Ismay to urge that "everything that was fit for battle" should be dispatched to the Far East. Then, with his eighty-strong party which included Beaverbrook and the Chiefs of Staff—Dill still representing the army while Brooke took over at the War Office—he boarded the great battleship *Duke of York*, sister of the lost *Prince of Wales*.

The passage was awful. Day after day, *Duke of York* ploughed through mountainous seas which caused her to pitch and roll. Max Beaverbrook, who had been invited partly to provide companionship for "the old man" and partly because he was alleged to be popular with Americans, wheezed that he was being borne across the Atlantic in "a submarine masquerading as a battleship." Churchill, almost alone among the passengers, was untroubled by seasickness. Patrick Kinna, while taking dictation, found his own misery worsened by the cigar smoke that choked the prime minister's cabin high in the superstructure. A stream of bad news reached the party at sea: the Japanese landed in northern Borneo on December 17, on Hong Kong island the next day. Churchill minuted the Chiefs of Staff on the fifteenth, urging the vital importance of ensuring that Singapore was held: "Nothing compares in importance with the fortress." Heedless of the pitching of the storm-tossed warship, he dictated a succession of long memoranda, setting out his views on the way ahead.

Supplies for Russia from both Britain and the United States must be sustained, he said, for only thus "shall we hold our influence over Stalin and be able to weave the mighty Russian effort into the general texture of the war." He proposed that American troops should be sent to Northern Ireland, to provide an additional deterrent against German landings. By 1943, he said, Britain would be "more strongly prepared against invasion than ever before." The possibility of a German descent on Britain continued to feature in his calculations. If Russia was knocked out, as still seemed likely, the Nazis could again turn west. Hitler must recognise the urgency of completing the conquest of Europe before America became fully mobilised. Churchill suggested that U.S. bombers should deploy in Britain, to join the growing air offensive against Germany. He expected Singapore to be defended for at least six months.

He interrupted his dictation to tell Kinna to make some sailors stop whistling outside his cabin. This was a distraction and vulgarity which he could not abide—he once said that an aversion to whistling was the only trait he shared with Hitler. Kinna duly retired, but was too nervous of his likely reception to address the offending seamen, who lapsed into silence spontaneously. Oblivious of the towering seas outside, the pitching of the huge ship, Churchill resumed composition of his *tour d'horizon*. He wanted the Americans to land in French North Africa in 1942. The following year, he anticipated launching attacks against some permutation of Sicily, Italy, Norway, Denmark, Holland, Belgium, France's Channel or Atlantic coasts or possibly the Balkans. In his memoranda, he made some wild assertions, for instance anticipating that, when the time came to invade the Continent, "the uprising of the local populations for whom weapons must be brought will supply the corpus of the liberating offensive." But he also looked with imaginative foresight to the creation of improvised aircraft carriers, which would indeed play a key role later in the war, and urged a carrier-borne air assault on Japan.

On December 21, he wrote a long letter to Clementine: "I do not know when or how I shall come back. I shall certainly stay long enough to do all that has to be done, having come all this way at so much trouble and expense." He told her that he had no patience with those who denounced Britain's unreadiness in the Far East: "It is no good critics saying 'Why were we not prepared?' when everything we had was already fully engaged." In this, he was surely justified. Those like Dill, who had favoured reinforcing Malaya at the expense of the Middle East, were mistaken. It would have been absurd to dispatch desperately needed aircraft, tanks and troops to meet a putative threat in the Far East, at the likely cost of losing Egypt to an enemy already at its gates. It is hard to imagine any redeployment of available British resources in the autumn of 1941 which would have prevented disaster. So far-reaching were British weaknesses of leadership, training, tactics, air support and will in Malaya and Burma that the Japanese were all but certain to prevail.

The heavy seas imposed delays which caused *Duke of York*'s passage to seem to its passengers interminable. Churchill fulminated at the waste of time, but was obliged to concede that he could not subdue the elements. A five-day crossing stretched to nine, then ten. The Chiefs of Staff delivered their comments upon Churchill's long strategic memoranda, which were discussed at a series of meetings under his chairmanship. They opposed a firm commitment to opening the major Second Front in Europe in 1943. Germany, they said, must first be weakened by intensified and protracted bombing. They urged acknowledgement of the fact that "the Japanese will be able to run wild in the Western Pacific" until Germany and Italy were disposed of. Churchill, who was undergoing one of his periodic bouts of scepticism about bombing, resisted any declaration of excessive faith in its potential. He warned against expecting the Americans to take as insouciant a view of Japanese Pacific advances as the Chiefs proposed. He said that it was essential to promote an offensive vision, rather than merely to advocate countermeasures against Axis thrusts. All this was very wise.

On December 22, *Duke of York* at last stood into Hampton Roads. The British party landed, and Churchill and his immediate staff boarded a plane for the short flight to Washington. Through its windows, they peered down through gathering darkness, fascinated by the bright lights of America's capital after the gloom of blacked-out London. There to meet the prime minister at the airport was Franklin Roosevelt, whose guest he became for the next three weeks. If this was a tense time for the British delegation, it was also an intensely happy one for Churchill. Who could deny his deserving of it, after all he had endured during the previous eighteen months? That first Anglo-American summit was code-named Arcadia, the paradise of ancient Greek shepherds. To the prime minister, Washington indeed seemed paradisiacal. Installed in the White House, he enthused to Clementine: "All is very good indeed; and my plans go through. The Americans are magnificent in their breadth of view."

From his first meeting with Roosevelt, he emphasised the danger that Hitler might seize Morocco, and thus the urgent need that Allied forces should preempt him. Less convincingly, he cited the French battleships *Jean Bart* and *Richelieu*, sheltering in North Africa, as "a real prize." He was galled when Dill suggested that shipping shortages might make it impossible to convey an American army across the Atlantic in 1942, and swept this argument aside. The two national leaders and their Chiefs of Staff discussed, then dismissed, arguments for creating a war council on which all the Allies and British dominions would be represented. It was agreed that while the dominions should be consulted, policy must be made between the Big Three.

This latter outcome was inevitable, but sowed the seeds of future unhappiness around the Empire, and especially in Australia. While in Washington, Churchill learned of the crippling of the battleships *Valiant* and *Queen Elizabeth* by Italian human torpedoes in Alexandria Harbour, together with the loss of two cruisers at sea. He was furious to hear that his deputy prime minister had informed the Australians and Canadians of the drastic weakening of the Mediterranean Fleet. "I greatly regret that this vital secret should be spread about the world in this fashion," he cabled Attlee. "We do not give our most secret information to the Dominions."

The British and American Chiefs of Staff held twelve joint meetings. To the relief of Churchill and his delegation, the U.S. leadership immediately confirmed the conclusion of earlier Anglo-American staff talks, that the Allies should pursue the policy of "Germany first." It is sometimes insufficiently recognised how far Allied decisions for 1942 were influenced by shipping imperatives. The British were shocked, in the first weeks after Pearl Harbor, to discover how few bottoms would be available in the year ahead, before the huge U.S. "Liberty Ship" building programme achieved maturity. Britain required thirty million tons of imports a year to sustain itself, which had to be borne across the Atlantic by merchant fleets much diminished by sinkings.

With the limited capacity available, there was much more scope for American action against the Germans, by supplying Russia and deploying U.S. troops in the west, than against the Japanese in the Pacific. The Asian war required three or four times the freighting effort of the European one, because of the distances involved. A merchant ship could make only three round-trips a year to the Pacific theatre. The "Germany first" strategy thus represented not only strategic sense, but also logistic necessity. Yet, given the much greater popular animosity towards Japan in the United States, it should never be taken for granted. Harold Macmillan observed later of the prime minister: "No one but he (and that only with extraordinary patience and skill) could have enticed the Americans into the European war at all." This overstated the case. But the U.S. commitment to the western conflict indisputably represented a diplomatic triumph for Britain.

When Roosevelt introduced the prime minister to a throng of American pressmen, Churchill roused cheers and applause by climbing onto a chair so they could see him better. Asked whether it was true that Singapore was the key to the Far East war, he parried skilfully: "The key to the whole situation is the resolute manner in which the British and American democracies are going to throw themselves into the conflict." How long would it last? "If we manage it well, it will only take half as long as if we manage it badly." His exuberance was increased by further optimistic signals from Auchinleck in North Africa about the progress of Crusader.

On Christmas Eve, standing beside Roosevelt on the balcony as the White House tree lights were illuminated before a huge crowd, he said: "I cannot feel myself a stranger here in the centre and at the summit of the United States. I feel a sense of unity and fraternal association which, added to the kindliness of your welcome, convinces me that I have a right to share your Christmas joys . . . Let the children have their night of fun and laughter. Let the gifts of Father Christmas delight their play. Let us grown-ups share to the full in their unstinted pleasures before we turn again to the stern task and the formidable years that lie before us, resolved that, by our sacrifice and daring, these same children shall not be robbed of their inheritance or denied their right to live in a free and decent world." He found his pulse racing after the balcony appearance, from which his words were broadcast: "It has all been very moving." That evening, it was also a struggle to overcome private dismay: he learned of the fall of Hong Kong.

Roosevelt, matching the prime minister courtesy for courtesy and jest for jest, taunted him at dinner about having fought on the wrong side in the Boer War. When Churchill was asked about the quality of U.S. food supplies to Britain, he complained: "too many powdered eggs." He cabled Auchinleck, urging that, now that the desert campaign seemed to be progressing so well, he should release an armoured brigade and four RAF squadrons for the Far East. On Christmas evening, he left the rest of the presidential party watching a movie, and stumped off upstairs murmuring about "homework." He was writing next day's speech to the U.S. Congress.

Washington Post reporter Hope Ridings Miller wrote: "Senators' . . . office telephones carried call after call from friends—wondering if there was some way, somehow, something could be done to obtain tickets for the biggest show on the season's calendar." It was late in the morning when Churchill, wearing a blue polka-dot bow tie, clambered to his feet in the chamber on Capitol Hill. He grinned, donned spectacles, blinked back the tears that so often filled his eyes at dramatic moments. Congressman

Frank McNaughton saw "a stubby, granite little man . . . dumpy, heavy-shouldered, massive-jawed, with a solid bald crown flecked with straggles of grey hair." Hands on hips, Churchill began to address the audience beyond the dense bank of microphones. "Smiling, bowing, and looking very much at home," wrote Miller, "the Prime Minister flushed slightly as the ovation ushering him in increased in volume and burst into an ear-splitting crescendo. Compared with that demonstration, the tone in which he began his speech was so low those of us in the press gallery had a difficult time catching all his opening lines . . . A consummate actor, who carefully times his speech so that each word and each syllable is given the exact emphasis it should have, Mr. Churchill also pauses at the proper time for applause . . . "

In the knowledge that Americans, and especially their legislators, were deeply wary of Britain as a suppliant, he said nothing of dependency, real though this was. Instead, he talked of partnership, shared burdens. He flourished his own American parentage: "I shall always remember how each Fourth of July my mother would wave an American flag before my eyes." He reached his peroration: "Lastly, if you will forgive me for saying it, to me the best tidings of all is that the United States, united as never before, has drawn the sword for freedom, and cast aside the scabbard." He unsheathed an imaginary blade, and brandished it aloft.

Then he sat down, sweating freely. As one man, the chamber rose. The applause echoed on and on, until at last with a little wave Churchill left the rostrum. Hope Ridings Miller reported: "I never saw Congress in a more enthusiastic mood, and some diplomats, who habitually sit on their hands at a joint Congressional meeting, lest one gesture of applause might be diplomatically misinterpreted, clapped louder and longer than anybody." Interior Secretary Harold Ickes called him "the greatest orator in the world . . . I doubt if any other Britisher could have stood in that spot and made the profound impression that Churchill made." It was just after one o'clock. The prime minister, pouring himself a whiskey in the Senate secretary's office, said to Charles Wilson, his doctor, "It is a great weight off my chest." At an informal lunch after his speech, he told congressmen: "The American people will never know how grateful we are for the million rifles sent us after Dunkirk. It meant our life and our salvation." If this was a flourish of flattery, it promoted a legend that Americans cherished. That night Wilson was alarmed to discover that Churchill had suffered an attack of angina pectoris. But there was nothing to be done, no change in the schedule to be considered. It would have been a political catastrophe, if the world saw Britain's elderly war leader flag.

Churchill used Roosevelt's personal train to travel to Ottawa to address the Canadian Parliament, where he achieved another wonderful success. Back at the White House, he wrote happily to Attlee, "We live here a big family, in the greatest intimacy and informality." Peerless phrases dropped from his lips in even the most banal circumstances. At the White House lunch on New Year's Day, as he transferred hash and poached egg to his plate, the egg slipped off. The prime minister restored it to the hash, and, with a glance at his hostess, said, "to put it on its throne." It was fortunate that conversation sparkled, for the food at the Roosevelt White House was notoriously awful. After the meal, in her sitting room Eleanor Roosevelt and her secretary Malvina "Tommy" Thompson compared notes on the two leaders with the First Lady's friend and confidant Joseph Lash. Lash said the prime minister had the richer temperament, but the president was a more dependable, steadier man in a crisis. " 'Tommy' clapped her hands and said she and Mrs. Roosevelt felt the same. The president was more hardheaded, they felt. He was less brilliant, but more likely to do the right thing. The president also gave the impression of being more under control, of never letting himself go."

It is striking how many of those who worked with Roosevelt deferred to his greatness, but disliked his personality. Diplomat Charles Bohlen, for instance, observed that despite the president's pose of informality, "the aura of the office was always around him." If Churchill's outbursts of ill temper sometimes irked colleagues, Roosevelt's associates were made uneasy by his bland geniality, his reluctance to display anger, or indeed to reveal any frank sentiment at all. Where Churchill sought clarity of decision by working on paper, Roosevelt preferred to do business verbally. No minutes were taken of his Cabinet meetings. This approach led to many confusions, on issues of war and domestic policy alike. The president prided himself on his powers of persuasion, and had raised to an art form the ability to send every visitor out of his presence confident that he had got what he wanted. Both Churchill and Roosevelt were often accused of betraying their own social class, but the president was a much more skilled politician. De Gaulle described him as "a patrician democrat whose every simple gesture is carefully studied."

Halifax wrote with condescension but some justice about Churchill's late-night sessions with the Chiefs of Staff at the White House: "Winston's methods, as I have long known, are exhausting for anybody who doesn't happen to work that way; discursive discussions, jumping like a water bird from stone to stone where the current takes you. I am sure the faults that people find with him arise entirely from overwhelming self-centredness, which with all his gifts of imagination make him quite impervious to other people's feelings." Some of Roosevelt's intimates were struck by Churchill's single-minded obsession with the war. The occupant of the White House, by contrast, was obliged to devote far more of his energies to domestic matters, and to managing Congress. "The difference between the President and the prime minister," wrote his secretary William Hassett, "is the prime minister has nothing on his mind but the war: the President must also control the government of the United States."

Churchill felt able to take more for granted with his own nation's legislature than did Roosevelt with his. Yet, while the Americans perceived Britain's government as entirely dominated by Churchill, the British took a legitimate pride in the effectiveness of their bureaucratic machine. Churchill's team were bemused by the whimsical fashion in which the U.S. government seemed to be conducted. Ian Jacob thought the Oval Office "one of the most untidy rooms I have ever seen. It is full of junk. Half-opened parcels, souvenirs, books, papers, knick-knacks and all kinds of miscellaneous articles lie about everywhere, on tables, on chairs, and on the floor. His desk is piled with papers; and alongside his chair he has a sort of bookcase also filled with books, papers, and junk of all sorts piled just anyhow. It would drive an orderly-minded man, or woman, mad." FDR's famous dog, Fala, had to be evicted from a meeting in the Cabinet Room for barking furiously during a Churchillian harangue.

Cadogan asked Halifax with mandarin disdain: "How *do* these people carry on?" They were unimpressed by Roosevelt as a warlord. Jacob wrote: "By the side of the Prime Minister he is a child in military affairs, and evidently has little realisation of what can and what cannot be done . . . To our eyes the American machine of Government seems hopelessly disorganised . . . They will have first to close the gap between their Army and Navy before they can work as a real team with us." Had any American senior officer read these words, he would have answered that it was pretty rich for a British soldier thus to patronise the United States and its armed forces when Britain's record since 1939 was of almost unbroken battlefield failure and since her economic survival rested upon American largesse. Criticisms of Roosevelt's working methods had substance, but ignored America's untold wealth and achievements.

The British, in the years ahead, would persistently underestimate U.S. capabilities, and feed American resentment by revealing their sentiments. They failed, for instance, to recognise the potency of Roosevelt's personal commitment to supplying Russia. Just as Churchill and Beaverbrook faced opposition on this issue in Britain, so the president was obliged to overcome critics at the top of the armed forces, in Congress and in the media who were fiercely reluctant to offer Stalin open cheques on the U.S.

Treasury. Roosevelt, like Churchill, stood head and shoulders above his military advisers in his understanding of the importance of supporting Russia's war. While American deliveries, like those of Britain, lagged far behind promises, without the exercise of the president's utmost personal authority the Soviet Union would have been denied food, commodities, vehicles and equipment that became vital to its war effort.

In Washington, the Allies agreed to a vast increase in U.S. weapons production—Beaverbrook made a useful contribution by urging the feasibility of this on Roosevelt. It would be more than two years before the full effects became apparent on the battlefield. The Americans, including George Marshall, were slow to grasp the length of the inevitable delay between decisions to arm and achievement of capability to unleash upon the enemy the vast war machine they planned to create. But a beginning was made at Arcadia. On January 5, Churchill flew to Florida for five days' warmth, rest and work. He revised the strategy papers he had composed on the voyage from Britain. Amid the obvious determination of the U.S. Chiefs of Staff to grapple with the German army, he committed himself to "large offensive operations" in Europe in 1943. This, even though news from the battlefronts was turning sour again. Rommel had been able to extricate seven German and Italian divisions from the desert battle, and was regrouping in Tripolitana. The Japanese were storming down the Malay Peninsula, prompting the first stab of apprehension about Singapore. Large reinforcements were being rushed to "the fortress," as Churchill so mistakenly called the island.

Then there were a few more days with Roosevelt. "They tell me I have done a good job here," Churchill said to Bernard Baruch. The financier replied: "You have done a one hundred per cent job. But now you ought to get the hell out of here." The visitor was in danger of outstaying his welcome. The president had grown bored with the relentless, self-indulgent sparring between the prime minister and Beaverbrook. While never lacking confidence in the superior might of the nation which he himself led, Roosevelt found that it became tiring to live alongside the Englishman's bombastic presence. He was glad to see his guests go. Churchill wrote in his memoirs: "The time had now come when I must leave the hospitable and exhilarating atmosphere of the White House and of the American nation, erect and infuriate against tyrants and aggressors. It was to no sunlit prospect that I must return." He knew with what dismay the British nation must greet the torrent of ill tidings from the Far East, which had yet to reach a flood.

The president said to the prime minister at their parting, "Trust me to the bitter end." Then Churchill took off in a Boeing Clipper flying boat, one of three such aircraft purchased from the Americans the previous year. The Clipper flew low and slow, but offered its passengers a magnificent standard of comfort and cuisine. Dinner, served between Bermuda and Plymouth, consisted of consommé, shrimp cocktail, filet mignon with fresh vegetables, dessert, coffee, champagne and liqueurs. Then the passengers were able to retire to bunks, though Churchill wandered restlessly during the night. They landed in Britain on the morning of January 17, after an eighteen-hour flight. That evening, the prime minister briefed the War Cabinet. "An Olympian calm" prevailed at the White House, he said. "It was perhaps rather isolated. The president had no adequate link between his will and executive action." The British found the State Department "jumpy." Cordell Hull had been enraged by the unheralded Free French seizure of the tiny Vichy-held islands of St.-Pierre and Miquelon, off Newfoundland, a development which wasted precious Anglo-American time and goodwill to resolve. Amery noted wryly that, in Churchill's report to the Cabinet, he did not trouble to mention his visit to Canada.

But the prime minister's mood was exultant, as well it might be. He had achieved a personal triumph in the United States such as no other Englishman could have matched. He told the king that, after many months of dating, Britain and America were at last married. If there was no doubt that henceforward Britain would be junior partner in the Atlantic alliance, Churchill had imposed his greatness on the American people, in a fashion that would do much service to his country in the years ahead.

There were important nuances about this first visit, however. First, at a time when most of the decision makers in both Britain and the United States still thought it likely that Russia would be defeated, they failed to perceive the extent to which the war against Hitler would be dominated by the struggle in the east. At the turn of 1941–42, Roosevelt and Churchill in Washington supposed that they were shaping strategy for the destruction of Nazism. They had no inkling of the degree to which Stalin's nation would prove the most potent element in achieving this. Though the United States was by far the strongest global force in the Grand Alliance, the Soviet Union mobilised raw military power more effectively than either Western partner.

As for Anglo-American relations, Charles Wilson wrote of Churchill: "He wanted to show the President how to run the war, and it has not quite worked out like that." Eden told the Cabinet: "There is bound to be difficulty in practice in harmonizing day-to-day Anglo-Russian co-operation with Anglo-American co-operation. Soviet policy is amoral: United States policy is exaggeratedly moral, at least where non-American interests are concerned." Despite the success of Churchill's Washington visit, it would be mistaken to suppose that all Americans succumbed to the magic of his personality. His great line to Congress—"What kind of people do they think we are?"—prompted widespread editorialising. But in the weeks that followed, by no means all of this was favourable to Britain. The *Denver Post* said sourly: "There is one lesson the United States should learn from England. That is to put our own interests ahead of those of everybody else." The *Chicago Tribune*'s attitude was predictably rancid: "It is unfortunate that Mr. Roosevelt has had the example of Mr. Churchill constantly before him as a guide. Mr. Churchill is a man of very great capacity in many directions, but as a military strategist he has an almost unbroken record of disappointments and failures."

Some of the foremost personalities at Arcadia found one another unsympathetic. Henry Morgenthau, the treasury secretary, thought Max Beaverbrook cocky to the point of impertinence. In the absence of the newly appointed Alan Brooke, the British Chiefs of Staff made a weak team. The Americans liked Charles Portal, but the airman rarely imposed himself. Admiral Dudley Pound seemed a cipher, whose fading health disqualified him from meaningful participation. The Americans were too polite to allude in the visitors' presence to Britain's resounding military failures, but these were never far from their minds when they discerned extravagant assertiveness in Churchill or his companions. They had respect for the Royal Navy and RAF, but scarcely any for the British Army. Scepticism about British military competence would persist throughout the war in the upper reaches of the U.S. Army, colouring its leaders' attitudes in every strategic debate.

As for the president and the prime minister, Hopkins said, "There was no question but that [Roosevelt] grew genuinely to like Churchill." This seems at best half true. Their political convictions were far, far apart. For all Franklin Roosevelt's irrepressible bonhomie, excessive doses of Churchill palled on him. A joke did the rounds in Washington, and indeed was featured in *Time* magazine, that the first question the president asked Harry Hopkins on his return from Britain in February 1941 was, "Who writes Churchill's speeches for him?" The prime minister sought to display courtesy by pushing the president's wheelchair each evening from the drawing room to the lift. Yet it seems plausible that this gesture was misjudged, that it merely emphasised the contrast between the host's enforced immobility and the guest's exuberant energy. British witnesses at the White House observed Churchill striving to overcome his own irrepressible instinct to talk, and instead trying to listen to the president. It is hard to believe that Roosevelt's profound vanity was much massaged by Churchill's presence in his home.

The president's respect for the British prime minister's abilities was not in doubt, any more than was his commitment to the alliance to defeat Germany and Japan. But he was a much cooler man than Churchill. "Even those closest to Roosevelt," wrote Joseph Lash, who knew him well, "were always asking, 'What does he really think? What does he really feel?' " At no time did Roosevelt perceive himself engaged with the prime minister in a matched partnership. He was no mere leader of a government but a head of state, who wrote to monarchs as equals. Churchill felt no deep sense of obligation to America for its provision of supplies. In his eyes, Britain for more than two years had played the nobler part, pouring forth blood and enduring bombardment in a lone struggle for freedom. Roosevelt had scant patience with such pretensions. He paid only lip service to Britain's claims upon the collective gratitude of the democracies. Churchill's nation was now mortgaged to the hilt to the United States. Sooner or later, the president had every intention of exercising his power as holder of his ally's title deeds.

Roosevelt had visited Britain several times as a young man, but never revealed much liking for the country. As president, he repeatedly rejected invitations to go there. He perceived hypocrisy in its pretensions as a bastion of democracy and freedom, while it sustained a huge empire of subject peoples denied democratic representation. Cooperation with Churchill's nation was essential to the defeat of Hitler. Thereafter, in the words of Michael Howard, Roosevelt "proposed to reshape the world in accordance with American concepts of morality, not British concepts of realpolitik." Roosevelt's acquaintance with foreign parts had been confined to gilded European holidays with his millionaire father and a 1918 battlefield tour. He nonetheless had a boundless appetite to alter the world. Eden was appalled when he later heard the president expound a vision of Europe's future: "The academic yet sweeping opinions which he built . . . were alarming in their cheerful fecklessness. He seemed to see himself disposing of the fate of many lands, allied no less than enemy." The president mentioned, *inter alia*, a liking for the notion that the French colonial port of Dakar should become a U.S. naval base. His hubris shocked not only the British, but also such wise Americans as Harriman.

Eden claimed that Churchill regarded Roosevelt with almost religious awe. Yet the foreign secretary almost certainly misread as credulity Churchill's supremely prudent recognition of necessity. In no aspect of his war leadership did the prime minister exercise a more steely self-discipline than in this relationship. "My whole system is founded on friendship with Roosevelt," he told Eden later. He knew that, without the president's goodwill, Britain was almost impotent. He could not afford not to revere, love and cherish the president of the United States, the living embodiment of American might. He dismissed doubts and reservations to the farthest recesses of his mind. For the rest of the war, he sought to bind himself to Roosevelt in an intimacy from which the president often flinched. Churchill was determined upon marriage. Roosevelt acknowledged the necessity for a ring; but was determined to maintain separate beds, friends and bank accounts. The prospect of ultimate divorce, once the war was won, held no terrors for him.

The second strand in that first alliance conference was the attitude of the U.S. Chiefs of Staff. They were appalled by the spectacle of Britain's prime minister establishing himself for weeks on end at the White House, engaged in strategic discussions with the president from which they were often absent. Marshall, an intensely moral man, deplored casual intermingling of professional and social intercourse—so much so that he always refused invitations to stay at Hyde Park, the Roosevelt estate on the Hudson River in upstate New York. So strict was his personal austerity that when he added a chicken run to his quarters at Fort Myer, he insisted upon paying personally for the materials used in its construction. Unfamiliar with the promiscuity of Churchill's conversation, he resented every moment of the visitor's intimacies with Roosevelt. "The British," wrote Henry Stimson, "are evidently taking advantage of the president's well-known shortcomings in ordinary administrative methods." Hopkins cautioned Roosevelt against agreeing to military decisions in the absence of Marshall. Yet, to the army chief of staff's fury, Roosevelt accepted Churchill's proposal that, if the Philippines fell, residual American forces should be redeployed to Singapore.

Marshall was even more hostile than Roosevelt to British imperial pretensions. And while from the outset the president's imagination was seized by the notion of a North African landing, Marshall's was not. He and his colleagues were irked by a perceived British assumption that they could now draw on United States manpower and weapons "as if these had been swept into a common pool for campaigns tailored to suit the interests and convenience of Great Britain," in the words of a Marshall biographer. "From the British standpoint it was easy to conclude that a course of action favorable to their national interest was simply good strategic sense and that failure of the Americans to agree showed inexperience, immaturity and bad manners." From the first day of the war, Marshall was bent upon engaging the Germans in northwest Europe at the earliest possible date and avoiding entanglement in British "sideshows."

The only British officer with whom Marshall forged a close relationship was Dill. Ironically, the discarded CIGS now became a significant figure in the Anglo-American partnership. By an inspired stroke, when Churchill went home he left behind in Washington a somewhat reluctant Dill, who was shortly afterwards appointed chief of the British military mission. Between the embassy and the mission—housed in the U.S. Public Health Building on Constitution Avenue—there were soon nine thousand British uniformed and civilian personnel in Washington. Dill also became the British representative on the newly created Combined Chiefs of Staff Committee when it met in Washington in the absence of Pound, Brooke and Portal. Halifax, as ambassador, achieved no intimacy with the Americans, and it was never plausible that he should do so. Dill was understandably bemused by his new appointment: "It is odd that Winston should want me to represent him here when he clearly was glad of an excuse to get me out of the CIGS job." But he became Marshall's confidant, a sensitive interpreter of the two nations' military aspirations. In the years that followed, Dill made a notable contribution to the Grand Alliance, calming transatlantic storms and explaining rival viewpoints. He prospered as a diplomat where he had failed as a director of strategy.

Churchill's first visit to Washington was thus a public triumph, but a less assured private one. Still, he was wise to bask while he could in the sunshine of the new American relationship. Back at home, many troubles awaited him. History perceives 1940, when Britain stood alone, as the pivotal year for the nation's survival. Yet 1942 would prove the most torrid phase of Churchill's war premiership. The British people, so staunch amid the threat of invasion, two years later showed themselves weary and fractious. Amid the reality of crushing defeats, they tired of promises of prospective victories. In peace or war, the patience of democracies is seldom great. That of Britain had been progressively eroded by bombardment, privation and battlefield humiliation. In the press, the Commons, and on the streets of Britain, Churchill now faced criticism more bitter and sustained than he had known since assuming office.

NINE

"The Valley of Humiliation"

1. Critics

THROUGHOUT HISTORY, societies have enthused about victorious overseas conflicts and recoiled from unsuccessful ones. The U.S. declarations of war represented the fulfilment of all Churchill's hopes since May 1940. Yet 1942 proved, until its last weeks, the most unhappy year of his premiership. It was not only that Britain suffered a further succession of defeats; it was that public confidence in the prime minister's leadership waned in a fashion unthinkable during the Battle of Britain. Even if it remained improbable that he would be driven from office, he was beset by critics who questioned his judgement and sought to constrain his powers. Between his return from the United States in late January and the Battle of El Alamein in November, there were no moments of glory, and almost unremitting bad news. The British Empire suffered the heaviest blows in its history, which only the American alliance rendered endurable.

On the train back to London after his flying boat landed from Washington, Churchill indulged a last flicker of complacency. He told his doctor: "I have done a good job of work with the President . . . I am sure, Charles, the House will be pleased with what I have to tell them." A glance at the day's newspapers disabused him. He laid down the *Manchester Guardian* without enthusiasm. "There seems to be plenty of snarling," he said. In the days that followed, ill tidings crowded forward. Naval losses in the Mediterranean meant that in the forthcoming months, Britain could deploy no battle fleet from Alexandria. Amid reports from Malaya that the British Army was falling back routed upon Singapore, Churchill enquired whether there was a case for writing off the "fortress" and diverting reinforcements and aircraft elsewhere. His message was copied in error to the Australian representative to the War Cabinet, Sir Earle Page—a man "with the mentality of a greengrocer," in Brooke's scornful phrase—who in turn forwarded it to Canberra. Prime Minister John Curtin responded with an indignant cable to Churchill, asserting that to abandon Singapore would be "an inexcusable betrayal."

Relations between the Australian government and London, never cordial, entered a new phase of acrimony. Churchill valued Australia's fighting men, but was contemptuous of its weak Labor government. He contrasted Australian pusillanimity—what would now be called "whingeing"—unfavourably with the staunchness of New Zealand. Throughout the war, he treated all the self-governing dominions as subject colonies, mere sources of manpower. Dominion politicians visiting London were accorded public courtesy and private indifference. Robert Menzies, the former Australian prime minister who was now opposition leader, commanded respect, but even Menzies had been moved to protest back in 1940, when his government heard of the Dakar operation only on reading about it in the press. The sole imperial figure to enjoy Churchill's confidence was Jan Smuts, South Africa's seventy-two-year-old prime minister. He was a man of notable intellect and good sense, a friend since the end of the Boer War and Churchill's peer in adventure and experience. It was Smuts, honoured with field marshal's rank in 1941, who said: "We should thank God for Hitler. He has brought us back to a realization of brute facts . . . He has, in fact, taken the lid off Hell, and we have all looked into it."

Churchill's impatience with the dominions was understandable. Their governments—with the notable exception of New Zealand's—often displayed a parochialism irksome to a British prime minister directing a global struggle for survival. Neither Canada nor Australia, for instance, introduced universal conscription for overseas service until the last stages of the conflict. But Churchill's condescension towards Canberra and Ottawa was no more likely to please sensitive colonial governments than his absolute dismissal of Indian opinion won friends in the subcontinent. "The PM is not really interested in Mackenzie King," wrote Charles Wilson about Canada's prime minister. "He takes him for granted."

The *New Statesman* complained, "Mr. Churchill has been unwilling to give so much as a gracious word to win the support of India and Burma." The prime minister's later reluctance to release scarce shipping to relieve the Bengal famine, which killed three million people, appalled both the viceroy and Leo Amery, secretary of state for India. When Amery wished to make a broadcast to explain British policy, the prime minister vetoed it, saying that such action was making too much of the famine and sounding apologetic. More than any other aspect of his wartime behaviour, such high-handedness reflected the nineteenth-century imperial vision of

Churchill's youth. As the Far East situation deteriorated, for four months there seemed a real possibility that Australia would be invaded. The Canberra government turned openly to the United States for protection, in default of reassurance backed by reinforcements which the threadbare "mother country" could not provide.

On January 27, amid increasing parliamentary criticism, Churchill faced the Commons. "It is because things have gone badly, and worse is to come, that I demand a Vote of Confidence," he said. This was a device designed to force his critics to show their hands, or flinch. Having won the subsequent division by a majority of 464 to 1, he walked beaming through the throng in the central lobby on the arm of Clementine, who had come to lend support. But he knew that this outcome represented no ending of his troubles. He was unwell, nagged by a cold he could not shake off. On February 9, Eden's private secretary Oliver Harvey told his chief that he should be prepared to take over the premiership, and noted in his diary: "I think he is." Beyond the risks inherent in Churchill's wartime travels, the health of a man of sixty-seven, labouring under huge strains, might collapse at any time. Such a contingency was never far from the consciousness of his close subordinates, who were also dismayed by unsurprising evidence of the strains under which he laboured. Brooke, less than two months in his job as CIGS, told Dalton at dinner on February 10: "Sometimes . . . the PM is just like a child who has lost his temper. It is very painful and no progress can be made with the business."

Churchill signalled Wavell, newly appointed as Anglo-American supreme commander in the Far East, urging that while the Russians on the Eastern Front and the Americans on Luzon, in the Philippines, were fighting so staunchly, it was essential that the army in Malaya should be seen to give of its best: "The whole reputation of our country and our race is involved." Two days later, on February 11, in response to continuing domestic criticism of his government and Beaverbrook's desire to resign, he offered Stafford Cripps, whom he despised but who had a large popular following, the Ministry of Supply. Churchill grumbled about Cripps's demand to sit in the War Cabinet: "Lots of people want to. You could fill the Albert Hall with people who want to be in the War Cabinet." Denied a seat, Cripps declined office.

There was a new shock on February 12. The German battle cruisers *Scharnhorst* and *Gneisenau* left Brest and steamed at full speed up the English Channel, assisted by fog. Churchill's secretary Elizabeth Layton entered the Cabinet Room at three p.m. to take dictation, where she found the prime minister "striding up and down, all on edge. He dictated four telegrams like a whirlwind, and then phoned this and phoned that. I wondered if I should go, and once did slip out, but was recalled. Did another telegram, he marched up and down, talking to himself, a mass of compressed energy. Presently he sat down and said, 'There's a bloody great battle going on out there.' I said, 'Do you think we might get them?' He said, 'Don't know. We winged 'em, but they aren't dead yet.' " The navy did not "get them." The German squadron reached Wilhelmshaven. Ultra informed Churchill that the ships had been severely damaged by mines on the last stage of their passage, but this was small comfort and could not be revealed because of its source. The British people saw only that the Royal Navy and RAF were unable to stop Hitler's capital ships passing with impunity through British home waters.

Headlines screamed, the public was affronted. The *Daily Mirror* asked on February 14: "Is it any longer true that we trust the Prime Minister, but do not trust his Government?" The *News Chronicle* likewise: "Have we not been hypnotised by Mr. Churchill's personality . . . into acquiescence in an inefficient war direction?" The *Daily Mail* wrote that there were two Churchills, "1. The Inspirer of the Nation. 2. The Controller of the War." The British people were perplexed by the second Churchill, who claimed "that it was the duty of Parliament and Press to maintain the Government with the implication that any weakening of his own position would be a weakening of its cause." The *Mail* rejected this view: "No man is indispensable." Sir William Beveridge wrote a major article for the *Times*, urging the creation of a "proper" War Cabinet of ministers without portfolios. A Glasgow secretary, Pam Ashford, wrote on March 5: "Defeatism is in the air, and . . . I feel it too." When Mass Observation quizzed its observers about the prime minister, the opinion-monitoring group was startled by the vehemence of criticism. A London clerk said: "I think it is time he went. After all, the only connection in which one thinks of Churchill now is with regard to high strategy, whatever that may be. High strategy stinks to high heaven . . . This view I have confirmed with quite a few people. His speeches are no longer listened to."

While this attitude was untypically strident, there was a yearning at every level of British society for a defence supremo who could deliver battlefield success, as the prime minister seemed unable to do. Many people sought a new deliverer, an aspiration no less strongly felt because it was unrealistic and unsupported by identification of an appropriate candidate. There was no appetite to change national leaders, but much enthusiasm for delegating Churchill's military powers. The prime minister said to his old friend Violet Bonham Carter: "I'm fed up . . . I feel very biteful and spiteful when people attack me." He was constantly urged to add talent to his Cabinet, "but where is the galaxy? I can't get the victories. It's the victories that are so hard to get."

On February 15, Singapore surrendered. This time there was no Dunkirk, no miraculous escape for the garrison. Almost thrice as many imperial troops fell into captivity as in France in 1940. Jock Colville, temporarily removed from Downing Street to train in South Africa as a fighter pilot, heard Churchill's broadcast addressing the disaster. He was deeply moved: "The nature of his words and the unaccustomed speed and emotion with which he spoke convinced me that he was sorely pressed by critics and opponents at home. All the majesty of his oratory was there, but also a new note of appeal, lacking the usual confidence of support . . . There was something about his voice and delivery which made me shiver." The broadcast was much less well received than most of Churchill's performances. In private, the prime minister was angry and depressed. "We have so many men in Singapore, so many men," he lamented. "They should have done better." At a Pacific War Council meeting, he said of the Japanese: "They moved quicker and ate less than our men."

He suggested to his naval aide, Capt. Richard Pim, that this might be the moment for him to surrender the premiership. Pim said: "But my God, sir, you cannot do that." It is unlikely that Churchill seriously considered resignation, but his despair was real enough. What use was it for him to display a warrior's spirit before the world if those who fought in Britain's name then showed themselves incapable of matching his rhetoric? In Norway, France, Greece, Crete, Libya and now Malaya, the British had been beaten again and again. Alan Brooke wrote in his diary: "If the army cannot fight better than it is doing at the present, we shall deserve to lose our Empire."

Some blame attached to Wavell, not for failing to achieve victory, but for declining to avow the inevitability of Singapore's fall and for not making an uncompromising recommendation to halt reinforcements and evacuate every possible man. Brooke had done exactly this in France in June 1940. The British 18th Division landed at Singapore on January 29, 1942, by which date there was no prospect of saving the campaign. Almost the entire army fell into captivity a fortnight later. It remains hard to understand why Churchill deluded himself that Singapore could be held. Every soldier knew that its fate must be decided in southern Malaya, that the island in isolation was indefensible, and the Chiefs of Staff made this plain to the prime minister on January 21. It was regrettable that commanders on the spot did not adopt a more trenchant tone. While Wavell's signals about Malaya were unfailingly pessimistic, they did not explicitly acknowledge that Singapore's demise was inevitable until it was too late to save any portion of its garrison. It was true that he exercised his short-lived command amid draconian signals from Churchill, demanding a last-man, last-round defence. But whereas it should have been possible to hold Crete, Singapore was doomed.

British and imperial forces in Malaya were ill-trained, poorly equipped and badly led at every level. They faced an enemy who commanded the air, but two years later German and Japanese soldiers displayed extraordinary resilience in the face of vastly stronger air forces than the Luftwaffe deployed in Greece or the Japanese in Malaya. It was the absence of any scintilla of heroic endeavour, any evidence of last-ditch sacrifice of the kind with which British armies through the centuries had so often redeemed the pain of defeats, that shocked Churchill. In Malaya, there was no legend to match that of Sir John Moore's retreat to Corunna in the Napoleonic Wars, of Rorke's Drift in Zululand, of the defence of Mafi-keng and Ladysmith in the Boer War. The Americans forged a propaganda epic, however spurious, out of their defence of the Bataan Peninsula between December 1941 and April 1942. The British salvaged nothing comparable from Southeast Asia. Their soldiers gave up pitifully easily, 130,000 surrendering after the loss of only around 3,000 killed. The *Times* of February 16 offered its readers crumbs of comfort for Singapore: "The sacrifice and the suffering and the incomparable gallantry of the defence were not wholly in vain." This was nonsense. There was only abject defeat, surrender to numerically inferior enemies who had proved themselves better and braver soldiers. It is brutal, but seems valid, to suggest that Malaya might have been defended with greater determination had British, Indian and Australian soldiers known the fate that awaited them in Japanese captivity.

Who could wonder that Churchill should be plunged into despair? "At the back of his mind and unconsciously, I believe," wrote Oliver Harvey shrewdly, "the PM is jealous of Stalin and the successes of his armies." Even if American aid enabled Britain to survive the war, how could the nation hold up its head in the world, be seen to have made a worthy contribution to victory, if its army covered itself with shame whenever exposed to a battlefield? Lack of shipping remained a massive constraint on deployments. John Kennedy wrote: "We have masses of reinforcements we cannot move." At any one moment of 1942, two thousand British and American merchantmen were afloat on the Atlantic shuttle, three or four hundred of them vulnerable to U-boat attack. In peacetime, a cargo ship took an average thirty-nine days to complete a round-trip between Europe and North America. Now, the same rotation took eighty-six days, with forty-three spent in port instead of a peacetime fourteen, mostly waiting for convoys. Dill cabled the Chiefs of Staff from Washington, saying that this seemed a time for the Allies to focus on essentials: security of the British Isles and United States and preventing a junction of German and Japanese forces on the Indian Ocean: "These simple rules might help us to stick to things that matter in these difficult days." Yet, as so often with British generals' strategic visions, this one was entirely defensive.

Churchill told the Commons on February 24: "The House must face the blunt and brutal fact that if, having entered a war yourself unprepared, you are struggling for life with two well-armed countries, one of them possessing the most powerful military machine in the world, and then, at the moment when you are in full grapple, a third major antagonist with far larger military forces than you possess suddenly springs upon your comparatively undefended back, obviously your task is heavy and your immediate experiences will be disagreeable." Many MPs nonetheless voiced discontent. James Griffiths, Labour member for the Welsh mining constituency of Llanelli, said that at the time of Dunkirk people had responded to the call. By contrast, "we believe that now there is a feeling of disquiet in the nation. We ought not to resent it." Commander Sir Archibald Southby, Epsom, spoke of the German "Channel dash" and the fall of Singapore as two events which "shook not only the Government but the British Empire to its foundations. Nay, it would be fair to say that they influenced opinion throughout the world. They produced the most unfortunate reverberations in the United States of America just at a time when harmony and understanding between the two nations was of paramount importance."

Sir George Schuster, Walsall, said he thought the public wanted to feel that it was being told the truth, and was beginning to doubt this. People had been assured that in Libya the British Army was now meeting the enemy on equal terms. Then, after Rommel's dramatic comeback, they heard that the Germans had a better antitank gun, that our guns were inadequate to pierce enemy armour. "That was a shock to public opinion. They felt they had been misled."

During lunch at Buckingham Palace that day, Churchill told the king that Burma, Ceylon, Calcutta, Madras and parts of Australia might well be lost. The defence of Burma had already begun badly. Brooke noted with his customary spleen that some politicians allowed the bad news to show. "This process does not make Cabinet Ministers any more attractive," he wrote to a friend. "But Winston is a marvel. I cannot imagine how he sticks it." Clementine wrote to Harry Hopkins, "We are indeed walking through the Valley of Humiliation."

In consequence of the disasters on the battlefield, Churchill was obliged to make changes in his government, more painful and embarrassing than some historians have acknowledged. Beaverbrook finally resigned. Stafford Cripps was given his seat in the War Cabinet, as lord privy seal and leader of the Commons. For the prime minister, this was a bitter pill. Accepting Cripps was a measure of the weakness of his position. The two men, wrote Eden wonderingly, had "always been as distant as a lion and an okapi." Churchill is alleged to have said of Libya: "There are miles and miles of nothing but arid austerity. How Cripps would like it!"

Cripps was fifty-two, a product of Winchester and New College Oxford, and nephew of the socialist intellectual Beatrice Webb. He became first a research chemist, then a successful commercial barrister. A pacifist in World War I, he was elected as a Labour MP in 1931 and served briefly in Ramsay MacDonald's government before refusing to join his coalition. A vegetarian and teetotaller, in the 1930s he became converted to Marxism, an uncritical enthusiast for the Soviet Union whose name was often coupled with that of Aneurin Bevan. In 1939, he was expelled from the parliamentary Labour Party after differences with Attlee. When Cripps served in Moscow between 1940 and 1942, Churchill was not displeased to note that Stalin showed much less enthusiasm for the ambassador, and for his company, than his British admirer displayed for the Soviet leader.

In many respects a foolish man, Cripps nonetheless became temporarily an important one in 1942. A fine broadcaster, his commitment both to the Soviet Union and to a socialist postwar Britain won him a large popular following. He spoke passionately, and without irony, of Russian workers "fighting to keep their country free," and of the alliance between "the free workers of England, America and Russia." Amid the mood of the times, such sentiments struck a powerful chord, contrasting with the stubborn conservatism of many other MPs—and of the prime minister. In a poll that invited voters to express a preference as prime minister if some misfortune befell Churchill, 37 percent of respondents named Eden, but 36 percent opted for Cripps.

Churchill was well aware that his new minister aspired to the premiership. For most of 1942, he felt obliged to treat Cripps as a potential threat to his authority. Amid so many misfortunes, some surprising people supported the lord privy seal's ambitions. Private conclaves of MPs, editors, generals and admirals discussed Churchill and his government in the most brutal terms. John Kennedy dined at Claridge's on March 5, 1942, with Sir Archie Rowlands of the Ministry of Aircraft Production and John Skelton, news editor of the *Daily Telegraph*: "The talk was very much about Winston and very critical. It was felt that Winston was finished, that he had played his last card in reforming the government. S[kelton] is very hostile to Winston and thinks Cripps should be put in his place. He feels that we shall lose the whole Empire soon and be driven back on G.B. It is easy to make a case for this." Averell Harriman wrote to Roosevelt on March 6:

> Although the British are keeping a stiff upper lip, the surrender of their troops at Singapore has shattered confidence to the core—even in themselves but, more particularly, in their leaders. They don't intend to take it lying down and I am satisfied we will see the rebirth of greater determination. At the moment, however, they can't see the end to defeats. Unfortunately Singapore shook the Prime Minister himself to such an extent that he has not been able to stand up to this adversity with his old vigor. A number of astute people, both friends and opponents, feel it is only a question of a few months before his Government falls. I cannot accept this view. He has been very tired but is better in the last day or two. I believe he will come back with renewed strength, particularly when the tone of the war improves.

The Battle of the Atlantic had taken a serious turn for the worse. In January, the German navy introduced a fourth rotor into its Enigma ciphering machines. This refinement defied British code breakers through the bloody year of convoying that followed. Charles Wilson, Churchill's doctor, noticed that the prime minister carried in his head every statistical detail of Atlantic sinkings. Nonetheless, Wilson wrote, "he is always careful to consume his own smoke; nothing he says could discourage anyone . . . I wish to God I could put out the fires that seem to be consuming him." Mary Churchill noted in her diary that her father was "saddened— appalled by events . . . He is desperately taxed." Cadogan wrote likewise: "Poor old P.M. in a sour mood and a bad way."

On March 6, Rangoon was abandoned. The next day, Churchill wrote to Roosevelt, urging that the Western Allies should concede to Russian demands for recognition of their 1941 frontiers—which Britain had staunchly opposed the previous year. The Americans demurred, but the prime minister's change of attitude reflected intensified awareness of the Western Allies' vulnerability. He was now willing to adopt the most

Germany triumphs in both west and east. (*above*) Blazing shore facilities on Crete in May 1941, and (*right*) one of some three million Russian soldiers who surrendered to the Wehrmacht during the first year of Operation Barbarossa

Friendship of state. (*above*) Harry Hopkins and his host pose outside Downing Street on January 10, 1941, with Brendan Bracken behind; (*left*) FDR and Churchill at Placentia Bay on August 10, the president leaning on the arm of his unlovable son Elliot

War in the desert. (*right*) British troops advance through a minefield. (*below*) Some of the tens of thousands of Italian prisoners who fell into British hands during Wavell's Operation Compass

Civilian chroniclers of the wartime experience: Vere Hodgson (*top left*) and George King (*top right*) in Home Guard battle dress

Whitehall diarists:
(*below left*) Sir John Kennedy;
(*below center*) Sir Alexander Cadogan;
(*below right*) Harold Nicolson

Clockwise from top left: Charles Wilson, Lord Moran; Hugh Dalton; Leo Amery; Cuthbert Headlam; Oliver Harvey; Lt. Gen. Sir Henry Pownall

Working on his train, with a secretary's "silent" typewriter at hand to take dictation

Viewing new aircraft with (*left to right*) Lindemann, Portal and Pound

Jock Colville's September 1941 farewell to Downing Street gathering, on the steps
to the garden. *Front row, left to right:* Colville, Churchill, John Martin, Tony Bevir;
(*back row, left to right*) Leslie Rowan, "Master" John Peck, Miss Watson, Commander
"Tommy" Thompson, Charles Barker

Return from Arcadia: Churchill briefly at the controls of the British plane that brought him home from Washington in January 1942

One of the many impassioned Second Front rallies held in Britain's cities in 1942–43

unwelcome expedients, if these might marginally strengthen Russia's resolve. Amid alarm that Stalin might be driven to parley with Hitler, eastern Poland became expendable. In the same spirit, Churchill cabled Moscow promising that if the Germans employed poison gas on the Eastern Front, as some feared was imminent, the British would retaliate as if such a weapon had been used against themselves. Western fears that Stalin might seek a separate peace persisted for many months.

Beyond the great issues on Churchill's desk, he was obliged to address myriad lesser ones. He warned about the risk of a possible German commando raid, launched from a U-boat, to kidnap the Duke of Windsor, now serving as governor-general of the Bahamas. The Nazis, said the prime minister, might be able to exploit the former king to their advantage. Having inspired the creation of the Parachute Regiment, which carried out its first successful operation against a German radar station at Bruneval, on France's northern coast, on February 28, Churchill pressed for the expansion of airborne forces on the largest possible scale. Four Victoria Crosses were awarded for the Royal Navy's March 28 attack on the floating dock at St.-Nazaire. This generous issue of decorations was designed to make the survivors feel better about the losses—five hundred men killed, wounded or captured. Propaganda made much of St.-Nazaire. The public was assured that the Germans had suffered heavily, though in reality their casualties were many fewer than those of the raiders. Meanwhile, ministers solicited Churchill about appointments, honours and administrative issues. Such nugatory matters were hard to address when the Empire was crumbling.

Churchill's obsession with capital ships persisted even in the third year of the war. He asserted that the destruction of the 42,000-ton *Tirpitz*, anchored in a Norwegian fjord where it posed a permanent threat to Arctic convoys, would be worth the loss of a hundred aircraft and five hundred men. On March 9, twelve Fairey Albacores of the Fleet Air Arm attacked the German behemoth, with clumsy tactics and no success. Churchill asked the first sea lord "how it was that 12 of our machines managed to get no hits as compared with the extraordinary efficiency of the Japanese attack on *Prince of Wales* and *Repulse*?" How not, indeed? Though British aircraft made an important contribution to interdicting Rommel's Mediterranean supply line in 1942, the RAF and Fleet Air Arm's record of achievement in attacks upon enemy surface ships remained relatively poor until the last months of the war. Churchill thought so, minuting Pound in the following year that it seemed "a pregnant fact" that the Fleet Air Arm had suffered only 30 fatalities out of a strength of 45,000 men in the three months to the end of April. The 1940 attack on Taranto and the 1941 crippling of the *Bismarck* were the only impressive British naval air operations of the war.

During the winter of 1941–42, Churchill had become unhappily conscious of the failure of British "precision bombing" of Germany. He was party to the important change of policy which took place in consequence, largely inspired by his scientific adviser. Lord Cherwell's intervention about bombing was his most influential of the war. It was a member of his Cabinet Statistical Office staff, an official named David Butt, who produced a devastating report based on a study of British bombers' aiming-point photographs. This showed that only a small proportion of aircraft were achieving hits within miles, rather than yards, of their targets. Cherwell convinced the prime minister, who was shocked by Butt's report, that there must be a complete change of tactics. Since, under average weather conditions, RAF night raiders were incapable of dropping an acceptable proportion of bombs on designated industrial objectives, British aircraft must henceforward instead address the smallest aiming points they were capable of identifying: cities. They might thus fulfil the twin objectives of destroying factories and "dehousing" workers, to use Cherwell's ingenuous phrase. No one in Whitehall explicitly acknowledged that the RAF was thus to undertake the wholesale killing of civilians. But nor did they doubt that this would be the consequence, though British propaganda for the rest of the war shrouded such ugly reality in obfuscation, not least from the aircrew conducting bomber operations at such hazard to themselves.

Churchill always considered himself a realist about the horrors and imperatives of war. Yet as recently as 1937, he had proclaimed his opposition to air attacks upon noncombatants, during a Commons debate on air-raid precautions: "I believe," he said, "that if one side in an equal war endeavours to cow and kill the civil population, and the other attacks steadily the military objectives . . . victory will come to the side . . . which avoids the horror of making war on the helpless and weak." Now, however, after thirty months of engagement with an enemy who was prospering mightily by waging war without scruple, Churchill accepted a different view. Bomber Command had failed as a rapier. Instead, it must become a blunt instrument. Operational necessity was deemed to make it essential to set aside moral inhibitions. For many months, indeed years ahead, bombing represented the only means of carrying Britain's war to Germany. The prime minister approved Cherwell's new policy.

On February 22, 1942, Air Chief Marshal Sir Arthur Harris became C-in-C of Bomber Command. Contrary to popular myth, Harris was not the originator of "area bombing." But he set about implementing the concept with a single-minded fervour which has caused his name to be inextricably linked with it ever since. The first significant event of Harris's tenure of command was a raid on the Renault truck plant in the Paris suburb of Billancourt. The War Cabinet hoped that this would boost French morale, which seemed unlikely when it emerged that more than four hundred civilians had been killed. On March 28, 134 aircraft carried out a major attack on the old German Hanse town of Lübeck. The coastal target was chosen chiefly because it was easy for crews to find. The closely packed medieval centre was, in Harris's contemptuous words, "built more like a fire-lighter than a human habitation." The raid left much of Lübeck in flames, and was judged an overwhelming success. Four successive attacks on the port of Rostock in late April achieved similar dramatic results, causing Goebbels to write hysterically in his diary, "Community life in Rostock is almost at an end." On May 30, Harris staged an extraordinary *coup de théâtre*. Enlisting the aid of training and Coastal Command aircraft, he dispatched 1,046 bombers against the great city of Cologne, inflicting massive damage.

The chief merit of the "Thousand Raid," together with others that followed against Essen and Bremen, lay less in the injury they inflicted upon the Third Reich—a small fraction of that achieved in 1944–45—than in the public impression of Britain striking back, albeit in a fashion which rendered the squeamish uncomfortable. Some 474 Germans died in the "Thousand Raid" on Cologne, but on June 2 the *New York Times* claimed that the death toll was 20,000. Churchill cabled Roosevelt: "I hope you were impressed with our mass air attack on Cologne. There is plenty more to come."

Throughout 1942 and 1943, British propaganda waxed lyrical about the achievements of the bomber offensive. Churchill dispatched a stream of messages to Stalin, emphasising the devastation. The British people were not, on the whole, strident in yearning for revenge upon Germany's civilian population. But many sometimes succumbed to the sensations of Londoner Vere Hodgson, who wrote: "As I lay in bed the other night I heard the deep purr of our bombers winging their way to Hamburg . . . This is a comfortable feeling. I turned lazily in bed and glowed at the thought, going back in my mind to those awful months when to hear noise overhead was to know that the Germans were going to pour death and destruction on us . . . One cannot help feeling that it is good for the Germans to know what it feels like. Perhaps they won't put the machine in motion again so light-heartedly."

Later in the war, when great Allied armies took the field, Churchill's enthusiasm for bombing ebbed. But in 1942 he enthused about the strategic offensive because he had nothing else. Again contrary to popular delusion, he never found Sir Arthur Harris a soulmate. The airman sometimes dined at Chequers, because his headquarters at High Wycombe was conveniently close. But Desmond Morton was among those who believed that the prime minister thought Harris an impressive leader of air forces, but an unsympathetic personality. Churchill said of Bomber Command's C-in-C after the war: "a considerable commander—but there was a certain coarseness about him." In the bad times, however—and 1942 was a very bad time—he recognised Harris as a man of steel, at a time when many other commanders bent and snapped under the responsibilities with which he entrusted them.

From the outset, area bombing incurred criticism on both strategic and moral grounds, both inside and outside Parliament. Clement Attlee, leader of the Labour Party and deputy prime minister, was a persistent private critic, on both moral and pragmatic grounds. He stressed the value of bombers in support of ground and naval operations. In the public domain, the *New Statesman* argued that it was perverse to heap praise on the fortitude of the civilian population of Malta in enduring Axis air attack, without perceiving the lesson for Britain's own forces attacking Germany. "The disaster of this policy is not only that it is futile," the distinguished scientist Professor A. V. Hill, MP for Cambridge University, told the House of Commons, "but that it is extremely wasteful, and will become increasingly wasteful as time goes on." But Hill's words reflected only a modest minority opinion.

There was a powerful case for accepting the necessity for area bombing. A major British industrial commitment was made to creating a massive force of heavy aircraft. This attained fulfilment only in the very different strategic circumstances of 1944–45. The most pertinent criticism of 1942–43 bombing policy was that the airmen's fervour to demonstrate that their service could make a decisive independent impact on the war caused them to resist, to the point of obsession, calls for diversions of heavy aircraft to other purposes, above all the Battle of the Atlantic. John Kennedy wrote in May 1942 that the bomber offensive "can be implemented only at severe cost to our command of the sea and our military operations on land. I have just been looking at an old paper of Winston's, written in Sept. 1940, which begins 'the Navy can lose us the war, but only the Air Force can win it . . . ' I am convinced that events will prove this to have been a profound delusion."

Cherwell supported Harris in resisting calls for the reinforcement of Coastal Command, but they were both surely wrong. Evidence is strong that even a few extra squadrons could have achieved more in fighting the U-boats, a deadly menace well into 1943, than they did over Germany in the same period. But the navy made its case without much skill or subtlety. Admiral Sir John Tovey, C-in-C Home Fleet, denounced the bomber offensive as "a luxury, not necessity." His words infuriated the prime minister, who was also irked by Tovey's reluctance to hazard his ships within reach of Norwegian-based German airpower. He described Tovey as "a stubborn and obstinate man," and was delighted when in May 1943 he was replaced by the supposedly more aggressive Adm. Sir Bruce Fraser. The admirals' difficulty was that, while their service's function of holding open the sea routes to the United States, Russia, Malta, Egypt and India was indispensable, it was also defensive. As Churchill said, the fleet was responsible for saving Britain from losing the war and played a more distinguished part than either of Britain's other services in 1942, but could not win it. The Admiralty damaged its own case by insisting that the RAF lavish immense effort, and accept heavy casualties, on bombing the impregnable U-boat pens of northwest France in and patrolling the Bay of Biscay. The sailors would have done better to emphasize the issue of direct air cover for the Atlantic convoy routes, which drastically impeded the operations of German submarines.

Churchill thought better of the Royal Navy as a fighting service than he did of most of its commanders. They seemed relentlessly negative towards his most cherished projects. He was justifiably angry that the admirals had ignored repeated urgings to master techniques for refuelling warships at sea, thus severely restricting the endurance of capital ships. But, even after the loss of *Prince of Wales* and *Repulse*, he remained cavalier about their vulnerability to air attack. Most of his naval commanders were fine professional seamen, whom Britain was fortunate to have. It was galling for them to have their courage implicitly and even explicitly impugned, when they were merely anxious to avoid gratuitous losses of big ships which would take years to replace. Nonetheless, like the generals, the admirals might have shown more understanding of the prime minister's fundamental purpose: to demonstrate that Britain could carry the fight to the enemy, and to do more than merely survive blockade and air bombardment.

Herein lay the case for the bomber offensive. Churchill seems right to have endorsed this, when Britain's armed forces were accomplishing so little elsewhere; but he was mistaken to have allowed it to achieve absolute priority in the RAF's worldwide commitments. Concentration of force is important, but so too is a prudent division of resources between critical fronts, of which the Atlantic campaign was assuredly one. By a characteristic irony of war, Churchill enthused most about bombing Germany during 1941–42, when it achieved least. Thereafter, he lost interest. In 1943, Bomber Command began to do serious damage to Ruhr industries, and might have achieved important results if the economic direction of Harris's operations had been more imaginative. In 1944–45, its impact on Germany's cities became devastating. But more intelligent American targeting policies enabled the USAAF to achieve the critical victories of the air war, against the Luftwaffe and German synthetic oil plants. The last volume of Churchill's war memoirs mentions Bomber Command only once, in passing and critically.

On April 1, 1942, Churchill wrote to Roosevelt: "I find it very difficult to get over Singapore, but I hope we shall redeem it ere long." Instead, however, bad news kept coming. On the fourth a Japanese battle fleet, ranging the Indian Ocean, launched planes to bomb Ceylon. In the days that followed, enemy aircraft sank two Royal Navy cruisers and the carrier *Hermes*. Mandalay fell, and it was plain that the British must withdraw across the Chindwin River out of Burma, into northeast India. Malta was in desperate straits, under relentless Axis air attack. Convoys to Russia suffered shocking losses from German air and U-boat attack. PQ13 in April lost five ships out of nine. Only eight ships of twenty-three dispatched in the next convoy reached their destination, fourteen having been turned back by pack ice. Churchill urged Stalin to provide more air and sea cover for the Royal Navy in the later stages of the Arctic passage, but the Russians lacked means and competence. There was also little goodwill. British sailors and airmen venturing ashore at Murmansk and Archangel were disgusted by the frigidity of their reception. Nowhere, it seemed, did the sun shine upon British endeavours, and the prime minister's spirits suffered accordingly: "CIGS says WSC is often in a very nasty mood these days," noted John Kennedy on April 7.

Even at this dire period, it was remarkable how many newspaper column inches were devoted to the needs and prospects of postwar reconstruction. This galled the prime minister. He expressed exasperation at having to bother with what he called "hypothetical post-war problems in the middle of a struggle when the same amount of thought concentrated on the question of types of aeroplane might have produced much more result." Yet many ordinary citizens found the war a less rewarding, more dispiriting experience than did Winston Churchill. The present seemed endurable only by looking beyond it to a better future.

Articles and correspondence constantly appeared in print, addressing one aspect or another of a world without war. As early as September 4,

1940, a letter writer to the *Times* named P. C. Loftus urged that "this nation not be found unprepared for peace as we were found unprepared for war." A correspondent signing himself "Sailor" wrote to the *New Statesman* on February 21, 1942: "Men wonder what they are fighting for. The old empty jingoisms about 'Freedom' and 'Homeland' no longer satisfy. There is a suspicion that all will not be well after the peace—that, after all, we are fighting for property and private interests." The prominent socialist intellectual Harold Laski complained of Churchill's refusal to declare a commitment to social change: "He does not seem to see that the steps we take now necessarily determine the shape of the society we shall enter when the war is over."

Gnawing dissatisfaction extended well beyond the confines of the political left. "This nation has become very soft," John Kennedy wrote sadly in his diary on February 23, 1942. "The people do not want to fight for the Empire. Mostly, I suppose, they do not care whether they have an empire or not so long as they have an easy and quiet life. They do not realise that German domination will be very unpleasant . . . I think something more is wanted on the political side. There is a great lack of any sense of urgency everywhere. We do not know what we are fighting for. The Atlantic Charter is not good enough an ideal up against the fanaticism of the Germans and the Japs." Officers commanding two army primary training centres told a morale investigator that the great majority of their recruits "lack enthusiasm and interest in the war and betray ignorance of the issues involved in it."

On March 6, 1942, an editorial in the *Spectator* declared: "The national fibre is today unmistakably different from what it was in those days of 1940 which the Prime Minister could speak of, in accents which carried universal conviction, as our finest hour. No one can pretend that we are living through our finest hour today." The writer, like his counterpart on the *New Statesman*, felt that the British people lacked a core of belief to move them, as the Russian people were moved: "Why do men and women in Britain today wait for inspiration from outside? Why are they listening for a voice? Have we no voice within us? Are we ignorant of what is needed?"

In May 1942, America's *Fortune* magazine published an entire issue about the postwar world. Henry Luce, proprietor of *Fortune*, invited Britain's foreign secretary to contribute an article about his own country's vision. Eden declined, prompting an official in the American Department of the Foreign Office, one C. R. King, to express dismay. It seemed to him a serious mistake to snub Luce. Yet he recognised the problem. Eden had no idea what to say: "I do not know that HMG have formulated (much less announced) any ideas on these problems beyond those that find expression in the Atlantic Charter." King added that there was wide agreement in the United States "that America will emerge, after total victory, militarily and economically supreme." The *Economist* challenged Churchill in an editorial: "When has the Prime Minister made one of his great and compelling speeches on the theme, not of world strategy, but of the hopes and fears of the British people? So long as he is silent, Conservatism, the dominant political attitude in Britain, is silent, and Americans inevitably believe that maybe the Conservatives are out to do nothing but conserve." The intellectuals' preoccupation with postwar Britain exasperated the prime minister when he was struggling to find means to avert the destruction of European freedom. But in this matter, his instincts were ill-attuned to those of the public.

Early in April, Churchill's honeymoon with Roosevelt was rudely interrupted. The prime minister had planned to go to India, to address its defence and constitutional future, but crises elsewhere made it seem inappropriate for him to leave London and travel so far. Stafford Cripps was dispatched in his stead, with a mandate to discuss with India's nationalist leaders prospective postwar self-government. Talks quickly collapsed. The Hindu-majority Indian National Congress rejected delay, and insisted upon immediate admission to political power. Cripps reported accordingly to London, and was told to come home. Churchill had expected, and indeed wished, no other outcome. He was content that the gesture had been made, and that it was Cripps who bore the odium of failure.

On April 11, however, Roosevelt cabled Churchill, urging that Cripps should remain in India and preside over the creation of a nationalist government. The president asserted that American opinion was overwhelmingly hostile to Britain on this issue: "The feeling is almost universally held that the deadlock has been caused by the unwillingness of the British Government to concede to the Indians the right of self-government . . . [if] minor concessions would be made by both sides, it seems to me that an agreement might yet be found." Many Americans explicitly identified India's contemporary predicament with that of their own country before the Revolution of 1776. "You're the top / You're Mahatma Gandhi!" wrote Cole Porter euphorically, reflecting the huge enthusiasm of his countrymen for the guru of the Indian independence movement. Such sentiment was wormwood to Churchill. At the best of times, he had little patience with the Indian people. His view was unchanged since he served among them as a cavalry subaltern in the 1890s. Leo Amery, the India secretary, found Churchill "a strange combination of great and small qualities . . . He is really not quite normal on the subject of India." The prime minister opposed, for instance, granting Indian commissioned officers disciplinary powers over British other ranks. He expostulated against "the humiliation of being ordered about by a brown man."

Churchill was ruthlessly dismissive of Indian political aspirations when the Japanese army was at the gates. He could scarcely be expected to forget that the Mahatma had offered to mediate Britain's surrender to Hitler, whom the standard-bearer of nonviolence and Indian freedom described as "not a bad man." Gandhi in 1940 wrote an open letter to the British people, urging them to "lay down arms and accept whatever fate Hitler decided. You will invite Herr Hitler and Signor Mussolini to take what they want of the countries you call your possessions. Let them take possession of your beautiful island with your many beautiful buildings. You will give all these, but neither your souls nor your minds."

Much worse, however, was the U.S. president's attempt to meddle with what the prime minister perceived as an exclusively British issue. It would never have occurred to Churchill to offer advice to Roosevelt about the future governance of America's Philippines dependency. He deemed it rank cant for a nation which had itself colonised the North American continent, dispossessing and largely exterminating its indigenous population, and which still practised racial segregation, to harangue others about the treatment of native peoples.

Here was an early, wholly unwelcome foretaste of the future. The United States, principal partner and paymaster of the alliance to defeat Fascism, was bent upon exercising decisive influence on the postwar global settlement. Churchill, who thought of nothing save victory and knew how remote this was in April 1942, found Roosevelt's heavy-handedness irksome. He lost no time in flagging both his determination to stand fast against the Indian National Congress's demands, and his sensitivity about American meddling. "Anything like a serious difference between you and me would break my heart," he wrote to the president on April 12, "and would surely deeply injure both our countries at the height of this terrible struggle." Roosevelt's belief that the day of empires was done would achieve postwar vindication with a speed even he might have found surprising. Britain's exercise of power over the Indian people between 1939 and 1945 was clumsy and ugly, and Churchill must bear some of the blame. But the prime minister was surely right in believing that a transfer of power in the midst of a world war was wholly unrealistic, especially when the Indian Congress's attitude to the Allied cause was equivocal.

The spring of 1942 brought some lifting of Allied spirits, especially after the U.S. Navy inflicted heavy damage on the Japanese in the May 4 Battle of the Coral Sea. Churchill changed his mind yet again about acceding to Russian demands for recognition of their territorial claims on Poland and the Baltic states. "We must remember that this is a bad thing," he told the Cabinet. "We oughtn't to do it, and I shan't be sorry if we don't." On May 5, British forces landed in Madagascar, seeking to preempt a possible Japanese coup. Churchill wrote to his son, Randolph: "The depression following Singapore has been replaced by an undue optimism, which I am of course keeping in proper bounds." He was much wounded by the criticisms that had fallen upon him since January. Before he made a national broadcast on May 10, he drafted a passage which he subsequently—and surely wisely—omitted to deliver, but which reflected the pain he had suffered in recent months:

Everyone feels safer now, and in consequence the weaker brethren become more vocal. Our critics are not slow to dwell upon the misfortunes and reverses which we have sustained, and I am certainly not going to pretend that there have not been many mistakes and shortcomings. In particular, I am much blamed by a group of ex-ministers for my general conduct of the war. They would very much like to reduce my power of direction and initiative.

Though I have to strive with dictators, I am not, I am glad to say, a dictator myself. I am only your servant. I have tried to be your faithful servant but at any moment, acting through the House of Commons, you can dismiss me to private life. There is one thing, however, which I hope you will not do; I hope you will never ask me or any successor you may choose to bear the burden of responsibility in times like these without reasonable authority and the means of taking decisions.

Hugh Dalton wrote on May 12, 1942: "Dinner with [Tory MP] Victor Cazalet, who thinks we cannot possibly win the war with the present PM. He has, however, no good alternative." King George VI, of all people, suggested to his prime minister at luncheon one day that the burden of also serving as defence minister was too much for him, and enquired gauchely what other aspect of public affairs he was interested in. Yet Churchill's difficulty henceforward was that the most formidable challenge to his authority came not from his British critics, but from the nation's overwhelmingly more powerful partner, the United States. When Harry Hopkins addressed MPs at the House of Commons on April 15, he sought to bolster Churchill's standing by asserting that the prime minister was "the only man who really understands Roosevelt." But the American also declared bluntly, as Harold Nicolson reported, that "there are many people in the USA who say that we are yellow and can't fight."

Dill mused in a letter to Wavell from Washington, "One trouble is that we want everything from them from ships to razor blades and have nothing but services to give in return—and many of the services are past services." A clever British official, Arthur Salter, wrote early in 1942: "It must be accepted that policy will increasingly be decided in Washington. To proceed as if it can be made in London and 'put over' in Washington, or as if British policy can in the main develop independently and be only 'co-ordinated' with America, is merely to kick against the pricks." The prime minister led a nation whose role in the war seemed in those days confined to victimhood, not only at the hands of the enemy, but also at those of its mighty new ally. He yearned inexpressibly to recover the initiative on some battlefield. His generals, however, offered no prospect of offensive action before autumn. Amid the deep public disaffection of spring and summer, this seemed to Churchill an eternity away.

2. Warriors and Workers

CHURCHILL was reconciled to the fact that Britain's defeats by Japan were irreversible until the tide of the war turned. Henceforward, recognising American dominance of Far East strategy, he devoted much less attention to the Japanese struggle than to the campaign against Germany. He remained bitterly dismayed by the failures of Auchinleck's forces in the Western Desert, where a paper comparison of strengths, showing significant British superiority, suggested that victories should be attainable. At a meeting with his military chiefs, he asserted repeatedly: "I don't know what we can do for that Army—all our efforts to help them seem to be in vain." Back in 1941, Cadogan, at the Foreign Office, wrote: "Our soldiers are the most pathetic amateurs, pitted against professionals . . . The Germans are magnificent fighters and their Staff are veritable Masters of Warfare. Wavell and suchlike are no good against them. It's like putting me up to play Bobby Jones over 36 holes. We shall learn, but it will be a long and bloody business." Yet a year later, there seemed no evidence that the British Army and its commanders had yet "learned." Cadogan wrote after the Far East disasters: "What will happen if the Germans get a footing here? Our army is the mockery of the world!"

Britain's generals were conscious of their service's low standing, but deemed it unjust that their own prime minister should sustain a barrage of harassment, criticism and even scorn against it. Especially between 1940 and 1942, they perceived themselves obliged to conduct campaigns with inadequate resources, in consequence of interwar defence policies imposed by the very Conservative Party which still dominated the government—though not, of course, by Churchill himself. Until 1943, and in lesser degree thereafter, the prestige of Britain's soldiers lagged far behind that of its sailors and airmen. Churchill's intemperate goading caused anger and distress to naval officers. He often threatened to sack dissenting or allegedly insufficiently aggressive admirals, including Sir Andrew Cunningham, Sir James Somerville of Force H and the Home Fleet's Sir John Tovey. But even when the Royal Navy suffered severe setbacks and losses, its collective honour and reputation remained unchallenged. The army, meanwhile, enjoyed a more secure social place in British national life than did its U.S. counterpart, and attracted into its smart regiments successive generations of aristocratic younger sons. But it was much less effective as a military institution. For every clever officer such as Brooke, Ismay or Jacob, there were a hundred others lacking skill, energy and imagination.

Churchill spent much of the first half of the war searching in mounting desperation for commanders capable of winning victories on land. Throughout his own long experience of war, he had been impressed by many heroes, but few British generals. In his 1932 work *Great Contemporaries*, he painted an unsympathetic portrait of Field Marshal Sir Douglas Haig, principal conductor of the nation's armies through the World War I bloodbath in France and Flanders:

> He presents to me in those red years the same mental picture as a great surgeon before the days of anaesthetics, versed in every detail of such science as was known to him: sure of himself, steady of poise, knife in hand, intent upon the operation: entirely removed in his professional capacity from the agony of the patient, the anguish of relations, or the doctrines of rival schools, the devices of quacks, or the first-fruits of new learning. He would operate without excitement, or he would depart without being affronted; and if the patient died, he would not reproach himself.

Churchill was determined that no British army in "his" war would be commanded by another such officer. Every general between 1939 and 1945 carried into battle an acute awareness of the animosity of the British people, and of their prime minister, towards the alleged "butchers" of 1914–18. In this baggage, indeed, may be found a source of the caution characteristic of their campaigns. Yet Britain's military limitations went much deeper than mere generalship. It might have been profitable for Churchill to divert some of the hours he devoted to scanning the countenances and records of commanders instead to addressing the institutional culture of the British Army. John Kennedy expressed the War Office's bafflement: "We manage by terrific efforts to pile up resources at the necessary places and then the business seems to go wrong, for lack of generalship and junior leadership and bad tactics and lack of concentration of force at decisive points."

Carl von Clausewitz laid down principles, rooted in his experience of the Napoleonic Wars, based on his perception that all European armies possessed approximately the same quality of weapons, training and potential. Thus, the Prussian believed that outcomes were determined by relative mass, and by the respective skills of rival commanders. If this was true in the early nineteenth century, it certainly was not in the Second World War. Allied and Axis armies displayed widely differing levels of ability and commitment. Superior weapons systems deployed by one side or the other sometimes produced decisive effects. Clausewitz distinguished three elements of war—policy, strategy and tactics. Churchill addressed himself with the keenest attention to the first two, but neglected the third, or rather allowed his commanders to do so.

Britain could take pride in its distaste for militarism. But its inability to deploy effective armies until a late stage of the Second World War was a grievous handicap. Even competent British officers found it hard to extract from their forces performances good enough to beat the Germans or Japanese, who seemed to the prime minister to try much harder. Conversely, Axis troops sometimes achieved more, especially in defence, than indifferent generalship by local commanders entitled Hitler or Hirohito to expect. Rommel, who in 1941–42 became a British obsession, was a fine leader and tactician, but his neglect of logistics contributed much to his own difficulties in North Africa. His triumphs over the British reflected the institutional superiority of his little German force as much as his own inspired opportunism. The Australian war correspondent Alan Moorehead, a perceptive eyewitness, wrote from the desert in August 1942, in an assessment laid before British readers while the war was still being fought: "Rommel was an abler general than any on the British side, and for this one reason—because the German army was an abler army than the British army. Rommel was merely the expression of that abler German army."

This seems to identify a fundamental Allied difficulty. Eighth Army's defeats in North Africa in 1941–42, almost invariably by German troops inferior in numbers and armoured strength, certainly reflected inadequate generalship. But they were also the consequence of deeper shortcomings of method and determination. The British public was increasingly conscious of these. Glasgow secretary Pam Ashford wrote on June 24, 1942:

"There is a general feeling that there is something wrong with our Forces . . . Mrs. Muir thought it was our generals who were not equal to the German generals, they get out-manoeuvred every time." Young laboratory technician and former soldier Edward Stebbing wrote, "The feeling is growing that we are having our present reverses in Libya and the Far East not merely because of inferiority in numbers and equipment, but also because the enemy are really too clever for us, or rather that we are too stupid for the enemy."

Ivan Maisky, the Russian ambassador in London, once observed to Hugh Dalton that he found British soldiers unfailingly stiff and formal, unlike their counterparts in the other services. The army, he suggested, lacked the Royal Navy's and RAF's collective self-confidence. This was so. General Pownall wrote after the Far East disasters:

> Our [career officers] regard [war] as an upsetting, rather exhausting and distinctly dangerous interlude in the happier, more comfortable and more desirable days of peace-soldiering . . . We need . . . a tougher Army, based on a tougher nation, an Army which is regarded by the people as an honourable profession to which only the best can gain admittance; one which is prepared and proud to live hard, not soft, in peace. One whose traditions are not based on purely regimental history but on the history of the whole British Army; where the competition is in efficiency, not in games or pipe-blowing and band concerts . . . Training must be harder, exercises must not be timed to suit meal-times. Infantry shouldn't be allowed to say that they are tired . . . We must cultivate mobility of mind as well as of body, i.e., imagination; and cut out the great hampering "tail" which holds back rather than aids the "teeth."

The regimental system was sometimes an inspirational force, but often also, as was implied by Pownall's remarks, a source of parochialism and an impediment to the cohesion of larger formations. German, American and Russian professional soldiers thought in divisions; the British always of the regiment, the cherished "military family." Until the end of the war, the dead hand of centralised, top-down command methods, together with lack of a fighting doctrine common to the entire army, hampered operations in the field. Techniques for the recovery of disabled vehicles from the battlefield—a vital skill in maximising combat power—lagged badly behind those of the Afrika Korps. British armoured units, imbued with a cavalry ethos, remained childishly wedded to independent action. In the desert as in the Crimea a century earlier, British cavalry charged—and were destroyed. This, when since 1940 the Germans had almost daily demonstrated the importance of coordinating tanks, antitank guns and infantry in close mutual support.

British unit as well as army leadership left much to be desired. On the battlefield, local elements seldom displayed initiative, especially if out-flanked. Troops engaged in heavy fighting sometimes displayed resolu-tion, but sometimes also collapsed, withdrew or surrendered more readily than their commanders thought acceptable. The sybaritic lifestyle of the vast rear headquarters nexus around Cairo shocked many visitors, espe-cially Americans but also including British ministers Oliver Lyttelton and Harold Macmillan. Here, indeed, was a new manifestation of the "château generalship" condemned by critics of the British Army in the First World War, and this time focused upon Shepheard's Hotel and the Gezira Club.

Sloth and corruption flourished in the workshops and bases of the rear areas, where tens of thousands of British soldiers indifferent to the progress of the war were allowed to pursue their own lazy routines, selling stores, fuel, and even trucks for private profit. "Petrol, food, NAAFI sup-plies, vehicle engines, tools, tyres, clothing—all rich booty—were pouring into Egypt, free for all who dared," wrote a disgusted colonel responsible for a network of ordnance depots, who was as unimpressed by the lack of "grip" in high places as by the systemic laziness and corruption he per-ceived throughout the rear areas of Middle East Command. It was a seri-ous indictment of the army that such practises were never checked. Even at the end of 1943, Harold Macmillan complained of the then Middle East C-in-C, Sir Henry "Jumbo" Maitland Wilson, that "the Augean stables are still uncleaned." Since shipping shortages constrained all Allied opera-tions, waste of matériel and supplies transported at such cost to theatres of war was a self-inflicted handicap. The Allies provided their soldiers with amenities and comforts quite unknown to their enemies. These became an acceptable burden in the years of victory, but bore heavily upon the war effort in those of defeat.

Throughout the conflict, in Britain's media there was debate about the army's equipment deficiencies, tactics and commanders. The government vacillated about how far to allow criticism to go. In December 1941, Tom Wintringham wrote an article for *Picture Post* entitled "What Has Hap-pened in Libya?" He attacked the army's leadership, tanks and guns. As a result, *Picture Post* was briefly banned from distribution in the Middle East and British Council offices worldwide. Few people doubted that what Wintringham said was true. The difficulty was to reconcile expression of realities with the need to sustain the morale of men risking their lives on the battlefield equipped with these same inadequate weapons, and sometimes led by indifferent officers.

In March 1942 the popular columnist John Gordon delivered a withering blast against Britain's service chiefs in Beaverbrook's *Sunday Express.* They were, he said, men who had achieved high rank merely by staying on in uniform in pursuit of "cushy billets" after the last war ended in 1918, while their betters earned civilian livings. "All this," noted a general who read Gordon's rant, "has a devastating effect on army morale. When soldiers are in a tight corner, how can they be expected to fight if they have been led to believe that their leaders are men of straw?"

Brooke, Alexander and others believed that some of the army's difficulties derived from the fact that its best potential leaders, who should have been the generals of World War II, had been killed in the earlier Great War. It may be of marginal significance that the German army husbanded the lives of promising junior officers with more care than did the British, at least until the 1918 campaigns, but it seems mistaken to make too much of this. The core issue was that Germany's military culture was more impressive. That of the prewar British Army militated against recruitment and promotion of clever, imaginative, ruthless commanders, capable of handling large forces—or even of ensuring that they were equipped with weapons to match those of the enemy. All too many senior officers were indeed men who had chosen military careers because they lacked sufficient talent and energy to succeed in civilian life. Brooke privately agreed with much of what John Gordon wrote. His own fits of melancholy were often prompted by reflections on the unfitness of the British Army to engage the Wehrmacht: "We are going to lose this war unless we control it very differently and fight it with more determination . . . It is all desperately depressing . . . Half our Corps and Divisional Commanders are totally unfit for their appointments, and yet if I were to sack them I could find no better! They lack character, imagination, drive and powers of leadership."

Harold Macmillan saw the wartime army at close quarters, and thought little of most of its senior officers. He accused both the British and U.S. Chiefs of Staff of surrounding themselves with a host of acolytes "too stupid to be employed in any operational capacity." Observing that one British commander was "a bit wooden," Macmillan continued:

> These British administrative generals, whose only experience of the world is a military mess at Aldershot or Poona, are a curiously narrow-minded lot. They seem to go all over the world without observing anything in it—except their fellow-officers and their wives . . . and the

various Services clubs in London, Cairo, Bombay, etc., but they are honourable, hard-working, sober, clean about the house and so on. At the end of their careers, they are just fit to be secretaries of golf clubs. War, of course, is their great moment. In their hearts (if they were honest with themselves) they must pray for its prolongation.

This was harsh, but not unjust. Churchill was imbued with a belief that the Admiralty's execution of Adm. Sir John Byng in 1757, for failing to relieve Minorca, had a salutary effect on the subsequent performance of the Royal Navy. He was right. Following Byng's shooting, from the Napoleonic Wars through the twentieth century, the conduct of British naval officers in the face of the enemy almost invariably reflected their understanding that while they might be forgiven for losing a battle, they would receive no mercy if they flinched from fighting one. After the sacking of General Sir Alan Cunningham in Libya, Churchill muttered to Dill about the virtues of the Byng precedent. The then CIGS answered sharply that such a view was anachronistic.

Dill could justly argue that displays of tigerish zeal such as the prime minister wanted were inappropriate to a modern battlefield, and frequently precipitated disasters. Neither Marlborough nor Wellington won battles by heroic posturing. But the prime minister was surely right to believe that generals should fear disgrace if they failed. The British Army's instinctive social sympathy for its losers was inappropriate to a struggle of national survival. Even the ruthless Brooke anguished over the dismissal of Ritchie, a conspicuous failure as Eighth Army commander in Libya: "I am devoted to Neil and hate to think of the disappointment this will mean to him." Some middle-ranking officers who proved notoriously unsuccessful in battle continued to be found employment: Ritchie was later allowed to command a corps in northwest Europe—without distinction. It would have been more appropriate to consign proven losers to professional oblivion, as the Americans often did. But this was not the British way, nor even Brooke's.

Fundamental to many defeats in the desert was an exaggerated confidence in manoeuvre and an inadequate focus on firepower. Until 1944, successive models of tank and antitank guns lacked penetrative capacity. It was extraordinary that, even after several years' experience of modern armoured warfare, British- and American-made fighting vehicles continued to be inferior to those of the Germans. Back in 1917, in the first flush of his own enthusiasm for tanks, Churchill had written to his former battalion second-in-command, Archie Sinclair, urging him to forsake any thought of a life with the cavalry, and to become instead an armoured officer: "Arm yourself therefore my dear with the panoply modern science of war . . . Embark in the chariots of war and slay the malignants with the arms of precision." Yet a world war later, Churchill was unsuccessful in ensuring that the British Army deployed armour capable of matching that of its principal enemy. From 1941 onwards, the British usually deployed more tanks than the Germans in the desert, sometimes dramatically more. Yet the Afrika Korps inflicted devastating attrition by exploiting its superior weapons and tactics.

Again and again MPs raised this issue in the Commons, yet it proved beyond military ingenuity or industrial skill to remedy. American tanks were notably better than British, but they too were outmatched by those of the Germans. Both nations adopted a deliberate policy of compensating through quantity for well-recognised deficiencies of tank quality. It is impossible to overstate the significance of this failure in explaining defeats. Nor was the problem of inadequate weapons restricted to tanks. In 1941, when the War Office was offered a choice of either one hundred 6-pounder antitank guns or six times that number of 2-pounders, it opted for the latter. By winter, Moscow was telling London not to bother sending any further 2-pounders to Russia, because the Red Army found them useless—as did Auchinleck's units in the desert. Only late in 1942 did 6-pounders become available in substantial numbers. The War Office struggled in vain to match the superb German 88mm dual-purpose antiaircraft and antitank gun, which accounted for 40 percent of British tanks destroyed in North Africa against 38 percent which fell to Rommel's panzers.

British tank and military vehicle design and production were nonstandardised and dispersed among a ragbag of manufacturers. Given that the RAF and Royal Navy exploited technical innovations with striking success, the failure of Britain's ground forces to do so, certainly until 1944, must be blamed on the army's own procurement chiefs. It was always short of four-wheel-drive trucks. Mechanical serviceability rates were low. Prewar procurement officers, influenced by the experience of colonial war, had a visceral dislike for platoon automatic weapons, which they considered wasteful of ammunition. The War Office of the 1920s dismissed Thompson submachine guns as "gangster weapons," but in 1940 found itself hastening to import as many as it could buy from the Americans. Only in 1943–44 did British Sten guns become widely available. Infantry tactics were unimaginative, especially in attack. British artillery, always superb, was the only real success story.

Until late in 1942, Eighth Army in North Africa was poorly supported by the RAF. Air force leadership was institutionally hostile to providing "flying artillery" for soldiers, and only sluggishly evolved liaison techniques such as the Luftwaffe had practised since 1939. Churchill strongly defended the RAF's right to an independent strategic function, asserting that it would be disastrous to turn the air force into "a mere handmaid of the Army." But it proved mistaken to permit the airmen such generous latitude in determining their own priorities. Close air support for ground forces was slow to mature. "In all its branches, the German war machine appeared to have a better and tighter control than our army," wrote Alan Moorehead. "One of the senior British generals said to the war correspondents . . . 'We are still amateurs. The Germans are professionals.' " This was an extraordinary admission in mid-1942. The army's performance improved during the latter part of that year. But, to prevail over the Germans, British and American forces continued to require a handsome superiority of men, tanks and air support.

There remained one great unmentionable, even in those newspapers most critical of Britain's military performance: the notion that man for man, the British soldier might be a less determined fighter than his German adversary. The "tommy" was perceived—sometimes rightly—as the victim of his superiors' incompetence, rather than as the bearer of any personal responsibility for failures of British arms. In private, however, and among ministers and senior officers, this issue was frequently discussed. George Marshall deplored the manner in which Churchill spoke of the army's other ranks as "the dull mass," a phrase which reflected the prime minister's limited comprehension of them. There was an embarrassing moment at Downing Street, when following a Cabinet meeting Randolph Churchill joined a discussion about the army, and shouted, "Father, the trouble is your soldiers won't fight." Churchill once observed of his son: "I love Randolph, but I don't like him." It was astonishing that, in the midst of debates about great matters, he indulged his son's presence, and expected others to do so. On this occasion, however, Randolph's intervention might have been hyperbolic, but it was to the point. Many British officers perceived their citizen soldiers as lacking the will and commitment routinely displayed by the Germans and Japanese. Underlying the conduct of Churchill's wartime commanders was a fundamental nervousness about what their men would, or would not, do on the battlefield.

Churchill understood that if British troops were to overcome Germans, they must become significantly nastier. This represented a change of view. In 1940 he favoured civility towards the enemy, reproaching Duff Cooper as minister of information for mocking the Italians: "It is a well-known rule of war policy to praise the courage of your opponent, which enhances your own victory when gained." Likewise, in January 1942, he declared his admiration for Rommel on the floor of the House of Commons: "a very daring and skilful opponent . . . and, may I say across the havoc of war, a great general." Progressively, however, the prime minister came to think it mistaken to suggest that Axis soldiers were honourable foes. Such courtesies encouraged British troops to surrender too readily. As the war matured, Churchill deplored newspaper reports of chivalrous German behaviour: "These beastly Huns are murdering people wholesale in Europe and have committed the most frightful atrocities in Russia, and it would be entirely in accordance with their technique to win a reputation for treating British and American soldiers with humanity on exceptional and well-advertised occasions."

In the spring and summer of 1942, Churchill was right to believe that the British Army's performance in North Africa was inadequate. Many of his outbursts about the soldiers' failures, which so distressed Brooke and his colleagues, were justified. It remains debatable whether remedies were available at a time when positions of military responsibility had perforce to be filled from the existing pool of regular officers. Most were captives of the culture to which they had been bred. Its fundamental flaw was that it required only moderate effort, sacrifice and achievement, and produced only a small number of leaders and units capable of matching the skill and determination of their enemies. The army's institutional weakness would be overcome only when vastly superior Allied resources became available on the battlefield.

At home among the civilians, wartime unity was a considerable reality. The majority of the British people remained staunch. Yet class tensions ran deep. Significant groups, above all factory workers, displayed disaffection. Sections of Britain's industrial workforce perceived no contradiction between supporting Churchill and the crusade against Nazism while sustaining the class struggle which had raged since the beginning of the century. Strikes were officially outlawed for the duration by the government's March 1941 Essential Work Order, but legislation failed to prevent wildcat stoppages, above all in coal pits, shipyards and aircraft plants, often in support of absurd or avaricious demands. At the depth of the Depression, in 1932, just 48,000 working days were lost to strikes in the metal, engineering and shipbuilding industries. In 1939, by contrast, 332,000 days were lost; in 1940, 163,000; 1941, 556,000; 1942, 526,000; 1943, 635,000; 1944, 1,048,000; and 1945, 528,000. This was a better record than that achieved in 1917, when stoppages in the same industries cost three million days of production. Nonetheless, it suggests a less than fulsome commitment to the war effort in some factories, also manifested by dockyard workers who, to the disgust of ships' crews, were guilty of systematic pilferage, including on occasion lifeboat rations.

Few workers broke ranks during the Dunkirk period. But as the war news improved, they perceived less urgency about the struggle for national survival. "I gather that production is not nearly good enough," wrote Tory MP Cuthbert Headlam in December 1940, "that the work people in airplane and other gov[ernment] factories are beginning to go ca'canny; that the dockers at the ports are giving trouble . . . communists active—I only hope that much of this gossip is exaggerated, but it is alarming nonetheless." In September 1941, when Churchill visited the Armstrong-Siddeley factory at Coventry, where Whitley bombers were being manufactured, he was warned that the plant was "a hotbed of communism." Jock Colville wrote: "I was disgusted to hear that their production tempo had not really grown until Russia came into the war." Nine thousand men at Vickers-Armstrongs in Barrow went on unofficial strike in a dispute over piecework rates. When a tribunal found against them, the strike committee held a mass meeting at a local football ground, and put forward a motion suggesting that the men should resume work "under protest." This was overwhelmingly defeated, and the dispute dragged on for weeks.

Of eight serious strikes in the aircraft industry between February and May 1943, six concerned pay, one was sparked by objections to an efficiency check on machine use, and one by refusal to allow two fitters to be transferred to different sections of the same shop. There were twenty-eight lesser stoppages prompted by disputes about canteen facilities, alleged victimisation of a shop steward, the use of women riveters, and refusal by management to allow collections for the Red Army during working hours. A report on the de Havilland factory at Castle Bromwich noted "a marked absence of discipline . . . slackness . . . difficulty in controlling shop stewards." Ernest Bevin reported that the aircraft industry "had failed to improve its productivity in proportion to the amount of labour supplies." A total of 1.8 million working days were lost during 1,785 disputes in 1943, a figure which rose to 3.7 million in 2,194 disputes in 1944.

"Strikes continue to cause much discussion," declared a 1943 Home Intelligence report. "The majority feeling is that strike action in wartime is unjustified . . . Fatigue and war-weariness, combined with the belief that we are 'out of the wood' and victory now certain, are thought by many to account for the situation." American seamen arriving in Britain were shocked by the attitudes they encountered among dockers. Walter Byrd, chief officer of the U.S. merchantman *James W. Marshall*, "made very strong criticism of the attitude of stevedores and other dockworkers in the port of Glasgow. He accused them of complete indifference to the exigencies of any situation, however urgent." Byrd complained to harbour security officers that many trucks and tanks were being damaged by reckless handling during off-loading. It was decided to dispatch some shipworkers to work in U.S. yards on British vessels. At a time when passenger space was at a premium, the service chiefs were enraged when these men refused to sail without their wives—and their demand was met: "I do not see why the country sh[oul]d not be mobilized and equality of sacrifice demanded," a senior army officer commented indignantly.

Of all wartime industrial disputes, 60 percent concerned wages, 19 percent demarcation, and 11.2 percent working arrangements. A strong Communist element on Clydeside was held responsible by management for many local difficulties. Some trades unionists adopted a shameless view that there was no better time to secure higher pay than during a national emergency, when the need for continuous production was so compelling. Those who served Britain in uniform were poorly rewarded—the average private soldier received less than a pound a week—but industrial workers did well out of the war. The Cost of Living Index rose from 88 in 1939 to 112.5 in 1945, while average wages rose from 106 to 164.

In the coal industry, wage increases were much steeper—from an indexed 109 to 222. But these did nothing to stem a relentless decline in production—by 12 percent between 1938 and 1944—which alarmed the government and bewildered the public. The mines employed 766,000 workers in 1939, 709,000 in 1945. Loss of skilled labour from the pits to the services provided an inadequate explanation for the fall in per capita output, since the German coal industry achieved dramatic increases under the same handicap. The official historians wrote later: "one can hardly overstress the effect of the Depression years upon the morale of the mining community . . . many miners . . . felt a sardonic satisfaction in finding themselves for once able to call the tune. Their attitude was not anti-social. It was only un-social . . . We have to consider how far these narrowed and embittered men could be expected to respond to inducements wrung from the authorities by the urgency of war."

In 1944, three million tons of coal production were lost by strikes. A team of American technical experts who studied Britain's mining industry reported to the government: "The center of the problem . . . is the bad feeling and antagonism which pervade the industry and which manifests itself in low morale, non-cooperation and indifference. In almost every district we visited, miners' leaders and mine owners complained of men leaving the mines early, failure to clear the faces and voluntary absenteeism." The Cabinet decided against publishing this report.

Class divisions sustained notable variations in communities' health. The southeast had prospered economically in the last years before war came, but other regions remained blighted by the Depression. In 1942, while four babies of every thousand born in southeast England died, seven perished in south Wales, the northwest and the northeast. Measles produced four times as many fatalities among children in the latter areas as in the former, and tuberculosis rates were much higher. A 1943 Ministry of Health study found that 10 percent of a sample of six hundred children were ill-nourished: "Many of the people had lived for years past in poverty and unemployment, and had given up the struggle to maintain a decent standard of housekeeping and cooking." The condition of many children evacuated from blitzed cities shocked those who received them. Of 31,000 registered in Newcastle, for instance, 4,000 were deficient in footwear, 6,500 in clothing. Authorities in Wales reported that among evacuees from Liverpool there were "children in rags," in a personal condition that "baffles description." Many of the families from which such offspring came perceived the war in less than idealistic terms.

Churchill had much greater faith in the British people than did ministers, which helps to explain his bitterness when they expelled him from office in 1945. Most Conservative politicians were fearful of the working class, conscious of deep popular discontent with the old order. Many voters would never forget the perceived betrayals of the Depression and the prewar foreign policy which had permitted the ascent of Hitler. Thoughtful Tories knew this. Halifax once wrote to Duff Cooper: "We [Chamberlain's ministers in early 1940] were all conscious of the contrast between the readiness of the Nation . . . to spend £9 million a day in war to protect a certain way of life, and the unwillingness of the administrative authorities in peace to put up, shall we say, £10 million to assist in the reconditioning of Durham unless they could see the project earning a reasonable percentage."

Many of Britain's "haves" were acutely nervous of its "have-nots," especially when popular enthusiasm for Russia was running high. Fear of "the reds," and of malign consequences from the boost the war provided to their prestige, was a pervasive theme among Britain's political class. Those with a taste for blunt speaking asserted that Russian Communists seemed to be conducting their war effort more impressively than British capitalists. Self-consciousness about this state of affairs was never far from the minds of either Churchill or his people in 1942–43. A deep, persistent discontent about perceived Western Allied inertia, contrasted with Soviet achievement, prevailed in many of the humblest homes in Britain.

TEN

"Second Front Now!"

ON APRIL 3, 1942, Roosevelt dispatched to London Harry Hopkins and George Marshall, bearing a personal letter from himself to the prime minister. "Dear Winston," this began, "What Harry and Geo Marshall will tell you all about has my heart and mind in it. Your people & mine demand the establishment of a front to draw off pressure on the Russians, & these peoples are wise enough to see that the Russians are to-day killing more Germans & destroying more equipment than you & I put together. Even if full success is not attained, the big objective will be. Go to it!"

The mission of Hopkins and Marshall was to persuade the British to undertake an early landing in France. This was the chief of staff of the U.S. Army's first encounter with Alan Brooke, and each man was wary of the other. They were a match in stubbornness, but little else. The Ulsterman was bemused when Marshall told him that he sometimes did not see Roosevelt for six weeks: "I was fortunate if I did not see Winston for 6 hours." The British were offered two alternative U.S. plans. The first called for a 1943 invasion by thirty U.S. and eighteen British divisions, with the strategic objective of securing Antwerp. Marshall, acutely mindful of the urgency of the Russians' plight, favoured the second and less ambitious option: an operation to be launched in September 1942 by mainly British forces, supported by two and one-half U.S. divisions—"no very great contribution," as Brooke observed acidly. The American general acknowledged that it might be impossible to indefinitely hold a beachhead on the Continent in the face of a rapid German buildup. He nonetheless considered that the benefits of drawing enemy forces from the Eastern Front at such a critical moment made even a short-lived incursion into France worthwhile.

It was almost intolerably galling for the British, after suffering German bombardment and siege through thirty-one months, for twenty-seven of which the Americans had sat comfortably in the dress circle, that they should now be urged to sacrifice another army in compliance with bustling U.S. impatience for action. Brooke wrote of Marshall: "In many respects he is a very dangerous man while being a very charming one!" The CIGS told his staff that the highest aspiration of any credible Anglo-American operation in France in 1942 would be to seize and hold the Cherbourg Peninsula across the twenty-mile width of its neck. Measured against the war in the east, said Brooke, where the Russians were fighting across a thousand-mile front, so feeble an initiative would make the Western Allies the laughingstock of the world. John Kennedy commented on Soviet demands for a French invasion: "The extraordinary thing is that the Russians seem to have no idea of our real strength. Or if they do, they are so obsessed with their own point of view that they do not care what happens to us." It was odd that a British general should expect anything else from Moscow. It was much more dismaying, however, to find the Americans prey to the same strategic fantasy, arguing the case for a sacrificial, even suicidal sortie into France, of a kind Japanese samurai might have applauded.

Churchill nonetheless responded enthusiastically to the president's letter, "your masterly document," as he called it. "I am in entire agreement in principle with all you propose, and so are the chiefs of staff. If, as our experts believe, one can carry this whole plan through successfully, it will be one of the grand events in all the history of war." Here, the prime minister set the tone for all British dealings with the Americans about the Second Front, as the invasion concept was popularly known—the "First Front" was, of course, in Russia. Though Churchill had not the slightest intention of leading an early charge back into Europe, he enthused to his visitors about the prospect. He accepted the need for Allied land forces to engage the enemy on the Continent, for he knew how dear this objective was to American hearts, especially that of George Marshall. Attlee and Eden joined the prime minister in declaring how warmly they welcomed Washington's plan. Churchill and his commanders then set about ensuring that nothing should be done to implement it, relying upon the difficulties to make the case for themselves.

In a series of meetings that began at Chequers, Marshall made his pitch. On April 14, he told Churchill and the British Chiefs that "within the next three or four months, we were very likely to find ourselves in the position when we were forced to take action on the continent." Mountbatten, now a member of the Chiefs' committee as head of Combined Operations, emphasised the dire shortage of landing craft. The prime minister cautioned that it was scarcely feasible to break off operations in all the other theatres in which Allied troops were engaged. Marshall, unimpressed by Britain's extravagant commitments, as he perceived them, in the Middle East, observed that "great firmness" would be needed to avoid "further dispersions."

The American visitors were generously plied with courtesies. They returned to Washington aware that Churchill and his commanders had doubts about a 1942 landing, but wrongly supposing that they were persuadable. Only slowly did Marshall and his colleagues grow to understand that British professions of principled enthusiasm were unmatched by any intention of early commitment. The chief of the army was too big a man to succumb to Anglophobia, as did some of his colleagues. But henceforward this stiff, humourless officer, who concealed considerable passion beneath his cool exterior, had a mistrust of British evasions, verbal and strategic, which persisted for the rest of the war. Churchill's nation, he considered, was traumatised by its defeats, morbidly conscious of its poverty and obsessed with fear of heavy casualties. The British refused to accept what seemed to the Americans a fundamental reality: that it was worth paying any price to keep Russia fighting.

Throughout the war, the military leaders of the United States displayed a strategic confidence much greater than that of their British counterparts. The fact that Americans were never obliged to face the prospect of invasion of their homeland, still less the reality of bombardment of their cities, removed a significant part of the tension and apprehension which suffused British decision making. American forces endured setbacks abroad, but never the storm of shell at home and abject defeats abroad which characterised British experience for three years. On the issue of the Second Front, Marshall's judgement was almost certainly gravely mistaken. The 1942 strategic view adopted by Churchill and Brooke was right. But the British damaged their relationship with the chief of staff of the army and his colleagues by persistent dissimulation. There was Churchill's cable to Roosevelt of April 17, acknowledging American enthusiasm for an early landing in France, and asserting that "we are proceeding with plans and preparations on that basis." As late as June 20 he was writing, albeit amid a thick hedge of qualifications: "Arrangements are being made for a landing of six or eight Divisions on the coast of Northern France early in September." The British prevaricated because they feared that frankness would provoke the Americans to shift the axis of their national effort westward, towards the Pacific. Indeed, Marshall once threatened to do this.

The debate was further complicated by the fact that Marshall's view accorded with that of the British and American publics. A host of ordinary people responded to the Russians' plight with a warmth and sympathy absent from the attitudes of British ministers and service chiefs. The *New Statesman* of February 14, 1942, quoted an army officer who had been a prewar Labour parliamentary candidate: "Everywhere there is a feeling that some groups of people—perhaps Big Business, perhaps the politicians—are thwarting our natural development. A few more Russian victories and Far East defeats may force Westminster to understand that the most deep-seated feeling in England today is one of envy—envy of the Russians, who are being allowed to fight all out." Envy was surely the wrong word to ascribe to public sentiment, but guilt there was in plenty among British people who felt that their own country was doing embarrassingly little to promote the defeat of the Axis.

On Sunday, March 29, forty thousand people massed in Trafalgar Square for a demonstration in support of a Second Front. Among other speakers, *Sunday Express* columnist John Gordon addressed the theme: "Strike in Europe now!" In April, the government lost two parliamentary by-elections, one in Rugby to an independent candidate standing on a "Second Front Now" ticket. On May 1 the left-wing weekly *Tribune* carried an unsigned article by Frank Owen, then undergoing armoured training as a soldier, headlined: WHY CHURCHILL? Its author posed the question: "Have we time to afford Churchill's strategy?"—meaning the delay to a Second Front. Brooke wrote in his diary, voicing sentiments which would persist through the next two years: "This universal cry to start a second front is going to be hard to compete with, and yet what can we do with some 10 divisions against the German masses? Unfortunately the country fails to realize the situation we are in." The Germans, operating with good land communications and a strong air force, could crush a miniature invasion without significantly depleting the vast Axis army, over two hundred divisions strong, engaged on the Eastern Front.

If Churchill could not escape the slings and arrows of critics ignorant of British military weakness, it was harsh that he also faced a barrage from one man who should have known better. Beaverbrook had resigned from the government allegedly on grounds of exhaustion. The shrewd civil servant Archie Rowlands believed, however, that the press lord perceived Churchill's administration failing, and wished to distance himself from its fate. Since Beaverbrook's visit to Moscow, this archcapitalist had become obsessively committed to Stalin's cause, and to British aid for Russia. His newspapers campaigned stridently for the Second Front, intensifying the pressure on Churchill.

Visiting New York as a semiofficial emissary of the British government, Beaverbrook addressed an audience of American newspaper and magazine publishers on April 23. He told them, "Communism under Stalin has won the applause and admiration of all the western nations." He asserted that there was no persecution of religion in the USSR, and that "the church doors are open." He urged: "Strike out to help Russia! Strike out violently! Strike even recklessly!" Here was rhetoric that went far beyond the courtesies necessary to placate Stalin and encourage his people, and which flaunted Beaverbrook's irresponsibility. Yet when Churchill telephoned the next day from London, instead of delivering the stinging rebuke which was merited, he sought to appease the erratic press baron by offering him stewardship of all Britain's missions in Washington. Happily this proposal was rejected, but it reflected Churchill's perception of his own political beleaguerment.

Beaverbrook preened himself before Halifax about the huge quantity of fan mail he claimed to be receiving. His egomania fed extravagant ambition. The ambassador recorded in his diary that Beaverbrook told him: "I might be the best man to run the war. It wants a ruthless, unscrupulous, harsh man, and I believe I could do it." It is possible that, at a time when there was widespread clamour for the Ministry of Defence to be divorced from the premiership, Beaverbrook saw himself in the former role. Yet he demonstrated notable naïveté about strategic realities, given that he was privy to so much secret information about British weakness. When challenged about the difficulties of providing air cover for an early landing in France, Beaverbrook asserted that this could be provided by Beaufighters. Any man who supposed that twin-engined aircraft like these could contest air superiority with German Bf-109s showed himself unfit to participate in strategic decision making. Monstrously, Beaverbrook threatened that his newspapers would campaign for recognition of Stalin's claims in eastern Europe and the Baltic states. Yet Churchill never lost faith in his friend, nor expelled him from his circle, as Clementine so often urged him to do. The prime minister's loyalty to "the Beaver" was as illdeserved as it proved unrewarding.

Molotov, Stalin's foreign minister, arrived in Britain for talks on May 21, 1942. Following his first encounter with the prime minister he reported to Moscow: "Concerning the second front, Churchill made a brief statement during the morning session, stating that the British and American governments are in principle committed to mounting such an operation in Europe, with maximum available resources, at the earliest possible date, and are making energetic preparations for this." After subsequent meetings, however, at which the British made much of the practical difficulties of staging an invasion of the Continent, he told Moscow that it would be rash to expect early action. Molotov was a grey bureaucrat so slavishly loyal to Stalin that during the purges of the 1930s, he signed an arrest order for his own wife. By such means he, almost alone among prominent old Bolsheviks, had escaped the executioners and clung to office. It must have strained to the limits Churchill's submission to political imperatives to entertain such a man at Downing Street and Chequers, which the Russian remembered chiefly, and contemptuously, for its lack of showers.

If further evidence was needed of Beaverbrook's mischief-making, Molotov reported on May 27, following two encounters with the press lord: "He advised me to push the British government [for an invasion], and assured me that Roosevelt is a proponent of the second front." Beyond Russian secretiveness, Churchill was also obliged to contend with Moscow's susceptibility to fantasies. Stalin appeared sincerely to believe that Japanese aircraft were being flown by German pilots, and that the British had for some unfathomable reason provided Japan with 1,500 combat aircraft.

Molotov's main business in London was to negotiate a treaty of alliance. He was dismayed by British refusal to meet the demands which Russia had been making ever since entering the war, for recognition of its hegemony not only over the Baltic states, but also over eastern Poland. Stalin, however, was less concerned. He cabled Molotov on May 24, telling him to accept the vaguely worded draft about postwar security offered by Eden: "We do not consider this a meaningless statement, we regard it as an important document. It does not contain that paragraph [proposed in a Russian draft] on border security, but probably this is not so bad as it leaves our hands free. We will resolve the issue of frontiers, or rather, of security guarantees for our frontiers . . . by force." Much more serious, in Russian eyes, was the perceived inadequacy of British arms shipments. Stalin emphasised the need for fighters and tanks, especially Valentines, which had proved best suited, or least unsuited, to Russian conditions. The British, however, remained evasive about increasing the strength of their convoys to Archangel. Joan Beaumont, one of the most convincing analysts of wartime Western aid to Russia, has written: "It is the irony of the commitment to the Soviet Union that while . . . consensus on its necessity grew in the first half of 1942, so also did the obstacles in the way of putting this into effect."

Grandiose American promises of aid—initially 8 million tons for 1942–43, half of this food—foundered on the Allies' inability to ship anything like such quantities. By the end of June 1943, less than 3 million tons had been delivered of a pledged 4.4 million. Joan Beaumont again: "Considerable though these achievements and sacrifices were, they seemed poor in contrast to the promises which had been made . . . At the time when the Russian need was greatest, the assistance from the West . . . was at its most uncertain." There was special Soviet bitterness about British refusal of repeated requests for Spitfires. The most strident of Russia's propagandists, Ilya Ehrenburg, denounced to his millions of Soviet readers the fact that the Allies were "sending very few aircraft, and not the best they have either." The Russians claimed to be insulted on discovering that some Hurricanes they received were reconditioned rather than new. Given the indifferent quality of planes and tanks provided, Moscow began to focus its demands upon trucks and food.

Molotov flew on from London to Washington, where the White House butler reported to Roosevelt that Russia's foreign minister had arrived with a pistol in his suitcase. The president observed that they must simply hope it was not intended for use on him. Following a meeting at the White House on May 30, Molotov displayed in his report to Moscow a frustration at Roosevelt's evasive bonhomie that would have struck a chord with the British. Dinner, the Russian complained, "was followed by a lengthy but meaningless conversation . . . I said that it would be desirable to engage at least 40 German divisions at the Western front in the summer and autumn of this year. Roosevelt and Marshall responded that they very much wanted to achieve this, but faced immediate shipping difficulties in moving forces to France." The Russian pleaded that, if there was no Second Front in 1942, Germany would be much stronger in 1943. "They offered no definite information." However, the president said that "preparations for the second front are under way . . . he, Roosevelt[,] is trying to persuade the American generals to take the risk and land 6 to 10 divisions in France. It is possible that it will mean another Dunkirk and the loss of 100,000–120,000 men, but the sacrifices have to be made to provide help in 1942 and shatter German morale."

Stalin cabled again on June 3, first rebuking Molotov for the brevity of his reports. The Soviet leader said that he did not want to be told mere essentials. He needed trivial details as well, to provide a sense of mood. "Finally, we think it absolutely necessary that both [British and American] communiqués contain paragraphs about establishing the second front in Europe, and state that full agreement had been reached on this issue. We also think it necessary that both communiqués should include specifics on deliveries of material from Britain and the USA to the Soviet Union."

Here were the same imperatives pressing Stalin as had weighed upon Churchill in 1940–41. First, and as the Russian leader acknowledged in his cables to Molotov, it was vital to persuade Hitler that there was a real threat of an Allied invasion of France, to deter him from transferring further divisions to the Eastern Front. Second, morale was as important to the peoples of the Soviet Union as to those of the democracies. Every gleam of hope was precious. Stalin nursed no real expectation that Anglo-American armies would land on the Continent in 1942. But, just as Churchill in 1940–41 promoted in Britain much higher expectations of American belligerence than the facts merited, so Stalin wished to trumpet to the Russian people Roosevelt's and Churchill's assurances that a Second Front was coming, even though he did not himself believe them. Should the British and Americans later breach such assurances, this would provide useful evidence of capitalist perfidy. For embattled Russia in the summer of 1942, "later" seemed scarcely to matter.

Back in London on June 9, Molotov met Churchill once more, before the signing of a treaty of alliance. If the Russian's purpose was to promote discord between London and Washington, he was by no means unsuccessful. The prime minister was much disturbed when Molotov told him of Roosevelt's aspirations for the postwar world, including international trusteeship for the Dutch and French empires in Asia, and enforced disarmament of all save the Great Powers. Then the foreign minister outlined his exchanges at the White House about the Second Front: "I mentioned among other things that Roosevelt agreed with the point of view that I had set forth, i.e., that it could prove harder to establish a second front in 1943 than in 1942 due to possible grave problems on our front. Finally, I mentioned that the president attached such great importance to the creation of a second front in 1942 that he was prepared to gamble, to endure another Dunkirk and lose 100,000 or 120,000 men . . . I stressed however that I thought the number of divisions which Roosevelt proposed to commit insufficient, i.e., six to ten.

"Here Churchill interrupted me in great agitation, declaring that he would never agree to another Dunkirk and a fruitless sacrifice of 100,000 men, no matter who recommended such a notion. When I replied that I was only conveying Roosevelt's view, Churchill responded: 'I shall tell him my view on this issue myself.' " Oliver Harvey recorded the same conversation: "Roosevelt had calmly told Molotov he would be prepared to contemplate a sacrifice of 120,000 men if necessary—our men. PM said he would not hear of it."

Molotov said years later: "We had to squeeze everything we could get out of [the Western Allies]. I have no doubt that Stalin did not believe [that a Second Front would happen]. But one had to demand it! One had to demand it for the sake of our own people. Because people were waiting, weren't they, to see whether help [from the Western Allies] would come. That sheet of paper [the Anglo-Soviet agreement] was of great political significance to us. It cheered people up, and that meant a lot then."

The Anglo-Soviet treaty signed on May 26 merely committed "the High Contracting Parties . . . to afford one another military and other assistance and support of all kinds." But in Moscow after Molotov's return from London, *Pravda* reported, "The Day is at hand when the Second Front will open." On June 19, the newspaper described a meeting of the Supreme Soviet, whose members were told that the accords reached between the Soviet Union, Britain and the United States reflected the fact 'that complete agreement had been achieved about the urgency of open-ing of the second front in Europe in 1942.' This announcement, said the paper, was received with protracted applause, as was a subsequent state-ment that "these agreements are of the highest importance for the nations of the Soviet Union, since the opening of the second front in Europe will create insurmountable difficulties for Hitler's armies on our front." All this was untrue, and well understood to be so by Stalin and Molotov. But among so many other deceits, what was one more, deemed so necessary to the spirit of the Russian people? And in this case, the Russians were entirely entitled to declare that the Americans, and in lesser degree the British, were making promises in bad faith.

Molotov, in old age, asserted that he found Churchill "smarter" than Roosevelt:

> I knew them all, these capitalists, but Churchill was the strongest and cleverest . . . As for Roosevelt, he believed in dollars . . . He thought that they were so rich and we so poor, and that we would become so weakened that we would come to the Americans and beg. This was their mistake . . . They woke up when they'd lost half of Europe. And here of course Churchill found himself in a very foolish predicament. In my opinion, Churchill was the most intelligent of them, as an impe-rialist. He knew that if we, the Russians, defeated Germany, then En-gland would start losing its feathers. He realized this. As for Roosevelt, he thought: [Russia] is a poor country with no industry, no grain, they are going to come and beg. There is no other way out for them. And we saw all this completely differently. The entire nation had been pre-pared for the sacrifices, for struggle.

This was, of course, a characteristic Soviet ex post facto exposition of what took place in 1942–43. But Molotov seems right to have perceived in the Americans' behaviour a fundamental condescension, of the same kind that underlay their attitude towards Britain. It was rooted in a belief that when the war was won, U.S. primacy would be unchallengeable by either ally.

Gen. Dwight Eisenhower wrote to his old friend George Patton on July 20, 1942: "This war is still young." For Americans, this was true. But the British, after almost three years of privation, defeat, intermittent bombardment and enforced inaction, saw matters very differently. Washington was seeking to browbeat Churchill into sacrificing yet another British army with token American participation, as a gesture of support for the Soviet Union. Marshall's cardinal mistake was failure to perceive that the scale of a battle in France was beyond the power of the Allies to determine. They might seek to launch a minor operation, but the Germans could mass forces to translate this into a major disaster. Marshall never acknowledged that even the fully mobilised U.S. Army of 1944–45 never became large enough to defeat even the one-third of Hitler's forces then deployed on the Western Front, until these had been drastically weakened by the Russians.

There was never the smallest possibility that the prime minister and his generals would accede to the U.S. proposal for 1942. "I do not think there is much doing on the French coast this year," the prime minister minuted the Chiefs of Staff on June 1. Britain in mid-1942 had fifteen divisions in the Middle East, ten in India and thirty at home, few of the latter battle-ready. None of the fifteen first-line infantry divisions in the Home Forces was fully equipped, while nine "lower establishment" formations were in worse case.

Churchill was enraged by a *Time* magazine article that described Britain as "oft-burned, defensive-minded," and wrote to Brendan Bracken: "This vicious rag should have no special facilities here." The British embassy in Washington reported to London: "Advocacy of a second front has increased largely as a result of the Russian reverses. An influential section of editorial opinion . . . has been insisting that the danger of such an operation now is more than outweighed by the greater danger likely to arise if it is delayed." The British were constantly provoked by manifestations of American ignorance about operational difficulties. A U.S. officer at dinner in London one night demanded of a British general why more fighters were not flown to Malta, to protect Mediterranean convoys. The visitor was oblivious of the fact, irritably explained by his host, that Malta was far beyond the range of Spitfires or Hurricanes flying from Gibraltar.

The British were increasingly troubled by the difficulties of conveying their views to an American leadership of which both the political and military elements seemed resistant to its ally's opinions. A British official in Washington wrote to London in May 1942: "No Englishman here has the close relationship with Hopkins and the President which are necessary. There is no one who can continually represent to the White House the

Prime Minister's views on war direction. The Ambassador does not regard it within his sphere. Dill dare not as he would ruin his relationship with the US chiefs of staff if he saw Hopkins too often." Brig. Vivian Dykes of the British military mission wrote: "We simply hold no cards at all, yet London expects us to work miracles. It is a hard life."

Churchill concluded that only another personal meeting with Roosevelt could resolve the Second Front issue, or, more appropriately, the alternative North African landing scheme—Operation Torch—in Britain's favour. He took off once more with Alan Brooke, in a Boeing flying boat. By the afternoon of June 19, he was being driven around Roosevelt's Hyde Park estate, tête-à-tête with his host. Here was exactly the scenario which Churchill wanted, and which the U.S. Chiefs of Staff deplored. Their commander-in-chief was communing alone with Britain's fiercely persuasive prime minister. Churchill wrote in his memoirs that the two men thus got more business done than at conferences. This was disingenuous. What he meant, of course, was that he was free from impassioned and hostile interventions by Marshall and his colleagues. At Hyde Park, the prime minister was enchanted to be treated as "family," though his staff sometimes overreached themselves in exploiting guest privileges. Private secretary John Martin was sternly rebuked by Roosevelt's telephonist, Louise Hachmeister, when she found him ensconced in her master's study, using the president's direct line to Washington.

On June 20 at Hyde Park, Churchill handed Roosevelt a masterly note on strategy. Arrangements for a landing in France in September were going forward, said the prime minister. However, the British continued to oppose such an operation unless there was a realistic prospect of being able to stay. "No responsible British military authority has so far been able to make a plan for September 1942 which has any chance of success unless the Germans become utterly demoralised, of which there is no likelihood. Have the American staffs a plan? If so, what is it? If a plan can be found which offers a reasonable prospect of success His Majesty's Government will cordially welcome it and will share to the full with their American comrades the risks and sacrifices . . . But in case no plan can be made in which any responsible authority has good confidence . . . what else are we going to do? Can we afford to stand idle in the Atlantic theatre during the whole of 1942?" It was in this context, urged Churchill, that a North African landing should be studied.

That evening, the president and the prime minister flew to the capital. They were together at the White House when a pink message slip was brought to Roosevelt, who passed it wordlessly to Churchill. It read: "Tobruk has surrendered, with 25,000 men taken prisoner." Churchill was initially disbelieving. Before leaving Britain, he had signalled to Auchinleck, stressing the importance of holding the port: "Your decision to fight it out to the end most cordially endorsed. Retreat would be fatal. This is a business not only of armour but of will power. God bless you all." Now, the prime minister telephoned Ismay in London, who confirmed the loss of Tobruk, together with 33,000 men, 2,000 vehicles, 5,000 tons of supplies and 1,400 tons of fuel. A chaotic defence, left in the hands of a newly promoted and inexperienced South African major general, had collapsed in the face of an unexpected German thrust from the southeast. The debacle was characterised by command incompetence, a pitiful indolence and lack of initiative among many units. Maj. Gen. Hendrik Klopper's last signal from Tobruk was an enigmatic study in despair: "Situation shambles . . . Am doing the worst. Petrol destroyed."

The prime minister was stunned, humiliated. It seemed unbearable that such news should have come while he was a visitor, indeed a suppliant, in Washington. Roosevelt, perceiving his guest's despondency, responded with unprecedented spontaneity, generosity and warmth. "What can we do to help?" he asked. After consultation with his Chiefs of Staff, the president briefly entertained a notion of dispatching a U.S. armoured division to fight in Egypt. On reflection, it was agreed instead to send the formation's three hundred Sherman tanks and one hundred self-propelled guns, for British use. This reinforcement, of quality equipment, was critical to later British victory at El Alamein. Roosevelt's gesture, which required the removal of new weapons from a U.S. combat formation, prompted the deepest and best-merited British gratitude of the war towards the president.

The U.S. historian Douglas Porch, one of the ablest chroniclers of the Mediterranean campaigns, believes that Churchill fundamentally misjudged American attitudes towards Britain's war effort. The prime minister wanted a victory in the Middle East, to dispel U.S. scepticism about British fighting capability. Porch argues, however, that "it was Britain's beleaguered helplessness that evoked most sympathy in Washington and helped to prepare the American people psychologically to intervene in the war." It was certainly true that Americans pitied British material weakness. Yet an enduring source of U.S. resentment, reflected in polls throughout much of the war, was a belief that the British were not merely poorly armed, but also did not try hard enough. It was one thing for the United States to provide food and arms to a defiantly struggling democracy. It was quite another, though, to see the British apparently content to sit tight in their island, conducting lethargic minor operations in North Africa, while the Russians did the real business, and paid the horrific blood price, of destroying Hitler's armies.

It was remarkable how much the mood in Washington had shifted since January. This time, there was no adulation for Churchill the visitor. "Anti-British feeling is still strong," the British embassy reported to London, "stronger than it was before Pearl Harbor . . . This state of affairs is partly due to the fact that whereas it was difficult to criticize Britain while the UK was being bombed, such criticism no longer carries the stigma of isolationist or pro-Nazi sympathies." Senator Allen Ellender of Louisiana declared sourly that "there was little point in supplying the British with war material since they invariably lost it all." Roosevelt's secretary William Hassett wrote in his diary: "These English are too aggressive except on the battlefront, as assertive as the Jews, always asking for a little more and then still more after that." Hassett claimed that the president found Churchill "a delightful companion," but added: "With a softie for president, Winnie would put rollers under the Treasury and open Second, Third, or Fourth Fronts with our fighting men."

As for the general public, an Ohioan wrote to the White House: "Tell that Churchill to go home where he belongs . . . All he wants is our money." An anonymous "mother of three" sought to address Britain's prime minister from California: "Every time you appear on our shores, it means something very terrible for us. Why not stay at home and fight your own battles instead of always pulling us into them to save your rotten necks?" A New Yorker's letter to a friend in Somerset, intercepted by the censors, said: "I knew when I saw your fat-headed PM was over here that there was another disaster in the offing." Such views were untypical—most Americans retained warm respect for Churchill. But they reflected widespread scepticism about his nation's willingness to fight, and doubt whether the prime minister's wishes matched American national interest. "All the old animosities against the British have been revived," wrote an analyst for the Office of War Information. "She didn't pay her war debts after the last war. She refuses to grant India the very freedom she claims to be fighting for. She is holding a vast army in England to protect the homeland while her outposts are lost to the enemy."

A further report later in the summer detected a marginal improvement of sentiment, but found confidence in the British still much below that of the previous autumn. It noted: "Phrases such as 'the British always want someone to pull their chestnuts out of the fire' and 'England will fight to the last Frenchman' have attained considerable currency." The OWI's July survey invited Americans to say which nation they thought was trying hardest to win the war. A loyal 37 percent chose the United States; 30 percent named Russia, 14 percent China, 13 percent offered no opinion. Just 6 percent identified the British as most convincing triers. A similar poll the following month asked which belligerent was perceived as having the best fighting spirit. Some 65 percent said America, but only 6 percent named Britain. The same survey highlighted Americans' stunning ignorance about the difficulties of mounting an invasion of Europe. A 57 percent majority said they thought the Allies should launch a Second Front "within two to three months." A similar 53 percent thought that such an operation would have a "pretty good" chance of success, while 29 percent reckoned the odds at fifty-fifty, and only 10 percent feared that an invasion would fail. A remarkable 60 percent of respondents thought not merely that an invasion of France should happen inside three months—they anticipated that it would.

U.S. Supreme Court Justice Felix Frankfurter wrote on July 9, 1942, to Stafford Cripps, who had expressed concern about Anglo-American relations: "The dominant underlying feeling is not bad . . . But there is a central difficulty. It is, as I see it, a lack of continuing consciousness of comradeship between the two peoples, not only in staving off an enemy that threatens everything we hold dear, but comradeship in achieving a common society having essentially the same gracious and civilized ends." Columnist Walter Lippmann expressed similar views to John Maynard Keynes. There was a need, suggested Lippmann, for a new political understanding between Britain and the United States about the future of its empire: "The Asiatic war has revived the profound anti-imperialism of the American tradition."

The Foreign Office was dismayed by remarks made by the Anglophile Wendell Willkie during a visit to Moscow. He told British ambassador Sir Archibald Clark Kerr that U.S. public opinion towards Britain was shaping "dangerously," that he, Willkie, was "scared" by it. Not one of the Americans he had met on his journey between Washington and Moscow, from truck drivers to ambassadors, had a good word for British behaviour abroad. He urged that the prime minister should make a speech on postwar policy, showing that he realised that "old-fashioned imperialism" was dead. Churchill, of course, had no intention of doing any such thing.

A July 6 report to the Foreign Office about the British embassy in Washington was almost flagellatory about the American view of Halifax's mission: "The Embassy . . . has a quite fantastically low reputation. It is regarded as snobbish, arrogant, patronizing, dim, asleep and a home of reactionary and generally disreputable ideas." The report then listed popular American objections to Britain, headed by its class system, which was alienating workers—"the British are going red"; imperialism; "British bunglers in high places: over-cautious, contemptuous of all new ideas and defensively minded, tired old men bored with their own task . . . British sitting safely in own island with 3.5 million men under arms, Brits always being defeated . . . Lend-Lease is stripping America to supply the British who have not even paid their [First] war debts . . . Anti-British sentiment is a part of the central patriotic American tradition . . . Anglophobia is a proof of vigorous Americanism, socially acceptable in a way anti-Catholicism and anti-semitism are not . . . All the Roosevelt-haters hate the English because they are held to be popular with the President."

British postal censorship reported to the Foreign Office on a cross section of U.S. opinion monitored in mail intercepts. From Newark, New Jersey, a man wrote to a friend in Britain: "Believe me we here are disgusted reading of British retreats and nobody blames the Tommy. We blame the Brass Hats for their inefficiency and being outmanoeuvred by Jerry every time." On September 11, a New Yorker wrote in the same vein: "There is no doubt that something is rotten about the British command everywhere . . . It isn't always lack of material—it is more often blind stupidity." Another New Yorker, posted to Australia, wrote to a British friend in Stoke-on-Trent: "English imperialism is responsible for more of our griefs and wars than you can shake a stick at. Incidentally I'm surprised to find that a great many Aussies hate the set-up in England more than I do! You IMPOSSIBLE English!"

Eden's parliamentary under-secretary, Richard Law, son of former prime minister Andrew Bonar Law, dispatched an extraordinarily emotional report to the Foreign Office during a visit to America. He claimed that in U.S. Army training camps "anti-British feeling was beyond belief . . . deliberately inculcated by certain higher officers, notably General [Brehon] Somervell, who mocked that Churchill lacked the 'sustained excitement' to execute a cross-Channel attack." Throughout the higher command of the U.S. Army, claimed Law, anti-British feeling was intense. There was violent jealousy of the prime minister, who was regarded as dominating and bamboozling the president. The American Chiefs of Staff "were about as friendly to the British as they would be to the German general staff if they sat round a table with them." This was an extravagant assessment of Anglo-American tensions. But it illustrates the scale of concern in British official circles in 1942, when the nation's military reputation was at its lowest ebb.

Churchill knew that his nation and his soldiers had to be seen to fight. If they could not engage in Europe, they must do so in the Middle East. The long periods of passivity which gripped Eighth Army in North Africa, however necessary logistically, inflicted immense harm upon both British self-esteem and the nation's image abroad. At a War Cabinet meeting presided over by Attlee, Bevin declaimed theatrically: "We must have a victory! What the British public wants is a victory!" When John Kennedy was summoned to Downing Street, the prime minister talked of current operations in North Africa, "then added a dig at the British Army (which unfortunately he can never resist) saying, 'if Rommel's army were all Germans [instead of part Italian], they would beat us.' " Later, the DMO reported the conversation to Brooke: "I told him what Winston had said about the Germans being better than our troops & he said he must speak to Winston about this. His constant attacks on the Army were doing harm—especially when they were made in the presence of other politicians, as they so often were." Yet so ashamed was Kennedy, as a soldier, about the fall of Tobruk that for some time he avoided his beloved "Rag"—the Army & Navy Club—to escape unwelcome questions about the army's lamentable showing.

While Churchill was in Washington in June, some American newspapers suggested that his government would fall. He was sufficiently disturbed by what he read to telephone Eden from the White House for reassurance that there was no critical threat to his leadership. Nothing important had changed, he was told, but Tory MP Sir John Wardlaw-Milne had tabled a censure motion in the Commons. Public opinion was fragile. "The people do not like him being away so much in such critical times," wrote a naval officer. A Mass Observation diarist, Rosemary Black, deplored Churchill's absence in America at a time when the British people were enduring so much bad news: "I myself felt pretty disgusted with him when I saw a photograph of him enjoying himself at the White House again. If only he'd keep those great gross cigars out of his face once in a way."

London voluntary worker Vere Hodgson, bewildered as was the rest of the nation by the fall of Tobruk, wrote crossly in her diary: "The enemy did not seem to understand what was expected of them, and failed to fall in with our plans. Grrr! As Miss Moyes says, it makes you see green, pink and heliotrope. I woke up in the middle of Sunday night, and thought of that convoy delivered with so much blood, sweat and losses to Tobruk on Saturday—to fall like ripe fruit into German mouths. I squirmed beneath the bedclothes and ground my teeth with rage." She added after the prime minister's broadcast two weeks later: "Mr Churchill's speech did not contain much comfort. He dominated us as he always does, and we surrender to his overpowering personality—but he knows no more than any of us why Tobruk fell!"

George King wrote to his son from Sanderstead in Surrey: "We heard yesterday that we have lost Tobruk; the same old story—rotten leadership. The Yanks will yet show us how to do the job. The 'red tabs' form the only rotten part of the British Army!" Lancashire housewife Nella Last, intensely loyal to Churchill, mused in bewilderment to her diary on June 25, 1942: "Where can soldiers go where they have a reasonable chance? Tobruk has gone—what of Egypt, Suez and India? Nearly three years of war: WHY don't we get going—what stops us? Surely by now things should be organised better in some way. Why should our men be thrown against superior mechanical horrors, and our equipment not standardised for easier management and repair? There is no flux to bind us— nothing. It's terrifying. Not all this big talk of next year and the next will stop our lads dying uselessly. If only mothers could think that their poor sons had not died uselessly—with a purpose . . . It's shocking."

A report of the Home Intelligence Division of the Ministry of Information declared: "Russian successes continue to provide an antidote to bad news from other fronts . . . 'thank God for Russia' is a frequent expression of the very deep and fervent feeling for that country which permeates wide sections of the public." Membership in Britain's Communist Party rose from 12,000 in June 1941 to 56,000 by the end of 1942. The British media provided no hint of the frightful cruelties through which Stalin sustained the Soviet Union's defence, nor of the blunders and failures which characterised its war effort in 1941–42.

In informed political and military circles, there was no scintilla of the guilt about Soviet sacrifices that prevailed among the wider public. From Churchill downwards, there was an overwhelming and not unreasonable perception that whatever miseries and losses fell upon the Russian people, the policies of their own government—above all the 1939 Nazi-Soviet Pact—were chiefly responsible. Brooke wrote disgustedly about British aid to Russia, "We received nothing in return except abuse for handling the convoys inefficiently." John Kennedy expressed bewilderment about public attitudes: "There is an extraordinary and misguided enthusiasm for the Russians. Stalin is more of a hero than the King or even Winston." A naval officer, Commander Andrew Yates, wrote to a friend in America: "Little as I formerly liked him, the man who killed a million Germans, Jo Stalin, becomes my friend for life." However, a Ministry of Information official cautioned against exaggerated fears that popular applause for Soviet military prowess equated with a mass conversion to Communism, such as some Tory MPs perceived: "That danger will never come through admiration of the achievements of another country, but only through dissatisfaction with our own—dissatisfaction savage enough to cherish a revolutionary programme."

Nonetheless, perceptions of the Red Army as braver and more willing to sacrifice than their own soldiers were a source of anger and shame among Churchill's people, which persisted throughout the summer of 1942. The public could not be told that Stalin's armies achieved their remarkable feats under draconian compulsion; that if Russian soldiers sometimes displayed more fortitude than British or American ones, this was chiefly because if they flinched they faced execution by their own commanders, a sanction imposed upon hundreds of thousands of Stalin's men in the course of the war. Debate about British military inertia and failure continued to dominate the press. "Reactionary attitudes are spreading," complained Communist Elizabeth Belsey. "*The Spectator* this week sounds much opposed to the 2nd front. What do all these people suppose Russia is to do without the 2nd Front? Continue fighting with faith instead of oil?"

Maggie Joy Blunt, a journalist of left-wing sympathies, wrote on August 7, 1942: "Why is not Mr. Churchill, rather than his critics, standing on the plinth of the Nelson column shouting for a Second Front and demanding greater efforts from every man and woman in the country? The desire to make that effort is there. The people would respond instantly to the right word from Churchill. We have the feeling, strongly, that Powers That Be wish to see Russian might crippled before they will move a finger to help. They do not want Russia to have any say in the peace terms. Capitalist interests are still vastly strong, and the propertied bourgeois, although a minority, have still an enormous influence on the conduct of our affairs and are terrified of the idea of Socialism. Socialism is inevitable." Londoner Ethel Mattison wrote to her sister in California on August 1: "When the Anglo-Soviet Alliance was signed, and . . . the Second Front was one of the main points . . . [it] rather tended to make people sit back and wait for it. However, the waiting has been so long and the Russians are suffering so terribly that it seems the idea must be pushed into realisation by the force of public opinion. Everywhere you go, in buses, trains and in lifts you hear fragments of conversation in connection with it."

The Russian press, unsurprisingly, devoted much space to the Second Front lobby. *Pravda* carried a story reporting the mass rallies in Britain in support of early action under the headline: ENGLISH PEOPLE ARE WILLING TO HELP THEIR RUSSIAN COMRADES. It quoted Associated Press correspondent Drew Middleton declaring after a tour of Britain that there was overwhelming public support for an invasion; that shipping difficulties could be overcome; that bombing of Germany was recognised as an insufficient support to Russia. *Pravda* described Second Front demonstrations in Canada. Through the months that followed, there was much more Moscow press comment on the same theme. On August 9 *Pravda* headlined: NO TIME TO LOSE—BRITISH PRESS ON THE SECOND FRONT. On August 15: TIME HAS COME TO ACT, SAY AMERICAN NEWSPAPERS. The next day, a report described a deputation representing 105,000 British workers from seventy-eight companies calling at Downing Street to present a Second Front petition to Churchill. On the nineteenth, *Pravda* headlined: ENGLISH PUBLIC ORGANISATIONS DEMAND OFFENSIVE AGAINST GERMANY, and on the twenty-third: WE HAVE NO RIGHT TO WAIT—ENGLISH TRADE UNIONS DEMAND OPENING SECOND FRONT.

The narrative of the Second World War presented by most historians is distorted by the fact that it focuses upon what happened, rather than what did not. Until November 1942, weeks and sometimes months passed without much evidence of activity by British land forces. Between June 1941 and the end of the war, British newspapers and BBC broadcasts were often dominated by reports of the struggle on the Eastern Front, where action appeared continuous. Countless editorials paid tribute to the deeds of "our gallant Russian allies." This goes far to explain why Russia commanded such admiration in contemporary Britain. Accounts of the eastern fighting were vague and often wildly inaccurate, but they coalesced to create a valid impression of vigorous, hideously costly and increasingly successful action by the Red Army. The battle for Stalingrad, which now began to receive massive coverage, intensified public dismay about the contrast between British and Russian achievements. "Every week of successful defence," reported the Ministry of Information on October 9, 1942, "confirms the popularity of the Russians and there is much uneasiness and unhappiness at the spectacle of our apparent inaction."

Ismay said that he admired Churchill as much for the courage with which he resisted a premature Second Front as for the vigour with which he promoted other projects. He observed that a lesser man might have given in to the vociferous lobbyists. He deplored the public's ignorance of the fact that real partnership with the Russians was impossible, given their implacable secretiveness. To understand the British public temper in World War II, it is necessary to recognise how little people knew about anything beyond the visible movements of armies and the previous night's bomber raids on Germany. Information which is commonplace in time of peace becomes the stuff of high secrecy in war: industrial production figures; weapons shortages; shipping movements and losses; details of aid to Russia or lack of it. Many reports in newspapers, especially those detailing Allied combat successes and enemy losses, were fanciful. The prime minister offered the nation only the vaguest and most general notion of its likely prospects. This was prudent, but obliged millions of people to exist for years in a miasma of uncertainty, which contributed decisively to the demoralisation of 1941–42.

A study of contemporary newspapers surprises a modern reader, because in contrast to twenty-first-century practise, greater attention was paid to events than to personalities, even that of Churchill himself. He received much less coverage than does a modern prime minister, and little detail about his personal life was revealed outside his inner circle. For security reasons, his travels were often unreported until he had left a given location. His speeches and public appearances were, of course, widely covered, but many days of the war passed without much press reference to the prime minister. While battlefield commanders such as Alexander and Montgomery became household names, other key figures remained almost unknown. Sir Alan Brooke, for instance, whose military role was second in importance only to that of Churchill, was scarcely mentioned in the wartime press.

Above all, accurate prophecy was rendered impossible by the fact that the condition of the enemy, the situation "on the other side of the hill," remained shrouded in mystery even to war leaders privy to Ultra secrets. Conditions in occupied Europe, as well as the state of Hitler's war machine, were imperfectly understood in London. It was widely reported that the Nazis were conducting appalling massacres, killing many Jews. But the concept of systematic genocide embracing millions of victims was beyond popular, and even prime ministerial, imagination. Entire books have been written about Churchill and the Holocaust, yet the fundamentals may be expressed succinctly: the prime minister was aware from late 1942 onwards that the Nazis were pursuing murderous policies towards the Jews.

British Jewish leaders sought to urge upon him that their people were being subjected to historically unprecedented horrors. He responded with words of deep sympathy, indeed passion, and in 1944 once urged that the RAF should do whatever was possible to check the slaughter. But he did not himself pursue the issue when told of "operational difficulties"— which meant that the airmen did not believe that attempts to destroy railway tracks in eastern Europe were as useful to the war effort as continuing the assault on Germany's cities. Churchill, in common with most of the U.S. and British war leaderships, perceived the killing of Jews in the context of Hitler's wider policy of massacre, which embraced millions of Russians, Poles, Yugoslavs, Greeks and other races. He believed that the only way to address these horrors was by hastening the defeat of Germany and liberation of the occupied nations. This assumption also guided sentiment among the public, which was told less than the Allied governments knew.

Ignorance about so many issues fed endless speculation, embracing a range of possibilities from the outbreak of peace within months, to indefinitely sustained conflict. When Harold Macmillan became British minister in the Mediterranean, he wrote: "the trouble . . . is that no one really has any idea as to the future course of the war. One minute people rush to an extreme of pessimism—and think it will never end. The next they become so excited by a favourable battle that they regard it as more or less over. And the experts cannot give us any guidance. The better they are, the less willing I find them (I mean men like Cunningham, Tedder and Alexander) to express a view." A contributor to *Punch* composed a poem about his own "befuddlement amid one bright star of England." This struck a chord with Alan Lascelles, assistant private secretary to King George VI, who wrote in his diary: "I suppose that, with the exception of some thirty or forty High Esoterics—the War Cabinet and its immediate minions—I get as much illumination on the drear fog of war as anyone in this country. Yet I am befogged, all right." For a humble citizen to keep going, it was necessary to hope blindly, because evidence for informed optimism was lacking.

In the first two days of July, Churchill faced a debate on the censure motion tabled against him in the Commons. Sir John Wardlaw-Milne destroyed his own case in the first minutes of his speech by proposing that the Duke of Gloucester, the king's notoriously thick-headed brother, should become Britain's military supremo. The House burst into mocking laughter, and Churchill's face lit up. He knew, in that moment, that he could put his critics to flight. But he was nonetheless obliged to endure a barrage of criticism. Aneurin Bevan spoke with vicious wit: "The prime minister wins debate after debate and loses battle after battle. The country is beginning to say that he fights debates like a war and the war like a debate." Bevan also asserted that arms factories were producing the wrong weapons; that the army was "riddled by class prejudice," and poorly commanded.

Then he delivered the sort of peroration which disgusted Churchill, but struck a powerful echo with the public: "For heaven's sake do not let us make the mistake of betraying those lion-hearted Russians. Speeches have been made, the Russians believe them and have broken the champagne bottles on them. They believe this country will act this year on what they call the second front . . . they expect it and the British nation expects it. I say it is right, it is the correct thing to do . . . Do not in these high matters speak with a twisted tongue." In the course of the vote of confidence debate, MPs voiced valid criticisms of the army's poor tanks and leadership. Much was said about the RAF's lack of dive-bombers, to which the British accorded exaggerated credit for German successes. Unsurprisingly, no one hinted that the British soldier was not the equal of his German counterpart, but there were fierce denunciations of the high command and class culture of the army, some of it from MPs less jaundiced than Bevan.

Americans were impressed that such strictures could be expressed. "Polyzoides" wrote in the *Los Angeles Times*: "The fact that, during one of the most critical periods in the history of the British Empire, there is still freedom of speech and criticism testifies to the greatness of the nation." Such high-minded sentiments provided, however, small comfort to the prime minister. Leo Amery wrote: "Winston is I think far too inclined to attribute to sheer personal malice the anxiety of various people to know what is really happening and makes no allowance either for the value in a democracy of telling our people the whole truth however unpalatable." A housewife diarist, Mrs. Clara Millburn, though a warm admirer of Churchill, was nonetheless impressed by the report of Wardlaw-Milne's performance in the Commons: "His speech sounds very good to us at first hearing." By contrast, she thought little of Oliver Lyttelton's opening speech for the government: "Everyone seems to want C as PM, but they do not think he has chosen wisely for his Cabinet." When the House divided, Churchill won by 475 votes to 25. "He is a giant among pygmies when it comes to a debate of this kind, and I think that everybody realizes it," wrote Tory MP Cuthbert Headlam, often a sceptic. But he added that, if the censure motion had been directed against the Ministry of Supply, he himself would not have voted against it. The next day, Mrs. Millburn wrote: "It is to be hoped that the PM takes some notice of the criticisms, for one feels some changes are necessary."

Churchill's Commons success did nothing to stifle wide-ranging and bitter criticism of the government's conduct of the war. The *Times*, in an editorial on July 10, though asserting that "no responsible body of opinion dreams of changing the national leadership," repeated its oft-made demand for a separation of the roles of prime minister and minister of defence. The paper returned to the charge on July 20, observing: "A British victory is urgently needed"; and again on the twenty-second: "All the evidence goes to show that the war machine is both cumbrous and unmethodical." In the *Times*'s letters column, a correspondent named Clive Garcia, writing from the Army & Navy Club, spoke of "a vicious circle to which we have now grown accustomed: first, disaster; then a debate on the conduct of the war, voicing profound apprehension; then a vote of confidence in the Government . . . then a pause until the next disaster." Meanwhile, asserted Garcia, "defects in the war machine go uncorrected."

Several other letter writers addressed intelligently and pertinently the inadequacy of British tanks. The *Times* commented on their strictures: "The simple question—though the answer may be complex—is how a great and inventive industrial country nearing the end of the third year of War has failed to supply its Army with weapons superior to those employed by the enemy, the nature of which was for the most part known?" An editorial in the *New Statesman* on July 29 asserted that the "military situation of the [Allies] is graver than at any time since 1940."

Within a few minutes of Churchill's return to Downing Street from the Commons on July 2, Leo Amery arrived with his son Julian, an army officer just back from Egypt. To the fury of Alan Brooke, who was also present, young Amery—"a most objectionable young pup," in the general's words—painted for the prime minister a picture of the desert army as demoralised, poorly equipped and bereft of confidence in its commanders. This confirmed Churchill's own views. In an unpublished draft of his war memoirs, he characterised the 1942 desert defeats as "discreditable" and "deplorable." In six months, Auchinleck's forces had been driven back six hundred miles. Worst of all, in Brooke's eyes, Captain Amery played to the strongest instincts of the prime minister by urging that Churchill should go himself to the Middle East and resolve the situation. "The cheek of the young brute was almost more than I could bear," wrote the CIGS. He had hoped himself to travel alone to Egypt, to address the army's difficulties. Now, instead, the prime minister was determined to intervene personally, then fly on to Moscow to confront Stalin.

But first, there was another visit to London by Hopkins, Marshall and King. Before they arrived, former CIGS Sir John Dill wrote to Churchill from Washington: "May I suggest with all respect that you must convince your visitors that you are determined to beat the Germans, that you will strike them on the continent of Europe at the earliest possible moment even on a limited scale, and that anything which detracts from this main effort will receive no support from you at all." The general mused tendentiously about a possible landing in France: "What does success mean? If invasion ultimately fails tactically but causes diversion from Russian front will it have succeeded?" Such maudlin reflections were unlikely to increase Churchill's confidence in Dill, who had gained some personal popularity in Washington because he was thought to favour an early Second Front. "Churchill, however, believes the other way," wrote Vice President Henry Wallace. "Apparently the ruling class in England is very anxious not to sacrifice too many British men. They lost so many in World

War I that they feel they cannot afford to lose more in World War II. They want to wait until the American armies have been sufficiently trained so that losses will be at least fifty-fifty. Dill does not belong to this school of thought." It was certainly true that some people in London believed the general had "gone native" in Washington.

To the prime minister's annoyance, following Marshall, King and Hopkins's arrival in London on July 19, they spent some hours communing with the newly appointed senior U.S. officer in Europe, Gen. Dwight Eisenhower, before calling at Downing Street. When Anglo-American discussions began, the visitors repeated their familiar demand for a 1942 beachhead in France. They clung stubbornly to two propositions which the British deemed monstrous. First, they thought that a "redoubt," such as Churchill had briefly favoured in June 1940, might be seized and held in northern France. Second, they considered that even if such an operation failed, the losses—destined to be overwhelmingly British—would be justified by the inconvenience imposed upon the Germans.

Brooke rehearsed familiar objections. The chief of staff of the U.S. army challenged him bluntly, demanding: "Well, how are we going to win this war? You cannot win it by defensive action." Churchill formally presented Marshall's proposal to the War Cabinet, which unanimously rejected it. There was little more to be said. The Americans remained deeply unhappy, but knew that they could not impose a scheme dependent almost entirely upon the sacrifice of British lives. Marshall had come to London with a brief from Roosevelt to make this final attempt to reconcile the British to an invasion of France; then, if he failed, to accept the North African plan. On July 22, the president cabled acquiescence in British rejection of an early assault on the Continent. With utmost reluctance, Marshall committed himself to what became the Torch landings of November 1942.

Now, the British were all smiles, and it was the Americans' turn to sulk. "Gil" Winant, the ambassador, usually mild-mannered, expressed vehement objections to the North African plan. The American visitors spent a final weekend at Chequers, with the prime minister at his sunniest, then returned to Washington, nursing frustration.

For most of August, Marshall continued to agitate against Torch. From the moment Churchill first mooted the North African scheme back in December, the chief of staff of the army had been willing to indulge it only if U.S. troops could land unopposed, with Vichy French acquiescence. The Americans were fearful that, if they were obliged to launch an amphibious assault, the Germans would swiftly reinforce North Africa through Franco's Spain, isolating any U.S. forces deployed east of the Straits of

Gibraltar. It is important to emphasise that, in the late summer of 1942, the American Chiefs believed that the British were doomed to lose Egypt. This would free Rommel's army to turn on a U.S. invasion force. Marshall not only disliked committing American soldiers to the Mediterranean theatre; he feared that a campaign there could fail. A cynic such as Alan Brooke might have contrasted unfavourably Marshall's insouciance about the perils of an abortive British descent on France with his sensitivity about the prospect of an unsuccessful American one on North Africa.

The Torch commitment represented one of Churchill's most important victories of the war. He had persuaded Roosevelt to impose a course of action on his Chiefs of Staff against their strongest wishes. As for the president, this was his most significant strategic intervention, one of the few occasions when he acted in earnest the part of commander-in-chief, instead of delegating his powers to his military advisers. The two national leaders displayed the highest wisdom. Roosevelt's decision was driven by the same political imperatives that Churchill recognised. Marshall later acknowledged this, saying of the U.S. Chiefs of Staff: "We failed to see that a leader in a democracy has to keep the people entertained. The people demand action." Fulfilment of this requirement was matched by the president's acknowledgement that if the British did not choose to land in France in 1942, they could not be made to do so. At this stage, also, Roosevelt was much more ready than in subsequent years to be influenced by Churchill's judgement. The United States would land only an initial seventy thousand men in North Africa, though thereafter these would be progressively reinforced. In 1942, a significant proportion of Marshall's available forces were committed to home defence of the United States, though it was hard to see who might mount an invasion.

The British sought to salve bruised U.S. Army sensibilities by offering a strong endorsement of its ambitions for a landing in France in 1943. But Marshall knew that once U.S. forces were fighting in the Mediterranean, it would be hard to get them out again in time for an invasion of France the following year. In the formal document decreeing the North African commitment, CCS 94, the Chiefs of Staff acknowledged "that it be understood that a commitment to [Torch] renders *Roundup* [an invasion of France] in all probability impracticable of successful operation in 1943." Only much later did some prominent American soldiers grudgingly concede that Churchill might have been right; that his and Roosevelt's commitment to Torch saved the Allies from a colossal folly. And this was only after the U.S. Army had experienced for itself the savage reality of fighting the Wehrmacht.

ELEVEN

Camels and the Bear

CHURCHILL TRAVELLED TO the Middle East in austere and dangerous discomfort. "What energy and gallantry of the old gentleman," marvelled Oliver Harvey, "setting off . . . across Africa in the heat of mid-summer." This was true enough, but masked the reality that for the rest of the conflict, Churchill was much happier in overseas theatres than amid the drabness of Britain, where he found scant romance and increasing pettiness and complaint. Though he cherished a vision of fortress Albion, its reality became increasingly uncongenial. Before his departure, the prime minister discussed with Eden whether another minister should join his party: "He felt the need for company, especially in Moscow." Here was a glimpse of Churchill's loneliness when he faced great challenges. He yearned for the comradeship of some peer figure, such as Beaverbrook or Smuts, in whom he could confide, with whom he could exchange impressions and jokes. This time, however, it was decided that he should take in his entourage only civil servants and soldiers, Alan Brooke foremost among them. They would be joined for the Moscow leg by Averell Harriman, whose presence was designed to ensure Russian understanding that what the British asserted, the Americans endorsed; and by Sir Archibald Wavell, who had served in Russia in 1919 and spoke the language.

They travelled aboard a Liberator bomber which possessed virtues of performance—range, speed and altitude—but none of the luxuries of the Boeing Clipper. Somewhat to the embarrassment of Britain's airmen, the safety of the prime minister was entrusted to a young Atlantic ferry pilot named Bill Vanderkloot, who hailed from Illinois. Vanderkloot was deemed to possess temperament, navigational skills and long-range experience which no available home-grown British pilot could match. The American admirably fulfilled expectations. His plane, however, was a cramped and unsuitable conveyance for an elderly man upon whose welfare, in considerable degree, the hopes of Western civilisation rested. It was so noisy that Churchill could communicate with his fellow passengers only by exchanging notes. The flight was long and cold. They made an African landfall over Spanish Morocco, then struck a course which took them well inland before turning east over the desert, flying high and using oxygen. In his mask, wrote one of the plane's crew, Churchill "looked exactly as though he was in a Christmas party disguise." He sat in the copilot's seat, reviving a host of youthful memories as they approached Cairo: "Often had I seen the day break on the Nile," during Kitchener's campaign against the Dervishes in 1898. Once on the ground, he began a long, painstaking grilling of soldiers and officials about the desert campaign, the army and its commanders.

All that he saw and heard confirmed his instincts back in London. Ever since 1939, visitors to Egypt had been dismayed by the lassitude pervading the nexus of headquarters, camps, villas, hotels and clubs that lay along the Nile. An air of self-indulgent imperialism, of a kind that confirmed the worst prejudices of Aneurin Bevan, persisted even in the midst of a war of national survival. "Old Miles [Lampson, British ambassador to Egypt] leads a completely peacetime existence, a satrap," wrote Oliver Harvey scornfully. "He does no work at all." The habits and complacency of peacetime also prevailed in many military messes. In 1941 Averell Harriman, no ascetic, was shocked by the indolence and luxury he saw around him on his first visit to Cairo. A year later, too many gentlemen still held sway over too few players. The former Republican presidential candidate Wendell Willkie, passing through Egypt, perceived a "lackadaisical" attitude to the war, which was "painful." Auchinleck had repeatedly disappointed Churchill's hopes. The good soldiers in the Middle East were tired. A staff officer wrote from Egypt in July 1942: "There seem to me to be too many people at home who have had no war—through no fault of their own—and too many people out here who have had too much war."

The desert army continued to suffer grave technical and tactical deficiencies. The cavalry ethos still dominated armoured operations, despite the frequent failures of British tanks' attempts to destroy German ones. "The Auk's" formations seemed unable to master the Afrika Korps' art of using antitank guns to stop British armour before committing its own panzers. The shoddiness of British industrial production was exposed when home-built tanks were off-loaded in Egypt. Their bolts proved to have been only hand-tightened at the factories, and most had been inadequately packed and loaded for ocean passage. Weeks of labour were necessary in the workshops of the Nile Delta before armoured vehicles were fit for action. American Grant tanks, which now equipped some British armoured units, mounted a 75mm sponson gun capable of destroying

German panzers, but were otherwise outmatched by them. New Shermans were still in transit from the United States.

Auchinleck's troops had been outfought again and again. British defeats in 1940–41 had been attributable to circumstances beyond commanders' control: prewar neglect, lack of air support and German superiority. The failures of late 1941 and 1942, however, reflected culpable weaknesses. The two ablest airmen in Cairo, Arthur Tedder and Arthur "Maori" Coningham, talked frankly to Churchill and Brooke about their perceptions of the army's shortcomings. Colonel Ian Jacob noted in his diary during the Cairo visit that there had been "far too many cases of units surrendering in circumstances in which in the last war they would have fought it out . . . The discipline of the Army is no longer what it used to be . . . There is lacking in this war the strong incentive of a national cause. Nothing concentrate has replaced the old motto 'For King and Country.' The aims set before the people . . . are negative, and it still does not seem to have been brought home . . . that it is a war for their own existence." War correspondent Alan Moorehead agreed:

In the Middle East there was, in August, a general and growing feeling [among the troops] that something was being held back from them, that they were being asked to fight for a cause which the leaders did not find vital enough to state clearly. It's simply no good telling the average soldier that he is fighting for victory, for his country, for the sake of duty. He knows all that. And now he's asking, "For what sort of victory? For what sort of a post-war country? For my duty to what goal in life?"

If this was indeed true—and Moorehead knew the desert army intimately—then the prime minister himself deserved some of the blame. It was he who, despite the urgings of ministers, refused to address himself to "war aims," a postwar vision. Instead, he held out to British soldiers the promise of martial glory, writing to Clementine from Cairo: "I intend to see every important unit in this army, both back and front, and make them feel the vast consequences which depend upon them and the superb honours which may be theirs." In supposing such things to represent plausible or adequate incitements for citizen soldiers, Churchill was almost certainly mistaken. But it was not in his nature to understand that most men cared more about their prospects in a future beyond war than about ribbons and laurels to be acquired during the fighting of it.

In Churchill's eyes the first priority in Egypt was, as usual, to identify new commanders. By August 6, after discussion with Smuts, whom he had asked to meet him in Cairo, he had made up his mind to sack Auchinleck.

The general received his dismissal ungraciously, and harboured bitterness for the rest of his life. Dill blamed Churchill for the Middle East C-in-C's failure, claiming that the prime minister "had ruined Auchinleck . . . he had dwarfed him just as he dwarfs and reduces others around him." This charge says more about Dill's limitations as a shop steward for unsuccessful British generals than about the prime minister's. Of course Churchill had harried Auchinleck. It has been suggested above that the general's failure in part reflected institutional weaknesses in the British Army. But "the Auk" had been the man in charge through a succession of operations abysmally conducted by subordinates of his choice. British failure to defeat the Afrika Korps at Gazala in May–June 1942 reflected gross command incompetence. It was surely right to dismiss Auchinleck.

Churchill's first impulsive thought for his replacement was Alan Brooke. The CIGS was much moved by the proposal, but wisely and selflessly rejected the chance of battlefield glory. He perceived himself as indispensable at the War Office—and he was right. The prime minister's next choice was Lt. Gen. William "Strafer" Gott, who had gained a reputation for dashing leadership from the front, but in whom Brooke lacked confidence. Since 1939, the prime minister had been convinced that Britain's armed forces lacked leaders with fire in their bellies. He sought to appoint to high command proven warriors, heroes. In this, he was often mistaken. Steely professionalism was lacking, rather than conspicuous personal courage. Many of Churchill's favourite warriors lacked intellect. Gott commended himself to the prime minister because he had made a name as a thruster, yet it is unlikely that he was competent to command Eighth Army. But fate intervened: en route to Cairo to receive his appointment, Gott's plane was shot down and he was killed. Instead, Brooke's nominee, Sir Bernard Montgomery, was summoned from a corps command in England to head Eighth Army. Churchill had met Montgomery on visits to his units, and was impressed by his forceful personality, if not by his boorish conceit. But, in accepting his appointment to the desert, the prime minister was overwhelmingly dependent on the CIGS's judgement. Gen. Sir Harold Alexander, a brave, charming but unassertive Guardsman who had recently presided over the British retreat from Burma, was appointed C-in-C Middle East. The prime minister, who found "Alex" congenial and reassuring, expected him to play a far more important role in shaping future operations than Montgomery. Several senior subordinate officers were also earmarked for sacking and replacement.

Having set in motion wholesale change at the top, Churchill departed from Cairo on the most taxing stage of this epic excursion. He was to meet the Soviet Union's warlord, and deliver the unwelcome news that the

Western Allies had determined against launching a Second Front in 1942. After a brief stopover in Tehran, on August 12 he made a ten-and-a-half-hour flight to Moscow, accompanied by his personal staff and Averell Harriman. A few hours after landing, Churchill was summoned to the Kremlin. He asked Harriman to accompany him: "I feel things would be easier if we all seemed to be together. I have a somewhat raw job."

In truth, and as surprisingly few historians show recognition of, Stalin was already aware of all that Churchill feared to tell him. Whitehall and Washington were alike deeply penetrated by Communist sympathisers. Among the most prominent, John Cairncross served as Lord Hankey's private secretary with access to War Cabinet papers until Hankey's sacking in 1942, when he was transferred to Bletchley Park. Anthony Blunt served in MI5, while Guy Burgess and Kim Philby worked for SIS. Donald Maclean had access to key Foreign Office material, especially concerning research on the atomic bomb. In the U.S. government—which was anyway lax about securing its secrets from the Russians—Harry Dexter White worked for Henry Morgenthau, Nathan Silvermaster for the Board of Economic Warfare, and Alger Hiss for the State Department. Harry Hopkins talked with surprising freedom, though surely not ill intent, to a key NKVD agent in the United States. Throughout the war, a mass of British and U.S. government reports, minutes and decrypted Axis messages was passed to Moscow by such people, through their controllers in London and Washington. As a result, before every Allied summit the Russians were vastly better informed about Anglo-American military intentions than vice versa. So much material reached Stalin from London that he rejected some of it as disinformation, plants by cunning agents of Churchill. When Kim Philby told his NKVD handler that Britain was conducting no secret intelligence operations in the Soviet Union, Stalin dismissed this assertion with the contempt he deemed it to deserve. Molotov and Lavrenty Beria, the Soviet intelligence and secret police chief, frequently concealed from their leader accurate intelligence which they believed would anger him.

Yet in August 1942, Stalin was thoroughly briefed about Western Allied strategy, thanks to the highly placed Soviet agents. He had been told of the fierce Anglo-American arguments about the Second Front. On August 4, Beria reported:

Our NKVD resident in London sent the following information received from a source close to the English General Staff: A meeting about the second front took place on 21 July 1942. It was attended by Churchill, Lord Mountbatten, General Marshall and others. General

Marshall sharply criticized the attitude of the English . . . He insisted
that the second front should be opened in 1942 and warned that if the
English failed to do this the USA would have to reconsider sending
reinforcements to Great Britain and focus their attention on the
Pacific. Churchill gave the following response to General Marshall:
"There is not a single top general who would recommend starting
major operations on the continent." A further meeting on the second
front took place on 22 or 23 July 1942. This was attended on the English side by Churchill, Mountbatten and the chiefs of staff; on the
American side by Marshall, Eisenhower and others. The participants
discussed a plan for the invasion of the continent which has been developed by English and American military experts . . . English chiefs of
staff unanimously voted against and were supported by Churchill who
declared that he could not vote against his own chiefs of staff. NKVD
resident in London also reported the following, based on information
from agents which had been also confirmed earlier by a source close to
American embassy: on 25 July the British war cabinet agreed that there
should be no second front this year.

A further August 12 NKVD intelligence brief to Stalin included a note
on the prime minister's political position: "Churchill departed for the
USSR in an atmosphere of growing domestic political crisis. The intensi-
fication of fighting on the Soviet-German front has had a marked effect
on British public opinion . . . Source believes Churchill will offer a number of concessions to the Soviet Union BERIA." Russian access to such
insights should not be taken to mean that Stalin was always correctly
informed. For instance, several times during the war, NKVD agents
reported to Moscow supposed parleys between the Western Allies and the
Nazi leadership. On May 12, 1942, Beria passed to Stalin a report from
the London resident on German attempts to start separate negotiations
with the English: "We know from a reliable source that an official from
the German embassy in Sweden has flown to England from Stockholm on
board a civilian aircraft." Like other such claims, this one was fallacious,
but it fuelled Soviet paranoia. NKVD information was entirely accurate,
however, about Britain's position on the Second Front. Moscow was told
that the prime minister's objections did not derive, as Stalin had supposed,
from political hostility to the USSR, but instead from pragmatic military
considerations.

Stalin had always displayed intense curiosity about Churchill, for a
quarter of a century the archfoe of Bolshevism. In June 1941, the Russian
leader was surprised by the warmth with which Britain's prime minister

embraced him as a cobelligerent. In the intervening fourteen months, however, little had happened to gain Stalin's confidence. Extravagant Western promises of aid had resulted in relatively meagre deliveries. The *Times* editorialist waxed lyrical on January 6, 1942, about the flow of British supplies to support the alliance with the Soviets: "The first result of this collaboration has been the splendid performance of British and American tanks and aeroplanes on Russian battlefields." This was a wild exaggeration of reality, based upon sunshine briefings of the media and Parliament by the British government. Not only were targets for shipments of aircraft and tanks to Russia unfulfilled, but much of the material dispatched was being sunk in transit.

Convoy PQ16 was the target of 145 Luftwaffe sorties, and lost 11 of its 35 ships. In July, when 26 out of 37 ships carrying American and British supplies were lost with PQ17, 3,850 trucks, 430 tanks and 250 fighters vanished to the bottom. Following this disaster the Royal Navy insisted on cancelling all further convoys for the duration of the Arctic summer and its interminable daylight. Churchill, pressed by Roosevelt, reinstated the September convoys and began moving supplies through Iran, where the British and Russians now shared military control. But the only important reality, in Moscow's eyes, was that aid consignments lagged far behind both Allied promises and Russian needs. Even more serious, the British had vetoed American plans for an early Second Front.

It is implausible that Stalin would have displayed a sentimental enthusiasm for his British allies, any more so than for any other human beings in his universe. He would never have acknowledged that his nation's predicament was overwhelmingly the consequence of his own awesomely cynical indulgence of Hitler back in 1939. But Russia's sense of outraged victimhood was none the less real for being spurious. The Soviets sought to bludgeon or shame the British and Americans into maintaining supply shipments and landing an army in Europe at the earliest possible date. Russia was counting her dead in the millions while the British cavorted in North Africa, paying a tiny fraction of the eastern blood sacrifice. In August 1942, Rostov-on-Don had fallen, Germany's armies were deep in the Caucasus and almost at the gates of Stalingrad. Posterity knows that Hitler had made a fatal mistake by splitting his principal summer thrusts in pursuit of the strategically meaningless capture of Stalin's name-city. The tide of the eastern war would turn decisively by the year's end. But Russians at the time could not see beyond cataclysm. They knew only that their predicament was desperate. They could no more regard Churchill's people as comrades-in-arms than might a man thrashing in a sea of sharks look in fellowship upon spectators cheering him on from a boat.

The prime minister wasted no time, at his first meeting with Stalin, before reporting the decision against a landing in Europe in 1942. He said that any such venture must be on a small scale, and thus assuredly doomed. It could do no service to Russia's cause. The British and American governments were, however, preparing "a very great operation" in 1943. He told Stalin of Torch, the North African invasion plan, observing that he hoped the secret would not find its way into the British press—a jibe at Ambassador Maisky's notorious indiscretions to journalists in London about operations to which he had been made privy. He spoke much about the RAF's bombing of Germany, describing the beginnings of a long campaign to systematically destroy Hitler's cities, with a ruthlessness he assumed the Soviet leader would applaud. "We sought no mercy," said the prime minister, "and we would show no mercy."

The substance of this first encounter, which lasted three hours and forty minutes, was made even less palatable by poor interpreting. All foreign visitors to the Kremlin were at first disconcerted that Stalin never looked into their eyes. Instead, this infinitely devious warlord, clad in a lilac tunic and cotton trousers tucked into long boots, gazed blankly at the wall or the floor as he listened and as he spoke. There were no immediate Soviet tantrums, though Stalin made plain his displeasure at the Second Front decision. "A man who is not prepared to take risks," he mocked, "cannot win a war." Given his prior knowledge of Churchill's "revelation," at this meeting he was making sport of the prime minister. But he did so with his usual supreme diplomatic skill, maintaining his visitors' suspense about what their host really knew or thought. When they parted and Churchill returned to his villa, he signalled Attlee in London: "He knows the worst, and we parted in an atmosphere of goodwill." Harriman cabled Roosevelt: "The prime minister was at his best and could not have handled the discussion with greater brilliance." The next day, August 13, Churchill conferred with Molotov about detailed aspects of Allied plans and aid to Russia.

That afternoon Brooke, Wavell and Tedder arrived, in a Liberator delayed by technical trouble. They were in time to attend the prime minister's second meeting with Stalin, and were shocked by their glacial reception. The Soviet leader began by handing Churchill a formal protest about the delay in launching the Second Front: "It is easy to understand that the refusal of the Government of Great Britain to create a second front in 1942 inflicts a moral blow to the whole of Soviet public opinion . . . complicates the situation of the Red Army at the front and compromises the plans of the Soviet command." What Churchill called "a most unpleasant discussion" ensued. He was resolute in making plain that the Allied decision was irrevocable, and thus that "reproaches were vain." Stalin taunted him with the destruction of PQ17: "This is the first time in history the British Navy has ever turned tail and fled from the battle. You British are afraid of fighting. You should not think the Germans are supermen. You will have to fight sooner or later. You cannot win a war without fighting."

Harriman slipped a note to Churchill: "Don't take this too seriously—this is the way he behaved last year." The prime minister then addressed Stalin with unfeigned passion about Britain's past defiance and future resolution, his stream of rhetoric flowing far ahead of the interpreters. Stalin laughed: "Your words are not important, what is vital is the spirit." Churchill accused Stalin of displaying a lack of comradeship. Britain, he reminded the Georgian, had been obliged to fight alone for a year. In the early hours of August 14, the two delegations parted as frigidly as they had met. "I am downhearted and dispirited," Churchill told his British colleagues. "I have come a long way and made a great effort. Stalin lay back puffing at his pipe, with his eyes half closed, emitting streams of insults. He said the Russians were losing 10,000 men a day. He said that if the British Army had been fighting the Germans as much as the Red Army had, it would not be so frightened of them."

After a few hours' sleep, the British communed among themselves. Churchill was smarting from the drubbing he had received. All his latent animosity towards the Soviets bubbled forth, revived by abuse from a leader who eighteen months earlier had been content to collude in Hitler's rape of Europe. He was also dismayed by an incoming signal from London, detailing heavy losses to the epic Pedestal convoy to Malta. Cabling Attlee to report the Russians' intransigence, he said that he made "great allowances for the stresses through which they are passing."

That night, the British attended a banquet, accompanied by the usual orgy of toasts. Hosts and guests feasted in a fashion grotesque in a society on the brink of mass starvation. But what was one more grotesquerie, amid the perpetual black pageant of the Kremlin? Stalin shuffled among the tables, as was his habit, clinking glasses and making jokes, leaving Churchill often lonely and perforce silent in his own place. When the Soviet warlord sat down once more, the prime minister said: "You know, I was not friendly to you after the last war. Have you forgiven me?" His host responded: "All that is in the past. It is not for me to forgive. It is for God to forgive." This literal translation obscures the proverbial meaning of the Russian phrase, probably missed by Churchill: "I will never forgive." The British delegation found it droll that Stalin, of all people, so often invoked the Deity, a habit he acquired as a young seminarian. He said of Torch:

"May God prosper this undertaking." The most notable success of the evening was a speech by Wavell in Russian.

Even the Soviets were impressed by the quantities of alcohol consumed by both their own leader and Churchill. One guest, unfamiliar with the prime minister's usual diction, wrote afterwards: "His speech was slurred as though his mouth was full of porridge." The Russians decided that Churchill must be perpetrating some shocking indiscretion when they saw Brooke tugging insistently at his sleeve, in a fashion no man would have dared do to Stalin. After the prime minister left the dining room, Stalin noticed that Alexander Golovanov, who commanded the Soviet air force's long-range bombers, was staring at him in some alarm. "Don't be afraid," said the Soviet leader, with unaccustomed docility. "I am not going to drink Russia away." He lapsed into silence for a few moments, then said, "When great affairs of state are at stake, alcohol tastes like water and one's head is always clear." Golovanov noted with respect that Stalin walked from the room steadily and unhurriedly.

Churchill left the banquet in sullen mood, deploring alike the food, his hosts' manners and the uncongenial setting. The next morning, a meeting between Brooke, Wavell and Stalin's senior officers proved abortive when the Russians flatly refused to disclose any details of their operations in the Caucasus, saying that they were authorised to discuss only the Second Front. The sole Soviet weapons system that inspired British enthusiasm was the Katyusha multiple rocket launcher, of which the visitors requested technical details. These were never forthcoming.

On Saturday, Churchill and his colleagues entered the big Kremlin conference room overlooking the Moskva River with considerable apprehension. The prime minister told Stalin that he had considered it his duty to inform him personally of the Second Front decision. Exchanges between the two sides were more fluent, because Churchill had now enlisted the services of Major Birse, a bilingual member of Britain's military aid mission. Stalin suddenly seemed more emollient. "Obviously there are differences between us," he said, "but . . . the fact that the meeting has taken place, that personal contact has been established . . . is very valuable." After more than an hour of talks, as they rose from the table Stalin suddenly, and apparently spontaneously, invited Churchill for drinks in his private apartment. There they adjourned for a further six hours of informal conversation, during which the prime minister believed that a better rapport was established. Stalin suggested a British landing in northern Norway, a proposal which Churchill could endorse with unfeigned enthusiasm. The Russian said that it would be helpful for Britain to dispatch trucks rather than tanks to the Red Army, though this request reflected ignorance of British military vehicle weaknesses. A suckling pig was brought in, which Stalin addressed avidly, and his guests sampled politely. A draft communiqué was agreed upon. At 2:30 a.m., Churchill parted from his host, with protestations of goodwill on both sides.

Back at his villa forty-five minutes later, the prime minister found that the Polish general Wladyslaw Anders had been awaiting him for many hours. "Ah! My poor Anders," said Churchill. "I have been detained by M. Stalin and now I must fly off. But you come along to Cairo and we shall have a talk there." Then he lay wearily down on a sofa, closed his eyes, and described to his party what had been said in Stalin's apartment. At 5:30 a.m., the British party took off for Cairo in four Liberators.

Churchill left Russia satisfied that his visit had achieved as much as was possible in bleak circumstances. He had displayed the highest gifts of statesmanship, placing a brave face upon bad tidings, never flinching when his host flourished the knout. Ian Jacob wrote: "No one but the Prime Minister could have got so far with Stalin, in the sense that we understand friendship. The thing that impressed me most about Stalin was his complete self-possession and detachment. He was absolutely master of the situation at all times . . . He had a gentle voice, which he never raised, and his eyes were shrewd and crafty."

Harriman was full of admiration for Churchill's patience in the face of Russian insults, for his restraint in withholding the obvious rejoinder to Stalin's mockery—that the Soviet Union had forged a devil's bargain with Nazi Germany in 1939. Yet the prime minister had scarcely enjoyed the Moscow experience. Jacob wrote: "Churchill was decidedly upset by the lack of comradeship that he had encountered. There was none of the normal human side to the visit—no informal lunches, no means of doing what he most liked, which was to survey at length the war situation in conversation, and to explore the mind of his interlocutor." Churchill nonetheless deluded himself that he had established a personal connection with Russia's leader. No man could achieve that, least of all a British aristocrat famously hostile to all that the Soviet Union stood for. Brooke wrote, "He appealed to sentiments in Stalin which I do not think exist there."

Churchill's faith in the power of his personality to alter outcomes was occasionally justified in his dealings with Roosevelt, but never with Stalin. The Russians dispensed a modicum of amiability and fellowship in the last stage of the prime minister's Moscow visit, because unremitting hostility might threaten the Anglo-American supply line. In August 1942, as at every subsequent summit, Stalin had two notable advantages. First, the

Western Allies would never press their own wishes beyond a certain point, because they feared that failure to indulge the Soviet warlord might provoke him to seek a separate peace with Hitler. While Stalin needed Anglo-American supplies, the Western Allies needed the Red Army more. Second, while visitors were obliged to improvise scripts as they went along, struggling to keep pace with apparent shifts of Soviet mood, Stalin's performance was precisely orchestrated from start to finish. He possessed almost complete knowledge of Allied military intentions, or lack of them, before Churchill landed in Moscow and delivered his budget of news at the Kremlin—and likewise at later 1943–45 meetings. Russia's leader was able to adjust every nicety of courtesy and insult accordingly. It is unlikely that Stalin made many, if any, genuinely spontaneous remarks or gestures while Churchill was in Moscow. He merely lifted or lowered British spirits as seemed expedient, with the assurance of an orchestral conductor.

The Russians missed no opportunity to work wedges between the British and Americans. One night when Churchill went to bed, Stalin urged Harriman to stay and talk. The diplomat pleaded exhaustion. When Harriman did find himself alone with the Russian leader, he was caressed with comparisons between U.S. and British prowess: "Stalin told me the British Navy had lost its initiative. There was no good reason to stop the convoys. The British armies didn't fight either—Singapore etc. The US Navy fought with more courage and so did the Army at Bataan. The British air force was good, he admitted. He showed little respect for the British military effort but much hope in that of the US." Stalin's words were not wasted. When Harriman reported back to Roosevelt in Washington, he thought the president was gratified by Churchill's discomfiture.

It is an outstanding curiosity of the Second World War that two such brilliant men as Winston Churchill and Franklin Roosevelt allowed themselves to suppose that the mere fact of discovering a common enemy in Hitler could suffice to make possible a real relationship, as distinct from an arrangement of convenience on specifics, between Britain, the United States and the Soviet Union. Stalin and his acolytes never for a moment forgot that their social and political objectives were inimical to those of their capitalist Western Allies. British politicians, generals and diplomats were, however, foolish enough to hope that they might achieve some comradeship with the Soviets, without forswearing their visceral loathing for them. Few senior Americans were as hostile to the Russians as were the British, partly because they were so confident of U.S. power, and correspondingly less fearful of Soviet ambitions. But the Americans, too—with such notable exceptions as Harriman—harboured delusions about their ability to make friends with the Russians, or at least to exploit U.S. might to bend the Soviet government to their will, which rational assessment of rival national purposes should have dispelled.

It is striking that Churchill's visit to Moscow failed to inspire any quickening of aid to Russia. Following the disaster to PQ17 in July, the British dispatched no further supplies to Archangel for two months, declining to risk another convoy in the relentless daylight of Arctic high summer. On and after September 20, twenty-seven of PQ18's forty ships arrived safely. Thereafter, for four months the Royal Navy was too preoccupied with supporting the Torch landings to dispatch any Arctic convoys at all. At horrific risk, thirteen merchant ships sailed independently and unescorted to the Kola Inlet. Just five arrived. By January 1943, only two further convoys, thirty merchantmen in all, had reached Russia safely. Thereafter, as Allied resources grew and German strength in northern Norway was weakened by diversions of Luftwaffe aircraft to other theatres, the picture changed dramatically. Massive consignments of vehicles, stores and equipment, most of American manufacture, were successfully shipped, half of them through Vladivostok. Such assistance made a critical contribution to the Red Army's advance to victory in 1944–45. But Stalin and his people were entitled to consider that they saved themselves until 1943 with only marginal foreign aid.

Soviet historians in comparatively modern times have continued to heap scorn upon the shortfalls of Western assistance. In 1978 Victor Trukhanovsky wrote: "The deliveries were curtailed not so much by the difficulties of escorting convoys . . . as Churchill and British historians like to claim, as by the fact that in Britain there were influential circles which did not like the alliance with the USSR and hindered the normal development of relations between the two alliances. Their influences affected the stance adopted by Churchill." Although in reality shortages of weapons and shipping, together with Soviet intransigence, were the principal inhibiting factors, it was true that few senior figures in Britain wanted the Soviets to emerge strengthened from the war. Extravagant early assurances given to Moscow by both Washington and London were broken. Churchill's promise to dispatch twenty, even forty British air squadrons to support the Red Army went unfulfilled. There were readily identifiable reasons for this. But Stalin saw only one reality: that while his own nation was engulfed in battle, blood and destruction, Britain remained relatively unscathed and America absolutely so.

Churchill was too wise to waste much consideration upon the moral superiority of Britain's position over that of the Soviet Union. All that now mattered to the British and Americans was that the three nations shared a common commitment to the defeat of Nazism. Nonetheless, it was hard to achieve even basic working relationships. Whatever courtesies Stalin accorded to such grandees as Churchill, Eden, Hopkins, Harriman and Beaverbrook, and whatever Soviet secrets he himself occasionally revealed to them, humbler Allied officers and diplomats were denied the most commonplace information. They were exposed to unremitting discourtesy on good days, to contemptuous abuse on bad ones. British and American sailors landing at Murmansk and Archangel suffered insults and humiliations. A later head of the British military mission to Moscow, Lt. Gen. Brocas Burrows, had to be replaced at the Soviets' insistence after their hidden microphones caught him describing them as "savages."

The prime minister and his colleagues, like Roosevelt and Marshall, knew that Russia must be given assistance because, to put the matter bluntly, each Russian who died fighting the Germans was one less Englishman or American who must do so. But it would have been asking too much to expect the Westerners to like the Russians. Policy made it essential to pretend to do so, just as Stalin sometimes offered a charade of comradeship. But the Soviets behaved as brutes both to their own people and to the Western Allies. Only the idealists of the left, of whom there were many in wartime Britain though rather fewer in America, sustained romantic illusions about Mother Russia. They were fortunate enough never to glimpse its reality.

Back in Cairo on August 17, Churchill briefly lapsed into exhaustion. After a rest, however, he quizzed Alexander about the prospective desert offensive, which there were hopes of launching in September. On the nineteenth, he drove 120 miles through sandy wastes landmarked with supply dumps and wired encampments to visit Montgomery at his headquarters and inspect troops. This was an outing which he thoroughly enjoyed. He claimed to detect a new mood among officers and men. His imagination surely ran ahead of reality, for the new regime had been in place only a week. But a perception of change buoyed his spirits. He slept in the plane back to Cairo, then attended a conference, dined and sat chatting to Brooke in the warm night air on the embassy lawn until two a.m. He commissioned the ambassador's wife, Lady Lampson, to undertake a shopping expedition on behalf of Clementine, buying Worth perfume, Innoxa and Chanel face cream, fifteen lipsticks—and silk to make the delicate underwear in which he loved to clothe himself.

A signal arrived from Mountbatten, describing the raid on Dieppe that had taken place that day. Of six thousand men engaged, mostly Canadian, a thousand had been killed and two thousand taken prisoner. More than a hundred aircraft had been lost in fierce air battles with the Luftwaffe. Yet the chief of Combined Operations reported, absurdly: "Morale of return-ing troops reported to be excellent. All I have seen are in great form." It was some time before Churchill fully grasped the disastrous character of the raid. Lessons were learned about the difficulties of attacking a hostile shore. Inflated RAF claims masked the reality that the Germans had that day shot down two British aircraft for every one which they themselves lost. Once more, a sense of institutional incompetence overlay the deba-cle. The invaders bungled the amphibious assault in every possible way, while the Germans responded with their accustomed speed and efficiency. After almost three years of war, Britain was incapable of conducting a lim-ited surprise attack against an objective and at a moment of its own choice. Mountbatten was successful in evading responsibility, much of which properly belonged to him—back in May, he had boasted to Molotov about "his" impending operation. But leaders and planners had failed at every level. Incredibly, Gen. Sir Archibald Nye, acting CIGS in Brooke's absence, was unaware that the raid was taking place. It is scant wonder that Churchill lacked confidence in his commanders, and remained morbidly fearful that Britain's war-making instruments were doomed to break in his hand.

Only Beaverbrook, still banging a drum for the Second Front, seemed unchastened by the experience of Dieppe. His *Evening Standard* asserted that the shipping problems impeding an early invasion could be overcome if the Chiefs of Staff displayed more guts, declared the raid to have been a near victory, and editorialised on August 21, 1942: "The Germans cannot afford any more Dieppes either on land or in the air . . . Two or three simultaneous raids on a large scale would be too much for the three soli-tary Panzer divisions in France." No general or minister doubted that such calls to arms were delivered at Beaverbrook's explicit behest. The pressures upon the prime minister not merely for action but for success were now greater than at any time since he assumed office.

TWELVE

The Turn of Fortune

CHURCHILL'S PURGE OF desert generals was greeted in Britain with unsurprising caution. So many newly promoted officers had been welcomed as Wellingtons, only to be exposed as duffers. The *Times*'s military correspondent observed that commanders in the Middle East "have changed so frequently that the subject can now be approached only with tempered enthusiasm." Through the months that followed, the British media displayed a wariness close to cynicism about Eighth Army's prospects. A *Times* editorial on August 26 observed that neither the RAF's bomber offensive nor the raid on Dieppe had "relieved the continuing sense of an inadequacy in the British military achievement at a time when our allies face a supreme crisis." Journalist Maggie Joy Blunt wrote in her diary on August 19, expressing dismay about Dieppe: "While I grumble young Russia waits in agony for our Second Front. Here in England we are divided, despondent and without faith, ruled by old men, governed by money. The old fears, the old distrust are deeply rooted." Such gloom was not confined to civilians. Brooke wrote later: "When looking back at those days in the light of after events one may be apt to overlook those ghastly moments of doubt which at the time crowded in on me."

Churchill, who read newspapers avidly, cannot have gained much pleasure from their scepticism about the command changes. However, he returned to London on August 24 exhilarated by what he had seen in the desert and by the perceived success of his visit to Stalin. His boundless capacity for optimism was among his greatest virtues, at a time when those around him found it easier to succumb to gloom. On the night of August 30 Rommel, desperately short of fuel, attacked at Alam Halfa. The British, forewarned by Ultra, inflicted a decisive repulse on the Afrika Korps. The prime minister now became passionately anxious that Montgomery's own offensive should be launched before the U.S. North African landings, provisionally scheduled for October. There was fresh trouble with Washington, where Marshall was urging Roosevelt to limit the scale of Torch, and to omit Algiers from its objectives. Churchill feared that he would have to defy medical advice and fly once more to see the president. Only on September 3 did Roosevelt accede to Churchill's imprecations, which were supported by U.S. generals Dwight Eisenhower and Mark Clark in London. Torch was to proceed on November 8, with landings at Casablanca, Oran and Algiers.

But while Allied warlords nursed private excitement about the prospect of great happenings, the public and body politic perceived only continuing inactivity. Churchill indulged an outburst of self-pity on September 24, telling Alan Brooke that he, the prime minister, "was the only one trying to win the war, that he was the only one who produced any ideas, that he was quite alone in all his attempts, no one supported him . . . Frequently in this oration he worked himself up into such a state from the woeful picture he had painted, that tears streamed down his face!"

It was inevitable that, having insisted upon assuming sole responsibility for direction of the war, Churchill should bear blame for the weaknesses which caused the armed forces so often to be seen to fail. Public dissatisfaction with Britain's wartime government attained its highest pitch during the last weeks before a dramatic change of fortune. Many ministers and generals, who readily accepted that only Churchill could be Britain's prime minister, were nonetheless convinced that he should divorce the premiership from the ministry of defence, delegating operational control of the war. But to whom? The mooted candidates were almost as unsuitable as had been the Duke of Gloucester. Leo Amery told Dill, home on leave, that he favoured appointing Wavell as "super–chief of staff . . . Dill agreed, but said nothing could get Winston to face up to it however bad the present arrangement may be." This exchange says little for the judgement of either man, but much about the mood in Whitehall towards the prime minister. Even Eden, Churchill's most trusted colleague, was convinced that he should relinquish the ministry of defence.

Churchill later described September and October 1942 as his most anxious months of the war. Amery complained after a Cabinet wrangle: "It is an awful thing dealing with a man like Winston who is at the same moment dictatorial, eloquent and muddle-headed." Beaverbrook, unswervingly mischievous and disloyal, told Eden on October 8 that the prime minister was "a 'bent' man, and couldn't be expected to last long . . . The future belonged to A.E." Influential Canadian diplomat Humphrey Hume Wrong, in London on a fact-finding mission, wrote in his diary: "The dominance of Churchill emerges from all these talks.

Cripps on the shelf, Attlee a lackey, Bracken the Man Friday of Churchill. It isn't as bad as the political gossips make out, but it's bad enough."

If Churchill's person was in Downing Street, his spirit was far away, in the drifting sands of Egypt. Montgomery was training troops, making plans, stockpiling ammunition, readying his new Sherman tanks. The foxy little general insisted upon launching Eighth Army's offensive according to his own timetable, heedless of the prime minister's impatience. A critical contribution to his campaign was already being made at sea. Guided by Ultra decrypts, the RAF and Royal Navy inflicted a series of devastating blows on the Italian tankers and supply ships fuelling and feeding the Afrika Korps. By late October, even before Eighth Army began its assault, the German logistical predicament in Egypt was desperate. The prime minister knew this from his Boniface decrypts, and dispatched a barrage of anxious, sometimes threatening, signals to Alexander. A British army strongly superior in men, tanks, guns and planes must surely be capable of defeating an enemy known to be almost immobilised for lack of fuel.

The operational value of Ultra material on the battlefield depended heavily on the receptiveness of individual commanders, and the quality of their intelligence chiefs. Some generals and admirals were astonishingly indifferent to the bounties they were offered. Montgomery was the first British desert commander to employ a top-class intelligence officer, in the person of Oxford academic Brig. Edgar Williams, and to heed his counsel. Ultra played a key role in enabling Montgomery to defeat Rommel's thrust at Alam Halfa. Adm. Sir Dudley Pound, first sea lord until 1943, often used intelligence poorly, most notoriously during the PQ17 Arctic convoy battle. By contrast, the Admiralty's Submarine Tracking Room was brilliantly conducted, and played a decisive role in the Battle of the Atlantic. In 1942, however, Bletchley's inability to crack the U-boat cipher rendered Allied convoys appallingly vulnerable. November saw the worst losses of the war: some 721,700 tons of Allied shipping were sunk. Then, suddenly and dramatically, the code breakers achieved another breakthrough, and once more provided the Royal Navy with means to track U-boat positions. From December onwards, convoys could again be routed away from the submarine wolf packs. Thanks overwhelmingly to intelligence, the tide of the Atlantic battle, as well as of the Mediterranean campaign to interdict supplies to Rommel, turned decisively against Germany.

Montgomery launched his attack at El Alamein on October 23. Brendan Bracken said: "If we are beaten in this battle, it's the end of Winston." This was histrionic: within a fortnight the Torch landings far behind Rommel's front would have rendered the German position in Egypt untenable. That is why Correlli Barnett, Douglas Porch and others have described El Alamein as "the unnecessary battle." But it was a desperately necessary one for the self-esteem of the British people. Bracken's words reflected the prevailing mood among even the prime minister's most loyal supporters. Churchill had presided over so many failures. There must be a success—a British success. Some postwar strategists have argued that, if Montgomery had merely waited for Torch, he could then have fallen upon Rommel's retreating army in the open, and achieved a far more devastating and less costly victory. But this was never a credible political option for Eighth Army—nor for the prime minister.

On the night of October 23, he attended a dinner for Eleanor Roosevelt at Buckingham Palace. A courtier wrote:

> Winston was like a cat on hot bricks, waiting for the news of the start of Alexander's offensive in Egypt. This . . . had begun at 8 pm our time, and I had to go out in the middle to get the news by telephone from No. 10. After a brief interval, nothing would content Winston but to go to the telephone himself. His conversation evidently pleased him, for he walked back along the passage singing "Roll Out the Barrel" with gusto, but with little evidence of musical talent. This astonished the posse of footmen through which he had to pass. I wondered what their Victorian predecessors would have thought had they heard Dizzy, or Mr. G[ladstone], singing "Knocked 'Em in the Old Kent Road" in similar circumstances.

Back in June, Auchinleck had chosen to halt his retreat and defend a line at El Alamein. South of a narrow stretch of desert, there less than forty miles wide, hills rendered the position impervious to flank attack. In contrast to most North African battlefields, there was little room for manoeuvre: it was necessary for an attacker to batter a path by frontal assault through minefields, wire and deep defences. In August, when Rommel attacked, these circumstances profited the British. Seven weeks later, they enabled 104,000 Germans and Italians to mount an unexpectedly staunch defence against 195,000 British troops and overwhelming firepower. Gen. Georg Stumme, acting as Axis commander during Rommel's absence on sick leave, was killed in the first days. Rommel returned. For almost a week, the British pounded and hammered at his positions. Churchill and the British people held their breath. The first news was good—but so it had often been before, to be followed by crushing disappointments. The British no longer dared to anticipate victory. One minister, Amery, wrote on October 26: "I am terribly anxious lest even with our

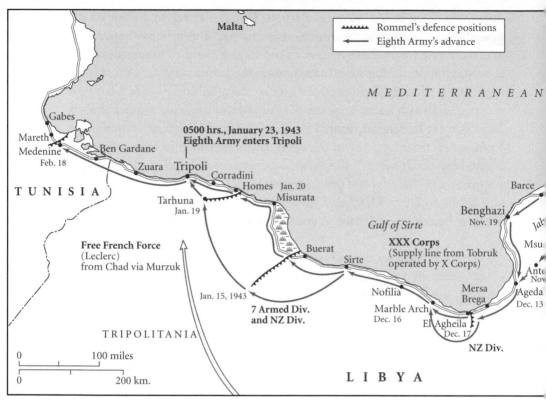

superior weight of tanks and artillery and aircraft it might yet prove another Passchendaele, and we spend ourselves in not quite getting through."

Churchill became seriously alarmed when, on October 28, Montgomery paused and regrouped. He dispatched a threatening minute to Brooke: "It is most necessary that the attack should be resumed before *Torch*. A standstill now will be proclaimed a defeat. We consider the matter most grave." British armies had been here so often before. Auchinleck had achieved comparable successes, only to see them crumble to dust. Then, on November 2, Montgomery launched his decisive blow, Operation Supercharge. "How minute and fragile one felt, trapped in this maelstrom of explosive fury!" wrote a bewildered young British platoon commander. "When we moved forward we scuttled like mice across the inhospitable sand . . . ready to sway and flatten ourselves to earth if a shell burst nearby . . . We were being fired upon. Though this was the very meaning of war, I felt a sense of outrage and betrayal. Someone had blun-

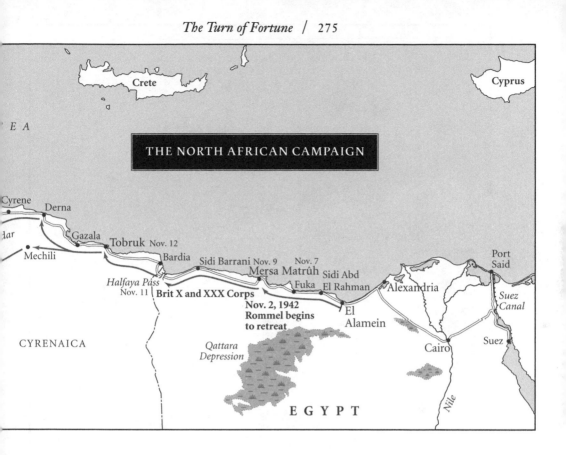

dered. How could the chaos conceivably resolve itself into a successful attack? Yet all the major battles of history must have seemed like this, a hopeless shambles to the individual in front, with a coherence only discernible to those in the rear."

Montgomery's men broke through. Ultra revealed to the British that Rommel considered himself beaten, and was in full retreat. Churchill rejoiced. At a Downing Street lunch he gleefully told guests, including MP Harold Nicolson: "There is more jam to come. Much more jam. And in places where you least expect it." After this coy hint at Torch, across the same lunch table he told Brendan Bracken to order the nation's church bells rung. When the proposal met doubts, he agreed to delay until November 15, to ensure that no accident befell Allied arms. Thereafter, he was determined that the British people should recognise just cause for celebration.

Brooke wrote in his diary: "If Torch succeeds we are beginning to stop losing this war." Early on Sunday, November 8, Allied forces landed in

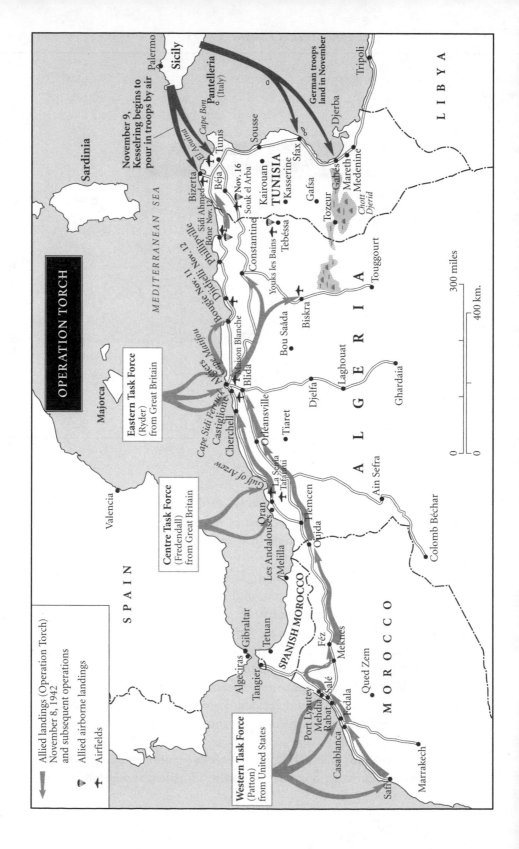

North Africa. Eisenhower's command was initially small, half the size of Montgomery's—107,000 men, 35,000 of them British. But the symbolic significance of this first commitment of American ground troops on a non-Pacific battlefield was immense. Though the invaders encountered some fierce resistance from Vichy forces, all the beachheads were swiftly secured. Churchill cabled congratulations to Marshall, adding wryly: "We shall find the problems of success not less puzzling though more agreeable than those we have hitherto surmounted together." The *Times* wrote of the prime minister's performance at the annual Mansion House dinner on November 10: "A sense of exaltation pervaded Mr. Churchill's speech. It was the speaker's due. In the toil and sweat and tears to which he summoned his country he has borne a leader's share." Dalton wrote on November 12: "The self-respect of the British Army is on the way to being re-established. Last week . . . a British general was seen to rush in front of a waiting queue at a bus stop and to leap upon the moving vehicle. One onlooker said he would not have dared to do this a week before."

Alexander and Montgomery became Britain's military heroes of the hour, and indeed of the rest of the war. The former was especially fortunate to find laurels conferred upon him, for his talents were limited. Hereafter, Alexander basked in Churchill's favour. He conformed to the prime minister's beau ideal of the gentleman warrior. While forces under his command would endure many setbacks, they never suffered absolute defeat. Montgomery was a much more impressive personality, a superb manager and trainer of troops, the first important British commander to display the steel necessary to fight the Germans with success. Montgomery's conceit was notorious. In one of his proclamations in the wake of a victory, he asserted that it had been achieved "with the help of God." In the United Services Club, an officer observed sardonically that "it was nice Monty had at last mentioned the Almighty in dispatches." Yet Churchill and Brooke knew that diffidence and modesty are seldom found in successful commanders. Montgomery had few, if any, of the attributes of a gentleman. This was all to the good, even if it rendered him less socially congenial to the prime minister than Alexander. Gentlemen had presided over too many British disasters.

"Monty's" professionalism was allied to a shrewd understanding of what could, and could not, be demanded of a British citizen army in whose ranks there were many men willing to do their duty, but few who sought to become heroes. He does not deserve to rank among history's great captains, but he was a notable improvement upon the generals who had led Britain's forces in the first half of the Second World War. A carapace of vanity armoured him against prime ministerial harrowing of the kind that so wounded Wavell and Auchinleck. In the autumn and winter of 1942, it was the newcomers' good fortune to display adequacy at a time when the British achieved a formidable superiority of men, tanks and aircraft.

"We are winning victories!" exulted London charity worker Vere Hodgson on November 29. "It is difficult to get used to this state of things. Defeats we don't mind—we have all developed a stoical calm over such things in England. But actually to be advancing! To be taking places! One has an uneasy sense of enjoying a forbidden luxury." Aneurin Bevan said nastily that the prime minister "always refers to a defeat or a disaster as though it came from God, but to a victory as though it came from himself." Throughout the war, Bevan upheld Britain's democratic tradition by sustaining unflagging criticism of the government. To those resistant to Welsh oratory, however, his personality was curiously repellent. A dogged class warrior, he harried Churchill across the floor of the Commons as relentlessly when successes were being celebrated as when defeats were lamented. Bevan drew attention to the small size of the forces engaged at El Alamein and to the dominance of Commonwealth troops in Montgomery's army. His figures were accurate, but his scorn was at odds with the spirit of the moment, which was full of gratitude, as was the prime minister. At a Cabinet meeting on November 9, Churchill offered the government's congratulations to the CIGS and secretary of state for the army's performance. This was, wrote Brooke sourly later, "the only occasion on which he expressed publicly any appreciation or thanks for work I had done during the whole of the period I worked for him."

For a generation after the Second World War, when British perceptions of the experience were overwhelmingly nationalistic, El Alamein was seen as the turning point. In truth, of course, Stalingrad—which reached its climax a few weeks later—was vastly more important. Montgomery took thirty thousand German and Italian prisoners in his battle, the Russians ninety thousand in theirs, which inflicted a quarter of a million losses on Hitler's Sixth Army. But El Alamein was indeed decisive for Britain's prime minister. On November 22, he felt strong enough to allow Stafford Cripps to resign from the War Cabinet, relegating him to the Ministry of Aircraft Production. Churchill said of Cripps to Stalin: "His chest is a cage, in which two squirrels are at war, his conscience and his career." Cripps had pressed proposals for removing the direction of the war from the prime minister's hands. Now, these could safely be dismissed, their author sidelined. His brief imposture as a rival to the national leader was over. In the ensuing thirty months of the German war, though the British people often grew jaded and impatient, never again was Churchill's mastery seriously questioned.

As Montgomery's forces continued to drive west across Libya, the prime minister looked ahead. Fortified by Ultra-based intelligence, he felt confident that the combination of Eighth Army's victory at El Alamein and the Torch landings ensured the Germans' expulsion from North Africa. No more than anyone else did he anticipate Hitler's sudden decision to reinforce failure, and the consequent prolongation of the campaign. In November 1942, it seemed plausible that the entire North African littoral would be cleared of the enemy by early 1943. What, then, for 1943? The Chiefs of Staff suggested Sicily and Sardinia. This prompted a contemptuous sally from Downing Street: "Is it really to be supposed that the Russians will be content with our lying down like this during the whole of 1943, while Hitler has a third crack at them?" Churchill talked instead of possible landings in Italy or southern France, perhaps even northwest Europe. Though he soon changed his mind, in November he still shared American hopes for Roundup, a major invasion of the Continent in 1943. He also remained mindful of his commitments to Stalin, and was acutely anxious not to be seen again to break faith. He told the War Office on November 23: "I never meant the Anglo-American Army to be stuck in North Africa. It is a springboard and not a sofa."

The Americans were unjust in supposing that Churchill always shared the extreme caution of his generals. On the contrary, the prime minister was foremost among those urging commanders to act more boldly. As he told the House of Commons on November 11, "I am certainly not one of those who need to be prodded. In fact, if anything, I am a prod. My difficulties rather lie in finding the patience and self-restraint through many anxious weeks for the results to be achieved." For most of the Second World War, Churchill was obliged to struggle against his military advisers' fear of battlefield failure, which in 1942 had become almost obsessive. Alan Brooke was a superbly gifted officer, who forged a remarkable partnership with Churchill. But, if Allied operations had advanced at a pace dictated by the War Office, or indeed by Brooke himself, the conflict's ending would have come much later than it did. The British had grown so accustomed to poverty of resources and shortcomings of battlefield performance that it had become second nature for them to expect the worst. Churchill himself, by contrast, shared with the Americans a desire to hasten forward Britain's creaky military machine. It was not that Britain's top soldiers were unwilling to fight. It was that they deemed it prudent to fight slowly. Oliver Harvey noted on November 14, with a cynicism that would have confirmed Stalin in all his convictions: "The Russian army having played the allotted role of killing Germans, our Chiefs of Staff think by 1944 they could stage a general onslaught on the exhausted animal."

This is an important and piercing insight upon British wartime strategy from 1942 onwards. There was a complacency, here explicitly avowed by Harvey, about the bloodbath on the Eastern Front. Neither Churchill nor Brooke ever openly endorsed the expressed desire of their colleagues to see the Germans and Soviets destroy each other. But they certainly wanted the vast attritional struggle in the east to spare the Western Allies from anything similar. Most nations in most wars have no option save to engage an adversary confronting them in the field. The Anglo-Americans, by contrast, were quarantined from their enemies by eminently serviceable expanses of water, which conferred freedom of choice about where and when to join battle. This privilege was exercised wisely, from the viewpoint of the two nations. The lives of their young men were diligently husbanded. But such self-interested behaviour, almost as ruthless as Moscow's own, was bound to incur Russian anger.

The Allied invasion of French colonial Africa provoked a political crisis. By chance, Adm. Jean Darlan, Vichy vice president and foreign minister, was in Algiers when the Americans arrived. He assumed command of French forces which, to the surprise and dismay of U.S. commanders, resisted their would-be liberators with considerable energy, inflicting some 1,400 American casualties. There was then a negotiation, however, which caused Darlan to order his troops to lay down their arms, saving many more American lives. He was rewarded by Eisenhower, Allied supreme commander of Torch, with recognition as France's high commissioner and de facto ruler of North Africa. The British, unconsulted, were stunned. Darlan had collaborated enthusiastically with the Germans since 1940. It had seemed plausible that he might lead the French navy against Britain—de Gaulle thought so. "*La France ne marchera pas,*" he told Churchill, "*mais la flotte—peut-être*"; "France will not march [on Britain]. But the fleet—perhaps." Now, Darlan's betrayal of Vichy demonstrated his moral bankruptcy. In his new role, he rejected requests for the liberation of Free French prisoners in North African jails, and indeed treated such captives with considerable brutality. Many exiled Frenchmen missed a great opportunity in November 1942 to sink their differences and throw themselves wholeheartedly into the struggle against the Axis. A British senior officer wrote aggrievedly: "Although the French hate the Germans, they hate us more." De Gaulle, Britain's anointed representative of "Fighting France," was, of course, outraged by the Darlan appointment, as was Eden. The Foreign Office had supported its lofty French standard-bearer through many outbursts of Churchillian exasperation, and in the face of implacable American hostility.

Throughout Churchill's life, he displayed a fierce commitment to France. He cherished a belief in its greatness which contrasted with American contempt. Roosevelt perceived France as a decadent imperial power which had lacked British resolution in 1940. Entirely mistakenly, given the stormy relationship between de Gaulle and Churchill, the president thought the general a British puppet. He was determined to frustrate any attempt to elevate de Gaulle to power when the Allies liberated France. The Americans had none of the visceral hatred for Vichy that prevailed in London. Since 1940 they had sustained diplomatic relations with Pétain's regime, which in their eyes retained significant legitimacy. Here was a further manifestation of British sensitivities born of suffering and proximity, while the United States displayed a detachment rooted in comfortable inviolability.

In November 1942, British political and public opinion reacted violently to Darlan's appointment. Just as the country was denied knowledge of Stalin's excesses, so it had been told nothing of de Gaulle's intransigence. British people knew only that the general was a patriot who had chosen honourable exile in London, while Darlan was a notorious Anglophobe and lackey of the Nazis. When Churchill addressed a secret session of the Commons about the North African crisis on December 10, the mood of MPs was angry and uncomprehending. In private, since Darlan's appointment on November 8, Churchill had wavered. He disliked the admiral intensely. But he was also weary of de Gaulle's tantrums. He deemed the solidarity of the Anglo-American alliance to transcend all other considerations. He spoke to the House with remarkable frankness— such frankness, indeed, that after the war much of what he said was omitted from the published record of his speeches to the Commons' secret sessions.

"In war," he said, "it is not always possible to have everything go exactly as one likes. In working with Allies it sometimes happens that they develop opinions of their own . . . I cannot feel that de Gaulle is France, still less that Darlan and Vichy are France. France is something greater, more complex, more formidable than any of the sectional manifestations . . . The House must not be left to believe that General de Gaulle is an unfaltering friend of Britain. On the contrary, I think he is one of those good Frenchmen who have a traditional antagonism ingrained in French hearts by centuries of war against the English . . . I could not recommend you to base all your hopes and confidence upon him."

He went on to explain to the Commons that Gen. Henri Giraud, whom the Americans thought a more suitable prospective national leader than de Gaulle, had been smuggled out of France by the Allies with the explicit intention that he should assume authority in North Africa. This purpose was confounded only when Giraud was rebuffed by senior French officers on the spot. Averell Harriman wrote: "I have always deemed it tragic that the British picked De Gaulle and even more tragic that we picked Giraud." On December 10 MPs, perhaps impressed by how fully Churchill confided in them, were placated by his arguments. In private, the British government redoubled its efforts to get Darlan removed from office. The Americans rejected London's proposal—an implausible one— that Harold Macmillan, British resident minister in the Mediterranean, should assume temporary authority in Algiers. Anglo-American relations were still steeped in acrimony on this issue when it was unexpectedly resolved. On December 24, a young French royalist burst into Darlan's office at the Summer Palace and shot him dead.

Responsibility for the assassination remains one of the last significant mysteries of the Second World War. The immediate perpetrator, one Fernand Bonnier de la Chapelle, was hurried before a firing squad two days later. Oliver Harvey, Eden's private secretary, expressed most undiplomatic dismay about the execution: "It shows how wrong you get if once you compromise with evil. You find yourself shooting a good man for doing what you should have done yourself." It was a relief to almost everyone else, however, that Bonnier de la Chapelle was extinguished without revealing details of his plot. That there was a plot is certain. A priest granted Bonnier de la Chapelle absolution for his action before he walked into the Summer Palace, and modern conspiracy theorists have not failed to notice that Brigadier Menzies, chief of the SIS, was in Algiers on Christmas Eve. The historian David Reynolds believes that the British were implicated. The most likely explanation, however, is that the killer was incited by a Free French group. Though there is no evidence of de Gaulle's personal complicity, the ruthless behaviour of his London organisation between 1940 and 1944 makes this credible.

While Darlan's murder was ugly, it lifted a heavy shadow from Anglo-American relations. General Giraud was installed in Darlan's place. After tortured negotiations between Churchill, Eden and de Gaulle in London, the two Frenchmen achieved a grudging and distant accommodation. Macmillan's attitude reflected that of many British politicians and diplomats: "One comes away, as always after conversations with De Gaulle, wondering whether he is a demagogue or a madman, but convinced that he is a more powerful character than any other Frenchman with whom one has yet been in contact." This widely shared view caused most British politicians and diplomats to conclude that de Gaulle must continue to be supported. Churchill kicked against such realism, demanding with extravagant verbosity that the general should be dumped. At the last, however, he sulkily acquiesced. De Gaulle remained recognised by London, though not by Washington, as the principal representative of France in exile.

On November 29, 1942, Churchill minuted the Chiefs of Staff: "I certainly think that we should make all plans to attack the French coast either in the Channel or in the Bay of Biscay, and that 12 July 1943 should be fixed as the target date." Throughout this period, he pressed Roosevelt repeatedly to expedite the U.S. buildup in Europe so that the invasion of France could take place in 1943. Astonishingly or even perversely, given his almost unflagging enthusiasm for attacking the supposed "soft underbelly" of the Axis, on December 1 Churchill wrote to Brooke: "It may be that we should close down the Mediterranean activities by the end of June with a view to *Round-Up* in August." The U.S. Chiefs of Staff were wholly justified in their belief that their British counterparts were unwilling to execute a 1943 cross-Channel attack. But they did an injustice to Churchill in supposing that he, too, had at this stage closed his mind. In the course of the next year, he vacillated repeatedly.

Marshall and his colleagues also underrated the professional skill and judgement of Brooke and his team. American practise was founded upon an expectation that means could always be found to fulfil chosen national objectives. Thus, Roosevelt's Chiefs of Staff decided upon a purpose, then addressed the practical problems of fulfilling it. The British Chiefs, by contrast, forever struggling against straitened resources, declined to endorse any course of action unless they could see how it was to be executed. Such caution irked Churchill as much as the Americans: "I do not want any of your own long-term projects," he often expostulated to Brooke, shaking his fist in the CIGS's face. "All they do is cripple initiative."

In December 1942, it seemed to Britain's service chiefs that it would be impossible to mass sufficient landing craft to support a D-Day in 1943. Pressure on shipping was unrelenting in every theatre. In addition, there were never enough troops. British relations with the Australian government were further strained in December by Canberra's insistence that 9th Australian Division should return home from North Africa, even though the threat of a Japanese invasion of Australia had been lifted. Churchill cabled Curtin, the Australian prime minister, that he did not consider this decision "in accordance with the general strategic interests of the United Nations," but Canberra remained implacable. Curtin's enthusiasm for leaving his men to fight at British discretion cannot have been enhanced by news that, while only 6 percent of the Allied troops at El Alamein were Australian, they suffered 14 percent of Montgomery's casualties in the battle.

And now the two North African campaigns faltered. The Allies were confounded by Hitler's decision to reinforce the theatre. While this was strategically foolish, it rendered much more difficult the immediate task of the British and U.S. armies. American commanders and troops lacked experience. Though the Allies had numerical superiority in men, tanks and aircraft, the Germans fought with their usual skill and persistence. Alexander was famous for his courtesy and charm in addressing the Americans, but in private he railed at their military incompetence.

His reservations about Eisenhower's soldiers were just, but it ill-became a British officer to express them. The British contingent in Ike's forces, designated as First Army, was led by Gen. Sir Kenneth Anderson. Anderson proved yet another in the long line of his nation's inadequate field commanders—"not much good," in Brooke's succinct words of dismissal. Operations in Tunisia dispelled any notion that First Army's men were entitled to patronise their U.S. counterparts. Eisenhower was more willing than most of his countrymen to hide frustrations about Allied shortcomings, but he wrote in his diary on January 5, 1943: "Conversations with the British grow wearisome. They're difficult to talk to, apparently afraid that someone is trying to tell them what to do and how to do it. Their practice of war is dilatory." A few days later, he added: "British, as usual, are scared someone will take advantage of them even if we furnish everything." In another entry, he described the British as "stiff-necked." Richard Crossman of Britain's Political Warfare Executive thought that "getting on with Americans is frightfully easy, if only one will talk quite frankly and not give the appearance of being too clever, but v[ery] few English seem to have achieved it." In North Africa, they were less than impressed by Eisenhower. Though Churchill's scepticism was later modified by necessity and experience, that winter he was sufficiently irritated by the general's perceived blunders to evade fulfilment of Ike's request for a signed photograph of himself.

At the beginning of December, the prime minister sketched a design for 1943 based upon his expectation that Tunisia would be occupied by the year's end, and North Africa cleared of Axis forces a month later. By Christmas, this timetable was wrecked. Eighth Army's westward advance against Rommel progressed much more slowly than Churchill had hoped in early November. The Russian convoy programme was further dislocated by the need to keep large naval forces in the Mediterranean. The British joint planners, unambitious as ever, favoured making Sardinia the Allies' next objective. The prime minister dismissed this notion, urging that Sicily was a much worthier target. But he had begun to perceive that a 1943 D-Day in France was implausible.

Churchill now wanted a conference of the "Big Three," to settle strategy. He loved summits, a coinage which he invented, not least because he believed that the force of his own personality could accomplish ends more impressive than his nation's real strength could deliver, in its fourth year of war. But Stalin declined a proposal to meet in Khartoum, saying that he could not leave Moscow. Roosevelt was often less enthusiastic than Churchill about personal encounters. Just as the prime minister hoped for disproportionate results from these, to the advantage of his own country, so the president knew that the wealth and might of the United States spoke more decisively than any words which he might utter at a faraway conference table. But he liked the idea of visiting this theatre of war, and accepted Churchill's proposal for a meeting to be held in liberated Casablanca, on the Atlantic coast of North Africa.

The prime minister arrived in the Liberator *Commando* on January 12, 1943. His identification for security purposes as "Air Commodore Frankland" seemed absurd from the moment he landed at Casablanca, where he was greeted by a glittering array of brass. Ismay muttered: "Any fool can see that is an air commodore disguised as the Prime Minister." The "air commodore" was then driven to his appointed residence, the Villa Mirador, inside the closely guarded perimeter where the conference was to be held. He cabled Attlee: "Conditions most agreeable. I wish I could say the same of the problems."

The American service chiefs flew from Washington to Bathurst, in west Africa, where George Marshall was persuaded to disembark in a beekeeper's hood, to ward off mosquitoes. This was abandoned when the chief of the army found the welcoming party clad only in shorts. The Americans flew on to Casablanca with a lavish inventory of tents, cooking equipment and trinkets suitable for Arabs, lest they should be forced down in the desert, together with snowshoes and cold weather clothing for a possible onward trip to Moscow. The British had their own embarrassments. They felt humiliated by their makeshift air transports, which obliged exalted passengers to disembark dirty and dishevelled from the bomb bays. Roosevelt reached Casablanca on January 14, and was installed in a villa close to that of the prime minister. Churchill greeted him exuberantly. The two great men talked, while their Chiefs of Staff embarked upon the bruising process of seeking an agreement which the president and prime minister could then be invited to endorse.

The Casablanca conference was the most important Anglo-American strategic meeting of the war, because it established the framework for most of the big things which were done thereafter. It represented the high point of British wartime influence, because it took place at a time when projected operations still depended on preponderantly British forces. Its deliberations were warmed by victories in Africa, and knowledge of looming Russian triumph at Stalingrad. At El Alamein, to some degree, the British Army had retrieved its fallen reputation. Churchill answered a question from correspondents about Eighth Army's pursuit of Rommel: "I can give you this assurance—everywhere that Mary went the lamb is sure to go." British staffwork for the conference was superb, aided by the presence offshore of a purpose-equipped command ship.

However powerful were the reservations of British service chiefs about their prime minister's strategic wisdom, an intimate working relationship ensured that they knew exactly what he wanted. By contrast, even after thirteen months of war the U.S. president was "still something of an enigma to his American advisers," in the words of Marshall's authorised biographer. " . . . Roosevelt imposed no unified plan." His military chiefs "still had twinges of doubt about Roosevelt's lack of administrative order, his failure to keep the Chiefs of Staff informed of private high-level discussions, and his tendency to ignore War Department advice in favour of suggestions from officials of other departments." Marshall knew from the outset that he would lose his battle for a 1943 cross-Channel attack. In advance of the summit, Roosevelt had displayed his customary opacity. However, he threw out enough hints to show that he, like the British, favoured the capture of Sicily. Adm. Ernest King, for the U.S. Navy, was overwhelmingly preoccupied with the Pacific campaign. Quite uncharacteristically, the chief of staff of the army was blustering in suggesting that an early invasion of France remained plausible.

In the Combined Chiefs' conference room at the Anfa Hotel, Alan Brooke echoed Churchill's recent protests to Roosevelt about the scale of the American Pacific buildup, which, said the British CIGS, threatened the agreed principle of "Germany first." The British thus wrong-footed Marshall, by pressing him to justify the weight of resources committed to the Japanese war, to the detriment of Europe. This was a telling counter against American arguments that the British were prevaricating. Brooke then argued—implausibly in the eyes of history, and even in the context of January 1943—that a massive combined bomber offensive against Germany, together with home-grown Resistance movements among the peoples of occupied Europe, might relegate an invasion of France to a mere mopping-up operation. The Americans pressed the British for early offensive action in Burma, to assist the cause of China. This was perceived as a vital priority in Washington, a negligible one in London.

British politicians and generals had thus far found little to enjoy about the Second World War. But many of those at Casablanca—with the exception of Brooke, who seldom relished anything about the conflict—found the conference congenial. Harold Macmillan described "a general atmosphere of extraordinary goodwill." The weather was still cool, but flowers bloomed everywhere amid the palm trees and bougainvillea. Notice boards gave details of meeting venues and timings, then, "when we got out of school at five o'clock, you would see field marshals and admirals going down to the beach to play with the pebbles and make sand castles . . . The whole spirit of the camp was dominated by the knowledge that two men were there who rarely appeared in public, but whose presence behind the scenes was always felt . . . It was rather like a meeting of the later period of the Roman empire . . . There was a curious mixture of holiday and business in these extraordinarily oriental and fascinating surroundings . . . The whole affair was a mixture between a cruise, a summer school and a conference."

Churchill, in the sunniest of moods in this sunny clime, wrote to Clementine on January 15 about the Chiefs of Staff's deliberations: "At present they are working on what is called 'off the record,' and very rightly approaching the problems in an easy and non-committal fashion on both sides." This reflected a wildly benign view. While courtesies were maintained, especially at social encounters, the first two days of conference sessions were tense and strained. Marshall asserted repeatedly that if the British were as serious as they professed about helping the Russians, they could only do this by executing Roundup, a landing in Europe in 1943. The British emphasised their principled support for Roundup, but insisted that resources were lacking to undertake such a commitment.

There was a punishing schedule for Symbol, as the conference was code-named. The Combined Chiefs of Staff held thirty-one meetings in eleven days. At later conferences in Quebec and elsewhere, some closed sessions took place, without the usual congregation of staff officers in attendance, to allow a degree of frankness and indeed rudeness between the principals in breaking deadlocks. Ian Jacob was always conscious of American reservations about Brooke: "I think CIGS's extremely definite views, ultra-swift speech and, at times, impatience, made them keep wondering whether he was not putting something over on them."

Moran wrote of Brooke "throwing down his facts in the path of understanding with a brusque gesture. In his opinion it was just common sense;

he had thought it all out. Not for a moment did it occur to him that there might be another point of view." At Casablanca Admiral King's temper, and passionate Anglophobia, periodically broke out. During one meeting, he asserted that American public opinion would never stand for certain courses. Brooke shrugged, and said, "Then you will have to educate them." King, nettled, responded: "I thank you [to remember that] the Americans are as well educated as the British."

Churchill and Roosevelt attended only the conference plenary sessions, which took place in the evenings at the president's villa. Churchill wrote to Attlee about Roosevelt: "He is in great form and we have never been so close." Harold Macmillan observed that the prime minister handled the plenary meetings "with consummate skill." Away from the big table, "his curious regime of spending the greater part of the day in bed and all the night up made it a little trying for his staff. I have never seen him in better form. He ate and drank enormously all the time, settled huge problems, played bagatelle and bezique by the hour, and generally enjoyed himself." Churchill was dismayed that the British Chiefs intended that a descent on Sicily should take place in September. This, he said, was much too late. While he did not accept the feasibility of a 1943 landing in France, he nonetheless wanted an alternative major Allied initiative by summer.

De Gaulle arrived, sulking, to meet Giraud. Churchill marvelled at his intransigence: "The PM stood in the hall watching the Frenchman stalking down the garden path with his head in the air," wrote his doctor, Charles Wilson. "Winston turned to us with a whimsical smile: 'His country has given up fighting, he himself is a refugee, and if we turn him down he's finished. Well, just look at him!' he repeated. 'He might be Stalin, with 200 divisions behind his words. I was pretty rough with him. I made it quite plain that if he could not be more helpful we were done with it . . . He hardly seemed interested. My advances and my threats met with no response." Tears came to Churchill's eyes as he said: "England's grievous offence in de Gaulle's eyes is that she has helped France. He cannot bear to think that she needed help. He will not relax his vigilance in guarding her honour for a single instant."

If the British were enjoying themselves at Casablanca, most of the Americans were not. Ian Jacob wrote disdainfully: "Being naturally extremely gullible, the Americans calmly repeat any hare-brained report they hear." John Kennedy wrote of their senior officers: "We feel that the Americans have great drive and bigger ideas than ours, but that they are weak in staff work and in some of their strategic conceptions. The Americans are extremely difficult to know. Under their hearty and friendly manner one feels there is suspicion and contempt in varying degrees according to personality." This was so. A biographer of Eisenhower has written: "Many American officers found their British opposite numbers to be insufferable not only in their arrogance but in their timidity about striking the enemy." One of Ike's divisional commanders, Maj. Gen. Orlando Ward, wrote in disgust that Americans in North Africa found themselves reduced to the status of "a pointer pup . . . If someone with a red mustache, a swagger stick and a British accent speaks to us, we lie down on the ground and wiggle."

Harriman was dismayed by the eagerness of the U.S. Chiefs of Staff, when in exclusively American company, to badmouth the British. In their hearts, he thought, Marshall and his colleagues recognised the intractability of mounting a cross-Channel attack in 1943 as surely as did the prime minister and Brooke. But, in Jacob's words, "they viewed the Mediterranean as a kind of dark hole, which one entered into at one's peril. If large forces were committed . . . the door would suddenly and firmly be shut behind one." They still seemed obsessed, in the eyes of the British Chiefs, with fears that the Germans might intervene in North Africa through Spain. They deplored the sensation that the British, and explicitly Churchill, were exerting greater influence upon their president's decisions than themselves.

The strategic deadlock was broken, in the end, by a combination of harsh realities and skilful diplomacy, in which Dill played a key role. In January 1943, the Americans had 150,000 troops in the Mediterranean theatre. The British in the region fielded three times as many soldiers, four times as many warships and almost as many aircraft as the United States. Once the North African campaign was wound up, formations immediately available for follow-up operations—located both in Britain and the Mediterranean—would comprise four French divisions, nine American—and twenty-seven British. Churchill's own soldiers, sailors and airmen continued to predominate in the conflict with Germany, albeit employing an increasing proportion of U.S. tanks and equipment. Until this balance of forces shifted dramatically in 1944, British wishes were almost bound to prevail. When Brooke grew close to despair at one point in the discussions, on January 18, during a lunchtime break, Dill first told him that agreement was closer than he supposed. Then he warned that if this could not be achieved between the Chiefs, Churchill and Roosevelt must be invited to arbitrate, which neither British nor American commanders wanted: "You know what a mess they would make of it!"

That same afternoon, the major differences were resolved. The British formally endorsed American commitments for the Pacific, and promised to launch an offensive in Burma after the monsoon. The two nations committed themselves to a massive air programme against Germany, the Combined Bomber Offensive, to create conditions for a successful invasion of France in 1944. They agreed to invade Sicily in the summer of 1943, and left further follow-up operations against Italy to be decided in the course of events. A face-saving sop was agreed to about a cross-Channel attack: if resources and landing craft proved available, there should be a major operation to seize a bridgehead in France in August 1943. It is unlikely that anyone present anticipated fulfilment of this condition, but lip service continued to be paid to it for months ahead, not least in cables to Stalin. Churchill and Roosevelt added a few token points of their own for the Combined Chiefs' formal endorsement. They reasserted the importance of convoys to Russia and aid to China; the Combined Chiefs of Staff were urged to try for a Sicilian landing as early as June; and the need was emphasised to hasten concentration of forces in Britain for an invasion of France.

Roosevelt thanked Dill for his role in brokering an Anglo-American deal. The British officer responded: "My object is to serve my country and to serve yours. I hope and I believe that our interests are identical and in every problem that arises I try to look at it not as a British or an American problem, but as an Anglo-American problem." Yet Dill, customarily much more temperate than Brooke in his judgements on all things American, later wrote to the CIGS about the president: "The better I get to know that man the more selfish and superficial I think him . . . of course, it is my job to make the most and the best of him."

The London *Times* adopted a complacent view of the status of Britain's leader at the Casablanca conference, news of which was given to the public only after the principals departed: "Mr. Churchill . . . takes his place at the President's side with equal and complementary authority. The light now beginning to break wherever allied forces are engaged shows his stature enhanced by the deep shadows through which his country has passed." There was a deceitful assertion in the newspaper's report that de Gaulle and Giraud "have come together in the utmost cordiality."

Churchill perceived Casablanca as a great success. He was charmed by Roosevelt's geniality, though Harriman claimed that he was distressed by the president's announcement to the press at the close of the conference that the Allies would insist upon the unconditional surrender of the Axis powers: "He was offended that Roosevelt should have made such a momentous announcement without prior consultation and I am sure he did not like the manner of it. I had seen him unhappy with Roosevelt more than once, but this time he was more deeply offended than before. I also had the impression that he feared it might make the Germans fight all the harder." These remarks have bewildered historians. In reality, the president had discussed unconditional surrender with Churchill before his announcement. The prime minister, in his turn, signalled prior warning to the War Cabinet in London.

If he was indeed irritated with Roosevelt, it was probably a matter of emphasis. There could be no possible negotiation with the Nazi regime, but Churchill might have liked to leave a margin of hope in the minds of prospective German anti-Nazis that their nation could expect some mercy if Hitler was deposed. Just before Pearl Harbor, in November 1941, Churchill reminded the Cabinet that, when Russia was invaded, "we had made a public statement that we would not negotiate with Hitler or with the Nazi regime." He added that he thought "it would be going too far to say that we should not negotiate with a Germany controlled by the Army. It was impossible to forecast what form of Government there might be in Germany at a time when their resistance weakened and they wished to negotiate." It is likely that in January 1943 his view had not changed much about the desirability of a constructive vagueness in the Allies' public position towards non-Nazi Germans, even following the vast accession of American strength, and the transformation of the war.

At Casablanca, Harriman told the president of Churchill's apparent distress about unconditional surrender. Roosevelt seemed unmoved. Likewise, at dinner with the prime minister, he mused aloud about independence for Morocco, compulsory education, fighting disease and other social crusades. Churchill displayed impatience. Harriman believed that Roosevelt talked as he did for the fun of provoking the old British Tory. "He always enjoyed other people's discomfort," wrote the U.S. diplomat. "It never bothered him very much when other people were unhappy." As at all their encounters, Churchill strove to create opportunities for tête-à-tête conversations with the president, but found it increasingly difficult to catch him alone. Roosevelt had grown wary of Churchill's special pleadings, impatient of his monologues, and was probably also mindful of Marshall's resentment about any strategic discussion from which the chief of staff of the army was absent.

In the months that followed Casablanca, such disaffected figures as Albert Wedemeyer made no secret of their anger at the manner in which a strategy had been approved by their president against the wishes of U.S. armed forces chiefs. They believed that British enthusiasm for Mediterranean operations was driven by imperialistic rather than military considerations. This remained their view through the ensuing two years. Such sentiments became known in Congress and the media, and were responsible for much cross-Atlantic ill temper. But Marshall, with notable statesmanship, acknowledged the decisions graciously. He strove against the anti-British sentiment widespread among America's soldiers, and wrote to the army's public relations chief shortly after Casablanca, urging him to counter the "insidious business of stirring up ill-feeling between the British and us."

The conference broke up with fervent expressions of goodwill on all sides. The prime minister and president drove for four hours to Marrakesh, where they installed themselves at the Villa Taylor. That evening, as the sun was setting amid the snowclad Atlas Mountains, Churchill climbed to the roof to savour the scene, which had much moved him on a peacetime visit six years earlier. Now, he insisted that the president must share the experience. Two servants locked hands to form a chair on which the president was carried up the winding stairs, "his paralysed legs dangling like the limbs of a ventriloquist's dummy," as Charles Moran noted cruelly. The prime minister murmured: "It's the most lovely spot in the whole world."

It seems open to doubt whether Roosevelt gained equal pleasure from an experience which emphasised his own incapacity. Churchill could be notably insensitive to the vulnerabilities of others. Amid delight about winning his battle for the Italian commitment at Casablanca, he allowed himself to express an enthusiasm for Britain's ally which few of Roosevelt's conference team would have reciprocated: "I love these Americans," he told his doctor, "they behave so generously." Yet never again would his enthusiasm be so unqualified. If there had been a period of real intimacy between America's president and Britain's prime minister in 1941–42, when Roosevelt in some measure deferred to Churchill's experience of war, thereafter their relationship became steadily more distant. Mutual courtesies and affectionate rhetoric were sustained. But perceptions of national interest diverged with increasing explicitness.

Before the two leaders parted, they dispatched a joint cable to Moscow, outlining the conference decisions. "Whatever we decided to undertake in 1943 would have to be represented to Stalin as something very big," wrote Ian Jacob. The Soviet warlord was now told that there would be a landing in Europe "as soon as practicable." Neither leader supposed, however, that their studied vagueness would fool Moscow. "Nothing in the world will be accepted by Stalin as an alternative to our placing 50 or 60 divisions in France by the spring of this year," observed Churchill. "I think he will be disappointed and furious." The prime minister was correct. To Marshal Georgy Zhukov, by now his most trusted commander, Stalin vented anger about the inadequacy of aid from the Western Allies: "Hundreds of thousands of Soviet people are giving their lives in the struggle against fascism, and Churchill is haggling with us about two dozen Hurricanes. And anyway those Hurricanes are crap—our pilots think nothing of them."

There was one important aspect of the Casablanca conference, and indeed of Allied strategy-making for the rest of the war, which was never expressly articulated by Western leaders, and is still seldom acknowledged by historians. The Americans and British flattered themselves that they were shaping policies which would bring about the destruction of Nazism. Yet in truth, every option they considered and every operation they subsequently executed remained subordinate to the struggle on the Eastern Front. The Western Allies never became responsible for the defeat of Germany's main armies. They merely assisted the Russians to accomplish this. For all the enthusiasm of George Marshall and his colleagues to invade Europe, it remains impossible to believe that the United States would have been any more willing than was Britain to accept millions of casualties to fulfil the attritional role of the Red Army at Stalingrad, Kursk, and in a hundred lesser bloodbaths between 1942 and 1945. The U.S. Army never attained a strength that would have enabled it to meet the main strength of the Wehrmacht in France or anywhere else, irrespective of the date chosen for D-Day. Roosevelt and Churchill enjoyed the satisfaction of occupying higher moral ground than Stalin. At Casablanca, they decided Anglo-American strategy. However, historians who claim that the president and prime minister "charted the course to victory" use grossly inflationary phrases. Stalin and his commanders did that.

Roosevelt took off for home on January 25. Churchill lingered, and in those surroundings which he loved created his only painting of the war, a view of the Atlas Mountains. Then he embarked upon one of his most energetic rounds of wartime travelling, which pleased chiefly himself. Brooke was obliged to cancel a cherished scheme for two days' sightseeing and a Moroccan partridge shoot, to accompany his master to Turkey. The Cabinet opposed this expedition, which ministers considered futile. Churchill overruled them, hankering to revive his grand design, which had foundered in 1941, to raise the Balkans against Hitler. He also rejoiced in the exhilaration of touring the Mediterranean as a victorious warlord after the humiliations and frustrations of earlier years.

Having arrived at the Cairo embassy early on January 26, he recoiled from the ambassadress's offer of breakfast tea, demanding instead white wine. Brooke described the scene with fastidious amazement: "A tumbler was brought which he drained in one go, and then licked his lips, turned to Jacqueline [Lampson] and said: 'Ah! that is good, but you know, I have already had two whiskies and soda and 2 cigars this morning!!' It was then only shortly after 7.30 am. We had travelled all night in poor comfort, covering some 2300 miles in a flight of over 11 hours, a proportion of which was at over 11,000 ft., and there he was, as fresh as paint, drinking wine on top of two previous whiskies and 2 cigars!!" In Cairo, Churchill held significant conversations with his former historical researcher, the Oxford don William Deakin, now an SOE officer handling Yugoslavia. Deakin described the modest help being dispatched to the royalist Gen. Draža Mihajlović and his Cetnik guerrillas. He briefed the prime minister for the first time about the significance of Josip Broz, "Tito," who led a rapidly growing force of some 20,000 insurgents whom SOE believed to be less Communist than they appeared. Deakin's views were supported by Ultra intercepts, already known to Churchill, revealing German belief that the Communists represented a much more substantial military threat than the Cetniks.

The prime minister endorsed approaches to Tito, and Deakin himself was soon parachuted to the Croat leader's headquarters. Unbeknown to the British, the partisan chief spent the spring of 1943 parleying with the Germans about a possible truce that would free his forces to destroy Mihajlović. Nazi intransigence, however, obliged the partisans to fight the Axis. The British, and especially officers of SOE, were guilty of persistent delusions about Tito's politics. But they were right about one big thing: Hitler's determination to defend Yugoslavia and its mineral resources caused him to deploy large forces in a country well suited to guerrilla operations. There, as nowhere else in occupied Europe outside Russian territory, internal resistance achieved a significant strategic impact.

The military contingent in Churchill's party set off for neutral Turkey clad in borrowed and absurdly ill-fitting civilian clothes. Their visit to President Ismet Inonu on January 30 was no more successful than the Cabinet had anticipated. The Turks were full of charm and protestations of goodwill. Always fearful of Stalin, they valued British good offices to dissuade the Russians from aggression on their northern border. In the stuffy railway carriage in which the two sides met, the British were half embarrassed and half impressed by Churchill's insistence on addressing the Ankara delegation in his fluent but incomprehensible French. It would have made no difference had he spoken in Chinese. The Turks were uninterested in joining the war. Why should they have done so? It might be true that the Allies now looked like winners. But, since the Anglo-Americans had no designs on Turkey, it was surely prudent for that impoverished nation to maintain its neutrality. Brooke fretted about the security risks to the prime minister on an ill-guarded train in the middle of nowhere. Local rumour had broadcast news of the visit far and wide. The CIGS searched out Churchill's detective, whom he discovered eating a hearty supper in the dining car: "I told him that the security arrangements were very poor and that he and his assistant must make a point of occasionally patrolling round Winston's sleeper through the night. He replied in an insolent manner: 'Am I expected to work all night as well as all day?' I then told him that he had travelled in identical comfort with the rest of the party, and that I was certainly not aware that he had even started working that day."

But the visit passed off safely until Churchill's Liberator, taxiing out on his departure, bogged down on the runway at Adana. The prime minister made comic personal attempts to direct recovery operations, with much gesticulation to the Turks about the plane's sunken wheel, before having recourse to a spare aircraft. Back in Cairo on February 1, he learned of the surrender of the German Sixth Army at Stalingrad. Cabling to congratulate Stalin, he enthused about "a heavy operation across the Channel in August," involving between seventeen and twenty British and U.S. divisions. The Russians could scarcely be blamed for adopting a cynical view of their allies when the prime minister sought to sustain this charade within days of settling an entirely different agenda at Casablanca. He flew on to Montgomery's headquarters outside Tripoli. In a natural amphitheatre at Castel Benito, he addressed soldiers of Eighth Army. "After the war," he said, "when a man is asked what he did it will be quite sufficient to say 'I marched and fought in the Desert Army.' And when history is written . . . your feats will gleam and glow and will be a source of song and story long after we who are gathered here have passed away." With tears in his eyes, he took the salute as 51st Highland Division, led by its bagpipers, passed in review before him through the streets of Tripoli. He visited the 2nd New Zealand Division and eulogised Freyberg, its commander.

In Algiers, on February 6, he told former Vichyite military leaders that "if they marched with us, we would not concern ourselves with past differences." At last, the British were successful in achieving recognition for de Gaulle in North Africa. General Giraud was replaced as principal French authority by a National Committee of uneasily mingled Gaullists and Giraudists. American distaste for de Gaulle persisted. But Washington grudgingly acknowledged that the Free French, whose soldiers had been fighting the Axis powers while Vichy's men collaborated with them, must be permitted some share in determining their nation's future.

At this, the end of Churchill's Mediterranean odyssey, he mused aloud about the possibility of his own death. Ian Jacob noted his remarks: "It would be a pity to have to go out in the middle of such an interesting drama without seeing the end. But it wouldn't be a bad moment to leave— it is a straight run-in now, and even the cabinet could manage it." His words were significant, for two reasons. First, he knew as well as any man how plausible it was that he should die on one of his wartime air journeys, as so many senior officers did. Two members of the Casablanca secretariat were killed when their plane was lost on the journey home, news which Brooke ordered to be temporarily withheld from Churchill when it came through on the eve of his own flight to Turkey. General Gott, the Polish general Wladyslaw Sikorski, Air Marshal Sir Trafford Leigh-Mallory, Adm. Sir Bertram Ramsay, and Arthur Purvis, the head of Britain's Washington purchasing mission, were only the most prominent figures killed on RAF wartime flights—interestingly, hardly any prominent USAAF passengers fell victim to similar misfortunes. Churchill observed, when a North African takeoff was delayed by magneto failure, that it was nice of the magneto to fail on the ground. So indeed it was.

He was right also to perceive that the most critical period of his leadership was at an end. Many dramas still lay ahead, but Britain no longer faced any danger of falling victim to Nazi tyranny. The course was set towards Allied victory. Back in London on February 11, 1943, making a Commons statement about Casablanca, he observed that Great Britain and the United States were formerly peaceful societies, ill-armed and unprepared. By contrast, "they are now warrior nations, walking in the fear of the Lord, very heavily armed, and with an increasingly clear view of their own salvation." Mindful of the resurgent U-boat threat in the Atlantic, he stressed the sea as the principal area of danger. In response to a foolish question about what plans existed for preventing Germany from starting another war, he replied that this would provide fit food for thought, "which would acquire more precise importance when the present unpleasantness has been ended satisfactorily."

It would be absurd to describe Churchill, in the early spring of 1943, as having become redundant. But after three years in which he had done many things which no other man could, he was no longer vital to Britain's salvation. If in 1940–41 he had been his nation's deliverer, in 1942–43 the Americans owed him a greater debt than they recognised, for persuading their president to adopt the Mediterranean strategy. His strategic judgement had been superior to that of America's Chiefs of Staff. Hereafter, however, his vision became increasingly clouded and the influence of his country waned. For the rest of the war, Churchill would loom much larger in the Grand Alliance as a personality than as leader of its least powerful element. Henceforward, never far from the minds of both Roosevelt and Stalin was a form of the brutal question which Napoleon asked about the Pope: "How many divisions have the British?"

THIRTEEN

Out of the Desert

IN 1943, to Winston Churchill and to many British, Russian and American people, it sometimes seemed that the Western Allies spent more time talking than fighting Hitler's armies. Granted, large forces of aircraft battered Germany in a bomber offensive of which much was made in newspapers and cables to Stalin. The Royal Navy, with growing strength and success, continued to wage a vital defensive struggle to hold open the Atlantic convoy routes. U.S. forces fought savage battles with the Japanese in the Pacific. But this was the last year of the war in which shortage of resources severely constrained Anglo-American ground action. In 1944, a vast array of ships, planes, weapons and equipment generated by U.S. industrial mobilisation flooded forth onto the battlefields, arming Allied forces on land, at sea and in the air on a scale such as the world had never seen. Until then, however, Churchill's and Roosevelt's armies engaging the Axis remained pathetically small in comparison to those of the Soviets.

The British committed thirteen divisions to North Africa, the Americans six. Of these formations, eight would land in Sicily. Some eleven British divisions in varying states of manning and with insufficient equipment remained at home, training for operations in France or wherever else the prime minister decided to commit them. Additionally, hundreds of thousands of British troops were scattered along the North African littoral, and throughout Egypt, Palestine, Syria, Iraq, Persia and India. These performed logistical and garrison functions of varying degrees of utility but were not, as Churchill often reminded Alan Brooke, killing Italians, Germans or Japanese. The U.S. Marine Corps was deployed in the Pacific, while Gen. Douglas MacArthur directed a modest army contingent in Australia and New Guinea. In 1943, the latter campaign was dominated by three Australian divisions. A huge Indian army in India, supplemented by British units, pursued desultory operations, but seldom that year deployed more than six divisions against the Japanese. At a time when Stalin and Hitler were pitting millions of men against each other in the east, it is scarcely surprising that the Russians viewed their allies' Mediterranean activities with contempt.

Most Anglo-American historians agree that a D-Day in France in 1943 would have been a disaster. It is only necessary to consider the ferocity of the resistance the Germans mounted in Normandy between June and August 1944 to imagine how much more formidable could have been their response to an invasion a year earlier, when Hitler's power was much greater and that of the Allies much less. But it infuriated the Russians that the British and Americans exercised to the full their luxury of choice, such as Stalin lacked after June 1941, about when to engage a major German army. It is possible that the Allies might have got ashore in France in 1943, and stayed there. But the casualties of the campaign that followed would have been horrendous, dwarfing those of northwest Europe in 1944–45. While the Russians fought most of their war beneath the triple goads of patriotism, compulsion and indifference to human cost, the Anglo-Americans were able to husband lives until their industrial resources could be deployed to overwhelming advantage. They chose to deploy far smaller frontline ground combat forces in proportion to their national populations than either Russia or Germany. David French, author of an acute study of the British Army, observes: "In absolute terms the British reduced their casualties simply by abstaining for long periods of the war from fighting the kind of intensive land battles in which they were bound to incur heavy losses."

On February 13, 1943, when it was still hoped that the North African campaign could be wound up within a month, Churchill was exasperated to hear that the Sicilian landing could not take place before July. He cabled Hopkins in Washington: "I think it is an awful thing that in April, May and June, not a single American or British soldier will be killing a single German or Italian soldier while the Russians are chasing 185 divisions around." He, like the British people, was acutely conscious of the Russians' losses and—increasingly—of their victories in the Caucasus, at Kharkov, and at Stalingrad. He cabled Stalin constantly about the progress of the RAF's bomber offensive, and assured him mendaciously that the French invasion plan was being "kept alive from week to week." When the Chiefs of Staff asked him to press Moscow for information about Russian military plans, he demurred: "I feel so conscious of the poor contribution the British and American armies are making . . . that I should not be prepared to court the certain rebuff which would attend a request for information." In a flush of impatience, he asked his Chiefs if the British could launch Husky, as the Sicily operation was now code-named, on their own. *No* was the firm reply. But in asking the question, Churchill discredited American suspicions that he was reluctant for his soldiers to fight.

February's defeat at the Kasserine Pass, in Tunisia, where a German thrust drove back in a rout superior U.S. forces, had no strategic significance. Within days, Eisenhower's troops regrouped and regained the lost ground. But it dealt a decisive blow to hopes of an early end of the campaign. On February 27, Alexander reported on the state of U.S. forces and the three French divisions, mostly colonial troops, now joining the campaign: "Americans require experience and French require arms . . . Hate to disappoint you, but final victory in North Africa is not (repeat not) just around the corner."

It was a perverse feature of the war that while the British people showed fervent admiration for Russian achievements, they seldom displayed the same generosity towards Americans. The Grand Alliance spawned a host of Anglo-Soviet friendship groups in Britain, but few Anglo-American ones. A Home Intelligence report of January 14, 1943, declared: "At the time of Pearl Harbor, public interest in the US received a momentary stimulus which soon declined and has (in marked contrast to the attitude to Russia and things Russian) remained low ever since." When news of the Kasserine battle was released in Britain, Violet Bonham Carter recorded in her diary a friend's story of meeting a vegetable seller in Covent Garden who said: "Good news today, sir!" "Have the Russians done well?" "No—the Americans have got the knock." This, asserted Bonham Carter, represented "the universal reaction" to news of the reverse that had befallen Eisenhower's army. A best-selling novel of the time was *How Green Was My Valley*. Attlee jested unkindly that Alexander in North Africa was now writing a sequel, *How Green Is My Ally*. Churchill deleted from a draft of his memoirs a February letter to the king, in which he wrote: "The enemy make a great mistake if they think that all the troops we have there are in the same green state as are our United States friends." Americans were irked to read the findings of a Gallup poll that asked British people which ally was making the greatest contribution to winning the war. Some 50 percent answered "Russia"; 42 percent "Britain"; 5 percent "China"; and just 3 percent "the United States."

The British knew that the war was a long way from ending, and were resigned to that prospect. But after more than three years of bombardment, privation and defeats, weariness had set in. It is hard to overstate the impact of the blackout on domestic morale. Year after year, throughout the hours of darkness the gloom of Britain's cities was relieved by no visible chink of light. As the novelist Anthony Powell observed, few people's tempers were as sound in 1943 as they had been in 1939. The British were morbidly sensitive to American triumphalism, of which echoes wafted across the Atlantic from these allies who still ate prodigiously and had never been bombed. Harold Macmillan wrote with lofty disdain about the Americans around him in the Mediterranean: "They all look exactly alike to me—like Japanese or Chinese."

Tory MP Cuthbert Headlam lamented news of a later U.S. battlefield success: "I am told that our efforts are scarcely noted in the American press. I fancy that the Americans after this war are likely to be more swollen-headed and tiresome than after the last; they may well be more troublesome to us than the Russians." In their hearts, all these men knew that their country could accomplish nothing without the United States, that only American supplies—albeit dearly purchased—made the defeat of Hitler possible. But it was sometimes hard to avoid indulging ungenerous sentiments amid British consciousness that the struggle was reducing their own society to penury, while America grew relentlessly in wealth and might. If many upper-crust British people hoped that the Soviets and Nazis would destroy each other in the course of the war, most Americans seemed equally enthusiastic about the prospect of the British Empire becoming a casualty of victory.

The Russians expressed renewed impatience about lack of progress in the Mediterranean. Stalin cabled Churchill: "The weight of the Anglo-American offensive in North Africa has not only not increased, but there has been no development of the offensive at all, and the time limit for the operations set by yourself was extended." The Soviet leader said that thirty-six German divisions were being redeployed from the west to the Eastern Front, an unimpressive testimonial to Anglo-American efforts. Churchill persuaded himself that this show of anger reflected the influence of the Soviet hierarchy. He still cherished delusions that he possessed a personal understanding with Stalin, interrupted only when other members of the Moscow politburo demanded a harsher line with the imperialists. Anglo-Russian relations worsened again when the Admiralty insisted on cancellation of its March convoy to Archangel. German capital ships posed a continuing threat off northern Norway, while British naval resources were strained to the limits by Mediterranean and Atlantic commitments. In early spring, for the last time in the war, Allied decryption of U-boat signals was interrupted, with shocking consequences for several Atlantic convoys—forty-two merchant ships were lost in March, against twenty-six in February.

Churchill sought to placate Moscow by promising a dramatic increase in aircraft deliveries via Iran, and 240,000 tons of supplies in August. But, once again, British assurances were unfulfilled because of shipping and convoying difficulties. Stalin cared nothing about these. Why should he have done? He saw only that his armies were being called upon to destroy those of Hitler, aided by more Western words than action. After the war, Brooke expressed surprise on rereading his own diary: "It is rather strange that I did not refer more frequently to the news from Russia." Indeed it was. Some 2.3 million Russian soldiers—and millions more civilians—died in 1943, while British and American forces fighting the Germans lost around 70,000 killed, including aircrew. In Moscow's eyes, it seemed characteristic that the Western Allies should again suspend supplies to Russia, where the real war was being fought, for the convenience of their own marginal operations in North Africa. Hugh Dalton asked Britain's Moscow ambassador, Sir Archibald Clark Kerr, if there was a danger of the Russians making a separate peace with Hitler: "He says he would not rule this out, if we continue to seem to them to be doing nothing to help."

Anglo-Soviet relations were further soured by the Germans' April announcement of the discovery of thousands of bodies of Polish officers killed by the Soviets in 1939 at Katyn, near Smolensk. On April 15 Churchill told General Sikorski, the Poles' leader in Britain: "Alas, the German revelations are probably true. The Bolsheviks can be very cruel." In the Commons smoking room, when Duff Cooper and Harold Nicolson mentioned Katyn to the prime minister, he answered tersely: "The less said about that the better." He urged Sikorski not to make much publicly of the story, to avoid provoking Moscow. Amid Polish rage, this warning went unheeded. The "London Poles" publicly denounced the Russians, who promptly severed relations with them and announced the creation of their own Polish puppet regime. Churchill warned Stalin sharply that Britain, in its turn, would not recognise Moscow's Poles. Lines were now drawn. Moscow was bent upon a postwar settlement that brought Poland into a Soviet-dominated buffer zone. Churchill expended immense energy and political capital throughout the next two years in efforts to prevent such an outcome. Yet nothing could alter geography: Warsaw lay much closer to the armies of Stalin than to those of Churchill and Roosevelt.

It might be supposed that, in those days, Churchill's daily existence was eased by the facts that many of the big decisions were taken, his critics had been put to flight by battlefield success, and Britain's survival was no longer in doubt. But there was no relaxation for a man who had chosen personally to direct the war effort, in the midst of a global struggle, and whose existence was entirely focused upon hastening Allied victory. Ian Jacob described him in bed of a morning: "Sawyers brings the breakfast; then Kinna is sent for to take something down; meanwhile the bell is rung for the Private Secretary on duty who is asked for news, & told to summon someone, say CIGS or Pug. Then it is the candle for lighting cigars that is wanted. Then someone must get Hopkins on the phone. All this while the PM is half-sitting, half-lying in his bed, breathing rather stertorously, & surrounded by papers."

Elizabeth Layton, one of Churchill's typists, remarked that he hated any of his staff to speak, unless they had something of substance to say: "There is nothing in the world he hates more than to waste one minute of his time," she wrote to her parents.

"He is so funny in the car; he may dictate, or he may just think for the whole hour, mumbling and grumbling away to himself; or he may be watching the various things we pass, suddenly making little ejaculations like 'Oh—look at the lambs,' or 'What kind of aeroplane is that'—to which little reply is expected. I think he knows now that I have learned not to waste his time by making any fool observations, which one might have felt obliged to break the silence by doing."

That weekend, Churchill was at his most benign. "We had good news about Tunisia," Layton wrote to her parents, "so the boss was in a good temper, and really I've seldom had such fun. He was very nice to us all and treated us like human beings for once! Poor man, don't think I ever blame him for not doing so—it is so understandable." The prime minister displayed no appetite for a respite from responsibility, and welcomed companionship only to provide himself with an audience. For all his sociability, paradoxically Churchill remained an intensely private person. Moran thought that he kept his own counsel, "sharing his secret thoughts with no one . . . There is no one to whom he opens his heart. Brooke is too cold and critical; he always seems to be doubtful of the P.M.'s facts and often throws cold water on his pet projects." Alexander, by contrast, was a skilled flatterer. The accommodating Guardsman listened patiently to the prime minister's monologues. When he himself responded, "he is always so reassuring," in Moran's words, "always so sure that the P.M.'s plans are right." The companionship of courtiers and visitors sufficed to assuage Churchill's restlessness only for short periods. He was driven by a hunger for movement, action and the company of other great men, with whom he could advance great matters.

It had become plain that, even if other factors proved favourable, landing craft would be lacking for a French D-Day in 1943. Lack of shipping also made it necessary to abort a proposed amphibious landing in Burma. Churchill wanted to ensure that the Americans persevered with his Mediterranean strategy, and were neither deflected towards the Pacific nor persuaded to hold back their forces for a later descent on France. He was shocked and angry when he learned that Eisenhower had said that news of two German divisions deployed in Sicily might make it necessary to abort Husky. On April 8, he minuted the Chiefs of Staff that he was bewildered about how the American general could therefore have professed himself so eager for a 1943 invasion of France across the Channel, "where he would have to meet a great deal more than two German divisions . . . I trust the chiefs of staff will not accept these pusillanimous and defeatist doctrines, from whomever they come."

John Kennedy wrote, as he watched the prime minister compose one such missive: "I had never seen him dictate before, and it was most interesting. He mouthed and whispered each phrase till he got it right, & then said it aloud to the typist." Churchill suggested another meeting with Marshall and Hopkins in North Africa in April, but neither the War Cabinet nor the Americans favoured such a rendezvous. Instead, he decided to go to Washington again. On May 4, he set off from London to Clydebank, and thence onward aboard the great liner *Queen Mary* to New York.

Throughout the first half of the war, Britain confronted predicaments rather than enjoying options. Henceforward, however, vastly improved circumstances conferred opportunities, and promoted dilemmas. The North African campaign was at last approaching a close. On May 8, British forces entered Tunis and the Americans took Bizerta. At Casablanca, the Americans had endorsed an overwhelmingly British vision for further Mediterranean operations. The two subsequent Anglo-American conferences of 1943, code-named Trident and Quadrant, were dominated by British efforts to sustain the U.S. commitment made in January. Some of the contortions of Marshall and his colleagues reflected a desire to gain control of the Allied agenda, to resist British wishes simply because they were British. It seemed to the Americans intolerable that, when their cash, supplies, aircraft, tanks and—soon—manpower would overwhelmingly dominate future Allied operations, Churchill and his colleagues should still seek to dictate the nature of these.

Each side also cherished its own delusions. For instance, the Americans were uninterested in amphibious operations in Southeast Asia, because these would contribute nothing towards fulfilling their only strategic interest in the region, that of assisting Chiang Kai-shek's ramshackle war effort in China. On Churchill's part, he sailed to America in May determined to resist entanglement in the fever-ridden jungles of Burma, eager instead for "an Asiatic *Torch*"—possible landings on Sumatra, Java or Malaya, all fanciful. Shrewd strategists, notably including the

British general Bill Slim, understood that the American drive across the central Pacific would be the key element in Japan's defeat. British operations in Burma were chiefly designed to "show willing" to the United States, which goes far to explain the prime minister's cynicism about most things to do with the Asian war.

Churchill and his commanders were justified in their insistence that operations in Sicily, and thereafter some further exploitation in Italy, were indispensable. He told the Chiefs of Staff at a meeting aboard the *Queen Mary* on May 10: "The greatest step we could take in 1943 . . . would be the elimination of Italy." But the British woefully underestimated the difficulties of conducting a campaign on the mainland, and the likely strength of German resistance. They were rash enough to urge upon the Americans a view, reflecting their experience against Mussolini's troops in North Africa, that occupying most of Italy would be easy.

The Anglo-American armies needed to learn manifold lessons about command structures, air support and large-scale opposed amphibious landings. These the Mediterranean provided in 1943. But, when the Russians were fighting huge and bloody battles in the east, it is unsurprising that American officers recoiled from the prospect that their own ambitions for the coming year should be so modest. Many senior figures in the U.S. Army doubted that the British were sincere about supporting a French D-Day even in the spring of 1944. Marshall and his colleagues, and indeed Roosevelt, were apprehensive that once the Allies got themselves into Italy, they would not be able to easily extricate the forces which it would be essential to shift to Britain before the end of the year.

During Churchill's first days in America, he visited Roosevelt's retreat at Shangri-La in the Blue Ridge Mountains, and delivered another magnificent oration to Congress on May 19. When Halifax, at the Washington embassy, fussed that after the war the Americans might demand repayment of Britain's Lend-Lease debt, Churchill said truculently: "Oh, I shall like that one. I shall say, yes by all means let us have an account . . . but I shall have my account to put in too, and my account is for holding the baby alone for eighteen months, and it was a very rough brutal baby . . . I don't quite know what I shall have to charge for it." He was dismayed, however, by a perceived decline in Roosevelt's health. "Have you noticed that the President is a tired man?" he demanded of Moran. "His mind seems closed; he seems to have lost his wonderful elasticity." While it was true that the president's health was declining, the real significance of his changed mood was that he was less amenable to Churchill's blandishments.

The prime minister would have been even more troubled had he known that at this very moment the president was secretly pursuing a bilateral meeting with Stalin, excluding Churchill, through the good offices of the prewar U.S. ambassador to Moscow, the egregious Joseph E. Davies. Davies, like Stafford Cripps, was a devoted admirer of the Soviet Union. During his time in Moscow, he sought to persuade his wife that volleys she heard as NKVD firing squads executed victims of the purges were mere construction workers' jackhammers. Davies formed a large art collection from works sold to him at knockdown prices by the Soviet authorities, looted from galleries or confiscated from murdered state enemies. His adulatory memoir of his time in Russia was made into a 1943 Hollywood movie, *Mission to Moscow*, using a script authorised by himself. In May, Roosevelt provided a USAAF aircraft to fly Davies to Moscow carrying prints of the film for Stalin's edification. Though this deplorable figure failed to arrange the encounter Roosevelt sought, the president's willingness to employ him reflected shameless duplicity towards Churchill.

The Combined Chiefs of Staff, meanwhile, were locked in close, tense, almost continuous sessions under Marshall's chairmanship. Brooke, on May 13, made remarks which stunned and appalled the Americans. Dismissing prospects of an early invasion of France, he said that "no major operations would be possible until 1945 or 1946, since it must be remembered that in previous wars there had always been some 80 French divisions available on our side . . . The British manpower position was weak." Marshall responded icily: "Did this mean that the British chiefs of staff regarded Mediterranean operations as the key to a successful termination of the European war?" Sir Charles Portal interjected, in a fashion surely designed to limit the damage done by Brooke's brutal assertion, that "if Italy was knocked out this year, then in 1944 a successful re-entry into NW Europe might well be possible." British scepticism, said Portal, focused on the notion that a force of twenty to twenty-five divisions could achieve important results across the Channel on the continent of Europe, which was quite impossible "unless almost the entire bulk of the German Army was in Russia or the Balkans."

Brooke once again emphasised that the Red Army alone possessed sufficient mass to engage the full weight of the Wehrmacht: "Russia was the only ally in possession of large ground forces and our strategy must aim to help her to the maximum possible effect." He wrote in his diary that night: "It was quite evident that Marshall was quite incapable of grasping the objects of our strategy nor the magnitude of operations connected with cross-Channel strategy." The CIGS found the Trident conference one of the most gruelling and depressing experiences of his war. The exchanges that day illustrated his extreme caution, indeed pessimism. Brooke's repu-tation as a strategist is significantly damaged by his remarks at the Com-bined Chiefs of Staff meeting on May 13. Though Marshall was often wrong in 1942–43, thereafter it was Brooke whose judgement was suspect. If the British view prevailed, it was hard to imagine that D-Day would take place in 1944. Never since December 1941 had the two allies' military leaderships seemed so far apart.

Yet as the Americans fought back, the British gave ground. At last, Brooke's team acknowledged a "firm belief" that conditions for an inva-sion of France would exist in 1944. On May 19 the British accepted a tar-get date of May 1, 1944, for a landing in northern France by twenty-nine divisions. Lt. Gen. Sir Frederick Morgan was appointed to lead the COSSAC ("chief of staff to the supreme Allied commander") staff, which would plan the invasion. The outcome, Churchill cabled to Attlee on May 21, was agreement that Britain should have "a free hand" in the Mediterranean until November 1943. Success in Sicily would be exploited to advance the elimination of Italy from the Axis until concentration and redeployment of forces for the French landings began. Brooke wrote, after a meeting with Roosevelt and Churchill at the White House on May 21, "I do not think they realised how near we were to a failure to reach agreement!" He observed four days later that such conferences were

the most exhausting entertainments imaginable. I am convinced they do a lot of good in securing great understanding between us, and yet— they fall short insofar as our basic convictions remain unaltered. King still remains determined to press Pacific at the expense of all other fronts. Marshall wishes to ensure cross-Channel operation at expense of Mediterranean. [I still feel] that Mediterranean offers far more hope of adding to final success. Portal in his heart feels that if we left him a free hand bombing alone might well win the war. And dear old Dudley Pound when he wakes up wishes we would place submarine warfare above all other requirements . . . And Winston?? Thinks one thing at one moment and another at another moment. At times the war may be won by bombing . . . At others it becomes essential for us to bleed our-selves dry on the Continent because Russia is doing the same. At oth-ers our main effort must be in the Mediterranean . . . with sporadic desires to invade Norway and "roll up the map in the opposite direc-tion to Hitler"! But more often he wants us to carry out ALL opera-tions simultaneously!

Churchill was at his most ebullient by the time he and Roosevelt parted. At a final press conference at the White House with Roosevelt on May 26, he delighted the assembled correspondents by clambering onto a chair and giving his famous two-fingered V sign. Then he boarded a Boeing Clipper for Algiers, via Gibraltar, accompanied by George Marshall and Brooke. The three travelled together, to brief Eisenhower about the conference decisions. En route, the aircraft was struck by lightning, awakening Churchill from a deep sleep. He wrote wryly: "I had always wondered why aircraft did not mind being struck by lightning. To a groundsman it would seem quite a dangerous thing." On the day of their later return from Gibraltar, a British plane, on much the same course, whose passengers included the film star Leslie Howard, was shot down by a German fighter, with the loss of all on board. If the hazards of many wartime flights were unavoidable, that of Churchill and his party to Algiers surely entailed extravagant risk. Had the chief of staff of the U.S. Army perished with the prime minister and CIGS, the blow to the Grand Alliance would have been terrible indeed. The party arrived safely, however. As they neared the Rock, Brooke was curiously moved to see the prime minister, wearing what he described as a yachting cap, peering eagerly down through the clouds with a cigar clenched between his lips, looking out for the first sight of land. The soldier, so often exasperated by his master, perceived this as a glimpse of his "very human & lovable side."

Churchill spent eight happy days in Tunisia and Algeria, on one of them addressing a great throng of British troops in the ancient amphitheatre at Carthage. "I was speaking," he told guests at dinner that night, "from where the cries of Christian virgins rent the air while roaring lions devoured them—and yet—I am no lion and certainly not a virgin." Eisenhower and Montgomery expressed confidence about planning for the Sicilian landing. Marshall, however, made it plain that he was determined to reserve judgement about future Italian operations until the outcome of the Sicilian campaign became clear.

On June 4, Churchill flew home to Britain in a Liberator. Four days later, he offered a survey of the war to the House of Commons which was justly confident, though Marshall and his colleagues might have disputed his sunny portrayal of Anglo-American relations: "All sorts of divergences, all sorts of differences of outlook and all sorts of awkward little jars necessarily occur as we roll ponderously forward together along the rough and broken road of war. But none of these makes the slightest difference to our ever-growing concert and unity, there are none of them which cannot be settled face to face by heart-to-heart talks and patient argument. My own relations with the illustrious President of the United States have become in these years of war those of personal friendship and regard, and nothing will ever happen to separate us in comradeship and partnership of thought and action while we remain responsible for the conduct of affairs." Here was, of course, an expression of fervent desire rather than of unfolding reality.

If Churchill expressed satisfaction about the progress of the war, Stalin did not. He cabled Roosevelt, copied to Churchill, to express dismay at Anglo-American postponements of D-Day, then wrote direct to the prime minister on June 24: "It goes without saying that the Soviet Government cannot put up with such disregard of the most vital Soviet interests in the war against the common enemy." Two days later, Churchill responded by dispatching one of his toughest messages of the war to the Russian leader: "Although until 22nd June 1941, we British were left alone to face the worst that Nazi Germany could do to us, I instantly began to aid Soviet Russia to the best of our limited means from the moment that she was herself attacked by Hitler. I am satisfied that I have done everything in human power to help you. Therefore the reproaches which you now cast upon your Western Allies leave me unmoved. Nor, apart from the damage to our military interests, should I have any difficulty in presenting my case to the British Parliament and nation." He was growing weary of the Russians, writing a fortnight later: "Experience has taught me that it is not worthwhile arguing with Soviet people. One simply has to confront them with the new facts and await their reactions."

Yet many British citizens sympathised with the Russian view. "I am the last to plead Stalin's case," Clark Kerr cabled from Moscow on July 1, but it seemed to the British ambassador that the weakness in the British position lay "not in our inability to open this second front but in our having led him to believe we were going to." Beaverbrook, still chronically disloyal, wrote to Henry Luce, overlord of *Time* magazine, on July 2: "In my view there is an undercurrent of uncertainty [in Britain] whether an attack on Italy can, so far as Russia is concerned, attain the proportions of a real Second Front. The public are convinced that the chance has now come to take the fullest advantage of Russian successes. And no operation in the West which left unaffected the German dispositions in the East would for long meet with popular favour." Surrey court reporter George King agreed with Beaverbrook: "When Mr. Churchill received the freedom of London last week," he wrote on July 7, "he said it seemed clear that 'before the leaves of autumn fall, real amphibious battles will be in progress.' One hopes so, because much as all must dread the casualties, the allies owe such an action to Russia and the slaves of Europe." Oliver Harvey wrote from the Foreign Office: "To some of the Government it is incredible, unforgivable, indeed inadmissible, that the Russian can be so successful. This is the attitude of the W[ar] O[ffice]."

On July 10, Allied forces landed in Sicily under the command of Britain's Sir Harold Alexander. In Washington and London, ministers and generals knew that Husky was marred by all manner of blunders, great and small. The airborne assault was shambolic. Anglo-American command arrangements remained confused throughout the campaign. Italian troops showed no desire to fight seriously, but the two German divisions on the island displayed their usual high professionalism in resisting the attacks of Alexander's much superior forces. The British and American publics, however, knew little about the bungles. They perceived only the overriding realities that the landings were successful, and that within weeks Axis forces were driven from Sicily. Brooke, who had been profoundly worried about Husky because it reflected a British design, experienced a surge of relief. Churchill, rejoicing, urged the Chiefs of Staff on July 13 to plan ambitiously for follow-up operations in Italy: "Why should we crawl up the leg like a harvest bug, from the ankle upwards? Let us rather strike at the knee." He wanted early amphibious landings, even before Sicily was cleared, directed against Naples and Rome. On July 16, he told Smuts: "I believe the President is with me: Eisenhower in his heart is naturally for it."

Macmillan pitied Eisenhower, attempting to fulfil his role as Mediterranean supreme commander amid a constant bombardment of cables marked "private, personal and most immediate," and emanating variously from the Combined Chiefs of Staff, Marshall, Roosevelt, Churchill direct, Churchill through the Foreign Office, or Eden through the Foreign Office. "All these instructions," observed Macmillan laconically, "are naturally contradictory and conflicting." He and Ike's chief of staff, Walter Bedell Smith, endeavoured to sort and reconcile such communications and decide which should be acted upon.

Even as Churchill enthused about the prospects in the Mediterranean, he began to waver again about Overlord, as D-Day in France would henceforward become known. On July 19 he told the Chiefs of Staff that he now had doubts whether the forces available in Britain by May 1, 1944, would suffice for a successful landing "in view of the extraordinary fighting efficiency of the German Army, and the much larger forces they could so readily bring to bear against our troops even if the landings were successfully accomplished. It is right for many reasons to make every preparation with the utmost sincerity and vigour, but if later on it is

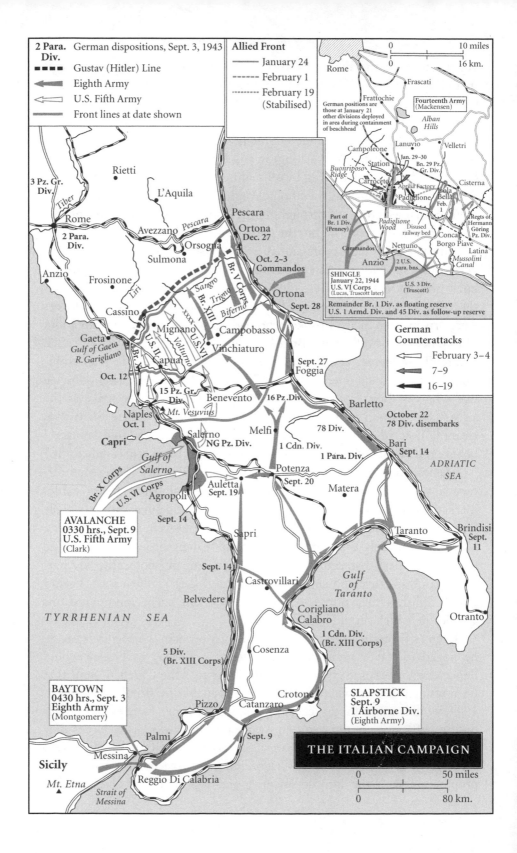

2 Para. Div. German dispositions, Sept. 3, 1943

▬▬▬ Gustav (Hitler) Line

◄━━ Eighth Army

◁━━ U.S. Fifth Army

━━━ Front lines at date shown

Allied Front

━━━ January 24

--- February 1

······ February 19 (Stabilised)

German positions are those at January 21 other divisions deployed in area during containment of beachhead

0 ____ 10 miles
0 ____ 16 km.

Rome
Frascati
Frattochie
Fourteenth Army (Mackensen)
Alban Hills
Campoleone Lanuvio Velletri
Jan. 29–30
Buonriposo Ridge Station Bn. 29 Pz. Gr. Div.
Carroceto Cisterna
Part of Br. 1 Div. (Penney) Aprilia Factory
Padiglione Wood Padiglione Isola Bella Feb. 1
Commandos *Padiglione Disused railway bed* Regts of Hermann Göring Pz. Div.
Nettuno Conca Borgo Piave
Anzio 2 U.S. para. bns. Latina
Mussolini Canal

SHINGLE January 22, 1944 U.S. VI Corps (Lucas, Truscott later) U.S. 3 Div. (Truscott)
Remainder Br. 1 Div. as floating reserve U.S. 1 Armd. Div. and 45 Div. as follow-up reserve

German Counterattacks
◁━━ February 3–4
◄━━ 7–9
◄━━ 16–19

3 Pz. Gr. Div.
Tiber
Rietti
L'Aquila
Pescara
Rome
Avezzano *Pescara*
Ortona Dec. 27
2 Para. Div.
Orsogna
Sulmona
Oct. 2–3 Commandos
Anzio
Frosinone
Liri
Sangro
Trigno
Br. V Corps
Br. XIII
Ortona Sept. 28
Cassino
Biferno
Gaeta
Gulf of Gaeta
R. Garigliano
xxxx U.S. VI
Mignano
Campobasso
Br. II
Volturno
Capua
Vinchiaturo
Sept. 27
Foggia
Oct. 12
15 Pz. Gr. Div.
Benevento
16 Pz. Div.
Barletto
October 22 78 Div. disembarks
Naples Oct. 1
Mt. Vesuvius
Salerno
HG Pz. Div.
Melfi
78 Div.
Bari Sept. 14
Capri
Gulf of Salerno
Br. X Corps
U.S. VI Corps
Agropoli
Auletta Sept. 19
1 Cdn. Div.
Potenza Sept. 20
Matera
1 Para. Div.
ADRIATIC SEA

AVALANCHE 0330 hrs., Sept. 9 U.S. Fifth Army (Clark)

Sept. 14
Sapri
Taranto
Brindisi Sept. 11

Sept. 14
Castrovillari
Gulf of Taranto
Belvedere
Corigliano Calabro
Otranto

TYRRHENIAN SEA

1 Cdn. Div. (Br. XIII Corps)

5 Div. (Br. XIII Corps)
Cosenza

BAYTOWN 0430 hrs., Sept. 3 Eighth Army (Montgomery)

Crotone
Pizzo Catanzaro

SLAPSTICK Sept. 9 1 Airborne Div. (Eighth Army)

Palmi
Sept. 9

Sicily
Messina
Mt. Etna
Reggio Di Calabria
Strait of Messina

THE ITALIAN CAMPAIGN

0 ____ 50 miles
0 ____ 80 km.

realised by all concerned that the operation is beyond our strength in May and will have to be postponed till August 1944, then it is essential that we should have this other consideration up our sleeves." He urged them to dust down Jupiter, his long-cherished scheme for a descent on northern Norway.

Oliver Harvey wrote admiringly in his diary on July 24 about the firmness with which Churchill had dismissed a proposal from Henry Stimson, visiting London, to advance the May 1 D-Day date: "On this, I'm thankful to say, the PM will refuse absolutely to budge. On military affairs he is instinctively right as he is wrong on foreign affairs. As a war minister he is superb, driving our own Chiefs of Staff, guiding them like a coach and four, applying whip or brake as necessary, with the confidence and touch of genius." Even though Stimson's proposal was indeed misguided, Harvey's accolade was ill-timed. Churchill's renewed foot-dragging showed him at his worst. For eighteen months, he had staved off Marshall's demands for early action in France. The British had the best of the arguments, at the cost of fuelling American mistrust and resentment. Back in May, Brooke had written, expressing exasperation with perceived American inconsistency of purpose, "Agreement after agreement may be secured on paper, but if their hearts are not in it they soon drift away again." Yet Marshall and his colleagues could have applied the same strictures to the British, with at least equal justice.

Lt. Gen. Sir Frederick Morgan, appointed by the Chiefs of Staff to lead Allied planning for Overlord, later became embittered when he perceived himself marginalised before D-Day eventually took place. Yet his postwar private observations cannot be wholly discounted. "I firmly believe," he told U.S. historian Forrest Pogue in 1947, "that [Churchill and his Chiefs] returned from Casablanca fully determined to repudiate the agreement that they had been forced there to sign with the Americans [for an invasion of France] . . . Apart from a mere dislike of the project, the British authorities proceeded to make every possible step to impede progress in NW Europe by diverting their forces, as unobtrusively as possible, to other theatres of war." Morgan expressed his conviction that his own appointment was made in the expectation that he would eventually be sacrificed "as a scapegoat when a suitable excuse should be found for withdrawing British support from the operation." Morgan cited the scepticism about Overlord of Admiral Cunningham, whom he quoted as saying, "I have already evacuated three British armies in the face of the enemy and I don't propose to evacuate a fourth." Morgan thought far more highly of the U.S. Chiefs of Staff and of Eisenhower than of the British leadership: The "Br. side . . . had suffered long series of disasters and had become 'casualty conscious' to a very high degree. Br manpower sit. In a state of bankruptcy. Inconceivable that Br. could play other than minor part in . . . reconquest of Europe from the Germans."

The Americans did not, of course, read the prime minister's July 19 minute to his Chiefs. But from the late summer of 1943 onwards, they perceived continuing British wavering about D-Day which they were now implacably—and rightly—committed to override. Churchill's hesitation about an invasion in 1944 reflected an apprehension about the fighting power of an Anglo-American army against the Wehrmacht which was unworthy of the Grand Alliance now that its means were growing so great, its huge mobilisation approaching maturity, and the Germans so much weakened by the Red Army. While a mere eight British and American divisions were fighting the only Allied land campaign against the Germans in Sicily, where the Allies lost six thousand killed, four million Russians and Germans had been locked in a death grapple at Kursk, which cost Hitler a decisive defeat and half a million casualties.

Churchill's new strategic vision embraced some wild notions. On July 25, Mussolini resigned and Italy's government fell into the hands of King Victor Emmanuel III and Marshal Pietro Badoglio. The Italian dictator's fall prompted Churchill to revive one of his favourite schemes, a descent on Italian-occupied Rhodes, designed to drag Turkey into the war. This ambition would precipitate a minor disaster later in the year, the Dodecanese campaign. Churchill's standing in American eyes would decline steadily between the summer of 1943 and the end of the war, and he himself bore a substantial share of responsibility for this. It is true that his wise warnings about the future threat posed by the Soviet Union were insufficiently heeded, but this was in significant part because the Americans lost faith in his strategic judgement.

He persuaded Washington that a new summit was now needed, to settle plans for Italy. This meeting, Quadrant, was to be held in Quebec. On August 5, 1943, he stood on the platform at Addison Road Station, in west Kensington, singing, "I go away / This very day / To sail across the sea / Matilda." Then his train slid from its platform northwards to Greenock, where his two hundred–strong delegation boarded the *Queen Mary*, once more bound for Canada. Churchill landed at Halifax on August 9, and remained in North America until September 14, by far his longest wartime sojourn there. Since it was plain that the big decisions on future strategy would be taken by Americans, as usual he sought to be on the spot, to deploy the weight of his own personality to influence them. While the Combined Chiefs of Staff began their debates in Quebec, Churchill travelled by train with his wife and daughter Mary to stay with Roosevelt. At

Niagara Falls, he told reporters: "I saw these before you were born. I was here first in 1900." A correspondent asked fatuously: "Do they look the same?" Churchill said: "Well, the principle seems the same. The water still keeps flowing over."

At Hyde Park it was stifling barbecue weather, and grilled hamburgers and hot dogs were served. Churchill fumed about reports of Nazi mass killings in the Balkans. He sought to interest the president in the region, with little success. Then the two leaders travelled to join the discussions of their Chiefs of Staff. The venue had been chosen to suit common Anglo-American convenience, without much heed to the fact that it lay on Canadian soil. Moran wrote that Canada's premier, Mackenzie King, resembled a man who has lent his house for a party: "The guests take hardly any notice of him, but just before leaving they remember he is their host and say pleasant things." Secretary of State Cordell Hull was permitted by Roosevelt to make one of his rare summit appearances at Quadrant, not much to his own satisfaction. Unwilling to share Churchill's late hours, one midnight Hull announced grumpily that he was going to bed. The prime minister expressed astonishment: "Why, man, we are at war!"

Stalin was making threatening demands for a Russian voice in the governance of occupied territories. He cabled from Moscow, demanding the creation of a joint military commission, which should hold its first meeting in Sicily. In Quebec, Churchill warned the Americans of "bloody consequences in the future . . . Stalin is an unnatural man. There will be grave troubles." He was correct, of course. Thereafter, the Russians perceived the legitimisation of their own conduct in eastern Europe. Since the Western Allies decreed the governance of territories which they occupied, the Soviet Union considered itself entitled to do likewise in its own conquests.

But the central issue at stake at Quebec was that of Overlord. The Americans were implacably set upon its execution, while the British continued to duck and weave. Wedemeyer wrote before the meeting that it was necessary for the U.S. Chiefs to advance a formula which would "stir the imagination and win the support of the Prime Minister, if not that of his recalcitrant planners and chiefs of staff." Marshall's biographer Forrest Pogue remarks of Churchill in those days: "As usual, he was full of guile." This seems to misread the prime minister's behaviour. Opportunism and changeability, rather than studied cunning, guided most of his strategic impulses. Yet there is no period of the war at which American dismay about British behaviour seems better merited than autumn 1943, as Eden and others acknowledged. Churchill and his commanders had always professed themselves committed to launching an invasion of Europe in 1944.

At the Casablanca and Washington conferences, the British had not argued against Overlord in principle, but merely fought for delay. Now, it seemed, they were altogether reneging.

Churchill opened at Quebec by reasserting principled support for an invasion. But he pressed for an understanding that if, in the spring of 1944, the Germans deployed more than twelve mobile divisions in France, the operation should not take place. Sir Frederick Morgan, director of the Anglo-American COSSAC staff planning the invasion, suggested that if the Germans appeared capable of deploying more than fifteen divisions against the beachhead in the two months following D-Day, a landing should be deemed impracticable. When the Germans flooded the river plains around Caen a few days before the conference began, COSSAC's operations division minuted: "The full implications of this have not yet been assessed, but it is quite possible that it will finally 'kill' *Overlord.*" Brooke made plain his continuing scepticism about the operation's feasibility.

The British case was that the immediate strategic priority was to seize the chances of the moment in the Mediterranean, rather than to stake everything upon a highly dangerous and speculative cross-Channel attack. In war, they argued, circumstances were always changing. They were more realistic than the Americans, in their understanding that a decision to enter Italy was irrevocable: "If we once set foot on the Italian mainland," wrote John Kennedy, "we are in for a big commitment . . . The Americans I am sure do not realise that limited operations in Italy eg against Naples, are impossible. We must either stop at the Straits of Messina or go the whole hog." On August 17, Churchill received a characteristically triumphalist signal from Alexander: "By 10 am this morning, the last German soldier was flung out of Sicily." The prime minister's enthusiasm for his favourite general seldom flagged, and he applauded the Sicilian operations as "brilliantly executed." Yet it had taken thirty-eight days for much superior Allied forces to expel less than three German divisions. Far from being "flung out" of the island, Gen. Albert Kesselring's troops had been inexcusably allowed to withdraw in good order across the Straits of Messina with most of their vehicles, guns and equipment.

At all the wartime conferences there was a notable contrast between the strains upon the principals, middle-aged and elderly men contesting great issues day and night, and the delights afforded to hundreds of attendant supporting staff who did not bear their responsibilities. The latter—staff officers, officials, clerks, ciphering personnel—worked hard at the summits, but also played hard. Duty officers were always in attendance upon the Teletype machines which rattled forth signals and reports around the clock. Typists composed minutes of that day's meetings, and planners prepared drafts for the next. But it seemed miraculous to these young men and a few women to be delivered for a few weeks from rationed, battered, darkened England, to bask in bright lights and prodigious quantities of food and drink, all of it free. Most danced and partied enthusiastically through the nights, while their great men wrangled. The English visitors revelled in shopping opportunities unknown in Britain for four years.

Events did more than changes of heart to patch up Anglo-American differences at Quebec. The known readiness of the new Italian government to surrender made it plain to Marshall and his colleagues that Allied forces in Sicily must advance into Italy. It seemed unthinkable to leave a vacuum, which the Germans could fill as they chose. The British, for their part, professed to endorse the Overlord plan presented by Morgan and the COSSAC team. There was much bickering about a cutoff date at which Allied divisions earmarked for France would have to be withdrawn from the Mediterranean, and thus about what objectives in Italy might feasibly be attained beforehand. Churchill, who dreamed of Allied armies driving towards Vienna, instead reluctantly endorsed a line from Livorno to Ancona by November, saying: "If we can't have the best, these are very good second bests." In the event, of course, Livorno and Ancona would not be taken until late June 1944. But in the heady days of August, the Allies still supposed that, once the Italians surrendered, the Germans would not make much of a fight for Mussolini's country.

When the conference ended on August 24, Ian Jacob wrote, "There seems to be general satisfaction, though I can't see what has been decided which takes us much beyond *Trident*." The "general satisfaction" was merely a matter of public courtesy. Brooke wrote, "The Quebec conference has left me absolutely cooked." He subsequently acknowledged that, at this time, he was close to a nervous breakdown. The Americans, for their part, were deeply unhappy about British conditionality towards Overlord. Churchill's team had not for a moment abandoned their determination to keep the Allies deeply engaged in Italy, even at risk to D-Day. After a brief break at a mountain camp for fly-fishing—not a pastime which Churchill indulged with much conviction—he travelled to Washington, where he spent the next five days urging the need to hasten operations in Italy. On September 3, Italian representatives signed the surrender document at Cassibile, in Sicily, while at dawn units of Eighth Army landed on the Italian mainland north of Reggio. Five days later, the British 1st Airborne Division seized the port of Taranto without opposition, which Churchill dubbed "a masterstroke" in a laudatory signal to Alexander.

On September 9, Mark Clark's Fifth Army staged an amphibious assault at Salerno, precipitating one of the bloodiest battles of the campaign, and a near disaster. "It was like fighting tanks barehanded," wrote an American infantry lieutenant colonel facing a panzer assault on the beachhead. "I saw riflemen swarm over the top of moving German tanks trying to shoot through slits or throw grenades inside. Other tanks would machine-gun them off. They ran over wounded men . . . and spun their treads." In the first hours, Clark was sufficiently panicked to order reembarkation, until overruled by Alexander. At painful cost, a perimeter was established and held. That day, as German forces raced to occupy key strategic positions across southern Italy, the Italian fleet set off toward Malta to surrender. Its flagship, the battleship *Roma*, was sunk en route by German bombers, once again demonstrating the Luftwaffe's skills against maritime targets. A mad Allied plan for a parachute assault on Rome was mercifully cancelled at the last moment. Even the Anglo-Americans at their most optimistic were forced to acknowledge that, against the Germans, such an adventure would prove disastrous.

Churchill was mortified that, once again, he was in Roosevelt's company when bad news came. He had held out to the president a prospect of easy victory in Italy. Now, instead, they learned of savage enemy resistance at Salerno. The British were naïve in anticipating that a surrender by Italy's government must of itself deliver most of the country into Allied hands. Brooke had told the Combined Chiefs of Staff on May 13: "He did not believe Germany would try to control an Italy which was not fighting." He and Churchill were importantly deceived by Ultra decrypts, which showed that the Germans intended to abandon most of Italy without a fight.

In the event, however, and as so often, Hitler changed his mind. This was a direct consequence of the Allied armies' poor showing, in German eyes, on Sicily and at Salerno. Anglo-American commanders and men exposed their limitations. Montgomery's performance was no more impressive than that of Mark Clark. The Germans were astonished by the ease with which some British and American soldiers allowed themselves to be taken prisoner. Kesselring, the German commander on the spot, concluded that defending Italy against such an enemy might be less difficult than he had previously supposed. He reported accordingly to Hitler. The führer responded by ordering a vigorous defence of the peninsula, a task Field Marshal Kesselring—appointed German supreme commander in Italy on November 6—undertook with extraordinary energy and effectiveness. Allied fumbling of the first phase of operations in Italy thus had critical consequences for the rest of the campaign.

In those days in America, Churchill became excited by a possible landing on the Dalmatian coast, using 75,000 Polish troops and possibly 2nd New Zealand Division. On September 10, Roosevelt departed for Hyde Park, leaving Britain's prime minister installed in America's capital: "Winston, please treat the White House as your home," said the president generously, urging him to invite whomever he liked. Churchill used this licence to the full, summoning Marshall to press upon him the case for hastening reinforcements to Italy. On September 14, at last he returned to Halifax, to board the battle cruiser *Renown* for home. His American hosts were glad to see him go. Their enthusiasm for his exhausting presence had worn as thin as their patience with his Mediterranean fantasies. Roosevelt's secretary William Hassett wrote after their visitor's previous Washington departure in May: "Must be a relief to the Boss for Churchill is a trying guest—drinks like a fish and smokes like a chimney, irregular routines, works nights, sleeps days, turns the clocks upside down . . . Churchill has brains, guts . . . and a determination to preserve the British Empire . . . He has everything except vision." This was a view now almost universal within Roosevelt's administration. Harry Hopkins told Eden, when the foreign secretary visited Washington, that the president—and indeed Hopkins himself—"loves W as a man for the war, but is horrified at his reactionary attitude for after the war." Hopkins spoke of the prime minister's age, "his unteachability."

The leaders of the United States were justly convinced that a cherry-picking approach to strategy was over. British evasions over a cross-Channel attack were no longer justifiable. If the Western Allies were to engage land forces on the continent of Europe in time to affect outcomes before the Russians defeated Hitler on their own, Overlord must take place in 1944. Henceforth, commitments in Italy must be adjusted to fit the overriding priority of the invasion of northwest Europe, and not vice versa. Marshall and his colleagues could scarcely be blamed for their exasperation at the prime minister's renewed pleas for a descent on northern Norway, and the fit of enthusiasm with which he was seized for operations in the eastern Mediterranean.

It was widely expected both in Washington and London that Marshall would command Overlord. Churchill had broken it to Brooke at Quebec that his earlier insouciant offer of this glittering appointment to the CIGS was no longer open. It was foolish of both the prime minister and the general to have supposed that a British officer might be acceptable for the role; and even more so of Brooke, by his own admission, to sulk for several months about his disappointment. He possessed a sublime, and exaggerated, conceit about his own strategic wisdom. He had grievously injured himself in American eyes by prevarications about Overlord, even more outspokenly expressed than those of the prime minister. Brooke had no just claim to command of an operation which for months he had denounced as premature.

Only an American could credibly lead this predominantly American crusade, but Roosevelt kept open until November his choice of appointee. Marshall wanted the job, sure enough. The chief of staff of the army indulged a brief fantasy that Sir John Dill might be his deputy, or even— if the British persuaded the president that one of their own should command—that the former CIGS might be supreme commander. Stimson wanted Marshall, because he believed that the chief of the army alone had the authority and strength of character to overcome the "mercurial inconstancy" of the prime minister.

There was always a paradox about Churchill as warlord. On the one hand, he had a wonderful instinct for the fray, more highly developed than that of any of his service advisers. Yet his genius for war was flawed by an enthusiasm for dashes, raids, skirmishes, diversions, and sallies more appropriate—as officers who worked with him often remarked—to a Victorian cavalry subaltern than to the director of a vast industrial war effort. The doctrine of concentration of force, an obsession of the Americans' and especially of Marshall's, was foreign to his nature. Though Churchill addressed his duties with profound seriousness of purpose, he wanted war, like life, to be fun. This caused the American service chiefs, earnest men all, not infrequently to think him guilty of frivolity as well as of pursuing selfish nationalistic purposes.

Brooke, meanwhile, was perhaps the greatest staff officer the British Army has ever known. But experience of fighting the Germans for four years with chronically inadequate resources had made him a cautious strategist, and by this stage of the war an unconvincing one. He shared the Americans' impatience, indeed exasperation, with Churchill's wilder schemes. But in the autumn of 1943 and indeed well into the winter, Brooke was joined to the prime minister in a common apprehension about Overlord. American resolution alone ensured that the operational timetable for D-Day was maintained. If Roosevelt and Marshall had been more malleable, the British would have chosen to keep larger forces in Italy, especially when Clark's and Montgomery's advances languished. D-Day would have been delayed until 1945.

The Allies were now committed to take the port of Naples, and exploit northwards to Rome. Thereafter, they had uneasily agreed that the future of the Italian campaign should be settled in the light of events. John Kennedy wrote on September 3: "It will be interesting to see whether the

Americans have judged the Mediterranean war better than we have." He himself bitterly regretted the scheduled diversion of forces from Italy to Overlord: "But we cannot dictate and I doubt if we could have done more to persuade the Americans. They are convinced that the landing in France is the only way to win the war quickly, & will listen to no arguments as to the mechanical difficulties of the operation or the necessity of weakening & drawing off the Germans by means of operations in the Medn." A month later, he was still writing about the arguments concerning "the Mediterranean versus *Overlord* strategy," but the War Office seemed resigned to the likely triumph of the latter: "In the end I suppose that we shall probably go into France with little opposition & the historians will say that we missed glorious opportunities a year earlier etc. etc."

Beaverbrook had tabled a new motion in the House of Lords calling for a Second Front. Now, he allowed himself to be wooed back into government as lord privy seal by Churchill's private assurance that the invasion was fixed for the following summer. Beaverbrook's recall exasperated many ministers. Churchill spoke passionately of his friend to W. P. Crozier of the *Manchester Guardian*: "I need him, I need him. He is stimulating and, believe me, he is a big man." Sir John Anderson felt it necessary to call the ministerial grumblers to order. "He says we must not make things too hard for the PM, who is conducting the war with great skill," recorded Dalton. "The PM was very unhappy during the period when Beaverbrook was not one of his colleagues. He is a sensitive artist, attaching great value to 'presentation' and the quality of the spoken word. He likes to have around him certain people, whose responses will not be jarring or unwelcome. He has valued Beaverbrook for this for many years. We must not, therefore, be too particular, even if things are sometimes not done in quite the most regular or orderly way." Beaverbrook's irregularities included, at this time, assisting Randolph Churchill to pay his debts. Though such subsidy certainly did not influence the prime minister's conduct towards him, it reflected a fundamentally unhealthy relationship, such as Beaverbrook contrived with many of his acquaintances.

The Americans found much more substantial cause for complaint about the prime minister's behaviour. Transatlantic debate remained dominated by British attempts to regard the Overlord commitment as flexible, and by U.S. insistence upon its inviolability. Given American primacy in the alliance which was now increasingly explicit, Churchill and Brooke must have known in their hearts that D-Day was almost certain to happen the following summer. But their attempts to suggest otherwise ate deeply into the fretwork of Allied trust. The Americans were wrong in supposing that Churchill's policy was directed towards ensuring that Overlord never took place at all. The huge and costly infrastructure already being created in Britain to support an invasion of France—not least Churchill's cherished Mulberry artificial harbours—disproved that allegation. The prime minister's "inconstancy" related exclusively to timing, but was none the less injurious for that. As for the British public, Surrey court reporter George King was unimpressed by Churchill's flowered phrases about the Italian campaign: "He says a Second Front is in existence, but I can't see it myself."

King's impatience with the progress of the war was widely shared. The left displayed astonishing venom towards the government. Communist Elizabeth Belsey, a highly educated woman of notable intellectual tastes as well as revolutionary fervour, remarked in a letter to her husband that the sudden death of Sir Kingsley Wood, the chancellor, "will save a piece of rope later on." In September 1943 she wrote that she and friends "amused ourselves making lists of the people who ought to be shot first when the time for shooting comes . . . [Walter] Citrine [TUC general secretary], Morrison, Halifax, [Lord] Londonderry, Lady Astor, [Sir James] Grigg and a heap more." She was disgusted by the hostility towards Russia displayed by the Polish exile government in London, and exulted at the deaths in a Gibraltar plane crash of its leader, General Sikorski, and the Tory MP Victor Cazalet: "No loss . . . I never did like having that Sikorski person on our side, did you?"

The Russians, of course, welcomed every manifestation of public dissatisfaction with Allied operations. On August 6, *Pravda* offered its readers one of its more temperate commentaries:

> It would be wrong to belittle the importance of allied military operations—the bombing of Germany by British and American air forces, and the importance of supplies and military material being provided to us. Nonetheless, only four German divisions opposed our allies in Libya, a mere two German divisions and a few Italian ones in Sicily. These statistics suffice to show the true scale of their operations as compared to those on the Soviet-German front where Hitler had 180 German divisions and about 60 divisions of his "allies" in the summer of 1942 . . . The armies of our British and American allies so far have had no serious encounters with the troops of Hitler's Germany. The Second Front so far does not exist.
>
> What is the Second Front? There is no cause to heed the waffling of certain people who pretend that they don't know what we are talking about; who claim that there is already not only a second front, but also, a third, a fourth, and probably even a fifth and a sixth front (including

the air and submarine campaigns, etc.). If we are to speak seriously about a second front in Europe, this would mean a campaign which, as comrade Stalin pointed out as early as the autumn of 1942, would divert, say, sixty German divisions and twenty of Germany's allies.

We know all the excuses used to justify delays . . . for example, arguments about [Hitler's] mythological "Atlantic Wall," and the allegedly insoluble shipping problem. The "impregnable Atlantic Wall" exists only in the minds of those who want to believe in such lies . . . After the success of the big allied landing in North Africa last year, and that of the allies' operation in Sicily, it seems ridiculous to cite "shipping problems" where a landing in Western Europe is concerned.

Amid the torrent of Soviet propaganda, bombast and insults, it was hard for British and American ministers and diplomats to know what Moscow's real views were. Long after the war, Molotov conceded to a Russian interviewer that Stalin was much more realistic than he ever acknowledged to Churchill and Roosevelt. The old Soviet foreign minister spoke gratefully of the Italian campaign:

Even such help was serviceable to us. After all, we were not defending England, we were defending socialism, you see. And could we expect them to help the cause of defending socialism? Bolsheviks would have been idiots to expect this! We just needed to be able to press them, to say "what villains you are!" . . . The [British] people of course realized that Russians were fighting while their own country wasn't. And not only did [the Anglo-Americans] hold back, they wrote and said one thing to us, but did something completely different. This made their own people see the truth and ask their own leaders: why are you playing tricks? This undermined faith in the imperialists. All this was very important to us.

In Britain, in 1943, there were more miners' strikes than at any time since 1900. The *Times* editorialised on September 3, amid another standstill in the pits: "The disposition to strike . . . may have some common origin. There is a too prevalent view that the war is going so well that effort in industry can be relaxed."

Trades unionist Jack Jones wrote to Brendan Bracken from Cardiff on October 3, 1943:

I think I may claim to know the mind of our workers, who are quite as loyal as the men and women of the Forces. Yet they strike! And at a time when it is more important than ever that they shouldn't. There may be even more disastrous stoppages through the coming winter.

Time itself induces war-weariness and frayed nerves, especially when what one is doing is unspectacular, out of the limelight and monotonous . . . A gnawing doubt is a sort of match ready to set aflame an undefined resentment against war conditions . . . What they want to steady them is a tonic. I remember during the last war the tonic effect on the South Wales miners of a visit and talk by L[loyd] G[eorge] . . . But this war dwarfs the last, and Mr. Churchill has had much more on his plate than ever L.G. had . . . My faith in Mr. Churchill's leadership is greater than ever. But I feel that now his capacity for inspiring others should, if it is humanly possible, be devoted to the steadying and inspiring of the splendid production line of our Home Front.

Churchill's failure to reach out explicitly to the industrial working class, beyond his national broadcasts and speeches, in part reflected disinclination. He preferred to address himself to the conduct of the war and foreign affairs; and in part, also, there was the fact that he had little to say to the factory people which they would wish to hear. He left to Ernest Bevin, in particular, the task of rallying Labour-voting miners and factory workers. He himself could not offer such people the vision of postwar Britain, and especially of socialist change, on which their hearts and minds were set. Churchill's single-minded commitment to victory lay at the heart of his greatness as a war leader. But for a growing number of his people, in the autumn of 1943 this was not enough.

In that season, between the Italian and Normandy campaigns, he made one of his last attempts to implement an explicitly British strategic initiative, against American wishes. He believed that the eastern Mediterranean offered opportunities for exploitation, which Washington was too blind to recognise. He therefore sought to address these with exclusively British forces. The consequence was a disaster, albeit minor in the scale of global war, which emphasised in the most painful fashion Germany's residual strength, together with the limitations of British power when the United States withheld its support.

FOURTEEN

Sunk in the Aegean

ONE OF THE most celebrated movie epics about the Second World War is Carl Foreman's *The Guns of Navarone*, based upon the 1957 thriller of that title written by Alastair Maclean. It depicts the landing of a British special forces team on a Greek island in the Aegean Sea. After stupendous feats of derring-do, they contrive the undoing of its German defenders, and safe passage for the Royal Navy's destroyers. Maclean's heroic fiction was rooted in an extraordinary series of episodes in the eastern Mediterranean in the autumn of 1943 which deserve to be better known to students of the war. This is not, however, because the saga ended in a British triumph, which it certainly did not, but because it provides a case study in a folly which was overwhelmingly Winston Churchill's responsibility. The story merits rehearsal and analysis, as an example of the consequences of the prime minister's capacity for rash boldness. If the scale of the campaign was mercifully small, the blunders were many and large. They help to explain why strategists who worked closely with Churchill sometimes despaired of his obsessions.

Rhodes and the much smaller islands of the Dodecanese to the north lie a few miles off the coast of Turkey, and are inhabited by Greeks. Italy had seized them in 1912. Three years later, France and Britain endorsed this shameless imperialist venture as part of the price for Italian accession to the allied cause in World War I. The islands, which possessed few merits save their barren beauty and strategic location, had been garrisoned by Italian forces ever since. They first attracted Churchill's attention in 1940. He believed, surely wrongly, that if the Allies could dispossess the Italians, such a visible shift of power in the eastern Mediterranean would induce Turkey to enter the war. At his behest, British commandos staged an abortive raid in February 1941. During the ensuing two years, the islands were recognised as beyond Allied reach. But as the Mediterranean skies brightened, Churchill's Aegean enthusiasm revived. At Casablanca, he urged upon the Americans the importance of seizing Rhodes and the Dodecanese, and tasked his own Chiefs of Staff to prepare a plan. In addition to troops, landing craft would be necessary, together with American fighters. The twin-engined Lightnings and British Beaufighters were the only planes with the range to provide air support over the Aegean from North African bases. The utmost "ingenuity and resource," urged Churchill, should be deployed to secure the Dodecanese.

Plans were made for two alternative scenarios: the first was a "walk in" to Rhodes with Italian acquiescence and the second was for Operation Accolade, an opposed invasion against German defenders. The priority of Sicily, however, meant that by late summer nothing had been done. John Kennedy wrote on August 13: "We shall have to shut down in the Aegean." The War Office assumed that the invasion of Italy, together with the commitment to Overlord, rendered operations there implausible. Instead, however, impending Italian surrender imbued the prime minister's Aegean ambitions with a new urgency. He remained convinced that an Allied coup there would precipitate Turkish belligerence. He ignored the irony that, because of the success of British deception plans designed to make Berlin suppose that the Allies might land in the Balkans, the Germans still deployed strong ground and air forces in the region.

The Americans were not interested in either the operation or the Turks as allies. They believed that British aspirations in the eastern Mediterranean were rooted in old-fashioned imperialism rather than contemporary strategy, and were resolutely opposed to any diversion of resources from Italy, never mind from Overlord. At the Quadrant conference in Quebec in August, they paid lip service to British enthusiasm for an Aegean initiative, but made it plain that whatever Churchill chose to do about Rhodes and the Dodecanese must be accomplished exclusively with the resources available to General Sir Henry "Jumbo" Maitland Wilson, now Middle East C-in-C in Cairo—"his jumbonic majesty," as Macmillan referred to this large and unimaginative dignitary. In other words, the British were on their own. There would be no USAAF Lightning fighters and precious few landing craft. At a time when concentration of force upon the Allies' central purposes seemed more important than ever before, U.S. leaders recoiled from an entirely gratuitous dispersal.

The prime minister was undeterred. He pressed Maitland Wilson to land on Rhodes anyway. The general, not one of his country's great military thinkers but compliant to Churchill's wishes, earmarked 4th Indian Division to execute Accolade. Then, however, it was decided that the Indians were needed in Italy. Maitland Wilson's cupboard was left almost bare of fighting units. He cabled Eisenhower on August 31: "Any enterprise

against Rhodes or Crete except an unopposed walk-in is now impossible."
The prime minister disagreed. The Germans were everywhere in retreat.
On the Eastern Front, they had just suffered devastating defeat at Kursk.
They had been expelled from Sicily. Italy was about to quit the war. On
every front, Ultra signal decrypts revealed German commanders bewail-
ing their flagging strength in the face of Allied dominance. Surely, in such
circumstances, even small forces boldly handled could crush the residual
German presence in the Aegean. While operations in the eastern
Mediterranean were to be conducted on a modest scale, they held special
lustre in the prime minister's eyes, because speed, dash and a touch of
piracy might yield an exclusively British triumph.

Urged on by London, Maitland Wilson resurrected Accolade, with
such ragbag forces as he could scrape together. On September 9, the
prime minister greeted news of the blossoming of his cherished project
with a notation: "Good. This is a time to play high. Improvise and dare."
Four days later, he cabled Maitland Wilson: "The capture of Rhodes by
you at this time with Italian aid would be a fine contribution to the general
war. Can you improvise the necessary garrison? ... What is your total
ration strength? This is the time to think of Clive and Peterborough, and
of Rooke's men taking Gibraltar ... " The prime minister's reference to
"ration strength" was, of course, a goad designed to remind the C-in-C of
the vast number of men under his command, scattered across hundreds of
thousands of square miles, and mostly employed on logistical or garrison
tasks. Churchill's stirring appeal to the memory of historic imperial triumphs ignored the fact that now Maitland Wilson's troops would face the
German army.

A fundamental doctrinal divide persisted throughout the war: the
British liked minor operations, while the Americans, with the marginal
exception of MacArthur, did not. U.S. strategic thinking, like that of the
Germans and Russians, was dominated by a belief in concentration of
force. The U.S. Army undertook very few raids such as the British, and
Churchill in particular, loved—Vaasgo, Bruneval, St.-Nazaire, Bardia,
Dieppe and many more. Special forces absorbed a dismayingly high proportion of Britain's most ardent warriors, volunteers attracted by the
prospect of early independent action rather than deferred encounters
within the straitjacket of a military hierarchy. Brooke deplored the prolif-
eration of army and marine commando units. He believed, probably
rightly, that their functions could have been as well performed by regular
units specially trained for specific tasks. The mushroom growth of British
special forces reflected the prime minister's conviction that war should, as
far as possible, entertain its participants and showcase feats of daring to

inspire the populace. In this, elite "private armies" fulfilled their purpose. But they ill-served the wider interests of the British Army, which was chronically short of good infantrymen for the big battlefields. Too many of Britain's bravest soldiers spent the war conducting irregular and self-indulgent activities of marginal strategic value.

Operations in the Mediterranean since 1940 had inspired the creation of a range of exotic units which basked in the prime minister's support and were led by social grandees or inspired eccentrics, often both. The Special Air Service (SAS), Special Boat Squadron (SBS), Long Range Desert Group (LRDG), Popski's Private Army, Special Interrogation Group and their kin provided much pleasure to the adventurous spirits who filled their ranks, and inflicted varying degrees of inconvenience upon the enemy. In the absence of more substantial forces, when Italy suddenly announced its accession to the Allied cause, Maitland Wilson turned to one of the "private armies," the Special Boat Squadron, to make the first moves in the Aegean. While its raiders began landing piecemeal on every island they could reach, the Middle East C-in-C dispatched its commander as an emissary to the Italians, to urge that they should turn on their local Germans without delay, and without waiting for British troops.

Maj. Earl Jellicoe, son of the World War I admiral, led the SBS with notable courage and exuberance. On the night of September 9, Jellicoe, abruptly plucked from the fleshpots of Beirut, was parachuted onto Rhodes with a wireless operator and an Italian-speaking Polish officer, who served under the nom de guerre of "Major Dolbey" and had never jumped before. Dolbey broke his leg on landing. Jellicoe, finding himself under fire as soon as he hit the ground, felt obliged to swallow the letter which he carried from Gen. Maitland Wilson to the Italian governor, Adm. Inigo Campioni. When the shooting stopped, however, Italian soldiers transported the British party to Campioni's quarters. There, with Dolbey interpreting amid acute pain from his shattered leg, Jellicoe set about persuading the governor to throw in his lot with the Allies.

At first, Campioni seemed enthusiastic. But when he learned that the British could hope to land only a few hundred men on Rhodes, while strong German forces were on the spot, his zeal ebbed. He was still prevaricating about active, as distinct from token, belligerence when the six-thousand men of the German assault division on Rhodes staged their own coup, overran the whole island and made prisoner its thirty-five-thousand-man Italian garrison. Jellicoe and Dolbey were fortunate that Campioni allowed them to sail away and avoid capture. Gen. Maitland Wilson wrote later that the admiral's spirit "was clearly affected by the delay and by the fact that the Germans were there while we were not."

The unfortunate Italian had the worst of all worlds. Having disappointed the British, he was later shot by the Germans.

Possession of Rhodes and its excellent airfields enabled Hitler's forces to dominate the Aegean. The only prudent course for the British was now to recognise that their gambit had failed, and to forsake their ambitions. Far from doing this, however, they set about reinforcing failure. If they could seize other nearby islands, they reasoned, these might provide stepping stones for an October landing on Rhodes, to reverse the verdict of September 11. This was a reckless decision, for which immediate blame lay with Maitland Wilson, but ultimate responsibility was Churchill's, who dispatched a stream of signals urging him on. Not only did the British lack strong forces to fight in the Dodecanese, but an opposed assault on Rhodes would have required a bloodbath, in pursuit of the most marginal strategic objective. The *Times* of September 18 reported the launching of operations in the Dodecanese, and commented: "Presumably the Germans will try to oust the allies by landing parachutists, but it is hoped . . . that the allied forces will be sufficient to thwart the German efforts. Thus the situation in the Aegean becomes pregnant with possibilities."

These were not, however, to the advantage of the British. What followed in September and October 1943 was a debacle, punctuated by piratical exploits and dramas, each one of which was worthy to become a movie epic. Patrols of the Long Range Desert Group, deprived of sands on which to fight since the North African campaign ended, began descending on the Dodecanese by landing craft, plane, naval launch, caique, canoe and boats of the superbly named Raiding Forces' Levant Schooner Flotilla. A company of the Parachute Regiment was flown into Kos by Dakota transports. Men of Jellicoe's SBS reached Kastellorizo in two launches, and thereafter deployed to other islands. Companies of the 234th Brigade, the only available British infantry force, were transported piecemeal to Kos and Leros as fast as shipping could be found to get them there.

A squadron of South African–manned Spitfires was deployed on Kos, which alone had an airfield. A British officer set up his headquarters there alongside that of the Italian garrison, their conspicuously hesitant new allies. An SOE officer landed on Samos, followed by several hundred troops. A general serving as military attaché in Ankara crossed from the Turkish coast. There were soon five thousand British personnel scattered through the archipelago. Command arrangements were chaotic, with almost absolute lack of coordination between army, navy and air force. But in those naïve early days, many of the newcomers relished the sensation of adventuring upon azure seas and islands steeped in classical legend. Amid

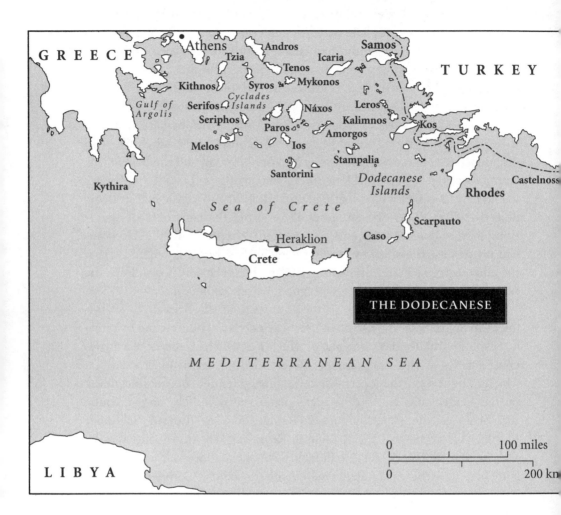

GREECE

Athens

Tzia

Andros

Tenos

Icaria

Samos

TURKEY

Kithnos

Syros

Mykonos

Gulf of
Argolis

Cyclades
Islands

Serifos

Náxos

Leros

Seriphos

Paros

Kalimnos

Kos

Amorgos

Melos

Ios

Kythira

Santorini

Stampalia

Dodecanese
Islands

Rhodes

Castelnoss

Sea of Crete

Scarpauto

Caso

Heraklion

Crete

THE DODECANESE

MEDITERRANEAN SEA

0   100 miles

0   200 km

LIBYA

barren hills, olive groves and little white-painted village houses, British buccaneers draped with submachine guns and grenades mingled with the local Greeks, breathed deep the Byronic air, pitched camps and waited to discover how the Germans would respond.

They were not long left in doubt. Hitler had no intention of relinquishing control of the Aegean. The Germans began to meet tentative British incursions by sea and air with their usual energy and effectiveness. Almost daily skirmishes developed, with RAF Beaufighters strafing German shipping, Luftwaffe planes attacking Kos, and LRDG patrols and elements of the SBS fighting detachments of Germans wherever they met them. An officer of yet another British intelligence group, MI9, was suddenly hijacked—and shot in the thigh—by pro-Fascist sailors on an Italian launch ferrying him between local ports. These men changed sides when they heard on the radio of Mussolini's rescue from mountain captivity by Otto Skorzeny's Nazi commandos. On several islands Germans, Italians and British roamed in confusion, ignorant of one another's locations or loyalties. Two British officers being held prisoner found their Austrian guard offering to let them escape if he might come too. Captors and captives often exchanged roles, as the tides of the little campaign ebbed and flowed.

The prevailing theme was soon plain, however. The Germans were winning. In Greece and the Aegean they deployed 362 aircraft, many of which were available to operate in the Dodecanese. The South African Spitfire squadron on Kos was hacked to pieces in the air and on the ground by Bf-109s. RAF Beaufighters lost heavily in antishipping strikes which inflicted little damage upon the enemy. German bombing demoralised the British—and still more, their new Italian allies—as well as destroying Dakotas shuttling to Kos. The Royal Navy was dismayed by the difficulties of sustaining supply runs to tenuously held islands while under German air attack. British troops in the area were a hotchpotch of special forces, intelligence personnel, gunners, infantry and "odds and sods" lacking mass, coherence and conviction. The main force, the 234th Brigade, had spent the previous three years garrisoning Malta, where its soldiers gained much experience of bombing, hunger and boredom, and none of battle. In the fifth year of the war, when in almost every other theatre the Allies were winning, in the eastern Mediterranean Churchill contrived to create a predicament in which British forces were locally vulnerable on land, at sea and in the air.

On the morning of October 3, the 680 soldiers, 500 RAF air and ground crews and 3,500 Italians on Kos awoke to discover that German ships offshore were unloading a brigade-strong invasion force whose arrival had been unheralded, and whose activities were unimpeded. It was a tribute to German improvisation that such an operation could be staged with little of the training or specialist paraphernalia which the Allies deemed essential for amphibious landings. The Germans mounted the Kos invasion with a scratch force, supplemented by a paratroop landing, against which the RAF launched ineffectual air strikes. The British defenders lacked both mobility and the will to leave its positions and mount swift counterattacks.

The island was twenty-eight miles long by six wide, with a local population of twenty thousand. Its rugged hills, impervious to entrenchment, rose to a height of 2,800 feet. In two days' fighting, 2,000 Germans supported by plentiful Stuka dive-bombers secured Kos for a loss of just 15 killed and 70 wounded. Some 3,145 Italians and 1,388 British prisoners fell into their hands, along with a mass of weapons, stores and equipment. Neither the Italians nor RAF personnel on the island showed much appetite for participation in the ground battle. It was a foolish delusion in London to have supposed that Italian troops, who for three years had shown themselves reluctant to fight the Allies, could any more readily be motivated to take on the Germans. The men of the Durham Light Infantry were outnumbered, inexperienced and never perceived much prospect of success. Churchill described the defence of Kos as "an unsatisfactory resistance." While this was true enough, responsibility rested overwhelmingly with those who placed the garrison there. The worst victims were the Italians, who paid heavily for their brief change of allegiance. On Kefalonia, in the Ionian Islands, the Germans had already conducted a wholesale massacre of four thousand "treacherous" Italian troops who surrendered to them. On Kos, the victors confined themselves to executing eighty-nine Italian officers. A few dozen determined British fugitives escaped by landing craft and small boat.

In the days and weeks following the loss of Kos, Churchill in vain pressed Eisenhower to divert resources from Italy to recapture it. A game of hide-and-seek persisted on other islands, between Hitler's units and British special forces. The Germans staged a further airborne landing on Astipálaia. Luftwaffe aircrew, accustomed to the depressed spirits of their countrymen who knew that the war was being lost, were amazed to find exuberant paratroopers in Junkers transports en route to a drop zone singing "*Kameraden*, today there is no going back." At this late stage of the war, the obliging British had provided the *Fallschirmjäger* with a field on which there were still victories to be won.

The Long Range Desert Group, whose men were not organised, trained or equipped to fight as infantry, suffered heavily in desultory battles. The main British force left in the Dodecanese was now based on Leros, an island much smaller than Kos and twenty miles farther north. When the British commander there heard that German prisoners on nearby Levitha had overpowered their captors and seized control, he packed fifty LRDG men onto two naval motor launches, and dispatched them to retake it. Once ashore, the LRDG fought a series of little actions with the Germans in which four raiders were killed and almost all the others captured. Just seven escaped at nightfall, by courtesy of the Royal Navy. Levitha remained firmly in German hands.

Churchill was dismayed by the unfolding misfortunes in the Aegean, as well he might be. Brooke wrote on October 6: "It is pretty clear in my mind that with the commitments we have in Italy we should not undertake serious operations in the Aegean . . . [but] PM by now determined to go for Rhodes without looking at the effects on Italy." Churchill chafed to travel personally to North Africa to incite the Americans to address themselves to Aegean operations. Cadogan wrote: "He is excited about Kos and wants to lead an expedition to Rhodes." The prime minister tried in vain to persuade Washington that Marshall should fly to meet him in Tunisia, there to be persuaded of the virtues of the Aegean commitment. On October 7, he wrote personally to Roosevelt: "I have never wished to send an army into the Balkans, but only by agents and commandos to stimulate the intense guerilla activity there. This may yield results measureless in their consequence at very small cost to main operations. What I ask for is the capture of Rhodes and the other islands of the Dodecanese . . . Leros, which at the moment we hold so precariously, is an important naval fortress, and once we are ensconced in this area air and light naval forces would have a fruitful part to play . . . I beg you to consider this." He argued that operations in the eastern Mediterranean were "worth at least up to a first-class division." The Americans disagreed. They transferred some Lightning squadrons to Libya, to operate in support of the Royal Navy in the Aegean. But, as other priorities pressed, after only four days these aircraft were withdrawn. Since the Germans were operating much superior Bf-109 single-engined fighters, it is anyway unlikely that the twin-engined Lightnings could have altered the local balance of airpower any more than did the RAF's Beaufighters. But the British were bitter that they were left to fight alone.

In London on October 8, the *Times* said of the fall of Kos: "It cannot be expected that every allied venture will be successful: but there is no denying that the state of affairs in the Dodecanese is causing disquietude." The paper asked pertinent questions about why stronger allied forces had not been committed. That day, Brooke wrote in his diary:

I am slowly becoming convinced that in his old age Winston is becoming less and less well balanced! I cannot control him any more. He has worked himself into a frenzy of excitement about the Rhodes attack, has magnified its importance so that he can no longer see anything else and has set his heart on capturing this one island even at the expense of endangering his relations with the President and with the Americans, and also the whole future of the Italian campaign. He refuses to listen to any arguments or to see any dangers! . . . The whole thing is sheer madness, and he is placing himself quite unnecessarily in a very false position! The Americans are already desperately suspicious of him, and this will make matters far worse.

All that Brooke said was true. That same day, October 8, Churchill wrote again to the Americans, addressing himself to both Eisenhower and the president: "I propose . . . to tell Gen. Wilson that he is free if he judges the position hopeless to order the garrison [of Leros] to evacuate . . . I will not waste words in explaining how painful this decision is to me." But Leros was not evacuated, as it should have been. Churchill cabled Maitland Wilson on October 10: "Cling on if you possibly can . . . If after everything has been done you are forced to quit I will support you, but victory is the prize."

On October 13, John Kennedy wrote: "It does seem amazing that the PM should spend practically a whole week on forcing forward his ideas about taking an island in the face of all military advice . . . Jumbo [Maitland Wilson] chanced his arm in occupying Kos and the other Aegean islands." Churchill cabled Maitland Wilson on October 14: "I am very pleased with the way you used such poor bits and pieces as were left to you. *Nil desperandum.*" And again to Maitland Wilson, copied to Eden: "Keep Leros safely." Churchill referred to Leros, absurdly, as a "fortress," even less meaningful in this case than when he had used the same word of Singapore and Tobruk. The C-in-C, desperate not to disappoint the prime minister, persevered. Given the scepticism of Brooke, why did not the CIGS assert himself, and insist upon withdrawal from the Aegean? The most plausible answer is that, when he was fighting Churchill almost daily about much bigger issues, notably including the prime minister's enthusiasm for an invasion of Sumatra, Leros seemed insufficiently important to merit yet another showdown. Win or lose, the campaign represented only a marginal drain on resources. Brooke could not hope to overcome the prime minister's passions on every issue. Instead he stood back, and watched the subsequent fiasco unfold.

For five further bloody weeks, the British struggled on in the Aegean. The battles which took place in that period at sea, in the air and on land more closely resembled those of 1941 than most Allied encounters with the Germans in 1943. The Royal Navy's cruisers, destroyers, submarines and small craft sought to sink German shipping and to bombard ports and shore positions, while subjected to constant air attacks by the Luftwaffe's Ju-88s. With the loss of the field on Kos, the RAF's nearest base was now three hundred miles away. Even old Stuka dive-bombers, powerless in the face of fighter opposition, became potent weapons when they could fly unchallenged.

There were many savage little naval actions in the narrow waters between the islands. On October 7, for instance, the submarine *Unruly* conducted an unsuccessful torpedo attack on a German troop convoy, then in frustration surfaced and engaged the enemy with its 4-inch deck gun until driven to submerge by the appearance of the Luftwaffe. *Unruly* later torpedoed a minelayer carrying 285 German troops. The cruisers *Sirius* and *Penelope* were caught by German bombers while attacking shipping, and *Penelope* was damaged. The destroyer *Panther* was sunk on October 8, and the cruiser *Carlisle* so badly damaged by bombers that after limping back to port she never put to sea again. The Luftwaffe sustained constant attacks on Leros's port facilities, so that British warships had to dash in, dump supplies, and sail again inside half an hour. The RAF's anti-shipping skills were still inferior to those of the Germans, and Beaufighter strikes cost the British attackers more heavily than their enemies. Even when raids were successful, such as one by Wellington bombers on the night of October 18, the results were equivocal: the Wellingtons dispatched to the bottom ships carrying 204 Germans, but also 2,389 Italian and 71 Greek prisoners. By October 22, a total of 6,000 Italian prisoners had drowned when their transports succumbed to British air strikes, while 29,454 Italian and British POWs had been successfully removed to the Greek mainland, and thence to Germany.

The cruisers *Sirius* and *Aurora* were badly damaged by Ju-88s, while German mines accounted for several British warships, including the submarine *Trooper*, which disappeared east of Leros. Almost every ship of the Royal Navy which ran the gauntlet to the Dodecanese, including launches, torpedo boats and caiques, had to face bombs, heavy seas in the worsening autumn weather, and natural hazards inshore. The destroyer *Eclipse* was sunk on October 23, while carrying two hundred troops and ten tons of stores. The navy reluctantly decided that it could no longer sail destroyers in the Aegean during daylight, in the face of complete German air dominance. The RAF continued to suffer heavily—in a single day's operations on November 5, six Beaufighters were destroyed, and four crews lost.

On October 31, the senior British airman in the Mediterranean, Air Chief Marshal Sir Arthur Tedder, wrote: "We are being pressed to throw good money after bad. The situation is fundamentally unsound." John Kennedy urged Alan Brooke on October 28 that "the price we were paying [for Leros was] too great and the return too small to justify retention." Brooke professed to agree, but told Kennedy that at that day's Chiefs of Staff meeting the decision had been made to hang on. It had now become too difficult to withdraw the garrison in the face of German air superiority. In his own diary, Brooke called Leros "a very nasty problem, Middle East [Command] have not been either wise or cunning and have now got themselves into the difficult situation that they can neither hold nor evacuate Leros. Our only hope would be assistance from Turkey, the provision of airfields from which the required air cover could be provided." Such aid was not forthcoming.

The final act of the Aegean drama began on November 12, when the Germans attacked Leros. The British garrison there, some 3,000 strong together with 5,500 Italians, had had several weeks to prepare for the inevitable. Nonetheless, when the moment came, everything that could go amiss did so. Before the landing the 234th Brigade was commanded by a short, red-faced and heavily moustached officer named Ben Brittorous, who embodied almost every deficiency of the wartime British Army. Brittorous was obsessed with military etiquette, and harassed officers and men alike about the importance of saluting him. In his weeks on Leros, he made himself loathed by his troops, and made few effective preparations to meet a German landing. When the Luftwaffe started bombing in earnest, he retired to his tunnel headquarters, and stayed there until relieved of his command a week before the German descent, to be replaced by a gunner officer, Brig. Robert Tilney. Tilney, newly promoted to lead in battle men whom he knew only slightly, was less disliked than Brittorous, but also seemed to lack conviction. He immediately redeployed his three infantry battalions around the island, with the intention of repelling a German landing on the beaches. Not only did this plan spread the defenders thin, but the brigade was very short of radios and telephones, so communication between Tilney and his units was tenuous, even before the Germans intervened.

On November 11, Ultra informed the British that a landing on Leros, Operation Typhoon, would be launched on the following day. Some 2,730 German troops were committed, a force inferior in size to that of the

Cairo, August 1942. *Front row, left to right:* Smuts, WSC, Auchinleck, Wavell; (*back row, left to right*) Tedder, Brooke, Harwood, Richard Casey

Arrival in Moscow: The bespectacled Molotov stands beside Harriman and Churchill in front of their Liberator.

A British fiasco is matched by a Soviet triumph. (*above*) A scene on the beach at Dieppe after the disastrous August 1942 raid. (*below*) Soviet troops advance towards their great victory at Stalingrad at the turn of the year.

Out of the desert at last. (*above*) The British advance at El Alamein in November 1942. (*left*) American war leaders at Casablanca in January 1943: Marshall and King sit on either side of Roosevelt, while behind them stand (*left to right*) Hopkins, Arnold, Somervell and Harriman.

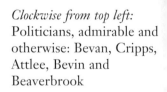

Clockwise from top left:
Politicians, admirable and
otherwise: Bevan, Cripps,
Attlee, Bevin and
Beaverbrook

Churchill with General Anderson at the Roman amphitheatre at Carthage, where he addressed men of Britain's desert army in May 1943

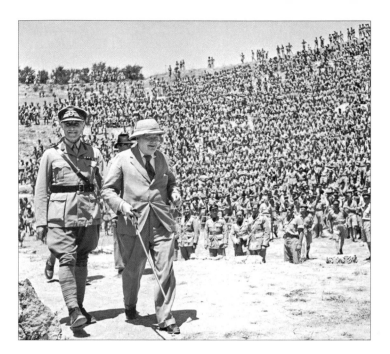

The agony of Italy: U.S. troops advance through characteristically intractable terrain.

Churchill's folly in the Dodecanese. (*above*) Beaufighters attack German shipping off Kos on October 3, 1943. (*below*) German troops land on the island, to achieve one of their last gratuitous military successes of the war.

At Algiers in June 1943 with (*left to right*) Eden, Brooke, Tedder, Cunningham, Alexander, Marshall, Eisenhower and Montgomery

With Clementine in the saloon of his special train in Canada in August 1943

The "Big Three" at Tehran on November 30, 1943, Churchill's sixty-ninth birthday, with the U.S. president visibly ailing

Churchill's last major personal strategic initiative of the war, t Anzio landing of January 1944

defenders. Yet the RAF and Royal Navy found themselves unable to do anything effective to interfere with enemy arrangements. Bad weather frustrated planned British bombing attacks on the Luftwaffe's Greek airfields. The commander of a Royal Navy destroyer flotilla in the area declined to brave a suspected minefield to attack the invasion convoy. The British official historian, Capt. Stephen Roskill, wrote later: "The enemy had boldly discounted any effective threat to the convoy by day, and by night he had concealed his vessels very skilfully; yet it seems undeniable that it should not have reached its destination virtually unscathed."

While the German main body landed from the sea, *Fallschirmjäger* staged another superbly brave and determined air assault. RAF strikes against the landing ships were notably less effective than the Luftwaffe's close support of the invaders. A fourth British battalion, landed to reinforce the 234th Brigade during the battle, failed to affect its outcome. Some of the island's defenders fought well, but others did not. The limited scale of British casualties indicates that this was no sacrificial stand. On Leros, from battalions of five hundred men apiece, the Royal West Kents lost eighteen killed in action, the Royal Irish Fusiliers twenty-two, the King's Own forty-five, the Buffs forty-two.

When the German parachutists landed, the defenders—in much superior numbers—should have launched an immediate counterattack on the landing zone before the invaders could reorganise. Instead, British infantry simply sat tight and fired from their positions. As the Germans advanced across the island, one British officer was dismayed to see men of the King's Own fleeing for their lives in the face of mortar fire. At 1800 on the first day, call sign Stupendous of the Long Range Desert Group signalled bitterly from Leros: "Lack of RAF support absolutely pitiful: ships sat around here all day, and Stukas just laughed at us." The defence lacked mobility and, more important, motivation and competence to match that of the Germans. Jeffrey Holland, who served as an infantry sergeant on Leros, wrote later: "As the battle progressed, it was evident that the enemy had deployed . . . first-class combat troops, who demonstrated consummate skill, courage and self-reliance." An SBS man wrote of one scene he observed: "We were amazed to see groups of British soldiers in open route order proceeding away from the battle area . . . The colonel stopped and interrogated them, and they said they had orders to retire to the south. Many were without arms, very dejected and exceedingly tired."

Brigadier Tilney lost control of most of his force at an early stage, and was enraged to find units retiring without orders. He threatened two battalion commanders with court-martial, for refusing to order their units into attack. Jeffrey Holland wrote: "The Germans moved quickly from one position to another, but never retreated; they seemed willing to accept a high rate of casualties. Their officers and NCOs exposed themselves to fire when directing an attack or defense. They seemed indifferent to the British fire which they sensed was tentative; neither well coordinated nor directed."

Some courageous British counterattacks were launched, in which a battalion commanding officer and several company commanders were killed. At midnight on November 14, Bletchley Park decrypted a German signal warning that the position of the invasion force on Leros was "critical," and that it was essential to get heavy weapons ashore immediately, to swing the battle. The Germans on Leros experienced nothing like the walkover they had enjoyed on Kos. But the defenders, having failed to take the initiative at the outset, never regained it. The terrain made it almost impossible for men to dig in, to protect themselves from bombing. Too often in World War II, British troops perceived enemy air superiority as a sufficient excuse to reconcile themselves to defeat.

Maitland Wilson kept alive Churchill's hopes of salvaging the battle, signalling on November 14 that British troops on Leros, though "somewhat tired," were "full of fight and well fed." To the end, the prime minister pressed for more energetic measures to support them. On the evening of the sixteenth, as he approached Malta en route to the Tehran conference, he signalled Air Chief Marshal Tedder: "I much regret not to see you tonight, as I should have pressed upon you the vital need of sustaining Leros by every possible means. This is much the most important thing that is happening in the Mediterranean in the next few days . . . I do not see how you can disinterest yourself in the fate of Leros." Tedder wrote scathingly afterwards: "One would have thought that some of the bitter lessons of Crete would have been sufficiently fresh in mind to have prevented a repetition . . . It seems incredible now, as it did then, that after four years' experience of modern war, people forgot that air-power relies on secure bases, weather, and effective radius of action."

At 1600 hours on November 17, the fifth day after the landing on Leros, Tilney surrendered. Some 3,000 British and 5,500 Italian soldiers became prisoners. Almost a hundred wounded men had been evacuated earlier. Several score bold spirits, including the inevitable and invincible Lord Jellicoe, escaped in small boats and eventually made their way to Turkey or small islands from which the navy rescued them. More than 3,000 British, Greek and Italian personnel were successfully evacuated from the nearby island of Samos before the Germans occupied this also. Including aircrew, the British lost around 1,500 killed in Aegean operations between September and November 1943—745 Royal Navy, 422 soldiers and 333 RAF. The Long Range Desert Group sacrificed more men in the Dodecanese than in three years of North African fighting. Five British infantry battalions were written off.

Hitler sent a congratulatory message to his Aegean commanders which was, for once, entirely merited: "The capture of Leros, undertaken with limited means but with great courage, carried through tenaciously in spite of various setbacks and bravely brought to a victorious conclusion, is a military accomplishment which will find an honourable place in the history of war." The British on Leros had advantages—notably that of holding the ground—which should have been decisive, even in the face of enemy air superiority. It was shameful that the German paratroopers were able to overcome larger numbers of defenders who knew that they were coming.

Adm. Sir Andrew Cunningham, now first sea lord, castigated the army: "I am still strongly of the opinion that Leros might have been held," he wrote later. Brigadier Tilney, a German POW until 1945, became principal scapegoat for the island's fall. Blame, however, properly ran all the way up through the chain of command to Downing Street. It was no more possible in 1943 than in 1941 for warships to operate successfully in the face of enemy air superiority. German aircrew were more proficient at attacking shipping than their British counterparts. British troops on Leros, as so often earlier in the war, showed themselves less effective warriors than their opponents. Far from being an elite, the 234th Brigade was a second-rate unit which conducted itself as well as might have been expected in the circumstances. The best apology that can be made for its performance is that it would have served little purpose for men to display suicidal courage, or to accept sacrificial losses, in a campaign which was anyway almost certainly doomed, and at a time when overall Allied victory was not in doubt.

If the defenders of Leros had repulsed the German assault in mid-November, British prestige might have profited, but the balance of power in the Aegean would have remained unchanged, and the agony would have been protracted. The Royal Navy would still have been left with an open-ended commitment to supply Leros under German air attack. As long as Rhodes remained in enemy hands, the British presence in the Dodecanese was strategically meaningless. Far from Leros offering a launching pad for a prospective assault on Rhodes, as Churchill insisted, it was merely a beleaguered liability. The Royal Navy suffered much more pain than it inflicted in the Aegean campaign, and achieved as much as could have been expected. In all, four cruisers, five destroyers, five minesweepers, two submarines and assorted coastal craft were sunk or badly damaged. The

RAF could not be blamed for the difficulties of conducting operations beyond the range of effective air cover, but its performance in the anti-shipping role was unimpressive. Some 113 aircraft were lost—the Beau-fighter squadrons suffered especially heavily, losing 50 percent of their strength. Once the airfields on Kos were gone, and with them any hope of operating single-engined fighters, the British should have cut their losses and quit.

In London, the news from the Aegean caused dismay and bewilderment in what was otherwise a season of Mediterranean victories. Cadogan at the Foreign Office wrote on November 16: "Bad news of Leros. Talk of, and plans for, evacuation brings back the bad days of '40 and '41. But it's on a smaller scale of course." A *Times* editorial on November 18 commented justly: "The fall of Leros should be a reminder that well-established principles of strategy cannot be neglected with impunity." A week later, the newspaper said that "this lamentable episode" raised issues about "the broad strategy of our whole Mediterranean campaign . . . on which British public opinion will require reassurance."

Britain's Aegean commitment was trifling in the grand scheme of the war, but represented a blow to national pride and prestige, precipitated by the personal decisions of the prime minister. Once more, he was obliged to confront the limitations of his own soldiers against the Germans—and the vulnerability of British forces without the Americans. John Kennedy described the operation as "a justifiable risk. [Maitland Wilson] could not know how strongly the Boche would resist." But four years' experience of making war against Hitler should have inoculated the prime minister and his generals against recklessness. Ultra intercepts warned London that the Luftwaffe was reinforcing the eastern Mediterranean, before British troops were committed. Churchill repeatedly deluded himself that bold-ness would of itself suffice to gain rewards. This might be so against an incompetent or feeble enemy, but was entirely mistaken against a su-premely professional foe who always punished mistakes. The daring of the prime minister's commitment was unmatched by the battlefield showing of those responsible for carrying it out. In the Aegean, as so often else-where, the speed of German responses to changing circumstances stood in stark contrast to faltering Allied initiatives.

Kennedy wrote that "the PM on paper has full professional backing for all that has been done." He meant that the Chiefs of Staff and Maitland Wilson formally endorsed the prime minister's commitments to the Aegean. In truth, however, almost all the higher commanders had allowed his wishes to prevail over their own better judgement. Brooke, unreason-ably, joined the prime minister in blaming the Americans for failing to provide support: "CIGS feels that the war may have been lengthened by as much as six months by the American failure to realise the value of exploiting the whole Mediterranean situation and of supporting Turkey strongly enough to bring her into the war." Yet why should the Americans have sought to save the British from the shipwreck of an adventure which they had always made it plain they did not believe in? There is, moreover, no reason to suppose that additional U.S. air support would have altered outcomes. Likewise, the British official historian seems mistaken in lamenting the diversion from the Aegean in the first days of the campaign of six Royal Navy fleet destroyers to escort battleships home to Britain. If the destroyers had remained, they would merely have provided the Luftwaffe with additional targets. Even had the British successfully seized Rhodes, it remains unlikely that Turkey would have entered the war, or that Turkish military assistance was worth much to the Allies.

Some of the same objections could be made to Churchill's 1943 commitment to the Aegean as to his earlier Balkan foray in 1915. The Dardanelles campaign, on which he impaled his First World War reputation, was designed to open the Black Sea route to arm Russia. Yet, even had the passage been secured, the World War I Allies were chronically short of weapons for their own armies, and had next to none to spare for shipment to the Russians. Likewise in 1943: even if Turkey had joined the conflict its army would have been entirely dependent on Anglo-American weapons and equipment. It was proving difficult to supply the needs of Russian, U.S., British and French forces. As the Americans anticipated, Turkey would more likely have become a hungry mouth for the Allies to feed than a threat to German purposes in the Balkans.

Churchill bitterly described the Aegean campaign as the Germans' first success since El Alamein. On November 21, he told his wife, Clementine, in a cable from North Africa: "Am still grieving over Leros etc. It is terrible fighting with both hands tied behind one's back." He was, of course, venting frustration that he had been unable to persuade the United States to support his aspirations. In his war memoirs, he described this as "the most acute difference I ever had with General Eisenhower." He cabled Eden from Cairo, also on November 21, to suggest that if questions were asked in Parliament about the Aegean, the foreign secretary should tell the House defiantly that the hazards of the operation were foreseen from the outset, "and if they were disregarded it was because other reasons and other hopes were held to predominate over them. If we are never going to proceed on anything but certainties we must certainly face the prospect of a prolonged war." This was lame stuff, to justify the unjustifiable.

Amazingly, at the meeting of the Combined Chiefs of Staff in Cairo on November 24, the prime minister renewed his pleas for an invasion of Rhodes. Marshall recalled: "All the British were against me. It got hotter and hotter. Finally Churchill grabbed his lapels ... and said: 'His Majesty's Government can't have its troops standing idle. Muskets must flame.'" Marshall responded in similarly histrionic terms: "Not one American soldier is going to die on [that] goddam beach." The U.S. Chiefs remained unwavering, even when Maitland Wilson joined the meeting to press the Rhodes case. The British, having lost to the Germans, now lost to the Americans as well. In a letter to Clementine on November 26, Churchill once more lamented the fall of Leros: "I cannot pretend to have an adequate defence of what occurred." Indeed, he did not. The Aegean campaign represented a triumph of impulse over reason that should never have taken place. It inflicted further damage upon American trust in the prime minister's judgement and commitment to the principal objectives of the Grand Alliance. It was fortunate for British prestige and for Churchill's reputation that it unfolded at a time when successes elsewhere eclipsed public consciousness of a gratuitous humiliation.

FIFTEEN

Tehran

IN THE EYES of the world, by the autumn of 1943 Churchill's prestige was impregnable. He stood beside Roosevelt and Stalin, the "Big Three," plainly destined to become victors of the greatest conflict in the history of mankind. "Croakers" at home had been put to flight by the battlefield successes denied to Britain between 1939 and 1942. Yet those who worked most closely with the prime minister, functionaries and service chiefs alike, were troubled by manifestations of weariness and erratic judgement. His government never lacked domestic critics. His refusal to seriously address issues of postwar reconstruction caused dismay. "His ear is so sensitively tuned to the bugle note of history," wrote Aneurin Bevan—for once justly—"that he is often deaf to the more raucous clamour of contemporary life." Eden agreed: "Mr. Churchill did not like to give his time to anything not exclusively concerned with the conduct of the war. This seemed to be a deep instinct in him and, even though it was part of his strength as a war leader, it could also be an embarrassment."

It was irksome for ministers responsible for addressing vital issues concerned with Britain's future to find their leader unwilling to discuss them, or to make necessary decisions. On November 29, 1943, Minister of Labour Ernest Bevin gained admission to the prime minister's bedroom, where so many remarkable scenes were played out in a setting sketched by Brooke: "The red and gold dressing gown in itself was worth going miles to see, and only Winston could have thought of wearing it! He looked rather like some Chinese mandarin! The few hairs were usually ruffled on his bald head. A large cigar stuck sideways out of his face. The bed was littered with papers and dispatches. Sometimes the tray with his finished breakfast was still on the bed table. The bell was continually being rung for secretaries, typists, stenographer, or his faithful valet Sawyers."

On this occasion, Bevin raised some issue of postwar planning. Churchill said crossly that he was just leaving to see Stalin, was preoccupied with other things, "and that it was really too much to go into detailed questions at the moment." Bevin was as angry as the prime minister. There was never a right time to catch Churchill to discuss matters which did not command his interest. Yet he was so often criticised for declining to seriously address postwar issues that it is salutary to compare his attitude with that of Hitler. The Nazis inflicted crippling economic, social and military damage upon their own empire by setting about forging a new "Greater Germany" while the war's outcome was still unresolved. Churchill's single-minded preoccupation with achieving victory may have dismayed his colleagues, but it seems a fault on the right side.

The British people acknowledged him as the personification of their war effort. As the dominance of the United States and the Soviet Union grew, his rhetoric and statesmanship were the most formidable weapons which his flagging nation could wield to sustain its place at the summit of the Grand Alliance. But in the last eighteen months of the war, while he received his share of the applause for Allied victories, he also suffered increasing frustrations and disappointments. At every turn, cherished projects were stillborn, favoured policies atrophied, because they could not be executed without American resources or goodwill, which were unforthcoming. This was by no means always to Britain's disadvantage. Some schemes, such as the Aegean campaign, did not deserve to prosper. But no man less liked to be thwarted than Churchill. Much happened, or did not happen, in the years of American ascendancy which caused the prime minister to fume at his own impotence.

His words remained as magnificent in the years of victories as they had been in those of defeats. He enjoyed moments of exhilaration, because he had a large capacity for joy. But the sorrows were frequent and various. He refused to abandon his obsession with getting the Turks into the war, cabling Eden, en route back from Moscow, that it was necessary to "remind the Turkey that Christmas was coming." He dismissed proposals summarily to depose the king of Italy, saying, "Why break off the handle of the jug before we get to Rome and have a chance of securing a new handle for it!" He told the Cabinet one day, amid a discussion about Soviet perfidy in publishing claims in *Pravda* that Britain had opened unilateral peace negotiations with the Nazis: "Trying to maintain good relations with a communist is like wooing a crocodile, you do not know whether to tickle it under the chin or beat it on the head. When it opens its mouth you cannot tell whether it is trying to smile, or preparing to eat you up."

In those months, Churchill's mind was overwhelmingly fixed upon the Mediterranean campaign. But it would have well served the interests of the British war effort had he also addressed another important issue which he neglected. Air Chief Marshal Sir Arthur Harris, C-in-C of Bomber Command, chose this moment to divert the bulk of his increasingly formidable force away from the Ruhr, where Lancasters and Halifaxes had been pounding factories for years, to attack Germany's capital. This was one of the major strategic errors of the RAF's war. The Berlin region was certainly industrially important, but was also far from Britain, heavily defended and often shrouded in winter overcast. This assault continued until April 1944, at a cost in RAF losses that became prohibitive, without dealing the decisive blow Harris sought—and which he had promised the prime minister. Bomber Command lost the "Battle of Berlin."

Much more significant, however, was the respite granted to the Ruhr. Adam Tooze's important recent research on the Nazi economy has shown that, in the autumn of 1943, the Ruhr's industries lay on the brink of collapse. If Bomber Command had continued its assault, instead of switching targets eastwards, the consequences for Hitler's war machine might have been dramatic. Allied intelligence about German production was poor. One of Harris's major mistakes as director of the bomber offensive was failure to grasp the importance of repeating blows against damaged targets. He allowed himself to be misled about his force's achievements by air photographs of devastated cities.

So, too, did the prime minister. To explain why he left the RAF to its own devices for much of the war, it is necessary to acknowledge how little reliable information was available about what bombing was, or was not, doing to Germany. The progress of Britain's armies was readily measured by following their advances or retreats on the map; that of the Royal Navy, by examining statistics of sinkings. But, once the Battle of Britain was won, the RAF's performance was chiefly judged by assessments, often spurious, produced by its own staff officers. Nobody, including Portal, Harris and Churchill, really knew what bombing was achieving, though soldiers and sailors believed it was much less than airmen claimed. The prime minister had a strong vested interest in thinking the best of British bombing. He trumpeted its achievements to the Americans, and even more to Stalin, to mollify their frustration about the meagre scale of Western ground operations. It would have been a major political embarrassment had evidence emerged that the strategic air offensive was doing less than Harris claimed.

Thus, between 1942 and the 1944 controversy about bombing the French rail network ahead of Overlord, Churchill never sought an independent assessment of what Bomber Command was contributing, though it consumed around one-third of Britain's entire war effort. Harris persuaded the prime minister that his aircraft wreaked havoc, as they did. But dramatic images of flame and destruction in the Reich were unaccompanied by rigorous analysis of German industry, about which intelligence was anyway sketchy and most of the RAF's data plain wrong. Harris, like his American counterparts, was left free to fight his battle as he himself saw fit, to pursue an obsessive attempt to prove that bombing could win the war without much input of accurate evidence or imagination. This was a serious omission on the part of the prime minister, and a missed opportunity for the Royal Air Force.

In this later period of the war, the fatigue of Churchill's people grew alongside American and Russian might. The Aegean campaign represented a minor demonstration of British vulnerability, but larger ones lay ahead. In the late autumn of 1943, four issues dominated Britain's military agenda: the campaign in Italy; the commitment to Overlord; residual possibilities of ambitious adventures in the Balkans; and Operation Buccaneer, a putative amphibious landing in Burma. On November 6, Sir Archibald Clark Kerr warned from Moscow of Russian fears that the British were still hostile to Overlord. Churchill responded: "I will do everything in human power to animate the forward movement on which my heart is set at this moment." But the words "forward movement" embraced a range of possible operations, some in the Mediterranean, of which Overlord was only one. Dalton wrote after a Cabinet meeting: "In an expansive moment Winston told us his apprehensions about the '*Overlord*' policy which the Americans have forced upon us, involving a dangerous and time-wasting straddle of our transport and landing craft between two objectives when we might have gone on more effectively in Italy and the Balkans."

For some weeks, Churchill had been pressing for a meeting with Roosevelt and Stalin, which he would dearly have liked to hold in London. It was surprising that the Russian leader rejected this notion out of hand, but the British felt snubbed when they learned that the president was likewise unwilling to visit their country. Such a rendezvous would play badly with the U.S. electorate in the forthcoming election year, claimed Roosevelt. After some dalliance, Tehran was found a mutually acceptable venue. Churchill sought an advance bilateral summit in Cairo, to which the Americans agreed. He sailed for the Mediterranean on the battle cruiser *Renown*, accompanied by his usual entourage and service chiefs, daughter Sarah and son, Randolph. Harold Macmillan boarded the great warship at Gibraltar: "We were greeted by her owner—or so he seemed—who was finding this an agreeable method of cruising." But Churchill was in poor health. Disembarking at Malta, he spent two days in bed at the residence of Lord Gort, the governor.

Gort was no slave to creature comforts. When Ismay visited the ailing prime minister, he was greeted by pathetic solicitations for enhanced rations and a bath: "Do you think you could bring me a little bit of butter from that nice ship? . . . I only want a cupful of hot water, but I can't get it." Churchill's bedroom overlooked a thoroughfare crowded with chattering Maltese. Moran recorded a touching moment: "From the street below came a great hubbub of voices. His brow darkened. He threw his legs out of bed, and striding across the room thrust his head through the open window, bawling: 'Go away, will you? Please go away and do not make so much noise.' "

The Chiefs of Staff held an unsatisfactory meeting, crowded into the prime minister's bedroom. A few days earlier, John Kennedy expounded in his diary on British policy for the encounter with the Americans: "We have now crystallised our ideas as to the strategy to be advocated." The Italian campaign should be continued; renewed efforts made to bring Turkey into the war through allied activism in the Balkans; and the United States urged "to accept a postponement of Overlord." The Adjutant General, Sir Ronald Adam, told a fellow officer: "The PM's stock is not high with the President at the moment, and the latter is being dragged rather unwillingly to Cairo . . . The PM has now gone very Mediterranean-minded, and the future of Overlord is again in the melting-pot."

Churchill chafed constantly about the slow progress of Allied operations in Italy. Winter weather had reduced campaigning to a crawl, and the Germans were resisting with their usual determination. "The pattern of battle seldom varied," wrote one veteran of the campaign, Fred Majdalany. "The Germans would hold a position for a time until it was seriously contested: then pull back a mile or two to the next defendable place, leaving behind a trail of blown bridges, minefields and road demolitions . . . The Allied armies would begin with a night attack—ford a stream or river after dark, storm the heights on the far side, dig themselves in by dawn, and hope that by that time the Sappers, following on their heels, would have sufficiently repaired the demolitions and removed the obstacles to permit tanks to follow up . . . The Germans, watching these proceedings, would attempt to frustrate them by raining down artillery and mortar fire."

The prime minister was infuriated that two British divisions had already been withdrawn from the line, in advance of their return home to prepare for D-Day. In a minute to the Chiefs on November 20, he complained of Italian operations being compromised by "the shadow of Over-lord." He said that Yugoslavia's partisans, whom he was eager to support more vigorously, were containing more Axis divisions than the British and American armies. He deplored American insistence on May 1 as the date for D-Day, "with inflexible rigidity and without regard to the loss and injury to the allied cause created thereby." The consequence of this "fixed target date," he said, was that "our affairs will deteriorate in the Balkans and that the Aegean will remain firmly in German hands . . . for the sake of an operation fixed for May upon hypotheses that in all probability will not be realized by that date." Churchill wanted all available resources directed, first, towards capturing Rome by January 1944 and, second, upon taking Rhodes later that month. None of this was likely to find favour with the Americans, nor deserved to.

The British delegation sailed on from Malta to Alexandria, and thence flew to Cairo, arriving on November 21. Macmillan, seeing Churchill for the first time in some months, perceived his powers diminished, yet still remarkable: "Winston is getting more and more dogmatic (at least out-wardly) and rather repetitive. One forgets, of course, that he is really an old man—but a wonderful old man he is too . . . It is amusing to watch how he will take a point and reproduce it as his own a day or two later. He misses very little, although he does not always appear to listen."

The first meeting of the Sextant conference took place on Novem-ber 23, and addressed the Far East. The U.S. contingent arrived in an irritable mood, because prior word of the gathering had leaked to corre-spondents, increasing the security risk. The British were galled by the attendance of Chiang Kai-shek and his wife, at American insistence. Much attention was given to Chinese issues. The British shared U.S. faith neither in China's value as an ally, nor in the massive commitment to pro-vide aid "over the Hump" of the Himalayas. They had not forgotten that, a few months earlier, Roosevelt had urged them to cede possession of Hong Kong to Chiang Kai-shek as a "gesture of goodwill." This caused Eden to observe to Harry Hopkins that he had not heard the president suggest any similar act of largesse at American expense. Smuts said emol-liently: "We are inclined to forget the President's difficulties. There is a very strong undercurrent against him. The things the Americans do are based partly on ignorance, partly on their determination to get power. We have learned hard lessons in the four years of the war. They have had no hard lessons. Yet we do not want to wait another four years while they learn them."

The British were right about the intractability of U.S. leaders on China, but their dismissive attitude increased Anglo-American tensions.

Churchill made much of plans to launch Orde Wingate and his Chindits on ambitious deep penetration missions in northern Burma. The Americans, however, regarded these as reflecting the characteristic British enthusiasm for sideshows, at the expense of major operations. They favoured Buccaneer, a big coastal landing in Burma. The British, however, now argued that Mediterranean action, not to mention Overlord, would be fatally compromised by diverting landing craft to the Bay of Bengal.

At the second plenary session on November 24, Churchill complained vigorously about the loss of Kos and Leros. He also said it was untrue that he favoured unlimited operations in Italy: he was committed to Overlord "up to the hilt." But he sought agreement that Allied armies should aim to reach a line between Pisa and Rimini. Eisenhower addressed the conference on the twenty-sixth. He was still only Mediterranean supreme commander, unaware that Overlord would soon become his personal responsibility. He said that he supported British aspirations both in the valley of the Po and the Aegean. "He [Eisenhower] stressed the vital importance of continuing the maximum possible operations in an established theatre since much time was invariably lost when the scene of action was changed." This was welcome to Churchill, if not to Marshall.

The conference's British administrators were at pains to offer hospitality matching that which the Americans had provided at Casablanca in January. But given Britain's impoverished state, they were embarrassed by their guests' locustlike response. The assembled throng of officials and service officers accounted for 20,000 cigarettes and 75 cigars. Each day, 500 beers, 80 bottles of whiskey, 12 of brandy, and 34 of gin were consumed. It was decided that at future summits, out of respect for the rationed people of Britain, those attending should at least be asked to pay for their own drinks.

Between sessions, Churchill took Roosevelt to see the Pyramids, and talked enthusiastically to his staff about the warmth of their relationship. Yet Eden described the Cairo conference as "among the most difficult I ever attended." British fortunes in the Far East were at their lowest ebb. Imperial forces were apparently incapable of breaking through into Burma in the face of a numerically inferior Japanese army. Given Roosevelt's rambling conversation, "W. had to play the role of courtier and seize opportunities as and when they arose. I am amazed at the patience with which he does this . . . Though the role of attendant listener was uncongenial to him, the Prime Minister played it faultlessly all these days, so that we came through without the loss of any feathers, if not with our tails up." But presidential needling of the prime minister was more pronounced than usual. Roosevelt reproached Churchill for allowing Eden to tell the king of Greece not to attempt to return home, once his country was liberated, until it was plain that his subjects wanted him. This was an odd intervention, given the Americans' subsequent hostility to the monarch. The British were furious with the president for encouraging Greek recalcitrance.

Churchill lamented to the British delegation Roosevelt's casual approach to business, observing that while he was "a charming country gentleman," his dilatory habits wasted time. The prime minister and his colleagues were surprised and irked by the Americans' failure to hold bilateral discussions with them before meeting Stalin. "PM and President *ought* to have got together, with their staffs, before meeting the Russians but that through a series of mischances has not happened," mused Cadogan. The British were slow to perceive that such evasion reflected policy rather than "mischances." This would be the president's first meeting with Stalin. Earlier in the year, Roosevelt had sought a meeting with the Soviet leader without Churchill present. When his initiative came to nothing, he coolly lied to the prime minister, asserting that the proposal had originated with Moscow, not himself. Roosevelt believed that he could forge a working relationship with Stalin, which must not be compromised by any appearance of excessive Anglo-American amity or collusion. It did not trouble him that to such an end Churchill must be discomfited.

Hopkins bemoaned the prime minister's "bloody Italian war" and warned Moran: "We are preparing for a battle at Tehran. You will find us lining up with the Russians." The doctor wrote wonderingly of the American attitude to Churchill: "They are far more sceptical of him than they are of Stalin." Hopkins's enthusiasm for the prime minister had diminished, and so too had his influence in his own country. Roosevelt's secretary wrote pityingly: "Poor Harry, the public is done with him. He is a heavy liability to the President." The U.S. delegation in Cairo leaked freely to correspondents. The *Washington Post* was among many newspapers which afterwards disclosed to the American public "the reported recalcitrance of Churchill" towards U.S. strategic wishes. No military agreements between the British and Americans had been reached by November 27, when Sextant adjourned for the principals to fly on to Tehran.

Churchill seldom showed much concern for his own security, but raised an eyebrow when his car was almost engulfed by crowds as the convoy approached the British legation in the Persian capital. Roosevelt had accepted lodgings in the Russian compound next door, and chose to meet Stalin for the first time alone. The opening session of the summit took place on the afternoon of November 28, in the Soviet embassy under

Roosevelt's chairmanship. It bears emphasis that, for every participant with a scintilla of imagination, these gatherings were awesome occasions. Even Brooke, tired and cynical, found it "quite enthralling" to behold the "Big Three" for the first time assembled together around a table. Those present knew that they were sharing in the making of history. Most strove to speak and act in a fashion worthy of the moment.

Churchill began by asserting his firm commitment to an advance to the Pisa-Rimini line in Italy; to a landing in southern France; and to Overlord, provided his preconditions about maximum German strength in the invasion area were met. "It will be our stern duty," he said, in a trumpet blast notably discordant with his haverings about the operation, "to hurl across the Channel against the Germans every sinew of our strength." Stalin enquired smoothly: "Who will command Overlord?" This was a brilliant shaft. He said that he could not regard any operation entirely seriously until a leader had been named to direct it. Though Eden found Stalin's personality "creepy" and chilling, like all the Western delegates the foreign secretary recognised a master of diplomacy: "Of course the man was ruthless and of course knew his purpose. He never wasted a word. He never stormed, he was seldom even irritated. Hooded, calm, never raising his voice, he avoided the repeated negatives of Molotov which were so exasperating to listen to. By more subtle methods he got what he wanted without having seemed so obdurate."

Roosevelt assured the Russian leader that a commander for Overlord would be appointed within days. Stalin—"Ursus Major," as Churchill christened "the Great Bear"—was satisfied. He even professed enthusiasm for the Italian campaign, despite his dismay that German divisions were still being transferred from the west to fight in Russia. Churchill praised the efforts of Tito's Communist partisans in Yugoslavia, which he assumed would please Stalin, and declared his eagerness to provide them with greater assistance. The Russian leader said that the Soviet Union would enter the war against Japan as soon as Germany was defeated, which gratified the Americans.

Early each morning of the summit, NKVD officers—who included Beria's son Sergo—presented Stalin with transcripts of conversations intercepted by microphones planted in the American residence. The Soviet leader expressed amazement at the freedom with which the Westerners talked among themselves, even though they must have realised that they were being overheard. Latterly, indeed, he began to wonder whether they were indeed so naïve that they did not guess: "Do you think they know that we are listening?" He was gratified to find Roosevelt speaking well of him. Once, noting the president's assertion that there was "no way to fool Uncle Joe," he grinned into his moustache and muttered: "The old rascal is lying." He was less amused by transcribed exchanges in which Churchill repeated to the president his reservations about Overlord. Young Beria was rewarded with a Swiss watch for the efficiency of his eavesdropping.

The most notorious episode at the conference arose from Stalin's brutal jest about shooting fifty thousand German officers once the war was won, followed by Roosevelt's rejoinder that forty-nine thousand would suffice. Elliott Roosevelt, one of the president's sons, rose to say that he cordially agreed with Stalin's proposal, and was sure that the United States would endorse it likewise. This caused Churchill to storm from the room in disgust. The Russians soothed the prime minister, but it was a grisly moment. When Stalin made his sally, Churchill knew him to be responsible for the cold-blooded massacre of at least ten thousand Polish officers—the true figure was almost thirty thousand—as well as countless of his own people. Moreover, the U.S. president's willingness to join the joke suggested a heartlessness which was real enough, and which shocked the British leader. Finally, Elliott Roosevelt's intervention was intolerable. It was a curiosity of the war that great men saw fit to take their children on missions of state. Randolph Churchill's presence in North Africa, and everywhere else, was an embarrassment. Jan Smuts and Harry Hopkins both brought their sons to Cairo for Sextant. But none matched the crassness of the president's offspring. Churchill knew that, to sustain the Anglo-American relationship, he must endure almost anything which Roosevelt chose to say or do. But that moment in Tehran was hard for him. Marshall said of Stalin at the conference: "He was turning his hose on Churchill all the time, and Mr. Roosevelt, in a sense, was helping him. He [FDR] used to take a little delight in embarrassing Churchill."

Cadogan recorded the distress of the British delegation when Roosevelt seemed willing to endorse almost everything Stalin proposed. When the future boundaries of Poland were discussed, Averell Harriman was dismayed by his president's visible indifference. Roosevelt wanted only enough to satisfy Polish-American voters, which was not much. Soviet eavesdroppers reported to Stalin Churchill's private warnings to Roosevelt about Moscow's preparations to instal a Communist government in Poland. According to Sergo Beria, Roosevelt replied that since Churchill was attempting to do the same thing by installing an anti-Communist regime, he had no cause for complaint.

The U.S. leader was much more interested in promoting Soviet support for the future United Nations organisation, an easy ball for the Russians to play. They indulged Roosevelt by ready acquiescence, though even Stalin expressed scepticism about the president's vision of China joining Russia, Britain and the United States to police the postwar world. Harriman perceived the danger of flaunting before the Russians Roosevelt's carelessness about eastern European borders. The relentless advance of Stalin's armies would have rendered it difficult for the West to stem Soviet imperialism. Churchill was by now reconciled to shifting Poland's frontiers westwards, compensating the Poles with German territory for their eastern lands to be ceded to Russia. That proposal represented ruthlessness enough. But the president's behaviour went further, making plain that Stalin could expect little opposition to his designs in Poland or elsewhere.

Roosevelt, bent upon creating a future in which the Great Powers acted in concert, seemed heedless of reality: that Stalin cared nothing for consensus, and was interested only in licence for pursuing his own unilateral purposes. Among the American team, Charles Bohlen and George Kennan of the State Department shared Harriman's misgivings about Roosevelt's belief that he shared a world vision with Stalin. The prime minister's fears for the future began to coalesce. "That the President should deal with Churchill and Stalin as if they were people of equal standing in American eyes shocked Churchill profoundly," wrote Ian Jacob.

Yet most of Roosevelt's delegation left the summit basking in a glow of satisfaction created by the formal commitment to Overlord, so long desired by both the United States and Soviet Union. The persistent evasiveness of the British on this issue irked even the most Anglophile Americans. The Tehran experience afterwards yielded one of Churchill's great sallies, no less pleasing for its misplaced self-belief. The meeting, he said, caused him to realise how small Britain was: "There I sat with the great Russian bear on one side of me, with paws outstretched, and on the other side the great American buffalo, and between the two sat the poor little English donkey who was the only one . . . who knew the right way home."

Stalin was highly satisfied with the Tehran talks. He perceived himself as getting all that he wanted. He thought the president a truth-teller, as Churchill was not, and told the Soviet high command on his return to Moscow: "Roosevelt has given a firm commitment to launch large-scale operations in France in 1944. I think he will keep his word. But if he does not, we shall be strong enough to finish off Hitler's Germany on our own." After Kursk, his confidence was justified.

Eden thought the 1943 meetings with the Russians the most satisfactory, or least unsatisfactory, of the war, before the steep deterioration of relations during 1944, when Soviet expansionism became explicit. But the

British delegation at Tehran deplored the manner in which the Big Three's discussions roamed erratically across a wilderness of issues, bringing none to a decisive conclusion save that Churchill would thereafter have found it difficult to escape the Overlord commitment. Cunningham and Portal declared the conference a waste of time. The British were especially dismayed that no attempt was made to oblige the Russians to recognise the legitimacy of the Polish exile government in London in return for Anglo-American acceptance of Poland's altered borders.

After Tehran, Churchill cannot have failed to understand how little Roosevelt cared for Britain, its interests or stature. Not for a moment did the prime minister relax his efforts to flatter and cajole the president. But it became progressively harder for him to address the United States than Russia. With Stalin, Churchill continued to seek bargains, but his expectations were pitched low. The American relationship, however, was fundamental to every operation of war; to feeding the British people; to all prospect of sustaining the empire in the postwar world. It seems extraordinary that some historians have characterised the relationship between Roosevelt and Churchill as a friendship. To be sure, the prime minister embraced the president in speech and correspondence as "my friend." "Every morning when I wake," he once said, "my first thought is how I can please President Roosevelt." But much of what FDR served up to Churchill between 1943 and 1945 was gall and wormwood.

From Tehran, while Roosevelt went home to Washington Churchill flew to Cairo. He was tired and indeed ill, yet meetings and dinners crowded in upon one another. He rebuked Mountbatten by signal for demanding the services of 33,700 fighting soldiers to address 5,000 Japanese in the Arakan region of Burma—"the Americans have been taking their islands on the basis of two-and-a-half to one. That your Generals should ask for six-and-a-half to one has produced a very bad impression." He dined at the embassy on December 10 with a party which included Smuts, Eden, Cadogan and Randolph Churchill, then took off at one a.m. for Tunisia. His York landed at the wrong airfield, where Brooke saw him "sitting on his suitcase in a very cold morning wind, looking like nothing on earth. We were there about an hour before we moved on and he was chilled through by then."

After another brief flight, they landed again, this time in the right place, and he was driven to Maison Blanche, Eisenhower's villa near Carthage. On December 11, he slept all day, then dined with Ike, Brooke, Tedder and others. He went to bed in pain from his throat. At four a.m., Brooke was awakened by a plaintive voice crying out "Hulloo, Hulloo, Hulloo." The CIGS switched on a torch and demanded crossly: "Who the hell is that?" His beam fell upon the prime minister in his dragon dressing gown, a brown bandage around his head, complaining of a headache and searching for his doctor. Next day Churchill had a temperature, and Moran telegraphed for nurses and a pathologist. He was diagnosed with pneumonia.

Through the days which followed, though he continued to see visitors and dispatch a stream of signals, he lay in bed, knowing that he was very ill. "If I die," he told his daughter Sarah, "don't worry—the war is won." On December 15, he suffered a heart attack. Sarah read *Pride and Prejudice* aloud to him. News of Churchill's illness unleashed a surge of sentiment and sympathy among his people. A British soldier in North Africa wrote in his diary: "We all hope and pray that he will recover. It would be a great thing if Mr. Churchill will live to see the victorious end to his great fight against the Nazis." On the afternoon of the seventeenth, Clementine Churchill arrived, escorted by Jock Colville, who had been recalled from the RAF to the Downing Street secretariat. The new antibiotics were doing their work. While the prime minister remained weak, and suffered a further slight heart attack, he no longer seemed in peril of death. On the nineteenth Clementine wrote to her daughter Mary: "Papa much better today. Has consented not to smoke and to drink only weak whisky and soda."

He was now fuming about the "scandalous . . . stagnation" of the Italian campaign, and especially about the failure to use available landing craft to launch an amphibious assault behind the German front. He urged Roosevelt to give swift consideration to British proposals for new command arrangements in the Mediterranean, now that Dwight Eisenhower had been named to direct Overlord. Roosevelt would almost certainly have given this role to Marshall, had the British been willing to agree that the chief of staff of the army should become super commander-in-chief of all operations against the Germans, in the Mediterranean as well as in northwest Europe. But Churchill and Brooke were determined to preserve at least one key C-in-C's appointment for a British officer. The president was unwilling to spare Marshall from Washington merely to lead Overlord. On those terms, he preferred to keep Marshall at home, as overall director of the U.S. war effort.

The British Chiefs of Staff wanted Maitland Wilson to succeed Eisenhower as Mediterranean supremo, and Air Chief Marshal Sir Arthur Tedder to become Ike's deputy for Overlord. Churchill favoured Alexander for British commander on D-Day—as also did Eisenhower. The War Cabinet demurred, urging Montgomery in deference to public opinion as well as military desirability. Surprisingly, Churchill acceded to their view.

This was certainly the right appointment, for Montgomery was a much superior general. But it was unusual for Churchill to allow himself to be baulked by ministers on a matter of such importance. Most likely, willingness to allow Alexander to remain in Italy reflected the importance which he attached to operations there. He believed, mistakenly, that "Alex" could provide the impetus he perceived as lacking. Macmillan strongly urged Alexander's appointment, noting that Maitland Wilson had been Middle East C-in-C for a year, yet had done nothing to galvanise the slothful British war machine in Egypt. The Americans finally acceded to British wishes for Alexander to take over in the Mediterranean, precisely because they attached much less importance to Italy than to Overlord.

On December 22, the British Chiefs of Staff signalled from London that they supported Churchill's proposal for a new amphibious assault in Italy. Initial planning assumed that there was only enough shipping to move a single division, while both Churchill and the Chiefs wanted to land two. On Christmas Day, Eisenhower, Maitland Wilson, Alexander, Tedder and Cunningham converged by air upon Carthage from all over the Mediterranean to discuss plans for Operation Shingle, a descent on the coast at Anzio, just south of Rome, provisionally scheduled for January 20. The meeting endorsed a two-division initial assault, subject to the proviso that it should not threaten the May date for Overlord.

On December 27, Churchill flew to Marrakesh for a prolonged spell of recuperation. "I propose to stay here in the sunshine," he wrote to Roosevelt, "till I am quite strong again." On his second day at the Villa Taylor, to his surprise and delight, he learned that the president had approved Shingle, subject only to renewed emphasis upon the sanctity of the French invasion date. This, however, was now to be put back a month, until June, at the insistence of Eisenhower and Montgomery. Having studied the D-Day plan for the first time, they were convinced that additional preparation, as well as a reinforced initial landing, were essential. The new date would fall in the first week of June. Churchill was hostile to the use of the word *invasion* in the context of D-Day: "Our object is the liberation of Europe from German tyranny . . . we 'enter' the oppressed countries rather than 'invade' them and . . . the word 'invasion' must be reserved for the time when we cross the German frontier. There is no need for us to make a present to Hitler of the idea that he is the defender of a Europe we are seeking to invade." This was, of course, one semantic dispute which he lost.

On January 4, 1944, he wrote to Eden: "I am getting stronger ever day . . . All my thoughts are on 'Shingle,' which as you may well imagine I am watching intensely." His convalescence in Marrakesh ended on January 14. He flew to Gibraltar, where Maitland Wilson and Cunningham gave him a final briefing on the Anzio plan. Then he boarded the battleship *King George V* to sail home. On the night of January 17 he landed at Plymouth, where he boarded the royal train, which had been sent to fetch him. Next morning, after an absence from England of nine weeks, he reached Downing Street. He cabled Roosevelt: "Am all right except for being rather shaky on my pins." Arriving at Buckingham Palace for lunch with the king, a private secretary asked if he would like the lift. "Lift?" demanded the indignant prime minister. He ran up the stairs two at a time, then turned and thumbed his nose at the courtier.

The House of Commons knew nothing of his return until MPs looked up in astonishment in the middle of Questions, then leapt to their feet and began shouting, applauding and waving order papers. Harold Nicolson described how cheer after cheer greeted him

> while Winston, very pink, rather shy, beaming with mischief, crept along the front bench and flung himself into his accustomed seat. He was flushed with pleasure and emotion, and hardly had he sat down when two large tears began to trickle down his cheeks. He mopped clumsily at himself with a huge white handkerchief. A few minutes later he got up to answer questions. Most men would have been unable, on such an occasion, not to throw a flash of drama into their replies. But Winston answered them as if he were the young Under-Secretary, putting on his glasses, turning over his papers, responding tactfully to supplementaries, and taking the whole thing as conscientiously as could be. I should like to say that he seemed completely restored to health. But he looked pale when the first flush of pleasure had subsided, and his voice was not quite as vigorous as it had been.

Churchill retained his extraordinary ability to hold the attention of the House through long, discursive assessments of the war. After one such, he suddenly leaned across to the Opposition and demanded casually: "That all right?" MPs grinned back affectionately. His mastery of the Commons, wrote Nicolson, derived from "the combination of great flights of oratory with sudden swoops into the intimate and conversational."

On the afternoon of January 19, Churchill presided at a Chiefs of Staff meeting, during which he urged commando landings on the Dalmatian coast, to progressively clear of Germans the islands off Yugoslavia. His hopes for Anzio were soaring. He spoke of forcing the Germans to withdraw into northern Italy, or even behind the Alps. Then Alexander's armies would be free to pursue towards Vienna, strike into the Balkans, or swing left into France. Two days later, as the American Maj. Gen. John Lucas's corps prepared to hit the beaches in Italy, the U.S. Fifth Army staged crossings of the Rapido River south of Rome. Churchill cabled to Stalin: "We have launched the big attack against the German armies defending Rome which I told you about at Tehran." By midnight on January 22, thirty-six thousand British and American troops and three thousand vehicles were ashore at Anzio, having achieved complete surprise.

Yet through the days that followed, news from Italy turned sour. The Rapido crossings proved a disaster. The Germans snuffed out each precarious American bridgehead in turn. Kesselring acted with extraordinary energy, recovering from his astonishment about Anzio to concentrate troops and isolate the invaders. Four Allied divisions were soon ashore, yet going nowhere. As the Germans poured fire into the shallow beachhead, British and American soldiers manning their foxholes and gun positions found themselves trapped in one of the most painful predicaments of the war. "We did become like animals in the end," said a soldier of the Sherwood Foresters. "You were stuck in the same place. You had nowhere to go. You didn't get no rest . . . No sleep . . . You never expected to see the end of it. You just forgot why you were there."

Casualties mounted rapidly, and so too did desertions. Nowhere from the beach to the front line offered safety from bombardment. The Luftwaffe attacked offshore shipping with new and deadly glider bombs. "It will be unpleasant if you get sealed off there and cannot advance from the south," Churchill wrote to Alexander on January 27. On February 8, he signalled to Dill in Washington, "All this has been a disappointment to me." It was true that German forces were tied down in Italy which would otherwise be fighting elsewhere. "Even a battle of attrition is better than standing by and watching the Russians fight. We should also learn a good many lessons about how not to do it which will be valuable in 'Overlord.'" But these were poor consolations for what was, indubitably, one of the big Allied failures of the war.

Anzio was the last important operation which sprang from the personal inspiration of the prime minister. Without his support, neither Eisenhower nor Alexander could have persuaded the American Chiefs of Staff to provide means for such a venture. It reflected his passion for what Liddell Hart called "the strategy of indirect approach," the exploitation of Allied command of the sea to sidestep the difficulties of frontal assault amid some of the most difficult terrain in the world. In principle Shingle was valid. But, to an extraordinary degree, commanders failed to think through a plan for what was to happen once the troops got ashore. In this, the weakness of the Anzio operation closely resembled that of Churchill's other notorious amphibious failure, at the Dardanelles in 1915—as American corps commander Maj. Gen. John Lucas suggested before it began. Alexander, as commander-in-chief, must bear responsibility for the inadequacy of strategic planning for Shingle. He and his staff grossly underestimated the speed and strength of the German response, believing that the mere threat to Kesselring's rear would cause him to abandon the defence of his line at Monte Cassino. They never identified the importance of quick seizure of the hills beyond the Anzio beaches, a far more plausible objective than a dash for Rome. The Americans, always sceptical, displayed better judgement about the landing's prospects than the British.

Moreover, all operations of war must be judged in the context of the forces available to carry them out. The Allies had insufficient shipping in the Mediterranean to put ashore an army large enough to risk a decisive thrust inland. Lucas has often been criticized for failure to strike swiftly towards Rome in the wake of his corps' successful landing. He was certainly a poor general. But had he done as the fire-eaters wished and dashed for the capital, he would have exposed a long, thin salient to counterattack. The Germans always punished excessive boldness, as they did nine months later at Arnhem. The likeliest outcome of a dash for Rome from Anzio would have been the destruction of Lucas's corps. As it was, despite four months of misery which the defenders of the Anzio perimeter now resigned themselves to endure, they were rewarded with belated success.

So bitter was the struggle on the coast, matched by the battle farther south for the heights of Monte Cassino, that the Allies experienced little joy in the capture of Rome when it came in June 1944. But what took place was preferable to what might have been had a more daring commander led the Anzio assault. Shingle confirmed the U.S. Chiefs of Staff in their conviction that Italy offered only poisoned fruits. "The more one sees of this peninsula, the less suited it seems for modern military operations," agreed Harold Macmillan. The campaign could not be abandoned, but henceforward the Americans viewed it as a liability. They would support no more of Churchill's adventures, in the Mediterranean or anywhere else.

Events in Italy in the winter of 1943–44 once more highlighted the gulf between the prime minister's heroic aspirations and the limitations of Allied armies fighting the Germans. "I gather we are still stronger than the enemy," he signalled to Alexander on February 10, "and naturally one wonders why over 70,000 British and Americans should be hemmed in on the defensive by what are thought to be at most 60,000 Germans"—in reality there were 90,000. He wrote to Smuts on February 27 that his confidence in Alexander was "undiminished," adding sadly: "Though if I had been well enough to be at his side as I had hoped at the critical moment, I believe I could have given the necessary stimulus. Alas for time, distance, illness and advancing years." If the generals of Britain and America had been Marlboroughs or Lees, if their citizen soldiers had displayed the mettle of Spartans, they might have accomplished in the Mediterranean such great deeds as Churchill's imagination conceived for them. But they were not and did not. They were mortal clay, doing their best against an outstanding commander, Kesselring, and one of the greatest armies the world has ever seen.

Churchill had been right, in 1942 and 1943, to force upon the Americans campaigns in the Mediterranean, when there was nowhere else they could credibly fight. He told the House of Commons on February 22: "On broad grounds of strategy, Hitler's decision to send into the south of Italy as many as eighteen divisions, involving, with their maintenance troops, probably something like half a million Germans, and to make a large secondary front in Italy, is not unwelcome to the Allies . . . We must fight the Germans somewhere, unless we are to stand still and watch the Russians." But by now there was a lameness about such an explanation. In 1944, Churchill's Italian vision was overtaken by that of Overlord, a huge and indispensable American conception. After Anzio, even the prime minister himself implicitly acknowledged this, and embraced the prospect of D-Day with increasing excitement. Though his enthusiasm for Mediterranean operations never subsided, he was obliged to recognise that the major battles in the west would be fought in France, not Italy.

In the spring of 1944, Churchill was full of apprehension not only about Overlord, but also about the mood of the British people. Several lost by-elections exposed voters' lack of enthusiasm for the government, and weariness with the war. After an Independent Labour candidate in West Derbyshire on February 18 defeated the Tory Lord Hartington, who campaigned with the prime minister's conspicuous endorsement, Jock Colville wrote: "Sitting in a chair in his study at the Annexe, the PM looked old, tired and very depressed and was even muttering about a General Election. Now, he said, with great events pending, was the time when national unity was essential, the question of annihilating great states had to be faced; it began to look as if democracy had not the persistence necessary to go through with it, however well it might have shewn its capacity of defence." In Churchill's Commons speech of February 22, he delivered a contemptuous jab at his critics, "little folk who frolic alongside the juggernaut of war to see what fun or notoriety they can extract from the proceedings." Five days later, writing to Smuts, he alluded to such people again: "Their chirpings will presently be stilled by the thunder of the cannonade." On March 25, to Roosevelt, he wrote ruefully, "We certainly do have plenty to worry us, now that our respective democracies feel so sure that the whole war is as good as won." Tory MP Cuthbert Headlam wrote in April 1944: "In the H of C smoking room a new leader is decided upon almost every other day."

There was much to vex Churchill, the burden made heavier because so few of the difficulties and hazards could be publicly avowed. Countless hours were devoted to Poland. The Polish exile government in London was obdurately opposed to changes in its frontiers—the shift of the entire country a step westward—which Churchill had reluctantly accepted. Its representatives persisted in proclaiming their anger towards Moscow about the Katyn massacres. What adherent of freedom and democracy could blame them? Yet so astonishing was the popularity of Russia in Britain that opinion surveys showed a decline in public enthusiasm for the Poles, because of their declared hostility to Moscow. Again and again, the prime minister urged the exiles to mute their protests. Since Russia would soon possess physical mastery of their country, Soviet goodwill was indispensable to any possibility that they might share in its postwar governance. Stalin lied flatly to Churchill, asserting that he had no intention of influencing Poland's internal politics, and that the Poles would be free to choose their own postwar rulers. But in a stream of cables and letters, the Soviet warlord vented his own anger, as real as it was base and monstrously hypocritical, about the London Poles' declarations of hostility to the Soviet Union.

It was plain to Churchill that the prospects of a free Poland were slender, and shrinking. Amid the exiles' rejections of his pleas for realism, his lonely battle to restore the nation to freedom was being lost. In all probability, nothing within the power of the Western Allies would have saved Poland from Stalin's maw. There was one dominant, intractable reality: the Soviet Union's insistence upon exacting its price for the twenty-eight million Russians who died in the struggle to destroy Nazism. On March 3, Eden asked Churchill to cable Moscow personally about the case of two Royal Navy seamen seized in Murmansk after a drunken brawl and sentenced to penal servitude in Siberia. The prime minister wrote to the foreign secretary: "I cannot send such a telegram which would embroil me with Bruin on a small point when so many large ones are looming up." Instead, he suggested to Eden that questions in Parliament might generate useful publicity about the case: "A little anti-Russian feeling in the House of Commons would be salutary at the present time." When Sir John Anderson wrote to Churchill urging that the Russians should be told of the Allies' "Tube Alloys" project—creation of the atomic bomb—Churchill scrawled in the margin of Anderson's minute: "On no account."

Eden wrote in his diary about Poland: "Soviet attitude on this business raises most disquieting thoughts. Is Soviet regime one which will ever co-operate with the West?" A few days later he added: "I confess to growing apprehension that Russia has vast aims and that these may include the domination of Eastern Europe and even the Mediterranean and the 'communising' of much that remains." In Italy, the Soviets refused to deal with the Allied Control Commission, and instead appointed their own ambassador with a mandate to embarrass the Anglo-Americans. It was painful for Churchill, who knew the truth about Stalin's tyranny and the perils posed by his ambitions, to be obliged to indulge the British people's romantic delusions, and to echo their gratitude for Russian sacrifices. Even as he was participating in an exceptionally harsh exchange of cables with Moscow on a range of issues, in a BBC broadcast on March 26 he nonetheless made a generous tribute to the Red Army. Its 1943 offensive, he said, "constitutes the greatest cause of Hitler's undoing." The Russian people had been extraordinarily fortunate to find, "in their supreme ordeal and agony a warrior leader, Marshal Stalin, whose authority enables him to combine and control the movements of armies numbered by many millions upon a front of nearly 2,000 miles, and to impart a unity and a concert to the war direction in the East which has been very good for Russia and for all her Allies." All this was true, but represented only a portion of reality.

Meanwhile, elsewhere, difficulties persisted with the French. Harold Macmillan wrote from Algiers: "I would much rather get what we want—if we can—through the French rather than by imposing it on the French. But it is a difficult hand for me to play . . . the trouble is that neither the President nor the PM has any confidence in de Gaulle." Churchill had adopted a jaundiced view ever since, at Brazzaville in the Congo in July 1941, the intransigent general gave an interview to the *Chicago Daily News* in which he suggested that Britain was "doing a wartime deal with Hitler." Churchill and Eden several times discussed the possibility that de Gaulle was mentally unhinged. The prime minister had become sick to death of his petulance and studied discourtesy. It seemed intolerable that Britain should struggle with Washington on behalf of Free France, which the Americans despised, and be rewarded only with ingratitude from its leader.

During Churchill's time in North Africa, he spent many hours with Macmillan and de Gaulle and other prominent Frenchmen, seeking to sustain a veneer of unity. His efforts were sabotaged by de Gaulle's unilateralism. At one moment, the general ordered the arrest of three prominent Vichyites in Algiers, which provoked an explosion of Churchillian exasperation. British politicians and diplomats exhausted themselves pleading before the prime minister the case for de Gaulle, a habitual offender facing a judge minded to don the black cap. After one exchange, Macmillan wrote: "Much as I love Winston, I cannot stand much more." Yet two days later, like almost every other close associate of the prime minister's, he relented: "He is really a remarkable man. Although he can be so tiresome and pig-headed, there is no one like him. His devotion to work and duty is quite extraordinary."

Churchill's commitment to restoring France to its rightful position as a great nation never wavered. For this, and for fighting the Americans so staunchly in support of its interests, the British government merited, though never received, its Gallic neighbour's enduring gratitude. In Quebec the previous year, Eden argued fiercely with Cordell Hull about the virtues of French resurrection: "We both got quite heated at one time when I told him we had to live twenty miles from France and I wanted to rebuild her as far as I could." Macmillan observed that while Roosevelt hated de Gaulle, Churchill's sentiments were more complex: "He feels about De Gaulle like a man who has quarrelled with his son. He will cut him off with a shilling. But (in his heart) he would kill the fatted calf if only the prodigal would confess his faults and take his orders obediently in future." Since this would never happen, however, there were many moments in 1943–44 when, but for Eden's loyalty to de Gaulle, Churchill would have cut the Frenchman adrift.

Even now, with two million men training and arming in Britain for the invasion, Churchill chose to sustain the dangerous fiction—dangerous because of the mistrust of himself which it fed among Americans—that Overlord still represented an option rather than an absolute commitment. In February he invited the Chiefs of Staff to review plans for Jupiter—an assault on northern Norway—if the French landings failed. He convened a committee to report to him weekly on the progress of D-Day preparations, and wrote to Marshall on February 15: "I am hardening very much on this operation as the time approaches in the sense of wishing to strike if humanly possible, even if the limiting conditions we laid down at Tehran are not exactly fulfilled." The conditional was still there, as it was in a message to Roosevelt which he drafted on March 25: "What is the latest date on which a decision can be taken as to whether 'Overlord' is or is not to be launched on the prescribed date? . . . If . . . 20 or 25 mobile German divisions are already in France on the date in question, what are we going to do?" This cable, which would have roused the most acute American dismay, was withheld after prudent second thoughts. But it reflected Churchill's continuing uncertainty, ten weeks before D-Day.

In the Mediterranean, Harold Macmillan wrote: "I am much distressed to see a worsening of Anglo-American relations generally since Eisenhower left and I am also not very hopeful of getting any new idea into the PM's mind at present." There was much debate and many changes of heart about Anvil, a prospective landing in the south of France originally scheduled to coincide with the descent on Normandy. The British, having favoured the scheme, now turned sour because of its inevitable impact on Allied strength in Italy. On March 21 Maitland Wilson signalled, recommending Anvil's cancellation. After protracted exchanges with Washington, most about landing craft, it was agreed to postpone the operation. Churchill became increasingly sceptical, and finally absolutely hostile. He favoured diversionary landings by commandos on the Atlantic coast of France. He also remained resolute in his enthusiasm for an invasion of Sumatra, exasperating his own Chiefs of Staff and especially Brooke. They opposed the scheme on its merits, and also knew that the Americans would never provide the necessary shipping. Washington was interested only in an offensive into upper Burma, to open a China passage. This, with deep reluctance, the British finally agreed to undertake.

Churchill's closest wartime colleagues, above all the Chiefs of Staff, emerged from the Second World War asserting the prime minister's greatness as a statesman, while deploring his shortcomings as a strategist. Yet no Allied leader displayed unbroken wisdom. Churchill's grand vision of the war was superb. Even acknowledging his anachronistic delusions about the future of the British Empire, he articulated the hopes and ambitions of the Grand Alliance as no other man, including Roosevelt, was capable of doing. His record as a warlord should be judged by what was done rather than by what was said. He indulged many flights of fancy, but insisted upon realisation of very few. The 1943 Aegean adventure was an exception rather than a commonplace.

If, as those who worked with him believed, in 1944–45 he was no longer what he had been in 1940–41, this is not to be wondered at. Smuts told Eden after a lunch of the prime minister's: "He may be mentally the man he was, he may be, but he certainly is not physically. I fear he overestimates his strength and he will wear himself out if he is not careful." The wise old South African, of whom Churchill mused that he was what he thought Socrates must have been like, took care to say this within earshot of the prime minister. Ismay was wryly amused by the sternness with which Smuts often urged on Churchill the care of his health, admonishing him for overstaying his bedtime. The prime minister responded "rather like a small boy being sent off by his mother."

For all Churchill's exhaustion and ill health, his personal fearlessness persisted. He loved to watch the Luftwaffe's occasional night attacks from a Whitehall roof. "The raids are very fine to look at now," he wrote to Randolph, who was in Yugoslavia, on April 4, "because of the brilliant red flares which hang seemingly motionless in the air, and the bright showers of incendiaries . . . sometimes I go to Maria's battery [Mary Churchill's antiaircraft position] and hear the child ordering the guns to fire." This was a lovely line. On March 4, Jock Colville described the prime minister on a Saturday at Chequers:

> Late at night, after the inevitable film, the PM took his station in the Great Hall and began to smoke Turkish cigarettes—the first time I have ever seen him smoke one—saying that they were the only thing he got out of the Turks. He keeps on referring to the point that he has not long to live and tonight, while the gramophone played the Marseillaise and Sambre et Meuse, he told Coningham, Harold Macmillan, Pug, Tommy and me that this was his political testament for after the war: "Far more important than India or the Colonies or solvency is the Air. We live in a world of wolves—and bears." Then we had to listen to most of Gilbert and Sullivan on the gramophone, before retiring at [three a.m.].

A mooted Easter meeting with Roosevelt on Bermuda was aborted because the president was ill—indeed, his health never recovered from the strains of the Tehran conference. Brooke, Moran and others anyway opposed any further long flights by the prime minister. His desire to see Roosevelt was driven more by restlessness and exaggerated faith in his own persuasive powers than by any real need for a summit. On April 4, 1944, Churchill told the House of Commons that 197,005 of the United Kingdom's people had perished since the war began in September 1939. This figure omitted many others who were posted merely as missing, but would never come home. The public, and even some of those closest to power, perceived the war as entering its final phase. Churchill himself never succumbed to such a delusion, above all in the shadow of Overlord. Another hundred thousand Britons had yet to die before victory would be won. He had to rouse himself, and his people, for new exertions.

SIXTEEN

Setting Europe Ablaze

THE SPRING and summer of 1944 witnessed a flowering, albeit imperfect in the prime minister's eyes, of one of his most cherished inspirations: resistance movements in occupied Europe and the Balkans. Back in 1940, Churchill famously ordered the minister of economic warfare, Hugh Dalton, to "set Europe ablaze." This instruction prompted the creation of the Special Operations Executive, a secret organisation charged with promoting resistance—explicitly terrorism, armed action by nonuniformed civilians—everywhere that the Axis held sway. By submarine and small boat, plane and parachute, British-trained agents descended on Europe, and later Southeast Asia, to establish contact with those willing to raise the banner of opposition to tyranny, albeit by means unsanctioned in the Geneva Conventions. Events in France have received most attention from postwar chroniclers, though the partisans in Yugoslavia achieved much greater strategic significance, as Churchill perceived from 1943 onwards.

The men and women of the SOE helped to create one of the enduring legends of World War II. It seemed then, as it still does today, especially heroic to risk torture and death alone, far behind enemy lines. Support for domestic insurrection represented a personal act of faith by the prime minister, which ran contrary to the views of many of his service advisers. He treasured a belief that the peoples of Europe could play an important part in their own liberation, declaring on June 10, 1941: "We shall aid and stir the people of every conquered country to resistance and revolt. We shall break up and derange every effort which Hitler makes to systematize and consolidate his subjugation." At the prime minister's behest, a War Office planning document the same month addressed the promotion of resistance movements: "Subjugated peoples must be caused to rise against their oppressors, but not until the stage is set. The 'attack from within' is the basic concept of such operations—and we should be able to do it in a bigger way than did the Germans. They had but a few Quislings to help them, and we have whole populations. The Patriots must be secretly organised and armed with personal weapons to be delivered to them by air if necessary."

Churchill anticipated that indigenous peoples would play a major part in their own liberation. If the United States entered the war, he wrote in a minute to Portal, the chief of the Air Staff, on October 7, 1941, there would be "simultaneous attacks by armoured forces in many of the conquered countries which were ripe for revolt." In a paper of June 15, 1942, he cited "rousing the populations" among the first objectives of Allied landings on the Continent. The mission of the SOE was to hasten such ripening and "rousing." In many books published even in the twenty-first century, accounts of what took place in the attempt to fulfil his vision are heavily coloured by romance. Reality was at least as interesting, but much more complex.

In June 1940, expressing to Canadian premier Mackenzie King his uncertainty about whether France would stay in the war, Churchill wrote: "I hope they will, even at the worst, maintain a gigantic guerrilla." In the event, through the first years of occupation, France and the rest of western Europe remained passive. Acts of violent opposition were sporadic. It took time for the trauma of defeat to be overcome, for like-minded defiant spirits to meet and coalesce into groups. The British were in no condition to offer assistance. Most important, only a tiny minority of people were willing actively to oppose the Germans. In the matter of resistance, as in so much else, Churchill's heroic enthusiasm struck little resonance with the mood of Europe's citizens, preoccupied with more humdrum concerns. They needed to feed their families, earn wages, preserve roofs above their heads. All these simple human purposes were put at risk—mortal risk—by any defiance of the occupiers.

Violent demonstrations flew in the face of national consensuses. It was not that people liked the Germans, but that acquiescence in their hegemony appeared to represent the only rational course. Such prominent figures as the French writer André Gide, who utterly rejected collaboration with the occupiers, nonetheless dismissed the notion of violent opposition. Until the Soviet Union and United States entered the war, Hitler's grasp upon his empire was beyond military challenge. Britain's prime minister uttered stirring words, echoed by broadcasters speaking from London in many languages to oppressed peoples, but no British army was capable of reentering the Continent. This made most people in Hitler's new dominions unwilling to threaten the welfare of their own communities by actions which promised retribution.

Even for those who wanted to fight, Churchill severely underestimated the difficulties of conducting guerrilla operations against an efficient and ruthless occupier in heavily urbanised regions of Europe. In Denmark, Holland, Belgium and large parts of France, there were few hiding places for armed bands. The Germans adopted policies designed to promote passivity. Any action against their forces brought down punishment upon entire communities. On May 27, 1941, Churchill sent a note to Lord Selborne, Dalton's successor at the Ministry of Economic Warfare, suggesting providing oppressed people with simple weapons and sticks of dynamite. Yet the use of "simple weapons" by such "oppressed people" provoked determinedly disproportionate German responses. On October 20 that year, an Alsatian Communist shot dead the German military commandant of Nantes, and made good his escape. Historian Robert Gildea has written: "Far from welcoming this assassination as the first step towards their liberation, the population of Nantes was horrified," not least because the dead German seemed to local bourgeois an unusually sympathetic personality though a ruthless anti-Semite. Ninety-eight civilian hostages were executed. This caused Maurice Schumann to broadcast from London on the BBC French Service, urging that such terrorist action should not be repeated. De Gaulle delivered the same message on October 23: "In war there are tactics. The war of the French must be carried out by those in charge, that is, by myself and the National Committee."

Churchill, however, dissented. He believed that it was essential to impose maximum pain and inconvenience upon the enemy. He deemed the deaths of hostages a necessary sacrifice for enabling the French people to show that they would not bow to tyranny, as most had indeed bowed since June 1940. He once told a meeting of the Cabinet Defence Committee that while acts of resistance prompted bloody reprisals, "the blood of the Martyrs was the seed of the church." The behaviour of Hitler's minions in occupied Europe had made the Germans hated as no other race had been hated, he said, and this sentiment must be exploited. He deplored any attempt to stifle resistance in the interests of innocent bystanders. "Nothing must be done which would result in the falling off of this most valuable means of harassing the enemy." This was an extension of the view he adopted when Britain was threatened with invasion. In 1940, Generals Paget and Auchinleck urged that the civil population should be told to stay at home, rather than risk their lives offering ineffectual resistance to the Germans with scythes and brickbats. The prime minister strongly disagreed. In war, he said, quarter is given not on grounds of compassion, but to deter the enemy from fighting to the end: "Here, we want every citizen to fight desperately and they will do so the more if they know that the alternative is massacre." What he expected from British civilians in 1940 he sought thereafter from those of occupied Europe.

Here was Churchill at his most ruthless. He was constantly fearful that, left to itself, Europe would lapse into subservience to Hitler's hegemony. It provoked his chagrin that few French people rallied to de Gaulle's standard not only in 1940, but through the years which followed. Usefully for Churchill's aspirations, Germany adopted towards most of its European empire policies so shamelessly selfish, as well as brutal, that even the rulers of Vichy France came progressively to understand that they could forge no partnership with their occupiers. Berlin wanted only economic plunder for the benefit of the Reich's citizens. Hitler's policies thus assisted those of Churchill.

Yet, at least until after D-Day, in 1944, reprisals convinced most people in the occupied countries that the cost of violent acts outweighed their value. The Norwegians, though strongly anti-German, conducted resistance with notable prudence. Norwegian special forces dispatched from Britain occasionally attacked important targets, such as the Rjukan heavy water plant, but local people avoided open combat. In Czechoslovakia, the May 27, 1942, killing of Reinhard Heydrich, "Protector" of Bohemia and Moravia, by Czechs parachuted in from Britain, prompted shocking reprisals, most notoriously the slaughter of the 198 men of the village of Lidice, whose women were sent to concentration camps. Local resistance groups were smashed. Many Czechs believe to this day that the assassination was mistaken, because it was purchased so dearly in innocent lives.

In France, the detonation of a roadside bomb in Marseilles prompted the Germans to demolish the entire *vieux quartier* of the city, making forty thousand people homeless. Terrasson, a pretty little town in south-central France, suffered heavily both from resistance activism and German reprisals. "The cycle is simple," its mayor, Georges Labarthe, wrote wretchedly to his mother in Paris in June 1944: "the *maquis* conduct an operation, the Germans arrive, the civil population pay the tariff, the Germans go away and the *maquis* reappear. Where there are casualties among the Germans, the retribution is terrible. I must confess that in these circumstances it is hard to be the representative and defender of the people."

In western Europe resistance achieved its greatest strength in wildernesses which mattered least to Hitler strategically—those most remote from potential invasion coasts. An overwhelming majority of people with large possessions—the aristocracy and the business community—collaborated with the occupiers, because they had most to lose. Many SOE agents captured by the Germans were betrayed by local inhabitants. British officers relied for assistance and shelter chiefly upon the little people of their societies—schoolteachers, trades unionists, peasant farmers. Only 20 percent of letters opened by French censors even late in the war, in the first six months of 1944, expressed approval of "terrorism." A typical comment was: "The *maquis* act in the name of patriotism, but fortunately the police are getting tough and I hope with all my heart that these youths are soon destroyed, for they commit all kinds of atrocities on innocent people." One of the best historians of wartime France, Julian Jackson, writes: "Other evidence exists that *maquis* violence was widely condemned." In the Jura, where terrible German acts of savagery took place in 1944, some local doctors refused to tend Resistance wounded. Many people refused fugitives shelter. Priests declined to say prayers for the dying. In Haute-Saône, the Vichyite prefect noted: "Less and less do the terrorists enjoy the complicity of the rural population." Extreme repression and unbridled brutality fuelled hatred but also fear. German policy was notably effective in suppressing dissent.

Churchill envisaged the peoples of Europe causing such trouble for the Germans that occupation became costly, even unviable. Yet untrained and ill-organised civilians could never aspire to defeat regular troops. "What is an army without artillery, tanks and air force?" demanded Stalin contemptuously about the Polish resistance. "In modern warfare such an army is of little use." He was by no means wrong. The objection of many decent and patriotic Europeans to resistance was that its sluggishly mounting tempo of violence sufficed to annoy the Germans, but imposed no crisis upon them. With brave and notable exceptions, it may be suggested that resistance was most enthusiastically supported by those, both British and people of the occupied nations, who had no personal stake in local communities vulnerable to reprisals.

Some senior British officers opposed the SOE's mandate on both pragmatic and ethical grounds. They perceived the unlikelihood of stimulating successful mass revolt, such as Churchill wanted, and were uncomfortable about promoting terrorism by armed civilians. The chief of the Air Staff, Portal, in February 1941 attempted to insist that one of the first SOE parties parachuted into France should wear uniform: "I think the dropping of men dressed in civilian clothes for the purpose of attempting to kill members of the opposing forces is not an operation with which the Royal Air Force should be associated," he told Gladwyn Jebb of the Foreign Office. "I think you will agree that there is a vast difference, in ethics, between the time-honoured operation of the dropping of a spy from the air, and this entirely new scheme for dropping what one can only call assassins." Such fastidiousness may seem ironic when displayed by one of the architects of area bombing. But it illustrates the sentiments of many senior service officers. Others, such as Sir Arthur Harris of Bomber Command, became fanatical foes of the SOE, because they resented the diversion of aircraft to support its networks.

Sir Stewart Menzies and his subordinates in the Secret Intelligence Service hated their amateur rivals, first, on Whitehall territorial grounds, and, second, because in the field ambushes and acts of sabotage excited the Germans and made more difficult discreet intelligence gathering by the SIS's agents. An early SOE hand in the Middle East, Bickham Sweet-Escott, wrote of his own introduction to cloak and daggery: "Nobody who did not experience it can possibly imagine the atmosphere of jealousy, suspicion, and intrigue which embittered relations between the various secret and semi-secret departments in Cairo during that summer of 1941." Matters were not much better a year later, when Oliver Lyttelton was dispatched to the Mediterranean as minister resident. He recorded: "I was disturbed . . . by the lack of security, waste and ineffectiveness of SOE." The same strictures were often voiced in London.

Between 1940 and 1943, the highest achievement of the SOE in most occupied countries was to keep agents alive and wireless transmitters functioning, with most success in rural areas. The Soviet Union's entry into the war prompted a dramatic accession of strength to resistance groups from Europe's Communists. A second critical development in France was Germany's 1943 introduction of massed forced labour, known as the Service du Travail Obligatoire (STO). Tens of thousands of young men fled into hiding in the countryside, to the maquis, to escape deportation to Germany. They formed bands under leaders of differing and often mutually hostile political hues. Most were preoccupied with feeding themselves through banditry which enraged its bourgeois victims, rather than with fighting the Germans. Many French people asserted bitterly after the war, in private at least, that the Germans behaved better than did Communist *maquisards*. There is a widespread delusion that resistance groups were commanded by SOE officers, but this was rarely so. Most British agents fulfilled a liaison role, exercising varying degrees of influence upon French group leaders through their control of cash and supply drops.

Above all, until the spring of 1944 resistance groups were poorly armed. Only then did the Allies possess sufficient aircraft and weapons to begin equipping *maquisards* wholesale. A whimsical November 1941 proposal from Lord Cherwell to drop containers of arms randomly across occupied Europe to encourage spontaneous acts of violence was rejected as a waste of scarce air resources. Until the last months before liberation, sabotage and guerrilla operations in most European countries—with the notable exception of Yugoslavia, of which more below—were on a relatively tiny scale. The so-called Armée Secrète, which recognised the authority of de Gaulle, generally respected instructions from London to remain passive until the approach of D-Day. Communist bands of the FTP—Franc-Tireurs et Partisans—adopted more activist tactics, with ruthless disregard for the interests of local people.

Churchill loved to meet British agents and Frenchmen, returned from their hazardous missions. He entertained at Downing Street Wing Commander Edward Yeo-Thomas—"the White Rabbit"—Jean Moulin and Emmanuel d'Astier de la Vigerie. Such encounters invariably prompted him to urge the RAF to divert more aircraft to aid their struggle. His personal enthusiasm for resistance was critical in overcoming the scepticism of conventional warriors. It was sometimes said of the "Baker Street Irregulars" that Britain was tipped on its side, and everything loose fell into the SOE. Many of its personnel, unsurprisingly, were individualists and eccentrics. Their perspicacity often failed to match their enthusiasm. They cherished extravagant faith in their unseen protégés in occupied Europe. A sceptic remarked of Col. Maurice Buckmaster, chief of the SOE's French Section: "He believed that all his geese were swans."

The SOE's most conspicuous security lapse was its failure, despite many warnings, to perceive that the Germans had so deeply penetrated its Dutch operations that almost every agent parachuted into Holland in 1942–43 landed into enemy hands. The revelation of this disaster, at the end of 1943, precipitated a crisis in the organisation's affairs. Its Whitehall foes, of whom there were many, crowded forward to demand curtailment of its operations and calls on resources. Menzies and his colleagues at the SIS argued that the debacle reflected the chronic amateurishness and lack of tradecraft prevailing at SOE's Baker Street headquarters and pervading its operations in the field. They were by no means wrong. The SOE since 1940 had indeed been learning on the job, at severe cost in lives and wasted effort. Meanwhile in September 1943, the army's exasperation with the SOE's Balkan operations, which it claimed were out of control, caused the C-in-C Middle East to demand that the organisation should be brought under his orders. This issue was still unresolved when the Dutch scandal broke.

On Churchill's return from Marrakesh in January 1944, the row was appealed to him for decision. He renewed the SOE's mandate (though rejecting its presumptuous demand for a seat on the Chiefs of Staff Committee), confirmed its independence, and ordered the RAF to release more aircraft for arms dropping. The organisation's internal historian wrote later: "There is no doubt that, in this critical phase of its development, SOE and the Resistance movements which it led were sustained very largely by the personal influence of Mr. Churchill." The prime minister took the view that the SOE's enthusiasm and activism outweighed its deficiencies. It was too late in the war to undertake wholesale restructuring. Much of the criticism of the SOE, he believed, derived from Whitehall jealousies. It was impossible to conduct a secret war of such an unprecedented kind without misfortunes which cost lives, as do all mistakes in conflict.

Thus, in the last months before liberation, relatively large quantities of arms—though pathetically small quantities of ammunition—began to reach resisters. The British estimated that some 35,000 active *maquisards* were in the field, though de Gaulle claimed a strength of 175,000 for France's secret army. The SOE believed that its *parachutages* provided weapons for 50,000. The intoxicating confidence thus created persuaded some groups to conduct disastrous pitched battles with the Germans. At Mont Mouchet on May 20, 1944, the regional Armée Secrète commander, Emile Coulaudon, ordered a mass concentration of his groups, six thousand strong. On June 10, the Germans attacked them. At least 350 *maquisards* perished, while the remainder dispersed and fled. Local communities suffered devastating reprisals.

Another act of folly, the brief liberation of the town of Tulle in the Corrèze by the Communist FTP for a few hours on June 9, caused SS panzergrenadiers to hang 99 innocent hostages from the lampposts in reprisal for the resistance massacre of the elderly Wehrmacht reservists who had garrisoned the town. At Oradour-sur-Glane the next day, 642 men, women and children were slaughtered, in reprisal for the abduction by *maquisards* of a popular SS battalion commander. That day, from London, Gen. Pierre Koenig, designated by de Gaulle as commander of the FFI—Forces Françaises de l'Intérieur—ordered a "maximum brake on guerrilla activities." Such a demand was at odds both with the mood of the moment and all previous instructions. It created confusion in the ranks of the Resistance. On June 17, Koenig issued a new order: "Continue elusive guerrilla activity to the maximum," while avoiding concentrations. This did not prevent the madness of the Vercors on July 21, where 640 *maquisards* and 201 local civilians were killed, as the Germans assaulted another ill-judged gathering of Resistance forces.

Around 24,000 FFI fighters died during the struggle for France. Thousands more, most of them civilians, perished in reprisals and executions of prisoners, for instance 11,000 in and around Paris; 3,673 in Lyons; 2,863 in the Limoges area; 1,113 in Lille; and similar proportions in lesser cities, together with thousands of others deported to German concentration camps, from which most never returned. It seems doubtful whether it was useful or prudent to arm the French Resistance on a large scale. Churchill's enthusiasm caused the maquis to become dangerous enough to enrage the Germans, but insufficiently powerful to defend themselves or their communities. Most *maquisards* had only pistols or Sten submachine guns with two or three magazines apiece. They lacked heavy weapons, ammunition and radio communications for sustained or large-scale engagements.

The courage and sacrifice of those who supported resistance, or even merely withheld support from Vichy, deserve the profound respect of posterity. But the moral achievement must be detached from cool analysis of the military balance. Postwar claims for the damage inflicted on the enemy by the French Resistance and its SOE sponsors were grossly exaggerated, as German war diaries make plain. Resistance historians, for instance, have claimed that the maquis inflicted hundreds of casualties upon the 2nd SS Das Reich Armoured Division on its march from southern France to Normandy in June 1944. German records, by contrast, reveal only thirty-five killed. The impact of maquis attacks on German communications that summer was infinitesimally smaller than that of Allied air attacks. Resistance fulfilled a striking moral function, especially important in resurrecting the postwar self-respect of occupied nations. Julian Jackson has written: "In the history of France, Resistance is more important as a social and political phenomenon than a military one."

The Balkans, however, were different. There, the terrain was much more favourable to guerrilla warfare. In Albania, Greece, Yugoslavia and also Italy, the prime minister perceived political circumstances and military opportunities which might yield dramatic benefits. New Zealand premier Peter Fraser urged caution, sensibly observing to Churchill that the Balkans was a region "of seething factions, who would turn to whoever would give them most support." But the prime minister believed that local passions could be harnessed to Allied purposes. It was remarked by critics that the enthusiasm of the prime minister and of the SOE's guiding lights reflected a "T. E. Lawrence complex," wild delusions about the prospect that a few personable British officers might influence the behaviour of entire Balkan societies, in support of British foreign policy objectives. American suspicions that imperialistic motives underpinned the SOE caused Roosevelt in October 1943 to advance to Churchill a clumsy request, swiftly dismissed by the prime minister, for Colonel Donovan of the American OSS to assume authority for all Allied special operations in the Balkans.

From 1943 onwards, the SOE lavished much effort upon Mediterranean countries, with mixed results. Some of its most flamboyant officers, men such as Billy Maclean and David Smiley, were dropped into the mountains of Albania to work with local partisans. Almost without exception, they loathed the country and its people. They found the Albanians far more eager to accept weapons and to steal equipment and supplies than to fight the Germans. "How pleased I shall be to return to civilisation again," one officer confided to his diary, "to be among people one can trust and not to be surrounded by dirt, filth and bad manners . . . It is not as if one was doing anything useful here or could do so. There is so little charity among these people that they cannot believe anyone would come all this way just to help them . . . They are boastful and vain with nothing to be boastful or vain about. They have no courage, no consistency and no sense of honour."

Enver Hoxha, the Albanian Communist leader who dominated guerrilla operations, was chiefly concerned to secure his own power base for a postwar takeover. It is easy to see why the Albanians, mired in poverty and a struggle for existence, showed so little enthusiasm for supporting the activist purposes of British missions. Guerrilla operations provoked the Germans to reprisals which the SOE's teams were quite incapable of deflecting. Young British officers in Albania hazarded their own lives with considerable insouciance. Local peasants, however, saw their homes, crops and families imperilled, for no discernible advantage save to pursue a misty vision of "freedom." Beyond a few useful acts of sabotage, in Albania the military achievements of resistance groups were slight.

Throughout the Balkans, internal political rivalries dogged British efforts to mobilise societies against their occupiers. In Greece and Crete, the population was overwhelmingly hostile to the Germans. The country had a long tradition of opposition to authority. Unfortunately, however, Greek society was racked by dissentions, the ferocity of which bewildered British officers thrust into their midst. There was no love for the king, nor for the Greek exile government backed by Churchill. Each guerrilla band cherished its own loyalties. Col. Monty Woodhouse, one of the most celebrated SOE officers who served among the Greeks, reported to Cairo: "No one is ever free from the struggle for existence; everything else is secondary to it. That is why no one outside Greece can speak for the Greeks." The British, on instructions from Cairo and ultimately from Churchill, were predisposed to support royalists. When Napoleon Zervas, leader of the relatively small Republican group EDES, told the SOE in 1943 that he backed the restoration of King George, he was rewarded by receiving twice the arms drops provided to the Communists of

EAM/ELAS, even though the Communists were six times more numerous, and were doing all the fighting. Zervas repaid British largesse by establishing a tacit truce with the Germans, and biding his time to pursue his own purposes. As so often in occupied Europe, political and military objectives pulled British policy in different directions.

In 1944, realities on the ground seemed to make it essential to provide arms to the Communists of ELAS, only some of which were employed against the Germans. Monty Woodhouse was recalled to Britain during the summer, and visited Churchill at Chequers to make the case for sustaining aid to ELAS. Woodhouse told the prime minister that if supplies to the Communists were cut off, "I very much doubt whether any of my officers will get out of Greece alive." Churchill brooded for a moment, then took Woodhouse by the arm and said, "Yes, young man, I quite understand." As the British officer left Chequers, the prime minister said at parting: "I am very impressed, and oppressed and depressed." Albeit hesitantly, Churchill directed that aid to the Communists should be maintained. British agents strove to persuade the Greeks to make common cause, but mutual hatreds were too strong. Moreover, every resistance attack on the Germans provoked reprisals on a scale as dreadful as those in Russia and Yugoslavia, overlaid upon widespread starvation.

Resistance in Greece became a more widespread popular movement than in western Europe. Some spectacular acts of sabotage were carried out by SOE teams, notably the 1942 destruction of the Gorgopotamos bridge. But "pundits overestimated what guerrillas could achieve," in the words of Noel Annan, who served on the Joint Intelligence Staff of the Cabinet Office. He asserts that such successes as the destruction of the Gorgopotamos came too late to be strategically useful, and made the planners in London overly optimistic. "It took months for our liaison officers to persuade ELAS to blow up the bridge. Had it been destroyed earlier it would have cut one of Rommel's supply lines when he stood at El Alamein. But it was not . . . The difficulties with ELAS should have warned the Foreign Office that ELAS's first objective was less to harass the Germans than to eliminate other guerrilla forces and their leaders." Nick Hammond, a British officer with the Greeks, wrote afterwards: "Armed resistance in the open countryside is something rarely undertaken. Only men of extreme, even fanatical enthusiasm will undertake the initiation and leadership of such a resistance, because it invites terrible reprisals on one's family, friends and fellow-countrymen."

In Greece and other occupied countries, the Germans economised on their own manpower by recruiting local collaborators for security duties. In France there were several brutal Pétainist militias, which until the summer of 1944 were notably more numerous than the maquis. The Croat Ustashi in Yugoslavia became a byword for savagery. Cossacks in German uniform, later the objects of much sympathy in the West for their enforced repatriation to Russia, played a prominent role in suppressing resistance groups in northern Italy and Yugoslavia, where their brutality was notorious. The Athens puppet government deployed its own "security battalions" against the guerrillas. A million Greeks lost their homes in consequence of German repression, and a thousand villages were razed. More than 400,000 Greek civilians died in the war, albeit most by mere starvation.

Bloodshed became relentless. Hitler's OKW (Oberkommando der Wehrmacht) headquarters ordered that fifty to a hundred hostages should be killed to avenge each German victim. At the end of October 1943, guerrillas in the northern Peloponnese achieved a notable coup, capturing and then killing 78 men of the 117th Jaeger Division. In consequences, 696 Greeks were executed, twenty-five villages burned. On May 1, 1944, 200 hostages were shot in Athens after an attack on a German general. On the fifth, 216 villagers were massacred in Klisura. On the seventeenth, 100 more hostages were executed in Khalkis. The tempo of such atrocities rose until the last day of the German presence in Greece. As the Wehrmacht withdrew, British officers sought with limited success to persuade the rival armed factions to harass the retreat. "We didn't inflict as much serious damage as we might have done," wrote Monty Woodhouse of the SOE. "But by that time, certainly in the case of EAM and ELAS, their sights were set on the future and not on the immediate future." It can convincingly be argued that much of what did and did not take place reflected domestic strife between Greeks, together with spontaneous acts of opposition to the occupiers, over which the British could exercise negligible influence.

In Italy, partisan warfare began to gather momentum after the Rome government's surrender of September 1943. Again, there were deep divisions between Communist and non-Communist bands. In June 1944, amid the euphoria of the breakthrough to Rome, broadcasts from Alexander's headquarters urged guerrilla bands, by now reckoned to be over 100,000 strong, to attack the Germans in their rear. The consequence was a surge of local assaults, followed by ghastly reprisals. As the Allied offensive in Italy bogged down in the autumn rains, on November 13 a new broadcast was made in Alexander's name, this time urging discretion. It was perceived at Allied headquarters that the call to arms had been delivered prematurely.

In the early spring of 1945, partisans resumed their harassment of the

Germans, and played a noisy part in the last phase of the Italian campaign. They sabotaged bridges and power and phone lines, and attacked German lines of communications. Alexander nonetheless felt obliged to issue a directive on February 4, formally abandoning any aspiration to create a mass partisan army, and substituting a commitment to selective sabotage. The problem was that resistance groups proved chronically resistant to direction from SOE missions: "Self-organised bands . . . are already getting out of hand." It was decreed that weapons should thereafter only be provided to those who could be trusted to use them against the Germans, rather than to promote their own local political ambitions. Headquarters of the 15th Army Group noted ruefully: "A Resistance movement may suddenly transfer itself from the credit to the debit side of the Allied ledger." Here was the nemesis of Churchillian hopes, though in the last weeks of the war Italian partisans seized many towns and villages on their own initiative.

Russia and Yugoslavia were the only countries where partisan warfare significantly influenced Hitler's deployments. In Russia, the Red Army sponsored large irregular forces to harass German lines of communication. Such Soviet operations were assisted by Stalin's indifference to casualties or victims of reprisals. In Yugoslavia, almost from the moment of their conquest in April 1941 the Germans faced local opposition. Field Marshal von Weichs ordered that German troops should shoot male civilians in any area of armed resistance, regardless of whether there was evidence of individual complicity. That October, after suffering a dozen casualties in a clash with partisans, the Germans massacred the entire two-thousand-strong male population of the town of Kragujevac in Serbia. Men and boys were shot in batches of a hundred, through a single day. Even wholesale brutality failed to suppress the Communist guerrillas, however, which grew to a strength of some 200,000. Hitler was determined both to secure the right flank of his Eastern Front and to maintain his hold on Yugoslavia's mineral resources. To achieve this, by 1944 twenty-one Axis divisions were deployed.

Michael Howard, a historian of British wartime strategic deception, believes that this commitment was far more influenced by fears of an Allied amphibious landing in Greece or Yugoslavia than by partisan activity, which could have been contained by much smaller forces. He argues that the German high command was importantly misled by a deception operation, code-named Zeppelin, which suggested an Allied army group in Egypt poised to move against the Balkans. As late as the spring of 1944, OKW in Berlin estimated that there were fourteen Allied divisions in Egypt and Libya, instead of the real three. At the time, however, it was the guerrillas' alleged successes which captured Churchill's imagination. News of Tito's doings, considerably exaggerated in the telling, excited him. Back in January 1943, when he was first briefed about Yugoslavia by his old researcher Bill Deakin, he had perceived possibilities which now seemed to be maturing. Here, at last, was the sort of popular revolt from which he hoped much.

In the autumn of 1943 the British, who had hitherto been supporting Gen. Draza Mihajlović's royalist Cetnik forces, concluded that Tito's partisans were conducting much more effective operations against the Germans, notably in Bosnia and Herzegovina. With persistent naïveté at best—and possibly deceit aforethought, since one of SOE's Cairo officers, James Klugmann, was an NKVD agent and others held strongly left-wing views—they convinced themselves that Tito's people were "not real communists." At the Tehran conference, the "Big Three" agreed that maximum support would be given to the Yugoslav partisans. It suited Stalin's interests to soft-pedal the ideological allegiance to Moscow of "the Jugs," as British soldiers called Tito's people. The Soviet warlord urged a partisan delegation—unsuccessfully—to forgo the red stars on their caps "to avoid frightening the English."

Churchill, in Cairo on his way back from Tehran, reasserted his enthusiasm for the Yugoslav commitment. Ignoring protests that it was inconsistent to support royalists in Greece and "reds" in Yugoslavia, he embraced the simple view that Tito's army would kill more Germans than Mihajlović's, and in this he was surely right. The axis of British effort shifted ruthlessly and dramatically. Beyond air drops and cargo plane landings, in 1944 it became possible to ship arms by sea to the Dalmatian coast. Tito's forces began to receive supplies in large quantities, which transformed their capabilities. Between 1943 and 1945, 16,470 tons of Allied arms were provided to Yugoslavia, against 5,907 tons dropped into Italy, and 2,878 tons sent to southern France.

A high-powered British mission, led by Brig. Fitzroy Maclean, MP, took over Bill Deakin's liaison role at Tito's headquarters in September 1943, and was soon joined by Maj. Randolph Churchill, MP. The partisans, while implacably ideologically hostile, recognised that the prime minister had sent his brightest and best to represent him in their camp. Partisan leader Milovan Djilas wrote: "Deakin was outstandingly intelligent . . . We found out that he was a secretary of a sort to Churchill and this impressed us, as much for the consideration shown to us as for the lack of favouritism among the British top circles when it came to the dangers of war." As for the dissolute Major Churchill, "we of course felt honoured, though it did occur to us that Randolph might be the grey eminence of the mission. But he himself convinced us by his behaviour that he was a secondary figure, and that his father had decided on this gesture out of his aristocratic sense of sacrifice and to lend his son stature. Randolph soon enchanted our commanders and commissars with his wit and unconventional manner, but he revealed through his drinking and lack of interest that he had inherited neither political imagination nor dynamism with his surname."

Djilas's perception of British behaviour, after almost three years in which the partisans had conducted an unaided struggle, was unsurprising and not unjust: "The British had no choice but either to carry out a landing in order to fight the Partisans, or else to come to an agreement with them on a rational, mutually profitable basis. They chose the latter, cautiously and without enthusiasm . . . Our own dogmatic ideological distrust kept us from understanding them, though it also preserved us from any hasty enthusiasm." The Americans never shared British warmth towards Tito. In April 1944, they angered Churchill by dispatching a mission to Mihajlović, which he ordered to be delayed in transit for as long as possible: "The greatest courtesy being used to our friends and Allies in every case," he wrote on April 6, "but no transportation." The U.S. team eventually reached the Cetniks, but the British were successful in deflecting Washington from sending supplies to them.

Tito's partisans never had the training, organisation or heavy weapons to defeat German forces in head-to-head combat. They were unable to evict the occupiers from any substantial towns. Nonetheless, they achieved control of large rural areas of Yugoslavia. Repeated German offensives, supported by the Luftwaffe, inflicted heavy casualties, above all on the civilian population, but failed to destroy Tito's army. More British officers were dropped to local headquarters, so that there were soon eleven missions and wireless transmitters on the ground. The SOE teams found themselves frustrated, because the partisans were indifferent to their proposals and advice, save about the mechanics of supply. The SOE's internal historian observed laconically: "It is a little doubtful whether the Missions served any purpose save to give adventurous occupation to a number of very tough young men . . . half a ton of ammunition and explosives would have been more effective than half a ton of British Liaison Officers." The allegiance of Tito's people was unequivocally to their own Communist movement. From 1942 to 1945, paralleling the struggle against the Germans, a bloody civil war was waged between partisans and Cetniks, in which the balance of atrocities was about even.

The British were unable to influence this, though Churchill made repeated efforts to reconcile Tito to the exiled King Peter. Even in June

1944, when the partisan leader had to flee from a German surprise attack and accept airborne evacuation to sanctuary at the Allied headquarters in Bari, Tito became no more biddable. The obliging British thereafter dispatched him to the offshore island of Vis, where he was secure from German assault and could prepare for a renewed partisan advance. Yet Tito's forces were unable to deliver a decisive blow against their occupiers, and were obliged to enlist the aid of the Red Army to dispossess the Cetniks of Serbia late in 1944. Unlike any guerrilla movement in western Europe, Yugoslav resistance diverted from the war's main battlefields significant enemy forces—though considerably less, if Michael Howard's interpretation of OKW documents is correct, than legend has suggested.

The political complexities of aiding resistance movements prompted exasperation among British ministers and field officers charged with reaching local accommodations. Harold Macmillan wrote in May 1944 that it was all very well for the prime minister to urge support for anti-German factions of widely varying political hues, but in an age of rapid communications, "the difficulty is that with . . . the universal listening to the radio, it is difficult [for the British] to be a Communist in Yugoslavia and a Royalist in Greece." Though the Greek Communists wanted British weapons they hated Churchill, because they knew that he wished to restore their king. Almost all the arms shipped to the Balkans in the course of the war, and likewise those provided to nationalists in Southeast Asia, were used later to advance anti-Western, anticapitalist interests. Churchill told Eden, "I have come to the conclusion that in Tito we have nursed a viper . . . he has started biting us."

Sir William Deakin has written: "Paradoxically, British influence on Resistance in Europe was at its strongest at the lowest point of our military strength and resources, and during the period of our own isolation [1940–42]." As resistance groups gained in confidence and the Germans began to withdraw, any gratitude they felt towards the British for supplying them with arms was outweighed by alienation from perceived British political objectives. A French historian of the Resistance, Henri Michel, has written: "Great Britain promised to the Resistance the return to a pre-war Europe, which the Resistance had rejected." This was an overstated generalisation, but reflected widespread sentiment.

By May 1944, during the approach to D-Day, 120 British and American heavy aircraft were committed to dropping arms to European resistance movements. An entire Balkan Air Force had been created, to supply Yugoslavia. The SOE had grown into an organisation staffed by more than eleven thousand soldiers and civilians, operating a network of training schools in Britain, the Mediterranean and India, and communicating with agents in some twenty countries. Its postwar internal history argued that no other force of its size contributed so much to the Allied war effort. Its agents and activities have stimulated a flood of postwar books and films, historical and fictional, which continues to this day. The romance of the story is indisputable, though service with the SOE in the field—again, contrary to popular myth—was actuarially less hazardous than fighting with an infantry battalion, never mind flying with Bomber Command. For instance, of 215 SOE personnel dropped into Yugoslavia, only 25 died. "F" Section lost a quarter of the 400 agents dispatched to France, but even this percentage compares favourably with the casualties of rifle companies in many campaigns.

It was unquestionably vital for the Allies to sustain contact between the free world and the occupied countries. The BBC's broadcasts in many languages kept alight candles of hope which played a moving and critical role in the lives of millions of people enduring tyranny. There remains no doubt of the merits of dispatching agents to gather intelligence, contact anti-German groups, establish networks and assist escaping Allied personnel. In 1944–45, partisans were often useful as guides and intelligence sources for the advancing Allied forces, but this was a marginal activity.

The important question about the SOE concerns the wisdom of its military policies. To the end of the war, while the Chiefs of Staff were eager for resistance groups to "make a mess," as one SOE officer in occupied France interpreted his orders, no coherent strategy was promulgated, based on a realistic assessment of what guerrillas might hope to achieve. Though useful work was done in France after D-Day, attacks on communications and German garrisons almost invariably hurt local populations more than the enemy. What else could have been expected?

The British Chiefs of Staff in 1944 urged that local resisters should be warned against provoking pitched battles with the Germans. Maj. Gen. Colin Gubbins, military head of the SOE, was formally rebuked when a bloody uprising took place in Slovakia, because his organisation appeared to have defied its orders and promoted it.

But the high command was thus attempting belatedly to reverse the policy pursued by the SOE, strongly encouraged by the prime minister, since 1940. Nor did Churchill share the generals' scruples. For instance, at a January 27, 1944, meeting with the Air Staff, the minister of economic warfare, Ismay and others, he expressed the desire to promote large-scale clashes between the French Resistance and the Germans. "He wished and believed it possible to bring about a situation in the whole area between the Rhone and the Italian frontier comparable to the situation in Yugoslavia. Brave and desperate men could cause the most acute embarrassment to the enemy and it was right that we should do all in our power to foster so valuable an aid to Allied strategy." On April 22, Churchill was urging on the Chiefs of Staff Operation Caliph, a scheme to land some thousands of British troops on the coast near Bordeaux simultaneously with D-Day. There was, he wrote, "a chance of a surprise descent into a population eager to revolt."

Though Caliph was never executed, Churchill was still eager to incite guerrillas to strike wholesale at the Germans. A million Yugoslavs died in strife which he explicitly, and surely wrongly, sought to replicate in southern France. Popular revolts, of which the last took place in Prague in May 1945, cost many lives to little useful purpose. Mark Mazower has written: "Only in the USSR did German counter-terror fail." Churchill's grand vision for revolt by the oppressed peoples of Europe was heroic, but could play no rightful part in industrialised war against a ruthless occupier. Deliverance relied upon great armies.

Any judgement on the resistance movement must weigh the balance between moral benefit and human cost, acknowledging that the military achievement was small. Col. Dick Barry, chief of staff to Gubbins, admitted afterwards: "It was only just worth it." The French people, for instance, took pride in the FFI's flamboyant demonstration when they took to the streets of Paris as the Germans retreated in August 1944. But the German decision to quit the capital was quite uninfluenced by the Resistance. In Crete in July 1944, against the orders of the SOE, local guerrillas embarked upon open attacks which provoked the Germans to execute a thousand innocent civilians, and burn thirty villages. The SOE's own historian wrote ruefully: "The game was not worth pursuing on these terms."

The most disastrous resistance epic of all was, of course, the Warsaw rising, which began in August 1944. There, Churchill's 1940 vision of an oppressed people breaking forth in revolt against their occupiers was dramatically fulfilled, though the SOE did not directly encourage the Polish initiative. But, in the absence of support from Allied regular forces, the Polish Home Army was comprehensively defeated. The British made much of their attempts, thwarted by Russian intransigence, to parachute arms to the Warsaw Poles. Gubbins was even rash enough to urge the Chiefs of Staff to accede to the urging of the Home Army's leaders that a Polish parachute brigade then in Britain should be dropped to aid the rebels. Even beyond the practical difficulties, it reflected lamentably on Gubbins's professional judgement that he endorsed such a romantic and futile notion. Parachute-dropped aid from Britain might have assuaged the frustration of Churchill and his people, but could not conceivably have altered the tragic outcome in Warsaw. Large-scale popular uprisings were doomed, unless conducted in concert with the advances of armies, which rendered them strategically irrelevant. The incitement of violent opposition in occupied countries made sense between 1940 and 1942, when every ruthless expedient had to be tried to avert Allied defeat. But it became irresponsible in 1944–45, when Allied victory was assured.

Among the occupied nations, postwar gratitude to Britain for the promotion of resistance was often equivocal. De Gaulle, with characteristic gracelessness, expelled SOE personnel from France as soon as he had power to do so. Georgios Papandreou, the Greek exile prime minister, told Harold Macmillan shortly before his country's liberation that the British should not disguise from themselves the fact that their prestige in the Balkans had fallen, while that of the Russians had risen, despite Allied victories in France and Italy: "Moreover, in our desire to attack the Germans we had roused and armed most dangerous Communist forces in Greece itself." Churchill's wartime enthusiasm for resistance groups was soured in 1944 and thereafter by the triumphs of several Communist and nationalist movements in their own countries. They seized power, or in some cases merely attempted to do so, throwing themselves into domestic struggles with greater determination than they had displayed against the Germans.

Towards the end of the war, Jock Colville describes how the controller of BBC European Services, the former diplomat Ivone Kirkpatrick, "gave a damning account of the inefficacy of both SOE and PWE [Political Warfare Executive], both of which have been loud in self-advertisement." Kirkpatrick observed that their failures confirmed his own beliefs in the importance of parliamentary scrutiny. Secret mandates rendered the SOE and PWE immune from the sceptical oversight their activities would otherwise have received. This is a criticism applicable to most secret intelligence organisations in war or peace, but Kirkpatrick knew enough of the SOE to render his view significant. "Special ops" recruited some remarkable men and women, and could claim useful sabotage achievements. But its essential purpose was misconceived. "The occupied nations believed with passion," in the words of Sir William Deakin, "and fought to construct their secret armies in the interior and exterior Resistance which would play a leading part in the last stage of liberation of their countries. But this was an obsessive dream."

The historian Thomas Arnold declared in 1842: "If war, carried out by regular armies under the strictest discipline, is yet a great evil, an irregular partisan warfare is an evil ten times as intolerable . . . letting loose a multitude of armed men, with none of the obedience and none of the honourable feelings of the soldier." It may be argued that Arnold's idealised view of warfare was rendered anachronistic by Hitler's tyranny, and by the need to mobilise every possible means of undoing it. Arnold, indeed, qualified his own assertion by saying that, if an invader breached the laws of conflict, "a guerrilla war against such an invader becomes justifiable." But nowhere, even in Yugoslavia, did resistance operations avert the need for regular forces to defeat those of the Nazis. France would not have been liberated one day later had the maquis never existed. The case for resistance, though by no means a negligible one, rests upon its contribution to the historic self-respect of occupied societies, to national legend.

The most baleful consequence of resistance was that it represented the legitimisation of violent civilian activity in opposition to local regimes, of a kind which has remained a focus of controversy throughout the world ever since. Not only the Germans, but also many citizens of occupied countries, endorsed the view that "one man's freedom-fighter is another man's terrorist." It is useful to recall that such a man as Portal perceived the SOE's personnel as terrorists. Though British agents were seldom directly concerned in the more ruthless actions of local groups, it was endemic to the nature of the struggle that partisans armed by London shot prisoners, sometimes wholesale; murdered real or supposed collaborators and members of rival factions; and often supported themselves through institutionalised banditry. A precedent was set by the wartime democracies' support for irregular warfare which could never be undone.

It would be an exaggeration to say that the SOE enabled dissident elements of several societies to overthrow their traditional social orders. The collapse of the Balkan monarchies was inevitable, cause for lament only to a Victorian sentimentalist such as the prime minister. In western Europe anti-Communist governments, decisively assisted by the presence of Anglo-American armies, were able to prevail in 1944–45. But the impact of the SOE's aid to resistance movements was significantly greater upon postwar societies than on military outcomes in the struggle against the Germans. Churchill came to recognise this. David Reynolds notes the remarkable fact that, in the six volumes of Churchill's war memoirs, the SOE is mentioned only once, in an appendix. " 'Setting Europe ablaze' had proved a damp squib," says the historian. It was fortunate for the peoples of many occupied countries that this was so.

SEVENTEEN

Overlord

IN THE FIFTH YEAR of Britain's war, all those concerned with its direction were desperately tired: "It's not the hard work, it's the hard worry," said Robert Bruce Lockhart, head of the Political Warfare Executive. To the British public, the wait for D-Day, the decisive milestone in the war in the west, seemed interminable. The Ministry of Information, in one of its regular opinion surveys, described domestic morale in the spring of 1944 as "poor," not least because of public apprehension about invasion casualties. "Spirits remain at a low level," reported the ministry's monitors on April 14. More and more workers flaunted disaffection. Industrial stoppages soared. February found 120,000 miners on unofficial strike in Yorkshire, 100,000 in Wales, and several hundred thousand more elsewhere. Even the president of the miners' union suggested that Trotskyite agitation was playing a part.

Miners' strikes abated in April after wages were increased, but there were also stoppages among gas workers and engineering apprentices. Some 730,000 man-hours were lost in one Scottish aircraft factory. At another firm in August 1944, 419,000 hours were lost when workers rejected a management proposal that women should manufacture textile machinery—the firm's normal business—while men continued to make aircraft components. On April 8, 1944, the British embassy in Washington reported to London about American public opinion: "Considerable disquiet is being evidenced over general political situation in England. This has centred mainly round Churchill's demand for a [parliamentary] vote of confidence, through continuing coal and shipyard strikes, alleged evidence of failures of party truce . . . are being taken as indications that all is by no means well. Press reports give impression that there is deep dissatisfaction over domestic policy and that British public no less than American is apprehensive over apparent lack of Allied unity."

The British and American peoples would have been even more alarmed had they known of the acrimony which overtook relations between Churchill and his Chiefs of Staff in the spring of 1944. Ironically, given that the prime minister's interest in the Japanese war was desultory, this was provoked by argument about operations in the Far East. Churchill became obsessed with the desire to commit all available British forces, including the powerful fleet earmarked to join the Americans in the Pacific, to a "Bay of Bengal" strategy for the recapture of Burma and Malaya. He was especially enthusiastic about a prospective landing on Sumatra, to provide a stepping-stone. He threatened to impose this plan on the Chiefs of Staff, against their implacable opposition, by exercising his prerogative as minister of defence. On March 21, Brooke wrote of a meeting with Cunningham and Portal: "We discussed . . . how best to deal with Winston's last impossible document. It is full of false statements, false deductions and defective strategy. We cannot accept it as it stands and it would be better if we all three resigned sooner than accept his solution."

It was a measure of the extravagance of Churchill's behaviour, and of the exhaustion of the Chiefs at this time, that they should have discussed resignation in the shadow of D-Day. The prime minister had never visited the Far East, knew nothing of conditions there, and seldom acted wisely in his occasional interventions in a hemisphere where Allied operations were overwhelmingly dominated by the United States. In the event, a compromise was fudged. The British proposed a campaign against the Japanese, launched from Australia through Borneo. A minor-key version of this was executed by Australian forces in the summer of 1945. Relations between the Chiefs of Staff and the prime minister steadied in the weeks following the awful March 1944 meetings, as the minds of these strained and weary men focused on the dominant reality of impending invasion of the Continent.

Churchill's misgivings about Overlord persisted until the invasion. D-Day planner Lt. Gen. Sir Frederick Morgan, his rancour increased by being denied an operational role in the invasion, said later: "Until the invasion of NW Europe was actually demonstrated to be successful, I believe [the prime minister] had the conviction it could not succeed." This is an overstatement and oversimplification, but there is no doubt of Churchill's unhappiness about Allied deployments. All through the spring of 1944, he chafed at the inadequate resources, as he perceived it, committed to Italy, and about continuing U.S. insistence upon Anvil, the planned Franco-American landing in southern France. Ironically, after so many clashes between Churchill and his Chiefs of Staff, they were now brought together by opposition to U.S. European strategy. "Difficulties again with our American friends," Brooke wrote on April 5, "who still persist in wanting to close down operations in Italy and open new ones in the south of France, just at the most critical moment." The same day, Churchill minuted the chiefs: "The campaign in the Aegean was ruined by stories of decisive battles in Italy. The decisive battles in Italy were ruined by pulling out seven of the best divisions at the critical time for Overlord."

On April 19, he talked of the invasion to Cadogan: "This battle has been forced upon us by the Russians and the United States military authorities." The diplomat, who spent some hours that day in meetings with the prime minister, was dismayed by his rambling: "I really am fussed about the PM," he wrote in his diary. "He is not the man he was twelve months ago, and I really don't know whether he can carry on." When the dominion prime ministers met in London on May 1 to begin a nine-day conference, Canadian premier Mackenzie King joined South Africa's Jan Smuts in paying tribute to Churchill's achievement in having deflected the Americans from a D-Day in 1942 or 1943. Churchill avowed to the dominion leaders that he himself would have "preferred to roll up Europe from the southeast, joining hands with the Russians. However, it had proved impossible to persuade the United States to this view. They had been determined at every stage upon the invasion in North-West Europe, and had consistently wanted us to break off the Mediterranean operations."

The range of problems besetting the prime minister was as daunting as ever, especially when others saw in him the same exhaustion as did Cadogan. "Struck by how very tired and worn out the prime minister looks now," wrote Colville on April 12. Churchill was full of fears about the cost of Overlord, though he wrote cheerfully to Roosevelt that day, asserting that he did not think losses would be as high as the pessimists predicted: "In my view, it is the Germans who will suffer very heavy casualties when our band of brothers gets among them." The prime minister had never liked Montgomery, whose egoism and crassness grated on him. Now, he told the War Office that the general must abandon his vainglorious round of public receptions and civic visits. In particular, Churchill recoiled from Monty's proposal to hold a "day of prayer" and to "hallow" Britain's armed forces in advance of D-Day at a grand religious service during which the king's coronation regalia would be paraded. Such an occasion, thought Churchill, would be more likely to demoralise the invasion forces than inspire them.

Intelligence warned that Hitler's secret weapons, flying bombs and rockets, would soon start to fall upon Britain. There was continuing difficulty with Washington about the Free French. The United States refused to concede authority in France to de Gaulle following the invasion. Churchill agreed that it would be prudent to keep the general in Algiers until the last moment before D-Day. He chafed unceasingly about the stalemate in Italy, both at Anzio and around Monte Cassino. Again and again, Allied forces suffered heavy casualties in assaults frustrated by Kesselring's stubborn defenders. Greek troops and sailors in Egypt mutinied, calling for Communist participation in their own leadership. An ugly armed confrontation took place. Churchill insisted on rejection of the mutineers' demands. The revolt was suppressed after a British officer was killed.

The Foreign Office and the service chiefs urged the prime minister to curb his telegraphic bombardment of Roosevelt about strategic issues. Churchill now favoured additional landings on the Atlantic coast simultaneous with Overlord. Dill cautioned him on April 24: "The president, as you know, is not military-minded." Appeals to Roosevelt were simply referred to Marshall, who could only be irked by attempts to circumvent him. The British lost an important battle with Washington about preinvasion bombing of French rail links. Churchill and the War Cabinet opposed extensive attacks, which were bound to kill many French civilians. Eisenhower and his staff insisted that a sustained interdiction campaign was essential, to slow the German post-D-Day buildup. Roosevelt and Marshall agreed, and were surely right. The RAF joined the USAAF to mount raids by night and day in the weeks before June 6, which inflicted damage of critical value to the Allied armies, at the cost of around 15,000 French lives. In the course of the whole war, Allied bombing killed 70,000 French people, against 50,000 British who died at the hands of the Luftwaffe.

Relations with the Russians had grown icy. Moscow accused the British of intriguing against them in Romania. Churchill wrote bleakly to Eden on May 8, "The Russians are drunk with victory, and there is no length they may not go." In the preceding six months, 191 British ships had carried more than a million tons of weapons and supplies to Russia, at last matching the scale of deliveries to the need. But there was no gratitude from Stalin. Wrangles about Poland persisted. Churchill again urged the London Poles to show themselves less intractable. He perceived how little leverage they possessed, with the Russians on the brink of overrunning their country, and Washington apparently indifferent.

The British won a notable victory that spring when they repulsed a Japanese offensive in northwest India, against Imphal and Kohima. This, however, increased tensions with the Americans. They intensified demands for a major offensive into northern Burma, to open the land route into China. Churchill deplored the prospect of a campaign in steaming, fever-ridden jungles, to no purpose that he valued. But, in the absence of U.S. shipping for amphibious landings in Southeast Asia, Slim's Fourteenth Army was indeed committed to invade northern Burma.

On May 14, there was belated good news from Italy. Alexander's Diadem offensive broke through the German line, a notable contribution being made by Gen. Alphonse Juin's French colonial forces. On the twenty-third, the Anglo-Americans launched their breakout from the Anzio perimeter. Churchill urged on Alexander the importance of cutting off Kesselring's retreat, a much more important objective than the seizure of Rome. General Mark Clark disagreed, however. His U.S. Fifth Army drove hard for the Italian capital, diverting only a single division to impede the enemy's withdrawal. So skilful were German disengagements, in Italy as later in northwest Europe, that it is unlikely Clark could have stopped Kesselring, even had he committed himself wholeheartedly to do so. But he did not. The liberation of Rome on June 4 prompted celebration among the Allied nations for a symbolic victory, but its strategic significance was small. As everybody concerned, from the prime minister downwards, should have perceived, the Italian capital was a mere geographical location. Kesselring was once more able to establish a defensive line. The Italian campaign continued as it had begun, in frustration and disappointment for its commanders and above all for its principal sponsor, Winston Churchill.

The prime minister seems quite wrong to have supposed that the Allied cause would have profited from an increased Italian commitment in 1944. For all Churchill's personal enthusiasm for Alexander, the Guardsman was an inadequate commander whose chief virtue was that he worked amicably with the Americans, as Montgomery did not. He seldom pressed a point, because he rarely had one to make. The terrain of Italy favoured the defence, which Kesselring conducted brilliantly. It was right for the Allies to take Sicily in July 1943, right to land and fight in Italy two months later. It was essential, once committed, to sustain a limited campaign there until 1945. But the Americans were correct, first to insist upon Overlord, then to accord its interests overwhelming priority. It is hard to believe that the forces later diverted to Operation Anvil would have achieved commensurate results if they had been retained in Italy. The Germans were too good, the battlefield unsuited to Allied purposes. Moreover, with the northern French rail net wrecked by bombing, Marseilles later proved a vital logistics hub for all of Eisenhower's armies, a channel for 40 percent of their supplies up to December 1944.

The prime minister thus expended capital in a struggle with Washington that he was bound to lose, and deserved to. He might have fared better in some of his trials of strength with the United States in 1944 had he not chosen to challenge his ally on so many fronts. On June 4, following the news of Rome's fall, he cabled Roosevelt: "How magnificently your troops have fought. I hear that relations are admirable between our own armies in every rank there, and here certainly it is an absolute brotherhood." It is necessary for great men at great moments to say such things to each other, but Churchill's rhetoric stretched truth to its limits. The U.S. journalist John Gunther put the matter more realistically when he wrote in a contemporary book about Overlord, "Lots of Americans and British have an atavistic dislike of one another."

The best that can be said about Anglo-American relations in 1944—and it is a very important best—is that at the operational level, the two nations' armed forces worked adequately together. Britain and the United States were the only major belligerents to sustain a real collaboration; Germany and Japan, and the Western Allies and Russia, did not. The men on the spot knew it was vital that it should be so. The Americans liked some senior British officers—Portal, Tedder, Morgan, Montgomery's chief of staff Freddie de Guingand—even if they found it hard to relate to others such as Brooke. Cunningham, for the Royal Navy, observed that he found it easier to get along with America's soldiers than with her sailors, above all King, the glowering chief of naval operations. The U.S. admiral never forgave the British for rejecting a request for the loan of an aircraft carrier for Pacific operations at a desperate moment in 1942, after the Americans had several times made their own flattops available to support British purposes in the European theatre. But while it is acknowledged that all alliance relationships are profoundly difficult, there remains much cause for admiration and gratitude for the manner in which the U.S. and British armed forces made common cause between 1942 and 1945. Eisenhower, who privately liked the British a good deal less than his geniality caused them to suppose, deserved much of the credit.

The troubles of the alliance were most conspicuous at its summit. Churchill, speaking of Allied deception plans, famously observed that truth is so precious that it must be protected by a bodyguard of lies. He might have said the same about his relationship with the United States. Benign deceits were indispensable. In May 1942, when criticism of his leadership was at its height, a letter writer to the *Times* suggested that instead of being prime minister, Churchill should fill "a place that has long been vacant in our body politic; it is the post of Public Orator." The proposal was mischievous, but this was a role which Churchill indeed filled to supreme effect, in conducting Britain's dealings with the United States. In his speeches between 1940 and 1945, he created a glorious fiction of shared British and American purposes. He never hinted to his own public, still less the transatlantic one, his frustrations and disappointments about the policies of Roosevelt, any more than he did about those of Stalin. Roosevelt, in his turn, largely reciprocated. The key to understanding the wartime Anglo-American relationship is to strip aside the rhetoric of the two leaders and acknowledge that it rested, as relations between states always do, upon perceptions of national interest. There was some genuine sentiment on Churchill's side, but none on Roosevelt's.

As D-Day approached, Churchill's attitude was bewilderingly complex, perhaps even to himself. He thrilled to a historic military operation, the success of which would go far to fulfil every hope he had cherished since 1940. He emphasised to his own people, as well as to the Americans, that Britain was wholeheartedly committed. He took the keenest interest in every detail of the invasion plans, and personally originated the Mulberry artificial harbours which were to be deployed off the Normandy coast. But he never ceased to lament the consequences of the huge commitment to Eisenhower's campaign for that of Alexander in Italy. He knew that the United States would dominate operations in northwest Europe once the Allies were ashore. The British war effort would attain its apogee on June 6. Thereafter, it must shrink before the sad gaze of its chieftain. At the British Army's peak strength in Normandy, Montgomery commanded 14 British, 1 Polish and 3 Canadian divisions in contact with the enemy. The U.S. Army in northwest Europe grew to 60 divisions, while the Red Army in mid-1944 deployed 480, albeit smaller formations. Seldom was less than two-thirds of the German army deployed on the Eastern Front. Throughout the last year of the war, Churchill was labouring to compensate by sheer force of will and personality for the waning significance of Britain's contribution.

For all his declarations of optimism to Roosevelt and Marshall, and at the May 15 final briefing before the king and senior Allied commanders at Montgomery's headquarters, St. Paul's School in West London, he nursed terrible fears of failure, or of catastrophic casualties. Every rational calculation suggested that the Allies, aided by surprise, airpower and massive resources, should get ashore successfully. But no one knew better than Churchill the extraordinary fighting power of Hitler's army and the limitations of the citizen soldiers of Britain and the United States, most recently exposed at Anzio. His imagination often soared to heights unattained by lesser mortals, but also plunged to corresponding depths. So often—in France and the Mediterranean, at Singapore, in Crete, Libya,

Tunisia, Italy—his heroic expectations had been dashed, or at least limply fulfilled.

If, for whatever reason, D-Day failed, the consequences for the Grand Alliance would be vast and terrible. Hitler's defeat would still be assured, but no new invasion could be launched until 1945. The peoples of Britain and the United States, already tired of war, would suffer a crippling blow to their morale, and to confidence in their leaders. Eisenhower and Montgomery would have to be sacked, replacements identified from a meagre list of candidates. And this was a U.S. presidential election year, so disaster in Normandy might conceivably precipitate defeat for Roosevelt. At Westminster and in Whitehall, there were already plenty of mutterings that Churchill himself was no longer physically fit to lead the country. "I'm fed up to the back teeth with work," he growled to his secretary Marion Holmes on the night of May 14, "so I'll let you off lightly." Though his fears about Overlord were unlikely to be fulfilled, and his apprehensions were magnified by his burdens and exhaustion, who could blame him for allowing them to fill his mind? What seems most remarkable is the buoyancy and good cheer with which, in the last weeks before D-Day, he concealed black thoughts from all but his intimates.

Alan Brooke invoked the authority of the king to dissuade Churchill from viewing the D-Day assault from a cruiser in the Channel. The prime minister felt that he had earned the right to witness this greatest event of the western war: "A man who has to play an effective part, with the highest responsibility, in taking grave and terrible decisions of war may need the refreshment of adventure," he wrote aggrievedly. Yet, beyond the risk to his safety, Brooke surely feared that, should there be a crisis on the day, Churchill would find it irresistible to meddle. It was for this reason that, since 1942, the CIGS had always sought to ensure that the prime minister was absent from any theatre where a battle was imminent. On the morning of June 6, had Churchill been aboard a warship in the Channel, he would have found it intolerable to stand mute and idle while—for instance—the Americans struggled on Omaha Beach. Commanders striving to direct the battle deserved to be spared from Churchillian advice and imprecations.

Thus, he was obliged to content himself with a round of visits to the invasion forces as they prepared for their moment of destiny. "Winston . . . has taken his train and is touring the Portsmouth area and making a thorough pest of himself!" wrote Brooke ungenerously. The day of June 4 found the prime minister aboard his railway carriage, parked a few miles from the coast in a siding at Droxford, in Hampshire, amid a revolving cast of visitors. Eden was irritated by the inconveniences of the accommodation, which had only one bath and one telephone: "Mr. Churchill seemed to be always in the bath and General Ismay always on the telephone. So that, though we were physically nearer the battle, it was almost impossible to conduct any business." Out of earshot of the prime minister, Ernest Bevin and the foreign secretary chatted amiably, though disloyally, about the possibility of sustaining the coalition government if "the old man" was obliged to retire. Bevin said he could work with Eden as prime minister, so long as the Tory committed himself to nationalising the coal mines, which the unions would insist upon. Smuts joined them, and asked what they had been discussing. When told Bevin's terms, "Socrates" said crisply: "Cheap at the price." It was a curiously tasteless discussion for the three men to hold, as half a million young men prepared to hurl themselves at Hitler's Atlantic Wall. But it reflected the new mood among Britain's politicians, who were looking to a future beyond Winston Churchill.

De Gaulle came, belatedly summoned from Algiers. The prime minister walked down the rail tracks to meet him, arms outstretched in welcome. The Frenchman ignored the offered embrace, and vented his bitterness that he himself was denied a role in the Allied return to his country. Churchill told him that the Americans insisted that his committee should not be granted its claim to the governance of liberated French territory. The British must respect U.S. wishes. He urged de Gaulle to seek a personal meeting with Roosevelt, in the hope that this might resolve their differences. The Frenchman later claimed that at Droxford Churchill told him that if forced to choose between America and France, Britain would always side with the United States. This was almost certainly false, or at least a wilful exaggeration. But de Gaulle's bitterness about being denied authority in France, a claim which he had striven for four years to justify, confirmed an animosity towards Britain which persisted for the rest of his life. Churchill exchanged cables with Roosevelt about the possibility of sending the Free French leader back to Algiers. In the event, he was allowed to remain. But Anglo-French relations were poisoned to a degree unassuaged by de Gaulle's subsequent elevation to power.

The Yugoslav partisan leader Milovan Djilas was with Stalin at his dacha outside Moscow when word came that the Allies would land in France the next day. The Soviet warlord responded with unbridled cynicism: "Yes, there'll be a landing, if there is no fog. Until now there was always something that interfered. I suspect tomorrow it will be something else. Maybe they'll meet up with some Germans! What if they meet up with some Germans? Maybe there won't be a landing then, but just promises as usual." Molotov hastily explained to the Yugoslav that Stalin did not really doubt that there would be an invasion, but enjoyed mocking the Allies. On this matter, after the prevarications and deceits of the previous two years, the Soviet leader had perhaps earned his jibes.

By the evening of June 5, Churchill was back in London. As Clementine departed for bed, she bade good night to her husband in his Map Room below Whitehall. He said: "Do you realize that by the time you wake up in the morning, twenty thousand young men may have been killed?" Unlike the Americans, with their unshakeable optimism, Churchill had borne the consequences of so many failures since 1940. It would be the crowning misery if British arms now failed to acquit themselves in a manner worthy of this crowning hour.

The D-Day landings of June 6 represented the greatest feat of military organisation in history, a triumph of planning, logistics and above all human endeavour. The massed airborne assault on the flanks which began in darkness, the air and naval bombardment followed by the dawn dash up the fire-swept shoreline by more than 100,000 American, British and Canadian engineers, infantrymen, armoured crews and gunners, achieved brilliant success. In a spirit that would have warmed the prime minister's heart, as one landing craft of the East Yorkshire Regiment approached the beach at La Brèche, company commander Major "Banger" King read *Henry V* aloud to his men:

> *On, on you noble English!*
> *Whose blood is fet from fathers of war-proof.*

At Colleville, the local mayor appeared on the sands to welcome the invaders, his person adorned by a gleaming brass fireman's helmet. At Omaha Beach, the U.S. 29th Division landed to meet the most savage resistance of the day. "As our boat touched sand and the ramp went down," an infantryman recalled later, "I became a visitor to hell." To Ernest Hemingway, serving as a war correspondent, the guns of the supporting battleships "sounded as though they were throwing whole railway trains across the sky." The invaders fought doggedly through flame and smoke, wire entanglements, pillboxes, minefields and gun positions, to stake out the claims of the Allied armies inside Hitler's Europe.

Hitler's Atlantic Wall was breached. Churchill spent the morning of

D-Day in his Map Room, following the progress of the landings hour by hour. To few men in the world did the battle mean so much. At noon, he told the House of Commons: "This vast operation is undoubtedly the most complex and difficult that has ever taken place." He lunched with the king, then returned for the afternoon to Downing Street, then at 6:15 felt able to tell the Commons that the battle was proceeding "in a highly satisfactory manner." Instead of the carnage which Churchill feared, just three thousand American, British and Canadian troops died on D-Day, together with about the same number of French civilians. By nightfall, in places the invaders had advanced several miles inland, securing perimeters which would soon be linked. A long and terrible struggle lay ahead, as invaders and defenders raced to reinforce their rival armies in Normandy. There were days when more Allied soldiers perished than on June 6. But the triumph of Overlord was assured.

Critically aided both by Anglo-American deception plans, which kept Hitler in expectation of further landings, and by preinvasion bombing, the German buildup proved much slower than had been feared. By nightfall on June 7, 250,000 of Eisenhower's men were ashore. Three evenings later, there were 400,000. Churchill warned Parliament of the need to avoid exaggerated optimism. Though "great dangers lie behind us, enormous exertions lie before us." On June 10, in a cable to Stalin he expressed extravagant hopes about Italy. Alexander, he proclaimed, was "chasing the beaten remnants of Kesselring's army swiftly northwards. He is on their tracks while mopping up the others." In truth, such a display of energy, so comprehensive a victory, was entirely beyond Alexander and his armies.

Two days later, on June 12, Churchill was at last allowed to visit the invasion beachhead in Normandy, an expedition which, of course, he adored. On the way to Portsmouth, he sought to tease a companion, Adm. Ernest King, a venture akin to striking a match on an iceberg: "Don't look so glum. I'm not trying to take anything away from the United States Navy just now." He was enchanted by the spectacle of the invasion coast, cabling again to Stalin: "It is a wonderful sight to see this city of ships stretching along the coast for nearly fifty miles and apparently safe from the air and the U-boats which are so near." Lunching with Montgomery, he expressed surprise that the Norman countryside seemed relatively unscathed: "We are surrounded by fat cattle lying in luscious pastures with their paws crossed." Before returning to England, the destroyer which carried him fired a few rounds towards German shore positions, at a range of six thousand yards. He declared his delight at sailing for the first time aboard a ship of the Royal Navy in action.

Back home, a grim welcome awaited. That night, German V-1 flying bombs began to fall on London. Churchill stood outside Downing Street, scanning the sky and listening to the growling motors of the "doodlebugs" overhead, whose sudden silence presaged descent and detonation. They were soon landing close by him. On Sunday, June 18, a V-1 killed sixty people during a service in the Guards' Chapel, three hundred yards from his study. During one noisy night of explosions and antiaircraft fire, at two a.m. he was dictating to his secretary Marion Holmes. "The PM asked if I were frightened. I said 'No.' How can one feel frightened in his company?" The first sea lord, Cunningham, was often a critic of the prime minister, but wrote in his diary after a meeting of the anti–flying bomb Crossbow Committee on June 19: "[Churchill] was at his best, and said the matter had to be put robustly to the populace, that their tribulations were part of the battle in France, and that they should be very glad to share in the soldiers' dangers."

In truth, however, the British people were much shaken by the V-1 offensive. They were almost four years older, and incomparably more tired, than they had been during the blitz of 1940. The monstrous impersonality of the doodlebugs, striking at all hours of day and night, seemed a refinement of cruelty. Mrs. Lylie Eldergill, an East Londoner, wrote to a friend in America: "I do hope it will soon be ended. My nerves can't take much more." Brooke was disgusted by the emotionalism of Herbert Morrison, the home secretary: "He kept on repeating that the population of London could not be asked to stand this strain after 5 years of war . . . It was a pathetic performance." The bombardment severely affected industrial production in target areas. In the first week, 526 civilians were killed, and thereafter the toll mounted. It was a godsend to morale that Rome's fall and D-Day had taken place before the V-1 offensive began. Hitler made an important mistake, by wasting massive resources on his secret weapons programme. The V-1s and subsequent V-2 rockets were marvels of technology by the standards of the day, but their guidance was too imprecise, their warheads too small, to alter strategic outcomes. The V weapons empowered the Nazis merely to cause distress in Britain. They might have inflicted more serious damage by targeting the Allied beachhead in Normandy.

Macmillan described Churchill one evening at Chequers at around this time: "Sitting in the drawing-room about six o'clock [he] said: 'I am an old and weary man. I feel exhausted.' Mrs. Churchill said, 'But think what Hitler and Mussolini feel like!' To which Winston replied, 'Ah, but at least Mussolini has had the satisfaction of murdering his son-in-law [Count

Ciano].' This repartee so pleased him that he went for a walk and appeared to revive." One of Brooke's most notorious diary entries about the prime minister was written on August 15:

> We have now reached the stage that for the good of the nation and for the good of his own reputation it would be a godsend if he could disappear out of public life. He has probably done more for this country than any other human being has ever done, his reputation has reached its climax, it would be a tragedy to blemish such a past by foolish actions during an inevitable decline which has set in during the past year. Personally I have found him almost impossible to work with of late, and I am filled with apprehension as to where he may lead us next.

Yet if Churchill was indeed old, exhausted and often wrong-headed, he was unchallengeable as Britain's war leader, and Brooke diminished himself by revealing such impatience with him. The prime minister possessed a stature which lifted the global prestige of his country far beyond that conferred by its shrinking military contribution. Jock Colville wrote: "Whatever the PM's shortcomings may be, there is no doubt that he does provide guidance and purpose for the Chiefs of Staffs and the F.O. on matters which, without him, would often be lost in the maze of inter-departmentalism or frittered away by caution and compromise. Moreover he has two qualities, imagination and resolution, which are conspicuously lacking among other Ministers and among the Chiefs of Staff. I hear him much criticised, often by people in close contact with him, but I think much of the criticism is due to the inability to see people and their actions in the right perspective when one examines them at quarters too close." All this was profoundly true.

Even in the last phase of the war, when American dominance became painfully explicit, Churchill fulfilled a critical role in sustaining the momentum of his nation. After D-Day, but for the prime minister's personal contribution, Britain would have become a backwater, a supply centre and aircraft carrier for the American-led armies in Europe. On the battlefield, there was considerable evidence that the British Army was once more displaying its limitations. The war correspondent Alan Moorehead, who served through the desert, Italy and into Normandy, enjoyed a close relationship with Montgomery. His view was noted after the war by Forrest Pogue: "By July, the American soldier [was] better than the English soldier. Original English . . . came from divisions which had been much bled. In first few days [I] went with Br. tanks. They stopped at every bridge because there might be an 88 around." These strictures might be a little harsh, but the Americans were justified in thinking the British, after five years of war, more casualty-averse than themselves.

In 1944–45, Churchill exercised much less influence upon events than in 1940–43. But without him, his country would have seemed a mere exhausted victim of the conflict, rather than the protagonist which he was determined that Britain should be seen to remain until the end. "So far as it has gone," Churchill told the Commons, "this is certainly a glorious story, not only liberating the fields of France after atrocious enslavement but also uniting in bonds of true comradeship the great democracies of the West and the English-speaking peoples of the world . . . Let us go on, then, to battle on every front . . . Drive on through the storm, now that it reaches its fury, with the same singleness of purpose and inflexibility of resolve as we showed to the world when we were alone." And so he himself sought to do.

EIGHTEEN

Bargaining with an Empty Wallet

FOR CHURCHILL, the weeks that followed D-Day were dominated by further fruitless wrangles with the Americans. Roosevelt sent him a head-masterly rebuke, drafted by Cordell Hull, for appearing to concede to the Russians a lead role in Romanian affairs, in return for Soviet acquiescence in British dominance of Greece. To the Americans, this attitude reflected the deplorable British enthusiasm for bilaterally agreed spheres of influence. Churchill replied irritably next day: "It would be quite easy for me, on the general principle of slithering to the left, which is so popular in foreign policy, to let things rip, when the King of Greece would probably be forced to abdicate and [the Communists of] EAM would work a reign of terror . . . I cannot admit that I have done anything wrong in this matter." If Roosevelt proposed to take umbrage about British failure to inform the White House about every cable to Stalin concerning Greece and Romania, then what of U.S. messages to Moscow concerning Poland, which the British were not made party to? Churchill concluded sadly: "I cannot think of any moment when the burden of the war has lain more heavily upon me or when I have felt so unequal to its ever-more entangled problems."

The prime minister still favoured landings on the Atlantic coast of France instead of Anvil and, even more dramatically, a major assault on Istria, the northeast Italian coast beyond Trieste, to take place in September. Brooke was cautious about this, warning that the terrain might favour the defence, and could precipitate a winter campaign in the Alps. But the Chiefs and their master were galvanised by an intercepted German signal on June 17. In this Hitler declared his determination to hold Apennine positions as "the final blocking line" to prevent the Allies from breaking into the northern Italian plain of the Po. Here, in British eyes, was compelling evidence of the German commitment to Italy, and thus of the value of contesting mastery there. The Americans—both Eisenhower and the U.S. Chiefs—were unimpressed. There followed one of the most acrimonious Anglo-American exchanges of the war.

The British Chiefs insisted that it was "unacceptable" for more Allied forces to be withdrawn from Italy. Eisenhower, as supreme commander, reasserted his commitment to the landings in southern France, and even more strongly rejected British notions, propounded in a plan drawn up by Maitland Wilson as Mediterranean C-in-C, for a drive from northeast Italy to the so-called Ljubljana Gap. On June 20 Ike wrote to Marshall that Maitland Wilson's plan "seems to discount the fact that Combined Chiefs of Staff have long ago decided to make Western Europe the base from which to conduct decisive operations against Germany. To authorize any departure from this sound decision seems to me ill-advised and potentially dangerous . . . In my opinion to contemplate wandering off overland via Trieste to Ljubljana repeat Ljubljana is to indulge in conjecture to an unwarrantable degree . . . I am unable to repeat unable to see how overriding necessity for exploiting the early success of Overlord is thereby assisted." The American Chiefs signalled on June 24 that Maitland Wilson's Trieste plan was "unacceptable." They confirmed their insistence that the three U.S. and seven French divisions earmarked for Anvil should be withdrawn from Italian operations.

Ill-advisedly, Churchill appealed against this decision to Roosevelt, while on June 26 the British Chiefs of Staff reaffirmed the "unacceptability" of the redeployment in a signal to their counterparts in Washington. Marshall remained immovable. On the twenty-eighth, Churchill dispatched a note to the president in which he wrote: "Whether we should ruin all hopes of a major victory in Italy and all its fronts and condemn ourselves to a passive role in that theatre, after having broken up the fine Allied army which is advancing so rapidly through the peninsula, for the sake of 'Anvil' with all its limitations, is indeed a grave question for His Majesty's Government and the President, with the Combined Chiefs of Staff, to decide." He himself, he said, was entirely hostile to Anvil. The next day, Roosevelt rejected Churchill's message: "My interests and hopes," he said, "center on defeating the Germans in front of Eisenhower and driving on into Germany, rather than on limiting this action for the purpose of staging a full major effort in Italy." Roosevelt added, in the midst of his own reelection campaign, that there were also political implications: "I should never survive even a slight setback in 'Overlord' if it were known that fairly large forces had been diverted to the Balkans."

Amazingly, Churchill returned to the charge. In a message to Roosevelt on July 1, after a long exposition of the futility of Anvil—"the splitting up of the campaign in the Mediterranean into two operations neither of which can do anything decisive, is, in my humble and respectful opin-ion, the first major strategic and political error for which we two have to be responsible"—he concluded: "What can I do, Mr. President, when your Chiefs of Staff insist on casting aside our Italian offensive campaign, with all its dazzling possibilities . . . when we are to see the integral life of this campaign drained off into the Rhone Valley? . . . I am sure that if we could have met, as I so frequently proposed, we should have reached a happy agreement." This was woeful stuff. It was supremely tactless for the prime minister to suggest to the president that, if he had been able to browbeat him face to face, he might have persuaded him to override his own Chiefs of Staff. To the British Chiefs, he expressed contempt for their American counterparts: "The Arnold-King-Marshall combination is one of the stupidest strategic teams ever seen. They are good fellows and there is no need to tell them this."

The Americans were unmoved by the barrage of cables from London. The British, with icy formality, acceded to the launch of Anvil—now renamed Dragoon—on August 15. This was the moment at which Churchill perceived his own flagging influence upon the U.S. president, and thus upon his country. "Up till Overlord," wrote Jock Colville later, "he saw himself as the supreme authority to whom all military decisions were referred." Thereafter, he became, "by force of circumstances, little more than a spectator." The prime minister afterwards told Moran: "Up to July 1944 England had a considerable say in things; after that I was con-scious that it was America who made the big decisions."

The British adopted a stubbornly proprietorial attitude to the Italian campaign, long after it had turned sour, and even after the dazzling suc-cess of Overlord. Marshall had made his share of mistakes in the course of the war—but so had Brooke and Churchill. Nothing in the summer exchanges between London and Washington justified the prime minister's condescension towards the U.S. Chiefs. Though Eisenhower is often, and sometimes justly, criticised for lack of strategic imagination, he and Mar-shall were assuredly right to insist upon the concentration of force in France.

Yet it was hard for Churchill to bow to the relegation of himself and his country from the big decisions. An American political scientist, William Fox, coined the word *superpower* in 1944. He took it for granted that Britain could be counted as one. The true measure of superpowerdom, however, is a capability to act unilaterally. This, Churchill's nation had lost. Dismay and frustration showed in his temper. Eden wrote on July 6: "After dinner a really ghastly defence committee nominally on Far East-ern strategy. We opened with a reference from W. to American criticism

ENGLAND

BELGIUM

GERMANY

CZECHOSLOVAKIA

OVERLORD

Rhine

Paris *Seine*

Dijon

Danube

Munich

AUSTRIA

Vienna

The Alps

Ljubljana

SWITZ.

Loire

FRANCE

Milan

YUGOSLAVIA

Bordeaux

Rhone

Turin

Po

Istrian Pen.

ANVIL

Genoa

ITALY

Rimini

Br. Eighth Army

ADRIATIC SEA

Marseilles

U.S. Fifth Army

Toulon

OVERLORD AND ANVIL

Corsica

Rome

SPAIN

Naples

Fr. II Corps

U.S. Seventh Army

⟵ American Landings (Anvil/Dragoon)
⟵---- British Plan

Sardinia

of Monty for over-caution, which W. appeared to endorse. This brought explosion from CIGS." Brooke wrote in his own diary:

A frightful meeting with Winston which lasted until 2 am!! It was quite the worst we have had with him. He was very tired as a result of his speech in the House concerning the flying bombs, he had tried to recuperate with drink. As a result he was in a maudlin, bad-tempered, drunken mood, ready to take offence at anything, suspicious of everybody, and in a highly vindictive mood against the Americans. In fact so vindictive that his whole outlook on strategy was warped. I began by having a bad row with him. He began to abuse Monty because operations were not going faster . . . I flared up and asked him if he could not trust his generals for 5 minutes instead of continuously abusing them and belittling them . . . He then put forward a series of puerile proposals, such as raising a Home Guard in Egypt to provide a force to deal with disturbances in the Middle East. It was not until midnight that we got onto the subject we had come to discuss, the war in the Far East! . . . He finished by falling out with Attlee and having a real good row with him concerning the future of India! We withdrew under cover of this smokescreen just on 2 am, having accomplished nothing beyond losing our tempers and valuable sleep!!

Eden commented later: "I called this 'a deplorable evening,' which it certainly was. Nor could it have happened a year earlier; we were all marked by the iron of five years of war." Accounts like that of Brooke, describing such passages of arms with Churchill, dismayed those who loved the prime minister, both his personal staff and family, when they were later published. The prime minister's former intimates took special exception to criticisms that his conduct of office was adversely affected by alcohol. The CIGS was coupled with Lord Moran, whose diary appeared in 1966, not only as a betrayer of the Churchillian legend but also as a false witness about his conduct. Yet the two men's views were widely shared. After listening to the prime minister for a time at a committee meeting, Food Minister Lord Woolton leaned over and whispered to Dalton like a naughty schoolboy: "He is very tight." Exhaustion and frustration probably influenced Churchill's outbursts more than brandy. But the evidence is plain: in 1944–45 he suffered increasingly from loss of intellectual discipline, sometimes even of coherence.

The pugnacity that had served his country so wonderfully well in earlier years became distressing when directed against his own colleagues, men of ability and dedication, who knew that they did not deserve to be so brutally handled. Churchill could rouse his extraordinary powers on great occasions, of which some still lay ahead. There would be many more flashes of brilliance and wit. But key figures in Britain's war leadership, instead of looking directly to him as the fount of all decisions, were now peering over his shoulder, towards a future from which they assumed that he would be absent. Eden, craving the succession, chafed terribly when the prime minister seemed unwilling to acknowledge his own political mortality. "Lunched alone with W," he wrote on July 17. "He was in pretty good spirits. My face fell when he said that when coalition broke up we should have two or three years of opposition and then come back together to clear up the mess!"

Yet there were still many moments when Churchill won hearts, including that of the foreign secretary, by displays of whimsy and sweetness. On August 4, when Eden called at Downing Street with his son Nicholas, on holiday from school at Harrow, the prime minister surreptitiously slipped into the boy's hand two pound notes, more than a fortnight's pay for an army private, with a muttered and of course vain injunction not to tell "*him*." Churchill's companions became bored when he recited long extracts from *Marmion* and *The Lays of Ancient Rome* across the dinner table at Chequers, but how many other national leaders in history could have matched such performances? He was moved to ecstasies by a screening of Laurence Olivier's new film of *Henry V,* not least because he was in no doubt about who was playing the king's part in England's comparable mid-twentieth-century epic. His impatience remained undiminished. Driving with Brooke from Downing Street to Northolt, their convoy encountered a diversion for road repairs. Churchill insisted on lifting the barriers and urging the cars along a footpath. The king himself would never do such a thing, the miscreant declared gleefully, for "he was *far* more law-abiding."

As for the war, by late summer 1944 the apprehension which dogged Churchill and his service chiefs through the spring was now supplanted by assurance that Germany's doom was approaching. But when? On this, the prime minister displayed better judgement than the generals. Until the end of September, they envisaged a final Nazi collapse by the turn of the year. Churchill, by contrast, told a staff conference on July 14: "Of course it was true that the Germans were now faced with grave difficulties and they might give up the struggle. On the other hand, such evidence as there was seemed to show that they intended to continue that struggle, and he believed that if they tried to do so, they should be able to carry on well into next year." His view remained unchanged even after the drama of the failed bomb plot against Hitler on July 20. This highlighted German internal opposition to Hitler—and its weakness.

Some illusions persist that the wartime Allies missed opportunities to promote the cause of "good Germans" who opposed Hitler, rejecting approaches from such men as Adam von Trott. Yet the British seemed right, first, to assume that any dalliance of this kind must leak, fuelling Soviet paranoia about a negotiated peace and, second, in believing that the anti-Hitler faction was both weak and flawed. Michael Howard has written: "We know that such 'right-minded people' did exist; but the remarkable thing is that . . . there should have been so few of them, and that their influence should have been so slight." Howard notes that most of the July 1944 bomb plotters were right-wing nationalists, who cherished grotesquely extravagant ambitions for their country's postwar polity. The principal objective of most of those who joined the conspiracy against Hitler, as the Foreign Office perceived at the time, was to enlist Anglo-American aid against the Russians. It is easy to understand why postwar Germans sought to canonise the July bomb plotters. But it would have represented folly for Churchill's government to dally with them, and there is no cause for historians to concede them exaggerated respect. A large majority of the July 20 conspirators turned against Hitler not because he was indescribably wicked, but because they perceived that he was leading Germany to defeat.

That July, in the face of new intelligence reports about the operations of the death camp at Auschwitz-Birkenau, Churchill wrote to Eden in the most explicit terms he used during the war about the nature of Nazi action against the Jews: "There is no doubt that this is probably the greatest and most horrible crime ever committed in the whole history of the world . . . It is clear that all concerned in this crime who may fall into our hands, including the people who only obeyed orders by carrying out the butcheries, should be put to death." Yet once again, the British dismissed the notion of bombing the death camps' facilities or transport links, partly on the grounds of inefficacy, that any damage could be readily repaired, and that anyway only the USAAF's day bombers were capable of the necessary precision, and partly on the spurious grounds that deportations of Jews from Hungary—reports of which prompted Churchill's note—appeared to have ceased.

Even at this stage, the scale of Nazi killings eluded British policymakers. An intelligence officer privy to Ultra decrypts who lectured to senior soldiers in 1944 about Germany's machinery of repression spoke in his briefings of killings in the thousands, not the millions, and did not explicitly mention Jews. Likewise the November 1943 joint Allied Moscow Declaration, warning of retribution against Germans who participated in "wholesale shooting of Italian officers or in the execution of French, Dutch, Belgian or Norwegian hostages or of Cretan peasants, or who have shared in the slaughter inflicted on the people of Poland or in territories of the Soviet Union," omitted Jews.

British and American intelligence possessed enough information by late 1944, from Ultra and escaped Auschwitz prisoners, to deduce that something uniquely terrible was being done to the Jews in Nazi-occupied Europe, if the right conclusions had been drawn from the evidence. The failure of either government to act has incurred brutal strictures from postwar critics. Yet Churchill, Roosevelt and their principal subordinates seem to deserve some sympathy for their admittedly inadequate responses. First, an instinctive reluctance persisted both in London and Washington to conceive a European society, even one ruled by the Nazis, capable of killings on the titanic scale exposed in 1945–46. Second, evidence about the massacre of Jews was still perceived in the context of other known mass killings of Russians, Poles, Greeks, Yugoslavs, Italians and other subject races. The British, especially, were wary of repeating the mistakes of the First World War, when reports of German atrocities, though real enough, were wilfully exaggerated for propaganda purposes. Such exploitation roused postwar anger among British people towards their own government.

Finally, given the known limitations of precision bombing even where good target intelligence was available, the case for specific action against the Nazi death machine seemed overborne by the overarching argument for hastening military victory to end the sufferings of all Europe's oppressed peoples. The airmen could be sure that any bombing of the camps would kill many prisoners. It is the privilege of posterity to recognise that this would have been a price worth paying. In the full tilt of war, to borrow Churchill's phrase from a different context, it is possible to understand why the British and Americans failed to act with the energy and commitment which hindsight shows to have been appropriate. Temperate historians of the period recognise a real doubt about whether any plausible air force action would substantially have impeded the operations of the Nazi death machine.

Again and again that summer, Churchill found his aspirations thwarted. He was eager that Britain should have the honour of hosting a summit, after he himself had travelled so far and often to dance attendance on Roosevelt and Stalin. He now proposed as a venue Invergordon, in Scotland, arguing that each leader could arrive there by battleship. The king would be able to entertain the Big Three at Balmoral. Stalin flatly refused to leave Russia. Even when Roosevelt agreed to a bilateral meeting, and after briefly professing enthusiasm for Invergordon, to Churchill's chagrin he finally decided that the conference should not take place in Britain. The president was unwilling, especially in a U.S. election year, to be seen as the guest of his nation's subordinate partner. A second visit to Quebec was scheduled for September.

Churchill's lonely struggle to save fragments of Polish freedom became ever less rewarding. He allowed himself a surge of hope when Stalin cabled on July 23, endorsing a "unification of Poles friendly disposed towards Great Britain, the USSR and the United States." Interpreting this—which Eden did not—as a sign that Stalin was willing to accommodate the "London Poles" in a new regime, Churchill told Roosevelt: "This seems to be the best ever received from Uncle Joe." But the significance soon became clear of Stalin's recognition of Moscow's puppet Polish National Committee, dubbed in London the "Lublin Poles." Stalin was bent on a Communist-dominated Polish government, with only token representation of other interests. Under extreme pressure from Churchill, the Polish exile prime minister in London, Stanislaw Mikolajczyk, agreed to fly to Moscow. But Mikolajczyk rightly anticipated that obeisance to Stalin would serve no purpose either for himself or his country's freedom.

On July 31, with Soviet forces only fifteen miles away across the Vistula, the Polish Home Army in Warsaw launched its uprising. Through the agonising weeks that followed, Churchill strove to gain access to Russian landing grounds to be used to dispatch arms to the Poles. The most earnest and humble pleas to Stalin—and in some of Churchill's cables, he was indeed reduced to begging—failed to move Moscow. The Russian leader believed that Churchill had deliberately provoked the Warsaw Rising to secure for the "London Poles" the governance of their country. Moscow was determined to prevent any such outcome. The prime minister had certainly since 1940 promoted an ideal of popular revolt, and some SOE officers encouraged Polish delusions. But he was in no way complicit in the launch of the Warsaw Rising, an explicitly local initiative. Though he sustained his campaign on behalf of Polish freedom for many months to come, he knew how great the odds were against success. While the Americans were not indifferent, they seemed so both in London and Moscow. The Red Army stood deep inside Poland, while Eisenhower's forces were far, far away.

Even more serious, from Churchill's viewpoint, was the frustration of his strategic wishes. He made a last, vain attempt to persuade the Americans against a campaign in Burma. Throughout the war, while Churchill was eager that British forces should be seen to regain Britain's colonies in the Far East, his interest in the military means by which this should be accomplished was sporadic and unconvincing. Most of his attention, and almost all his heart, focused upon the German war, even as Slim's imperial army prepared to advance towards the Chindwin frontier of Burma.

Until almost the last day before the landing in southern France on August 15, Churchill argued doggedly against "the Anvil abortion," pleading for alternative assaults on the Atlantic coast of France, or in northeast Italy. "I am grieved to find that even splendid victories and widening opportunities do not bring us together on strategy," he wrote to Hopkins in Washington on August 6. The British failed to perceive that the arguments for getting into southern France were less persuasive in rousing U.S. determination than those for getting every possible man out of Italy.

As Churchill railed in the face of so many difficulties and disappointments, he adopted a familiar panacea: personal activity. In a fashion imbued with pathos, because it marked his transition from prime mover to spectator, he became for some weeks a battlefield tourist. During his travels he conducted some business. But his journeys represented a substitute for implementing policy, rather than a means of doing so. On July 20 he flew to Normandy, where 1.4 million Allied troops were now deployed. On August 5, he again toured the battle zone and met commanders. Both trips delighted him, for he savoured proximity to the music of gunfire as much as ever. He underrated the scale and speed of the developing German collapse in France, and the new strategic opportunities which would follow. He expected months more fighting before Allied troops reached the borders of Germany. Had he understood that dramatic change in the circumstances of Eisenhower's armies was imminent, with the collapse of German resistance in France, he would probably have remained at hand, to dispatch a flood of imprecatory messages to Roosevelt, Marshall, Eisenhower and Brooke. As it was, however, he departed for the Mediterranean.

On August 11, he landed in Algiers. Summoning de Gaulle for a meeting, he was infuriated when the Frenchman, seething with indignation about the Allies' refusal to grant him authority in his own country, declined to attend. Randolph Churchill, recuperating after a plane crash in Yugoslavia, met his father and heard a stormy denunciation of de Gaulle. Afterwards, in an unusually statesmanlike intervention, Randolph urged pity: "After all, he is a frustrated man representing a defeated country. You as the unchallenged leader of England and the main architect of victory could well afford to be magnanimous." Churchill wrote to Clementine: "I feel that de Gaulle's France will be a France more hostile to England than any since Fashoda [in 1898]."

Nonetheless, under relentless pressure from Eden, Churchill supported de Gaulle's cause against the Americans. Before D-Day, Admiral Leahy, Roosevelt's chief of staff who had served as U.S. ambassador to Vichy, told the president that the Allies would find Marshal Pétain their most appropriate French negotiating partner, because of his popularity with his own people. In the weeks following the invasion, this delusion was confounded by French Resistance fighters who seized power in liberated areas, and displayed overwhelming support for de Gaulle. The men of Vichy were consigned by their countrymen to prison or oblivion. Late in August, the general was allowed to return to France, where he became the country's de facto ruler. Two months later, albeit with the deepest reluctance, Washington recognised his leadership of a French provisional government.

On August 12, Churchill flew to Italy, where he installed himself in Maitland Wilson's residence, the Villa Rivalta, overlooking the Bay of Naples. He remained in Italy for more than two weeks, bathing several times in the sea, much to his pleasure, and conducting meetings. He continued to fume about the diversion of forces to France. In those days of mid-August, 100,000 men were being transferred in landing ships from Italy. Offshore in a launch one sunny morning, Churchill found himself hailed by thousands of troops lining the rails of vessels on passage to the Côte d'Azur. He acknowledged their cheers, but wrote in his memoirs, "They did not know that if I had had my way, they would have been sailing in a different direction." As for the Italian people, after years of proclaiming the need for firmness, if not harshness, toward Mussolini's nation, the sight of smiling Italian faces now softened his heart, rekindling his lifelong instinct towards mercy.

He met Tito, flown in from Yugoslavia, and feted him considerably. The Communist leader returned to his headquarters so enchanted by the prime minister that some of his partisan comrades were alarmed. Dismissing their warnings of the British leader's duplicity, the Yugoslav enthused: "It isn't as simple as you think! Yes, Churchill is an imperialist, an anti-Communist! But you won't believe it, his eyes were filled with tears when he met me. He almost sobbed, 'You're the first person from enslaved Europe I have met!' Churchill even told me that he had wanted to parachute into Yugoslavia, but he was too old!" One partisan shook his head and muttered to another, "The English are clever: an escort of warships and naval manoeuvres in honour of the Old Man [Tito], and I see that it's had its effect on him!"

On August 16, Churchill watched the Dragoon landing from an assault vessel a few miles offshore. In a letter to Clementine, he portrayed the splendour of the armada "all spread along twenty miles of coast with poor St. Tropez in the centre." The invaders met little opposition, and were soon racing northeastward to a linkage with Eisenhower's armies on September 12. The prime minister spent hours in talks about Mediterranean policy with Macmillan, Maitland Wilson and others. British handling of Italian affairs was unimpressive, and perceived as such by the Americans. Churchill and Eden acquiesced in the return from Moscow of exiled Communist leader Palmiro Togliatti, and his inclusion in the Italian government in exchange for its recognition by the Russians. Dogged British resistance to the participation of Count Carlo Sforza, a former foreign minister who had been living in the United States and was esteemed by the Americans, annoyed Washington intensely. London was taken unawares when Marshal Badoglio was ejected from the Italian leadership in June 1944. Thereafter, British struggles to create and sustain a Rome government acceptable to Churchill and his colleagues incurred constant criticism from the U.S. State Department and media. The Americans' own ideas were naïve, but founded in a commitment to Italian rights of self-determination, which they perceived the British as flouting in their old imperialistic way.

Increasingly Churchill's attention focused upon Greece, where he perceived serious danger of a Communist takeover. The guerrillas of EAM/ELAS, armed by the SOE, were the best-organised force in the country. As the Germans began to withdraw from southern Greece, Churchill ordered that British troops should be readied to fly into Athens the moment the enemy abandoned the city, to forestall a Communist coup. It was hard to find men, when the Allied armies in Italy had been so much depleted for Dragoon, but forces for Greece, the prime minister insisted, had to be found. Some airborne units were earmarked.

Then he advanced towards the front, dressed in army summer rig with medal ribbons and a solar topee that would have looked absurd on any other man. Alexander drove him to a hilltop on which he could hear small-arms fire, watch machine gunners flail the enemy amid showers of empty cases spinning away into the dust and see tanks grinding into action. The outing provided him with as much happiness as any experience in the last months of the war. He was in the midst of a British army which, if not immediately triumphant, was indisputably predominant, in the company of a general whom he deemed a paladin. Alexander received far fewer reproaches for slow progress than did Montgomery. Churchill blamed the misfortunes of the joyless, bloody Italian theatre exclusively upon the Americans. They, he believed, had stripped Alex's army of the means with which it might have changed the fate of Europe and spared the Balkans from Soviet domination. Many of those engaged in the struggle, and bearing its sacrifices, shared his opinion. A humble Eighth Army signaller wrote in his diary on August 27, 1944, "I feel sure this is a secondary front and therefore being denied the vital necessities of war."

On August 29, Churchill landed back in Britain with a temperature of 103 degrees, and a patch on his lung which caused his doctors to prescribe another course of antibiotics. He had achieved nothing of substance in the Mediterranean, nor in Normandy, save to assuage a growing sense of his own impotence, and to indulge his passion for witnessing great events. Foreign Office official Oliver Harvey muttered scornfully about the prime minister "fooling about in Italy." Amid the miseries and slaughter inflicted on London by the flying-bomb offensive, Churchill faced greater personal risk at home than in Normandy or the Mediterranean. Though his government had much to do, most of the tasks were uncongenial to him. More and more of his ministers' time was occupied with preparing for peace. At worst, victory could not be more than a year or two away. The British people looked with eagerness mingled with uncertainty towards a future without war. Yet the prime minister's interest in domestic matters was spasmodic and perfunctory. David Reynolds notes that in Churchill's memoirs, he makes no mention of the 1944 Butler Education Act, the most important piece of domestic legislation passed during his wartime premiership. Ismay once observed, "The PM can be counted on to score a hundred in a Test Match, but is no good at village cricket." The issues of postwar reconstruction, the mundane concerns of the careworn British people, required ministers to take the field in many village cricket matches.

Winning the war, and securing the place of the British Empire in the new world, were Churchill's unaltering preoccupations. Because the Americans perceived the prime minister as the embodiment of his country, they failed to recognise that many younger British people, some of them in government, saw as surely as did Roosevelt and his compatriots that the day of empire was done. For those obliged to work with Churchill, difficulties mounted. His flagging health, rambling monologues and refusal to address business which did not stimulate his interest posed great difficulties. Leo Amery complained: "Our Cabinet meetings certainly get more and more incoherent, though I notice that there is much more talking by everybody, often simultaneously, than there used to be when Winston held the field entirely by himself . . . What makes me so tired at Cabinets is the same feeling that one has in a taxi wishing to catch a train with a driver who dawdles and misses every green light."

The philosopher and historian Isaiah Berlin wrote: "Churchill is pre-occupied by his own vivid world, and it is doubtful how far he has ever been aware of what actually goes on in the heads and hearts of others. He does not react, he acts; he does not mirror, he affects others and alters them to his own powerful measure . . . His conduct stems from great depth and constancy of feeling—in particular, feeling for and fidelity to the great tradition for which he assumes a personal responsibility, a tradition which he bears upon his shoulders and must deliver, not only sound and undamaged but strengthened and embellished, to successors worthy of accepting the sacred burden." This seems profoundly true of Churchill's behaviour in the last months of the war. Two or three years earlier, he had power to shape events as well as popular perceptions of them. Now, the world was going on its way with ever less heed for his grandiose antique vision, though it could still be moved by his words.

Through the autumn, the miseries of Poland provided a running theme, as the Nazis suppressed the Warsaw Rising with familiar savagery. Not only Stalin, but also Roosevelt, resisted Churchill's impassioned pleas to press Moscow about the Warsaw Home Army. The Americans wanted Siberian bases for their B-29 bomber operations against Japan, and were unwilling to provoke the Russians about what they perceived as lesser matters. On August 26, the president rejected an appeal from Churchill that the United States and Britain should dispatch a strongly worded joint protest to Moscow about Poland. Roosevelt wrote: "I do not consider it advantageous to the long-range general war prospects for me to join with you in the proposed message to Uncle J." On September 4 the prime minister, still unwell, felt obliged to rise from his sickbed to calm a Cabinet whose members were sincerely angered by events in Warsaw. While he welcomed spontaneous media expressions of dismay, he urged that ministers should remain temperate about Russian behaviour.

Churchill was still ailing when he boarded the *Queen Mary* at Greenock on September 6, bound for Quebec. Brooke remarked that he seemed "old, unwell and depressed. Evidently found it hard to concentrate and kept holding his head between his hands." Conditions belowdecks for most of the crossing were oppressively hot. After the austerities of British diet, on the liner the customary sybaritic fare was provided for the prime minister's party. Jock Colville described their meals as "gargantuan in scale and epicurean in quality; rather shamingly so." There was the usual glittering table talk, faithfully recorded by the three notable diarists aboard—

Colville, Brooke and Moran. The prime minister said that he would not regret the loss of any Labour colleague from his government save Bevin, the only one whose character and capacity he esteemed. He lamented the fact that he no longer felt that he had a message to deliver to the British people: "All he could now do was to finish the war, to get the soldiers home and to see that they had houses to which to return. But materially and financially the prospects were black."

He found time to read, first Trollope's *Phineas Finn*, then *The Duke's Children*, which describes a Victorian political grandee's embarrassments with his offspring. The latter novel can scarcely have failed to prick Churchill, at a time when his own son's marriage to his wife, Pamela, was breaking up. She had conducted a notable affair with Averell Harriman, a future husband, and was later unkindly described as having become "a world expert on rich men's bedroom ceilings." Earlier that year, Churchill achieved one of his few moments of intimacy with Brooke, when the two men discussed tête-à-tête over supper their difficulties with their respective grown-up children.

But, while the prime minister struggled to recruit his strength, as usual he spent many hours on the *Queen Mary* preparing for the summit. He minuted the Chiefs of Staff during their passage that Britain should "not yield central and southern Europe entirely to Soviet ascendancy or domination." This was, he said, an issue of "high political consequences, but also has serious military potentialities." He expressed distress that the British and imperial armies were nowhere advancing the nation's standard as he would have wished. One-third of their strength, in northwest Europe, was deployed under U.S. command; one-third in India was about to launch an offensive in Burma, "the most unhealthy country in the world under the worst possible conditions," merely to appease America's China ambitions; and the remaining one-third in Italy had been emasculated for Dragoon. Had he known, he said, that the Americans would use their monopoly of landing ships unilaterally to enforce strategy, he would have ensured that Britain built her own. He was appalled to hear that Mountbatten was demanding 370,000 men and 24,000 vehicles from Europe before launching an assault against Rangoon. He still craved an amphibious landing on the Istrian Peninsula, "in the armpit of the Adriatic."

Churchill arrived in Quebec by overnight train on the morning of September 11, within a few minutes of the president. They drove together from the station to the Citadel. The next day, Colville heard the prime minister say that he would that evening discuss postwar occupation zones in Germany with Roosevelt. The private secretary, knowing Churchill had not studied the relevant papers, offered to read them aloud to him in his bath. This procedure proved only partially successful, because of Churchill's tendency to submerge himself from time to time, missing key passages of the brief. The prime minister cabled to the War Cabinet in London that the conference had opened "in a blaze of friendship." There was indeed a blaze of courtesies, but not of agreed policies. In Churchill's opening exposition of events, he sought to flatter the Americans by saying that the results of the detested Dragoon were "most gratifying." Roosevelt interrupted him, observing mischievously—even maliciously—that "some of the credit for the conception was due to Marshal Stalin." Churchill then talked much about Italy, and the merits of striking for Vienna. He seemed oblivious of American boredom and indifference. Cunningham, the first sea lord, thought Roosevelt "looked very frail, and hardly to be taking in what was going on."

The two leaders wasted considerable time discussing the plan of Henry Morgenthau, the Treasury secretary, for pastoralising postwar Germany. The president, knowing that Churchill was increasingly fearful about how Britain could pay its bills when Lend-Lease ended, said that deindustrialising the Ruhr would remove Britain's principal competitor in Europe. Great economic opportunities could thus shine upon the British people. This notion prompted a spasm of enthusiasm in Churchill. Cherwell, in one of his baleful interventions, urged the scheme's merits. On September 15, both leaders formally endorsed the Morgenthau Plan, to the horror of both Cordell Hull and Anthony Eden, who said the British Cabinet would never accept it. Roosevelt quickly recognised that he had made a mistake. The Morgenthau Plan was forgotten—except by Nazi propagandists, when the story leaked. In the last months of the war, many Germans believed Goebbels when he told them that, if they bowed to defeat, they would be condemned to become slave labourers in a peasant economy. The Treasury secretary's foolish initiative at Quebec motivated some enemies to fight even more desperately than they might otherwise have done, even to the last ditch.

The final formal session of the conference took place on September 16. Churchill proclaimed his commitment to dispatch a major fleet to join the Pacific campaign, as soon as the European war allowed. He made much of this, heedless of the fact that the Royal Navy's ships were as worn and battered as their crews. They lacked ventilation systems appropriate to Pacific conditions. And carrier operations, the dominant feature of the campaign, were the least impressive British naval combat skill. At the closing press conference of the summit, appearing as usual beside the president, the prime minister trumpeted Britain's commitment to the Pacific

theatre. He prompted laughter among the assembled American correspondents when he said: "You can't have all the good things to yourselves.
You must share." He then waxed lyrical about the virtues of summitry:
"When I have the rare and fortunate chance to meet the President of the
United States, we are not limited in our discussions by any sphere . . . The
fact that we have worked so long together, and the fact that we have got to
know each other so well under the hard stresses of war, makes the solution
of problems so much simpler, so swift and so easy it is."

This was flummery. In truth, even after two days with Roosevelt at
Hyde Park before boarding the *Queen Mary* in New York on Septem-
ber 20 for the voyage home, Churchill knew how little he had achieved.
"What is this conference?" he rumbled to Moran. "Two talks with the
Chiefs of Staff; the rest was waiting to put in a word with the President."
The British had been dismayed to note the absence of Harry Hopkins
from Quebec. Even when their favourite American sage appeared at Hyde
Park, it was plain that Hopkins no longer enjoyed his old intimacy with
Roosevelt. Especially in a U.S. election year, he represented baggage
which the president did not wish to be associated with, not least because
Hopkins was perceived by his countrymen as too susceptible to British
special pleading. Now that the British saw that his influence was gone,
their old affection ebbed shamelessly. Brendan Bracken dismissed him as
"weak" and "useless." Yet there is no reason to suppose that Hopkins was
moved by pique when he warned Halifax, in Washington, that a Republican victory in the imminent presidential election might serve British
interests better than the return of Franklin Roosevelt. To this, the "historic partnership" had descended.

Churchill was in mellow mood on the voyage home, but saw nothing
in which to rejoice. The Warsaw Rising was all but over, despite belated
and almost entirely unsuccessful arms drops to the defeated Home Army
by 110 USAAF Flying Fortresses, which were grudgingly permitted to
refuel in Russia. Eden had failed to persuade the Quebec conference to
recognise the French National Committee as the nation's government.
Churchill told Colville that following the events of recent years, "my illusions about the French have been greatly corroded." It was another month
before de Gaulle's obvious primacy among his countrymen obliged Washington to relent.

On September 28, back in London, Churchill reported to the Commons. With barely permissible nationalistic hyperbole, he described Normandy as "the greatest and most decisive single battle of the whole war."
He hailed Burma as "the campaign of Admiral Mountbatten," a slight
upon Gen. Bill Slim, the fine commander conducting the British offen-

sive. He sought to make the best of defeat at Arnhem, seeing cause for celebration in an unaccustomed display of boldness by the Allies, even though the airborne assault had failed to secure a Rhine crossing. At the beginning of October, British troops began to move into southern Greece behind the retreating Germans. Churchill made a renewed plea to Roosevelt for the transfer of three U.S. divisions from France to Italy—and received the inevitable refusal.

It was against the background of repeated American snubs that Churchill now embarked upon his most controversial wartime journey. He determined to fly to Moscow for bilateral talks with Stalin. It is impossible to perceive this mission as other than a gesture of desperation. Having failed to enlist American support for any of the purposes which now mattered most to him, instead he sought to achieve them by going head-to-head with the Russians. Yet Stalin bargained only for advantage. Britain could offer nothing of interest to him. He well understood that the Americans had distanced themselves from Churchill's nation. The prime minister's behaviour can only be explained by acknowledging that he still nursed an exaggerated self-belief in his ability to reach personal understandings with Stalin. There was a pathos about his flight to Moscow in October 1944, well understood by those who worked most closely with the tired old prime minister.

He paused briefly in Italy, hearing from his commanders a tale of inadequate resources and sluggish progress. He saw Georgios Papandreou, and embarrassed the Greek prime minister by subjecting him to a long lecture on the virtues of monarchy. On October 9 he arrived in Moscow and was driven to Molotov's dacha, his residence for the visit. At the first meeting with Stalin, he plunged immediately into a demand that Britain should have the principal voice in determining the future of Greece. He soon made it plain to the Soviet warlord that he spoke for himself, for Britain, and not for its transatlantic partner. Stalin observed silkily that Roosevelt "demanded too many rights for the United States of America, leaving too little for the Soviet Union and Great Britain." Churchill produced what he called a "naughty document." This was the draft of what became known as the "percentages agreement," in American eyes the most notorious piece of chicanery in Churchill's premiership. In Romania, Russia was to be recognised as having a 90 percent interest, while "the others" had 10 percent. In Greece, these figures were to be reversed. In Yugoslavia and Hungary, interests would be shared fifty-fifty. In Bulgaria, Russia would have a 75 percent interest, "the others" 25 percent. Churchill pushed this half sheet across the table to Stalin, who glanced at it, added a large blue tick, and passed the paper back across the table.

During the hours and days that followed, there was much general talk between the two men: about Greece and Yugoslavia, where Stalin agreed with Churchill that they should seek to prevent civil war between rival ideologies; about Italy, where the prime minister requested that Moscow should not "stir up Italian communists"; and about monarchs—Churchill said that nowhere would Britain seek to reenthrone a ruler against the will of the people. He made it plain that Britain would not support mass executions of defeated Nazis, though he hoped that as many as possible would be killed on the battlefield. He asserted his belief that no ideology should be imposed on small states, which must be free to decide their own destinies. Meanwhile, Eden haggled with Molotov about details of the percentages agreement, with the Russian foreign minister demanding, for instance, 90 percent influence in Bulgaria.

On October 11, Churchill sought to resolve such matters in a long missive to Stalin which he drafted, then showed to Averell Harriman, now U.S. ambassador in Moscow. Harriman said that Roosevelt and Cordell Hull would certainly repudiate the letter, if it was sent. Instead, the prime minister telegraphed to the president, urging the importance of acting swiftly to prevent an eruption of civil wars in the Balkans. Already, Communist partisans in Albania had rejected the return of King Zog, exiled from the country since 1941.

Then Churchill's delegation set forth for the British embassy, to host a dinner for Stalin and Molotov. There, Stalin told his host that it had not been policy, but military realities, which had prevented the Red Army from succouring the Warsaw Poles. The prime minister asked Lazar Kaganovich, the commissar for railways, how he made his nation's transport trains run on time. When an engine driver failed in his duty, said Kaganovich with a wolfish grin . . . then he drew his hand across his throat. Churchill rarely displayed anxiety about his own safety, but in Moscow he was furious to discover that his plane was left overnight in the hands of Russian guards. He insisted that thereafter a member of its RAF crew must remain aboard the aircraft around the clock. It is hard to suggest that this represented paranoia.

As always at these meetings, talking continued into the small hours. The Russian mood seemed unreservedly benign. Churchill cabled to Roosevelt about "an extraordinary atmosphere of goodwill." To Clementine, he wrote on October 13: "The affairs go well. We have settled a lot of things about the Balkans & prevented hosts of squabbles that were maturing. The two sets of Poles have arrived & are being kept for the night in separate cages . . . I have had v[er]y nice talks with the Old Bear. I like him the more I see him. Now they respect us here & I am sure they wish to work with us. I have to keep the President in constant touch & this is the delicate side."

In almost all of this Churchill was mistaken. Unaccustomed Russian civility, even warmth, was inspired by a new self-confidence, born of battlefield triumph. Virtually none of the assurances Stalin offered had substance. He had no intention of honouring them. What he wanted in the Balkans, he would take. Stalin could always raise a laugh from his obeisant courtiers by saying, as he often did: "We fucked this England!" The prime minister could claim only one success which proved enduring: Greece. Stalin recognised the strength of British sentiment about the country, together with the reality of Western Allied dominance of its airspace and surrounding seas. All the rest of the Balkans was within the Soviets' grasp. Though strife lay ahead in Greece, the Russians made no attempt to promote Communist victory. Thus far, and thus far only, Churchill may have accomplished something useful in Moscow.

His most notable failure was the attempt to save Poland. He summoned from London a Polish exile delegation, led by Prime Minister Mikolajczyk, who attended under threat from Churchill. Days of icy roundtable discussion followed, with the Russians half amused and half embarrassed by the slavish puppet show put on by their own "Lublin Poles." Churchill wrote to the king from Moscow, "Our lot from London are, as Your Majesty knows, a decent but feeble lot of fools, but the delegates from Lublin seem to be the greatest villains imaginable." Between sessions, Churchill made desperate efforts to induce the London Poles to accept the proposed new frontiers for their country, which would cede territory to Russia in exchange for land carved from eastern Germany. Blandishments and threats alike failed to move Mikolajczyk and his colleagues, who remained obdurate. Stalin dismissed a compromise proposal advanced by the British. When the Polish leader returned to London and put the final Soviet offer to his colleagues, it was decisively rejected. He then resigned as prime minister. Churchill found himself accepting commiserations from Stalin, because "his" Poles had rejected a deal. It was apparent that, in these circumstances, Moscow's appointees would rule the country.

It would have suited Stalin to gain Mikolajczyk's acquiescence both in the new borders and in accepting a marginal role in the new government. But, since there was no possibility that non-Communists would be granted real influence, far less power, the London Poles lost nothing and preserved their honour by rejecting Stalin's proposals. Churchill, however, was left to nurse despondency and failure. He thought the Poles almost demented in their refusal to make terms with Moscow. When

General Anders, Polish corps commander in Italy, expressed hopes that the Allies would free Poland by force once Germany was beaten, Churchill said despairingly: "This is crazy. You cannot defeat the Russians." In his perception, Mikolajczyk's stubbornness had handed his country to Stalin. "The Poles' game is up," he said tersely to Moran. Better, he thought, to accept a Russian mess of pottage than nothing at all.

Posterity should surely be moved in recognising that Churchill cared so much about Poland, where Britain had no selfish interest whatever. He waged a long, thankless struggle on behalf of the nation which had become the victim of Nazi aggression at the outbreak of the Second World War. It seemed to him unbearably tragic that impending Allied victory should merely offer a new servitude to the people on whose behalf Britain had declared war on Germany. Yet this was the case, and would have been so even had Roosevelt entered the lists in support of Churchill. The Russians were on the Vistula, while the Anglo-Americans were not yet at the Rhine. "Far quicker than the British and also the Americans," Sir William Deakin has written, "the Russians grasped the inner logic of the situation, namely that at the final victory the fate of the occupied countries of Europe . . . would be decided neither by the Resistance leaders themselves on the spot nor their representatives . . . in London and Moscow, but along a frontier between the armies of the Western Allies on the one hand and the Russians on the other."

The Moscow visit ended with the usual round of banquets. Churchill told Stalin that he favoured some grouping of Poland, Hungary and Czechoslovakia after the war, which the Russian leader cared for not at all. Stalin surprised Churchill by expressing a passionate hatred for Switzerland. But the Russians displayed no hostility to the British, as they had so often done in the past. On the contrary, Churchill and Stalin talked with freedom and, on the Russian side, unembarrassed mendacity. On October 18, Churchill addressed a press conference at the British embassy. The next morning, Stalin not only came to the airfield in the rain to see the prime minister off, but condescended to inspect the interior of his York aircraft. The two men parted with every evidence of cordiality. On the afternoon of October 22, Churchill landed back in Britain.

The world was allowed to suppose that his Moscow visit was merely a routine meeting of allies. It inspired in Churchill a brief surge of illusion, that he had forged an understanding with Stalin which might yield fruits such as he had failed to harvest from Roosevelt. The U.S. president, by contrast, was irked. He was in no doubt about Churchill's purpose. Britain's prime minister was attempting to achieve what the United States was absolutely committed to resist: the creation of spheres of influence in postwar Europe and the Balkans. The divide between British and American policy had never been greater since December 1941.

For all their public expressions of mutual regard, it is hard to suppose that, by this time, Churchill or Roosevelt cherished much private affection for each other. Their objectives were too far apart. The president's world vision was more enlightened than that of the old imperialist prime minister, yet even less realistic. He pinned his faith for the future upon the new United Nations organisation, the rise of Chiang Kai-shek's China, and a working partnership between America and the Soviet Union. His motives were exalted. Churchill's impassioned commitment to freedom excluded the world's black and brown races, as that of the president did not—though he shocked his own staff by domestic references to "the nigger vote." But, while Churchill had a quixotic strand of personal humility intermixed with his vanity, Roosevelt had none. His faith in his own power, as well as that of his nation, was unbounded. His unwillingness to acknowledge his own mortality, which was even more pressing than that of men threatened by death on the war's battlefields, was a grievous omission in the last months of his presidency. He might at least have ensured, as he did not, that Vice President Harry Truman was admitted to the secrets of the Grand Alliance.

It seems mistaken to be surprised, however, by Washington's cavalier treatment of both Britain and its prime minister. Beyond the new hubris of the United States, on many matters of strategy and policy the British had displayed poor judgement in 1944. They were wrong about Overlord, about Italy both militarily and politically, and were dilatory and confused about the Japanese war. On the battlefield their soldiers performed adequately rather than impressively. Churchill allowed himself to be distracted into pursuit of self-indulgent whims, such as a proposal that some aged British naval guns mounted at Dover should be shipped to the Continent to aid Eisenhower's campaign. British attempts to ignore their own impoverishment and retain a giant's role in the world inspired pity among their American friends, contempt among their American enemies. Churchill told Smuts: "You must remember . . . that our armies are only about one-half the size of the Americans and will soon be little more than one third . . . It is not as easy as it used to be for me to get things done." Churchill often asserted that, far from owing a huge cash debt to the United States when the war was over, Britain should be recognised as a creditor, for its lone defence of freedom in 1940–41. This was never plausible. When the war ended, the world would assess Britain's rightful place by reading its bank statement. Informed British people recognised this, and feared accordingly.

On October 27, Churchill reported to the Commons on his visit to Moscow. He now commanded an affection among MPs which transcended partisan loyalties. "How much depends on this man nowadays," wrote Tory MP Cuthbert Headlam, for so long a sceptic. "Without Winston's prestige and personality, where should we be with Roosevelt and Stalin? They are tiresome enough as things are—but how could Anthony Eden, or Attlee, stand up to them? No—I have never been a Winstonian, but I do realize that today if a man ever be indispensable, Winston is that man."

When Attlee told MPs that Churchill was again in Moscow, Labour members were seen shaking their heads in mingled admiration and sympathy, saying: "He oughtn't to do it. Poor old boy, he really oughtn't to do it." There was a readiness to indulge him, almost unique in parliamentary experience: "He is not of course as vigorous or pugnacious as in 1940," wrote Harold Nicolson. "But he has no need to be. He is right to take the more sober tone of the elder statesman." Conservatives who had spurned Churchill in 1940 recognised him in 1944 as offering the only political hope for their party, which was profoundly unpopular in the country. The old ruling class perceived that the electorate yearned for its dispossession, as soon as ballot papers were offered to them at a general election. In Nicolson's words: "The upper classes feel that all this sacrifice and suffering will only mean that the proletariat will deprive them of all their comforts and influence, and then proceed to render this country and Empire a third-class State." Yet the prime minister himself was far from immune from the effects of public alienation. Nicolson was shocked one day to notice scrawled graffiti in a station lavatory: "Winston Churchill is a bastard." When he remarked upon it to an RAF officer standing beside him, the airman shrugged, saying, "Yes. The tide has turned. We find it everywhere."

"But how foul. How bloody foul!"

"Well, you see, if I may say so, the men hate politicians."

"Winston a politician! Good God!"

On October 27, the prime minister delivered a brilliant speech about his experiences in Moscow. Then he adjourned to the smoking room, and addressed the barman: "Collins, I should like a whisky and soda—single." After sitting down for a moment, he struggled out of his armchair and returned to the bar. "Collins, delete the word 'single' and insert the word 'double.' " "Then," in the words of an MP, "grinning at us like a schoolboy, he resumed his seat." Here was another of those impish miniatures which help to explain why love for Churchill ran so strong among most of those who worked with him. For all Alan Brooke's exasperation with his master at this time, he wrote fondly of a scene that winter, as the two men visited the snowbound French battlefront in the Vosges. The prime minister arrived for lunch with de Gaulle "completely frozen, and almost rolled up on himself like a hedgehog. He was placed in a chair with a hot water bottle at his feet and one in the back of his chair. At the same time good brandy was poured down his throat to warm him internally. The results were wonderful, he thawed out rapidly and when the time came produced one of those indescribably funny French speeches which brought the house down."

But the British people had by now hardened their hearts towards their rulers, even the greatest. Many felt less gratitude to those presiding over victory in the most terrible conflict in history than implacable resentment against the politicians whom they held responsible for getting them into it in the first place. Even if Churchill had not himself been among the guilty men of the 1930s, he was now their political standard-bearer. And for all his giant stature as Britain's war leader, millions of voters sensed that his interest in the humdrum domestic troubles of peace was perfunctory. An anonymous officer of the Second Army, fighting in Holland, wrote in the *Spectator* about the mood of the British soldier under his command: "[He] is fighting for the future of the world and does not believe in that future . . . He asks a lot of the future, but he doesn't expect to get any of it." The writer perceived his men as chronically mistrustful of all authority, institutions and politicians, but Tories most of all: "It is, perhaps, encouraging that Tommy, 1944, will not be foozled by facile talk of a land fit for heroes. He wants deeds, not words." Few among such men perceived Winston Churchill as the national leader likely to fulfil such hopes once victory came.

NINETEEN

Athens:
"Wounded in the House of Our Friends"

GERMAN WITHDRAWAL from the Balkans precipitated a crisis for
Churchill which severely damaged his standing in America, engaged him
in bitter political dispute at home, and provided the last perilous military
adventure of his life. Experience at the end of World War II demonstrated
that it is much more difficult to order the affairs of liberated nations than
of defeated ones. This is because it is undesirable, if not impossible, to
arbitrate their affairs with the same ruthlessness. If Washington's twenty-
first-century neoconservatives had possessed a less muddled understanding of the experience of 1944–45, had studied more closely Allied
difficulties managing liberated territories in the Roosevelt-Churchill era,
they might have inflicted less grief upon the world in our own times by
their blunders in Iraq and Afghanistan.

In almost every European country freed from German domination,
former resistance groups armed by the SOE sought to assert themselves
in governance. In France, only de Gaulle's extraordinary personal authority and the presence of the Anglo-American armies—together with
Stalin's abstention from mobilizing his followers in a country where political instability might damage Soviet interests—made it possible to contain
the Communists of the FTP. Many ex-*maquisards* were hastily drafted
into the new French army, for service under Eisenhower. In neighbouring
Belgium, the exiled government which returned from London in September found itself facing a strong challenge from left-wingers, including
Communist resistance members. Having played a modest role in Belgian
liberation, they now, to the alarm of the authorities, refused to be disarmed. There was anger about the Belgian government's alleged reluctance to impose retribution upon those who had served the German
occupation regime. On November 25, leftist trades unionists staged a big
demonstration in Brussels and appeared bent upon forcing entry to government buildings. Police overreacted, firing on the demonstrators and

wounding forty. In the weeks that followed, tensions ran high. The British Army, strongly backed by Churchill, was determined to tolerate neither a threat to its lines of communications with the battlefront nor any attempted Communist takeover. British troops deployed in Brussels in large numbers.

This action restored a resentful peace, but prompted hostile press comment. U.S. correspondents, especially, deplored the use of force to suppress "heroic resistance fighters," of whatever political persuasion. Churchill displayed insensitivity in his support for the restoration of long-exiled governments to societies traumatised and radicalised by the experience of occupation. However, American enthusiasm for self-determination underrated both the malevolence of the Communists and the danger of anarchy overtaking the liberated nations.

In Albania and Yugoslavia Communist partisan movements set about seizing control as the Germans fell back. No other political element was strong enough to stop them, and in Serbia Tito enjoyed direct assistance from the Red Army. "Tito is turning very nasty," Churchill told Smuts on December 3. The Yugoslav partisans demanded the expulsion of the British from the Dubrovnik coastal area. At the same time, in eastern Europe, the "Lublin Poles" proclaimed themselves the provisional government of their country, with no offer of participation for the exiled administration in London. All this made Churchill acutely anxious about the future of Greece. In the first days following German withdrawal, arriving British troops were greeted with unbridled enthusiasm. When Eden visited Athens on October 26, his car was mobbed by cheering crowds. Lord Moyne, accompanying him, said brightly: "It is good that there is one country where we are so popular."

The Greek honeymoon ended abruptly. Armed factions roamed city streets, amid well-founded reports that Communists were slaughtering alleged "reactionaries." The Papandreou government struggled to assert its control of the country while the Communists of EAM/ELAS refused to demobilise, and guerrilla bands converged on Athens. The British strove to reinforce their weak forces in the capital, scouring the Mediterranean for men. "Everything is degenerating in the Greek government," the prime minister wrote to Eden on November 28, "and we must make up our minds whether we will assert our will by armed force, or clear out altogether." Two days later, he reached a predictable decision: "It is important to let it be known that if there is a civil war in Greece we shall be on the side of the Government we have set up in Athens, and that above all we shall not hesitate to shoot."

The next day, December 1, the six Communist and socialist ministers in the Athens regime resigned en bloc, and called a general strike. On December 3, frightened and ill-disciplined police fired on a demonstration. One policeman and eleven demonstrators were killed. Furious crowds besieged Athens police stations. The police, like other elements of the Papandreou government's makeshift security forces, were widely perceived by Greeks as having collaborated with the German occupiers. The historian Mark Mazower has written: "Despite Churchill's belief that he had forestalled a communist attempt to seize power, there is no sign that the uprising in Athens was anything other than a spontaneous popular movement which took the [Communist] party leadership by surprise." At first, the guerrillas of EAM/ELAS concentrated their fire on Greek government forces. But, when they perceived British troops furthering the cause of their right-wing foes, they started shooting at the "liberators."

The nuances of this situation eluded British commanders on the spot. They merely perceived their authority violently challenged. It should also be noticed, as it was not by most American observers at the time, that all over Greece the Communists were conducting murderous purges of bourgeois opponents, often along with their families. Churchill was bitterly angry. He assessed the Greek situation, and Communist intentions, through the prism of developments in Poland, Albania, Yugoslavia and Belgium.

The Greek crisis broke while the Belgian one was still making headlines. Churchill was harshly misjudged by Americans, who supposed that he sought an undemocratic outcome in Greece. His mistake was that, for two turbulent months, he conceded to the Greek king, George II, exiled in London, a veto on constitutional arrangements. So intemperate were Churchill's expressions of hostility to the Communists of EAM/ELAS that Clementine felt moved to write him a note of warning:

> My darling Winston,
> Please do not before ascertaining full facts repeat to anyone you meet what you said to me this morning i.e. that the Communists in Athens had shown their usual cowardice in putting the women & children in front to be shot at. Because altho' Communists are dangerous, indeed perhaps sinister people, they seem in this War on the Continent to have shown personal courage . . .
> Your loving & devoted Clemmie

Clementine's words were significant, because they reflected widespread sentiment in Britain as well as America. Allied propaganda throughout the Nazi occupation had made much of the Communist role in resistance, portraying EAM/ELAS, like Tito's partisans in Yugoslavia, as heroic freedom fighters. Not only was their contribution to the anti-Nazi struggle exaggerated, but reports of their atrocities, well-known to SOE officers on the ground, were suppressed. Many people on both sides of the Atlantic thus viewed the Greek left in roseate hues.

Worse, Churchill's lingering desire to salvage the Greek monarchy, despite overwhelming evidence of its unpopularity, compromised his own authority. Almost all his ministers, including Eden and Macmillan, were unwilling to offer even vestigial support to George II. They were also conscious of the rickety character of the Papandreou regime, an unconvincing foundation for the restoration of democracy. Churchill's instinct was probably right, that if the Allies had done nothing the Communists would have seized Greece with the same ruthlessness they were displaying everywhere else in eastern Europe and the Balkans. But clumsy diplomacy caused the British to be seen, above all in Washington, as would-be imperialist oppressors of a liberated people. Lincoln MacVeagh, the U.S. minister in Athens, criticised the British for "handling this fanatically freedom-loving country as if it were composed of natives under the British raj."

On December 5, Edward Stettinius, who had just replaced Cordell Hull as U.S. secretary of state, raised the stakes by publicly criticising British policy in Greece and also in Italy, where the British were at loggerheads with the Americans about whether Count Sforza should be permitted a role in the new Rome government. Stettinius said: "We expect the Italians to work out their own problems of government along democratic lines without influence from outside. This policy would apply to an even more pronounced degree with regard to governments of the United Nations in their liberated territories." Whatever the merits of the argument, it was deeply unhelpful of Stettinius, and damaging to Churchill, thus publicly to have distanced the United States from Britain.

A marked shift in American media sentiment was taking place. Conservative commentators, hitherto bitterly sceptical about British foreign policy, now showed themselves sympathetic to Churchill's efforts to check the onset of European Communism. The liberal press, however, deplored what it perceived as new manifestations of British imperialism. It is a striking reflection upon the mood of those days that perceived British misconduct in Greece and Italy provoked much more comment and protest in the United States than did Russia's ruthless handling of its newly occupied eastern European territories.

Many American papers asserted the right of resistance movements, whatever their political complexion, to a voice in the governance of their countries. A State Department opinion survey stated: " 'Liberal' papers, pleading for a greater representation for Resistance forces, were critical of Churchill's alleged attempt to maintain a reactionary regime against the wishes of the Greek people." William Shirer of CBS urged that the United States back up its words by taking action in opposition to British "toryism." The State Department said: "Substantially universal approval has greeted the proposition that the composition of governments in Italy and in 'liberated territories' is an internal affair . . . Representatives of Greek-American organizations visited the State Department to protest British intervention in Greece . . . The Department also received numerous letters from organizations and individuals protesting British policy and applauding the United States's [December 5] declaration."

Many American newspapers perceived the Soviets and British as tarred with the same brush, both seeking to impose their selfish wills on free peoples. Isolationists blamed Britain, and explicitly Churchill, for "seeking to bury the Atlantic Charter" with its declared right to self-determination. The Raleigh, North Carolina, *News & Observer*, for instance, cited "the shooting of Greeks for no greater crime than opposing a Government which seeks to bring back a discredited King" as being "not only a mistake but a tragedy." There were increasing demands, echoed in Congress, for a revision of Lend-Lease legislation to link U.S. aid to Britain and Russia with less high-handed foreign policies in those countries. The *Chicago Sun*, urging Lend-Lease revision, observed that "Washington has both the right and obligation to let the British government know that we do not propose to aid the enemies of democracy in Italy, Greece, or elsewhere through Lend-Lease or any other means."

A Princeton poll in December found that Americans thought Britain likely to be a much less trustworthy postwar ally than China. On December 13, 1944, the U.S. press reported anti-British student protests and marches at Harvard, Radcliffe, Wellesley and Northeastern. In Boston, students waved placards proclaiming: AMERICANS SUPPORT CHURCHILL AS WAR LEADER, NOT TORY. The protesters issued a statement: "We are not against Churchill as a war leader, but against his reactionary policy in Belgium, Italy, and Greece." U.S. trades unionists also demonstrated against British policy.

An attack on the prime minister by H. G. Wells was widely reported. "Churchill must go," the aged British literary sage wrote in *Tribune*: "Winston Churchill, the present would-be British Führer, is a person with a range of ideas limited to the adventures and opportunities of British political life . . . Now he seems to have lost his head completely . . . When the British people were blistered with humiliation by the currish policy of the old Conservative gang in power, the pugnacity of Winston brought him to the fore. The country liked fighting and he delighted in fighting. For want of a better reason he became the symbol of our national will for conflict, a role he has now outlived." Thomas Stokes wrote in the *Los Angeles Times* on December 12: "What we are seeing is the opening of the big battle between the right and the left for the control of postwar Europe. There's Great Britain on one side and Russia on the other, with the United States as a sort of arbiter or umpire trying to establish some middle course, and being in the difficult position of the harassed liberal who is caught in the crossfire from each side."

For Churchill, the only positive news coming out of Greece was that the Russians appeared to be holding back. "This is good," he wrote to Eden, "and shows how Stalin is playing the game." For once, the prime minister's optimism was justified. Throughout the unfolding imbroglio in Greece there was no sign that Moscow sought to meddle. Churchill, indeed, was moved to assert that on this issue he found the Russians much more biddable than the Americans. Stalin acknowledged spheres of influence, however broadly he sought to draw his own. Roosevelt did not.

On December 8, 1944, there was a stormy Commons debate about Greece, in which Emanuel Shinwell and Aneurin Bevan, men of the left, led the attack on the government. Churchill, who once more chose to remind the House that it could dismiss him if it so wished, won a vote of confidence by 279 votes to 30. But many MPs remained dissatisfied. Harold Nicolson thought the prime minister misread the mood of the House, which "at its best was one of distressed perplexity, and at its worst of sheer red fury." Harold Macmillan, who attended the debate, saw the prime minister afterwards in the Downing Street Annexe. He found him tired and petulant: "He rambled on in rather a sad and depressed way. The debate had obviously tired him very much, and I think he realised the dangers inherent in the Greek policy on which we are now embarked. He has won the debate, but not the battle of Athens."

Churchill seemed to have dug in his heels. He cabled Rex Leeper, the British ambassador in Greece, on December 10: "In Athens as everywhere else our maxim is 'no peace without victory.' " Yet Lt. Gen. Ronald Scobie, commanding British troops in Greece, signalled that he lacked sufficient men to hold the capital, never mind to enforce the prime minister's desired disarmament of the guerrillas. Alexander was now Mediterranean C-in-C, having replaced Maitland Wilson, who was dispatched to become the British military representative in Washington following the sudden death of Sir John Dill. Churchill urged Alexander to find more troops for Greece.

Relations with the Americans took a sharp turn for the worse. On

December 5, Churchill had signalled to Scobie, urging him to adopt a ruthless policy towards the Communist guerrillas: "Do not hesitate to fire at any armed male in Athens who assails the British authority or Greek authority . . . act as if you were in a conquered city where a local rebellion is in progress." Jock Colville sent this message at five a.m., when amid exhaustion he forgot to mark it "GUARD"—not to be shown to Americans. Adm. Ernest King, on his own initiative and even before learning of Churchill's draconian signal, ordered that U.S. shipping should not be used to supply or reinforce the British in Greece. Churchill cabled Harry Hopkins on December 9: "It grieves me very much to see signs of our drifting apart at a time when unity becomes even more important, as dangers recede and faction arises." Hopkins persuaded Admiral King to rescind his order, apparently without reference to Roosevelt. But a *Washington Post* editorial declared on December 9: "The American people simply do not relish the spectacle of Sherman tanks going into action against the men who held the pass in war-stricken Hellas." Correspondent Barnet Nover attacked Churchill for his harsh words about the Greek Communist guerrillas: "What suddenly transformed those patriots into 'bandits'?"

A malevolent hand in the U.S. administration leaked Churchill's draconian directive to Scobie to columnist Drew Pearson, who published it in the *Washington Post* on December 11. The ensuing anti-British tirade caused Churchill to draw unfavourable contrasts with Moscow's useful silence. "I think we have had pretty good treatment from Stalin in Greece," he wrote to Eden, "much better in fact than we have had from the Americans." The *Post* editorialised on December 6 that "the use of force carries within it the seeds of its destruction." On the eighth, a *Post* article by Marquis Childs argued: "Winston Churchill and the clique around him want to believe that you can put a little paint and a little varnish on the old order and prop it up in place again. It won't prop. That's the meaning of the news out of Brussels and Athens . . . the course that is being followed in Greece and Belgium is the best way to ensure communism in the end."

Walter Lippmann wrote in the *Washington Post* of December 14 that problems had arisen in Greece "because Mr. Churchill is trying to apply the great principle of legitimacy in government without a correct appreciation of the unprecedented condition of affairs which the Nazi conquest and occupation have created." The problem facing those trying to reconstruct Europe is "how to fuse the legitimacy acquired by Resistance movements with the legitimacy inherited by the old governments." This was an accurate analysis of Churchill's dilemma, lacking only an answer to it. Events in Greece, and elsewhere, were critically influenced by the outcome of policies promoted by the prime minister himself through the SOE. It was only possible for ELAS to mount a challenge to the Greek government and its British sponsors because London had provided the Communists with arms.

Halifax cabled gloomily from the Washington embassy, "Our version of the facts is largely disbelieved." On the ground in Athens, Scobie's units faced increasingly violent pressure from ELAS guerrillas. Open insurgency was breaking out. Alexander signalled: "British forces are in fact beleaguered in the heart of the city." Both Macmillan and Leeper, at the British embassy, believed that Churchill failed to grasp the complexities of the situation. However distasteful were the Communists, the Greek right was at least as much so. Macmillan urged the prime minister to accept that the king—"the real villain of the piece"—must remain exiled in London, while the primate of Athens, Archbishop Damaskinos, should be appointed regent, to reconcile the warring factions. Macmillan had little time for the Greek prime minister: "We do not wish to start the Third World War against Russia until we have finished the Second World War against Germany—and certainly not to please M. Papandreou." The British in Athens, who perceived a regency as offering by far the best chance of a settlement acceptable to the Greek people, were enraged by the perceived duplicity of the Greek prime minister, who urged George II to reject a regency.

Men of the British Army who found themselves seeking to sustain by force the Athens regime were as divided as the rest of the world about the merits of their cause. Capt. Phillip Zorab, for instance, hated the Communists and everything that he saw and heard of their doings: "These ELAS guerrillas don't care who they hit," he wrote in a letter home, "and I have four first-hand reports of atrocities committed by them on other Greeks . . . Greeks now know that when we said that political differences would not be settled by use of arms, we meant it." Other British soldiers, however, were deeply troubled by the role in which they found themselves cast. Major A. P. Greene, like Zorab a gunner, told his family:

> I thought a good deal before writing this letter, because it contains some pretty definite views. But they must be aired or ten years of principles go for naught. Briefly I think our country is being misled on the subject of Greece. I have just finished reading Churchill's speech, and I disagreed with it vehemently. Greece is a country with no background of real democracy in its modern history . . . We, the preachers of non-intervention, are forcing on Greece the government we want, and think it wants . . . Churchill's speech was, to me, a political false-

hood . . . People at home should know that it is the *Manchester Guardian* and not Churchill that represents the opinion of 80% of the army here. Whether they be regulars or volunteers, high ranking officers or privates, the vast majority want no part in what, to them, is a face-saving war of Churchill's own making.

Greene acknowledged that all the local factions were guilty of atrocities, "but I think the bulk of Greek youth wants socialism . . . I shall stay until I'm so heartily sick of assisting in the installation of a fascist regime in Greece that I summon up enough courage to resign." He was right in believing that the wartime experience had radicalised Greek youth, as it appears to have radicalised him. Yet if Churchill's support for restoring the monarchy was mistaken, he was surely justified in his revulsion against allowing power to fall by default into Communist hands, as would have been most likely to happen in the absence of British military intervention.

On December 17, Alexander signalled that another infantry division might be needed to hold Athens, a shocking prospect since the formation would have to be withdrawn from the Italian front. Two days later, 563 RAF personnel at the British air headquarters at Kifissia, outside Athens, surrendered to ELAS after a battle in which 57 airmen had been killed or wounded. During the month's fighting in Athens, the British Army lost 169 killed, 699 wounded and 640 missing—mostly prisoners—an appalling scale of casualties for what began as a postliberation security operation, equivalent to the loss of two infantry battalions to the Allied order of battle. Macmillan wrote in his diary on December 21: "Poor Winston! What with Greece, Poland and the German breakthrough on the Western Front, this is going to be a grim Christmas." By the twenty-second, with strife intensifying, Churchill was at last becoming persuadable about the possibility of a regency, and keeping the king out of Greece pending a referendum on his future. But he said crossly to Cadogan: "I won't instal a Dictator." In truth, the prime minister was dithering. An almost daily barrage of hostile questions in the Commons sustained pressure on the government. He cabled to Smuts: "I have had endless trouble about Greece where we have indeed been wounded in the house of our friends. Communist and Left-wing forces all over the world have stirred in sympathy with this new chance and the American Press reporting back has to some extent undermined our prestige and authority in Greece. There would be no chance of our basing a British policy upon the return of the King. We must at all costs avoid appearing to be forcing him on them by our bayonets."

"Setting Europe ablaze."
(*left*) Instructing French
maquisards on the use of
the sten submachine gun,
supplied in large quantities
to the French Resistance
by SOE in 1944

(*below*) An SOE mission
looking suitably flamboyant
in occupied Yugoslavia

Images of D-Day:
Operation Overlord,
June 6, 1944, climactic
moment of World War I
in the west

With his unworthy favourite Alexander in Italy, August 26, 1944

In Paris on Armistice
Day, November 11, 1944,
an unusually affable
moment with De Gaulle

In Athens on December 26,
1944, meeting the warring
Greek factions in conference
with Eden (*far left*),
Archbishop Damaskinos,
Alexander and Macmillan,
while gunfire raged in the
streets outside

At Yalta in February 1945: The USN's Admiral King engages in sober conversation with Brooke, Ismay and Marshall.

One of the Valentine tanks supplied by Britain to the Red Army enjoys a moment of triumph as it carries victorious Russian soldiers through the streets of Sofia, the Bulgarian capital.

Last set piece of the western campaign: Churchill stands at a vantage point overlooking the Rhine with Brooke and Montgomery before the British crossing in March 1945.

he sublime consummation
Churchill's war leadership of
tain: (*above*) On the balcony
Buckingham Palace with the
al family on VE Day, May 8,
5; (*below*) he addresses his
on, and the world, from
wning Street.

With Truman and Stalin at Potsdam on July 17, 1945. Though he did not know it, Winston Churchill had only nine more days to serve as Britain's wartime prime minister.

Much grief—even perhaps the bloody strife in Greece—might have been averted if Churchill had reached this conclusion months earlier, and explicitly proclaimed it to the Greek people. But it was hard to resolve the affairs of half a world emerging from the horrors of Nazi occupation amid the new reality of Soviet expansionism. If British policy was sometimes misjudged, so too was American. The British embassy in Washington reported to London about U.S. media opinion: "Indignation with Britain has given way to a kind of disgruntled and disenchanted cynicism which says that it was foolish ever to have supposed that the European, and in particular Russian and British, leopards could really have been expected to change their spots as the result of a few idealistic words from America."

What now was to be done? On the afternoon of Saturday, December 23, Churchill drove to Chequers, where a large family party was assembled for Christmas. He had scarcely arrived before he declared his determination to abandon the celebration and travel to Athens. His decision caused consternation, above all to Clementine. This was one of the very rare moments of the war at which she broke down, fleeing upstairs in floods of tears. Her husband had just turned seventy, and in poor health. Private secretary John Martin wrote in his diary: "Glad I am not going on an expedition of which I disapprove, the prize not being worth the risks." Late on Christmas Eve Churchill and his entourage, including Anthony Eden, drove to Northolt and took off for Italy in a new American C-54 Skymaster. "Make it look British," Churchill urged when the plane was delivered, and the aircraft had been refitted to an extraordinary standard of comfort for the times. Its principal passenger complained only that the clock in his private compartment ticked too loudly, and insisted upon disconnection of an electrically heated lavatory seat.

What did Churchill hope to achieve in Athens? It seemed to him, rightly, essential to Britain's global prestige, and above all to relations with the United States, that he should succeed in stabilising Greece. It was implausible that this could be achieved under Papandreou. Some broadly based coalition government was needed. His advisers believed that Archbishop Damaskinos might provide the necessary sheet anchor, and supervise the creation of such a regime. Yet Churchill was mistrustful of surrendering the country to some wily local prelate. As ever, he wanted to see, and then to be seen to act, for himself. Early in the afternoon of Christmas Day, his Skymaster landed at Kalamaki Airfield.

One of the welcoming party observed cynically that the visitors "had the air of men to whom a brilliant idea had been vouchsafed after the third glass of port upon which they had immediately decided to act but which they could now no longer very clearly recall." Macmillan found the prime minister "in a most mellow, not to say chastened mood." A two-hour conference took place in the plane, the interior of which became icy cold. Churchill's shivering typist, Elizabeth Layton, was increasingly fearful for "Master's" health. The security situation was much worse than had been recognised in London, with snipers active in many parts of the Greek capital. Towards evening, a convoy of armoured cars took the party on a long, tense, uncomfortable journey to Phaleron, where they were transferred by launch to the light cruiser *Ajax*, a veteran of the 1939 river Plate battle, which was anchored offshore, safely beyond small-arms range.

Her captain warned the exalted visitor that it might be necessary to disturb his tranquillity by firing the ship's main armament in support of British ground forces. Churchill, of course, enthused at the prospect: "Pray remember, Captain, that I come here as a cooing dove of peace, bearing a sprig of mistletoe in my beak—but far be it from me to stand in the way of military necessity." Shortly afterwards Macmillan, Leeper, Papandreou and Damaskinos boarded the ship. The spectacle of the prelate in full canonical dress, complete with black silver-knobbed staff, brushing past sailors in the ship's companionways who were celebrating Christmas in fancy-dress, impressed the British as irresistibly droll.

Churchill was captivated by the jolly archbishop, who made plain his revulsion towards the Communists and the atrocities they had committed. The prelate, the prime minister told MPs later, "struck me as a very remarkable man, with his headgear, towering up, morally as well as physically, above the chaotic scene." Colville wrote: "We are now in the curious topsy-turvy position of the prime minister feeling strongly pro-Damaskinos . . . while [Eden] is inclined the other way." The next morning, the visitors rose to survey the battlefield—what Churchill called "the pink and ochre panorama of Athens and the Piraeus, scintillating with delicious life and plumed by the classic glories and endless miseries and triumphs of its history." The shore was bathed in bright sunshine. "One can see the smoke of battle in the streets west of the Piraeus," wrote Colville, "and there is a constant noise of shellfire and machine-guns. We had a splendid view of Beaufighters strafing an ELAS stronghold."

Osbert Lancaster, an artist then serving as press attaché at the British embassy, described the arrival the next afternoon of Churchill, once more borne by armoured car from the harbour through the drab, dusty, bullet-scarred streets. The prime minister wore the uniform of an RAF air commodore: "The change in his appearance since I had last seen him at close quarters some three years previously was marked. His face seems to have been moulded in lard lightly veined with cochineal and he badly needed a haircut. But the sound of mortaring and rifle-fire, combined with the historic associations of the countryside through which he had just passed, were clearly already having a tonic effect and he was distinguished from all his companions by an obvious and unswerving sense of purpose none the less impressive for being at the moment indeterminate." The latter intimation of confusion was unwarranted. The British had already convened a conference of all the warring parties, to meet under Churchill's auspices but Damaskinos's chairmanship.

The embassy resembled a besieged outpost during the nineteenth-century Indian Mutiny. Power was cut off, while gunfire provided orchestration. Some fifty staff, many of them women, had been subsisting for nine days on army rations in conditions of acute discomfort. The ambassador's wife, whom Harold Macmillan found more impressive than her husband, directed domestic operations with a courage and energy likewise worthy of a Victorian imperial drama. Fortunately for the inmates, ELAS guerrillas had only small arms, so the British remained safe if they avoided exposing themselves at doors and windows. Between meetings with commanders, Churchill met and applauded the embassy staff, for whom he afterwards arranged an immediate issue of decorations.

At four p.m., representatives of the Greek factions assembled around a long table in the freezing, otherwise barren conference room of the Foreign Office. The rattle of musketry punctuated the proceedings, with voices sometimes drowned out by rocket and mortar concussions. Churchill seated himself in the centre, flanked by Archbishop Damaskinos, Eden and Macmillan. At one end were American, Russian and French representatives. The Greeks filled in around them, leaving space at a vacant end for the Communists, who were late. Churchill and the prelate spoke brilliantly and at length, with long pauses for interpretation, before news arrived of the absentees, "three shabby desperados." The Communists had been delayed arguing with British security guards about their demand to bring weapons into the conference chamber. On their appearance, Churchill wrote to Clementine later, "after some consideration I shook the ELAS delegates' hand[s] and it was clear from their response that they were gratified." He repeated much of his opening harangue: "Mr. Eden and I have come all this way, though great battles are raging in Belgium and on the German frontier, to make this effort to rescue Greece from a miserable fate and raise her to a point of great fame and repute . . . Whether Greece is a monarchy or a republic is a matter for Greeks and Greeks alone to decide. I wish you all that is good, and good for all."

Alexander said, "Instead of me putting my brigades into Greece, I should like to see Greek brigades coming to help me in Italy in the war against our common enemy." Macmillan was disgusted by the oily platitudes offered by the Communists, who extolled their own desire for peace: "I thought it all very disingenuous, especially remembering the frightful atrocities these men are committing both on our troops and on harmless fellow-countrymen throughout Greece. Winston was much moved, however." Then the foreigners rose and left the table, to enable the Greeks to negotiate with one another.

Once they were outside, their exchanges provided several notable vignettes. The prime minister engaged the head of the Russian military mission in conversation: "What's your name? Popov? Well, Popov, I saw your master the other day, Popov! Very good friends your master and I, Popov! Don't forget that, POPOV!" Even the colonel's limited English enabled him to comprehend Churchill's attempt to brandish his relationship with Stalin. Then it was explained that the delay in the proceedings had been caused by the need to disarm the Communist delegates. The prime minister looked thoughtful and withdrew a pistol from his own pocket, growling complacently: "I cannot tell you the feeling of security one enjoys, knowing that one is the only armed man in such an assembly as that!" He replaced the weapon in his overcoat before retreating with his entourage by armoured car to the embassy, and thence to Phaleron. When his typist Elizabeth Layton seated herself at the opposite end of the naval barge's cabin to the prime minister, Churchill said: "No, come and sit by me." To Alexander's wry amusement, the two travelled back across the chilly water to the *Ajax*, cosily enfolded together in a huge rug.

The next day, the archbishop came to the British embassy to report on progress of the noisy, bitter talks at the Foreign Office. At one point, apparently, Gen. Nikolaos Plastiras—whom Churchill insistently addressed as "Plaster-Arse"—shouted at a Communist: "Sit down, butcher!" The prime minister was in high spirits, having been taken by Alexander to a vantage point from which the general explained the Athens battlefield. Macmillan saw this as a reprise of Churchill's famous appearance at a London shoot-out with terrorists, during his 1911 incarnation as home secretary: "Of course this affair is a sort of 'super Sidney Street,' and he quite enjoyed having the whole problem explained to him by a master of the military art." When the ELAS delegates asked to see Churchill privately, he was eager to accept. But Macmillan and Damaskinos persuaded him that it was essential now to leave the Greeks to sort out their own affairs. That evening, the archbishop announced Papandreou's resignation as prime minister. His last act in office was to cable to King George II in

London, declaring the united endorsement of Greece's politicians for a regency. Churchill wrote to Clementine: "This Wednesday has been an exciting and not altogether fruitless day. The hatreds between these Greeks are terrible. When one side have all the weapons which we gave them to fight the Germans and the other, though many times as numerous, have none, it is evident that a frightful massacre would take place if we withdrew."

Lack of both electricity and camera flashbulbs made it necessary to hold the prime minister's parting photo session in the embassy garden, much to the dismay of those responsible for his safety. Access was possible only by traversing a short walkway from the drawing room, on which he was visible to the world from Constitution Avenue. Attempts to hustle him behind the safety of the garden wall were frustrated by an onrush of photographers, which caused the prime minister to halt on the walkway. To the dismay of the press attaché behind him, "a short crack followed by a shower of plaster announced that a bullet had hit the wall two feet above our heads. Summoning all my courage, I . . . gave the infuriated Prime Minister a sharp shove in the back, precipitating him smartly down the steps into the comparative safety of the garden." On December 28, Churchill flew out of Athens for Naples. He had yearned to linger, and again to meet the Greeks. Macmillan, however, persuaded him that his duty was to return to London and reconcile King George of the Hellenes to the regency. Churchill allowed himself to be buckled into his seatbelt on the Skymaster, acknowledging that "even the most eminent persons are subject to the laws of gravity." As the plane taxied, he suddenly ordered it to halt. He insisted on passing down to the ground party an amendment to the British final communiqué. Then he took off for Italy, and home.

Back in London the next afternoon, the prime minister twice met the king of the Hellenes, at 10:30 p.m. and 1:30 a.m. At 4:00 a.m., George II at last agreed to the regency. Churchill retired to bed, after a working and travelling day that had lasted twenty-two hours. General Plastiras became prime minister, though he was obliged to resign soon afterwards, following the leak of a letter revealing that in 1941 he had offered himself to the Nazis as leader of a collaborationist Greek government. On the night of January 4, 1945, the firepower of the British Army and diminished confidence in their own prospects persuaded the Communist guerrillas to retire to the countryside. An uneasy armistice was agreed to between the factions. Violence in Athens subsided, though it required the deployment of ninety thousand British troops to secure the country. Greece remained in a state of civil war between 1946 and 1949, but a non-Communist—

indeed, bitterly anti-Communist—government survived until the Americans relieved the British of responsibility for Greek security.

Churchill's visit was significant chiefly because it reconciled him to a course of action which all the other British players had already endorsed. The decisive factor in Greece was Stalin's abstention. It suited Moscow to acknowledge the principle that whichever ally liberated an occupied country should determine its subsequent governance. The ELAS guerrilla leaders were vastly more impressed by the silence of Colonel Popov, Stalin's man in Athens, than by the eloquence of Britain's prime minister. In Greece, Churchill received his sole reward for the Moscow "percentages agreement," which Americans so much disliked. So tormented and riven was Greek society in the wake of the occupation that it is hard to imagine any course of action which might have brought about the peaceful establishment of a democratic government. What emerged was probably the least bad outcome, in which no one could take just pride.

Churchill's dramatic venture into personal diplomacy commanded less world attention than it might otherwise have done, because it coincided with the Battle of the Bulge in Belgium and Luxembourg. According to a State Department survey, the overriding U.S. media impression of British action remained unfavourable: "Anglo-American differences and British military action in Greece during early December received more than twice as much front page space as Churchill's mission to Athens . . . Predominant editorial opinion throughout the crisis was never categorically opposed to British leadership in Greece and the Mediterranean, but strongly objected to the possible imposition of an unrepresentative and unpopular government on the Greek people, and to the possible creation of a closed British sphere of interest." Drew Pearson's final column of 1944 unfavourably compared Churchill's "outgrown imperialism" with more enlightened attitudes elsewhere in the British body politic. Criticism of British shortcomings at home and abroad was now a running theme in the U.S. press. Virginius Dabney wrote in the *New York Times* on December 31 that opinion in the American south, traditionally friendly to Britain, was turning hostile: "The development which has provoked most adverse comment is Winston Churchill's policy in Greece and Italy. Even in this strongly pro-British region criticism is being heard, not only of Churchill but of the British people."

The British did not receive this bombardment in silence. On December 30, after a surge of U.S. comment which added allegations of "slacking" to other charges against America's ally, the *Economist* delivered a counterblast:

What makes the American criticisms so intolerable is not merely that they are unjust, but that they come from a source which has done so little to earn the right to postures of superiority. To be told by anyone that the British people are slacking in their war effort would be insufferable enough to a people struggling through their sixth winter of black-out and rations and coldness—but when the criticism comes from a nation that was practising Cash-and-Carry during the Battle of Britain, whose consumption has risen during the war years, which is still without a national service act—then it is not to be borne.

There is still a great deal of wishful thinking in Britain, even in the highest quarters, to the effect that good behaviour on our part will procure some great prize, such as an Anglo-American alliance . . . It is as well to be brutally frank: there is no more possibility of any of these things than of an American petition to rejoin the British Empire . . . What, then, is the conclusion for British policy towards America? Clearly it is not that any quarrels should be picked . . . But let an end be put to the policy of appeasement which, at Mr. Churchill's personal bidding, has been followed, with all the humiliations and abasements it has brought in its train.

Following the *Economist's* outburst, the State Department recorded "an orgy of recrimination between the American and British presses." The Washington embassy reported to London the following week on U.S. attitudes: "The general reaction is that although the British attack was not unprovoked and the British cannot have been expected to take the flood of criticism poured by the United States press and radio lying down, yet the British are surely much too touchy and the tone of their retort is much too harsh." Though a January 14 *Life* magazine editorial described the *Economist's* criticisms as well-merited, many U.S. publications remained hostile. Office of War Information and State Department surveys in the early months of 1945 found that Americans consistently rated the British more blameworthy than the Russians for the difficulties of the Grand Alliance.

The State Department study noted: "Despite recent press comment sympathetic to the British, a confidential opinion poll indicates that dissatisfaction with the British has increased among the public at large. The tabulation shows that mass opinion, dissatisfied with the way in which Russia, Britain and the United States are cooperating, blames chiefly Britain . . . The 'nationalist' press, even in comment praising Field-Marshal Montgomery and the British people, continued to charge that the 'British and Russians are playing power politics against each other in the middle of this war, while we, at least at this moment, do most of the fighting.' "

Churchill found little to celebrate in what he called the "new, disgusting year" of 1945. Russian intransigence was familiar, but overbearing American behaviour filled a bitter cup. Tempers were frayed to the limit, in government and among the British people. Eden wrote on January 12: "Terrible Cabinet, first on Greece . . . Whole thing lasted four and a half hours. Really quite intolerable. I was in a pretty bloody temper . . . for everyone started taking a hand in drafting messages for me." Churchill found it much harder to sustain relative inactivity in Downing Street than to undertake initiatives abroad, even if these were ill-rewarded. One morning he told his typist Marion Holmes, "You know I cannot give you the excitement of Athens every day."

There seemed no limit to the troubles sent to vex him. Montgomery gave an outrageously hubristic press conference following his modest personal contribution to the Bulge battle. This excited new American hostility and correspondingly exasperated the prime minister. Churchill was obliged to recognise that there was no more chance of restoring King Peter of Yugoslavia to his throne than King Zog of Albania or King Carol of Romania to theirs. Roosevelt agreed to Stalin's proposal for a February summit at Yalta, in the Crimea, causing Churchill to cable: "I shall be waiting on the quay. No more let us falter! From Malta to Yalta! Let nobody alter!" In reality, however, the British complained bitterly about the inconvenient venue. They remained resentful that Roosevelt was unwilling to visit their own country, or to accept Churchill's alternative suggestion of a meeting in Iceland. The prime minister sent congratulations to Stalin on the Russian Vistula offensive, all the more fulsome because of his anxiety for Soviet goodwill in Greece and Poland. Brooke expressed relief that Churchill seemed finally reconciled to the fact that there could be no Adriatic amphibious landing, nor a drive on Vienna. Churchill brusquely dismissed de Gaulle's demand that he should attend the Yalta conference in the name of his country. "France cannot masquerade as a Great Power for the purposes of war," he told Eden.

The prime minister said to Marian Holmes, "You wouldn't like my job—so many different things come up which have to be settled in two or three minutes." At a time when many of his own ministers were wearying of Churchill, Holmes paid a tribute which reflected the passionate affection and loyalty he retained among his personal staff: "In all his moods— totally absorbed in the serious matter of the moment, agonized over some piece of wartime bad news, suffused with compassion, sentimental and in tears, truculent, bitingly sarcastic, mischievous or hilariously funny—he was splendidly entertaining, humane and lovable." While ministers and commanders complained with increasing impatience about the prime minister's failing concentration and outbursts of irrationality, he remained a unique repository of wisdom. Consider, for instance, his words to Eden, who had been pressing him about arrangements for postwar Germany:

It is a mistake to try to write out on some little pieces of papers what the vast emotions of an outraged and quivering world will be either immediately after the struggle is over or when the inevitable cold fit follows the hot. These awe-inspiring tides of feeling dominate most people's minds . . . Guidance in these mundane matters is granted to us only step by step, or at the utmost a step or two ahead. There is therefore wisdom in reserving one's decisions as long as possible and until all the facts and forces that will be potent at the moment are revealed.

Likewise, on January 18 he delivered to the House of Commons a report on the war situation which some thought was as glittering a display of oratory as he had produced since 1940. In a two-hour speech, he said of Greece:

The House must not suppose that, in these foreign lands, matters are settled as they would be here in England. Even here it is hard enough to keep a Coalition together, even between men who, although divided by party, have a supreme object and so much else in common. But imagine what the difficulties are in countries racked by civil war, past or impending, and where clusters of petty parties have each their own set of appetites, misdeeds and revenges. If I had driven the wife of the Deputy Prime Minister out to die in the snow, if the Minister of Labour had kept the Foreign Secretary in exile for a great many years, if the Chancellor of the Exchequer had shot at and wounded the Secretary of State for War . . . if we, who sit here together, had back-bitten and double-crossed each other while pretending to work together, and had all put our own group or party first and the country nowhere, and had all set ideologies, slogans or labels in front of comprehension, comradeship and duty, we should certainly, to put it at the mildest, have come to a General Election much sooner than is now likely. When men have wished very much to kill each other, and have feared very much that they will be killed quite soon, it is not possible for them next day to work together as friends with colleagues against whom they have nursed such intentions or from whom they have derived such fears.

Churchill said to Colville in those days, speaking of the South African prime minister, "Smuts and I are like two old love-birds moulting together on a perch, but still able to peck." He "pecked" to incomparable effect. After his difficult passages with MPs about Greece in December, he had now restored his position. Yet he told at least one considerable untruth to the Commons on January 18, denying that events in the Mediterranean were in any way influenced by rival notions about "spheres of influences." In reality, in his gratitude for Stalin's forbearance on Greece, he was desperate to be seen to keep his own side of the Moscow bargain. He was exasperated to hear that British diplomats in Romania had been protesting about Soviet actions there, and wrote angrily to Eden: "Why are we making a fuss about the Russian deportations in Romania of Saxons and others? It is understood that the Russians were to work their will in this sphere. Anyhow, we cannot prevent them." He told Colville on January 23: "Make no mistake, all the Balkans, except Greece, are going to be bolshevized; and there is nothing I can do to prevent it. There is nothing I can do for poor Poland either."

If Churchill often displayed greatness on great matters, his ministers and commanders were increasingly sensitive to "the old man's" limitations. His rambling dissertations at Cabinet meetings, often about papers which he had not troubled to read, exasperated colleagues. So, too, did his willingness to invite and accept ill-informed opinions across the table from Brendan Bracken and Beaverbrook, in preference to the considered views of Cabinet committees. Clement Attlee wrote him a note of protest about his behaviour, which fired the prime minister's wrath, but which his own staff and Clementine agreed to be both courageous and just. Attlee had typed the note with his own fumbling fingers, to ensure that no other eyes saw it. Yet Churchill vented his spleen by reading it aloud down the telephone to Beaverbrook. Private secretary John Martin said: "That is the part of the prime minister which I do not like." Jock Colville agreed. The prime minister was eventually persuaded to reconsider his first thought, of an angry riposte to Attlee. He responded temperately. Then he said: "Let us think no more of Hitlee or of Attler: let us go and see a film." If he was sometimes roused to stand high upon his dignity, he seldom retained the posture for long. While he sometimes behaved unworthily, he had earned the right to be readily forgiven.

TWENTY

Yalta

ALMOST EVERY DAY of the war that he was not travelling, Churchill visited his Map Room. Capt. Richard Pim, RN, the lanky Welshman who presided there, was a key figure in the Downing Street entourage, often accompanying the prime minister on his journeys to maintain the flow of battlefield news he craved. Churchill still intervened constantly in matters of detail concerning the armed forces. Britain's falling troop strength was a preoccupation. He deplored the dissolution of some units to fill the depleted ranks of others. There were wearisome wrangles about the respective manpower claims of the army, RAF and coal mines. Churchill was anxious that soldiers dispatched to the Far East at the end of the German war should receive additional pay. He followed with the keenest interest the commitment of Germany's new advanced U-boats to the Atlantic, British progress towards producing jet fighters to match those of Hitler, and efforts to counter the V-2 rocket bombardment which continued to inflict distress on southern England.

But these were all minor matters, by comparison with the great strategy decisions of earlier years. The Allied armies were advancing across Europe with little opportunity for the prime minister to influence their courses. He hailed successes, chafed in familiar fashion at setbacks and delays, but knew that power resided at Eisenhower's headquarters and in Washington. Oliver Harvey wrote, somewhat patronisingly, "As the purely military problems simplify themselves, the old boy's tireless energy leads to ever closer attention to foreign affairs." Almost all Churchill's thoughts were now fixed upon the postwar settlement of Europe, which might be critically influenced by the Yalta summit. "I have great hopes of this conference," he told the House of Commons, "because it comes at a moment when a good many moulds can be set out to receive a great deal of molten metal." Nonetheless, he complained to Harry Hopkins, who was in London, that if the Allies had spent ten years researching a possible rendezvous, they could not have devised a less convenient one than the Crimea. It was farcical that a desperately sick U.S. president should be obliged to travel six thousand miles to suit the whims of Soviet doctors, who had allegedly told Stalin not to venture abroad. As for the prime minister himself, on January 29 he arrived at Malta, the Anglo-American staging point for Yalta, with a temperature of 102 degrees.

The Combined Chiefs of Staff held an unpleasant preliminary meeting, its atmosphere poisoned by personality clashes entwined with the campaign in northwest Europe. Montgomery's boorish behaviour towards Eisenhower sustained friction. Brooke was distressed to find that Marshall refused even to enter into argument with the British about strategy. America's course was set, for a measured advance to the Elbe. Franklin Roosevelt arrived aboard the cruiser *Quincy* on February 2. If Churchill was feverish, the British were shocked to perceive in the leader of the United States the wreck of a man. It was a grim prospect, to set off for a summit with an American president unfit for important business. After the delegations' first dinner together at Malta, Eden fumed about lack of serious discussion: "Impossible even to get near basics. I spoke pretty sharply to Harry [Hopkins] about it . . . pointing out that we were going into a decisive conference and had so far neither agreed about what we would discuss nor how to handle matters with a Bear who would certainly know his mind." Human sympathy for Roosevelt was eclipsed by dismay about the implications of his incapacity to defend the interests of the West.

The Allied leaders' arrival in the Crimea on February 3 was inauspicious. After the planes carrying the great men landed, Roosevelt had to be assisted into a jeep to inspect a Russian guard of honour, with Churchill walking beside him. There followed a nightmare six-hour trip to Yalta, along terrible roads. The prime minister looked around without enthusiasm. "What a hole I've brought you to!" he said to Marian Holmes. Later, he described the resort bleakly as "the Riviera of Hades." Generals found themselves billeted four to a room, colonels in dormitories of eleven. From national leaders downwards, all complained about the shortage of bathrooms. On February 4, there was a preconference dinner of the principals. Eden wrote: "A terrible party, I thought. President vague and loose and ineffective. W., understanding that business was flagging, made desperate efforts and too long speeches to get things going again. Stalin's attitude to small countries struck me as grim, not to say sinister." Security around the Soviet leader was so tight that he arrived for a photo session almost invisible amid a phalanx of armed guards.

Despite all the criticism of Churchill in the United States during the past months, few Americans at Yalta doubted the power of his personality.

C. L. Sulzberger wrote in the *New York Times* that among the "Big Three," Roosevelt was "certainly blander than either of his colleagues," while Churchill, "with his romantic conceptions, his touch of mysticism, his imperialism, his love of uniforms and color, is something of a Renaissance figure. He combines more talents than either Stalin or Roosevelt— more than almost any political figure who has ever attained his stature."

Polls in America continued to report widespread personal respect for the prime minister, and a renewed faith that Britain would prove a reliable postwar ally. But enthusiasm for Churchill's country was importantly qualified. Most Americans—70 percent—were implacable in their belief that at the end of the war the British should repay the billions they had received in Lend-Lease supplies. Even when told that their ally lacked means to do this, 43 percent of respondents said that they must do so anyway. It was a perverse and unhelpful compliment to Britain that the United States, its leaders and people alike, still overestimated the wealth of Churchill's nation. Few grasped the extent of its moral, strategic and financial exhaustion. Finally, of course, the war had done nothing to diminish U.S. anti-imperialism. A March OWI survey reported: "During the past year, Britain . . . has been under severe attack by an active minority for its alleged failure to play its proper role in the 'Big Three Team' . . . During December and January dissatisfaction with Big Three cooperation was . . . directed chiefly at Britain . . . [which was] chiefly blamed for 'not living up to the Atlantic Charter.' "

The attitude of the unusually large anti-British minority found striking expression in a widely publicised article in the *Army and Navy Journal.* In a stinging passage, equally critical of Russian and British policy, the journal accused Britain of "showing greater preoccupation in Italy, Greece and Albania to protect her life-line through the Mediterranean to India than in achievement of the prime objective of our American armies—prompt defeat of Germany." The survey concluded: "A shift in the allocation of chief blame from Russia to Britain is revealed by recent polls."

All this should be considered in the context of the miracle that, thanks to the statesmanship of George Marshall, Dwight Eisenhower, Alan Brooke, Winston Churchill, Franklin Roosevelt and finally Harry Truman, the Western Allies preserved to the end of the war a façade of unity. Given the shortcomings of every alliance in history, the Anglo-American working relationship remains remarkable. But Roosevelt made policy during the last months of his life in the knowledge that the American people supported his own postwar vision, and felt scant sympathy for that of Churchill. Britain could draw upon only a meagre credit balance of sentiment in the United States.

The Western leaders' first meeting with Stalin, at the Livadia Palace, where the conference convened, briefly revived Churchill's spirits. Stalin, the affable host, deployed some of his limited repertoire of English phrases: "You said it!," "So what?," "What the hell goes on around here?" and "The toilet is over there"—all except the last presumably garnered from watching American movies. Churchill wrote later, describing the sensation of finding himself one of the three most powerful men on earth, now gathered together: "We had the world at our feet, twenty-five million men marching at our orders by land and sea. We seemed to be friends." Such romantic illusions were soon banished. For the British at least, the Yalta experience became progressively more distressing.

Churchill opened on an entirely false note, by expounding to the first plenary session his hopes for an Allied drive from northeast Italy through the "Ljubljana Gap." This idea had been dead for months in the minds of everyone save the prime minister. It seemed otiose now to revive it. With Eisenhower's armies approaching the Rhine, Churchill sought to flatter the Russians by inviting their advice on large-scale river crossings. Stalin, in his turn, asked Roosevelt and Churchill what they would like the Red Army to do—for all the world as if their answer might cause him to alter his deployments. He declared sanctimoniously that he had considered the launching of Russia's vast January offensive "a moral duty," after the Anglo-Americans requested action to relieve pressure from the German offensive in the Ardennes. In reality, it is unlikely that the timing of the Soviet assault was advanced by a single day in deference to Western wishes.

Churchill told Stalin that Eisenhower's forces wanted the Red Army to do only one thing: keep going. The Soviets always knew, however, that British dollops of flattery masked a fundamental hostility to their objectives, while the U.S. president was much less intractable. "Our guards compared Churchill to a poodle wagging its tail to please Stalin," wrote Sergo Beria. "We shared friendly feelings towards Roosevelt which did not extend to Churchill." Yet, Soviet cynicism was evenly apportioned between the two. Molotov quoted an unnamed colleague who said of Roosevelt: "What a crook that man must be, to have wormed his way to three terms as president while being paralyzed!" Soviet eavesdroppers laughed heartily when they heard Churchill complain that he could not sleep at night because of the bedbugs.

Each day, the principals met at four p.m. for sessions which lasted four or five hours. In between, there were lunches, dinners, and tense national consultations among the delegations. Stalin was astonishingly amiable, as well he might be, as the most conspicuous profiteer from the war. Roosevelt drifted in and out of consciousness of the proceedings. When he engaged, it was most frequently to press for delay—for instance, in settling German occupation zones—or to accede to Soviet views. Again and again, the British found themselves isolated. Churchill opposed the "dismemberment" of Germany, to which Stalin was committed, and also argued against imposing extravagant reparations on the vanquished. He reminded the conference of the failure of such a policy in 1919: "If you want your horse to pull your cart, you had to give him some hay." But the Americans and Russians had already settled on a provisional figure of $20 billion, of which the Soviet Union was to receive half.

The Americans joined with the Russians in resisting Churchill's proposal to give France a seat on the Allied Control Commission in Germany. At British insistence, however, France was grudgingly conceded a zone of occupation. Churchill's bilateral meetings with Roosevelt were fruitless. At lunches and dinners, platitudes were exchanged, but no business was done. The combination of Roosevelt's mortal languor and disinclination to indulge Britain was fatal to Churchill's hopes. There is little doubt that, at Yalta as at Tehran, the president deliberately sought to reach out to Stalin by distancing himself from the prime minister. It is hard to suggest that this tactic did Western interests substantial harm, for Stalin's course was set. But it certainly conferred no discernible advantage.

Churchill, returning to his villa on the night of February 5, was irked to find that no intelligence brief had arrived from London. John Martin wrote: "It has gone to my heart to hear 'Colonel Kent' calling again and again for news and being offered only caviar." That night, before he went to sleep, Churchill said to his daughter Sarah: "I do not suppose that at any moment in history has the agony of the world been so great or widespread. To-night the sun goes down on more suffering than ever before in the World." Churchill's fund of compassion towards the enemy, incomparably greater than that of his peers at Yalta, was among his most notable qualities. "I am free to confess to you," he wrote to Clementine, "that my heart is saddened by the tales of the masses of German women and children flying along the roads everywhere in 40-mile long columns to the West before the advancing Armies. I am clearly convinced that they deserve it; but that does not remove it from one's gaze. The misery of the whole world appals me and I fear increasingly that new struggles may rise out of those we are successfully ending." Amid such phrases, allegations crumble against Churchill the "war lover."

The U.S. president and British prime minister have often been criticised for agreeing at Yalta to transfer to Stalin all Soviet subjects detained in Europe. Of those who returned, even from German captivity, some were shot and most were dispatched to labour camps. Almost all who had served in enemy uniform were liquidated. Yet, on the repatriation issue, it is impossible to see how the Anglo-Americans could have acted otherwise. The Soviet Union had borne the overwhelming burden of the land war against Hitler. The Western Allies were still soliciting the assistance of the Red Army, to complete the defeat of Japan. The price of Soviet military aid, of so much Russian blood spilt while so much American and British blood was saved, was acquiescence in a large measure of Soviet imperialism. Churchill expressed to the Soviet warlord his anxiety for the return of British POWs, whom the Russians were liberating in increasing numbers. In a world which, as Churchill so vividly described, was consumed by suffering, it was hard for the Anglo-Americans to demand much priority of sympathy for Soviet subjects who had served the Nazi cause. The integrity of Allied purposes in the Second World War was inescapably compromised by association with the tyranny of Stalin, to defeat that of Hitler. Once this necessary evil was conceded, lesser ones remorselessly followed. Among them was the surrender of hundreds of thousands of perceived Soviet renegades.

The foremost business of Yalta, above all in Churchill's eyes, was the future of Poland. Stalin wanted recognition of its new frontiers—the so-called Curzon Line in the east, the Oder-Neisse in the west. Churchill made plain that he was now less concerned with territory than with the democratic character of the new Polish government. He sought to exchange Western recognition of the frontiers Moscow wanted for some shreds of domestic freedom for the Poles. He could not, he said, accept that Moscow's "Lublin Poles" represented the will of the nation. Stalin riposted that the new Warsaw regime was as representative of the Polish people as was de Gaulle's new government of France. Roosevelt sought to adjourn the session, but Churchill insisted that the Polish issue must be resolved. The president observed impatiently that "Poland had been a source of trouble for over 500 years." The prime minister said: "We must do what we can to put an end to the trouble." Here was another exchange sorely damaging to British purposes. Roosevelt's apparent indifference was once more flaunted before Russian eyes.

Overnight, however, some reinforcement was secured for the Polish cause. Roosevelt signed a letter to Stalin, saying that the United States— like Britain—could not recognise the Polish government as then composed. At the conference's third plenary session on February 7, the president described the Polish issue as of "very great importance." There was more talk of occupation zones in Germany. Agreement was reached about respective states' voting rights at the proposed new United Nations.

On February 8, Churchill reasserted the urgency of settling the Polish question. Molotov said that the new communist government had been "enthusiastically acclaimed by the majority of the Polish people." Churchill pressed for immediate free elections, which prompted Stalin to again raise comparisons with France, where no poll was scheduled. Then, however, the Russian leader conceded that an election might be held in Poland within a month. There was still no visible anger in the conference chamber. There followed, indeed, more exchanges of compliments between the principals. But that night Churchill said bleakly: "The only bond of the victors is their common hate" towards Hitler.

Anglo-American leverage with Stalin derived solely from Lend-Lease supplies. Even had Roosevelt threatened to suspend shipments unless the Western powers gained satisfaction about Poland, the Russians would not have bowed. Stalin had shown himself implacable in imposing his territorial demands since 1941, when Western aid was much more important than in 1945. From start to finish, he grasped the fact that the Anglo-Americans needed Russia's vast human sacrifice more than Russia needed Western supplies. Even had the president himself been willing to exercise such pressure—as, of course, he was not—neither the American nor the British people would have supported sanctions. Popular enthusiasm for a common front against the Axis still ran high. Attempts to impose Western wishes upon the heroic Russians would have commanded sympathy only with a small minority of people who grasped the reality of looming eastern European servitude.

At the fifth plenary session on February 9, Churchill said that diplomatic observers must monitor the Polish election. The Russians responded smoothly that this was perfectly acceptable to them, but the Warsaw government must be consulted: the presence of such observers might wound the Poles by implying that they were not trusted. Likewise, when Churchill said that a British ambassador should be sent to Warsaw, the Russians deferred the matter to Polish arbitration. With his usual serpentine skill, Stalin reminded the prime minister of his debt to Moscow by asserting that he had "complete confidence" in British policy in Greece.

Next day, the tenth, Roosevelt caused consternation to the British by announcing that he would leave Yalta on the following morning. When the president had cabled the prime minister back in January, asserting his intention to spend only five days at Yalta, Churchill expostulated to his staff that even the Almighty had allowed himself seven to make the world. Now, in British eyes, the summit had yet to achieve decisive conclusions. But the president was correct; even had he lingered, it was unlikely anything further would have been accomplished. The chasm between Russian intentions and Western aspirations in eastern Europe was unbridgeable. Nonetheless, an agreement had been reached about Poland which, if Stalin kept his word, might sustain some fig leaf of democracy. Churchill professed satisfaction. He could do little else. He spent February 12 as a tourist, visiting British battlefields of the Crimean War, and gazing on the ruins of Sebastopol. The next day, he rested aboard the British liner *Franconia*, anchored off the coast at his pleasure, then flew to Athens.

The contrast could not have been greater between his previous visit, amid gunfire, and the hysterical applause with which he was received on the afternoon of February 14. Vast crowds thronged the streets of the Greek capital, offering a vindication that was sweet to him. He elected to make a further brief stop in Cairo. "A wandering minstrel I," he sang to himself, a ditty from his beloved Gilbert and Sullivan, "a thing of threads and patches." He landed back in Britain on February 20. Beaverbrook was among those who offered extravagant congratulations on his alleged "success" at Yalta, which "followed so swiftly on the heels of the Greek triumph, that you now appear to your countrymen to be the greatest statesman as well as the greatest warrior."

Even by Beaverbrook's standards, this was a travesty. In the House of Commons, there was profound anxiety about the outcome of Yalta, and its implications for the Poles. The concluding communiqué by the Big Three had asserted that Poland's provisional government should be "reorganized on a broader democratic basis with the inclusion of democratic leaders from Poland itself and from Poles abroad." The new government "shall be pledged to the holding of free and unfettered elections as soon as possible . . . In these elections all democratic and anti-Nazi parties shall have the right to take part." The cession of eastern Poland to Russia was acknowledged, in return for indeterminate territorial compensation in the west, which should "thereafter be determined at the peace conference."

Churchill told the War Cabinet that he was "quite sure" Stalin "meant well to the world and to Poland." Likewise, facing fierce criticism in the House on February 27, he cited the fact that "most solemn declarations have been made by Marshal Stalin and the Soviet State" about Polish elections. "I repudiate and repulse any suggestion that we are making a questionable compromise or yielding to force or fear . . . The Poles will have their future in their own hands, with the single limitation that they must honestly follow . . . a policy friendly to Russia. That is surely reasonable." Fortified by the fulfilment of Stalin's promise of noninterference in Greece, he clung to the hope that the Soviet warlord would keep his word about Poland: "I know of no government which stands to its obligations, even in its own despite, more solidly than the Russian Soviet Government.

I decline absolutely to embark here on a discussion about Russian good faith."

Over a drink in the smoking room afterwards with Harold Nicolson and Lord De La Warr, he said that he did not see what else he could have done at Yalta, save accept Stalin's assurances. On the night of February 28, he told Jock Colville that he would refuse to be cheated over Poland, "even if we go to the verge of war with Russia." He voiced aloud his fear that he might be deceived by Stalin, as Neville Chamberlain had been deceived by Hitler—then dismissed it. He was exultant when an amendment on Poland moved by Tory right-wingers in the Commons was defeated by 396 votes to 25. But eleven ministers abstained, and one resigned. Eden, lacking confidence in Russian good faith, remained deeply depressed. General Anders, for the Poles, told Brooke that "he had never been more distressed since the war started . . . He could see no hope anywhere."

Back in Moscow, Stalin expressed satisfaction about the outcome of Yalta. Unsurprisingly, he spoke more warmly of Roosevelt than of Britain's prime minister. "Churchill wants a bourgeois Poland to be the USSR's neighbour," he told Zhukov, "a Poland that would be hostile to us. We cannot allow this. We want to ensure a friendly Poland once and for all, and that is what the Polish people want, too." *Pravda*'s political columnist told Russian readers with satisfaction, "We see unprecedented unanimity in the United States and England in welcoming the resolutions of the Crimea Conference." The paper asserted that American and British commentators treated the protests of Polish émigrés with the contempt which these deserved.

No course short of war with Russia would have saved Polish democracy in 1945, and by February only a compound of vanity and despair could have caused Churchill to pretend otherwise. The Soviet Union believed that, having paid overwhelmingly the heaviest price to achieve the defeat of Hitler, it had thus purchased the right to determine the polity of eastern Europe in accordance with its own security interests. To this day, Roosevelt's admirers declare that he displayed greater realism than Britain's prime minister in recognising this. The Western Allies lacked power to contrive any different outcome. Churchill, who had fought as nobly as any man in the world to deliver Europe, was now obliged to witness not the liberation of the east, but the mere replacement there of one murderous tyranny by another.

TWENTY-ONE

The Final Act

IN THE LAST MONTHS of Churchill's war premiership, his satisfaction about the Nazis' imminent downfall was almost entirely overshadowed by dismay at the triumph of Soviet hegemony in eastern Europe. He wrote to a Tory MP on March 6, "We are now labouring to make sure that the Yalta Agreement about Poland and free elections is carried out in the spirit as well as in the letter." In reality, of course, Yalta was flouted in both. Almost daily, news reached Downing Street of savage Soviet oppression in Poland, including the imprisonment of sixteen prominent Poles who had attended a meeting under a safe-conduct from the Red Army, and the deportation to labour camps of thousands of non-Communists. Beria's NKVD conducted a war of repression against Polish democrats which persisted until the end of the German war, and after. Churchill drafted a fierce cable to Stalin, for which he invited American approval: "All parties were exercised," he wrote, "about the reports that deportations, liquidations and other oppressive measures were being put into practice on a wide scale by the Warsaw administration against those likely to disagree with them."

The dying Roosevelt vetoed this message, and thereafter repeatedly rejected Churchill's imprecations for the United States to adopt a harsher policy towards Moscow. The president proposed a "political truce" in Poland, which the British believed would merely strengthen the Soviet puppet regime. "I cannot agree that we are confronted with a breakdown of the Yalta Agreement," Roosevelt wrote on March 15. " . . . We must be careful not to give the impression that we are proposing a halt to the land reforms [collectivisation] imposed by the new Polish government." A stream of messages followed from Churchill to Roosevelt, emphasising the prime minister's perception of the urgency and gravity of the Polish situation. Most went unanswered. The British persisted with their efforts, but received scant comfort from Washington, and none from Moscow.

Events on the battlefield had a momentum of their own, which Churchill could not influence. At this very late hour, he made a brief attempt to assert British influence by exchanging Tedder with Alexander. He wrote to his field marshal on March 1, as if this was a done deal: "I have written privately to Eisenhower to tell him that you will be replacing Tedder as Deputy Supreme Commander about the middle of this month and that I propose Tedder shall replace you in the Mediterranean." The purported justification was that Alexander's presence in northwest Europe would ease tensions between Eisenhower and Montgomery. In reality, Churchill wanted his favourite to assume control of the entire Allied ground battle for the last phase of the German campaign. The proposal was mistaken from every possible standpoint, not least Alexander's unfitness for the role. The Americans swiftly quashed it. Churchill received no more satisfaction from Washington when he remonstrated about Eisenhower's signal to Stalin, assuring him that the Western armies would stay away from Berlin. The Americans were not listening. If their manner towards Churchill was increasingly brusque, on the points of military substance it is impossible to doubt that they were right.

Churchill made one further intervention on strategic bombing policy, which has cast a baleful shadow over the historiography of the Second World War. On March 28, he minuted Portal and the Chiefs of Staff Committee:

It seems to me that the moment has come when the question of bombing of German cities simply for the sake of increasing the terror, though under other pretexts, should be reviewed. Otherwise we shall come into control of an utterly ruined land . . . The destruction of Dresden remains a serious query against the conduct of Allied bombing . . . I feel the need for more precise concentration upon military objectives, such as oil and communications behind the immediate battle-zone, rather than on mere acts of terror and wanton destruction, however impressive.

Portal, the standard-bearer of the Royal Air Force, was affronted by these remarks, as well he might have been. He persuaded Churchill to withdraw them, substituting a fresh document which omitted such phrases as "acts of terror." The new minute began in more pedestrian terms: "It seems to me that the moment has come when the question of the so-called 'area bombing' of German cities should be reviewed from the point of view of our own interests . . . " This sanitised version was signed on April 1. Churchill was anyway in no doubt that he had ordered a halt to area attacks on cities. He was thus dismayed, soon afterwards, to learn that five hundred Lancasters of Bomber Command had devastated Potsdam. Some five thousand civilians were alleged to have perished, because the population had neglected air-raid precautions, supposing that the city's architectural treasures granted it immunity from bombardment. Churchill wrote crossly to Archibald Sinclair, the secretary for air, and Portal, "What's the point of going and blowing down Potsdam?" Portal replied that the Luftwaffe's operational headquarters had been transferred there, and that the attack was "calculated to hasten the disintegration of enemy resistance."

The truthful answer to Churchill's question was that a huge force of British heavy bombers existed, and there was deep reluctance to stand them down as long as German resistance continued. The Red Army had begun to fight the last great battle of the European war for Berlin, a few miles from Potsdam. Churchill's attitude, displayed in his draft note to Portal of March 28, was characteristic in its impulsiveness, even irrationality. Earlier in the war, he had been a committed supporter of area bombing, though once delivered from the desperate predicament of 1940–41 he never shared the exaggerated faith of the airmen that this could win the war. When the great land campaigns began in Italy and France, he lost interest in Bomber Command. Its contribution might be useful, but was plainly not decisive. It may sound flippant to suggest that Britain's prime minister was oblivious of the operations of hundreds of heavy aircraft, dealing nightly death and destruction to some of the greatest cities in Europe. Yet amid the huge issues crowding in upon him each day, the air offensive receded into the background—as also, it must be said, did the issue of the Nazi death camps and possible RAF operations to impede their activities. In Churchill's mind, the fate of the Jews was entwined with that of millions of other European captives of Hitler. The best means of securing their delivery was to win the war as swiftly as possible. Amid the deep shock of the scenes at Bergen-Belsen when it was liberated by the British Army in April, the prime minister hastened to dispatch a delegation of MPs and peers to the concentration camp, to take formal heed of its horrors. But even in the light of unfolding evidence of genocide, the prime minister perceived the camps in the broader context of the Nazi tyranny.

So vast was the scale of the war by 1944–45, so diverse its manifestations, that no human being, even Winston Churchill, could address every aspect with the commitment which some modern critics believe should have been expected of him. How could it have been otherwise? He interested himself in a wider range of affairs than any national leader in history. But many things, including air policy in the last year of the war, were neglected. Commanders were left to do as they thought best. The only important bombing controversy to which Churchill seriously addressed himself from 1942 onwards was that concerning the 1944 assault on the French road and rail network before D-Day, which he was persuaded reluctantly to endorse.

Throughout the war, the direction of the strategic air offensive was impeded by the fact that its achievements were shrouded in mystery. The airmen's extravagant claims could be assessed only through problematic interpretation of aerial photography, with limited assistance from Ultra signal decrypts. In December 1941, Mr. David Butt's Cabinet Office report caused the prime minister to accept that the RAF's campaign against Germany, so prodigious in its demands on national resources, was not achieving commensurate results. Thus the decision was made to change policy, to conduct "area bombing" of cities, in place of ineffectual precision attacks on military and industrial targets. "In the full tilt of war," observed Churchill in old age, "it was the only means of hitting back. I was of course ultimately responsible . . . But later I was not so sure of the effectiveness of the bludgeon." Until June 1944, however, when great Allied armies became committed to the battlefield, the prime minister found it convenient to promote the view that strategic bombing was making an important contribution to the defeat of the enemy. If it was not, then many people—among whom Stalin was the most important—would have asked whether Britain was playing anything like a large enough part in fighting the war.

In attempting to distance himself from the bombing of Dresden, as Churchill did on March 28, 1945, he ignored his own request to Sinclair at the Air Ministry, just before Yalta, to launch major air attacks in eastern Germany, to assist and impress the Russians, who expressed an eagerness for such support. Dresden had featured for years on Bomber Command target lists. It had been left unscathed only because it was a low priority, and a long haul from British airfields. Throughout the war, none of Britain's senior airmen showed much aesthetic sensitivity. Portal had advocated heavy bombing of Rome when the city still belonged to Mussolini. Harris had assured the chief of the Air Staff that he had "no false sentiments" about dispatching his bombers against one of the greatest cultural centres in the world. Only American opposition deflected attacks. Churchill's personal intervention was responsible for causing Dresden, together with Chemnitz and Leipzig, to be pushed up the February target schedule, and largely destroyed on the night of February 13–14. It is unsurprising that no one at Bomber Command headquarters voiced concern about the fate of baroque churches before unleashing the Lancasters.

The prime minister, however, had not thought much before making his own, almost casual request to Sinclair. Throughout the war, a host of matters briefly engaged his attention, then receded. It is implausible, but just possible, that by March 28 he had genuinely forgotten that he had urged the RAF to attack eastern German cities. The key to understanding the destruction of Dresden, so often misinterpreted as a unique atrocity, is that amid daily global carnage, the attack order had much less significance to those responsible than it seems to posterity to have merited.

In the aftermath of Dresden, however, the raid was the subject of widespread comment—and some criticism. Following a press conference at Eisenhower's headquarters about bombing policy on February 16, an AP correspondent named Howard Cowan filed a dispatch stating: "The Allied air commanders have made the long-awaited decision to adopt deliberate terror bombing of German population centres as a ruthless expedient to hastening Hitler's doom." This story received prominent play in American newspapers, though it was censored in British ones. U.S. Secretary of War Henry Stimson demanded an enquiry into Dresden, which prompted Gen. "Hap" Arnold of the USAAF to respond: "We must not get soft. War must be destructive and to a certain extent inhuman and ruthless." In Britain, though there was no widespread outcry, questions were asked in the Commons by the government's inveterate critic Labour MP Richard Stokes. For the first time in many months, Churchill addressed himself seriously to the issue of area bombing. He perceived that it was indeed wanton to continue the destruction of great cities, when the Germans were so close to collapse. With his usual instinct for mercy towards the vanquished, he wished to halt the process. This was both right and humane. The prime minister injured himself, however, by attempting in his draft minute to Portal to make this judgement retrospective, to condemn the Dresden decision to which he had been an implicit, if not absolutely explicit, party.

He also gave a formidable hostage to history, by declaring that Bomber Command's campaign was terroristic. No one in the upper reaches of Britain's war machine had ever privately doubted that this was so, but ministers and airmen took elaborate pains to avoid acknowledging it. This was not Churchill's first mention of terror, in the context of bombing. He used the word much earlier, in a memorandum to the War Cabinet in November 1942, about policy towards Italy. "All the industrial centres should be attacked in an intense fashion," he wrote, "every effort being made to terrorise and paralyse the population."

In war as in peace, there is unlikely to be much cause for pride in a policy about which it is deemed necessary to deceive one's own people. The reputations of Churchill and Bomber Command alike were damaged by the exchanges of March–April 1945. The prime minister, who of all men should know, had put his signature to a document, albeit subsequently withdrawn, declaring Britain's strategic air offensive to have been terroristic. He had then been privy to an administrative sleight of hand designed to suppress this admission of the truth.

Churchill's writings, dating back to World War I, make plain that he thought air bombardment of civilians barbaric. In the early part of World War II, when Germany had already ravaged half the cities of Europe and Britain had no other plausible means of attacking Hitler's Reich, he suppressed his instincts and endorsed the bomber offensive. That decision seems both inevitable and justifiable. It is a gross abuse of language to identify area bombing as a "war crime," as do some modern critics. The policy was designed to hasten the defeat of Germany by destroying its industrial base, not wantonly to slaughter innocents. Yet it remains a blot on the Allied conduct of the war that city attacks were allowed to continue into 1945, when huge forces of aircraft employed sophisticated technology against negligible defences, and German industrial output could no longer much influence outcomes. Both the operational necessity to attack cities—because the RAF was capable of nothing else—and the strategic purpose of such operations were gone. Yet the assault was maintained because, until Churchill's belated intervention, nobody thought to tell the air forces to stop, or rather to restrict themselves to residual military targets.

Here was a classic example of technological determinism. The weapons existed, and thus they continued to be used. The pity of Churchill's March 28 memorandum, not least from the viewpoint of some 150,000 German civilians who perished under air attack in 1945, was that it had not been written several months earlier. Yet it is hard not to sympathise with the exhausted old prime minister, bearing the troubles of the world upon his shoulders, for being slow to act. The record of his conduct towards Hitler's people shows an overarching instinct towards mercy, remarkable in the leader of a nation which had suffered so much at German hands since 1939. Churchill's 1945 papers contain many charitable reflections and directions about the treatment of Germans. These should be set in the balance against the undoubted excesses of the bomber offensive, and his own responsibility for them.

In the last weeks of the European war, Churchill undertook two more battlefield joyrides. Much to his own satisfaction, he relieved himself in the

Siegfried Line on March 3, with an aside to photographers: "This is one of the operations connected with this great war which must not be reproduced graphically." He performed the same ceremony in the Rhine three weeks later, on a visit to watch Montgomery's great river crossing with Alan Brooke. As he gazed down upon the vast panorama from a chair set out for him on a Xanten hilltop, he said: "I should have liked to have deployed my men in red coats on the plain down there and ordered them to charge." Then he added, not without satisfaction: "But now my armies are too vast." At the sound of aircraft, he sprang to his feet: "They're coming! They're coming!" He watched fascinated as the great armada passed overhead, thousands of multicoloured parachutes blossoming forth above the German riverbank. He was hurried unwillingly to the rear by the generals when desultory German shells began to fall. Brooke wrote: "It was a relief to get Winston home safely . . . I honestly believe that he would really have liked to be killed on the front at this moment of success. He had often told me that the way to die is to pass out fighting when your blood is up and you feel nothing."

At a lunch at Chequers a few days later, Churchill told his cousin Anita Leslie how much he had enjoyed his outing: "I'm an old man and I work hard. Why shouldn't I have a little fun? At least, I thought it was fun but one has to hate seeing brave men die . . . " Leslie was driving an ambulance for the Free French. "With childish longing in his voice Winston asked what the French thought of him. 'They do like me? They are fond of me? Give them my love.' " If these were the words of a sentimental old man, his flagging interest in daily business reflected the condition of an exhausted one. "The PM is now becoming an administrative bottleneck," wrote Colville.

There was a last spasm of frustration about his inability to influence military operations. When he learned that Eisenhower had signalled to Stalin that the Anglo-American armies would make no attempt to close upon Berlin, he expressed strong displeasure that such a communication should have been made without reference to the British or U.S. governments. As Russian behaviour rapidly worsened, he urged that the Anglo-American armies should advance as far eastwards as possible and stay there, heedless of agreed occupation zones, until Moscow showed some willingness to keep its side of the Yalta bargain. Meanwhile, Russian paranoia that the West would make its own peace deal with the Germans intensified. Zhukov visited the Kremlin on March 29. Stalin walked to his desk, leafed through some papers, picked one out and handed it to his marshal. "Read this," he said. It was a report based upon information from "foreign sympathisers" who claimed that representatives of the Western

Allies were conducting secret talks with emissaries of Hitler about a separate peace. Berlin's overtures had been rejected, said the letter, but it remained possible that the German army would open its Western Front to give the Allies passage to Berlin. "What do you think?" asked Stalin, continuing without waiting for Zhukov's answer: "I do not believe Roosevelt will violate the Yalta agreement. But as for Churchill—that man is capable of anything."

The Americans indeed showed no interest in diplomatic brinkmanship with the Kremlin. Though Roosevelt was persuaded to send a last challenging missive to Stalin about Poland, Washington would precipitate no confrontation. When Heinrich Himmler sought to parley with the Western Allies, Churchill reported the fact to Stalin, who had dispatched a stream of angry and indeed insulting cables to London and Washington about U.S. negotiations in Switzerland with SS general Karl Wolff, concerning a German surrender in Italy. Now, the Russian leader sent a notably emollient message to Churchill: "Knowing you, I had no doubt that you would act in just this way."

The prime minister found the cable waiting in Downing Street on returning from dinner with the French ambassador on the night of April 25. It prompted a spasm of maudlin goodwill towards Stalin. Jock Colville noted in dismay that Churchill, not entirely sober, sat for ninety minutes in the Annexe, talking enthusiastically to Brendan Bracken about the cable, and then spent a further ninety minutes doing the same before the young private secretary: "His vanity was astonishing and I am glad U[ncle] J[oe] does not know what effect a few kind words, after so many harsh ones, might well have on our policy towards Russia . . . No work was done and I felt both irritated and slightly disgusted by this exhibition of susceptibility to flattery. It was nearly 5am when I got to bed." Three days later, Churchill cabled Stalin, offering a further olive branch: "I have been much disturbed at the misunderstanding that has grown up between us on the Crimea agreement about Poland." There was no misunderstanding, of course. Stalin was bent upon asserting Soviet hegemony over Poland, and that was an end of the matter.

Back in December 1941, when Eden cabled Churchill from Moscow urging the necessity for acceptance of Russia's demands for recognition of its pre-Barbarossa 1941 frontiers, the prime minister replied: "When you say that 'nothing we and the US can do or say will affect the situation at the end of the war,' you are making a very large assumption about the conditions which will then prevail. No one can foresee how the balance of power will lie, or where the winning armies will stand. It seems probable however that the US and the British Empire, far from being exhausted, will be the most powerful armed and economic bloc the world has ever seen, and that the Soviet Union will need our aid for reconstruction far more than we shall need theirs." By 1945, the frustration of such hopes was plain. The Soviets were vastly stronger, the British much weaker, than Churchill had anticipated. The U.S. commitment to perceived common Anglo-American interests, in Europe or anywhere else, was more tenuous than it had ever been.

In the cold light of day, the prime minister understood this. On May 4 he wrote to Eden, then in San Francisco for the inaugural meeting of the United Nations, about the evolving situation in eastern Europe as he saw it:

> I fear terrible things have happened during the Russian advance through Germany to the Elbe. The proposed withdrawal of the United States Army to the occupational lines which were arranged . . . would mean a tide of Russian domination sweeping forward 120 miles on a front of 200 or 400 miles. This would be an event which, if it occurred, would be one of the most melancholy in history. After it was over and the territory occupied by the Russians, Poland would be completely engulfed and buried deep in Russian-occupied lands . . . The Russian frontier would run from the North Cape in Norway . . . across the Baltic to a point just east of Lubeck . . . half-way across [Austria] to the Izonzo river behind which Tito and Russia will claim everything to the east. Thus the territories under Russian control would include the Baltic Provinces, all of Germany to the occupational line, all Czecho-slovakia, a large part of Austria, the whole of Yugoslavia, Hungary, Roumania, Bulgaria, until Greece in her present tottering condition is reached . . . This constitutes an event in the history of Europe to which there has been no parallel . . . All these matters can only be settled before the United States Armies in Europe are weakened . . . It is to this early and speedy showdown and settlement with Russia that we must now turn our hopes. Meanwhile I am against weakening our claim against Russia on behalf of Poland in any way.

The Allies now found themselves in a bewildering and uncharted new world; Roosevelt was gone. Following the vast shock of his death on April 12, Churchill briefly entertained the notion of flying to Washington for the funeral. Finally, he decided that he was needed in London, an out-come that was also probably influenced by personal disinclination. The prime minister's enthusiasm for the president had waned dramatically. There had been so many slights. Some were relatively trivial, such as a

March decision by Washington to halt meat exports to Britain. Some were more serious, such as the imposition of draconian curbs on postwar British civil aviation in accordance with the terms of Lend-Lease. Above all, of course, there was American unilateralism on eastern European issues. Roosevelt's greatness was not in doubt, least of all in the mind of Churchill. But it had been deployed in the service of the United States, and only incidentally and reluctantly in the interests of the British Empire or even of Europe. "We have moved a long way," wrote Moran in February, "since Winston, speaking of Roosevelt, said to me in the garden at Marrakesh 'I love that man.' "

Now, Churchill had to deal with the wholly unknown figure of Harry Truman. In the first weeks of the new president's tenure, though his inexperience was manifest, there were welcome indications that he was ready to deal much more toughly with the Russians than had Roosevelt in his last months. But no more than his predecessor was the newcomer at the White House willing to risk an armed clash with the Soviet Union for the sake of Poland or any other eastern European nation. At this stage, Washington believed, there was no virtue in empty posturing when the Red Army stood on the Elbe. Nor did Churchill's combativeness towards Moscow find much resonance among his own people. For four years, the British had embraced the Russians as heroes and comrades-in-arms, ignorant of the absence of reciprocal enthusiasm. Beyond a few score men and women at the summit of the British war machine, little was known of Soviet perfidy and savagery. No more in Britain than in the United States was there any stomach for a Churchillian crusade against a new enemy.

VE Day was proclaimed on May 8, 1945. On the afternoon of the seventh, the Chiefs of Staff gathered at Downing Street for a moment of celebration. Churchill himself set out a tray and glasses, then toasted Brooke, Portal and Cunningham as "the architects of victory." Ismay wrote in his memoirs: "I hoped that they would raise their glasses to the chief who had been the master-planner; but perhaps they were too moved to trust their voices." This was disingenuous. Brooke and Cunningham, if not Portal, nursed complex emotions towards the prime minister. Others, including Ismay and the Downing Street staff, forgave rough handling, amid their love and admiration for Churchill. The field marshal and the admiral found this more difficult. Brooke wrote on May 7: "I can't feel thrilled, my main sensation is one of infinite mental weariness! A sort of brain lethargy which refuses to register highlights, and remains on an even dull flat tone." The next day he added, with some bitterness: "There is no doubt that the public has never understood what the Chiefs of Staff have been doing in the running of this war . . . The PM has never enlightened them much, and has never once in all his speeches referred to the Chiefs of Staff." A few months earlier, Brooke had written of Churchill: "Without him England was lost for a certainty, with him England has been on the verge of disaster again and again. And with it all no recognition hardly at all for those who help him except the occasional crumb intended to prevent the dog straying too far from the table."

Brooke was envious of the greater power and fame enjoyed by Marshall, his American counterpart. A man of considerable vanity, he overrated his own talents, and was ungenerous in his estimate of Churchill's. But a significant part of his achievement as CIGS—and it was a remarkable achievement—lay in his willingness to fight Churchill day or night when he believed him wrong. While Brooke was a cautious soldier who might not have prospered as a field commander, he had provided a superb foil for the prime minister, preserving him from many misfortunes. His contribution to Britain's war effort had been substantial. Like the hedgehog, in 1942–43 he understood one big thing: that the Allies must not prematurely engage large elements of the Wehrmacht. He was unable to accept that the price of serving a towering historical figure was to be obscured by his shadow.

Clementine was visiting Russia on behalf of the Red Cross on VE Day, much to the sorrow of both Churchills. At three p.m., the prime minister broadcast to the British people: "Yesterday morning at 2.41am at Headquarters, General Jodl, the representative of the German High Command, and Grand Admiral Doenitz, the designated head of the German State, signed the act of unconditional surrender of all German land, sea and air forces in Europe to the Allied Expeditionary Force, and simultaneously to the Soviet High Command . . . The German war is therefore at an end." He recalled Britain's lonely struggle, and the gradual accession of great allies: "Finally almost the whole world was combined against the evil-doers, who are now prostrate before us. We may allow ourselves a brief period of rejoicing; but let us not forget for a moment the toil and efforts that lie ahead. Japan, with all her treachery and greed, remains unsubdued . . . We must now devote all our strength and resources to the completion of our task, both at home and abroad. Advance, Britannia! Long live the cause of freedom! God save the King." His secretaries and staff lined the garden of Downing Street to clap him to his car. He grinned, responding, "Thank you so much, thank you so much." Then he drove to the House of Commons, to repeat to MPs the speech which he had made to the nation.

A few grumblers muttered that they would have liked to hear from him some expression of gratitude to the Deity. It is interesting to speculate whether Churchill offered any private expression of indebtedness to a higher power at that afternoon's Commons Service of Thanksgiving at St. Margaret's, Westminster. Jock Colville believed that the events of the war, especially the Battle of Britain, moved Churchill a considerable distance from defiant atheism towards faith. The prime minister once remarked to Colville that he could not help wondering whether the government above might be a constitutional monarchy, "in which case there was always a possibility that the Almighty might have occasion to send for him."

From a balcony in Whitehall that evening, Churchill addressed the vast, cheering crowd: "My dear friends, this is your hour. This is not victory of a party or of any class. It's a victory of the great British nation as a whole. We were the first, in this ancient island, to draw the sword against tyranny . . . " The crowd sang "Land of Hope and Glory" and "For He's a Jolly Good Fellow" as Churchill returned to the Downing Street Annexe, to spend the rest of the evening with Lord Camrose, proprietor of the *Daily Telegraph*. In his company, the prime minister cast aside the exuberance of the afternoon, once more rehearsing his dismay about Soviet barbarism in the east. At 1:15 a.m., when Camrose left, Churchill returned to his secretaries and papers.

Pravda asserted triumphantly that "the significance of the link-up of the Red Army and the allied Anglo-American forces is as great politically as militarily. It offers further proof that provocations by Hitler's people designed to destroy the solidarity and brotherhood-in-arms between ourselves and our allies . . . have failed." Yet Churchill spent the first days of European peace plunged in deepest gloom about the fate of Poland. On May 13, he cabled Truman:

> Our armed power on the continent is in rapid decline. Meanwhile what is to happen about Russia[?] I have always worked for friendship with Russia but, like you, I feel deep anxiety because of their misinterpretation of the Yalta decisions, their attitude towards Poland, their overwhelming influence in the Balkans excepting Greece, the difficulties they make about Vienna . . . and above all their power to maintain very large armies in the field for a long time.
>
> What will be the position in a year or two, when the British and American armies have melted . . . and when Russia may choose to keep two or three hundred [divisions] on active service? An iron curtain is drawn down upon their front . . . Surely it is vital now to come to an understanding with Russia, or see where we are with her before we

weaken our armies mortally, or retire to the zones of occupation. I should be most grateful for your opinion or advice . . . To sum up, this issue of a settlement with Russia before our strength has gone seems to me to dwarf all others.

Truman answered: "From the present point of view, it is impossible to make a conjecture as to what the Soviets may do when Germany is under the small forces of occupation and the great part of such armies as we can maintain are fighting in the Orient against Japan." The president agreed with Churchill that a tripartite meeting with Stalin had become urgently necessary.

Yet what if talking to Stalin got nowhere, as was highly likely? Within days of Germany's surrender, Britain's prime minister astounded his Chiefs of Staff by enquiring whether Anglo-American forces might launch an offensive to drive back the Soviets by force of arms. Churchill was enthused by the robust attitude of Truman, whose tone suggested a new willingness to respond ruthlessly to Communist flouting of the Yalta terms. Brooke wrote after a War Cabinet meeting on May 13: "Winston delighted, he gives me the feeling of already longing for another war! Even if it entailed fighting the Russians!" On the twenty-fourth, the prime minister instructed the Chiefs of Staff that, with the "Russian bear sprawled over Europe," they should consider the military possibilities of pushing the Red Army back eastwards before the Anglo-American armies were demobilised. He requested the planners to consider means to "impose upon Russia the will of the United States and British Empire" to secure "a square deal for Poland." They were told to assume the full support of British and American public opinion, and were invited to assume that they could "count on the use of German manpower and what remains of German industrial capacity." The target date for launching such an assault would be July 1, 1945.

The Foreign Office—though not Eden himself—recoiled in horror from Churchill's bellicosity. One of Moscow's Whitehall informants swiftly conveyed tidings to Stalin of an instruction from London to Montgomery about contingency planning. Zhukov wrote in his memoirs:

We received reliable information that while the final campaign was still in progress Churchill sent a secret telegram to Marshal Montgomery instructing him carefully to collect German weapons and material and store them in such a way that would permit retrieving them easily in order to distribute among German units with which they would have to cooperate if the Soviet advance had continued. We had to make a harsh statement at the next session of the Allied Control Commission. We stressed that history knew few examples of such perfidy and betrayal of allies' obligations and duty. We declared that we thought that British government and army leadership deserved the most serious condemnation. Montgomery attempted to refute the Soviet statement. His colleague American General [Lucius] Clay was silent. Apparently, he was familiar with this instruction by the British Prime Minister.

Zhukov's story was founded in a reality unacknowledged in detail in Britain until the relevant papers were released by the National Archive in 1998. Alan Brooke and his colleagues faithfully executed the prime minister's wishes, to examine scenarios for initiating military action against the Russians. The report prepared by the War Cabinet Joint Planning Staff required feats of imagination from its creators unprecedented in Churchill's premiership. In the preamble, the drafters stated their assumption that, in the event of hostilities between the Russians and the Western Allies, Russia would ally itself with Japan. "The overall or political object is to impose upon Russia the will of the United States and British Empire." Yet the planners immediately pointed out that the scope of any new conflict initiated by the Western powers would not thereafter be for them to determine: "Even though 'the will' of these two countries may be defined as no more than a square deal for Poland, that does not necessarily limit the military commitment. A quick success might induce the Russians to submit to our will . . . but it might not. That is for the Russians to decide. If they want total war, they are in a position to have it."

The planners observed that even if an initial Western offensive was successful, the Russians could then adopt the same tactics they had employed with such success against the Germans, giving ground amid the seemingly infinite spaces of the Soviet Union: "There is virtually no limit to the distance to which it would be necessary for the Allies to penetrate into Russia in order to render further resistance impossible . . . To achieve the decisive defeat of Russia . . . would require . . . (a) the deployment in Europe of a large proportion of the vast resources of the United States [and] (b) the re-equipment and re-organisation of German manpower and of all the Western European allies."

The planners concluded that Western airpower could be used effectively against Soviet communications, but that "Russian industry is so dispersed that it is unlikely to be a profitable air target." They proposed that 47 Anglo-American divisions might credibly be deployed in an offensive, 14 of these armoured. More than 40 divisions would have to be held back for defensive or occupation tasks. The Russians could meet an Allied thrust with 170 divisions of equivalent strength, 30 of them armoured. "It is difficult to assess to what extent our tactical air superiority and the superior handling of our forces will redress the balance, but the above odds would clearly render the launching of an offensive a hazardous undertaking." The planners proposed two main thrusts, one on the northern axis Stettin-Schneidemühl-Bydgoszcz, the second in the south on an axis Leipzig-Poznań-Breslau. They concluded, "If we are to embark on war with Russia, we must be prepared to be committed to a total war, which will be both long and costly."

They warned in an annexe that Moscow could probably call upon the aid of local Communists in France, Belgium and Holland to conduct an extensive campaign of sabotage against Western lines of communications. The word *hazardous* is used eight times in the planning document, to describe the proposed Anglo-American operations. Annexe IV addressed likely German attitudes to an invitation to participate in hostilities between Russia and the West: "The German General Staff and Officer Corps are likely to decide that their interests will be best served by siding with the Western Allies, although the extent to which they will be able to produce effective and active co-operation will probably be limited at first by the war-weariness of the German Army and of the civil population." It was dryly suggested that German veterans who had fought on the Eastern Front might be reluctant to repeat the experience. However, addressing the issue of morale among Anglo-American soldiers invited to fight the Russians, the planners displayed astonishing optimism. They claimed that their men might be expected to fight with little diminution of the spirit they had displayed against the Germans—this, though Alexander in Italy had already annoyed the prime minister by reporting that his troops were reluctant to engage Tito's Communists.

The Chiefs of Staff were never under any delusions about the military, never mind political, impracticability of launching an offensive against the Russians to liberate Poland. The CIGS wrote on May 24: "The idea is of course fantastic and the chances of success quite impossible. There is no doubt that from now onwards Russia is all-powerful in Europe." On the thirty-first, the Chiefs "again discussed the 'unthinkable war' against Russia . . . and became more convinced than ever that it is 'unthinkable!' " The debate cannot have failed to rouse, in the minds of those privy to the secret, echoes of 1918–19, when Churchill insisted upon committing to Russia an abortive Allied military expedition designed to reverse the verdict of the 1917 Bolshevik revolution.

Passing the planners' report to the prime minister on June 8, Ismay wrote: "In the attached report on Operation 'UNTHINKABLE,' the Chiefs of Staff have set out the bare facts, which they can elaborate in discussion with you, if you so desire. They felt that the less was put on paper on this subject the better." The Chiefs themselves appended a comment to the report: "Our view is . . . that once hostilities began, it would be beyond our power to win a quick but limited success and we should be committed to a protracted war against heavy odds. These odds, moreover, would become fanciful if the Americans grew weary and indifferent and began to be drawn away by the magnet of the Pacific war."

Churchill responded on June 10:

> If the Americans withdraw to their zone and move the bulk of their forces back to the United States and to the Pacific, the Russians have the power to advance to the North Sea and the Atlantic. Pray have a study made of how then we could defend our Island, assuming that France and the Low Countries were powerless to resist the Russian advance to the sea. What naval forces should we need and where would they be based? What would be the strength of the Army required, and how should it be disposed? How much Air Force would be needed and where would the main airfields be located? . . . By retaining the codeword "UNTHINKABLE," the Staffs will realize that this remains a precautionary study of what, I hope, is still a purely hypothetical contingency.

In the original draft of this note, Churchill's final words were "a highly improbable event." He altered these in his familiar red ink, to make implementation of Unthinkable seem remoter still.

On July 11, the Chiefs' Joint Planning Committee responded to the prime minister's enquiries about the implications of a possible Soviet advance to the Channel, following demobilisation of Eisenhower's armies. Russian naval strength, they concluded, was too limited to render an early amphibious invasion of Britain likely. They ruled out a Soviet airborne assault. It seemed more likely, they suggested, that Moscow would resort to intensive rocket bombardment, on a scale more destructive than that of the German V-1s and V-2s. To provide effective defence against a long-term Russian threat, they estimated that 230 squadrons of fighters, 100 of tactical bombers and 200 of heavy bombers would be necessary.

The Unthinkable file was closed a few days later, when another cable arrived from Truman. He rejected the arguments for renouncing or even delaying Anglo-American withdrawal to the occupation zones agreed to at Yalta. Washington had decided there was no case. The prime minister was obliged to recognise that there was not the slightest possibility that the Americans would lead an attempt to drive the Russians from Poland by force, nor even threaten Moscow that they might do so. It was also unimaginable that Churchill's own government and fellow countrymen would have supported such action. In June 1945, his perception of the Soviet Union was light-years apart from that of his nation. Most British people were much less impressed by the perils facing Poland than by the wartime achievement of their Russian comrades-in-arms, whom they had learned to regard with enthusiasm. Churchill was obliged hereafter to undertake a dramatic reversal of view. If the Western Allies could not liberate Poland by force, then a new political attempt must be made to persuade Stalin to compromise about its future. Turning aside from his brief dalliance with Unthinkable, the prime minister committed himself to renewed efforts to exploit his supposed relationship with Stalin in pursuit of Polish interests.

It was fortunate for Churchill's reputation that his speculation about confronting Russia in arms was not revealed in detail for another half century. In the years following the end of the war, it became progressively apparent to the Chiefs of Staff, and to the Western world, that it was necessary for the Western Allies to adopt the strongest possible defensive measures against further Soviet aggression in Europe. On August 30, 1946, Field Marshal "Jumbo" Maitland Wilson reported from Washington that the U.S. Chiefs of Staff had become sufficiently fearful of possible conflict with the Russians to favour commencing military planning for such a contingency. In London, the Unthinkable file was taken out and dusted down. Military preparations for a conflict with the Soviet Union became a staple of the Cold War, though at no time was it ever deemed politically acceptable or militarily practicable to attempt to free eastern Europe by force of arms. In May and June 1945, Churchill's warrior instincts were still astonishingly powerful. But the society in which he lived had only just sufficient ardour to finish the Japanese war. There was none whatsoever for engaging new enemies, whatever the principled merits of the cause.

Labour leader Clement Attlee at first favoured sustaining the coalition government and delaying a general election until the defeat of Japan. His party, however, was minded otherwise. On May 23 the coalition was dissolved, after five years and thirteen days of office. There was an emotional farewell gathering of ministers at Downing Street. Then Churchill set about forming a new ministry, without Labour and Liberal members. An election was called for July 6, which almost every pundit anticipated that the Tories would win. The nation's gratitude to Winston Churchill, it was assumed, outweighed its undoubted alienation from the Conservative Party.

Yet, for those who sought evidence about the mood of the British people, much had been available since 1939. On July 3, 1940, the American general Raymond Lee had lunched in London with an unnamed Tory MP who asserted his conviction that even if Britain won the war, Labour would govern afterwards. By 1945, roosting time had come for many old chickens. Anthony Eden, widely perceived as the brightest star of his Tory generation, disliked his own party even more than did Churchill. He wrote during a visit to Greece about his sense of remoteness from British soldiers he met, and his doubts about how to reach them on the hustings:

> It would be the highest honour to serve and lead such men. But how is one to do it through party politics? Most of these men have none, as I believe that I have none. And how is this General Election to express any of this, for they could not be farther from the men of Munich in their most extreme form, for whom I have to ask the electors to vote. It is hell. Curiously enough W[inston] doesn't seem to feel any of this and is full of the lust for electoral battle, and apparently content to work with men afterwards, with many, probably most, of whom he doesn't agree. No doubt he is confident that he can dominate them, but I feel a responsibility to ask the electorate to vote for them.

British soldier Edward Stebbing had written back in November 1940, "There are . . . many who think that this war will only be worth fighting if there is a new order of things to follow." Everything that had happened since strengthened this belief in the minds of many British people. In December 1944 the *Wall Street Journal* displayed notable prescience, identifying popular anger in Britain towards Churchill's Greek policy with a deeper rejection of old Tory imperialism: "It is clear that the Churchill government will last out the war in Europe, but the chances of its return to office when the election after victory is held are more doubtful. It is not very likely that Mr. Lloyd George's [1919] 'khaki election [victory]' will be repeated."

The Mayhews were an upper-middle-class Norfolk family, of whom in 1945 one younger scion, Christopher, was standing as a Labour candidate in the county against a Tory who was a former member of a notorious right-wing movement—the Link. Mayhew's uncle, Bertram Howarth, secretary of the British Association for the Advancement of Science, wrote in a family newsletter: "[I am] in the throes of a mental political upheaval.

I believe I have voted Conservative all my life, but unless something epoch-making happens between now and the General Election, I can't do it again." His wife, Ellie, district commandant of the local Women's Voluntary Service, felt likewise: "Personally I cannot vote for our sitting [Tory] member; he is stupid, elderly and reactionary . . . He was the sole MP to vote against the Beveridge Report. So I shall have to be a Liberal." When Churchill spoke optimistically about his election prospects to General Bill Slim, home on leave from Burma, Slim responded with characteristic bluntness: "Well, Prime Minister, I know one thing. My Army won't be voting for you."

A tide of sentiment was sweeping British people of all classes, driven by determination to build a new future rather than cherish pride in the past. Churchill himself said back in 1941, of the state school boys who occupied many of the RAF's cockpits: "They have saved this country; they have the right to rule it." Labour's Aneurin Bevan told one of his many election audiences, "We have been the dreamers, we have been the sufferers, now we are the builders." Churchill was applauded everywhere he went during his June 1945 election tours, and public admiration for him was very real. But with the wisdom sometimes displayed by democracies, few people allowed this to influence their votes. Churchill's election broadcasts were harshly combative. He deployed against the threat of socialism all the impassioned verbiage which he had mobilised for so long against the nation's enemies. Even many supporters thought his tirades ill-judged, and there were moments when he himself seemed to agree.

Clementine wrote to her daughter Mary on June 20: "Papa broadcasts tonight. He is very low, poor Darling. He thinks he has lost his 'touch' and he grieves about it." Londoner Jennifer McIntosh wrote to her sister in California on July 4: "One of the most extraordinary things has been the terrific slump in the Churchill prestige . . . I wish you could have heard his election broadcasts—they were deplorable, the last one pitifully cheap." Likewise, Oliver Harvey at the Foreign Office perceived Churchill as conducting "a jingo election which is terrifying in its inappropriateness." Churchill was much more a social conservative than he was a political Conservative. He lacked real sympathy for or interest in the party which he nominally led at the hustings. He anticipated that the election outcome would represent a vote of confidence in his own war leadership, rather than a verdict on the Tories' fitness to rule.

But the war was almost ended. While the rival candidates campaigned, most of the complexities of occupying Germany and sustaining the struggle against Japan were addressed without interventions from the prime minister. Addicted to tidings from battlefields, he often stumped into the secretaries' room at Downing Street to demand: "Any news come in?" Told, perhaps for the sixth time in a day, that there was none, he said irritably: "I won't have it . . . I must have more regular reports. It's your business to keep me informed." Yet opportunities were now few to order the movements of armies, fleets or air forces. He directed Alexander to act vigorously to expel Tito's partisans from Trieste and northeastern Italy, to which they laid claim. When the C-in-C warned that British troops were much less enthusiastic about fighting Yugoslavs than Germans, Churchill dismissed his fears—and ordered a display of force. Faced with this, the Yugoslavs withdrew behind the Izonzo River. The prime minister again used British troops to force the French to withdraw from Syria, which was handed over to an indigenous Arab government. France occupied an area of northwestern Italy which it claimed. Here, too, Churchill acted ruthlessly and successfully, insisting upon removal of de Gaulle's forces.

In Southeast Asia, Slim's Fourteenth Army was mopping up the last of the Japanese in Burma, and preparing for an amphibious assault on Malaya, scheduled for September. Captain Pim diligently moved the relevant pins and arrows on the walls of the Map Room at Downing Street, but the prime minister's heart was never deeply engaged. He remained preoccupied with the fate of Europe, and with urging upon the new U.S. president the need to adopt firm policies towards the Russians.

On May 18, the Churchills entertained to lunch at Downing Street the Russian ambassador, Fyodor Gusev. When Clementine and other guests left the table, the prime minister unburdened himself to the Soviet emissary. It seems worth relating at length Gusev's account of the meeting, as evidence both of Churchill's sentiments and of the manner in which these were reported to Moscow. The prime minister began by describing the importance he attached to a new summit meeting at which "either we shall achieve an agreement on future cooperation between our three nations, or the Anglo-American community will become united in opposition to the Soviet Union. It is difficult to anticipate the possible consequences of this second scenario." Gusev wrote:

> Here Churchill raised his voice, saying "We are full of grievances." I asked him what he had in mind. Irritably and in heightened tones, he began to catalogue the issues: 1) Trieste. Tito has "sneaked up to Trieste and wants to seize it." Churchill laid his hands on the table and showed how Tito was sneaking up to Trieste. "We will not allow"— Churchill roared—"the resolution of territorial disputes by seizure . . . We and the Americans are united in our resolution that all territorial issues should be resolved through a peace conference." I remarked that

as far as I knew Tito did not intend to resolve any territorial issues. Churchill ignored me and continued: "Armies are confronting each other. Grave trouble can break out at any time unless goodwill is displayed." 2) Prague. Churchill declared that we did not allow British representatives into Prague. "Our accredited ambassador has been prevented from entering Czechoslovakia," he said. I remarked that only the previous day Czech government representatives had travelled from London to Prague on a British aircraft. Churchill continued: "You wish to claim exclusive rights for yourselves in every capital occupied by your troops. The British government cannot understand such a Soviet attitude and cannot justify it to the British people, mindful that we are under mutual obligations to display friendship and cooperation . . . We, the British, are a proud nation and cannot allow anyone to treat us in this way."

Churchill would not listen to my comment on this and continued: 3) Vienna. "You do not allow us to enter Vienna. The war is over, but our representatives cannot inspect quarters for our soldiers." [Gusev launched into an exposition of the Soviet position which the prime minister cut short:] "Why will you not allow our representatives to enter Vienna? Now the war is over, what possible consideration can justify the refusal of the Soviet government to admit our representatives to Vienna?" There were more brusque exchanges about the Soviet establishment of a puppet regime in Austria, then Churchill turned to the German capital: "You do not allow us into Berlin. You want to make Berlin your exclusive zone."

I declared that Churchill's statement was groundless as we have an agreement on occupation zones and control of greater Berlin. Churchill again repeated that he is willing to allow any number of Soviet representatives to go anywhere. Churchill moved on to Poland and spoke with even greater anger. Things were going from bad to worse where the Polish issue was concerned, he said. He saw no hope for a satisfactory resolution of it: "We have endorsed Polish delegates, and you have imprisoned them. Parliament and the public are deeply concerned" . . . Churchill thinks that forthcoming debates in Parliament will demonstrate the great indignation of the British nation, and he will find himself at a loss about how to satisfy public opinion. Churchill then vaguely hinted that a satisfactory outcome of the Polish issue might lead to a resolution of the issue of the Baltic States.

Churchill did not want to hear my comments and moved on to characterize the gravity of the general situation. "Your front stretches from Lubeck to Trieste. You allow no one to enter the capitals which you control. The situation in Trieste is alarming. Polish affairs have reached a dead end. The general climate is at boiling point." I told Churchill that he was familiar with the Soviet government's position—that it makes no claims on territory or on the European capitals. Our front does not stretch as far as Trieste. Marshal Tito's troops may be there, but we are not responsible for Marshal Tito. He and the Yugoslav people have won themselves a place of honour among the United Nations by their struggle.

Churchill said: "I know that you are a great nation. By your struggle you have won an equal status among the great powers. But we, the British, are also a proud nation and we will not allow anyone to abuse us and trample upon our interests. I want you to understand that we are profoundly concerned by the current situation. I have ordered that demobilization of the Royal Air Force should be delayed." He then abruptly terminated the conversation, apologized for his frankness and departed to discuss with Attlee the forthcoming parliamentary elections.

The Soviet ambassador appended to this dispatch a personal commentary on the meeting:

Churchill was extraordinarily angry, and seemed to be making an effort to keep himself under control. His remarks were full of threats and blackmail, but it was not just blackmail. Following his radio broadcast of 13 May, the English press has adopted a stronger anti-Soviet line in reporting European events. It seeks to interpret all the emerging problems in terms of the USSR's attitude. Churchill's speech was an instruction to the press. Polish agents are conducting a bold anti-Soviet campaign in parliamentary circles and demand new debates on the Polish issue. Eden had already announced in the House of Commons that a foreign affairs debate will take place after the holidays. We may expect this to develop into a big anti-Soviet demonstration intended to pressure and threaten the USSR. So far we have no precise information on the purpose of Eisenhower's and Montgomery's forthcoming visit to London, but we have reason to think that they have been summoned to discuss and evaluate the allies' military position. We should recognise that we are dealing with an adventurer who is in his element at war, who feels much more at ease in the circumstances of war than those of peace.

Gusev's account of this meeting is unlikely to have been shown to Stalin, because Churchill's bluntness would have displeased him. In any event, it could have exercised not the smallest influence upon Moscow's policies. The Russians knew that the Americans shared little of the prime minister's passion about eastern Europe. For all Churchill's bluster and his mutterings to the Chiefs of Staff about the possibility of launching Operation Unthinkable, neither Western nation was ready to challenge the Russians by force. The old statesman's diatribe merely vented his personal bitterness and frustration. He knew in his heart that the tyranny established by the Red Army could not be undone either through diplomacy or by force of arms.

After polling day on July 6, there was a three-week pause before the election result was announced, to allow the overseas service vote to be counted. Churchill flew to southwestern France for his first holiday since 1939, at a château owned by a Canadian well-wisher. Then, on July 15, he took a plane onward to Berlin, for the last great Allied conference, the closing episode of his own war.

Churchill professed confidence about the election outcome. This was shared by Stalin who believed he would be returned to power with a parliamentary majority of at least eighty. Nonetheless, in a most honourable display of his respect for democracy, Churchill invited Clement Attlee, the possible prime minister–in–waiting, to join the British delegation at Potsdam. The Labour leader was waiting to greet him at his appointed villa, 23 Ringstrasse, along with Montgomery, Alexander and Eden. On July 16, Churchill held his first two-hour meeting with Harry Truman. He emerged much encouraged by what he saw and heard. Truman spoke much more toughly than had Roosevelt in his last months. Later, the prime minister toured the ruins of Berlin, and gazed without animosity upon the Germans foraging amid the rubble. "My hate had died with their surrender," he wrote later. "I was much moved by their desolation, and also by their thin haggard looks and threadbare clothes." Staring at the remains of Hitler's bunker, he reflected that this was how Downing Street would have looked had matters turned out differently in 1940. But he quickly wearied of tourism. Now as ever, what seized his imagination was the opportunity to discuss great issues with the most powerful men on earth, if not as their equal in national might then at least as their acknowledged peer in personal stature.

The Potsdam conference, of which the first formal session took place on July 17, achieved no meaningful decisions or conclusions. Churchill said of himself: "I shall be only half a man until the result of the poll."

Diplomat John Peck noted with some foreboding that, when the prime minister and Attlee inspected a parade of British troops in Berlin, Attlee received the louder cheers. Opening a soldiers' club, Churchill said: "May the memory of this glorious pilgrimage of war never die!" Yet many of his audience, men of Montgomery's armies, viewed both their recent past and future prospects in much more pragmatic terms.

Churchill's first responsibility was to take the measure of Harry Truman, and to lay before the new president his fears for Britain and the world. Truman, in his turn, felt a certain apprehension about the encounter. Harry Hopkins, in Moscow late in May, told Zhukov as he bade farewell before flying to London to see Churchill: "I respect the old man, but he is difficult. The only person who found talking to him easy was Franklin Roosevelt." Now, in Potsdam, Churchill described to Truman his fears for British solvency, when the country owed £3 billion of external debt. He expressed his hopes of American support. They talked much of eastern Europe, from which the news daily grew worse. Churchill was very excited by news, which reached the president at Potsdam, of the successful atomic bomb test at Alamogordo, New Mexico. He encouraged the president to disclose to Stalin "the simple fact that we have this weapon"—a significant and optimistic use of the plural possessive.

Churchill agreed, without consulting his cabinet colleagues, that the Americans would employ the atomic bomb against Japan without further reference to London. He urged that Britain and the United States should maintain the closest postwar military links, with reciprocal basing rights around the world. When Truman took refuge in bromides, and declined an explicit commitment, Churchill sallied in disappointment: "A man might make a proposal of marriage to a young lady, but it was not much use if he was told that she would always be a sister to him." He was rash enough to indulge a tirade against China and its pretensions, which of course irked the Americans. Brooke was indignant that the U.S. Chiefs of Staff discussed strategy for the final phase of the Pacific war in the absence of the British. What else could he have expected? The most significant British role was to endorse, and marginally to modify, the so-called Potsdam Declaration to Japan, warning of dire consequences if she failed forthwith to surrender to the Allies.

Brooke was exasperated by Churchill's exuberant display of enthusiasm about the news of "Tube Alloys"—the atomic bomb project. The CIGS displayed an extraordinary failure of understanding when the prime minister discussed the issue with his Chiefs of Staff over lunch on July 23. "I was completely shattered by the PM's outlook!" wrote the CIGS.

He had absorbed all the minor American exaggerations, and as a result was completely carried away. It was now no longer necessary for the Russians to come into the Japanese war, the new explosive alone was sufficient to settle the matter. Furthermore we now had something in our hands which would redress the balance with the Russians! The secret of this explosive, and the power to use it, would completely alter the diplomatic equilibrium! Now we had a new value which redressed our position (pushing his chin out and scowling), now we could say if you insist on doing this or that, well we can just blot out Moscow, then Stalingrad, then Kiev, then Kuibyshev, Karkhov [*sic*], Stalingrad, Sebastopol etc. etc. And now where are the Russians!!! I tried to crush his over-optimism based on the results of one experiment, and was asked with contempt what reason I had for minimizing the results of these discoveries. I was trying to dispel his dreams and as usual he did not like it. But I *shudder* to feel that he is allowing the half-baked results of one experiment to warp the whole of his diplomatic perspective!

If the prime minister failed to perceive the strategic limitations of nuclear weapons, his senior military adviser displayed in this encounter an extraordinary ignorance about the greatest scientific undertaking of the war, indeed the most momentous in history. Here was a manifestation of the manner in which even exalted Allied directors of strategy were slow to grasp the significance of the Bomb. Back in 1940–41, British scientists' theoretical nuclear research was well ahead of their American counterparts'. Following the joint commitment to build an atomic bomb, and the transfer of all relevant British material and personnel to the United States, the Americans adopted an increasingly ruthless proprietorial policy towards nuclear research. It had been agreed that the project should be a partnership. But Sir John Anderson, the responsible minister, soon reported to Churchill that the Americans were concealing information from the British in a "quite intolerable" fashion. At Quebec in May 1943 a new agreement was reached between Britain's prime minister and the U.S. president, subsequently confirmed in writing at Hyde Park in August. At Hyde Park again in September 1944 Churchill persuaded Roosevelt belatedly to sign a document agreeing that Anglo-American nuclear cooperation and exchange of information should continue after the war. But the Americans none the less displayed little inclination to regard atomic research as a shared venture—and impoverished Britain was in no condition to build a bomb of its own. After the war, successive British governments were reduced to pleading with Washington for the honouring of the nuclear agreements struck between Roosevelt and Churchill.

The social nuances of Potsdam were endless. During an Allied reception at Churchill's villa, the host offered a toast to Marshal Zhukov. The Russian, caught by surprise, responded by addressing the prime minister as "comrade." Then, alarmed by the perils of being heard to use such fraternal language to an archcapitalist, he hastily amended this to "comrade-in-arms." The next day in Stalin's office, the soldier was indeed taunted about the readiness with which he had made a comrade of Churchill. Only Stalin, among the Russians, allowed himself freedom to take personal liberties with the Western Allies.

Churchill spent much time—there was one session of five hours—alone with the Soviet warlord. Stalin was in the highest humour. He perceived himself as the foremost victor of World War II. Not for decades would it become apparent that the Soviet Union's devastation, and the economic consequences of subordinating all other interests to Russia's vast military machine, had sown the seeds of the Communist system's eventual collapse. In July 1945 the world, like the Soviet leader himself, perceived only that he presided over the greatest power on the European continent, one that was militarily unassailable. Stalin professed to confide in Churchill as if he was an old friend, apologising for Russia's failure to publicly display its gratitude for British wartime supplies, and promising that he would make amends at some suitable moment. At a banquet given by Churchill, the tyrant amazed guests by circling the table and collecting autographs on the menu: "His eyes twinkled with mirth and goodwill." He flattered the prime minister shamelessly—and was rewarded with Churchill's beaming benevolence. Eden wrote in dismay: "He is again under Stalin's spell. He kept repeating 'I like that man.' " Yet the Soviet warlord, inevitably, conceded nothing. The puppet Polish leadership was brought to Potsdam at Churchill's urging, and listened stonily to his arguments that non-Communists should be included in the Warsaw government, and that Poland should moderate its western frontier expectations.

Churchill never doubted the malevolence of Soviet intentions in eastern Europe, and indeed around the world. But he sustained residual delusions that he himself might influence Stalin, and thus fulfil purposes from which the full commitment of the United States was withheld. Sergo Beria, son of the NKVD chief, wrote: "Of all the western leaders Churchill had the best understanding of Stalin and succeeded in seeing through almost all of his manoeuvres. But when he is quoted as suggesting that he gained an influence over Stalin I cannot help smiling. It seems amazing that a person of such stature could so delude himself."

Stalin could be dispossessed of his vast trove of booty only by force of arms. He knew that the Western Allies lacked stomach or means for such a trial. Thus, he felt at liberty to divert himself in the company of the old imperialist, who indeed perhaps amused him, as he amused the world. Britain lost nothing by Churchill's dalliance with Stalin at Potsdam and elsewhere, because nothing could have been said or done to change outcomes. But it was a sad end to so much magnificent wartime statesmanship by the prime minister that the lion should lie down with the bear, roll on his back and allow his chest to be tickled. Far back in October 1940, Churchill had observed that "a lot of people talked a lot of nonsense when they said wars never settled anything; nothing in history was ever settled except by wars." In July 1945, it was impossible to pretend that the affairs of Europe had been satisfactorily "settled" by Allied victory in the Second World War.

On July 25, the British delegation left the Americans and Russians to confer, and returned to Britain to discover the election outcome. Churchill landed back at Northolt that afternoon, expecting to return to Potsdam two days later. Even the Russians assumed this: "no one in our conference delegation had the slightest doubt that he would be reelected," recalled Admiral Kuznetsov. At Downing Street, Captain Pim had reorganised the Map Room to display poll results as they came in—a somewhat generous interpretation of his naval duties, on behalf of a political party leader. On the morning of the twenty-sixth, Churchill settled himself in front of Pim's boards, remaining there throughout the day with the companionship of Beaverbrook and Brendan Bracken. It was soon plain that the Conservatives had suffered a disaster. In the new House of Commons, Labour would hold 393 seats. The Tories' numbers fell from 585 to 213. The Conservative government was at an end. Churchill had lost his parliamentary majority. He could no longer serve as prime minister. At seven p.m., he said quaintly to Pim: "Fetch me my carriage, and I shall go to the Palace." He resigned his office. Clement Attlee assumed the mantle, formed his own government and returned to Potsdam in Churchill's stead. The Russians were bewildered by Churchill's defeat. "I still cannot comprehend how this could happen that he lost the election!" said Molotov later. "Apparently one needs to understand the English way of life better . . . In Potsdam . . . he was so active."

The fallen leader strove to act manfully. On his return to Downing Street from Buckingham Palace, he said to his private secretary Leslie Rowan: "You must not think of me any more; your duty is now to serve Attlee, if he wishes you to do so. You must therefore go to him, for you must think also of your future." Rowan broke down and cried. When

Moran said something about voters' ingratitude, Churchill responded: "Oh no, I wouldn't call it that, they have had a very bad time." Yet the misery of his predicament cut to his heart. For nearly six years, he had inhabited a universe of fevered action. An almost unbroken stream of reports, minutes, cables and issues for decision flowed through his study, the Map Room, the Cabinet Room, his bedroom and even his bathroom day and night. Now, instead, with devastating abruptness, there was nothing. The vacancy seemed almost unendurable. "The rest of my life will be holidays," he said to Moran. "It is a strange feeling, all power gone."

Churchill moved from Downing Street into Claridge's Hotel. He was confronted with all manner of domestic problems such as he had been allowed to ignore for six years, not least the need to pay bills. His personal finances during the war years remain somewhat opaque. He received a monthly salary of £449 from the Treasury, for his services as prime minister. In addition, his books generated substantial income. There was some postwar political controversy about the fact that, throughout the war, he gained handsome royalties from sales of collections of his prime ministerial speeches. For instance *Into Battle*, the first volume, generated £11,172, of which sum the prime minister instructed his bank to divert half to the account of his son, Randolph. He received a huge amount, £50,000, in October 1943 for the film rights of his biography of Marlborough and a further £50,000 in April 1945 from Alexander Korda for film rights to his *History of the English-Speaking Peoples*. He was able to adopt a lofty attitude about book contracts and delivery dates with his publisher, Macmillan, because one of its most influential directors was a member of his government. An old friend, Sir Henry Strakosch, who died in 1943, bequeathed the prime minister £20,000 in his will. Yet punitive wartime taxation, more than 80 percent, absorbed a large part of these sums. Even on a care-and-maintenance basis, Chartwell, his home in Kent, incurred costs. Randolph, the monstrous pelican in the family, represented a major drain on his purse. As prime minister, he contributed about £35 a month for his personal share of the costs of Chequers. What is undisputed is that he emerged almost penniless from his experience as the saviour of his nation.

Smuts said, more than two years earlier, "Winston's mind has a stop in it at the end of the war." Churchill grumbled: "I do not believe in this brave new world . . . Tell me any good in any new thing." Even had he won the election, the great conflict with which he would be inseparably identified for the rest of human history had barely three weeks to run. The nugatory military decisions still at the discretion of a British national leader could exercise little influence upon the manner in which its final operations were conducted. Thereafter, while Churchill might have enjoyed retaining the trappings of power, as all prime ministers do, he was quite unsuited to address the challenges of peace. Isaiah Berlin wrote: "Churchill sees history—and life—as a great Renaissance pageant: when he thinks of France or Italy, Germany or the Low Countries, Russia, India, Africa, the Arab lands, he sees vivid historical images—something between Victorian illustrations in a child's book of history and the great procession painted by Benozzo Gozzoli in the Riccardi Palace . . . No man has ever loved life more vehemently and infused so much of it into everyone and everything that he has touched."

Yet by July 1945 the British people hungered for simpler and more immediate things. They had played their parts in the most terrible global drama in history. Now they were eager to quit the stage, to address themselves to their own private and social purposes, which Churchill only dimly understood, and was unsuited to assist them to fulfil. Alexandre Dumas wrote: "*Il y a des services si grands qu'on ne peut les payer que par l'ingratitude.*" The electorate had performed a service to Churchill, as well as to itself, by parting company with its great war leader when there was no more war for him to lead. He was profoundly glad for his nation that its struggle was approaching a conclusion, but deeply grieved for himself. At noon on July 27, he held his final cabinet—"a pretty grim affair," in Eden's words:

> After it was over I was on my way to the front door when W. called me back and we had half an hour alone. He was pretty wretched, poor old boy. Said he didn't feel any more reconciled this morning, on the contrary it hurt more, like a wound which becomes more painful after the first shock. He couldn't help feeling his treatment had been scurvy. "Thirty years of my life have been passed in this room. I shall never sit in it again. You will, but I shall not," with more to the same effect.

As he left Chequers after a final weekend with his family and intimates, he wrote in its visitors' book: "FINIS." Three weeks later, on August 15, Japan's surrender brought an end to the Second World War.

Churchill had wielded more power than any other British prime minister had known, or would know again. In 1938, he seemed a man out of his time, a patrician imperialist whose vision was rooted in Britain's Victorian past. By 1945, while this remained true, and goes far to explain his own disappointments, it had not prevented him from becoming the greatest war leader his country had ever known, a statesman whose name rang across the world like that of no other Englishman in history. Himself believing Britain great, for one last brief season he was able to make her so. To an extraordinary degree, what he did between 1940 and 1945 defines the nation's self-image even into the twenty-first century.

His achievement was to exercise the privileges of a dictator without casting off the mantle of a democrat. Ismay once found him bemoaning the bother of preparing a speech for the House of Commons, and obviously apprehensive about its reception. The soldier said emolliently: "Why don't you tell them to go to hell?" Churchill turned in a flash: "You should not say those things: I am the servant of the House." General Sikorski remarked at Chequers that the prime minister was a dictator chosen by the people. Churchill corrected him: "No, I am a privileged domestic, a *valet de chambre*, the servant of the House of Commons." It should be a source of wonder and pride that such a man led Britain through the war, more than half believing this. It was entirely appropriate that he led a coalition government, for he was never a party man. He existed, sui generis, outside the framework of conventional politics, and never seemed any more comfortable with the Conservative Party than it was with him. A. G. Gardiner wrote of Churchill back in 1914: "He would no more think of consulting a party than the chauffeur would of consulting the motor car." The same was true in 1945.

As for Churchill's war direction, it is not difficult to identify his strategic errors and misplaced enthusiasms. Anatole France wrote, *"Après la bataille, c'est là que triomphent les tacticiens."* Yet the outcome justified all. The defining fact of Churchill's leadership was Britain's emergence from the Second World War among the victors. This, most of his own people acknowledged. No warlord, no commander in history has failed to make mistakes. As Tedder observed, "War is organised confusion." It is as easy to catalogue the mistakes of Alexander the Great, Caesar and Napoleon as it is those of Churchill. Both Britain's most distinguished earlier war leaders, Pitt the Elder and Younger, were responsible for graver strategic follies than himself.

Historians and biographers have a duty to present evidence for the prosecution, to identify blunders and shortcomings. But before the jury retires, it is necessary to strip away nugatory matter, and focus upon essentials. Churchill towers over the war, standing higher than any other single human being at the head of the forces of light, as many Americans recognised. Mark Sullivan wrote in the *New York Herald Tribune* on May 11, 1945: "Churchill's greatness is unexcelled . . . Churchill's part in this world war reduces the classic figures of Rome and Greece to the relatively inconsequent stature of actors in dramas of minor scope . . . Churchill was the fighting leader, and his own poet." Anyone who attempts the difficult feat of imagining British wartime history deprived of his presence will find it sadly shrunken in stature. Even Brooke was once moved to complain, "Dull cabinet without PM." To an extraordinary degree, one man raised his nation far above the place in the Grand Alliance which its contribution in troops, tanks, ships and planes could have justified from 1943 onwards. It is a mistake to assess Churchill's war leadership in isolation. When it is measured against that of Roosevelt or Stalin, not to mention Hitler, Mussolini or Tojo, his failures and shortcomings shrink dramatically. No honourable course of action existed which could have averted his nation's bankruptcy and exhaustion in 1945, nor its eclipse from world power amid the new primacy of the United States and Russia.

Churchill possessed the ability, through his oratory, to invest with majesty the deeds and even failures of mortal men. More than any other national leader in history, and aided by the power of broadcast communications, he caused words to become not mere assertions of fact or expressions of intent, but acts of governance. "His countrymen have come to feel that he is saying what they would like to say for themselves if they knew how," wrote Moran. " . . . Perhaps for the first time in his life, he seems to see things through the eyes of the average man. He still says what he is feeling at the moment, but now it turns out that he is speaking for the nation."

In reality, as this book has sought to show, Churchill did not command the respect and trust of all the British people all of the time. But he empowered millions to look beyond the havoc of the battlefield, and the squalor of their domestic circumstances amid privation and bombardment, and to perceive a higher purpose in their struggles and sacrifices. This was, of course, of greater importance in averting defeat in 1940–41 than later, when the Allies were able to commit superior masses of men and matériel to securing victory. Churchill's rhetoric has played a significant part in causing the struggle against Hitler to be perceived by posterity as "the good war." He explained the struggle as no one else could, in terms mankind could comprehend and relate to, now as then. Even most American historians, when chronicling the wartime era, are more generous in their use of quotations from the words of Winston Churchill than from those of their own president, Franklin Roosevelt.

He cherished aspirations which often proved greater than his nation was capable of fulfilling. This, too, has been among the principal themes of this narrative. But it seems inconsistent to applaud his defiance of reason in insisting that Britain must fight on in June 1940, and then to denounce the extravagance of his later demands upon its people and armed forces. The service chiefs often deplored his misjudgements and intemperance. Yet his instinct for war was far more highly developed than their own. If they were often right in pleading that the time was not ripe to fight, left to their own devices they would have been intolerably slow to fight at all. While Brooke was an officer of remarkable qualities, like many soldiers he was a limited human being. He deluded himself in claiming, as he did after the conflict, that Western strategy had evolved in accordance with his own conception. While this may have been so in 1942–43, thereafter the European war was brought to a conclusion in consequence of Soviet exertions aided by American supplies, with significant assistance from the strategic air offensive and Eisenhower's armies. In the west, major military operations—which means the northwest Europe campaign—conformed to an American design, to which the foremost British contribution was to delay the invasion of the Continent until conditions were overwhelmingly favourable.

Britain produced few outstanding military commanders in the Second World War, a reflection of the institutional debility of the British Army, which also afflicted its tactics, choice of weapons and battlefield performance. The Royal Navy was Britain's finest fighting service, its performance tarnished only by the limitations of the Fleet Air Arm. The Royal Air Force also made an outstanding contribution, but like the USAAF it suffered from the obsessive reluctance of its higher commanders to subordinate their independent strategic ambitions to the interests of naval and ground operations.

It is often and justly remarked that Churchill enjoyed war. He revered heroes. Yet away from the battlefield, he seldom found such men congenial companions. Few generals are highly cultured men or notable conversationalists, capable of illuminating a conference room or dinner table to Churchill's standard. In his peacetime life, even after the two world wars, old warhorses played little part. Many people supposed that he himself would have coveted a Victoria Cross. This was surely true in his youth. But when his daughter Mary asked in his old age whether he felt that anything was missing from his wondrous array of laurels, he said nothing of medals, but instead answered slowly: "I should have liked my father to have lived long enough to see that I made something of my life."

During the war years, his commanders far more often disappointed his hopes than fulfilled them. He was forever searching for great captains, Marlboroughs and Wellingtons, yet towards the end he grew impatient even with Alexander, his unworthy favourite. He valued both Brooke and Montgomery, but never warmed to them, save as instruments of his will. Neither the British Army nor its chieftains fulfilled his soaring warrior ideal, and it was never plausible that they should. Much of the story of

Churchill and the Second World War is of Britain's leader seeking from his nation's torpid military culture greater things than it was capable of achieving. He inspired it to accomplish more than it dreamed possible in June 1940, but never as much as he wanted. Such is the nature of the relationship between many great leaders and their peoples, who know themselves mortal clay. Had Britain—or America—produced legions of warriors such as those of wartime Germany and Japan, they would have ceased to be the kind of liberal democracies the war was fought to preserve.

If Churchill's rhetoric and personality had been less remarkable, if he himself had not been so lovable, some of his military decisions might have been more harshly judged both by his contemporaries and by posterity. As it was, he was able to weave spells in the House of Commons and in his writings, which deflected even the best-merited criticisms. The only charge against him which stuck with the public, and lost him the general election of 1945, derived from his indifference to forging a new society. Moran wrote in 1943: "With Winston war is an end in itself rather than a means to an end." The British people understood his indifference to humdrum domestic issues, and thus acted as sensibly in evicting Churchill from Downing Street in 1945 as they had done by supporting his installation there in 1940.

Macmillan was at least half right in asserting that only Churchill could have secured the commitment of American power to the Mediterranean and Europe in the year following Pearl Harbor. Without his personal influence, the lure of the Pacific might have proved irresistible to Roosevelt and his Chiefs of Staff. If the Americans in 1944–45 came to regret their engagement in the Mediterranean, in 1942–43 it is impossible to perceive how else the Western Allies' armies could have played some part in fighting Hitler's armies.

There is an escapable pathos about Churchill's predicament in the last year of the war, because almost all his ambitions were frustrated, save for victory over the Axis. His engagement with armies became almost exclusively that of a tourist, because he could no longer much influence their movements. For such a mighty warrior, this was a source of unhappiness. The limits to his powers of negotiation with Roosevelt and Stalin were set by economic and strategic realities. But he accomplished the little that a British leader could.

Churchill's view of the British Empire and its peoples was unenlightened by comparison with that of America's president, or even by the standards of his time. This must be set in the balance against his huge virtues. He excluded brown and black peoples from his personal vision of freedom. Yet almost all of us are discriminatory, not necessarily racially, in the manner and degree in which we focus our finite stores of compassion. In this as in many other things, Churchill displayed mortal fallibility. Most great national leaders are cold men, as Roosevelt ultimately was, for all his capacity to simulate warmth. Churchill, despite monumental egoism, displayed a human sympathy that was none the less impressive because he often neglected intimates and servants, and failed to extend his charity to imperial subject races.

Any assessment of Churchill's wartime contribution must include words of homage to his wife. Clementine provided a service to the world by her manifold services to her husband, foremost among which was to tell him truths about himself. He was a domestic and parental failure, as most great men are. It would be disruptive to any family to accommodate a lion in the drawing room. Without ever taming Winston, Clementine managed and tempered him as far as any mortal could, while sustaining her husband's love in a fashion which moves posterity. Whatever he might have been without his indomitable wife, it would surely have been something less than he was.

History must take Churchill as a whole, as his wartime countrymen were obliged to do, rather than employ a spokeshave to strip away the blemishes created by his lunges into excess and folly. If the governance of nations in peace is best conducted by reasonable men, in war there is a powerful argument for leadership by those sometimes willing to adopt courses beyond the boundaries of reason, as Churchill did in 1940–41. His foremost quality was strength of will. This was so fundamental to his triumph in the early war years that it seems absurd to suggest that he should have become more biddable, merely because in 1943–45 his stubbornness was sometimes deployed in support of misjudged purposes.

He was one of the greatest actors upon the stage of affairs whom the world has ever known. Familiarity with his speeches, conversation and the fabulous anecdotage about his wartime doings does nothing to diminish our capacity to be moved to awe, tears and laughter by the sustained magnificence of his performance. He was the largest human being ever to occupy his office. If his leadership through the Second World War was imperfect, it is certain that no other British ruler in history has matched his direction of the nation in peril or, please God, is ever likely to find himself in circumstances to surpass it.

Acknowledgements and References

My first debt is to Richard Johnson of HarperCollins in London and Ash Green at Knopf in New York, for showing the confidence to commission this work, when less optimistic souls might have judged that there was no more usefully to be said about Winston Churchill. Robert Lacey of HarperCollins is a superb editor who contributes immeasurably to the coherence of my books; likewise Andrew Miller at Knopf. Michael Sissons and Peter Matson have been my agents for longer than they care to remember, and have always been wonderfully supportive.

Dr. Lyuba Vinogradov has been responsible for research and translation in Moscow on this book, as for my earlier *Armageddon* and *Nemesis*. It has today become much more difficult to access Soviet archives than it was a decade ago, but Lyuba achieved a remarkable amount by scouring published document collections. I am especially grateful to her for translating hundreds of pages of material concerning Churchill and the Allies from the wartime Soviet press.

Edward Young, whom I met when he was assisting Douglas Hurd with his biography of Peel, has done important and extraordinarily energetic research for me in U.S. archives. He is on the threshold of becoming a distinguished historian in his own right. As usual, I owe thanks to the peerless staff of the London Library, whose patience and goodwill are invaluable. Allen Packwood and his team at the Churchill Archive Centre in Cambridge have been tirelessly helpful, a great tribute when they contend with a column of Churchill scholars threading daily through their doors. Beyond generosity with his time while I was visiting Churchill College, Allen was generous enough to read my draft manuscript and make helpful comments and corrections.

William Spencer and his colleagues at the British National Archive, together with their American counterparts at the National Archive in Washington—Tim Nenninger most conspicuous among them—show how magnificently great collections function when staffed by men and women who really care. The Imperial War Museum's library and manuscript archive become ever more important, now that most 1939–45 eyewitnesses are dead. The Liddell Hart Archive at King's College, London, holds many important papers, and I am especially grateful for access to Sir John Kennedy's diary. I am indebted to copyright holders who have given permission for extracts from their material to be quoted in my text, including Antonia Yates for the papers of Capt. Andrew Yates.

Anyone who writes about Winston Churchill must pay tribute to Sir Martin Gilbert, his official biographer, whose work laid the foundations for all who follow. Gilbert's massive life, accompanied by the equally fascinating companion document collections, represents one of the great scholarly achievements of our time. Future writers and biographers will owe Sir Martin a further debt when he completes his forthcoming volumes of war papers for 1942–45.

Professor Sir Michael Howard, OM, CH, MC, and two other old friends, Godfrey Hodgson and Don Berry, have read my draft manuscript. Both made immensely helpful suggestions and proposed amendments, most of which I have acted upon. I am indebted to Antony Beevor for focusing my attention on Operation Unthinkable, and for the time and advice of Professor David Reynolds, Professor Robert Gildea, Professor Christopher Andrew and Chris Bellamy. In the United States, Dr. Williamson Murray made many helpful suggestions about the text, based upon his own exhaustive knowledge of the period. Dr. Tami Biddle of the U.S. Army War College is extraordinarily generous with her own material, in this case pointing me to Harris's and Slessor's 1941 reports from Washington and to important material on Allied relationships in the collection at Carlisle. The contribution of my secretary, Rachel Lawrence, is always indispensable, not least in collating notes and references. So too is that of my infinitely long-suffering wife, Penny, who feels doomed forever to share my spirit existence, focused upon 1939–45. She deserves to believe that some day we shall progress towards a real life in our own times.

In the references below, collections are abbreviated as follows: British National Archive, BNA; U.S. National Archive, USNA; Churchill Archive Centre, CAC; Imperial War Museum, IWM; the Liddell Hart Archive at King's College, London, LHA; and U.S. Army Military History Institute, USAMHI. After much vacillation, I have omitted references to some documents which have been for many years in the public domain, and which are clearly identified and dated in the text. All direct quotations from Churchill not otherwise sourced are to be found in the two volumes of Martin Gilbert's biography covering the war years.

Notes

INTRODUCTION

3   "He had once conceived": Boswell, p. 1100.

3   Andrew Roberts has painted: Roberts, *Masters*.

4   The most vivid wartime memory: Author interview, 1992.

4   he told his staff: Colville, December 12, 1940.

5   "Everything depended upon him": Wheeler-Bennett, *Action*, p. 236.

5   "He was not mad": Knight, p. 366.

5   "may overstate his indispensability": Wrigley, p. 85

7   "It would be easy by a cunning": LHA, MS diary of Maj. Gen. Sir John Kennedy (hereafter "Kennedy diary, LHA"), January 26, 1941.

9   "Churchill so evidently": Lees-Milne, p. 69, August 19, 1972.

9   "I wish I were twenty": Nicolson, p. 37, September 9, 1939.

CHAPTER ONE: THE BATTLE OF FRANCE

12   "It was a marvel": Reynolds, *In Command*, p. 126.

12   "If there is going to be a war": Baldwin to Lord Davidson, in Young, p. 112.

13   "several fishing rods": IWM, Sir C. Nicholson Papers, p. 9.

13   "I don't think WSC will be": Quoted in Roberts, *Masters*, p. 199, undisclosed source, May 13, 1940.

13   "It's all a great pity": Butler Papers, G11, quoted in ibid., p. 209.

13   "If I had to spend my whole life": Broad and Fleming, eds., p. 51.

13   "Events are moving so fast": *New Yorker*, May 12, 1940.

13   "Elizabethan zest for life": Harold Nicolson, *Spectator*, May 17, 1940.

13   "How Winston thinks that he can be Prime Minister": Amery, p. 615, May 11, 1940.

14   "conscious of a profound": Churchill, *Second World War*, 1:526.

14   "David, sir, David!": Sebag-Montefiore, p. 59.

15   "British troops have landed in Iceland": Sir Michael Howard, personal recollection to the author, December 28, 2008.

16   "Perhaps the darkest day in English history": Channon, p. 248.

16   In May 1940, while few influential figures: Rhodes-James.

16   " 'Keep your eye on Churchill' ": Gardiner, *Pillars*, p. 77.

18   "additional complication": *Collier's*, January 1939.

18   "the poor tank": *News of the World*, April 14, 1938.

18 "the submarine will be mastered": Gilbert, *War Papers*, Churchill to Neville Chamberlain, March 25, 1939.
18 "I feel we may compare the position": Gilbert, *War Papers*, 1:568.
18 "It may well be": Speech to the St. George's Association, April 24, 1933.
18 "I am beginning to come round": Amery, p. 584, March 14, 1940.
19 "Winston has not been nearly bold": Amery, p. 617, May 11, 1940.
19 "head of school's fag": Private information to author.
19 "So at last that man": Headlam, p. 197, May 10, 1940.
19 "The new War Cabinet": Bond, p. 131.
19 "perfectly futile for war": Roskill, *Hankey*, 3:464.
19 "May I wish you every possible": Wheeler-Bennett, *Action*, p. 219.
20 "seemed well satisfied": Eden, p. 98.
20 "In Winston's eyes": Moran, p. 275.
21 "He proved in this one short speech": *Philadelphia Inquirer*, May 14, 1940.
21 "That smart, tough, dumpy little man": *Time*, May 27, 1940.
21 "We have for twenty years": Richardson, p. 77.
22 "purely physical soldiers": Lee, p. 216, January 9, 1941.
22 "not too happy about the military": Colville, p. 131, May 14, 1940.
22 "I think myself that the battle": Kimball, 1:37, May 15, 1940.
23 "The summer landscape": Quoted in Horne, pp. 286–87.
24 "Harold, I think it would be wise": Nicolson, p. 86, May 17, 1940.
24 "superb confidence": Wheeler-Bennett, *Action*, p. 219.
24 "What a beautiful handwriting": Colville, p. 184, July 3, 1940.
24 Embracing his staff as: Wheeler-Bennett, *Action*, p. 219.
25 "I went up to my father's bedroom": Quoted in Gilbert, *Finest Hour*, p. 358.
25 "It must be remembered that the defence": BNA, INF1/264, May 19, 1940.
26 "Militarily, I did not see how": Eden, p. 107, May 24, 1940.
26 "About time number 17": Ibid.
27 "sole remaining bargaining counter": Kimball, 1:40, May 20, 1940.
28 "the government should at once": *New Statesman*, May 25, 1940.
28 "Nobody minds going down": Pownall, 1:327.
28 "Can nobody prevent him": Ibid., 1:333, May 23, 1940.
30 "Everything is complete confusion": Cadogan, p. 189, May 25, 1940.
30 A Gallup poll showed Americans: Gallup, May 29, 1940.
31 "too rambling and romantic": Cadogan, p. 190, May 26, 1940.
32 "He is still thinking of his books": Colville, p. 132, May 16, 1940.
32 he "would be addressing": Ibid., p. 118, May 7, 1940.
32 "so great . . . it is madness": Quoted in Lawlor, p. 96.
32 "It is not the descendants": Harold Nicolson, *Spectator*, May 17, 1940.
32 "I think they're going to beat us": Sheridan, p. 91.
34 "The decision affected us all": Ismay, p. 131.
36 "It is a drop in the bucket": Morgenthau diary, Morgenthau Papers, Franklin D. Roosevelt Library, Hyde Park, N.Y.
36 "The least costly solution in both life": New York *Herald Tribune*, May 24, 1940.
37 "I thought Winston talked": Halifax diary, Borthwick Institute, York, May 27, 1940.
38 "His world is built upon the primacy": Berlin, p. 6.
39 "Some of Mr. Churchill's broadcasts": Waugh, pp. 222–23.

CHAPTER TWO: THE TWO DUNKIRKS

40 "And so here we are back": Pownall, 1:351–52.

41 "on reasonable conditions": Reynolds, *In Command*, p. 170.

41 "He was quite magnificent": Dalton, May 28, 1940.

42 "I hope you realise your distinction": Horsfall, p. 142.

42 "There was a limit to what any of us": Private information to the author, 2001.

42 "It does seem to me incredible": Hichens, p. 81.

43 "No one in the room": Ian Jacob, "His Finest Hour," *Atlantic*, March 1965.

43 "the Luftwaffe, badly weakened": Potsdam Institute for the Study of Military History, 2:291.

44 "A dejected-looking old man": Ismay, p. 133.

45 "he could count on no artillery": Karslake, p. 124.

47 "The political object of the re-constituted BEF": C. P. Stacey, p. 278.

47 "the Breton redoubt": L. F. Ellis, p. 298.

47 "People who go to Italy": Colville, p. 152, April 10, 1940.

48 "Reynaud was inscrutable": Eden, p. 116.

48 "Mr. Churchill appeared imperturbable": De Gaulle, *L'Appel* (Plon: 1999), p. 54.

48 "That woman . . . will undo": Ismay reported conversation in Kennedy diary, LHA, March 3, 1941.

48 "M. Reynaud felt that while Mr. C": Foreign Relations of the United States, 1940–41. pp. 4–115.

49 "Normally I wake up buoyant to face": Eden, p. 182, December 19, 1940.

51 "Churchill, who objected": Colville, p. 232.

52 "If the French will go on fighting": Ibid., pp. 155–56, June 14, 1940.

52 "it was impossible to make a corpse feel": Brooke, p. 81, June 14, 1940.

53 "It is a desperate job being faced": Ibid., p. 83, June 15, 1940.

53 "Much equipment had been": Stacey, p. 284.

53 "The lack of previous training": Quoted in Karslake, p. 262.

54 "Their behaviour was terrible!": Ibid.

54 "repeating poetry, dilating on the drama": Colville, pp. 157–58, June 15, 1940.

54 "told one or two dirty stories": Ibid.

54 "less violent, less wild": Ibid., p. 170, June 25, 1940.

55 "We are France!" Lacouture, p. 240.

56 "Mr. Churchill finds that there are not enough French": *Le Matin*, June 24, 1940.

56 "When a flood comes the water flows over": Brooke, p. 69, May 25, 1940.

56 "My reason tells me that it now be": Nicolson, p. 96, June 15, 1940.

57 "This period was one of carefree": Fleming, pp. 88, 92.

57 "Here lies the material of a whole army": Potsdam Institute, Bock diary, June 2, 1940.

57 An American correspondent reported home: *New Yorker*, June 17, 1940.

CHAPTER THREE: INVASION FEVER

59 "Thank heavens they have": Horsfall, p. 153.

59 "Winston Churchill has told us": IWM, G. W. King, 85/49/1, June 16, 1940.

59 "Now we know that we have got to": Hichens, p. 90.

60 "Now I suppose it's our turn": Patrick Mayhew, ed., p. 77.

60 "[Captain] Bill Tennant came in": CAC, Edwards diary, REDW1/2.

62 "one thing that strikes me": Lee, p. 5, June 17, 1940.

62 "It is no secret that Great Britain": Quoted in Lash, p. 197.

62 "The great majority of Americans": *Philadelphia Inquirer*, May 23, 1940.

63 Richard E. Taylor of Apponaugh: IWM, Misc 200/3160.

63 "I have a feeling . . . that in the England": Somerset Maugham, *Time*, October 21, 1940.

63 "Propaganda is all very well": Colville, p. 175, June 28, 1940.

63 "One queer thing": Lee, p. 23, May 25, 1940.

63 "I don't know what we'll fight": Kennedy diary, LHA, November 12, 1942, story recounted by Walter Elliott.

64 "when so many interesting things": CAC, Martin diary, MART1, p. 12.

64 "You ought to have cried 'Shame' ": Colville, p. 135, May 19, 1940.

65 "We should have had an enormous army": Kennedy diary, LHA, May 27, 1941.

65 "I went on my knees": Halifax diary, Borthwick Institute, York, February 8, 1941.

66 "It was a terrible decision": Moran, p. 316, July 9, 1945.

67 Oran, a painful necessity: See, for instance, Payne, passim.

68 "But all contingent upon": BNA, PREM3/131/1, June 27, 1940.

68 "You will observe that the document": BNA, PREM 3/131/2.

68 "Am profoundly shocked and disgusted": Ibid.

68 "Please remember the serious nature": Ibid.

68 "This declaration would take the form": Ibid.

69 "There are difficulties which appear": CAC, Bevin Papers, Ernest Bevin to Professor W. K. Hancock, BEVNII/4/1, November 13, 1940.

69 "if the Government of Eire": Kimball, 1:106, December 7, 1940.

69 "Winston was in great form": Ironside, July 6, 1940.

70 "strikes me as tired": Gilbert, *War Papers*, 2:132, June 10, 1940.

70 "They paid lip-service": Fleming, p. 80.

70 "The menace of invasion": Ibid., p. 307.

71 "Hitler must invade or fail": Colville, p. 195, July 14, 1940.

71 Not until March 1941: Hinsley, 1:429, 451.

71 "in wonderful spirits": Brooke, p. 92, July 17, 1940.

72 "Radio sets were not then very": Henry Fairlie, "The Voice of Hope," *New Republic*, January 27, 1982, p. 16.

72 "Gradually we came under the spell": Hodgson, p. 5.

72 "sent shivers (not of fear)": Nicolson, p. 93, June 5, 1940.

72 "Mr. Churchill is the only man": *New Yorker*, August 25, 1940.

72 "Like a great actor": Berlin, p. 22.

72 "It is certainly his hour": Headlam, p. 213.

72 "I won't go on about the war": IWM, Papers of Mrs. E. Elkus.

73 she had saved her wages: CAC, Eade Papers, 2/2, September 11, 1942.

73 "Romans in Rome's quarrel": CAC, Martin diary, p. 7.

CHAPTER FOUR: THE BATTLE OF BRITAIN

74 "*Il y a beaucoup de puérilités*": Boswell, p. 876.

75 "I shall always associate that garden": Colville, p. 505, August 24, 1944.

75 "Winston wept": CAC, Martin diary, p. 29.

75 "The odds today have been unbelievable": Barclay, pp. 51–52.

76 "This sounds very peculiar today": IWM, Alec Bishop MS, 98/18/1.

77 "a farrago of operational": Colville, p. 288, November 7, 1940.
77 "It is the sneaks and stinkers": BNA, PREM3/220/48.
78 Jones spent twenty minutes: Jones, p. 101.
78 "Here was strength": Ibid., p. 107.
79 "a little ruffled": Colville, p. 211, August 7, 1940.
79 "Don't speak to me": Ismay, pp. 179–80.
80 "He paweth in the valley": John Kennedy, *Business of War*, p. 62.
80 "I try myself by court martial": Colville, p. 231, August 27, 1940.
80 "glaucous, vigilant, angry": Nicolson, p. 127, November 20, 1940.
81 "There goes the bloody British Empire": Colville, p. 340, January 24, 1941.
82 "Gimme 'Pug'!": Nel, p. 74.
82 "whether very great men": Colville, p. 389, May 20, 1941.
82 "an unscrupulously rough-and-tumble fighter": Lee, p. 77, October 10, 1940.
82 "You know, I may seem to be very fierce": CAC, Martin diary, p. 4.
82 "Ll[oyd] G[eorge] was purely external": Amery, p. 1034, March 26, 1945.
82 "It's very naughty of the PM": Moran, p. 287.
82 "the formidable ramparts": Moran, p. 324.
83 "Darling Winston": quoted in Soames, ed., *Speaking*, p. 454.
83 "to find himself subjected to a flow": Wheeler-Bennett, *Action*, p. 53.
84 "He has more wit than humour": Moran, p. 226, September 21, 1944.
84 "collapsed between the chair": Colville, p. 319, December 15, 1940.
84 "Winston feasts on the sound": Moran, p. 8, December 12, 1941.
84 "No one could predict": Wheeler-Bennett, *Action*, p. 177.
85 "the ferment of ideas": Ibid., p. 150.
85 "almost certain invasion": Channon, p. 266, September 16, 1940.
87 "like all the other soldiers": Neville Chamberlain diary, July 1, 1940.
87 "the nakedness of our defences": Brooke, p. 90, July 2, 1940.
87 "not satisfied that . . . the co-operation": BNA, CAB69/1.
88 "I feel an immense joy": Hichens, p. 99.
88 On August 25: Elmhirst, p. 51.
89 "Thank God . . . the defeatist opinions": Lee, p. 108, September 15, 1940.
89 "usual vigorous rhetorical good sense": Dalton, p. 80.
90 "I am on top of": Elmhirst, p. 53.
92 "That man's effort is flagging": Colville, p. 261, October 11, 1940.
92 "The club is burning, sir": CAC, Martin diary, p. 32.
93 "a farmer driving pigs": Colville, p. 217, August 10, 1941.
94 "For something like a year": Thompson, p. 41.
94 "One can now say confidently": *Dokumenty Vneshnei Politiki*, pp. 361, 387.
94 Lothian's "wild" appeal: Nicolson, p. 104, July 22, 1940.
94 "[He] was very interesting about the City": Lee, p. 165, December 8, 1940.
95 "Feeling in the Carlton Club": Channon, p. 268.
95 "I think it's a good thing that we've suffered": IWM, Green Papers, 99/9/1, letter of September 4, 1940.
96 "this was the sort of war which would suit": Colville, p. 262, October 12, 1940.
96 "We . . . soon adapt ourselves": Trollope, p. 102.
96 "if one looked on all this": Colville, p. 240, September 16, 1940.
96 "Malaya, the Australian government's intransigence": Eden, p. 214, January 21, 1941.
96 "We [have] got to admit that Germany": Colville, p. 312, October 13, 1940.
97 "the narrowest, most ignorant": Colville, p. 406, June 22, 1941.

CHAPTER FIVE: GREEK FIRE

99   saw no prospect beyond stalemate: See Bond, pp. 119–59.

99   "sit tight and defend ourselves": Dalton, p. 87.

99   "They say no one knows": Lee, p. 54, September 12, 1940.

100   "in a month's time": Ibid., p. 10, July 3, 1940.

100   "If Hitler were to postpone invasion": Nicolson, p. 103, July 20, 1940.

100   "I have heard a good many members": Diary, November 14, 1940, quoted in Garfield, p. 18.

100   "At our weekly meeting last night": CAC, Bevin Papers, letter from F. Price, BEVN6/59, September 22, 1940.

100   "Winston, why don't we land a million men": CAC, Eade Papers, 2/2, March 6, 1941.

100   "We will go easy at first": Gibb, pp. 40–41.

101   "the discharge of bombs is pitifully small": BNA, PREM3/21/1.

101   "No more than anyone else did he see clearly": Pownall, 2:8, November 2, 1940.

101   "As the PM said goodnight to the Air Marshals": Colville, p. 266, October 13, 1940.

102   "He was always, in effect": Attlee to New York City press conference, February 1, 1946.

102   "These military men v[er]y often fail": Soames, ed., *Speaking*, p. 23, May 30, 1909.

102   "The book is full of abuse of politicians": Ibid., p. 357, February 19, 1932.

102   "A series of absurd conventions became established": Churchill, *World Crisis*, vol. 2, part 3, chapter 10, pp. 1131, 1134–35.

103   "I am so glad you were able to find the means": Churchill to Tovey, April 7, 1941.

103   "by 300 determined men": Colville, p. 286, November 3, 1940.

106   "He lay there in his four-post bed": Ibid., p. 285, November 3, 1940.

106   "as if it were the only source of information": Nicolson, p. 121, October 17, 1940.

106   " 'How are you?' ": Ibid.

107   "You should not telegraph at Government expense": Gilbert, *Finest Hour*, pp. 905–6.

107   "I purred like six cats": Churchill, *Second World War*, 2:480.

107   "At long last we are going to throw off": Ismay, p. 195.

107   "If, with the situation as it is": BNA, PREM3/288/1.

109   "Off we went across the unknown country": Barnett, *Desert Generals*, pp. 37–65.

110   "For the first time the possibility": Harvey diary, p. 149, February 22, 1941.

110   "Mr. Churchill's speech has rather sobered me": Hodgson, pp. 122–23, February 11, 1941.

110   "We cannot, from Middle East resources": Eden, p. 168.

110   "The weakness of our policy": Ibid., p. 170, November 3, 1940.

111   "We were near the edge of the precipice": Kennedy diary, LHA, January 26 and February 11, 1941.

111   "He thinks Greece is lost": Sherwood, *White House Papers*, 1:239–40.

112   "Found Wavell waiting for me at 9am": Eden, p. 131, August 13, 1940.

113   Churchill and his generals failed to perceive: Hinsley, et al., 1:260.

114   "I hope, Jack": Eden, p. 240.

114   "General Wavell should regain unit ascendancy": BNA, CAB120/10, April 14, 1941.

115 "I think it is desperate": Kennedy diary, LHA, April 10, 1941.

115 "CIGS is miserable": Ibid., April 11, 1941.

115 "Chiefs of staff overawed & influenced": Ibid.

115 "I am afraid of a disaster": Menzies, p. 120.

116 "Aren't you going to listen to Winston Churchill?": Broad and Fleming, eds., p. 133, April 27, 1941.

116 "All that the country really wants": Nicolson, p. 162, April 13, 1941.

116 "He himself took a depressed view": Roskill, *Hankey*, 3:506, May 13, 1941.

117 "We hold our breath": Hodgson, p. 177, May 25, 1941.

118 "The difference between the capability": IWM, 92/12/1, Belsey Papers.

119 Churchill, a few months later: Colville, p. 443, September 28, 1941.

119 "Once more Germany gives the impression": Sebastian, p. 343, April 9, 1941.

119 "You've lost the game": Pauli, p. 137.

119 "the utter darkness": Brooke, p. 379, February 4, 1943.

119 "The PM in conversation will steep himself": Menzies, p. 169, March 1, 1941.

120 Churchill observed crossly: CAC, Eade Papers, 2/2, July 24, 1941.

120 "was right when he asserted": Potsdam Institute, 3:555.

121 "As far as I can make out": BNA, PREM4/17/2, March 20, 1941.

121 "He said some very harsh things about Wavell": Colville, p. 394, June 3, 1941.

121 "that fine commander whom we cheered": BBC broadcast, April 27, 1941.

121 "I understand he has a great deal": Soames, ed., *Speaking*, p. 480, May 13, 1943.

121 Wavell's best biographer, Ronald Lewin: Lewin, *The Chief.*

121 "My trouble is that I am not really interested in war": Pownall, 2:95.

122 "Now I'm going to waste a morning": Kennedy diary, LHA, September 14, 1939.

122 "They are a pretty fair lot of gangsters": Pownall, 2:19, June 3, 1941.

122 "It is a bad feature of the present situation": Kennedy diary, LHA, July 9, 1942.

122 "When he is in the right mood": Kennedy diary, LHA, February 9, 1941.

123 "It is a strange thing": Brooke, p. 647, January 20, 1945.

123 "At times you could kiss his feet": CAC, A. V. Alexander Papers, AVAR6/1, diary, June 10, 1942.

123 Capt. Stephen Roskill, the official historian: See Roskill, *Churchill*, p. 279.

123 "I . . . have to confess to an inherent difficulty": Cunningham, pp. 578, 580.

124 "I never saw him ruffled": Richards, pp. 202–3.

124 "I am thankful I have so little to do with him": Kennedy diary, LHA, December 5, 1941.

124 "Ismay is such a devotee of PM's": Ibid., April 10, 1941.

125 "Is there any evil except in intent?": IWM, Alec Bishop unpublished MS, 98/18/1.

125 "The chief difficulty is understanding what he says": CAC, Martin diary, p. 10.

126 "In truth it is only a sham of a parliament": Davie and Chisholm, p. 664, May 14, 1941.

127 "If you see that you are about to be captured": Wilson, p. 16 and passim.

127 "Moran was seldom, if ever": Wheeler-Bennett, *Action*, p. 110.

128 "He always retained unswerving independence of thought": Colville, p. 125.

129 "The people strike me": Lee, p. 243, April 16, 1941.

129 "Young man": John Kennedy, *Business of War*, p. 236.

129 "War," he wrote, "consists of fighting": quoted in Reynolds, *In Command*, p. 244.

129 "I suppose you realise that we shall lose the Middle East": Kennedy diary, LHA, June 21, 1941.

CHAPTER SIX: COMRADES

130 "There is nothing straightforward about this war": Garfield, p. 129.
132 "None of this conflicts with our main interest": Gilbert, *War Papers*, 1:147–49, September 25, 1939. On this issue, see, for instance, Carlton, passim.
132 "That the Russian armies should stand": BBC broadcast, October 10, 1939.
133 "a sentiment widely felt": Colville, p. 436, September 3, 1941.
133 "They think they are dealing with normal people": Pownall, 2:36, July 17, 1941.
133 "I don't suppose that the 'conquest' ": Headlam, p. 157, June 22, 1941.
133 "One feels that God is on our side": Ibid., p. 258.
134 "I glory in all this": IWM, 85/49/1, G. W. King MS, July 30, 1941.
134 "The Russians have not been too nice": Hodgson, p. 185, June 22, 1941.
134 "Somehow I think Stalin": Ibid., p. 190, July 2, 1941.
134 "I was agreeably surprised . . . that Churchill received Russia": IWM, 92/12/1, Belsey letters, June 25, 1941.
135 "It's impossible to say how long Russian resistance": Pownall, 2:30, June 29, 1941.
135 "I don't believe Winston is at heart": Ibid., p. 31, June 30, 1941.
136 "Why the authorities at home": Cunningham, p. 350.
137 "It was quite evident that all of the Britishers": Lee, p. 416.
137 "Britain's radio spies are at work": *Daily Mirror*, February 14, 1941.
137 "The danger of enemy": Hinsley, 2:671.
138 "almost a pariah in London": Lee, p. 317, June 23, 1941.
139 "an obstinate, high-minded man": Quoted in Reynolds, *In Command*, p. 256.
140 "The British government, by its passive": Bellamy, p. 415.
140 "We would like to inform you on the contents": *Ocherki Istorii Rossiikoi Vneshney Radvedki*, pp. 143–44.
141 "In order to enable Russia to remain": Hansard, September 30, 1941.
141 "Hitler is throwing all he has got into the Eastern battles": IWM, 85/49/1, G. W. King MS.
143 "I can still remember with what close attention": Kumanyov, p. 300.
143 "Now I have to bring to light the fact": Roskill, *Hankey*, 3:533.
144 Chris Bellamy, among the best-informed Western historians: Bellamy, p. 446.
144 "The effect upon us psychologically": *Observer*, August 17, 1941.
144 "My main feeling is one of bitter": Quoted in Garfield, p. 172, October 9, 1941.
144 "the rising temper of the British people": Gilbert, *War Papers*, 3:1372, October 25, 1941.
144 "Things are pretty hard here": CAC, CHAR1/362.
145 "The fundamental difficulty is that altho": Kennedy diary, LHA, July 7, 1941.
145 "Would that the two loathsome monsters": Pownall, p. 50, October 29, 1941.
145 "The Labour ministers": Harvey, p. 179, October 27, 1941.
145 "In two years struggle with the greatest military Power": Gilbert, *War Papers*, 3:1204, September 12, 1941.
145 "Winston's attitude to war is much more realistic": Menzies, p. 99, March 31, 1941.
145 "The Army must do something": Kennedy diary, LHA, October 9, 1941.
145 "Winston is in a difficult position": Ibid., October 13, 1941.
146 "Yes, I am afraid Moscow is a gone coon": Ibid., October 11, 1941.

CHAPTER SEVEN: THE BATTLE OF AMERICA

147 "I wonder if the Americans realise how late": Kennedy diary, LHA, May 25, 1941.

147 "rushing vast quantities of weapons": Hull, 2:967.

148 "The United States Administration is pursuing": Eden, p. 176.

148 "after the victory was won with our blood": Kimball, 1:102.

149 "I have never realised so strongly as now": Quoted in Kynaston, 3:472.

149 "Our desperate straits alone": Eden, p. 135.

149 "I have never liked Americans, except odd ones": Quoted in Roberts, *Holy Fox*, p. 280.

149 "The heavy labour of toadying": Ibid., p. 278.

149 "I only said that I thought you might hate it": Eden, p. 182.

150 During a trip to Detroit: *Christian Science Monitor*, May 12, 1941, p. 15 and November 11, 1941, p. 8.

150 "pretty hopeless—the old trouble of being unable": Harvey, p. 20, July 15, 1941.

150 "because he couldn't get on with these Americans": Dalton, p. 272, August 25, 1941.

150 "They really are a strange and unpleasing people": Headlam, p. 270, August 15, 1941.

150 "no great enthusiasm for the US": BNA, FO371/34114.

150 "it wouldn't really pay us for the US": LHA, Slessor Papers, Box XIIC.

150 "when one is dealing with a people so arrogant": RAF Museum, Hendon Harris Papers, folder H98, September 15, 1941.

151 "It is just a little humiliating": Dalton, p. 247, July 10, 1941.

151 "the average man's . . . unfavourable view": Planning Committee minutes, BNA, INF1/249, June 4, 1941.

151 "Donovan . . . is extremely friendly to us": Kennedy diary, LHA, March 7, 1941.

152 "a possible America": Watt, p. 161.

152 "he quite understood the exasperation": Colville, p. 283, November 1, 1940.

152 "I was . . . only a Second Lieutenant": Pilipel, p. 16.

152 "Had he been pure English aristocracy": Hodgson, pp. 189–90, July 2, 1941.

153 "Here's a telegram for those bloody Yankees": Colville, p. 136, May 19, 1940.

153 By late 1941, Churchill ran second: Richard L. Coe, *Washington Post*, January 11, 1942.

154 "I believe that we really can keep out": Sherwood, *White House Papers*, 1:125.

154 "a walking corpse": *Time*.

154 "He can work only seven hours a day": *Time*, March 10, 1941.

154 "of the exact state of England's need": Sherwood, *White House Papers*, 1:239.

155 "I suppose you could say—but not out loud": Ibid., 1:237.

155 "We seek no treasure": Chandros, pp. 165–66.

156 "Hopkins was, I think, very impressed": Quoted in Gilbert, *Finest Hour*, pp. 997, 999.

156 "I have never had such an enjoyable time": Lee, p. 220.

156 "Apparently the first thing that Churchill asks for": Ickes, p. 181.

157 "He finished with really glorious words of comfort": Hodgson, pp. 195–96, July 27, 1941.

157 "Winston is completely certain of America's full help": Menzies, p. 64, February 22, 1941.

158 "It is never very easy for the British": *Books & Bookmen*, October 1977, in a review of Joseph P. Lash's *Roosevelt and Churchill, 1939–41* (Andre Deutsch, 1977).

158 "Personally I am very sorry to see America turning": IWM, M. P. Troy Papers, 95/25/1, January 1, 1941.

158 "As soon as the Lend-Spend, Lend-Lease": Harriman and Abel, p. 5.

159 "We can't take seriously requests": Ibid., p. 15.

159 "He resented this so much": Lee, p. 307, June 9, 1941.

159 By contrast Col.—soon to be a lieutenant general: Pogue, *Marshall: Ordeal and Hope*, pp. 133–34.

159 "if rather than when continued to dominate": Ibid., p. 139.

160 "I was deeply worried the president": Harriman and Abel, p. 18.

160 "I must attempt to convince": Ibid., p. 18.

160 "The PM is much smaller than I expected": Ibid., p. 61.

160 "the PM bluntly stated": Ibid., p. 28.

161 "believing that we shall get the Americans": Amery, p. 689, May 19, 1941.

161 "The great difficulty is re-educating": Harriman and Abel, p. 57.

161 "The idea of being our armoury": Headlam, p. 234, December 31, 1940.

161 "The great thing is not to antagonise the United States": Nicolson, p. 153, March 21, 1941.

161 "Well, yes": Lee, p. 357, July 26, 1941.

162 "frightened of nothing but Japan": Cadogan, p. 393, July 21, 1941.

162 "A wonderful story is unfolding": Quoted in Gilbert, *War Papers*, 3:810.

163 "a disorderly day's rabbit-shooting": BNA, PREM4/27/9, March 13, 1941.

163 "I must say I do not think our friend": BNA, PREM3/485/6, folio 16.

163 "with a retinue which Cardinal Wolsey might have envied": Colville, p. 424, August 3, 1941.

164 "Working in H[arry] H[opkins]'s cabin this morning": CAC, Geoffrey Green, GREE1.

165 "really incapable of a personal friendship with anyone": Quoted in Davis, p. 212.

167 "Not a single American officer": CAC, Jacob diary, JACB1/10, August 11, 1941.

167 "It would be an exaggeration to say that Roosevelt and Churchill": Sherwood, *White House Papers*, 1:364.

168 "My God, this is history!": CAC, Geoffrey Green, GREE1, August 10, 1941.

168 the occasion must fulfil the fantasies of a "pressman": CAC, Jacob diary, August 10, 1941.

168 That afternoon, Churchill took a launch: CAC, Martin diary, p. 60.

168 "Am I going to like it?": Ibid., p. 62.

169 "It was hard to tell whether Churchill": Wheeler-Bennett, *Action*, p. 206.

169 "a very interesting and by no means unfruitful meeting": CAC, Churchill Papers, CHAR1/362/28-32, August 29, 1941.

169 "Roosevelt is all for coming into the war": Pownall, 1:374.

170 "nothing dressed up very nicely": Kennedy diary, LHA, August 24, 1941.

170 "There was a statement of War Aims": Hodgson, p. 201, August 15, 1941.

170 "I ought to tell you that there has been a wave of depression": Gilbert, *War Papers*, 3:1125, August 28, 1941.

170 "The PM said that after the joint declaration": Colville, p. 434, August 30, 1941.

170 He even questioned—as did some: Harvey, p. 210, August 31, 1941.

171 "The attitude of the people he had been with": Quoted in Lee, p. 376, August 24, 1941.

171 "It will not be possible for the whole British Army": Gilbert, *War Papers*, 3:1202.

171 "plans were worked out to establish": Trukhanovsky, p. 273.

172 "the Food Account was very high": CAC, Churchill Papers, CHAR1/379/12-20.

173 "Oh, Miss, you'll never guess what he did next . . . ": Nel, pp. 43–45.

174 "Now run inside and type like HELL": Ibid., p. 67.

174 "Winston was depressed at outset": Eden, p. 294, September 22, 1941.

174 "in the event of a collision between Japan": BNA, HWI/25.

174 "Make sure they have all they want on extreme priority": Hinsley et al., 3:655, appendix 3.

175 "Another Prayer from the prime minister": CAC, Edwards diary, REDW2/3, August 24–25, 1941.

175 "There is nothing like having something that can catch and kill anything": Kimball, 1:165, November 2, 1941.

176 "People are wondering why you don't do something offensively": Harriman and Abel, p. 109, October 20, 1941.

176 "Whatever may happen on the Russian front": Pownall, 2:41.

176 Camrose was sufficiently impressed: Quoted in Hartwell, p. 316.

176 On the nineteenth, Churchill told guests during a lunch: CAC, Eade Papers, November 11, 1941.

177 "A. E. is much perplexed": Harvey, p. 179, October 10, 1941.

178 "Winston's methods were frequently repulsive to him": Brooke, p. 192, October 20, 1941.

178 "too much impressed by the enemy's will": John Kennedy, *Business of War*, p. 78.

179 "his ability to shake himself like a dog": Kennedy diary, March 19, 1942.

180 "If they declare war on us": Winant, pp. 196–97.

180 "tired and depressed": Harriman and Abel, p. 111.

181 "Saturated and satiated with emotion": Quoted in Reynolds, *In Command*, p. 264.

CHAPTER EIGHT: A GLIMPSE OF ARCADIA

182 "Well then, this war is over": Billotte, p. 187.

182 "We simply can't be beaten": Nicolson, p. 197, December 11, 1941.

182 "Though I do not wish anyone to be bombed": Hodgson, p. 232, December 9, 1941.

182 "While the public are prepared to make": BNA, INF1/292.

185 "I do not know when or how I shall come back": Soames, ed., *Speaking*, p. 460, December 21, 1941.

186 "All is very good indeed": Ibid., p. 461, December 24, 1941.

187 "No one but he": Macmillan, p. 294, November 16, 1943.

188 "Senators' . . . office telephones carried call": *Washington Post*, December 27, 1941.

189 "the greatest orator in the world": Ickes, December 26, 1941.

189 "It is a great weight off my chest": Moran, p. 23.

190 "to put it on its throne": Lash, p. 15.

190 " 'Tommy' clapped her hands": Ibid., p. 16.

190 "the aura of the office was always around him": Bohlen, p. 210.

190 "a patrician democrat whose every simple gesture": Amery, p. 882, April 15, 1943.

191 "The difference between the President": Hassett, p. 171.

191 "one of the most untidy rooms": CAC, Jacob diary, JACB1/12.

191 "How *do* these people carry on?": Cadogan, p. 586.

191 "By the side of the Prime Minister he is a child": CAC, Jacob diary, JACB1/14.

191 "They will have first to close the gap": Ibid., p. 90.

192 "They tell me I have done a good job here": Ickes, February 1, 1942.

192 "The time had now come when I must leave": Churchill, *Second World War*, 3:625.

193 Amery noted wryly: Amery, p. 242, January 17, 1942.

193 "He wanted to show the President": Moran, p. 21.

193 "There is bound to be difficulty in practice": Eden, p. 319, January 28, 1942.

194 "There is one lesson the United States should learn": *Denver Post*, February 6, 1942.

194 "It is unfortunate that Mr. Roosevelt": *Chicago Tribune*, February 2, 1942.

194 "Who writes Churchill's speeches for him?": *Time*, book review section, p. 94, March 17, 1941.

195 "Even those closest to Roosevelt": Lash, p. 195.

195 "proposed to reshape the world": Michael Howard, *Books & Bookmen*, October 1977.

195 "The academic yet sweeping opinions": Eden, p. 374.

195 "My whole system is founded on friendship": Ibid., p. 323.

196 "The British," wrote Henry Stimson, "are evidently taking advantage": Stimson diary, Sterling Memorial Library, Yale, January 11, 1942.

196 "as if these had been swept into": Pogue, *Marshall: Ordeal and Hope*, p. 265.

197 "It is odd that Winston should want me": Quoted in Danchev, p. 10.

CHAPTER NINE: "THE VALLEY OF HUMILIATION"

198 "There seems to be plenty of snarling": Moran, p. 28.

198 "with the mentality of a greengrocer": Brooke, p. 212, December 19, 1941.

199 "We should thank God for Hitler": John Kennedy, *Business of War*, p. 318.

199 "The PM is not really interested in Mackenzie King": Moran, p. 20.

199 "Mr. Churchill has been unwilling to give": *New Statesman*, January 31, 1942.

199 When Amery wished: Bayley and Harper, p. 234.

200 "I think he is": Harvey, February 9, 1942.

200 "Sometimes . . . the PM is just like a child": Dalton, p. 368.

200 "The whole reputation of our country and our race is involved": Harvey, February 9, 1942.

200 "Lots of people want to": Bonham Carter, p. 236, February 11, 1942.

200 "striding up and down, all on edge": Layton Papers, quoted in Gilbert, *Road to Victory*, p. 56.

201 "Defeatism is in the air, and . . . I feel it too": Garfield, p. 223.

201 "I think it is time he went": MO report, quoted in Mosley, p. 241.

201 "I'm fed up . . . I feel very biteful": Bonham Carter, p. 236, February 11, 1942.

202 "The nature of his words and the unaccustomed speed": CAC, Colville MS diary, February 16, 1942.

202 "We have so many men in Singapore": Nicolson, p. 211, February 12, 1942.

202 "But my God, sir, you cannot do that": Pim Papers, quoted in Gilbert, *Road 202Victory*, p. 62.

202 "If the army cannot fight better": Brooke, p. 231, February 18, 1942.

203 "At the back of his mind and unconsciously": Harvey, p. 91, February 5, 1942.

203 "We have masses of reinforcements": Kennedy diary, LHA, February 3, 1942.

204 "These simple rules might help us": Dill to Brooke, March 5, 1942.

204 "This process does not make Cabinet Ministers": Bryant, 1:375.

205 "We are indeed walking through the Valley of Humiliation": Hopkins Papers,

Georgetown University, Washington, D.C., Box 4, folder 1, Accession 1, Series 1, correspondence.

205 "always been as distant as a lion and an okapi": Eden, p. 539.

205 "fighting to keep their country free": Cripps, BBC broadcast, February 6, 1942.

206 "The talk was very much about Winston": Kennedy diary, March 5, 1942.

206 "Although the British are keeping a stiff upper lip": Harriman and Abel, p. 126.

206 "he is always careful to consume": Moran, p. 32.

206 "saddened—appalled by events": Quoted in Gilbert, *Road to Victory*, p. 69.

206 "Poor old P.M. in a sour mood and a bad way": Cadogan, p. 440, March 4, 1942.

207 "a pregnant fact": Roskill, *Churchill and the Admirals*, p. 232.

208 "I believe," he said, "that if one side in an equal war": Hansard, November 16, 1937.

209 "built more like a fire-lighter": Conversation with the author, June 21, 1977.

209 "I hope you were impressed": Kimball, 1:504, June 1, 1942.

209 "As I lay in bed the other night": Hodgson, p. 407. August 15, 1943.

210 "a considerable commander—but there was a certain coarseness about him": Brown, p. 201.

210 perverse to heap praise: *New Statesman*, Februry 28, 1942.

210 "The disaster of this policy": Hansard, February 24, 1942.

210 "can be implemented only": Kennedy diary, LHA, May 31, 1942.

211 "a stubborn and obstinate man": Roskill, *Churchill and the Admirals*, p. 130.

212 "I find it very difficult to get over Singapore": Kimball, 1:438.

212 "CIGS says WSC is often in a very nasty mood these days": Kennedy diary, LHA, April 7, 1942.

212 "hypothetical post-war problems": Amery, p. 785, March 8, 1942.

213 "He does not seem to see that the steps": *New Statesman*, April 11, 1941.

213 "This nation has become very soft": Kennedy diary, LHA, February 23, 1942.

213 "lack enthusiasm and interest in the war": BNA, WO163/52, Quarterly Morale Report.

214 "that America will emerge, after total victory": BNA, FO371/30656.

213 "When has the Prime Minister made one": *Economist*, December 19, 1942.

214 "The feeling is almost universally held": Kimball, *Churchill and Roosevelt*, 1:446.

214 "a strange combination of great and small qualities": Amery, p. 746 (November 19, 1941) and p. 750 (November 25, 1941).

215 "the humiliation of being ordered about": Ibid., p. 822, July 27, 1942.

215 "lay down arms and accept whatever fate": Tendulkar, 5:291.

215 "Anything like a serious difference between you": Kimball, 1:449.

216 "We must remember that this is a bad thing": Cadogan, p. 450, May 7, 1942.

216 "The depression following Singapore": CAC, Churchill Papers, CHAR1/369/5-8, May 2, 1942.

216 "Everyone feels safer now": Ibid.

217 "there are many people in the USA": Nicolson, p. 222, April 15, 1941.

216 "One trouble is that we want everything": BNA, CAB122/96, April 7, 1942.

216 "It must be accepted that policy will increasingly": Salter, pp. 185–86.

217 "I don't know what we can do for that Army": Kennedy diary, LHA, June 11, 1942.

217 "Our soldiers are the most pathetic amateurs": Cadogan, p. 374 (April 29, 1941) and p. 389 (June 18, 1941).

217 "What will happen if the Germans get a footing here?": Ibid., p. 433, February 9, 1942.

218 "He presents to me in those red years": Churchill, *Great Contemporaries*, p. 144.
219 "We manage by terrific efforts to pile up resources": Kennedy diary, LHA, July 31, 1942.
219 "Rommel was an abler general than any on the British side": Moorehead, p. 418.
220 "There is a general feeling that there is something wrong": Garfield, p. 260.
220 "The feeling is growing that we are having": Ibid., p. 212, February 10, 1942.
220 Ivan Maisky, the Russian ambassador in London: Dalton, November 18, 1941.
220 "Our [career officers] regard [war]": Pownall, 2:98.
221 "Petrol, food, NAAFI supplies": Stanford, p. 110 and passim.
221 "the Augean stables are still uncleaned": Macmillan, p. 322, December 8, 1943.
222 "All this," noted a general who read Gordon's rant, "has a devastating effect on army morale": Kennedy diary, LHA, March 5, 1942.
222 "We are going to lose this war unless we control it": Brooke, p. 243, March 31, 1942.
222 "too stupid to be employed in any operational capacity": Macmillan, p. 313, December 2, 1943.
222 "These British administrative generals": Ibid., p. 347, January 1, 1944.
223 Following Byng's shooting: See Rodger, 2:272 and passim.
223 Churchill muttered to Dill about the virtues of the Byng precedent: Kennedy diary, LHA, December 5, 1941.
223 "I am devoted to Neil": Brooke, p. 270, June 22, 1942.
223 Fundamental to many defeats in the desert: French, passim.
224 "Arm yourself therefore my dear": Quoted in Gilbert, *Churchill: A Life*, 4:63.
225 "a mere handmaid of the Army": BNA, PREM3/499/9, Churchill to Attlee, July 29, 1942.
225 "In all its branches, the German war machine": Moorehead, p. 409.
225 "Father, the trouble is your soldiers won't fight": Eden, p. 378, October 6, 1942.
225 "I love Randolph, but I don't like him": Brown, p. 148.
226 "a very daring and skilful opponent": Hansard, January 29, 1942.
226 "These beastly Huns": McLaine, p. 139.
227 "I gather that production": Headlam, p. 231, December 5, 1940.
227 "I was disgusted to hear that their production tempo": Colville, p. 441, September 26, 1941.
227 Of eight serious strikes in the aircraft industry: BNA, AVIA10/269.
227 "a marked absence of discipline": BNA, CAB102/406.
227 "had failed to improve its productivity": BNA, CAB70/6.
227 "Strikes continue to cause much discussion": BNA, INFI/282, October 1943.
228 Byrd complained to harbour security officers: BNA, FO371/34115.
228 "I do not see why the country sh[oul]d not be mobilized": Kennedy diary, LHA, March 12, 1942.
228 Of all wartime industrial disputes: Inman, p. 365.
228 The Cost of Living Index rose from 88: Ibid., passim.
228 "one can hardly overstress the effect": Court, p. 325.
228 "The center of the problem . . . is the bad feeling": BNA, CAB123/21.
229 "Many of the people had lived for years past": Ministry of Health report, Cmd.6468.
229 "children in rags": Titmuss, p. 115.
229 "We [Chamberlain's ministers in early 1940] were all conscious": Quoted in McLaine, p. 104.

CHAPTER TEN: "SECOND FRONT NOW!"

230 "I was fortunate if I did not see Winston for 6 hours": Brooke, p. 247, April 10, 1942.

230 "no very great contribution": Ibid., p. 246, April 9, 1942.

231 "In many respects he is a very dangerous man": Ibid., p. 249, April 11, 1942.

231 The CIGS told his staff: Kennedy diary, LHA, April 5, 1942.

231 "The extraordinary thing is that the Russians seem": Ibid.

231 "I am in entire agreement in principle": Kimball, 1:448, April 12, 1942.

232 "we are proceeding with plans and preparations on that basis": Ibid., 1:459, April 17, 1942.

232 "Arrangements are being made for a landing": Ibid., 1:515.

232 "This universal cry to start a second front": Brooke, p. 243, March 30, 1942.

234 "I might be the best man to run the war": Halifax, March 31, 1942.

234 "Concerning the second front, Churchill made a brief statement": Rzheshevsky, pp. 113, 190.

235 "We do not consider this a meaningless statement": Ibid., p. 157.

235 "It is the irony of the commitment to the Soviet Union": Beaumont, p. 99.

235 "Considerable though these achievements and sacrifices were": Ibid., p. 142.

236 "sending very few aircraft, and not the best they have either": Ibid., p. 147.

236 "They offered no definite information": Rzheshevsky, p. 231.

236 "preparations for the second front": Ibid., p. 222.

236 "Finally, we think it absolutely necessary": Ibid., p. 250.

236 First, and as the Russian leader acknowledged: Chuev, p. 258.

237 "I mentioned among other things": Ibid., p. 319.

237 "Roosevelt had calmly told Molotov": Harvey, p. 244, June 10, 1942.

237 "We had to squeeze everything we could get": Chuev, p. 66.

238 "the High Contracting Parties . . . to afford one another": *Pravda*, June 14, 1942.

238 found Churchill "smarter": Chuev, p. 26.

238 "I knew them all, these capitalists": Ibid., pp. 65–67.

239 "This vicious rag should have no special facilities here": BNA, PREM4/26/8, June 7, 1942.

239 "Advocacy of a second front has increased": Nicholas, p. 58, July 25, 1942.

239 A U.S. officer at dinner in London: Kennedy diary, LHA, April 5, 1942.

240 "No Englishman here has the close relationship": BNA, CAB109/47, Birley to Jacob.

240 "We simply hold no cards at all": Dykes diary, October 12, 1942, quoted in Danchev, p. 20.

240 Private secretary John Martin was sternly rebuked: Hassett, p. 68.

240 "No responsible British military authority": CAC, JACB1/14.

241 "it was Britain's beleaguered helplessness": Porch, p. 208.

242 "Anti-British feeling is still strong": Nicholas, p. 38, May 14, 1942.

242 "there was little point in supplying the British": Ibid., p. 49, June 27, 1942.

242 "These English are too aggressive": Hassett, June 20 and 24, 1942.

242 "a delightful companion": Ibid., June 20, 1942.

242 "I knew when I saw your fat-headed PM": BNA, FO371/30656.

242 "All the old animosities against the British": USNA, RG84, Box 5.

242 "Phrases such as 'the British always want someone' ": USNA, RG208, Box 11, Survey of Int. Material, OWI Survey No. 113, June 10, 1942.

242 The OWI's July survey invited Americans: Ibid., OWI Survey No. 114, July 1, 1942.

243 Some 65 percent said America: Ibid., OWI Survey No. 117, August 29, 1942.
243 "The dominant underlying feeling is not bad": BNA, FO371/30656.
243 "the Asiatic war has revived": Lippmann Papers, Yale, April 18, 1942.
243 "old-fashioned imperialism": BNA, FO371/30656, Clark Kerr dispatch, September 28, 1942.
243 "The Embassy . . . has a quite fantastically low reputation": BNA, FO371/30656, July 6, 1942.
244 "were about as friendly to the British": Ibid., October 5, 1942.
244 "We must have a victory!": Harvey, p. 249, June 22, 1942.
245 "I told him what Winston had said": Kennedy diary, LHA, July 18, 1942.
245 "The people do not like him being away": IWM, Cons Shelf P, Yates letters, June 22, 1942.
245 "I myself felt pretty disgusted with him": Quoted in Mosley, p. 254.
245 "The enemy did not seem to understand": Hodgson, p. 293, June 23, 1942.
245 "Mr Churchill's speech did not contain much comfort": Ibid., p. 298, July 5, 1942.
245 "We heard yesterday that we have lost Tobruk": IWM, G. W. King 85/49/1, June 22, 1942.
246 "Where can soldiers go": Lash, *Roosevelt and Churchill, 1939–1941*, p. 209, June 25, 1942.
246 "Russian successes continue to provide": BNA, INF1/292, January 26 through February 1, 1942.
246 "We received nothing in return": Brooke, p. 223, January 27, 1942.
246 "There is an extraordinary and misguided": Kennedy diary, LHA, March 23, 1942.
246 "Little as I formerly liked him": IWM, Cons Shelf P, January 2, 1942.
246 "That danger will never come through admiration": McLaine, p. 210.
247 "Reactionary attitudes are spreading": IWM, Belsey 92/12/1, August 8, 1942.
247 "Why is not Mr. Churchill": Garfield, *Private Battle*, p. 274.
247 "When the Anglo-Soviet Alliance was signed": IWM, Papers of Mrs. E. Elkus.
247 ENGLISH PEOPLE ARE WILLING TO HELP THEIR RUSSIAN COMRADES: *Pravda*, August 5, 1942.
248 "Every week of successful defence": BNA, INF1/284.
250 "the trouble . . . is that no one really has any idea": Macmillan, p. 46, March 20, 1943.
250 "I suppose that, with the exception of some thirty or forty": Lascelles, p. 41, July 24, 1942.
251 "The fact that, during one of the most critical periods": *Los Angeles Times*, June 28, 1942.
251 "Winston is I think far too inclined": Amery, p. 818, July 6, 1942.
251 "His speech sounds very good to us": Millburn, p. 144, July 1, 1942.
251 "He is a giant among pygmies": Headlam, p. 322.
251 "It is to be hoped that the PM takes some notice": Millburn, p. 145, July 2, 1942.
252 "The simple question—though the answer may be complex": *Times* (London), July 1, 1942.
252 "a most objectionable young pup": Brooke, p. 276, July 3, 1942.
252 "discreditable" and "deplorable": Reynolds, *In Command*, p. 302.
252 "The cheek of the young brute": Brooke, p. 276, July 3, 1942.
252 "May I suggest with all respect that you must convince": BNA, AIR8/1074, Dill, JSM 300, Aide Memoire on Future Operations, July 16, 1942.

252 "Churchill, however, believes the other way": Wallace diary, May 25, 1943, quoted in J. M. Blum, ed., *The Price of Vision* (Houghton Mifflin, 1973).

253 "Well, how are we going to win this war?": Kennedy diary, LHA, July 18, 1942.

254 "We failed to see that a leader in a democracy": Pogue, *Organizer of Victory*, p. 330.

CHAPTER ELEVEN: CAMELS AND THE BEAR

255 "What energy and gallantry of the old gentleman": Harvey, p. 253, July 30, 1942.

255 "He felt the need for company, especially in Moscow": Eden, p. 338.

256 "looked exactly as though he was in a Christmas party disguise": Winfield, p. 69.

256 "Often had I seen the day break on the Nile": Churchill, *Second World War*, 3:412.

256 "Old Miles [Lampson, British ambassador to Egypt]": Harvey, p. 307, October 14, 1943.

256 "There seem to me to be too many people": IWM, 4/27/1, Papers of Lt. Gen. Sir Charles Gairdner, July 8, 1942.

257 "far too many cases of units surrendering": Richardson, p. 119.

257 "In the Middle East there was, in August": Moorehead, p. 412.

257 "I intend to see every important unit": Soames, ed., *Speaking*, p. 467, August 9, 1942.

258 The general received his dismissal ungraciously: Kennedy diary, LHA, August 23, 1942.

259 "Our NKVD resident in London": *Ocherki Istorii Rossiikoi Vneshney Razvedki*, August 4, 1942.

260 "Churchill departed for the USSR": Ibid., August 12, 1942.

260 "We know from a reliable source": Ibid.

263 "I am downhearted and dispirited": Moran, p. 68, August 13, 1942.

263 "You know, I was not friendly to you": Harriman and Abel, p. 161.

264 "May God prosper this undertaking": Moran, p. 138.

264 "Don't be afraid": Golovanov, p. 345.

265 "No one but the Prime Minister": Richardson, p. 144.

265 "Churchill was decidedly upset": Wheeler-Bennett, *Action*, pp. 215–16.

265 "He appealed to sentiments in Stalin": Brooke, p. 300, August 13, 1942.

266 "Stalin told me the British Navy": Harriman and Abel, p. 161.

266 When Harriman reported back to Roosevelt: Ibid., p. 169.

267 "The deliveries were curtailed": Trukhanovsky, pp. 283–84.

268 "savages": Harriman and Abel, p. 352.

268 He commissioned the ambassador's wife: CAC, Churchill Papers, CHAR1/379/12-20.

CHAPTER TWELVE: THE TURN OF FORTUNE

270 "have changed so frequently that the subject": *Times* (London), August 19, 1942.

270 "While I grumble young Russia waits": Garfield, p. 280.

270 "When looking back at those days": Brooke, p. 314, August 24, 1942.

271 "was the only one trying to win the war": Ibid., p. 324, September 24, 1942.

271 "super–chief of staff . . . Dill agreed": Amery, p. 830, August 25, 1942.

271 Churchill later described September and October: Moran, p. 85.

271 "It is an awful thing dealing with a man": Amery, p. 838, September 24, 1942.

271 "a 'bent' man, and couldn't be expected": Harvey, p. 264, October 9, 1942.

271 "The dominance of Churchill emerges": Hume Wrong diary, November 11, 1942.

272 "If we are beaten in this battle, it's the end of Winston": Moran, p. 91.

273 "the unnecessary battle": Porch, p. 290.

273 "Winston was like a cat on hot bricks": Lascelles, pp. 66–67, October 23, 1942.

273 "I am terribly anxious lest even with our superior weight": Amery, p. 840, October 26, 1942.

275 "How minute and fragile": Craig, p. 79.

275 "There is more jam to come": Nicolson, p. 260, November 6, 1942.

275 "If Torch succeeds we are beginning to stop losing this war": Brooke, p. 338, November 4, 1942.

277 "A sense of exaltation pervaded Mr. Churchill's speech": *Times* (London), November 11, 1942.

277 "The self-respect of the British Army": Dalton, p. 519.

277 "it was nice Monty had at last mentioned": Kennedy diary, LHA, August 1, 1942.

278 "We are winning victories!": Hodgson, p. 331.

278 "the only occasion on which he expressed publicly": Brooke, p. 340, November 9, 1942.

279 "Is it really to be supposed that the Russians": Harvey, p. 268, November 10, 1942.

279 "I never meant the Anglo-American Army": Gilbert, *Road to Victory*, p. 260.

279 "The Russian army having played the allotted role": Harvey, p. 270, November 14, 1942.

280 "*La France ne marchera pas*": Colville, p. 311, December 13, 1940.

280 "Although the French hate the Germans": Kennedy diary, LHA, November 18, 1942.

281 "In war," he said, "it is not always possible": Gilbert, *Road to Victory*, p. 277.

282 "I have always deemed it tragic that the British": Harriman and Abel, p. 173.

282 "It shows how wrong you get if once you compromise with evil": Harvey, p. 279, December 26, 1942.

282 The historian David Reynolds believes that the British: Reynolds, *In Command*, p. 330.

282 "One comes away, as always after conversations with De Gaulle": Macmillan, p. 101, June 1, 1943.

283 "I do not want any of your own long-term projects": Brooke, p. 376, January 31, 1943.

284 "not much good": Ibid., p. 364, January 20, 1943.

284 "Conversations with the British grow wearisome": Eisenhower, 1:98.

284 "getting on with Americans is frightfully easy": Dalton, p. 722.

286 "still something of an enigma": Pogue, *Marshall: Organizer of Victory*, p. 5.

286 "a general atmosphere of extraordinary goodwill": Macmillan, p. 8, January 26, 1943.

287 "At present they are working on what is called 'off the record' ": Soames, ed., *Speaking*, p. 473, January 15, 1943.

287 "I think CIGS's extremely definite views": CAC, Jacob diary, JACB1/19.

288 "Then you will have to educate them": Pogue, *Marshall: Organizer of Victory*, p. 7.

288 "with consummate skill": Macmillan, p. 9, January 26, 1943.

288 "The PM stood in the hall watching the Frenchman": Moran, pp. 97–98, January 22, 1943.

288 "Being naturally extremely gullible": CAC, Jacob diary, JACB1/19.

288 "We feel that the Americans have great drive": Kennedy diary, LHA, January 14, 1943.

289 "Many American officers found their British opposite numbers": Ambrose, p. 146.

289 "a pointer pup . . . If someone with a red mustache": Orlando Ward Papers, USAMHI Carlisle, diary, January 1943.

289 "they viewed the Mediterranean as a kind of dark hole": CAC, Jacob diary, JACB1/19.

289 "You know what a mess they would make of it!": Brooke, p. 362.

290 "My object is to serve my country": Roosevelt Papers, Hyde Park, PPF 8832.

290 "The better I get to know that man": LHA, Alanbrooke Papers, 14/39/B, February 9, 1944.

290 "Mr. Churchill . . . takes his place at the President's side": *Times* (London), January 27, 1943.

290 "He was offended that Roosevelt": Harriman and Abel, p. 188.

291 "we had made a public statement": BNA, CAB65/24, November 27, 1941.

291 "He always enjoyed other people's discomfort": Harriman and Abel, p. 191.

292 "Whatever we decided to undertake in 1943": CAC, Jacob diary, JACB1/19.

292 "Hundreds of thousands of Soviet people": Zhukov, 2:314.

293 "A tumbler was brought": Brooke, p. 370, January 26, 1943.

294 "I told him that the security arrangements were very poor": Ibid., p. 374, January 30, 1943.

295 "if they marched with us, we would not concern ourselves with past differences": Churchill, *The Second World War*, 4:647–48.

295 "It would be a pity to have to go out in the middle": CAC, Jacob diary, JACB1/19.

296 "they are now warrior nations, walking in the fear": Hansard, February 11, 1943.

CHAPTER THIRTEEN: OUT OF THE DESERT

298 "In absolute terms the British reduced their casualties": French, p. 284.

299 "Americans require experience": Quoted in Gilbert, *Road to Victory*, p. 360.

299 "Good news today, sir!": Bonham Carter, p. 260, March 10, 1943.

299 *How Green Is My Ally:* Dalton, p. 557.

299 "The enemy make a great mistake": Reynolds, *In Command.*

299 Some 50 percent answered: Gallup poll, June 1, 1943.

300 "They all look exactly alike to me": Macmillan, p. 256, October 14, 1943.

300 "I am told that our efforts": Headlam, p. 410, June 26, 1944.

301 "It is rather strange": Brooke, p. 464, October 28, 1943.

301 "He says he would not rule this out": Dalton, p. 551, February 8, 1943.

301 "The less said about that the better": Nicolson, p. 291, April 20, 1943.

301 "Sawyers brings the breakfast": CAC, Jacob diary, JACB1/19.

302 "There is nothing in the world he hates": Quoted in Gilbert, *Road to Victory*, p. 356, letter of March 17, 1943.

302 "He is so funny in the car": Layton letter, April 7, 1943, quoted in Gilbert, *Road to Victory*, p. 375.

302 "We had good news": Ibid., pp. 374–75.

302 "sharing his secret thoughts with no one": Moran, p. 198, August 4, 1944.

302 "he is always so reassuring": Ibid., p. 209, August 20, 1944.

303 "I had never seen him dictate before": Kennedy diary, LHA, April 6, 1943.

304 "Oh, I shall like that one": Quoted in Birkenhead, p. 537.

304 "Have you noticed that the President is a tired man?": Moran, p. 116, May 25, 1943.

305 "unless almost the entire bulk of the German Army": BNA, CAB120/83.

305 "It was quite evident that Marshall was quite incapable": Brooke, p. 406, May 18, 1943.

306 "the most exhausting entertainments imaginable": Ibid., pp. 409–11, May 24 and 25, 1943.

307 "I had always wondered why aircraft": Churchill, *Second World War,* 4:727.

307 "very human & lovable side": Kennedy diary, LHA, December 8, 1943.

307 "I was speaking," he told guests at dinner that night, "from where the cries of Christian virgins rent the air": Brooke, p. 416, June 1, 1943.

308 "Experience has taught me that it is not worthwhile arguing": BNA, CAB120/683, July 25, 1943.

308 "I am the last to plead Stalin's case": CAC, CHUR4/301/187, fs272-4, p. 276.

308 "In my view there is an undercurrent of uncertainty": Library of Congress MS Div., H. R. Luce Papers, Box 1, folder 7.

308 "When Mr. Churchill received the freedom of London": IWM, 85/49/1, King Papers.

309 "To some of the Government it is incredible": Harvey, p. 304, February 10, 1943.

309 "All these instructions": Macmillan, p. 167, July 29, 1943.

311 "On this, I'm thankful to say": Harvey, p. 342, July 24, 1943.

311 "Agreement after agreement may be secured on paper": Brooke, p. 398, May 4, 1943.

311 "I firmly believe": USAMHI, Carlisle, OCMH, Forrest Pogue notes of 1947 interview with Morgan for *The Supreme Command.*

313 "The guests take hardly any notice of him": Moran, p. 130, August 18, 1943.

313 "stir the imagination and win the support": Pogue, *Marshall: Organizer of Victory,* p. 241.

313 "As usual, he was full of guile": Ibid., p. 244.

313 Yet there is no period of the war at which American dismay: Harvey, p. 357, October 24, 1943.

314 "The full implications of this have not yet been assessed": BNA, WO205/33.

314 "If we once set foot on the Italian mainland": Kennedy diary, LHA, August 13, 1943.

315 "The Quebec conference has left me absolutely cooked": Brooke, p. 450, August 30, 1943.

315 He subsequently acknowledged that: Ibid., p. 466, November 1, 1943.

316 "It was like fighting tanks": Quoted in Atkinson, *Day of Battle,* p. 207.

316 "He did not believe Germany would try to control": BNA, CAB120/83.

317 "Must be a relief to the Boss for Churchill is a trying guest": Hassett, pp. 169, 315.

317 "loves W as a man for the war": Harvey, p. 238 (March 11, 1943) and p. 239 (March 29, 1943).

318 The chief of staff of the army indulged a brief fantasy: See Pogue, *Marshall: Organizer of Victory,* p. 318.

318 "mercurial inconstancy": Ibid., p. 320.

319 "But we cannot dictate and I doubt if we could have done more": Kennedy diary, LHA, September 3, 1943.

319 "In the end I suppose that we shall probably go into France": Ibid., September 26, 1943.

319 Beaverbrook had tabled a new motion: Hansard, September 23, 1943.

319 "I need him, I need him": Taylor, p. 500.

319 "He says we must not make things too hard for the PM": Dalton, p. 660, October 29, 1943.

320 "He says a Second Front is in existence": IWM, G. W. King, 85/49/1, August 22, 1943.

320 "will save a piece of rope later on": IWM, 92/12/1, Belsey letters, September 12 and 23, 1943.

320 "No loss . . . I never did like having that Sikorski person on our side, did you?": Ibid., letters of May 1 and September 23, 1943.

320 "It would be wrong to belittle the importance of allied military": *Pravda*, August 6, 1943.

321 "Even such help was serviccable to us": Chuev, p. 39.

321 "I think I may claim to know the mind of our workers": BNA, INF1/220.

CHAPTER FOURTEEN: SUNK IN THE AEGEAN

324 "his jumbonic majesty": Macmillan, p. 425, April 19, 1944.

325 "Good. This is a time to play high": Churchill, *Second World War*, 5:182.

325 He believed, probably rightly, that their functions: Brooke, p. 185, September 25, 1941.

326 "was clearly affected by the delay": Wilson dispatches, 1946, quoted in Holland, p. 33.

331 "It is pretty clear in my mind": Brooke, p. 458, October 6, 1943.

331 "He is excited about Kos": Cadogan, p. 565, October 7, 1943.

331 "I have never wished to send an army into the Balkans": Kimball, 2:498.

331 "worth at least up to a first-class division": BNA, FO954/32.

332 "I am slowly becoming convinced that in his old age": Brooke, p. 459, October 8, 1943.

332 "I propose . . . to tell Gen. Wilson that he is free": BNA, FO954/32.

332 "It does seem amazing that the PM": Kennedy diary, LHA, October 13, 1943.

334 "We are being pressed": Tedder, *With Prejudice*, p. 484.

334 "the price we were paying [for Leros was] too great": Ibid., October 28, 1943.

334 "a very nasty problem, Middle East [Command]": Brooke, p. 464, October 28, 1943.

335 "The enemy had boldly discounted": Roskill, *War at Sea*, vol. 3, pt. 1, p. 202.

335 "Lack of RAF support absolutely pitiful": IWM, LRDG 2/3.

335 "As the battle progressed, it was evident that the enemy": Holland, p. 135.

335 "We were amazed to see groups of British soldiers": Rogers, p. 203.

335 "The Germans moved quickly from one position to another": Holland, p. 148.

336 At midnight on November 14: Bennett, p. 398, appendix 13.

336 "I much regret not to see you tonight": Quoted in Tedder, p. 485.

336 "One would have thought that some of the bitter lessons": Ibid., p. 486.

337 "I am still strongly of the opinion that Leros": Cunningham, p. 582.

338 "Bad news of Leros": Cadogan, p. 576, November 16, 1943.

338 "The fall of Leros should be a reminder": *Times* (London), November 24, 1943.

339 "CIGS feels that the war may have been lengthened": Kennedy diary, LHA, November 7, 1943.

339 Likewise, the British official historian seems mistaken: Molony, 5:541.

339 "Am still grieving over Leros etc": Soames, ed., *Speaking,* p. 485, November 21, 1943.

339 "the most acute difference I ever had with General Eisenhower": Churchill, *Second World War,* 5:199.

339 "and if they were disregarded it was because other reasons": Ibid., 5:198–99.

340 "All the British were against me": Pogue, *Marshall: Organizer of Victory,* p. 307.

340 "I cannot pretend to have an adequate defence of what occurred": Soames, ed., *Speaking,* p. 487, November 26, 1943.

CHAPTER FIFTEEN: TEHRAN

341 "His ear is so sensitively tuned": Foot, p. 326.

341 "Mr. Churchill did not like to give his time to anything": Eden, p. 441.

341 "The red and gold dressing gown": Brooke, p. 223, January 27, 1942.

342 "and that it was really too much to go into detailed questions at the moment": Dalton, p. 676, November 30, 1943.

342 "remind the Turkey that Christmas was coming": Brooke, p. 467, November 3, 1943.

342 "Why break off the handle of the jug": Ibid., p. 468, November 8, 1943.

342 "Trying to maintain good relations": Ibid., p. 516, January 24, 1944.

343 Adam Tooze's important research: Tooze, p. 625 and passim.

344 "In an expansive moment Winston told us": Dalton, p. 947, October 18, 1943.

344 "We were greeted by her owner": Macmillan, p. 293, November 15, 1943.

345 "From the street below came a great hubbub of voices": Moran, pp. 156–57, November 18, 1943.

345 "We have now crystallised our ideas": Kennedy diary, LHA, November 7, 1943.

345 "The PM's stock is not high": Pownall, 2:119.

345 "The pattern of battle": Fred Majdalany, *Cassino: Portrait of a Battle* (Cassell, 1999), p. 33.

346 "Winston is getting": Macmillan, p. 304, November 25, 1943.

346 This caused Eden to observe: Sherwood, *White House Papers,* 2:717.

346 "We are inclined to forget the President's difficulties": John Kennedy, *Business of War,* p. 317, at lunch on November 19, 1943.

347 "W. had to play the role of courtier": Eden, pp. 424, 426.

348 "PM and President *ought*": Cadogan, p. 579, November 28, 1943.

348 "bloody Italian war": Moran, p. 159.

348 "We are preparing for a battle at Tehran": Ibid., p. 160.

348 "They are far more sceptical of him than they are of Stalin": Ibid.

348 "Poor Harry, the public is done with him": Hassett, p. 161, March 9, 1943.

348 "the reported recalcitrance of Churchill": Selden Menefee, *Washington Post,* January 13, 1944.

348 "quite enthralling": Brooke, p. 483, November 28, 1943.

349 "Of course the man was ruthless": Eden, p. 514.

349 "Do you think they know that we are listening?": Beria, p. 124.

350 "He was turning his hose on Churchill": Marshall interview, November 15, 1956, cited in Pogue, *Organizer of Victory,* p. 313.

350 Cadogan recorded the distress: Cadogan, p. 580, November 29, 1943.

350 Soviet eavesdroppers reported to Stalin: Beria, p. 126.

351 "That the President should deal with Churchill": Wheeler-Bennett, *Action,* p. 210.

351 "Roosevelt has given a firm commitment": Zhukov, 3:94.

352 Cunningham and Portal declared the conference: Moran, p. 168.

352 "Every morning when I wake": Coote Papers, January 27, 1944, quoted in Gilbert, *Road to Victory*, p. 646.

352 "the Americans have been taking their islands": December 9, 1943.

352 "sitting on his suitcase in a very cold morning wind": Bryant, *Triumph of the West*, p. 114.

353 "If I die," he told his daughter Sarah: Quoted in Gilbert, *Road to Victory*, p. 606.

353 "We all hope and pray": IWM, diary of W. A. Charlotte, 93/19/1.

353 "Papa much better today": quoted in Gilbert, *Road to Victory*, p. 613.

354 Macmillan strongly urged: Macmillan, p. 322, December 8, 1943.

354 "Our object is the liberation of Europe": Churchill to Chiefs of Staff, January 2, 1944.

355 "while Winston, very pink": Nicolson, pp. 344–45, January 18, 1944.

355 "That all right?": Ibid., p. 321, September 9, 1943.

356 "We did become like animals in the end": Quoted in d'Este, *Fatal Decision*, p. 316.

357 as American corps commander Maj. Gen. John Lucas: See Atkinson, *Day of Battle*, p. 354.

357 "The more one sees of this peninsula": Macmillan, p. 429, April 23, 1944.

358 "Sitting in a chair in his study": Colville, p. 474, February 18, 1944.

359 "Their chirpings will presently be stilled": Hansard, February 27, 1944.

359 "In the H of C smoking room": Headlam, p. 403, April 25, 1944.

360 "On no account": Gilbert, *Road to Victory*, p. 715, March 21, 1944.

360 "Soviet attitude on this business": Eden, p. 439, March 4, 1944.

360 "I confess to growing apprehension that Russia": Ibid.

360 "I would much rather get what we want": Macmillan, p. 124 (June 15, 1943) and p. 126 (June 18, 1943).

361 "Much as I love Winston": Ibid., p. 335 (December 23, 1943) and p. 338 (December 25, 1943).

361 "We both got quite heated at one time": Eden, August 20, 1943.

361 "He feels about De Gaulle": Macmillan, p. 335, December 23, 1943.

362 "I am much distressed to see": Ibid., p. 389, March 4, 1944.

362 "He may be mentally the man he was": Eden, p. 442, May 1, 1944.

363 "rather like a small boy": Kennedy diary, LHA, September 24, 1942.

363 "The raids are very fine": CAC, Churchill Papers, CHAR1/381/11-18.

363 "Late at night": Colville, p. 476, March 4, 1944.

CHAPTER SIXTEEN: SETTING EUROPE ABLAZE

364 "Subjugated peoples must be caused": Pownall, 2:21.

365 "simultaneous attacks by armoured forces": Gilbert, *War Papers*, 3:1313.

365 "I hope they will, even at the worst, maintain a gigantic guerrilla": Gilbert, *Finest Hour*, p. 473.

366 On May 27, 1941, Churchill sent: BNA, CAB120/827.

366 "Far from welcoming": Gildea, p. 165.

366 "Nothing must be done": Cabinet Defence Committee, August 2, 1943.

366 "Here, we want every citizen to fight": Colville, pp. 192–93, July 12, 1940.

367 Berlin wanted only economic plunder: See, for instance, Mazower, *Hitler's Empire*, passim.

367 "The cycle is simple": Quoted in Hastings, *Das Reich*, pp. 148–49.

368 "Other evidence exists that *maquis* violence was widely condemned": Julian Jackson, *France*, p. 534 and passim.

368 "I think the dropping of men": AHB/1D3/1588, quoted in M. R. D. Foot, *SOE in France* (HMSO, 1966), p. 153.

369 "Nobody who did not experience it can possibly imagine": Sweet-Escott, p. 73.

369 "I was disturbed . . . by the lack of security": Chandos, p. 239.

369 "Many French people": Hastings, *Das Reich*, passim, interviews by the author.

369 A whimsical November 1941 proposal: Astley and Wilkinson, p. 117.

370 "He believed that all his geese": Hastings, *Das Reich*, p. 35.

370 "There is no doubt that, in this critical phase": Mackenzie, p. 415.

372 German records, by contrast, reveal only thirty-five killed: Hastings, *Das Reich*, p. 278.

372 "In the history of France": Julian Jackson, *France*, p. 387.

372 "of seething factions, who would turn to whoever would give them most support": BNA, CAB99/28.

373 "How pleased I shall be to return to civilisation again": Quoted in Bailey, *Wildest Province*, p. 134.

373 "No one is ever free from the struggle for existence": Quoted in Mackenzie, p. 486, May 26, 1944.

374 As so often in occupied Europe, political and military objectives: Mazower, *Inside Hitler's Greece*, passim.

374 "I am very impressed, and oppressed and depressed": IWM, audio archive, quoted in Bailey, ed., *Forgotten Voices*, p. 250.

374 "pundits overestimated what guerrillas could achieve": Annan, p. 75.

374 "Armed resistance in the open countryside": Hammond, p. 180.

375 "But by that time, certainly in the case of EAM and ELAS": Bailey, ed., *Forgotten Voices*, p. 251.

376 "Self-organised bands . . . are already getting out of hand": Quoted in Molony, vol. 6, pt. 3, p. 210.

376 "A Resistance movement may suddenly transfer itself": Ibid.

376 Michael Howard, a historian of British wartime strategic deception: See Howard, 5:135–55.

377 "Deakin was outstandingly intelligent": Djilas, p. 253.

377 "we of course felt honoured": Ibid., p. 368.

378 "The British had no choice": Ibid., p. 348.

378 "It is a little doubtful whether the Missions": Mackenzie, p. 434.

379 "the difficulty is that with . . . the universal listening": Macmillan, p. 445, May 1 through 23, 1944.

379 "I have come to the conclusion": BNA, PREM4/381C/341 and 4/369/438, December 19, 1944.

379 "Paradoxically, British influence on Resistance in Europe": CAC, Deakin Papers, *A Note on Resistance* MS, DEAK16, p. 25.

380 "He wished and believed it possible to bring about a situation": War Cabinet paper, quoted in Mackenzie, p. 612.

381 "Only in the USSR did German counter-terror fail": Mazower, *Hitler's Empire*, p. 485.

381 "It was only just worth it": To the author, interview, March 4, 1980.

381 "The game was not worth pursuing": Mackenzie, p. 483.

381 Gubbins was even rash enough: Astley and Wilkinson, p. 202.

382 "Moreover, in our desire to attack the Germans": Macmillan, p. 545, October 9, 1944.

382 "gave a damning account": Colville, p. 581, April 3, 1945.

382 "The occupied nations believed with passion": CAC, Deakin Papers, DEAK16, p. 24.

382 "If war, carried out": Thomas Arnold, *Lectures on Modern History* (Longman, 1874), pp. 160–61.

383 David Reynolds notes the remarkable fact that: Reynolds, *In Command*, p. 175.

383 " 'Setting Europe ablaze' had proved a damp squib": Ibid., p. 176.

CHAPTER SEVENTEEN: OVERLORD

384 "It's not the hard work, it's the hard worry": Dalton, p. 714, April 29, 1944.

384 "Spirits remain at a low level": BNA, INF1/293.

384 "Considerable disquiet": Nicholas, ed., p. 345.

385 "We discussed . . . how best": Brooke, p. 533, March 21, 1944.

385 "Until the invasion": USAMHI, Carlisle, OCMH Forrest Pogue notes of 1947 interview with Morgan for *The Supreme Command*.

386 "Difficulties again with our American": Brooke, p. 537, April 5, 1944.

386 "This battle has been forced upon us": Cadogan, p. 621, April 19, 1944.

386 "preferred to roll up Europe from the south-east": BNA, CAB99/28.

386 "Struck by how very tired and worn out": Colville, p. 484, April 12, 1944.

386 "In my view, it is the Germans": Kimball, 3:87, April 12, 1944.

388 So skilful were German disengagements: See, for instance, Atkinson, *The Day of Battle*, passim.

389 "How magnificently your troops have fought": Kimball, 3:163, June 4, 1944.

389 "Lots of Americans and British": Gunther, p. 59.

389 "a place that has long been vacant": Mr. T. Bowman, *Times* (London), May 30, 1942.

391 "A man who has to play": Churchill, *Second World War*, 5:551.

391 "Winston . . . has taken his train": Brooke, p. 553, June 4, 1944.

392 "Mr. Churchill seemed to be always in the bath": Eden, p. 452, June 4, 1944.

392 "Cheap at the price": Ibid., p. 454.

392 "Yes, there'll be a landing": Djilas, *Wartime*, p. 39.

394 "Don't look so glum": Pogue, *Marshall: Organizer of Victory*, p. 394.

394 "We are surrounded by fat cattle": Brooke, p. 557, June 12, 1944.

395 "The PM asked if I were frightened": Holmes diary, quoted in Gilbert, *Road to Victory*, p. 813.

395 "[Churchill] was at his best, and said the matter": Cunningham diary, quoted in ibid.

395 "I do hope it will soon": IWM, Papers of Mrs. E. Elkus, letter of September 2, 1944.

395 "He kept on repeating": Brooke, p. 563, June 27, 1944.

395 "Sitting in the drawing-room": Macmillan, p. 474, June 25, 1944.

396 "We have now reached the stage": Brooke, p. 581, August 15, 1944.

396 "Whatever the PM's shortcomings": Colville, p. 489, May 13, 1944.

396 "By July, the American soldier": USAMHI, Carlisle, OCMH Forrest Pogue notes of January 21, 1947, interview with Alan Moorehead for *The Supreme Command*.

CHAPTER EIGHTEEN: BARGAINING WITH AN EMPTY WALLET

398 Roosevelt sent him a headmasterly rebuke: Kimball, 3:201, June 22, 1944.
398 "I cannot think of any moment": Ibid., 3:202, June 23, 1944.
399 "Whether we should ruin all hopes": Ibid., p. 219, June 28, 1944.
399 "My interests and hopes": Ibid., pp. 222–23, June 24, 1944.
400 "What can I do, Mr. President": Ibid., p. 229, July 1, 1944.
400 "The Arnold-King-Marshall combination is one of the stupidest": PM's personal minute to CoS, D.218/4, quoted in Gilbert, *Road to Victory*, p. 843, July 6, 1944.
400 "Up till Overlord": Colville, p. 574, March 20, 1945.
400 "Up to July 1944 England": Moran, July 5, 1954.
400 "After dinner a really ghastly defence committee": Eden, p. 461, July 6, 1944.
402 "A frightful meeting with Winston": Brooke, p. 566, July 6, 1944.
402 "I called this 'a deplorable evening' ": Eden, p. 462, July 6, 1944.
402 "He is very tight": Dalton, p. 473, April 29, 1944.
403 "Lunched alone with W": Eden, p. 463, July 17, 1944.
403 On 4 August, when Eden called: Ibid., p. 467, August 4, 1944.
403 "he was *far* more law-abiding": Brooke, p. 673, March 23, 1945.
403 "Of course it was true that the Germans": BNA, CAB79/77.
404 "We know that such 'right-minded people' ": Howard, *Liberation or Catastrophe*, p. 75.
404 "There is no doubt": BNA, FO371/42809.
404 An intelligence officer: See Richard Breitman, *Official Secrets* (Penguin, 1999), p. 216.
406 "This seems to be the best ever": Kimball, 3:261, July 29, 1944.
408 "After all, he is a frustrated man": CAC, Randolph Churchill to Winston Churchill, Churchill Papers, CHAR1/381/42-44, August 11, 1944.
408 "I feel that de Gaulle's France will be a France more hostile": Soames, ed., *Speaking*, p. 501, August 17, 1943.
408 "They did not know that if I had had my way": Churchill, *Second World War*, 5:84.
409 "The English are clever": Djilas, p. 401.
409 "all spread along twenty miles of coast": Soames, ed., *Speaking*, p. 500, August 17, 1944.
410 "I feel sure this is a secondary": IWM, diary of W. A. Charlotte, 93/19/1.
410 "fooling about in Italy": Harvey, p. 355, August 26, 1944.
410 David Reynolds notes: Reynolds, *In Command*, p. 395.
410 "The PM can be counted on to score": Colville, p. 595, May 1, 1945.
410 "Our Cabinet meetings certainly get more": Amery, p. 994 (August 9, 1944) and p. 1020 (November 23, 1944).
411 "Churchill is preoccupied by his own": Berlin, pp. 13, 15.
411 "I do not consider it advantageous": Kimball, 3:296.
411 "old, unwell and depressed": Brooke, p. 589, September 8, 1944.
411 "gargantuan in scale": Colville, p. 509, September 6, 1944.
412 The prime minister said that he would not regret: Ibid.
412 "All he could now do was to finish the war": Colville, p. 510, September 7, 1944.
412 Earlier that year, Churchill: Brooke, p. 525, February 25, 1944.
412 "high political consequences, but also has serious military potentialities": Churchill to Chiefs of Staff, September 9, 1944.
414 Brendan Bracken dismissed him: Colville, p. 555, January 23, 1945.
414 Yet there is no reason to suppose: BNA, FO371/38550/AN4451.
414 "my illusions about the French": Colville, p. 517, September 20, 1944.

416 "The affairs go well": Soames, ed., *Speaking*, p. 306, October 13, 1944.

417 "We fucked this England!": Chuev, p. 75.

417 "Our lot from London are, as Your Majesty knows": BNA, CAB120/165.

418 "The Poles' game is up": Moran, p. 249, October 17, 1943.

418 "Far quicker than the British": CAC, Deakin Papers, DEAL16, p. 14.

419 "You must remember . . . that our armies": BNA, PREM4/337/23, December 3, 1944.

420 "How much depends on this man": Headlam, p. 435, December 13, 1944.

420 "He oughtn't to do it": Nicolson, p. 406, October 9, 1944.

420 "He is not of course": Ibid., p. 352, February 22, 1944.

420 "The upper classes feel that all this sacrifice": Ibid., p. 356, March 27, 1944.

420 "Winston Churchill is a bastard": Ibid., p. 347, February 7, 1944.

420 "Collins, I should like a whisky and soda": Ibid., pp. 408–9, October 27, 1944.

421 "completely frozen": Brooke, p. 625, November 13, 1944.

421 "[He] is fighting for the future of the world": *Spectator*, November 24, 1944.

CHAPTER NINETEEN:
ATHENS: "WOUNDED IN THE HOUSE OF OUR FRIENDS"

423 "It is good that there is one country": Eden, October 26, 1944.

424 "Despite Churchill's belief": Mazower, *Inside Hitler's Greece*, p. 352.

424 "My darling Winston": Soames, ed., *Speaking*, p. 507, December 4, 1944.

425 "We expect the Italians to work out their own problems": Foreign Relations of the United States, *Conferences at Washington, 1942*, 3:1162.

425 " 'Liberal' papers, pleading for a greater representation": USNA, RG59, Box 11, State Department Surveys of Public Opinion on International Affairs, 1943–1975.

426 "Substantially universal approval has greeted the proposition": USNA, RG59, Box 11, Survey No. 17, December 23, 1944.

426 "seeking to bury": Ibid.

426 A Princeton poll: USNA, RG59, Box 11, Princeton Poll, December 23, 1944.

426 "Winston Churchill, the present": *Tribune*, December 1944.

427 "This is good": Churchill to Eden, November 23, 1944.

427 "at its best was one of distressed": Nicolson, p. 416, December 8, 1944.

427 "He rambled on": Macmillan, p. 600, December 8, 1944.

429 "Our version of the facts is largely disbelieved": BNA, CAB121/559.

429 "We do not wish to start the Third World War": Macmillan, p. 612, December 19, 1944.

429 "These ELAS guerillas don't care": IWM, 06/110/1, letter of January 7, 1945.

430 "but I think the bulk of Greek youth wants socialism": IWM, 86/61/1, letters of December 5 and 12, 1944, and February 5, 1945.

430 "Poor Winston!": Macmillan, December 21, 1944, p. 613.

430 "I won't instal a Dictator": Cadogan, p. 689, December 21, 1944.

431 "Indignation with Britain has given way": Nicholas, p. 481, December 24, 1944.

431 "Glad I am not going on an expedition": CAC, Martin Papers, MART/2, December 24, 1944.

431 "had the air of men to whom a brilliant idea": Osbert Lancaster, *Spectator*, November 12, 1965.

432 "in a most mellow, not to say chastened mood": Macmillan, p. 616, December 25, 1944.

432 "struck me as a very remarkable man": Hansard, January 18, 1945.

432 "We are now in the curious": Colville, p. 540, December 26, 1944.

432 "the pink and ochre panorama of Athens": Hansard, January 18, 1945.

432 "One can see the smoke of battle": Colville, p. 540, December 26, 1944.

432 "The change in his appearance": Lancaster, *Spectator*, November 12, 1965.

433 "three shabby desperados": Colville, p. 541, December 26, 1944.

433 "after some consideration I shook": Soames, ed., *Speaking*, p. 509, December 26–27, 1944.

434 "I thought it all very disingenuous": Macmillan, p. 619, December 26, 1944.

434 "I cannot tell you the feeling of security one enjoys": Lancaster, *Spectator*, November 12, 1965.

434 "Sit down, butcher!": Macmillan, p. 619, December 27, 1944.

434 "Of course this affair is a sort of 'super Sidney Street' ": Ibid.

435 "This Wednesday has been an exciting": Soames, ed., *Speaking*, p. 509, December 28, 1944.

435 "a short crack followed by": Lancaster, *Spectator*, November 12, 1965.

436 "Anglo-American differences and British military action": USNA, RG59, Box 11, State Department Surveys of Public Opinion on International Affairs, 1943–1975.

437 "an orgy of recrimination": USNA, RG59, Box 11, p. 500, January 21, 1945.

437 "The general reaction is that although the British attack": Nicholas, p. 494, January 7, 1945.

437 Office of War Information and State Department surveys: USNA, RG59, Box 11, Survey No. 22.

437 "Despite recent press comment sympathetic to the British": USNA, RG59, Box 11, State Department Surveys of Public Opinion on International Affairs, 1943–1975, No. 19.

438 "Terrible Cabinet, first on Greece": Eden, p. 506, January 12, 1945.

438 "You know I cannot give you": Quoted in Gilbert, *Road to Victory*, p. 1138.

438 "France cannot masquerade as a Great Power": Churchill to Eden, January 19, 1945.

438 "You wouldn't like my job": Holmes diary, January 14, 1945, quoted in Gilbert, *Road to Victory*, p. 1148.

438 "In all his moods": Holmes letter to Gilbert, February 12, 1985, quoted in ibid.

439 "It is a mistake to try to write out": Churchill to Eden, January 4, 1945.

440 "Smuts and I are like two old love-birds": Colville, p. 553, January 17, 1945.

440 "Why are we making a fuss": BNA, FO954/26/382.

440 "Make no mistake, all the Balkans": Colville, p. 555, January 23, 1945.

440 "Let us think no more of Hitlee": Ibid., p. 554, January 20, 1945.

CHAPTER TWENTY: YALTA

441 "As the purely military problems": Harvey, p. 365, November 11, 1944.

441 "I have great hopes of this conference": Hansard, January 18, 1945.

442 "Impossible even to get near basics": Eden, p. 511, February 2, 1945.

442 "What a hole I've brought you to!": Holmes diary, February 3, 1945, quoted in Gilbert, *Road to Victory*, p. 1172.

442 "A terrible party, I thought": Eden, p. 512, February 4, 1945.

443 "Big Three": *New York Times*, February 4, 1945.

443 "During the past year, Britain": USNA, RG59, Box 1, Opinion Studies, Special Poll, March 22, 1945.
444 "We had the world at our feet": Quoted in Gilbert, *Road to Victory*, p. 1174.
444 "Our guards compared Churchill to a poodle": Beria, p. 137.
444 "What a crook that man must be": Chuev, p. 76.
444 Soviet eavesdroppers laughed heartily: Beria, p. 138.
445 "It has gone to my heart": CAC Martin Papers, MART2.
445 "I do not suppose that at any moment in history": Sarah Churchill, *Keep on Dancing*, pp. 75–76.
445 "I am free to confess to you": Soames, ed., *Speaking*, p. 512, February 1, 1945.
446 "We must do what we can": BNA, CAB120/170.
448 "followed so swiftly on the heels": BNA, PREM4/77/1B/359.
449 "even if we go to the verge of war": Colville, p. 566, February 28, 1945.
449 He voiced aloud his fear: Ibid., p. 562, February 23, 1945.
449 "he had never been more distressed": Brooke, p. 665, February 22, 1945.
449 "Churchill wants a bourgeois Poland": Zhukov, 3:216.
449 "We see unprecedented unanimity": *Pravda*, February 18, 1945.

CHAPTER TWENTY-ONE: THE FINAL ACT

450 "I cannot agree that we are confronted": Kimball, 3:568.
452 "calculated to hasten the disintegration": BNA, PREM3/12/2, April 20, 1945.
453 "In the full tilt of war": Browne, p. 248.
453 Portal had advocated heavy bombing of Rome: BNA, AIR8/436.
456 "It was a relief to get Winston home": Brooke, p. 678, March 26, 1945.
456 "I'm an old man and I work hard": Leslie, pp. 142–43.
456 "The PM is now becoming": Colville, p. 592, April 24, 1945.
457 "What do you think?": Zhukov, 3:224.
457 "His vanity was astonishing": Colville, April 26, 1945.
457 "I have been much disturbed at the misunderstanding": April 29, 1945.
458 "I fear terrible things have happened": BNA, FO954/20.
459 "We have moved a long way": Moran, p. 277, February 7, 1945.
459 "I hoped that they would raise their glasses": Ismay, p. 394.
459 "I can't feel thrilled, my main sensation": Brooke, p. 688, May 7, 1945.
459 "There is no doubt that the public has never understood": Ibid., p. 689, May 8, 1945.
460 "Without him England was lost for a certainty": Ibid., p. 590, September 10, 1944.
461 "in which case there was always a possibility": Colville, p. 128.
461 "the significance of the link-up of the Red Army": *Pravda*, April 29, 1945.
462 "From the present point of view": BNA, FO954/26c.
462 "Winston delighted, he gives me": Brooke, p. 690, May 13, 1945.
462 "Russian bear sprawled over Europe": Ibid., p. 693, May 24, 1945.
462 "We received reliable information": Zhukov, 3:322.
463 "The overall or political object is to impose upon Russia": BNA, CAB120/691.
464 "The idea is of course fantastic": Brooke, p. 693, May 24, 1945.
464 "again discussed the 'unthinkable war'": Ibid., p. 695, May 31, 1945.
465 "In the attached report": Ibid.
466 In London, the Unthinkable file was taken: BNA, FO954/26c.

467 On July 3, 1940, the American general: Lee, p. 10, July 3, 1940.

467 "It would be the highest honour": Eden, p. 522, February 16, 1945.

467 "There are . . . many who think that this war": Stebbing, November 27, 1940, quoted in Garfield, p. 24.

467 "It is clear that the Churchill government": *Wall Street Journal*, December 13, 1944.

467 "[I am] in the throes of a mental political upheaval": Mayhew, ed., pp. 234–35.

468 "Well, Prime Minister, I know one thing": Quoted in Levin, *Standardbearer*, p. 246.

468 "They have saved this country": Colville, p. 433, August 30, 1941.

468 "We have been the dreamers": Foot, p. 505.

468 "One of the most extraordinary things": IWM, Papers of Mrs. E. Elkus.

468 "a jingo election which is terrifying": Harvey, p. 383, June 10, 1945.

469 "I won't have it . . . I must have": Moran, p. 319, July 10, 1945.

471 "Churchill was extraordinarily angry": Rzheshevsky, pp. 519–24.

472 "My hate had died with their surrender": Churchill, *Second World War*, 6:545.

472 "I shall be only half a man": Moran, p. 313, July 8, 1945.

473 "I respect the old man, but he is difficult": Zhukov, 3:325.

474 "He had absorbed all the minor American": Brooke, p. 709, July 23, 1945.

475 During an Allied reception: Zhukov, 3:336.

475 "He is again under Stalin's spell": Eden, July 17, 1945.

475 "Of all the western leaders Churchill": Beria, p. 135.

476 "a lot of people talked a lot of nonsense": Colville, p. 273, October 22, 1940.

476 "no one in our conference delegation": Kumanyov, p. 303.

476 "I still cannot comprehend": Chuev, p. 85.

476 "You must not think of me any more": Wheeler-Bennett, *Action*, p. 262.

477 "The rest of my life will be holidays": Moran, p. 353, July 27, 1945.

477 he contributed about £35: CAC, Churchill Papers, CHAR1/379/12-20.

477 "Winston's mind has a stop in it": Eden, p. 350, November 9, 1942.

477 "I do not believe in this brave new world": Moran, p. 224, September 20, 1943.

478 "Churchill sees history—and life": Berlin, pp. 4, 12.

478 "After it was over I was on my way": Eden, p. 551, July 27, 1945.

479 "Why don't you tell them to go to hell?": Nicolson, p. 238, August 7, 1942.

479 "No, I am a privileged domestic": Kennedy diary, LHA, February 16, 1941.

479 "He would no more think of consulting a party": Gardiner, *Prophets*, p. 234.

480 "Dull cabinet without PM": Brooke, p. 388, March 8, 1943.

480 "His countrymen have come to feel": Moran, p. 13, December 23, 1941.

481 "I should have liked my father": Mary Soames to the author, May 23, 2004.

Select Bibliography

The published literature on Winston Churchill is enormous. My own library includes more than a hundred titles by or about him, and over a thousand books on World War II, many of which have been marginally useful in writing this book. It seems meaningless, however, to catalogue them all. The list below details only works extensively consulted or explicitly quoted in my own text.

Addison, Paul. *Churchill on the Home Front, 1900–1955*. Cape, 1992.
Aglan, Alya. *La Résistance sacrifiée: Le Mouvement Libération-Sud 1940–1944*. Flammarion, 1999.
Ambrose, Stephen. *Eisenhower: The Soldier*. Allen & Unwin, 1984.
Amery, Leo. *The Empire at Bay: The Leo Amery Diaries, 1929–1945*. Edited by John Barnes and David Nicolson. Hutchinson, 1988.
Andrews, Christopher, and Oleg Gordievsky. *KGB*. Hodder & Stoughton, 1990.
Annan, Noel. *Changing Enemies*. HarperCollins, 1995.
Astley, Joan Bright. *The Secret Circle: A View of War at the Top*. Hutchinson, 1971.
Astley, Joan Bright, and Peter Wilkinson. *Gubbins and SOE*. Leo Cooper, 1993.
Atkinson, Rick. *An Army at Dawn*. Henry Holt, 2004.
———. *The Day of Battle*. Henry Holt, 2007.
Attlee, Clement. *As It Happened*. Viking, 1954.
Bailey, Roderick. *The Wildest Province*. Cape, 2008.
———, ed. *Forgotten Voices of the Secret War*. Ebury Press, 2008.
Barclay, George. *Fighter Pilot*. William Kimber, 1976.
Barker, Elisabeth. *Churchill and Eden at War*. Macmillan, 1978.
Barnett, Correlli. *The Desert Generals*. Allen & Unwin, 1983.
———. *The Audit of War*. Macmillan, 1986.
Bayly, Christopher, and Tim Harper. *Forgotten Armies: The Fall of British Asia, 1941–45*. Penguin, 2004.
Beaumont, Joan. *Comrades in Arms*. Davis-Poynter, 1980.
Bellamy, Chris. *Absolute War*. Macmillan, 2007.
Bennett, Ralph. *Ultra and Mediterranean Strategy*. Hamish Hamilton, 1989.
Beria, Sergo. *My Father Beria: In the Corridors of Stalin's Regime* (Moi oets Beriya: V koridorakh stalinskoi vlasti). Moscow, 2002.
Berlin, Isaiah. *Personal Impressions*. Hogarth Press, 1980.
Best, Geoffrey. *Churchill: A Study in Greatness*. Hambledon, 2001.
———. *Churchill and War*. Hambledon, 2005.

Billotte, Pierre. *Le Temps des Armes*. Plon, 1972.

Birkenhead, The Earl of. *Halifax: The Life of Lord Halifax*. Hamish Hamilton, 1965.

Blum, John Morton. *Years of War, 1941–1945: From the Morgenthau Diaries*. Houghton Mifflin, 1977.

Bohlen, Charles E. *Witness to History, 1929–1969*. Norton, 1973.

Bond, Brian. *Liddell Hart: A Study of His Military Thought*. Cassell, 1977.

Bonham Carter, Violet. *Champion Redoubtable: The Diaries of Violet Bonham Carter*. Edited by Mark Pottle. Weidenfeld & Nicolson, 1998.

Boswell, James. *The Life of Samuel Johnson*. Everyman, 2004.

Brendon, Piers. *Winston Churchill: An Authentic Hero*. Methuen, 1984.

Broad, Richard, and Suzie Fleming. *Nella Last's War*. Sphere, 1983.

Brooke, Alan. *War Diaries, 1939–1945: Field Marshal Lord Alanbrooke*. Edited by Alex Danchev and Daniel Todman. Weidenfeld & Nicolson, 2001.

Browne, Anthony Montague. *Long Sunset: Memoirs of Winston Churchill's Last Private Secretary*. Cassell, 1995.

Bryant, Arthur. *The Turn of the Tide*. Collins, 1957.

———. *Triumph of the West*. Collins, 1959.

Butcher, Harry C. *Three Years with Eisenhower*. Heinemann, 1946.

Butler, J. R. M. *Grand Strategy*, Vol. 2. HMSO, 1957.

———. *Grand Strategy*, Vol. 3, Parts 1 and 2. HMSO, 1964.

Cadogan, Alexander. *The Diaries of Sir Alexander Cadogan*. Edited by David Dilks. Cassell, 1971.

Calder, Angus. *The People's War*. Cape, 1986.

Carlton, David. *Churchill and the Soviet Union*. Manchester University Press, 2000.

Chandos, Lord (Oliver Lyttelton). Bodley Head, 1962.

Channon, Henry. *Chips: The Diaries of Sir Henry Channon*. Edited by Robert Rhodes James. Weidenfeld & Nicolson, 1967.

Charmley, John. *Churchill: The End of Glory*. Harcourt Brace, 1993.

———. *Churchill's Grand Alliance: The Anglo-American Special Relationship, 1940–1957*. Harcourt Brace, 1995.

Chuev, Feliks. *140 Conversations with Molotov* (Sto sorok besed s Molotovym). Terra, 1991.

Churchill, Sarah. *Keep On Dancing*. Weidenfeld & Nicolson, 1981.

Churchill, Winston S. *The World Crisis*, 2 vols. Odhams, 1927.

———. *Speeches, 1938–45*. 5 vols. Vol. 1 edited by Randolph Churchill. Vols. 2–5 edited by Charles Eade. Cassell, 1941–45.

———. *The Secret Session Speeches*. Edited by Charles Eade. Cassell, 1946.

———. *The Second World War*. 6 vols. Cassell, 1948–54.

———. *Great Contemporaries*. Leo Cooper, 1990.

———. *My Early Life*. Touchstone, 1999.

Clarke, Peter. *The Cripps Version*. Allen Lane, 2002.

Clausewitz, Carl von. *On War*. Edited by Michael Howard and Peter Paret. Princeton, 1976.

Colville, John. *The Fringes of Power: Downing Street Diaries, 1939–1955*. Hodder & Stoughton, 1985.

Court, W. H. B. *Coal*. Longman, 1951.

Craig, Norman. *The Broken Plume*. IWM, 1982.

Cunningham, Andrew Browne. *A Sailor's Odyssey*. Hutchinson, 1951.

Dalton, Hugh. *The War Diaries of Hugh Dalton*. Edited by Ben Pimlott. Cape, 1986.

Danchev, Alex. *Very Special Relationship: Field Marshal Sir John Dill and the Anglo-American Alliance*. Brasseys, 1986.

Davie, Michael, and Anne Chisholm. *Beaverbrook*. Hutchinson, 1992.

Davis, Kenneth S. *FDR: The War President*. Random House, 2000.

de Gaulle, Charles. *War Memoirs*. Vol. 1, *Call to Honour, 1940–42*. Collins, 1955.

———. *War Memoirs*. Vol. 2, *Unity, 1942–44*. Weidenfeld & Nicolson, 1959.

D'Este, Carlo. *Fatal Decision: Anzio and the Battle for Rome*. HarperCollins, 1991.

———. *Eisenhower: A Soldier's Life*. Henry Holt, 2002.

———. *Warlord: Winston Churchill at War, 1878–1945*. Harper, 2008.

Djilas, Milovan. *Wartime*. Secker & Warburg, 1980.

Dokumenty Vneshnei Politiki, 1940–22.12.41. Moscow, 1999.

Dykes, Vivian. *Establishing the Anglo-American Alliance: The Second World War Diaries of Brigadier Vivian Dykes*. Edited by Alex Danchev. Brassey's, 1990.

Eden, Anthony. *The Eden Memoirs: The Reckoning*. Cassell, 1965.

Ehrman, John. *Grand Strategy*. Vols. 5 and 6. HMSO, 1956.

Eisenhower, Dwight David. *The Papers of Dwight David Eisenhower*. Vol. 1, *The War Years*. Edited by Alfred D. Chandler, Jr. Johns Hopkins, 1970.

Ellis, L. F. *The War in France and Flanders*. HMSO, 1953.

Elmhirst, Sir Thomas. *Recollections*. Privately published, 1991.

Fisk, Robert. *In Time of War*. Andre Deutsche, 1983.

Fleming, Peter. *Invasion 1940*. Hart-Davis, 1957.

Foot, Michael. *Bevan*. McGibbon & Kee, 1962.

Foreign Relations of the United States. *The Conferences at Malta and Yalta, 1945*, Washington, D.C., 1955.

———. *The Conferences at Cairo and Tehran, 1943*. Washington, D.C., 1961.

———. *The Conferences at Washington, 1942*. Vol. 3. Washington, D.C., 1961.

———. *The Conferences at Washington, 1941–1942, and Casablanca, 1943*. Washington, D.C., 1968.

———. *The Conferences at Washington and Quebec, 1943*. Washington, D.C., 1970.

———. *The Conference at Quebec, 1944*. Washington, D.C., 1972.

Fraser, David. *Alanbrooke*. Collins, 1997.

French, David. *Raising Churchill's Army*. Oxford, 2000.

Gardiner, A. G. *Prophets, Priests and Kings*. London, 1914.

———. *The Pillars of Society*. Dent popular edition, 1916.

Garfield, Simon. *Private Battles: How the War Almost Defeated Us*. Ebury, 2006.

Gibb, Andrew. *With Winston Churchill at the Front*. Gowans & Gray, 1924.

Gilbert, Martin. *Finest Hour: Winston S. Churchill, 1940–41*. Heinemann, 1983.

———. *Road to Victory: Winston S. Churchill, 1942–45*. Heinemann, 1986.

———. *Never Despair: Winston S. Churchill, 1945–1965*. Heinemann, 1988.

———. *Churchill: A Life*. 8 vols. Henry Holt, 1991.

———. *The Churchill War Papers*. 3 vols. Heinemann, 1993–2000.

———. *In Search of Churchill*, John Wiley, 1994.

Gildea, Robert. *Resistance, Reprisals and Community in Occupied France*. Transactions of the Royal Historical Society, 6th series, 2003, pp. 163–85.

Golovanov, Alexander. *The Long-Range Bomber Force: Memoirs of the Chief Marshal of Aviation*. Tsentrpoligraf, 2007.

Gunther, John. *D-Day*. Hamish Hamilton, 1944.

Haffner, Sebastian. *Churchill*. Haus, 2003.

Hammond, Nicholas. *Venture into Greece*. William Kimber, 1983.

Harriman, W. Averell, and Elie Abel. *Special Envoy to Churchill and Stalin, 1941–1946*. Random House, 1975.

Harris, Sir Arthur. *Bomber Offensive*. Collins, 1947.

Harrison, Mark, ed. *The Economics of World War II*. Cambridge, 1998.

Hartwell, Lord. *William Camrose: Giant of Fleet Street.* Weidenfeld & Nicolson, 1992.

Harvey, Oliver. *The War Diaries of Oliver Harvey, 1941–1945.* Edited by John Harvey. Collins, 1978.

Hassett, William. *Off the Record with FDR.* Allen & Unwin, 1960.

Hastings, Max. *Bomber Command.* Michael Joseph, 1979.

———. *Das Reich: The 2nd SS Panzer Division's March to Normandy, June 1944.* Michael Joseph, 1981.

———. *Overlord: D-Day and the Battle for Normandy.* Michael Joseph, 1984.

———. *Armageddon: The Battle for Germany, 1944–45.* Macmillan, 2004.

———. *Nemesis: The Battle for Japan, 1944–45.* HarperCollins 2006.

Hastings, Max, with Len Deighton. *The Battle of Britain.* Rainbird, 1980.

Headlam, Cuthbert. *Parliament and Politics in the Age of Churchill and Attlee: The Headlam Diaries, 1935–51.* Edited by Stuart Ball. Cambridge, 1999.

Hichens, Antony. *Gunboat Command.* Pen & Sword, 2007.

Higgins, Trumbull. *Winston Churchill and the Second Front. 1940–1943,* Oxford University Press, 1957.

Hinsley, F. H., et al. *British Intelligence in the Second World War.* 4 vols. HMSO, 1979–1990.

Hodgson, Vere. *Few Eggs and No Oranges: The Diaries of Vere Hodgson.* Persephone, 1999.

Holland, Jeffrey. *The Aegean Mission.* Greenwood Press, 1988.

Holmes, Richard. *In the Footsteps of Churchill.* BBC, 2006.

Horne, Alastair. *To Lose a Battle.* Macmillan, 1969.

Horsfall, John. *Say Not the Struggle.* Roundwood, 1977.

Howard, Michael. *Grand Strategy.* Vol. 4, *1942–43.* HMSO, 1972.

———. *British Intelligence in the Second World War.* Vol. 5, *Strategic Deception.* HMSO, 1990.

———. *Liberation or Catastrophe?: Reflections on the History of the Twentieth Century.* Continuum, 2007.

Hull, Cordell. *Memoirs of Cordell Hull.* Hodder & Stoughton, 1948.

Ickes, Harold L. *The Secret Diary of Harold L. Ickes.* Simon & Schuster, 1953–54.

Inman, P. *Labour in the Munitions Industries.* HMSO and Longmans, 1957.

Ironside, Lord. *The Ironside Diaries.* Edited by R. Macleod and D. Kelly. Constable, 1962.

Ismay, Lord. *The Memoirs of General the Lord Ismay.* Heinemann, 1960.

Jackson, Julian. *France: The Dark Years.* Oxford, 2001.

Jackson, Sir William, and Lord Bramall. *The Chiefs: The Story of the United Kingdom Chiefs of Staff.* Macmillan, 1992.

Jefferys, Kevin. *The Churchill Coalition and Wartime Politics.* Palgrave Macmillan, 1993.

Jenkins, Roy. *Churchill.* Macmillan, 2001.

———. *Franklin Delano Roosevelt.* Times Books, 2003.

Jones, R. V. *Most Secret War: British Scientific Intelligence, 1939–1945.* Hamilton, 1978.

Karslake, Basil. *The Last Act.* Leo Cooper, 1979.

Keegan, John. *Churchill.* Weidenfeld & Nicolson, 2002.

Kennedy, David. *Freedom from Fear: The American People in Depression and War, 1929–45.* Oxford, 1999.

Kennedy, Sir John. *The Business of War.* Hutchinson, 1957.

Kersaudy, François. *Churchill and de Gaulle.* Collins, 1981.

———. *Norway 1940.* Collins, 1990.

Kershaw, Ian. *Hitler: Hubris, 1889–1936.* Allen Lane, 1998.

———. *Hitler: Nemesis, 1936–45.* Allen Lane, 2000.

———. *Making Friends with Hitler.* Allen Lane, 2004.

———. *Fateful Choices: Ten Decisions That Changed the World, 1940–41.* Allen Lane, 2007.

Kimball, Warren, ed. *Churchill and Roosevelt: The Complete Correspondence.* 3 vols. Princeton, 1984.

Knight, Nigel. *Churchill Unmasked.* David & Charles, 2008.

Kumanyov, G. A. *Close to Stalin* (Ryadom so Stalinym). Moscow, 1999.

Kynaston, David. *A History of the City of London.* Vol. 3. Chatto & Windus, 1999.

Lacouture, Jean. *De Gaulle: The Rebel, 1890–1944.* Collins Harvill, 1990.

Langworth, Richard M., ed. *Churchill by Himself.* Ebury, 2008.

Lascelles, Sir Alan. *King's Counsellor: The Diaries of Sir Alan Lascelles.* Edited by Duff Hart-Davis. Weidenfeld & Nicolson, 2006.

Lash, Joseph P. *Roosevelt and Churchill, 1939–1941: The Partnership That Saved the West.* Norton, 1976.

Lavery, Brian. *Churchill Goes to War: Winston's Wartime Journeys.* Conwey, 2007.

Lawlor, Sheila. *Churchill and the Politics of War, 1940–41.* Cambridge, 1994.

Lee, Raymond. *The London Observer: The Diaries of General Raymond Lee, 1939–41.* Edited by James Leutze. Hutchinson, 1972.

Lees-Milne, James. *The Diaries of James Lees-Milne.* John Murray, 2007.

Leslie, Anita. *A Story Half Told.* Hutchinson, 1983.

Lewin, Ronald. *Slim: The Standardbearer.* Leo Cooper, 1977.

———. *The Chief.* Hutchinson, 1980.

———. *Churchill as Warlord.* Scarborough, 1982.

Lukacs, John. *The Duel: Hitler Versus Churchill.* Oxford, 1990.

———. *Five Days in London, May 1940.* Yale, 2001.

Lysaght, Charles Edward. *Brendan Bracken.* Allen Lane, 1979.

Mackenzie, William. *The Secret History of SOE.* St. Ermins Press, 2000.

Macmillan, Harold. *War Diaries.* Macmillan, 1984.

Martin, Sir John. *Downing Street: The War Years.* Bloomsbury, 1991.

Mayhew, Patrick, ed. *One Family's War.* Hutchinson, 1985.

Mazower, Mark. *Inside Hitler's Greece.* Yale. 1993.

———. *Hitler's Empire.* Penguin, 2008.

McLaine, Ian. *Ministry of Morale.* Allen & Unwin, 1979.

Meacham, Jon. *Franklin and Winston: Portrait of a Friendship.* Granta, 2004.

Menzies, Robert. *Dark Days: The Diaries of Robert Menzies.* Edited by A. W. Martin and Patsy Hardy. National Library of Australia, 1993.

Millburn, Clara. *Mrs. Millburn's Diaries.* Harrap, 1979.

Molony, C. J. C. *The Mediterranean and Middle East.* 6 vols. HMSO, 1973.

Moorehead, Alan. *African Trilogy.* Cassell, 1998.

Moran, Lord. *Winston Churchill: The Struggle for Survival, 1940–1965.* Constable, 1966.

Morgan, Sir Frederick E. *Overture to Overlord.* Doubleday, 1950.

Morgan, Ted. *Churchill, 1874–1915.* Cape, 1982.

———. *Franklin Roosevelt.* Simon & Schuster, 1992.

Mosley, Leonard. *Backs to the Wall: London Under Fire, 1939–45.* Weidenfeld & Nicolson, 1971.

Nel, Elizabeth. *Mr. Churchill's Secretary.* Hodder, 1958.

Nicholas, H. G., ed. *Washington Despatches.* Weidenfeld & Nicolson, 1981.

Nicolson, Harold. *The Diaries of Harold Nicolson, 1939–45.* Edited by Nigel Nicolson. Weidenfeld & Nicolson, 1967.

Ocherki Istorii Rossiikoi Vneshney Razvedki (Studies on the History of the Soviet Foreign Intelligence Service). Moscow, 2007.

Overy, Richard. *War and Economy in the Third Reich.* Oxford, 1995.

———. *Why the Allies Won.* Norton, 1997.

———. *Russia's War.* Penguin Press, 1998.

———. *The Dictators: Hitler's Germany and Stalin's Russia.* Norton, 2004.

Pauli, Kurt. *Von Serbien bis Kreta.* Steirische Verlagsanstatt, 1942.

Payne, Stanley G. *Franco and Hitler.* Yale, 2007.

Pickersgill, J. W., and D. F. Forster. *The Mackenzie King Record.* Vols. 1 and 2. University of Toronto, 1968.

Pile, Gen. Sir Frederick. *Ack-Ack: Britain's Defence Against Air Attack.* Harrap, 1949.

Pilipel, Robert H. *Churchill in America.* NEL, 1977.

Pogue, Forrest C. *The Supreme Command.* Washington, D.C., 1954.

———. *George C. Marshall: Education of a General, 1880–1939.* Viking, 1964.

———. *George C. Marshall: Ordeal and Hope, 1939–42.* Viking, 1965.

———. *George C. Marshall: Organizer of Victory, 1943–45.* Viking, 1973.

Porch, Douglas. *Hitler's Mediterranean Gamble.* Weidenfeld & Nicolson, 2004.

Portelli, Alessandro. "The Massacre of Civitella Val Di Chianti: Myth and Politics, Mourning and Common Sense," in *The Battle of Valle Giulia: Oral History and the Art of Dialogue.* Wisconsin, 1997.

Postan, M. M. *British War Production.* HMSO, 1952.

Potsdam Institute for the Study of Military History. *Germany and the Second World War* (9 volumes published in translation by Oxford 1990–2008).

Pownall, Henry. *Chief of Staff: The Diaries of Lieutenant-General Sir Henry Pownall.* Edited by Brian Bond. 2 vols. Leo Cooper, 1972, 1974.

Ramsden, John. *Man of the Century: Winston Churchill and His Legend since 1945.* HarperCollins, 2002.

Ray, John. *The Battle of Britain: New Perspectives.* Arms & Armour Press, 1994.

Reynolds, David. *The Creation of the Anglo-American Alliance, 1937–1941.* University of North Carolina Press, 1982.

———. *From World War to Cold War.* Oxford, 2002.

———. *In Command of History: Churchill Fighting and Writing the Second World War.* Penguin, 2004.

Reynolds, David, Warren F. Kimball, and A. O. Chubarian, eds. *Allies at War: The Soviet, American and British Experience, 1942–45.* Palgrave Macmillan, 1994.

Rhodes-James, Robert. *Churchill: A Study in Failure, 1900–39.* World, 1970.

Richards, Denis. *Portal of Hungerford.* Heinemann, 1977.

Richardson, Charles. *From Churchill's Secret Circle to the BBC: The Biography of Lieutenant General Sir Ian Jacob.* Brassey's, 1991.

Roberts, Andrew. *The Holy Fox: A Life of Lord Halifax.* Weidenfeld & Nicolson, 1991.

———. *Masters and Commanders.* Penguin, 2008.

Robinson, Derek. *Invasion 1940.* Constable, 2005.

Rodger, N. A. M. *The History of the Royal Navy.* Vol. 2. Penguin, 2005.

Rogers, Anthony. *Churchill's Folly.* Cassell, 2003.

Roosevelt, Elliott. *As He Saw It.* Duell, Sloan and Pearce, 1946.

Rose, Norman. *Churchill: An Unruly Life.* Simon & Schuster, 1995.

Roskill, Stephen. *The War at Sea.* 3 vols. HMSO, 1960.

———. *Hankey: Man of Secrets.* 3 vols. Collins, 1974.

———. *Churchill and the Admirals.* Collins, 1977.

Royal Historical Society Proceedings. *Record of the Churchill Conference at the Institute for Historical Research, January 2001.* Cambridge, 2001.

Rzheshevsky, O. A. *Stalin and Churchill: Meetings, Conversations, Discussions* (Stalin I Cherchil: Vstrechi, besedy, diskussi). Moscow, 2004.

Salter, Arthur. *Slave of the Lamp*. Weidenfeld & Nicolson, 1967.

Sayers, R. S. *Financial Policy, 1939–45*. HMSO, 1956.

Sebag-Montefiore, Hugh. *Dunkirk*. Penguin, 2006.

Sebastian, Mikhail. *Journal, 1935–44*. Heinemann, 2001.

Sheridan, Dorothy, ed. *Wartime Women*. Heinemann, 1990.

Sherwood, Robert. *The White House Papers of Harry L. Hopkins*. Vols. 1 and 2. Eyre & Spottiswoode, 1948.

———. *Roosevelt and Hopkins: An Intimate History*. Harper, 1950.

Slessor, Sir John. *The Central Blue*. Cassell, 1956.

Slim, Field Marshal Viscount. *Defeat into Victory*. Cassell, 1956.

Soames, Mary. *Clementine Churchill*. Cassell, 2002.

———, ed. *Speaking for Themselves: The Personal Letters of Winston and Clementine Churchill*. Doubleday, 1998.

Sokolov, Vladimir, and Pyotr Stegny. *Bridges and Barriers II, Rodina No. 5*. Moscow, 2003.

Stacey, C. P. *The Canadian Army, 1939–45*. E. Cloutier, 1955.

Stafford, David. *Roosevelt and Churchill*. Overlook Press, 2000.

Stanford, J. K. *Tail of an Army*. Phoenix House, 1966.

Strong, Kenneth. *Intelligence at the Top*. Cassell, 1968.

Sweet-Escott, Bickham. *Baker Street Irregular*. Methuen, 1965.

Taylor, A. J. P. *Beaverbrook*. Simon & Schuster, 1972.

Tedder, Lord. *With Prejudice*. Cassell, 1966.

Tendulkar, D. G. *Mahatma*. 5 vols. New Delhi, 1988.

Thompson, R. W. *Churchill and Morton*. Hodder & Stoughton, 1976.

Thorne, Christopher. *Allies of a Kind*. Hamish Hamilton, 1978.

Thurlow, Richard. *Fascism in Britain: A History, 1918–1985*. Oxford, 1987.

Titmuss, Richard. *History of the Second World War: Problems of Social Policy*. HMSO, 1950.

Tooze, Adam. *Wages of Destruction: The Making and Breaking of the German War Economy*. Allen Lane, 2006.

Trollope, Anthony. *Autobiography*. Trollope Society, 1999.

Trukhanovsky, V. G. *Winston Churchill* (Uinston Cherchil. Politicheskaya Biograpiya). Progress Publishers, 1978.

Wallace, Henry. *The Price of Vision: The Diary of Henry A. Wallace 1942–1946*. Edited by John Morton Blum. Houghton Mifflin, 1973.

Watt, D. C. *Succeeding John Bull*. Cambridge, 1980.

Waugh, Evelyn. *Men at Arms*. Chapman & Hall, 1952.

Wheeler-Bennett, Sir John. *John Anderson Viscount Waverley*. Macmillan, 1962.

———, ed. *Action This Day: Working with Churchill*. Macmillan, 1968.

Wieviorka, Olivier. *Une Certaine Idée de la Résistance: Défense de la France, 1940–1949*. Seuil, 1995.

Wilmot, Chester. *The Struggle for Europe*. Collins, 1952.

Wilson, Thomas. *Churchill and the Prof*. Cassell, 1995.

Winant, John G. *A Letter from Grosvenor Square*. Hodder and Stoughton, 1948.

Winfield, Ronald. *The Sky Belongs to Them*. Kimber, 1976.

Wrigley, Chris. *Churchill*. Haus, 2006.

Young, Kenneth. *Stanley Baldwin*. Weidenfeld & Nicolson, 1976.

Zhukov, G. K. *Vospominaniya i Razmyshlenita* (Memories and Reflections). 3 vols. Moscow, 1992.

Index

Page numbers in *italic* refer to maps.

Abbeville, *17*, 28, *29*, *35*
Abyssinia, 104, 105, 109, 120
Adam, Ronald, 345
Admiralty, British, 41, 123–4, 160, 174, 180, 183, 211, 300; Byng execution and, 223; Churchill's calls to, 83, 93, 124; Submarine Tracking Room of, 272
Admiralty House, 19, 24–5
Aegean campaign, 323–40, *328*, 342, 344, 346, 362, 386
Africa, 71, 100, 104–10; British colonies in, 33, 105; British successes in, 107, 109, 110, 113; French colonies in, 67; Italian colonies in, 104; *see also* North Africa; *specific countries*
Afrika Korps, 178, 270; British troops compared with, 220, 224, 256; institutional superiority of, 219; Italians in, 245; in Libya, 110, 114, 258, 320; Montgomery's campaign and, 272–5, *274–5*
"aid to Britain" committee, 63
aircraft industry, aircraft, 34, 40, 90, 142, 210, 441; British shortage of, 146; fighter vs. bomber production in, 71; Japanese, 235; in Operation Crusader, 178; sent to Soviets, 142, 171, 236, 261; strikes in, 8, 227, 384; from U.S., 147
Aircraft Production Ministry, British, 76, 278
Air Force, Italian, 80, 106
Air Force, U.S., 60
Air Ministry, British, 91, 453

Air Staff, British, 46, 380, 453
Ajax (British light cruiser), 432, 434
Alam Halfa, 270, 272
Albania, 105, 114, 372, 373, 417, 423, 424, 443
Albery, Irving, 21
Alexander, A. V., 19, 25–6
Alexander, Harold, 222, 250, 268, 272, 284, 299, 353–8, 472; appointed C-in-C Mediterranean, 354; appointed C-in-C Middle East, 258; celebrity of, 179, 249, 277; Churchill's correspondence with, 356; Churchill's relationship with, 302, 481; Greek policy and, 427, 429, 430, 433–4; Husky and, 309, 314; Italian campaign and, 315, 316, 354, 356, 357–8, 388, 390, 394, 409–10; Overlord and, 353; resistance movements and, 375, 376; Shingle and, 354, 356, 357–8; Tedder replaced with, 451; Yugoslavs and, 464, 469
Algeria, *276*, 307
Algiers, 271, *276*, 360, 361, 387, 392; Churchill in, 295, 307, 407–8; Darlan in, 280, 282
Allenby, Edmund, 105
Allied Control Commission, 360, 445, 463
Allied Expeditionary Force, 460
Allied Moscow Declaration (1943), 405
Allied Supplies Executive, 143
Allied Supreme War Council, 45, 48–51
All-Ireland Defence Force, 68

Amery, Julian, 252
Amery, Leo, 7, 105, 133, 199, 252, 271;
  on Cabinet meetings, 410–11; on
  Churchill, 13, 18, 19, 82, 193,
  214–15, 251, 271; on North African
  campaign, 273–4
Amiens, 26, 28, 29, 35
Anders, Wladyslaw, 265, 418, 449
Anderson, John, 122, 319, 359–60, 474
Anderson, Kenneth, 284
Anglo-American alliance, 3, 5–6, 36,
  457–8; Arcadia and, 183–97; Atlantic
  Charter and, 168, 170, 213, 214, 443;
  Casablanca conference and, 285–93;
  collaboration in, 389; Dill's role in,
  197; façade of unity in, 443; French
  policy and, 280–3; junior partner in,
  193; Operation Unthinkable and, 6;
  postwar domination and, 171; Soviet
  interference in, 266; Tehran
  conference and, 348–51; tensions in,
  362, 386–90, 399–400, 418–19,
  422–9; Trident and, 303–7
Anglo-Soviet agreement (1942), 235,
  237–8, 247
Annan, Noel, 374
anti-Americanism, 149–54, 163, 288–9,
  299–300
anti-British sentiment, 158, 159, 242–4,
  288, 289, 292, 425, 426, 428, 436
anti-Communism, 32, 133, 383
antitank weapons, 18, 64, 106, 143, 204,
  221, 223, 224, 256
Anzio, 310, 354–8, 387, 388
appeasement, appeasers, 18, 24, 31, 65,
  76, 94, 112
Arcadia, see Washington conference
  (Arcadia; 1941)
Archangel, 143, 144, 171, 212, 267, 268,
  300
Ardennes forest, 14, 17, 21, 444
Armageddon (Hastings), 8
Armée Secrète, 370, 371
Armstrong-Siddeley factory, 227
Army, Belgian, 17, 20, 26, 29, 30, 35
Army, British, 30, 56, 124, 135, 250, 346,
  419, 441, 461–4, 481–2; Bergen-
  Belsen liberated by, 452; in Berlin,
  473; in Brussels, 423; colonial
  reinforcements for, 25, 30; in Crete,
  117–19; Dill made head of, 77;
  dismal performance of, 4–5, 12–13,
  42, 88, 105, 114, 115, 118, 119, 122,
  124, 202, 203, 204, 217–26, 244–6,
  252, 256–7; failure to fight of, 135,
  142, 171, 225, 242, 244, 266, 299; in
  Far East, 198, 200, 203, 441; French's
  views on, 298; German Army
  compared with, 13, 15, 40, 57, 116,
  118–19, 203, 219, 220, 223–6, 245,
  251, 256, 309, 390; in Greece, 423,
  424, 426–30, 435; institutional
  culture and, 8, 175, 218, 258, 481;
  lack of peacetime conscription for,
  22; Norwegian deployment of,
  11–13, 21, 44; Overlord and, 309,
  311, 390, 394; post-Battle of France
  role of, 103–4; in proposed offensive
  against Soviets, 463–4; Red Army
  compared with, 220, 246–7, 263, 297,
  298; renewed esteem of, 277, 286;
  special forces in, 325–6, 330; U.S.
  Army compared with, 218, 220,
  396–7; U.S. view of, 194, 304; in
  World War I, 218, 221, 222; see also
  British Expeditionary Force; Eighth
  Army, British; specific troops
Army, Dutch, 17, 20
Army, French, 20, 22, 26, 27, 41, 53, 135;
  casualties of, 57; new, 422; see also
  specific armies
Army, German, 103, 171, 192, 297, 301;
  Allied use considered for, 462–3, 464;
  British Army compared with, see
  Army, British, German Army
  compared with; Dunkirk evacuation
  and, 43; invasion threat and, 66,
  69–70, 87–8; Italian campaign and,
  310, 316, 345, 353, 356, 357, 358,
  376, 388, 394; Overlord and, 309,
  314, 387, 390; in Sicily, 309, 312,
  314, 320, 325; U.S. Army compared
  with, 239; see also specific panzer
  divisions, army groups, and corps
Army, Italian, 104–5, 192, 304, 309, 320
Army, Japanese, 203, 219, 225, 347
Army, Soviet, see Red Army
Army, U.S., 60, 159, 171, 191, 194, 226,
  253, 266, 346, 390, 458, 461–4; anti-
  British feeling in, 244; British Army
  compared with, 218, 220, 396–7;
  D-Day and, 304; German Army

compared with, 239; Italian campaign and, *310*, 316, 318, 390; Overlord and, 394; proposed offensive against Soviets, 463–4; Red Army compared with, 297, 298; Torch and, 254, *276*, 277, 299; Wehrmacht compared with, 293

Army Air Forces, U.S. (USAAF), 166, 175, 212, 296, 324, 387, 404, 414, 454, 481

Army Group A, German, *17*, *35*, *43*, *86*

Army Group B, German, *17*, *35*

Army Group C, German, *17*

Arnhem, 415

Arnold, Henry "Hap," 166, 400, 454

Arnold, Thomas, 382–3

Arras, 26, 28, *29*, *35*

Ashford, Pam, 201, 219–20

Asia, 71, 237; *see also* Far East; *specific places*

Astor, Lady, 320

Athens, 8, 116, 375, 409, 422–40; Churchill in, 431–5, 448; Eden in, 423

Atlantic, 120–1, 187, 211; as British lifeline, 52, 67, 101, 109, 136; British shipping losses in, 106, 172, 187; French coast landings of, 387, 398, 407; merchantmen travel times in, 203–4

Atlantic, Battle of the, 127, 141, 169–70, 174, 175, 206, 210, 296, 297; code breaking in, 272

Atlantic Charter, 168, 170, 213, 214, 426, 443

Atlantic Wall, 87, 392, 393

atomic bomb, 259, 360, 473–4

Attlee, Clement, 19, 33, 40, 55, 122, 184, 205, 244, 272, 420; bombing policy and, 210; on Churchill, 102; Churchill's communications with, 190, 262, 263, 285, 288, 306, 440; elections and, 466, 472, 476; at Postdam conference, 472, 473, 476; Second Front and, 231

Auchinleck, Claude, 177–8, 217, 224, 241, 252, 256–8, 366; Churchill's problems with, 139, 166, 278; Churchill's sacking of, 257–8; Crusader and, 139, 178, 183, 188; El Alamein and, 273; Montgomery compared with, 274

Augusta (U.S. cruiser), 164, 166, 169

Auschwitz-Birkenau, 404, 405

Australia, 187, 198–9, 200, 204, 297, 385

Australian troops, 37, 114, 120, 199, 203, 283, 297, 385; in Tobruk, 129, 139

Austria, 458, 470

Badoglio, Pietro, 312, 409

Baku, 132, 183

Baldwin, Stanley, 12, 16, 46, 64, 93, 149, 155–6

Balfour, Arthur J., 155–6, 172

Balkans, 110, 111, 185, 293, 305, 313, 324, 339, 399, 410, 415–17, 419, 461; Allied activism in, 324, 331, 344, 345; collapse of monarchies in, 383; German withdrawal from, 422, 423; Hitler's defensive purpose in, 113–14; resistance movements in, 364, 370, 372–81; rise of Russian prestige in, 382; in World War I, 339; *see also specific places*

Baltic states, 184, 216, 234, 235, 458

Barclay, George, 75

Bardia, *108*, 109, 325

Barnett, Correlli, 273

Barry, Dick, 381

Baruch, Bernard, 152, 192

Bastille Day (1940), 71–2

Bataan Peninsula, 203, 266

BBC, 15, 33, 55, 85, 132–3, 137, 141, 147, 157, 170, 248, 360; foreign language broadcasts of, 366, 380

Beaufighters, 234, 324, 329, 331, 333, 334, 338

Beaumont, Joan, 235–6

Beaverbrook, Lord, 19, 24, 50, 76–7, 122, 172, 271, 440; Arcadia and, 184, 192, 194; Churchill's correspondence with, 71; Churchill's relationship with, 76–7, 80, 126, 132, 165, 184, 192, 234, 255, 319, 476; defeatism of, 99; as minister of supply, 141–4, 161, 200; resignation of, 200, 205, 233; Second Front and, 142, 233–5, 269, 308, 319; Soviet policy and, 141–4, 191, 233–5, 268

Beda Fomm, *108*, 109

Bedell Smith, Walter, 309

BEF, *see* British Expeditionary Force

Belgium, *17*, 55, 61, 113, 185, 405,
    422–3, 424, 436, 464; BEF in, 14,
    21–4, *29*; Germans in, 14, 15, 19, 21,
    29; government in exile of, 149, 422;
    resistance movements in, 366, 422;
    surrender of, 40; *see also* Army,
    Belgian
Bellamy, Chris, 144
Belsey, Elizabeth, 118, 134, 247, 320
Bengal famine, 199
Benghazi, *108*, 114
Bergen-Belsen, 452
Beria, Lavrenty, 140–1, 259–60, 450
Beria, Sergo, 349–50, 444, 475
Berlin, 451, 452, 456, 470, 472, 473;
    bombing of, 88–9, 343
Berlin, Isaiah, 38, 72, 411, 478
Bermuda, 34, 184, 363
Bernays, Rob, 9
Bevan, Aneurin, 61, 134, 205, 250–1,
    256, 278, 341, 427, 468
Beveridge, William, 201
Bevin, Ernest, 19, 69, 99, 100, 122, 227,
    322, 412; on Churchill's retirement,
    392; on need for victory, 244–5;
    postwar planning and, 341–2
Bevir, Tony, 125
Billancourt raid, 209
Birkenhead, F. E. Smith, Lord, 165
Bismarck (German battleship), 120–1,
    163, 164, 167, 208
Bizerta, *276*, 303
Black, Rosemary, 245
Blenheim Palace, 129, 155
Bletchley Park, 259; code breakers at, 6,
    78–9, 136, 137, 174, 206, 272, 300,
    336
Blunt, Anthony, 259
Blunt, Maggie Joy, 247, 270
Bock, Fedor von, *17*, 57
Boeing Clippers, 192–3, 255, 307
Boer War, 188, 203
Bohlen, Charles, 190, 351
Bolsheviks, Bolshevism, 16, 131, 235,
    301, 321
Bomber Command (Hastings), 8
bombing: area, 209–11, 451–5; precision,
    208, 405; terror and, 454; war crime
    and, 455; *see also specific places*
Bonham Carter, Violet, 201–2, 299
Boniface, 78, 272

Bonnier de la Chapelle, Fernand, 282
Bordeaux, 54, 381, *401*
Borrow, George, 34
Boulogne, 28, *29*, *35*
Bracken, Brendan, 19, 24, 46, 154, 155,
    158, 239, 275, 414, 440, 457;
    Churchill's relationship with, 126–7,
    476; on El Alamein, 272–3; Jones's
    correspondence with, 321–2
Bremen, bombing of, 209
Brest, 52, 53
Briare, 47–9
Bridges, Edward, 5, 19, 24, 125
Britain, Battle of (1940), 4, 27, 49, 58,
    74–99, 109, 120, 148, 175, 198, 343,
    461; Churchill's tactical interventions
    in, 77–8; first day of, 70, 75; Sealion
    in, *86*, 88
British Empire, 204, 362, 410, 457–8,
    459, 463, 482; *see also* Great Britain;
    specific places
British Expeditionary Force (BEF),
    21–34; in Battle of France, 8, 14, *17*,
    26–8, 30–4, *35*, 40–7, 51, 57, 58, 64;
    in Belgium, 14, 21–4, *29*; casualties
    of, 57; evacuation of, 8, 24, 26, 28,
    30, 31, 33, 34, 40–4, 46, 61, 64, 202;
    new (second), 8, 30, 41, 45–6, 47, 51,
    53–4, 65, 111
Brittany, 45, 47, 49, 51
Brittorous, Ben, 334
Brooke, Alan, 7, 9, 22, 56, 71, 82, 119,
    123, 135, 178–9, 197, 198, 218, 226,
    249, 252–5, 284, 297, 363, 389, 412,
    442, 443, 481; Aegean and, 331–2,
    334, 338–9; on army, 202, 222, 245,
    325; on atomic bomb, 473–4;
    becomes Home Forces C-in-C, 70; at
    Casablanca conference, 286–90; on
    Churchill, 89, 200, 204–5, 245, 271,
    278, 332, 341, 352–3, 385, 391, 396,
    402, 411, 420–1, 438, 456, 460, 462,
    473–4, 480; Churchill's
    correspondence with, 283;
    Churchill's relationship with, 279,
    302, 318, 362, 412, 481; considered
    as replacement for Auchinleck, 258;
    Dill replaced by, 178–9, 184, 194;
    gloom of, 270; Husky and, 309;
    invasion threat and, 87, 88; Italian
    campaign and, 316, 331, 332, 386,

398; on Julian Amery, 252; at meeting with Roosevelt, 240; Middle East travels and, 252, 255, 257, 258, 268; Montgomery's correspondence with, 274; on Morrison, 395; Overlord and, 317–18, 319, 391; at Potsdam conference, 473–4; at Quebec conference (1943), 314, 315, 317; return to France of, 46, 51; on Ritchie, 223; Sandys as viewed by, 126; second Dunkirk and, 8, 52, 53, 202; Second Front and, 230–3, 253, 254; Soviet policy and, 142–3, 246, 280, 301, 462, 463; Stalin-Churchill meeting and, 262, 264, 265; at Tehran conference, 349; Turkey visit of, 293, 294–5; on U.S. inconsistency, 311; VE Day and, 459–60; at Washington conference (1943), 305–7

Brooke, Benita, 179
Bruce, Stanley, 37
Bruneval, 207, 325
Brussels, *17*, 21, 149, 422–3
Buckingham Palace, 204, 273, 355
Buckmaster, Maurice, 370
Bulgaria, 415, 416, 458
Bulge, Battle of the (1944), 436, 438
Burgess, Guy, 259
Burma, 199, 289, 302, 303, 304, 352, 385, 407, 414–15, 469; Buccaneer and, 344, 347; cause of China and, 287, 362, 387–8, 412; likelihood of British loss of, 186, 204, 212
Burrows, Brocas, 268
Butler, R. A., 13, 40–1
Butler Education Act (1944), 410
Butt, David, 208, 453
Byng, John, 223
Byrd, Walter, 227–8

C-54 Skymaster, 431, 435
Cadogan, Alexander, 30, 191, 217, 338, 352, 386, 430; Atlantic Charter and, 168; on Churchill, 31, 37, 162, 206, 331; at Tehran conference, 350
Cairncross, John, 140, 259
Cairo, 221, 256–8, 268, 283–94, 295, 339–40, 352, 369, 377, 448; bilateral summit in (Sextant; 1943), 344–8,

350; Dill and Eden in, 106, 111–12, 114
Calais, 28, *29*, 30, 34, *35*
Campioni, Inigo, 326–7
Camrose, Lord, 172, 176, 461
Canada, 125, 187, 199, 247; Churchill in, 189–90, 191; troops from, 268, 390, 393
Carol, King of Romania, 438
Carthage, 307, 352–4
Casablanca, 271
Casablanca conference (Symbol; 1943), 285–93, 295, 296, 303, 311, 314, 323–4, 347
Caucasus, 132, 171, 261, 298
Cazalet, Victor, 216, 320
censorship, British postal, 244
Central War Rooms, 76, 80
Centre Task Force, British, *276*
Cetnik guerrillas, 294, 377, 378, 379
Chamberlain, Neville, 13, 19, 27, 32, 93, 112, 155–6, 172, 449; Battle of France and, 22, 24, 33, 37, 45, 46; Churchill's eulogy for, 97–8; death of, 79, 95, 97–8; fall of, 12, 16, 21, 25, 27, 43; German settlement advocated by, 40; Greek policy and, 105; House of Commons addressed by (May 7, 1940), 11–12; Irish policy of, 67, 68; peace making and, 94; as prime minister, 9, 11–12; Roosevelt rebuffed by, 25; Soviet policy and, 132
Channon, Henry "Chips," 16, 85
Charles I, King of England, 51–2
Chartwell, 26, 69–70, 477
Chemnitz, bombing of, 453
Chequers, 54, 71, 84, 92, 93–4, 96–7, 103, 110, 132, 363, 395–6, 431, 478; bombing threat at, 155; expenses at, 172–3, 477; security at, 54, 76; telephone calls at, 54, 83; visitors at, 157, 160, 170, 172, 173, 180, 210, 231, 235, 253–4, 374, 456, 479
Cherbourg Peninsula, 231
Cherwell, Frederick Lindemann, Lord, 27, 77, 168, 369, 413; bombing and, 208, 210–11; Churchill's relationship with, 126, 127, 177
Chiang Kai-shek, 303, 346, 419

Chiefs of Staff, British, 6, 11, 78, 87, 103, 104, 115, 122–5, 159, 222, 279, 362, 370, 451; Aegean and, 324, 334, 338; Anvil and, 385–6, 399; Arcadia and, 184, 186, 187, 190, 194; Battle of France and, 22, 25, 47, 55; Casablanca conference and, 285–90; Churchill's acrimonious relations with, 385; Churchill's first meeting with, 19–20; Churchill's guiding of, 311, 396; daily meetings of, 123; Dill's cable to, 204; Far East and, 202; future strategy paper of, 101; Greek policy and, 111; Husky and, 298–9, 303, 309; invasion of France and, 283, 303, 309, 311, 312, 345–6, 353–4, 361; invasion threat and, 34, 136; Italian campaign and, 354, 398, 399, 400; Jupiter and, 311, 361; in Malta, 345; Morgan's views on, 311–12; resignation considered by, 385; resistance groups and, 380, 381; Second Front and, 231, 239, 269; Soviet policy and, 136–7, 138, 141, 142, 146, 298, 412, 462–6; U.S. Chiefs compared with, 283; VE Day and, 459–60; at War Cabinet meetings, 122, 123; Washington conference and, 305

Chiefs of Staff, U.S., 139, 222, 240, 241, 296, 311, 340, 466, 473, 482; anti-British feeling of, 244; Arcadia and, 184, 187, 192, 196; Casablanca conference and, 285–90; invasion of France and, 263, 313; Italian campaign and, 399, 400; Shingle and, 356, 357; Torch and, 254

children, 70, 229

Childs, Marquis, 428

China, 242, 290, 299, 426, 473; Burma offensive and, 287, 362, 388, 412; Cairo conference and, 346; U.S. relations with, 303, 412, 419

Churchill, Clementine, 64, 77, 95, 100, 160, 165, 173, 200, 268, 312, 393, 395, 431, 440, 468, 469; Beaverbrook disliked by, 76, 234; in Carthage, 353; husband's communications with, 82–3, 102, 121, 185, 186, 257, 287, 339, 340, 408, 409, 416, 424, 433, 435, 445; in

Russia, 460; services provided to husband by, 483

Churchill, Jack, 152

Churchill, Jennie, 189

Churchill, Mary, 206, 312, 353, 363, 468, 481

Churchill, Randolph, 24–5, 225, 319, 344, 350, 352, 477; de Gaulle and, 407–8; father's correspondence with, 144–5, 169, 216, 363; marital problems of, 412; Yugoslav resistance and, 377–8

Churchill, Sarah, 344, 353, 445

Churchill, Winston Spencer: abundance of writing about, 3–4; ambition of, 19, 95, 312, 324; American behavioural traits of, 152; anti-Americanism attributed to, 153, 154; anxiety of, 416, 423, 438, 446; appearance of, 189, 256, 307, 355, 358, 386, 432–3; arrogance of, 5, 199–200; as averse to whistling, 185; as battlefield tourist, 407–10, 455–6; becomes prime minister, 4, 8, 12–13, 16, 19, 20, 25; bombing decisions and, 8, 186, 208–12, 249, 343, 404, 451–5; British people's relationship with, 4, 5, 62, 88, 89, 90, 94, 101, 133, 358; broadcasts to British of, 25, 26, 61, 71–2, 85, 116, 121, 132–3, 136, 141, 170, 202, 216, 245, 480; broadcast to Americans of, 162–3; changeability of, 16, 84, 105, 313; cigar smoking of, 14, 73, 165, 173, 184, 245, 293, 317, 341, 353; close calls of, 49–50, 307, 348; Cold War and, 6; confidence of, 24, 26, 30, 61, 78, 81, 89, 94, 102; courage of, 49, 85, 248; critics of, 5, 174, 197–217, 250, 251, 278, 319, 341–2, 396, 402, 436, 442, 445, 448; cronies' influence on, 126–8; as defence minister, 4, 13–14, 15, 18, 22, 103, 271; depression of, 202, 216, 358, 374, 411, 427; diplomatic role of, 5–6, 24, 431–6; discourtesy and intemperance of, 81–3, 122, 218, 481; drinking of, 165, 264, 288, 293, 317, 353, 402, 420, 421, 457; emotion of, 5, 44–5, 46, 75, 92, 355, 408; exhaustion of, 395–6, 402, 456; exuberance of, 9, 13,

44, 54, 71, 81, 107, 119, 342; fanciful ideas and projections of, 103, 136, 303, 312, 318, 362; finances of, 477; as first lord of the Admiralty, 12, 19, 67; flagging influence of, 400, 405–7; generosity of spirit of, 96–8, 121; genius of, 81, 85; greatness of, 3, 6, 9, 85, 178, 179, 193, 322, 362, 440, 478, 479; health problems of, 189, 200, 345, 352–5, 362–3, 410, 411, 442; imagination of, 390–1, 396; impatience of, 152, 153, 170, 199, 272, 403; invasion threat and, 30, 31, 34, 64–6, 69–71, 75–6, 85, 88, 89, 97, 109, 135; lack of vision of, 317, 341–2, 362, 410, 482; lifestyle of, 172–3; loneliness of, 77, 80, 255, 263; loss of intellectual discipline and coherence of, 402–3; misjudgements and follies of, 8, 10, 15, 16, 18, 46, 52, 54, 95, 113, 119, 323–40, 480; musings on death of, 295–6, 353; newspaper reading of, 83, 106, 198, 270; painting of, 293; patience of, 152, 265; Pearl Harbor and, 180–1; political leadership of, 61, 102; popularity of, 89, 93–4; posts filled by, 18–19, 24; predictions of fall of, 245, 403; privacy of, 302; promiscuity of conversation of, 128, 194, 196; as Public Orator, 389–90; as redundant, 296; relationship with his generals of, 4–5, 96–7, 101, 105, 109, 112–13, 121, 217–18, 223, 279, 481; rhetorical style of, 155–6, 480, 482; as saviour of civilisation, 80–1, 255; self-discipline of, 24, 98, 195–6; self-indulgence of, 5, 172–3; self-pity of, 81, 271; strategic memoranda of (1941), 185–6, 192; strategy concerns of (fall 1940), 99–102; stubbornness of, 5, 205; tardiness of, 79, 82; theatricality and showmanship of, 37, 51–2, 152, 168, 403, 483; Ultra access of, 78, 113, 137, 201, 279, 316; war as viewed by, 9, 18, 48–9, 119, 129, 145, 179, 191, 208, 212, 481; warlord paradox of, 318; war memoirs of, 4, 12, 14, 69, 117, 139, 181, 192, 212, 240, 252, 299, 339, 408, 410; as warrior, 18, 80, 202, 466; wisdom of, 99; wit of, 13, 26, 64, 84, 173, 179, 403; work routine of, 173–4, 190, 301–2, 303, 317; in World War I, 12, 16, 19, 100–1, 102, 339, 357, 455; *see also specific people and topics*

Ciano, Count, 395–6
Citrine, Walter, 320
Clark, Bennett Champ, 139
Clark, Kenneth, 151
Clark, Mark, 271, *310*, 316, 318, 388
Clark Kerr, Archibald, 243, 301, 308, 344
Clausewitz, Carl von, 219
Clay, Lucius, 463
coalfields, coal industry, 8, 228, 441
Coastal Command, British, 209, 210–11
Cold War, 6, 466
Colfox, Philip, 20–1
Cologne, bombing of, 209
Colville, John "Jock," 9, 24, 47, 52, 54, 64, 79–84, 106, 125, 152, 153, 353, 440, 449; on Churchill, 79, 80, 82, 83, 84, 128, 202, 358, 363, 386, 396, 400, 432, 456, 457, 461; on German-Soviet conflict, 133; Greek policy and, 119, 428, 432; on Ismay, 22; on Moran, 127–8; on Placentia Bay meeting, 163; on production, 227; Quebec conference (1944) and, 411–14; on royals, 79; on summer of 1940, 74–5
Colville, Lady Cynthia, 96
Combined Chiefs of Staff, 309, 316, 340, 399, 442; Casablanca conference and, 286, 287, 290; Quebec conference (1943) and, 312, 313; Trident and, 305, 306
Combined Chiefs of Staff Committee, 197
Combined Intelligence Centre, 80
Combined Operations, 176, 231
Communism, 132–4, 227, 228, 229, 246, 320, 342, 387, 422–30; Beaverbrook's views on, 233–4; in Belgium, 422–3, 464; in France, 366, 371, 422, 464; in Greece, 373–4, 382, 409, 417, 423–5, 428, 429, 430, 433–6; in Holland, 464; in Italy, 409, 416; in Poland, 350, 406, 447; resistance movements and, 366, 369, 370, 371, 373–4, 376, 378, 379, 382, 398, 429; sympathizers with, 6, 140, 259; in Yugoslavia, 294, 349, 423, 464

Communist Party, British, 138, 144, 246
concentration camps, 367, 371–2, 404–5,
    452
concentration of force, doctrine of, 318,
    324, 325, 400
Congress, U.S., 51, 62, 158, 180, 191,
    291; Churchill's speeches to, 188–9,
    194, 304; Lend-Lease and, 155, 157,
    426; Neutrality Act and, 36, 148;
    Roosevelt opposition in, 157, 171; *see
    also* House of Representatives, U.S.;
    Senate, U.S.
Coningham, Arthur "Maori," 257, 363
Conservative Party, British, *see* Tories
Cooper, Duff, 24, 110, 137, 225, 229,
    301
Cork and Orrery, Lord, 21
COSSAC (chief of staff to the supreme
    Allied commander), 306, 314, 315
Coulaudon, Emile, 371
Courtaulds company, 149
Cowan, Howard, 454
Craigavon, Lord, 67–9
Craigie, Robert, 181
Creagh, Michael, 109
Crete, 25–6, 54, 106, 116–20, 136, 202,
    325, *328*, 336, 405; fall of, 117–20;
    resistance movements in, 373, 381
Crewe, Lord, 125
Cripps, Stafford, 79, 132, 200, 205–6,
    272; Frankfurter's correspondence
    with, 243; in India, 214; Soviet Union
    and, 142, 205, 305
Cromwell, Oliver, 3
Crossbow Committee, 395
Crossman, Richard, 284
Croydon, bombing of, 88
Crozier, W. P., 319
Cunningham, Alan, 178, 223
Cunningham, Andrew B., 80, 118, 121,
    123–4, 135–6, 218, 250, 311, 337,
    352, 459; Churchill plan problems
    and, 385; on getting along with
    Americans, 389; on Roosevelt, 413;
    Shingle and, 354, 355
Curtin, John, 139, 198–9, 283
Czechoslovakia, 115, 367, 418, 458, 470

D'Abernon, Lord, 39
Dabney, Virginius, 436

Dakar, 67, 195, 199
Dalmatian coast, 317, 355, 377
Dalton, Hugh, 7, 19, 41, 71, 89, 99, 200,
    216, 220, 301, 319, 364, 402; anti-
    Americanism and, 150, 151; on army,
    277; on Overlord, 344
Daluege, Kurt, 137
Damaskinos, Archbishop, 429, 431–4
Dardanelles campaign (1915), 339, 357
Darlan, Jean-François, 44, 280–2
Davies, Joseph E., 305
Deakin, William, 294, 377, 379, 382, 418
Defence Committee, British, 30, 107,
    122, 142, 161, 366; cigars distributed
    at, 173; Japan policy and, 174
de Gaulle, Charles, *29*, 48, 50–1, 71, 182,
    280–3, 414, 421, 422, 446, 469;
    African colonies and, 67; Churchill's
    relationship with, 281, 282–3, 360–1,
    392, 407–8; Giraud's meeting with,
    288, 290; in London, 54–6, 281, 282;
    North African recognition for, 295;
    Overlord and, 386–97; resistance
    movements and, 366, 367, 370, 371,
    382; on Roosevelt, 190; U.S. views
    on, 281, 360, 361, 387, 392, 408; wife
    of, 55; Yalta conference and, 438
de Guingand, Freddie, 389
de la Vigerie, Emmanuel d'Astier, 370
De La Warr, Lord, 449
democracy, 1, 31, 66, 93, 99, 158, 161,
    195, 251, 254, 278, 425, 468, 482;
    Churchill's views on, 358–9, 472; in
    Greece, 425, 436; in Poland, 447–50
Denmark, 20, 185, 366
de Valera, Eamon, 67–9
Dieppe raid (1942), 268–9, 270, 325
Dill, John, 23, 77, 85, 101, 124, 223, 271,
    387; Arcadia and, 184, 186, 187, 197;
    Auchinleck's failure and, 258; Battle
    of France and, 47, 53; becomes head
    of British Army, 31; Casablanca
    conference and, 289, 290; as chief of
    British military mission, 197, 240,
    252, 253; Churchill's
    communications with, 107, 252, 356;
    Churchill's distrust of, 70; Churchill's
    sacking of, 117, 178–9; death of, 427;
    Far East and, 185–6; gloom of, 115,
    116–17, 178; Greek policy and,
    105–6, 111–12, 114, 115; invasion

threat and, 87; on losing the Middle East, 129; Overlord and, 318; at Placentia Bay meeting, 166, 167
Disraeli, Benjamin, 81
Ditchley, 155, 156
Djilas, Milovan, 377–8, 392–3
Dodecanese Islands, 8, 103, 312, 323–40, *328*
Doenitz, Grand Admiral, 460
"Dolbey, Major," 326
Donovan, William "Wild Bill," 151, 372
Dowding, Hugh, 22, 65; Battle of Britain and, 75, 77, 90, 91
Downing Street, 225, 245, 337, 353, 355; staff at, 172, 173; visitors to, 235, 252, 275, 370, 469
Draft Renewal Bill, U.S., 163
Dresden, bombing of, 453, 454
Droxford, 391–2
Duke of York (British battleship), 184–6
Dumas, Alexandre, 478
Dunkirk, 5, 7, *17*, *29*, 40–58, 65, 89, 115, 189, 204, 227; first evacuation from, 26, 28, 30, 31, 33, 34, 40–4, 46, 52, 64; perimeter of, 34, *35*, 41; Pownall's report on, 43, 44; second, 8, 52–3, 64, 202; Second Front and, 236, 237; wreckage at, 57
Dunkirk spirit, 61
Durham Light Infantry, 330
Dykes, Vivian, 240

EAM (Greek resistance group), 374, 375, 398, 409, 423–5
eastern Europe, 234, 249, 313, 360, 423, 425, 448, 449, 450, 458, 459, 466, 472, 473, 475; *see also specific places*
Eastern Front, 135, 137, 143, 145, 161, 200, 207, 248, 280, 300, 304, 390, 464; Kursk on, 293, 312, 325; Second Front and, 230, 231, 236
East Yorkshire Regiment, 393
Economic Warfare Ministry, British, 366
Economist, 214, 436–7
Eden, Anthony, 19, 26, 49, 54, 85, 99, 103, 122, 150, 156, 161, 245, 309, 416, 420; Aegean and, 332, 339; becomes foreign secretary, 112; in Briare, 47–8; in Cairo, 11–12, 106, 114, 352; at Cairo conference, 346,

347–8; at Chequers, 173; on Churchill, 20, 174, 271, 341, 392, 400, 402, 403, 475; on Churchill-Cripps relationship, 205; Churchill's communications with, 70, 110, 183, 184, 339, 342, 354, 387, 404, 423, 427, 428, 439, 457; Churchill's relationship with, 112; considered as Tory leader, 95; considered for prime minister, 200, 205, 392; elections and, 467; on food, 172; French rulers and, 280, 282, 361, 408, 414, 438; Greek policy and, 106, 110, 111–12, 114, 423, 425, 431–4, 438; on harmonizing alliance partners, 193–4; homosexual allegations about, 112; Iraq policy and, 120; Japan policy and, 162; Lend-Lease and, 149; Middle East travels and, 255; on Norway plans, 177; Overlord and, 313, 392; Persian incursion and, 139; Polish policy and, 360, 406, 457, 471; postwar world and, 213–14, 235, 317; at Potsdam conference, 472, 475; at Quebec conference (1943), 361; at Quebec conference (1944), 413, 414; on Roosevelt-Churchill relationship, 195–6; Second Front and, 231; Soviet policy and, 132, 133, 138, 140, 141, 184, 268, 351, 359, 462; at Tehran conference, 349; on U.S., 148; Western Desert offensive and, 107; at Yalta conference, 442
Eden, Nicholas, 403
EDES (Greek resistance group), 373–4
Edwards, Ralph, 60–1, 175
Edward VIII, King of England, *see* Windsor, Duke of
Egypt, 107, *108*, 115, 117, 131, 186, 211, 254, *275*, 354; British Army in, 129, 221, 241, 252, 256–8, 272, 297; Churchill in, 252, 256–8, 268, 293–4, 295, 339–40, 352, 377, 448; Greek mutiny in, 387; Italian assault on, 85, 105; Zeppelin and, 376
Ehrenburg, Ilya, 236
18th Division, British, 202
Eighth Army, British, 4, 244–5, 256–8, 268, 270, *401*; Churchill's address to, 295; command changes in, 178, 223, 257–8;

Eighth Army, British *(continued)*
Commonwealth troop dominance in,
278; defeats of, 219–20, 252, 257; in
Italian campaign, *310*, 315, 410; in
North African campaign, 272–5,
274–5, 279, 284, 286; poor RAF
support for, 224–5
Eire, 67–9
Eisenhower, Dwight, 239, 253, 260, 307,
309, 311, 352, 362, 388, 398–9, 406,
407, 409, 419, 422, 441–4, 451, 454,
456, 471, 481; Aegean and, 324–5,
330, 332; Anvil/Dragoon and, 399,
409; at Cairo conference, 347;
Churchill's correspondence with,
332, 451; Churchill's relationship
with, 339; Husky and, 303, 307;
Overlord and, 347, 353, 354, 387,
390, 391, 394; Shingle and, 354, 356;
Torch and, 271, 277, 280, 284, 299;
Trieste plan and, 399
El Alamein, Battle of (1942), 4, 198, 241,
272–3, *275*, 279, 283, 286, 374; as
turning point, 278
ELAS (Greek resistance group), 374, 375,
409, 423–5, 429–30, 433, 434, 436
Elbe River, 442, 458, 459
Eldergill, Lylie, 395
Ellender, Allen, 242
Embick, Stanley, 159
emotion, "three-inch pipe" theory of, 56,
130–1
English Channel, *17*, 34, 45, 47, 63,
65–6, 283, 391; Battle of Britain and,
75, *86*, 87, 91, 93; German battle
cruisers in, 200–1, 204
Enigma ciphering machines, 206
Ernle-Drax, Reginald, 87
Essen, bombing of, 209
Essential Work Order (1941), 226
Evening News, 28, 106

Far East, 136, 146, 167, 178, 184–8, 200,
220, 233, 385, 441; British Army in,
198, 200, 203, 441; Cairo conference
and, 346, 347; RAF in, 183;
Roosevelt's views on, 180; U.S.
strategic dominance and, 217; Wavell
and, 200, 202–3; *see also specific
countries*

FFI (Forces Françaises de l'Intérieur),
371, 381
Fifth Army, U.S., *310*, 316, 356, 388,
401
51st Highland Division, 51, 295
52nd Division, British, 53–4
Finland, Soviets in, 132, 135, 148
1st Airborne Division, British, *310*, 315
First Army, British, 284
First Army, French, 14, 15, *17*, 28, *29*, 43
1st Canadian Division, 45, 47, 52, 53,
310
Fleet Air Arm, British, 87, 175, 183,
207–8, 481
Fleming, Peter, 57, 70
Ford, Edward, 42
Foreign Office, British, 73, 107, 162,
243–4, 259, 280, 309, 338, 387, 434,
462; bomb plot against Hitler and,
404; resistance movements and, 374
Foreman, Carl, 323
Forester, C. S., 164
Fortune, 62, 213–14
Fourteenth Army, British, 388, 469
4th Indian Armoured Division, 107, 109,
110
4th Panzer Division, *29*, *35*, 43
Fox, William, 400
France, 100, 135, 145, 185, 297, 339,
405, 452; Allied invasion of (1944),
87, 289, 290, 298, 306; *see also*
Operation Overlord; bombing of rail
network in, 343, 387, 388, 453;
Churchill in, 26, 394, 407, 410, 472;
Churchill's Bastille Day broadcast
and, 71–2; Churchill vs. Roosevelt
view of, 281, 361; collapse of
Germans in, 407; colonial holdings
of, 50, 195, 237, 280, 469; colonial
troops of, 299, 388; Communism in,
366, 371, 422, 464; de Gaulle's return
to, 408, 446; fall of, 34, 37, 40, 41, 44,
47, 48, 51, 54, 57–8, 59, 61, 64, 65,
88, 132; German zone of occupation
given to, 445; greatness of, 20, 281,
361; mass forced labor in, 369;
morale in, 209; 1943 cross-channel
attack considered for, 283, 285, 286,
288, 289, 290, 295, 298, 302, 303,
305–6; resistance movements in,
364–72, 374–5, 380, 381, 408;

Second Front and, 230, 231, 236, 239, 243, 252, 253, 254; southern, 279, 349, 362, 377, 381, 399, 407; *see also* Operation Anvil/Dragoon; U-boat pens in, 211; in World War I, 19, 55; Yalta conference and, 438; *see also* Free French; Vichy French; *specific places*

France, Anatole, 479

France, Battle of, 11–58, 61, 64, 113, 202; Maginot Line in, *17*, 20, 23, 76; map of Dunkirk perimeter in, *35*; map of German advance in, *29*; map of May 1940 deployments in, *17*; *see also* Dunkirk

Franco, Francisco, 67, 120

Frankfurter, Felix, 158, 243

Fraser, Bruce, 211

Fraser, Peter, 372

freedom, 131, 168, 189, 195, 213, 214, 419, 482–3; Poland and, 6, 359, 406, 418, 446, 464; of speech, 251

Free French, 55–6, 67, 71, 193, 280–3, 295, 360–1, 366, 456; troops of, 120, *274*; U.S. views on, 386–7, 392

Freeman, Wilfrid, 166

French, David, 298

French National Committee, 414

Freyberg, Bernard, 117, 118, 119, 295

FTP (Franc-Tireurs et Partisans), 370, 422

Gallipoli campaign, 11, 12, 16

Gamelin, Maurice, 14, 28

Gandhi, Mahatma, 214, 215

Garcia, Clive, 251–2

Gardiner, A. G., 16, 479

Gazala, *108*, 258

George II, King of Greece, 348, 373, 398, 424, 425, 426, 429, 430, 434–5

George VI, King of Great Britain and Northern Ireland, 13, 76, 193, 246, 299, 403, 406; Churchill's correspondence with, 28, 46, 417; Churchill's meetings with, 79, 204, 216, 355, 390, 394; Hopkins and, 153, 158; Overlord and, 390, 391

German General Staff and Officer Corps, 464

German High Command, 460

Germany, 458, 468, 472; postwar vision for, 96, 412–13, 439, 445, 446, 465; in World War I, 101, 405

Germany, Nazi, 4–5, 9, 36, 128, 161, 162, 185–7, 195, 213, 219–25, 260–3, 267, 277–80, 297–301, 304, 319–22, 399, 444, 450–4, 459–65, 469, 482; Aegean campaign and, 324–7, 329–31, 333–40, 346; Allied invasion of France and, 298; Balkans withdrawal of, 422, 423; in Battle of France, *17*, 19–28, *29*, 31–4, *35*, 43–8, 52, 53, 54, 56; British invasion threat from, *see* Great Britain, invasion threat and; Combined Bomber Offensive against, 286, 290, 297, 320; in Crete, 117–18; doom date for, 403–4; equipment shortages of, 130; fall of Poland to, 11, 20, 113, 115, 418; French collapse of, 407; in Greece, 110, 114, 116, 117, 203, 375, 409, 415, 424; Hess peace mission and, 120; Holocaust and, 249–50, 404–5; in Indian Ocean, 204; industries in, 140, 208, 212, 228, 343, 455, 462; Italian campaign and, *310*, 316, 345, 353, 356, 357, 358, 376, 388, 394, 398; Japan's relations with, 174, 235, 389; Morgenthau Plan and, 413; in North Africa, 129, 161, 192, 204, 240–1, 253, 284, 289, 299; *see also* Afrika Korps; in occupation of Norway, 11–13, 15; Overlord and, 309, 314, 387, 390, 393, 394; in Persia, 139; RAF offensive against, 88–9, 101, 140, 171, 208–12, 298, 343, 451–5; resistance movements and, 364–76, 378–81; Second Front and, 233, 236, 239, 240, 320–1; Soviet pact with (1939), 131, 184, 246, 261, 265; Soviet subjects returned from, 445–6; Soviet Union invaded by, 71, 92, 114, 129–44, 291, 308; Stalin's brutal jest about mass executions in, 350; strategy for destruction of, 193; in Syria, 120; Torch and, *276*; unconditional surrender and, 290–1, 460; war on U.S. declared by, 183; Warsaw rising and, 411; in Yugoslavia, 110, 113, 114, 294, 355, 374; *see also specific people and topics*

"Germany first" policy, 186, 187, 197, 286

Ghormley, Robert, 97

Gibraltar, 33, 64, 136, 239, 307, 320, 325, 344, 355

Gibraltar, Straits of, 253–4

Gide, André, 365

Gildea, Robert, 366

Giraud, Henri, *17*, 281–2, 288, 290

Gloucester, Duke of, 250, 271

Gneisenau (German battle cruiser), 200–1

Goebbels, Joseph, 65, 111, 209, 413

gold, 79, 148, 149, 151

Golovanov, Alexander, 264

Gordon, John, 222, 233

Gorgopotamos bridge, 374

Göring, Herman, 43, 75, 88, 90, 92

Gort, Lord, *17*, 21–2, 26, 27, 28, 43, 139, 177, 345; Dunkirk evacuation and, 30, 40, 41, 43, 44

Gott, William, 258, 296

Grand Alliance, 193, 197, 296, 299, 307, 312, 340, 342, 362, 391, 419, 437, 480

Graziani, Rodolfo, 104–5

Great Britain: anti-Americanism of, 149–54, 163, 299–300; anti-Communism in, 32; coalition government dissolved in, 466; economic opportunities for, 413; elections in, 358, 466–8, 472, 476–7, 482; evacuation of coastal civilians in, 109; food issues in, 149, 161, 172–3, 188, 459; German settlement advocates and, 27, 31–4, 37–8, 40–1, 151, 215, 260; Hess peace mission and, 120; Holocaust and, 249–50, 404–5, 452; home defences of, 21, 22, 45, 47, 64, 85, 87–93, 97, 109, 135, 136, 171, 242; industrial workers in, 8, 226–9, 321–2, 384; intelligence services in, 71, 77–80, 103, 113, 137, 176, 405; *see also* Home Intelligence, British; invasion threat and, 30, 31, 34, 64–6, 69–71, 75–6, 80, 85, 87, 89, 91, 92–3, 97, 99–100, 103, 109, 133–6, 171, 176, 197, 366; legend of, 91, 92, 98, 129, 203; Lend-Lease aid to, 139, 148–9, 155, 157, 158, 161, 171, 244, 304, 413, 443, 459; Luftwaffe bombing of, 64, 70, 73, 74, 75, 80, 88–93, 109; morale problems in, 25, 32, 59, 61, 89, 100, 161, 197, 204, 270, 299, 384, 395; Nazi perception of, 65; nuclear research in, 474; odds of winning the war of, 60; oil needs of, 104; Pacific commitment of, 413–14; people of German education and origin in, 177; Persian incursion of, 139; postal censorship in, 244; postwar vision for, 165, 171, 205, 212–14, 243, 257, 322, 410; public mood swings in, 7–8, 250, 358; public's ignorance in, 248–50; resolve of people of, 27, 38; Second Front and, 140, 142, 172, 230–54; sense of humiliation in, 4; small size of, 351; Soviet demands of, 137, 171, 206–7, 216, 235; Soviet popularity in, 6, 138, 232–3, 246, 248, 299, 308, 359, 360; threat of German air attack on, 21, 25, 48; U.S. assistance to, *see* United States, British assistance from; U.S. bombers in, 185; war costs in, 79; war machine in, 122–9; war matériel shortages of, 64, 106, 130, 135, 144, 146, 297; *see also specific people and topics*

Great Contemporaries (Churchill), 218

Great Depression, 165, 226, 228, 229

Greece, 54, 105–7, 110–19, 130, 202, *328*, 329, 398, 422–40, 443; British matériel sent to, 106; British troops in, 423, 424, 426–30, 435; Communism in, 373–4, 382, 409, 417, 423–5, 428, 429, 430, 433–6; German operations against, 110, 114, 116, 117, 203, 375, 409, 415, 424; liberation of, 348; RAF in, 113, 114, 118, 430; resistance movements in, 372–7, 382, 409, 425, 429; Soviet non-interference in, 417, 427, 436, 440, 447, 448; Soviet policy and, 415, 416, 428, 429, 436, 438, 440, 458, 461

Green, Geoffrey, 164, 168

Green, Muriel, 32

Green, Yolande, 95

Greene, A. P., 429–30

Greenwood, Arthur, 19, 33, 40, 122

Gretton, John, 21

Griffiths, James, 204

Grigg, James, 112, 320
Gubbins, Colin, 380, 381
Guderian, Heinz, 14–15, *29*
guns, 64, 70, 76, 106, 118, 148, 224, 241, 419; British Sten, 224; Churchill photo with, 93; rifles, 64, 70, 80, 106, 143, 169, 189; Thompson submachine, 224
Guns of Navarone, The (movie), 323
Gunther, John, 170, 389
Gusev, Fyodor, 469–72

Hachmeister, Louise, 240
Hackett, Walter, 15
Haig, Douglas, 218
Halifax, Lord, 12, 13, 16, 18–19, 41, 50, 78, 152, 229, 243, 320, 414; anti-Americanism of, 149–50, 163; Arcadia and, 190, 191; on Beaverbrook, 234; at Cabinet meetings, 31, 33, 34, 37, 40–1, 45; Churchill's extravagant rhetoric and, 155–6; Churchill's relationship with, 38; considered as Tory leader, 95; German settlement and, 31, 33, 34, 37–8, 40–1, 94; Greek policy and, 429; lack of intimacy with Americans of, 197, 240; made British ambassador to Washington, 112; new troop deployments to France resisted by, 45, 46
Hammond, Nick, 374
Hankey, Lord, 19, 32, 116–17; Soviet policy and, 141, 143, 259
Harriman, Averell, 141, 142, 158–61, 167, 180, 195, 268, 282, 412, 416; in Cairo, 256; Casablanca conference and, 289, 290, 291; Churchill's correspondence with, 176; in Moscow, 255, 259, 262, 263, 265; at Tehran conference, 350, 351
Harriman, Kathleen, 160, 161
Harris, Arthur, 150–1, 208–12, 343–4, 369, 453
Hartington, Lord, 358
Harvey, Oliver, 110, 145, 150, 200, 203, 237, 282; on Churchill, 311, 410, 441, 468; on Middle East, 255, 256; on Russian army, 279–80, 308–9
Hassett, William, 191, 242, 317

Headlam, Cuthbert, 19, 72, 133, 150, 227, 251, 300, 359, 420
Health Ministry, British, 229
Hemingway, Ernest, 393
Henry V (Shakespeare), 393
Hess, Rudolf, 76, 120
Heydrich, Reinhard, 367
Hichens, Robert, 42–3, 59, 60, 88
Hill, A. V., 210
Hill, Kathleen, 172
Himmler, Heinrich, 457
Hiss, Alger, 259
history, Churchill's views on, vii, 9, 31–2, 51–2, 61, 97, 102, 119
History of the English-Speaking Peoples (Churchill), 477
Hitler, Adolf, 16, 48, 143, 161, 178, 184, 219, 229, 266, 294, 300, 360, 392–5, 446, 447, 449, 457; Aegean and, 329, 337, 338; Africa policy of, 71, 110, 114, 129, 186, 279, 284; Asia policy of, 71, 174; Atlantic Wall of, 87, 392, 393; Balkans policy of, 113–14; Battle of France and, 11, 15, 23, 31, 32, 43–4; Beaverbrook as viewed by, 76; British invasion threat and, 64, 65, 70, 71, 76, 80, 85, 88, 91, 92, 100, 133, 136, 176; Churchill compared with, 9, 81, 82, 139, 185, 342, 480; Churchill's defiance of, 56, 98, 138; Directive No. 17 of, 73; failed bomb plot against, 404; fall of Crete and, 118; Italian campaign and, 316, 398; obsession with the east of, 65, 71, 92, 100, 110, 129–30, 131, 135, 141, 170, 193, 261, 298; possibility of British negotiations with, 5, 27, 31–4, 37–8, 40–1, 215, 291, 360, 404; possibility of Soviet negotiations with, 207, 301; Reichstag speech of, 73; resistance movements and, 364–7, 375, 376, 383; Second Front and, 236, 320–1; secret weapons of, 386; Smuts's view of, 199; Stalin as match for, 134; Vichy French and, 66
Hoare, Samuel, 24, 76
Hobart, Percy, 77
Hodgson, Vere, 72, 110, 117, 134, 152, 157, 170, 245; on bombing of Germany, 209; on Pearl Harbor, 182; on winning victories, 278

Hogg, Quintin, 16
Holland, *17*, 51, 55, 87, 185, 237, 405, 421, 464; Germans in, 14, 15, 16, 19; government in exile of, 149; resistance movements in, 366, 370; *see also* Army, Dutch
Holland, Jeffrey, 335–6
Hollis, Leslie, 124, 125
Holmes, Marion, 391, 395, 438–9, 442
Holocaust, 249–50, 404–5, 452
Home Forces, British, 31, 64, 70, 87, 97, 109, 239
Home Intelligence, British, 25, 150, 182, 227, 246, 299
Homer (Chapman), 42
Hong Kong, 184, 188, 346
Hood (British battle cruiser), 120, 164
Hopkins, Harry, 111, 153–60, 171, 194, 239, 240, 268, 303, 317, 414, 473; at Cairo conference, 350; Churchill's communications with, 298, 407, 428; Clementine's correspondence with, 205; House of Commons addressed by, 216–17; in London, 153–6, 216–17, 230, 252, 253, 441–2; Placentia Bay meeting and, 163, 164, 170; on Roosevelt-Churchill relationship, 194, 216; Tehran conference and, 348; Yalta conference and, 441–2
Horsfall, John, 41–2
House of Commons, British, 16, 18–21, 28, 224, 476; Aegean and, 339; anti-Soviet feeling in, 359; bombing policy and, 454; censure motion against Churchill in, 245, 250; Chamberlain's address to (May, 7 1940), 11–12; Churchill and, 12, 13, 21, 61, 66, 89, 96, 177, 178, 183, 198, 200, 204, 208, 216, 226, 250–1, 278, 307–8, 355, 358, 363, 394, 397, 414–15, 420, 427, 430, 439, 440, 441, 448; Churchill's speeches in, 18, 20, 46, 51–2, 59–60, 95, 97–8, 106, 118, 121, 141, 279, 281–2, 296, 358, 402, 479, 482; Greek policy and, 427, 430; Hopkins's address to, 216–17; Polish policy and, 448, 449, 471; Yalta conference and, 441, 448
House of Lords, British, 12, 32, 140, 319

House of Representatives, U.S., 157, 163, 170
Howard, Leslie, 307
Howard, Michael, 158, 195, 376, 379, 404
Howarth, Bertram, 467–8
Howarth, Ellie, 468
Hoxha, Enver, 373
Hull, Cordell, 51, 147, 193, 313, 361, 398, 413, 416, 425
Hungary, 404, 415, 418, 458
Hurricanes, 141, 143, 236, 292; RAF, 70, 75, 91, 136, 239
Hyde Park, N.Y., 196, 240, 313, 317, 414, 474

Iceland, 15, 120, 163, 168, 438
Ickes, Harold, 156, 189
imperialism, 199–200, 419, 467, 478; SOE and, 372; Soviet, 446; U.S. view of, 243, 281, 291, 324, 409, 425, 436
In Command of History (Reynolds), 3
India, 25, 131, 199, 211, 212, 239, 297, 379, 387, 412, 443; self-government for, 16, 214–15, 242; troops from, 25, 203
Indian National Congress, 214, 215
indirect approach, strategy of, 356
Indomitable (British carrier), 175, 183
Information Ministry, British, 24, 64, 246, 248, 384
Inonu, Ismet, 294
Into Battle (Churchill), 477
Iran, 171, 261, 300; *see also* Persia
Iraq, 116, 119–20, 121, 297, 422
Ireland, united, 67–9
Ironside, William Edmund, 22, 23, 26, 30, 31, 69–70, 178
Ismay, Hastings, 79–80, 82, 107, 124–5, 218, 241, 380, 392; Battle of France and, 22, 26, 28, 47, 51; Casablanca conference and, 285; on Churchill, 128, 248, 362–3, 410, 459, 479; Churchill's correspondence with, 171; Far East policy and, 184; on Pétain, 44; Soviet policy and, 141, 464–5
Istria, 398, 412
Italy, 25–6, 80, 101–10, 118, 177, 185, 186, 225, 245, 380, 443, 469; Aegean

and, 323–7, 329, 333, 334; in Africa, 85, 104–5, 107, 161, 273; Allied campaign in, 279, 304–9, *310*, 314–22, 331, 332, 344–7, 349, 353–8, 360, 362, 375, 376, 385–8, 390, 391, 394, 398–400, 408, 409–10, 412, 413, 415, 419, 430, 452, 454; Communism in, 409, 416; German surrender in, 457; in Greece, 105–6, 114; mediation for peace and, 31, 37, 41, 44; post-liberation government in, 409, 425, 426; RAF bombing of, 44, 49, 113; resistance movements in, 372, 375–6, 377; surrender of, 315, 316, 324, 325; war entered by, 44, 47; war on U.S. declared by, 183

Jackson, Julian, 368, 372
Jacob, Ian, 21, 84, 125, 127, 142, 218, 295, 351; on army, 257; Casablanca conference and, 287, 288, 289, 292; on Churchill's morning routine, 301–2; on Churchill-Stalin meeting, 265; Dunkirk evacuation and, 43, 44; on Oval Office, 191; Placentia Bay meeting and, 167, 169; on Quebec conference (1943), 315
James, Robert Rhodes, 16
Japan, 4, 65, 104, 160, 167, 175, 176, 187, 195, 217, 286, 297, 347, 352, 385, 411, 419, 446, 460, 462, 466, 468, 482; atomic bomb used against, 473–4; British ships destroyed by, 183, 184, 207, 212; Churchill's fear of, 161–2, 174; defeat of, 304; expansionism of, 24, 184, 188, 202–3; German relations with, 174, 235, 389; in India, 387; in Indian Ocean, 204, 212; Malaya attacked by, 180, 183, 186, 192, 203; Pearl Harbor attacked by, 180–3; Soviet relations with, 162, 184, 349, 446, 463; surrender of, 478; U.S. oil embargo against, 169
Jebb, Gladwyn, 368
Jefferis, Millis, 77
Jellicoe, Earl, 326, 327, 336
Jenkins, Roy, 3
Jews, 249–50, 404–5, 452

Job, book of, 80
Jodl, General, 460
Johnson, Samuel, 3, 74
Joint Intelligence Committee, British, 66
Joint Planning Staff, British, 6
Jones, Herbert, 62–3
Jones, Jack, 321–2
Jones, R. V., 77–8
Juin, Alphonse, 388
Jupiter, 311, 361

Kaganovich, Lazar, 416
Karslake, Henry, 53–4
Katyn massacre, 301, 359
Keats, John, 154
Kennan, George, 351
Kennedy, John, 22, 64–5, 101, 111, 145, 178, 203, 213, 345; on Aegean, 324, 332, 334, 338; on bomber offensive, 210; Casablanca conference and, 288–9; on Churchill, 7, 206, 212, 245, 303, 332; on Ismay, 124; on Italian campaign, 314, 318–19; on losing the Middle East, 115, 129; on politician-services rift, 122; on poor performance of army, 219; on Second Front, 231; on Soviet popularity, 246; on U.S., 147
Kennedy, Joseph, 54, 153, 154, 155
Kenya, 105, 109
Kesselring, Albert, 276, 314, 316, 387, 394; Anzio and, 356, 357, 358
Keyes, Roger, 71
Keynes, John Maynard, 243
King, "Banger," 393
King, C. R., 213–14
King, Ernest, 166, 167, 252, 253, 389, 400; Casablanca conference and, 286, 288; Churchill's teasing of, 394; Greek policy and, 428
King, George, 59, 60, 134, 141, 245–6, 308, 320
King, Mackenzie, 173, 199, 313, 365, 386
King George V (British battleship), 355
Kinna, Patrick, 184, 185, 301
Kirkpatrick, Ivone, 382
Klopper, Hendrik, 241
Klugmann, James, 377
Knight, Nigel, 5

Koenig, Pierre, 371
Korda, Alexander, 477
Korizis, Alexander, 115
Kos, 327–33, *328*, 336, 338, 347
Kragujevac massacre, 376
Kursk, 293, 312, 325, 351
Kuznetsov, Admiral, 476

Labarthe, Georges, 367
Labour Party, British, 12, 16, 19, 40, 94, 132, 145, 322, 412, 420; Cripps in, 205; elections and, 358, 466–8, 472, 476
Lambert, George, 95
Lampson, Jacqueline, 268, 293
Lampson, Miles, 107, 256
Lancaster, Osbert, 432–3
Landemore, Mrs., 173
Lascelles, Alan, 250
Lascelles, Tommy, 82
Lash, Joseph, 190
Laski, Harold, 213
Last, Nella, 13, 116, 246
Law, Richard, 244
Layton, Elizabeth, 173, 174, 200–1, 302, 432, 434
Leahy, William, 138, 408
Lee, Raymond, 63, 89, 94, 99–100, 128–9, 156, 159, 161, 467; on Churchill, 82; on defeatism, 62, 89; on Soviet ambassador, 138
Leeper, Rex, 427, 429, 432
Lees-Milne, James, 9
Lees-Smith, Hastings, 59–60
LeHand, Marguerite, 165
Le Havre, 49, 51, 53
Leigh-Mallory, Trafford, 296
Leipzig, bombing of, 453
Lend-Lease aid, 139, 148–9, 154, 158, 161, 171, 183, 244, 304, 413, 426, 443, 447, 459; Congress and, 155, 157
Leningrad, 134, 183
Leopold, King of Belgium, 40
Leros, 327, *328*, 331–9, 347
Leslie, Anita, 456
Levitha, 331
Lewin, Ronald, 121
Liberal Party, British, 16, 19, 68, 466

Liberator bombers, Churchill's use of, 255–6, 265, 285, 295, 307
Libya, 105, 116, 204, 223, *276*, *328*, 331, 376; Afrika Korps in, 110, 114, 258, 320; British defeats in, 202, 220; Churchill on, 205; Italians in, 104; Montgomery's campaign in, *274*, 279; Operation Compass in, *108*, 109
Liddell Hart, Basil, 14, 19, 99, 356
Lidice massacre, 367
Life, 159, 437
Lindbergh, Charles, 36, 182
Lindemann, Frederick, *see* Cherwell, Frederick Lindemann, Lord
Linlithgow, Lord, 149
Lippmann, Walter, 243, 428
Ljubljana, *401*
Ljubljana Gap, 399, 444
Lloyd, Lord, 105
Lloyd George, David, 32, 40, 76, 82, 155–6, 172, 322, 467
Lockhart, Robert Bruce, 384
Loftus, P. C., 213
London, 64, 344; bombing of, 76, 80, 88–9, 90, 96, 363, 395, 410; Churchill-Roosevelt meeting in, 165; de Gaulle in, 54–6, 281, 282; dominion prime ministers' meeting in (1944), 386; Harriman in, 160; Hopkins in, 153–6, 216–17, 230, 252, 253, 441–2; Italian ambassador in, 31; Japanese embassy in, 24; Marshall in, 230–1, 252, 253; Menzies in, 113, 115; Molotov in, 234–7; Poles in, 301, 320, 352, 359, 387, 406, 417; Pownall in, 43; Reynaud in, 31; Soviet ambassador in, 94; Stimson in, 311; U.S. embassy in, 63, 99
Londonderry, Lord, 320
Long Range Desert Group (LRDG), 32, 327, 329, 330–1, 335, 337
Lothian, Lord, 34, 73, 94, 148
Low Countries, 25, 65; *see also* Belgium; Holland; Luxembourg
Lübeck, bombing of, 209
Lublin Poles, *see* Polish National Committee
Lucas, John, 356
Luce, Henry, 213, 308

Luftwaffe, 15, 20, 103, 106, 212, 225, 267, 268, 387, 452; in Aegean, 329, 330, 333–4, 335, 338, 339; in Battle of Britain, 64, 70, 73, 74, 75, 77–8, 80, 87–93, 96, 109, 120; in Crete, 117, 119; Dunkirk evacuations and, 40, 43, 45; Great Britain bombed by, 64, 70, 73, 74, 75, 80, 88–93, 109; Greece bombed by, 114, 203; Italian campaign and, 316, 356; losses of, 75, 90, 92, 135, 140; in Mediterranean, 113, 118; Messerschmitt Bf-109s of, 91–2, 234, 329, 331; navigational aids of, 77–8; night flights of, 77, 89, 90, 92, 93, 109, 136, 363; in North Africa, 178; resistance movements and, 378; threat of British attack from, 21, 25, 48, 155
Luxembourg, 14, *17*, 436
Lyme Bay, *86*, 87
Lyttelton, Oliver, 174, 221, 251, 369

MacArthur, Douglas, 297, 325
MacDonald, Ramsay, 68, 205
McIntosh, Jennifer, 468
Maclean, Alistair, 323
Maclean, Billy, 373
Maclean, Donald, 140, 259
Maclean, Fitzroy, 377
Macmillan, Harold, 250, 282, 300, 310, 324, 357, 360–3, 409, 482; army as viewed by, 221, 222–3; at Casablanca conference, 287, 288; on Churchill, 187, 344, 346, 361, 379, 395–6, 427, 432; Greek policy and, 425, 429, 430, 432–5; on resistance movements, 379, 382
MacVeagh, Lincoln, 425
Maginot Line, *17*, 20, 23, 76
Maisky, Ivan, 94, 138, 140, 171, 220, 262
Maitland Wilson, Henry, 324–7, 332, 336, 338, 340, 354, 408, 409; Anvil and, 362; made British military representative in Washington, 427; Shingle and, 354, 355; Soviet policy and, 466; Trieste plan of, 399
Malaya, 162, 198, 200, 202, 210, 303, 385, 469; Dill's views on, 185–6;

Japanese attacks on, 180, 183, 186, 192, 203
Máleme airfield, 117
Malta, 33, 118, 136, 140, 175, 211, 212, 239, 263, 316, 329, 336; Churchill in, 345–6, 442
Mansion House dinner (1942), 277
Manston, German bombings of, 75
Map Room, 393, 394, 441, 469, 476
March, Juan, 120
Margesson, David, 18–19, 179
Marine Corps, U.S., 297
Marlborough, Duke of, 153, 223, 477
Marrakesh, 292, 354–5, 459
Marseilles, 367, 388, *401*
Marshall, George, 36, 159, 192, 240, 268, 283, 309, 331, 340, 347, 353, 442, 443, 460; Arcadia and, 196–7; Casablanca conference and, 285, 286, 287, 289, 291–2, 293; Churchill's communications with, 277; concentration of force and, 318, 400; control of Allied agenda sought by, 303; Eisenhower's correspondence with, 399; invasion of France and, 311, 317, 318, 361, 387, 390; Italian campaign and, 315, 317, 399, 400; in London, 230–1, 252, 253; morality of, 196; at Placentia Bay meeting, 166, 167; Second Front and, 230–2, 236, 253, 259–60; at Tehran conference, 350; Torch and, 253–4, 271; at Washington conference, 305–7
Marthe, Crown Princess of Norway, 165
Martin, John, 34, 73, 75, 82, 85, 92, 125, 240, 431, 440, 445
Martin, Kingsley, 61
Marvell, Andrew, 51–2
Masters and Commanders (Roberts), 3
Matin, Le, 56
Mattison, Ethel, 247
Maugham, Somerset, 63
Mayhew, Christopher, 467
Mayhew, Paul, 60
Mazower, Mark, 381, 424
McNarney, Joseph, 159
McNaughton, Andrew, 53
McNaughton, Frank, 189

Mediterranean, 31, 104, 105, 110, 115, 117–20, 129, 291, 303, 305, 347, 357, 379, 423, 436, 443; British vs. Americans in, 289; Churchill as battlefield tourist in, 407–10; Churchill's emphasis on, 175, 296, 306, 314, 317, 322–40, 344, 345, 358, 386, 399–400, 409, 482; eastern, 322–40, *328;* Eden's reports from, 112; Eisenhower as supreme commander in, 309; Eisenhower's successor in, 353–4; German operations in, 100, 113, 117, 118, 119, 319; Italian aircraft in, 80; map of, *xiv–xv;* operations against Italy in, 25–6; Overlord vs., 319; RAF in, 135–6, 207, 239; Rommel's supply line in, 207, 272; Royal Navy in, 91, 113, 117, 136, 140, 156, 187, 198, 284, 323, 329, 331; SOE and, 373; Soviet view of, 298, 360; spheres of influence and, 440; Tedder made C-and-C in, 451; U.S. forces in, 254, 289, 300, 304; *see also specific places*
Menzies, Robert, 9, 37, 113, 115, 119, 139, 145, 157, 199
Menzies, Stewart, 78–9, 174, 282, 369, 370
Mers el-Kébir, 66–7
Messina, Straits of, *310,* 314
Meuse, 14, *17,* 21, 23, *29*
Michel, Henri, 379
Middle East, 37, 104, 133, 135, 171, 185–6, 232, 239, 241, 244; British aid to Greece and, 110, 111; Churchill in, 252, 255–8, 268; command changes in, 178, 257–8, 270; evacuation considered for, 115; loss of, 129, 178; tank and aircraft shortage in, 146; *see also specific places*
Middle East Command, 85, 144, 221, 334
Middleton, Drew, 247
Mihajlović, Draža, 294, 377, 378
Mikolajczyk, Stanislaw, 406, 417–18
Millburn, Clara, 251
Miller, Hope Ridings, 188, 189
Mission to Moscow (movie), 305
Molotov, Vyacheslav, 131, 234–8, 262, 269, 321, 349, 415, 416, 476; on Overlord, 393; at White House, 236, 237; Yalta conference and, 444, 447

Monckton, Walter, 60
Monnet, Jean, 158
Monte Cassino, 357, 387
Montgomery, Bernard, 22, 388, 437, 442, 451, 463, 471, 472, 481; appointed head of Eighth Army, 258; celebrity of, 179, 249, 277; Churchill and, 268, 295, 402, 410, 462; conceit of, 277, 386, 438; Husky and, 307; in Italian campaign, *310,* 316, 318; North African campaign of, 270, 272–5, *274–5,* 277–9, 283–4, 286; Overlord and, 353–4, 386, 390, 391, 394; Rhine crossing of, 456; Torch and, 273, 274
Mont Mouchet, 371
Moore, John, 203
Moore, Thomas, 177
Moore-Brabazon, John, 133
Moorehead, Alan, 219, 225, 257, 396
Moran, Charles Wilson, Lord, 9, 82, 84, 193, 198, 199, 206, 348, 363, 400, 477, 480, 482; on Brooke, 287–8, 302; on Churchill in Malta, 345; Churchill's health problems and, 189, 353; on Churchill's privacy, 302; Churchill's relationship with, 128; Colville's views on, 127–8; on de Gaulle, 288; on Mackenzie King, 313; Quebec conference (1944) and, 412, 414; on Roosevelt, 292, 459
Morgan, Frederick, 306, 311–12, 314, 315, 385, 389
Morgenthau, Henry, 36, 149, 152, 165, 173, 194, 259
Morgenthau Plan, 413
Morocco, 186, *276*
Morris-Jones, Henry, 16
Morrison, Herbert, 122, 320, 395
Morton, Desmond, 94, 127, 210
Morton, H. V., 167
Moscow, 183, 205, 243, 406; Churchill in, 252, 255, 259–68, 415–18, 420; Davies in, 305; Kremlin in, 262–5, 456–7
Moulin, Jean, 370
Mountbatten, Lord Louis, 176, 231, 259–60, 268–9, 352, 412, 414
Moyne, Lord, 140, 423
Murmansk, 130, 143, 144, 146, 212, 268; Royal Navy seamen seized in, 359

Murrow, Ed, 155
Mussolini, Benito, 25, 177, 215, 304, 329, 395–6, 453; ambition of, 110; British settlement with, 33; Churchill compared with, 81, 82, 480; Churchill's debt to, 104; mediation with Hitler and, 31, 37; resignation of, 312; war declared by, 47

Naples, 309, *310*, 314, 318, *401*, 408, 435
Napoleonic Wars, 203, 219, 223
Narvik, 21, 27, 118
Navy, French, 31, 47, 54, 186, 280; British destruction of, 66–7
Navy, German, 66, 118, 206; "Channel dash" of, 200–1, 204
Navy, Italian, 107, 316
Navy, Soviet, 465
Navy, U.S., 60, 97, 166, 167, 175, 191, 216, 266, 394; air squadrons of, 175; Pacific buildup of, 286
Netherlands, *see* Holland
Neutrality Act, U.S., 23, 36, 148
Newall, Cyril, 23
Newfoundland, 34, 163–9, 193
New Statesman, 28, 61, 199, 210, 213, 233, 252
New Yorker, 13, 62, 72
New York Herald Tribune, 36, 97, 479
New York Times, 36, 138–9, 209, 436, 443
New Zealand, 114, 117, 119, 199
Nicolson, Claude, 30
Nicolson, Harold, 13, 24, 31, 56–7, 72, 94, 100, 182, 275, 301, 420, 449; on achieving victory, 116; on Churchill in House, 355, 427; on Churchill's remoteness, 80
Ninth Army, French, 21, *29*, *86*
NKVD, 259–60, 305, 349, 377, 450
Norman, Montagu, 149
Normandy, 52, 298, 362, 372, 390, 391, 394, 395, 414; Churchill's visits to, 394, 407, 410
North Africa, 104–9, *108*, 143, 161, 224–5, 226, 244–5, 261, 280–303, 331, 350; British defeats in, 219–20, 252, 257; Churchill in, 4, 252, 256–8, 268, 285–95, 339–40, 344–8, 352–5,

360; French in, 50, 280–2, 295; Germans in, 129, 161, 192, 204, 240–1, 253, 284, 289, 294; *see also* Afrika Korps; Italians in, 104, 304; Montgomery's campaign in, 270, 272–5, *274–5*, 283–4, 286, 297–303; Operation Compass in, 107–9, *108*, 111, 114; Operation Crusader in, 139, 178, 183, 188; Operation Torch in, *see* Operation Torch; U.S. in, 185, 196, 253–4, 297, 303; *see also specific countries*
Northern Ireland, 67–9, 185
Norway, 11–16, 44, 65, 111, 202, 211, 300, 405; advocacy of British landing in (1941), 138, 142; Churchill's interest in descent on, 138, 177, 185, 264, 311, 317, 361; convoys to Russia and, 143, 267; German occupation of, 11–13, 15, 18, 20; government in exile of, 55, 149; Narvik operations in, 21, 27, 118; resistance movements in, 367; *Tirpitz* in, 164, 207
Nover, Barnet, 428
Nye, Archibald, 269

O'Connor, Richard, 107, 109, 110
Office of War Information, U.S. (OWI), 242–3
oil, 104, 113, 132, 169, 183, 212
OKW (Oberkommando der Wehrmacht), 375, 376, 379
Operation Accolade, 324, 325
Operation Anvil/Dragoon, 362, 385–6, 398–400, *401*, 407, 412, 413; Churchill's viewing of, 409
Operation Barbarossa, 130–46
Operation Battleaxe, 121
Operation Buccaneer, 344, 347
Operation Caliph, 381
Operation Compass, 107–9, *108*, 111, 114
Operation Crusader, 139, 178, 183, 188
Operation David, 14
Operation Dynamo, 34
Operation Husky, 298–9, 303, 306, 307, 312, 314, 315, 316, 320, 321, 324, 325, 388

Operation Overlord, 309, 311–15, 317–22, 324, 343, 344, 352, 363, 384–97, 399, 400; British concerns about, 311–15, 318–20, 344–7, 350, 361–2, 385–6, 419; casualties in, 393, 394; Churchill's complex attitude toward, 390–1; command of, 317–18; date change for, 354; deception plans in, 394; Ike's deputy for, 353–4; invasion vs. liberation in, 354; Italian campaign taken over by, 358; map of, *401*; military organisation of, 393; Omaha Beach in, 391, 393; as priority, 317, 319; Tehran conference and, 349, 350, 351
Operation Roundup, 254, 279, 283, 287
Operation Sealion, *86*, 88
Operation Shingle, 354–8
Operation Supercharge, 274–5
Operation Tiger, 115
Operation Torch, 240, 267, 272–7, *276*, 279, 284, 299, 321; Marshall's dislike of, 253–4; political crisis provoked by, 280–3; Stalin and, 262, 263–4
Operation Typhoon, 334–5
Operation Unthinkable, 6, 465–6, 472
Operation Victor, 109
Oradour-sur-Glane, 371
Oran, 66–7, 271
Owen, Frank, 233

Pacific War Council, 202
Page, Earle, 198
Paget, Bernard, 64, 366
Palestine, 25, 105, 297
Pantelleria, 103
Panter-Downes, Mollie, 13, 62, 72
Papandreou, Georges, 382, 418, 423–5, 429, 431–4
Parachute Regiment, British, 207, 327
Paris, *17*, 22, 23, 37, 43, 64, 371, *401*; British embassy in, 44, 45; Churchill in, 23, 44–5, 71; defence of, 44; fall of, 24, 31, 52; German drive on, 46–8, 52; German retreat in, 381
Park, Keith, 89
Patton, George, 239, *276*
Pauli, Kurt, 119
Peake, August Charles, 170

Pearl Harbor, 6, 158, 180–3, 187, 242, 299, 482
Pearson, Drew, 428, 436
Peck, John, 473
percentages agreement, 415–16
Persia, 104, 139, 183, 297
Pétain, Philippe, 31, 44, 48, 49, 55, 66, 67, 120, 281, 408
Pétainist militias, 374–5
Peter, King of Yugoslavia, 378, 438
Philadelphia Inquirer, 21, 62–3
Philby, Kim, 259
Philippines, 175, 196, 200, 203, 215
Phillips, Tom, 174–5
Pim, Richard, 202, 441, 469, 476
Piraeus, 114, 432
Pisa-Rimini line, 347, 349
Pittman, Key, 62
Placentia Bay meeting (1941), 163–71, 177
Plastiras, Nikolaos, 434, 435
Pogue, Forrest, 311, 313, 397
Poland, 6, 53, 59, 145, 405, 424, 430, 461–4; borders of, 351, 352, 359, 417, 446, 457; elections in, 447, 448, 450; fall of, 11, 20, 113, 115, 418; government in exile of, 55, 301, 320, 352, 359, 418; Katyn massacre and, 301, 359; resistance movement in, 368, 381–2, 406; Soviet relations with, 132, 184, 207, 216, 235, 301, 320, 350, 351, 352, 359, 360, 368, 387, 398, 406, 411, 416–18, 438, 440, 446–50, 457, 458, 459, 461, 462, 466, 470, 471, 475; troops from, 317, 390; Yalta conference and, 446–50
Polish Home Army, 381, 406, 411, 414
Polish National Committee (Lublin Poles), 406, 417, 423, 446
Popov, Colonel, 434, 436
Popski's Private Army, 326
Porch, Douglas, 241, 273
Portal, Charles, 124, 197, 305, 352, 385, 459; bombing and, 343, 451–3; resistance movements and, 365, 368; U.S. relations with, 124, 194, 389
Porter, Cole, 214
Portes, Comtesse de, 48, 51
Portsmouth, 53, *86*, 87, 391
Potsdam, bombing of, 452

Potsdam conference (1945), 472–6
Potsdam Declaration to Japan, 473
Potsdam Institute, 120
Pound, Dudley, 18, 47, 49, 123, 194, 197, 207, 272; at Placentia Bay meeting, 166, 167
Powell, Anthony, 299–300
Pownall, Henry, 7, 28, 40, 101, 121, 169; on army, 220; on Cabinet, 122; Dunkirk report of, 43, 44; on invasion threat, 135; on Soviet Union, 133, 135, 145
PQ convoys, 143, 212, 261, 263, 266, 267, 272, 284, 290, 297, 300
Pravda, 238, 247–8, 320–1, 342, 461
Prince of Wales (British battleship), 163–4, 168, 169, 175; destruction of, 183, 184, 207, 211
prisoners of war (POWs): British, 116, 117, 119, 202, 203, 268, 316, 330, 336, 446; German, 90, 278; Greek, 333; Italian, 107, 109, 278, 330, 333, 336; U.S., 316
Purvis, Arthur, 296
PWE (Political Warfare Executive), 382

Quebec conference (Quadrant; 1943), 287, 303, 312–15, 324, 361, 474
Quebec conference (1944), 406, 411–14
Queen Mary (liner), 303, 304, 312, 411–12, 414

RAF, *see* Royal Air Force, British
Raiding Forces' Levant Schooner Flotilla, 327
Ramsay, Bertram, 296
Ramsgate, *86*, 87
Red Army, 132, 138, 142, 227, 248, 262–7, 304, 360, 376, 390, 444, 462, 472; Anglo-American link-up with, 461; British Army compared with, 220, 246–7, 263, 297, 298; in fight for Berlin, 452; Finland and, 132, 135; Harvey's views on, 279–80, 308–9; losses of, 145, 263, 292; Pacific war and, 446; in Poland, 406, 416, 450;

U.S. Army compared with, 297, 298; Wehrmacht vs., 135, 305, 312; Western supplies for, 144, 224, 264–5, 267; in Yugoslavia, 379, 423
Reggio Di Calabria, *310*, 315
Reid, Whitelaw, 97
Reinhardt, Georg, 14–15
Renown (battle cruiser), 317, 344
Republicans, 36, 154, 157, 414
Repulse (British ship), 175, 183, 207, 211
resistance movements, 364–83; liberated nations and, 422–6; *see also specific countries and groups*
Reynaud, Paul, 22, 30, 41, 47–51, 53, 54–5, 60; Churchill's meetings with, 23, 31, 44–5, 48–51; resignation of, 55
Reynolds, David, 3, 12, 282, 383, 410
Rhine River, 415, 418, 444, 456
Rhodes, 312, 323–7, *328*, 331, 332, 337, 340, 346
Rhone River, 380, *401*
Rhone Valley, 400
Ritchie, Neil, 178, 223
Roberts, Andrew, 3
Romania, 113, 387, 398, 415, 440, 458
Rome, 309, *310*, 316, 318, 342, 346, 354, 356, *401*; Allied capture of, 357, 388, 389, 395; bombing considered for, 177, 453
Rommel, Erwin, 110, 114, 129, 136, 178, 192, 204, 219, 224, 226, 245, 254; Alam Halfa attacked by, 270, 272; Mediterranean supply lines of, 207, 272, 374; Montgomery's campaign and, 272–5, *274–5*, 284
Roosevelt, Eleanor, 173, 190, 273
Roosevelt, Elliott, 350
Roosevelt, Franklin D., 6, 25, 36, 99, 139, 149, 151–60, 162–71, 180, 235–40, 296, 309, 341, 411–20, 457; on Anglo-American alliance, 5; Battle of the Atlantic and, 174; Churchill compared with, 165, 190–2, 195, 362, 480, 483; Churchill's communications with, 22–3, 27, 63, 69, 148, 162, 163, 175, 206–7, 209, 212, 214, 230–1, 232, 283, 331, 332, 354, 355, 359, 372, 386, 387, 389, 392, 398, 399–400, 411, 438;

Roosevelt, Franklin D. *(continued)*
Churchill's meetings with, 163–71,
183–97, 240–1, 245, 285–93, 303–7,
312–17, 323–4, 344–52, 361, 363,
377, 405–6, 411–14, 438, 441–9, 473,
474; Churchill's relationship with,
167, 194–6, 214–15, 216, 241, 265,
266, 290–1, 292, 304–5, 307–8, 317,
352, 390, 419, 445, 458–9, 473, 482;
Churchill's wooing of, 152, 164–5,
166, 169, 196; death of, 419, 458–9;
destruction of French warships and,
66; foreign travels of, 165, 195;
France as viewed by, 281, 360, 361;
French appeals to, 50, 51; handicap
of, 194, 292, 444; Harriman's
communications with, 206, 262, 266;
health problems of, 304, 363, 413,
442; Hopkins's report to, 111; Lend-
Lease and, 157, 158; mistresses of,
165; Morgenthau Plan and, 413;
Overlord and, 318, 349, 350, 351,
361, 390; Pearl Harbor and, 180,
482; Polish policy and, 411, 446, 450,
457; postwar world and, 165, 237,
350–1; Second Front and, 230–1,
232, 235, 236, 237, 240, 253, 254;
Soviet Union and, 130, 138, 146,
261, 268, 305, 308; Stalin meeting
pursued by, 305, 348; Stalin's
communications with, 308; supply
"loans" of, 148; Torch and, 254, 271;
Truman compared with, 472
Roskill, Stephen, 123, 335
Rostock, bombing of, 209
Rouen, 45–6
Rowan, Leslie, 125, 476
Rowlands, Archie, 206, 233
Royal Air Force, British (RAF), 8, 30, 34,
41, 56, 96, 103, 124, 135–6, 176, 194,
201, 207, 220, 224–5, 270, 272, 416,
420, 441, 467, 471, 481; in Aegean,
324, 329–30, 331, 333, 334, 335, 337,
338; Air Striking Force of, 43; army
action refused by, 118–19; Battle of
Britain and, 74, 75, 85, 87–92; Battle
of France and, 21, 22, 23, 26–7, 43,
46, 47, 48, 57, 65; Beaufighters of,
324, 329, 331, 333, 334, 338; bomber
attack and, 66, 74; Bomber
Command of, 88–9, 92, 140, 208–12,
343–4, 380, 452–5; in bombing of
Italy, 44, 49, 113, 177; Dunkirk
evacuations and, 43, 45; 11 Group of,
79, 91; in Far East, 183; Fighter
Command of, 43, 65, 75, 76, 77, 79,
80, 89–92; German offensive of,
88–9, 101, 140, 171, 208–12, 298,
343, 451–5; in Greece, 113, 114, 118,
430; Harris's U.S. difficulties and,
150–1; Hurricanes of, 70, 75, 91,
136, 239; in Iraq, 120; Jewish
slaughter and, 249; losses of, 75, 90,
113, 135, 140, 268, 269, 296, 337;
night attacks of, 140, 208, 209, 248,
387; in Operation Crusader, 178;
Overlord and, 387; resistance
movements and, 368, 369, 370; Sofia
bombed by, 113; Spitfires of, 91, 136,
239; U-boat positions and, 273; value
of publicity and, 92
Royal Dutch Shell oil company, 51
Royal Irish Fusiliers, 59, 335
Royal Navy, British, 8, 27, 30, 34, 41, 47,
56, 103, 136, 176, 183, 194, 201, 210,
220, 224, 263, 272, 394, 481; in
Aegean, 323, 329, 331, 333, 335, 336,
337, 339; aircraft carriers of, 136;
Battle of Britain and, 80, 85, 87;
Churchill's relations with
commanders of, 123–4, 211; courts-
martial and, 163–4; in Crete, 117; in
Dunkirk evacuation, 41, 42–3, 65; in
Far East, 174–5; Force H of, 66;
losses of, 65, 101, 117, 207, 336; in
Mediterranean, 91, 113, 117, 136,
140, 156, 187, 198, 284, 329, 331;
Murmansk seizure and, 359; Pacific
commitment of, 413–14; Pittman's
views on, 62; Placentia Bay meeting
and, 166–7; PQ convoys and, 212,
261, 266, 267, 297; in St.-Nazaire
attack, 207; Torch landings and, 267;
see also specific ships
Royal Scots Fusiliers, 100–1
Rucker, Arthur, 32
ruling class, British, 5, 7, 12, 152, 252–3,
420; anti-Communism of, 133;
Churchill disdain of, 32, 38–9, 94–5;
compromise peace and, 27, 32, 94;
Nazi perception of, 65
Rundstedt, Karl Rudolf Gerd von, *17*, 43

Russia, czarist, 339
Russian Revolution (1917), 32

Sackville-West, Vita, 72
St.-Nazaire, 41, 53, 207, 325
St.-Valéry-en-Caux, 51
Salerno, *310*, 316
Samos, 327, *328*, 336
Sandys, Duncan, 126
Sardinia, 103, 279, 284
Savoy of the Other Club, 172, 173
Sawyers (Churchill's valet), 173, 301
Scharnhorst (German battle cruiser),
    200–1
Schumann, Maurice, 366
Schuster, George, 204
Scobie, Ronald, 427–9
Scotland, 120, 156, 171, 384, 406
Seal, Eric, 32, 54, 156
Sebastian, Mikhail, 119
Second Army, French, *17*, 21, *29*
Second Front, 140, 172, 186, 230–54,
    259–64, 269, 270, 308, 320–1; air
    cover for, 234; Beaverbrook and, 142,
    233–5, 269, 308, 319
2nd New Zealand Division, 295, 317
2nd SS Das Reich Armoured Division,
    372
Secret Intelligence Service, British (SIS),
    75, 78–9, 369, 370
Sedan, *17*, 19, 21
Selborne, Lord, 366
self-determination, 409, 416, 423, 426
Senate, U.S., 36, 157, 168
Serbia, 379, 423
Service du Travail Obligatoire (STO),
    369
7th Armoured Division, 107, 109, 110,
    274
Seventh Army, French, 14, 15, *17*, *29*
Sextant, *see* Cairo, bilateral summit in
Seymour, Charles, 63
Sforza, Count Carlo, 409, 425
Sherwood, Robert, 63, 167
Shinwell, Emanuel, 427
shipbuilding industry, strikes in, 8
Shirer, William, 426
Siberia, 359, 411
Sicily, 103, 121, *276*, *310;* as Allied
    target, 185, 279, 285, 286, 288, 290,

297, 298–9, 304; *see also* Operation
    Husky
Siegfried Line, *17*, 456
Sikorski, Wladyslaw, 110, 296, 301, 320,
    479
Silsby, Eleanor, 72–3
Silvermaster, Nathan, 259
Simmons, Roscoe Conkling, 153
Sinclair, Archibald, 19, 55, 223–4, 452,
    453, 454
Singapore, 54, 160, 184–5, 188, 192, 196,
    332; abandonment considered for,
    198–9; fall of, 202–3, 204, 206, 212,
    216
Sixth Army, German, 278, 295
6th Australian Division, 107, 109
Skelton, John, 206
Skorzeny, Otto, 329
Slessor, James, 150
Slim, Bill, 304, 388, 407, 414–15, 468,
    469
Smiley, David, 373
Smith, F. E., 172
Smuts, Jan, 47, 165, 176, 199, 255, 257,
    386, 392, 440, 477; in Cairo, 350,
    352; Churchill's correspondence
    with, 357–9, 419, 423, 430; on
    Churchill's health, 362–3
Snyder, J. Buell, 170
socialism, 165, 205, 247, 322, 423–4,
    468
SOE, *see* Special Operations Executive
Sofia, bombing of, 113
Somaliland, 105, 109
Somervell, Brehon, 244
Somerville, James, 66, 218
South Africa, 9, 47, 149, 176, 199,
    202; Spitfires manned by, 327,
    329
Southampton (British cruiser), 156
Southby, Archibald, 204
Southeast Asia, 303, 364, 379, 388
Soviet High Command, 460
Soviet Union, 4, 60, 129–47, 161, 182–5,
    200, 211, 226, 227, 242, 258–68,
    297–301, 308–9, 325, 342, 404, 405,
    411–20, 425–8, 456–66, 469–72; as
    ally, 6, 143, 389; Balkans prestige of,
    382; Britain's dealings with, 131–8,
    171–2, 175, 178, 250, 252, 258–68,
    270, 359–60, 387, 398, 404, 437–8;

Soviet Union (continued)
    brunt of war borne by, 146, 171, 193,
    229, 230, 233, 241, 246, 247, 268,
    279–80, 292, 293, 298, 301, 304, 358,
    360, 446; Churchill's concerns about,
    312, 313, 410, 412; Churchill's
    consideration of action against,
    461–6; collapse of, 475; Cripps's
    commitment to, 205; defeat expected
    for, 137–8, 167, 170, 176, 193;
    demands of, 137, 171, 206–7, 216,
    235; entry into war of, 365, 369; in
    Finland, 132, 135, 148; in Germany,
    451, 452, 453, 459; Greek policy of,
    415, 416, 417, 427, 428, 429, 436,
    438, 440, 447, 448, 458, 461; Hess
    peace mission and, 120; intelligence
    of, 140–1; Italy's relations with, 409;
    Japan's relations with, 162, 184, 349,
    446, 463; Katyn massacre and, 301,
    359; morale in, 236–7; Nazi invasion
    of, 71, 92, 114, 129–44, 291, 308;
    Nazi pact with (1939), 131, 184, 246,
    261, 265; oil in, 132, 183; Overlord
    and, 344, 349, 350, 386; in Persia,
    139; Poland and, see Poland, Soviet
    relations with; postwar world and,
    350–1; Potsdam conference and,
    475–6; public mood swings in, 7;
    railways in, 416; resistance
    movements in, 374, 376, 381;
    Romania's relations with, 387, 398,
    415, 440, 458; Roundup and, 287;
    Second Front and, 140, 230–9,
    247–8, 250, 259–63, 270, 308, 320–1;
    separate peace threats and, 171–2,
    207, 301; Stalingrad battle and, 248,
    261, 278, 286, 293, 295, 298; Tehran
    conference and, 348–51, 377;
    territorial expansion of, 184, 234,
    313, 446, 447, 458; Turkey's relations
    with, 294; Unthinkable and, 6,
    465–6, 472; Western aid to, 6, 130,
    138, 139, 141–4, 146, 171, 183, 185,
    187, 191–2, 212, 235–6, 246, 261,
    264–7, 284, 292, 300–1, 308, 339,
    387, 447; Yalta conference and, 438,
    442–50, 456–7, 462; see also Red
    Army, specific people
Spain, 24, 64, 67, 120, 253, 289
Spanish Morocco, 256, 276

Spears, Edward, 44, 47–50
Special Air Service (SAS), 326
Special Boat Squadron (SBS), 326, 327,
    329, 335
Special Interrogation Group, 326
Special Operations Executive (SOE), 5,
    8, 327, 429; establishment of, 71;
    resistance movements and, 294, 364,
    365, 367–73, 375–83, 406, 409, 422,
    425
Spectator, 13, 213, 247, 421
Spitfires, 236, 327, 329; RAF, 91, 136, 239
Spring, Howard, 167
SS, 137, 371
Stalin, Joseph, 132, 134, 138–42, 146,
    205, 212, 278, 279, 295–8, 341, 343,
    376, 442–51, 472, 480; advantages of,
    265–6; Beaverbrook's meetings with,
    142; British elections as viewed by,
    472; Casablanca conference and, 285,
    290, 292, 293, 295; Churchill's
    communications with, 295, 298, 300,
    308, 356, 394, 398, 406, 438, 450, 457;
    Churchill's jealousy of, 203;
    Churchill's meetings with, 252,
    258–68, 270, 344, 348–51, 406,
    415–18, 438, 462; Churchill's
    relationship with, 260–1, 263, 265,
    268, 300, 352, 387, 390, 434, 457, 466,
    475, 482; cruelties of, 246, 247, 281,
    350, 360, 446; Greek policy and, 428,
    436, 440, 447, 448; Overlord and,
    392–3, 394; percentages agreement
    and, 415–16; Polish policy and, 351,
    359, 406, 411, 446–50, 457; Potsdam
    conference and, 475–6; Roosevelt's
    communications with, 308;
    Roosevelt's pursuit of meeting with,
    305, 348; Second Front and, 140,
    233–7, 259–63, 308, 321; separate
    peace fears about, 207, 266; Soviet
    subjects transferred to, 445–6; spheres
    of influence and, 427, 440; supply
    needs of, 171; Tehran conference and,
    348–51, 377; territorial ambitions of,
    184, 234, 313, 446, 447; Truman's
    meeting with, 462; wartime
    achievements of, 4, 6; Yalta conference
    and, 438, 442–50, 456–7
Stalingrad, battle for, 248, 261, 278, 286,
    293, 295, 298

Stark, Harold, 166
State Department, U.S., 139, 193, 259, 351, 409; Greek policy and, 425–6, 436, 437
Stebbing, Edward, 100, 101, 130, 144, 220, 467
Stettinius, Edward, 425
Stimson, Henry, 157, 159, 196, 311, 318, 454
Stokes, Richard, 454
Stokes, Thomas, 427
Strakosch, Henry, 477
Strangeways, David, 14
strikes, 8, 226–8, 321–2, 384, 424
Student, Kurt, 117, 118
Stumme, Georg, 273
submarines, 18, 333; German, 69, 101, 136, 170, 174, 183, 203, 207, 211, 212, 272, 296, 300, 394, 441
Sullivan, Mark, 479
Sulzberger, C. L., 443
Sumatra, 303, 332, 362, 385
Sunday Express, 151, 222, 233
superpower, coining of word, 400
Supply Ministry, British, 251
Sweden, 20, 260
Sweet-Escott, Bickham, 369
Swing, Raymond Gram, 151
Switzerland, 418, 457
Swordfish biplane torpedo bombers, 107
Symbol, *see* Casablanca conference (Symbol; 1943)
Syria, 116, 120, 121, 297, 469

tanks, 85, 109, 115, 116, 223–4, 289; of BEF, 25, 53, 57; for British home defence, 64; British loss of, 121; British shortage of, 106, 135, 146; of Germans, 221, 223, 224, 316; Grant, 147, 256–7; inadequacy of, 251, 252, 256; in Operation Crusader, 178; Sherman, 147, 241, 257, 272; for Soviet Union, 138, 142, 143, 144, 171, 235, 236, 261, 264
Taranto, 107, 208, *310*, 315
Tavistock, Lord, 32
Taylor, Richard E., 63
Tedder, Arthur, 250, 253–4, 257, 262, 334, 336, 352, 389, 451, 479

Tehran conference (1943), 336, 344, 348–52, 363, 377
Tennant, Bill, 60
Tenth Army, French, *29*, 51
Terrasson, 367
Thompson, Malvina (Tommy), 160
Tilney, Robert, 334–7
Time, 21, 62, 93, 154, 159, 194, 239
Times, 15–16, 20, 201, 203, 213, 251–2, 270, 321, 389; on Aegean, 327, 331, 338; on Casablanca conference, 290; on Mansion House dinner, 277
Tirpitz (German ship), 164, 174, 175, 207
Tito (Josip Broz), 294, 349, 377, 378–9, 408–9, 423, 458, 464; Trieste and, 469–70, 471
Tizard, Henry, 77–8
Tobruk, 54, *108*, 109, 110, 121, 129, *274*, 332; Australian defence of, 129, 139; fall of, 240–1, 245–6
Togliatti, Palmiro, 409
Tooze, Adam, 343
Tories (Conservative Party), 11, 12, 19, 27, 33, 94–5, 133, 214, 218, 229, 247, 420, 421; anti-Americanism of, 150; Churchill hated by, 16, 21, 132; elections and, 358, 466–8, 476
Toulon, 67
Tours, 50–1
Tovey, John, 164, 211, 218
trade unions, 422–3, 426
Treasury, British, 79
Trident, *see* Washington conference (Trident; 1943)
Trieste, 469, 471
Trieste plan, 399
Tripoli, 114, 121, *274*, 295
Trollope, Anthony, 96
Trott, Adam von, 404
Troy, Melville, 158
Trukhanovsky, Victor, 267
Truman, Harry, 419, 443, 459, 469; Churchill's communications with, 461–2, 465; Potsdam conference and, 472–3
Tulle, 371
Tunis, *276*, 303
Tunisia, *274*, *276*, 284, 299, 302, 307, 331, 352

Turkey, 105, 107, 111, 293–6, 312, 327, *328*, 336; entry into war of, 323, 324, 339, 342, 345
Twain, Mark, 152
29th Division, U.S., 393
234th Brigade, British, 327, 329, 334, 335, 337

U-boats, *see* submarines
Ultra, 78, 113, 117, 130, 136, 137, 201, 249, 279, 294, 316, 325; Aegean and, 334, 338; Afrika Korps and, 178, 270, 272, 275; Holocaust and, 404–5
United Nations, 350–1, 419, 425, 446, 471
United States, 44, 45, 47, 60, 62, 128, 147–75, 211–17, 266–8, 297–300, 342, 386–94, 396–400, 405–20, 453, 461–6, 482; Aegean and, 331, 338–9, 340; Anvil/Dragoon and, 362, 385–6, 398–400, *401*, 412, 413; Arcadia and, 182–97; Australia's relations with, 200; British assistance from, 23, 25, 27, 30, 34, 36, 62, 63, 64, 73, 99, 121, 138, 139, 146–9, 166, 168, 169, 183, 188, 241, 242; British children shipped to, 70; British overseas bases surrendered to, 69; British payments to, 79, 121, 139, 148–9, 157, 304, 413, 443; Churchill's decline in standing in, 6, 242, 312, 422–9, 436; Churchill's popularity in, 6, 93, 94; Churchill's visits to, 152, 183–97, 240–1, 245, 303–7, 317, 414; Churchill's wooing of, 6, 54, 63, 97, 147, 152–8, 160, 169, 170, 180, 196, 482; dominance of, 385, 396–7, 400, 457–8; election of 1944 in, 391, 406, 414; entry into war of, 6, 25, 50, 69, 99, 143, 158, 170, 174, 176, 180–3, 198, 365; fall of Singapore and, 204; French arms contracts with, 55; Germany and Italy's declaration of war on, 183; Greek policy and, 105, 111, 119, 422–31; Hess peace mission and, 120; Holocaust and, 405; home defence of, 254; industry in, 182, 297; Irish issues and, 67, 69; morality of, 193–4, 195; oil of, 104; Overlord and, 318, 349, 350, 351, 361, 386, 391–3; Pacific buildup and battles of, 286, 297, 302–4, 473, 482; in Philippines, 175, 196, 200; Portal's dealings with, 124; postwar world and, 165, 171, 215, 238; Quebec conference (1943) and, 287, 303, 312–15, 324, 361; Quebec conference (1944) and, 411–14; resistance movements and, 378, 379, 406; sale of British businesses in, 149; Second Front and, 230–47, 252–4, 259–60; Soviet demands and, 206; Soviet supplies from, 130, 139, 143–4, 171, 183, 185, 191–2; Soviet Union as viewed by, 138–9; Tehran conference and, 344, 348–52, 363, 377; Trident and, 303–7; Trollope's visit to, 96; war advocates in, 36; war matériel shortages in, 130, 144, 297; war opposition in, 30, 36, 138, 154, 166; wartime boom in, 151; winning the war dependent on, 6, 25, 101, 147, 182, 183, 196; Yalta conference and, 438, 441–50, 457, 462, 465; *see also* Anglo-American alliance; *specific people*
Unruly (British submarine), 333
Urey, Harold, 63

V-1 flying bombs, 395, 465
V-2 rockets, 395, 441, 465
Vanderkloot, Bill, 255
VE Day, 459–61
Vercours, 371
Versailles Treaty, 36, 62
Vichy French, 66–7, 120, 193, 253, 280–2, 295, 361, 367, 372; Operation Torch and, 277, 280
Vickers, Geoffrey, 16
Victor Emmanuel III, King of Italy, 312, 342
Vienna, 413, 438, 461, 470
Viscose rayon-manufacturing company, 149
Vistula offensive, 418, 438

Wales, 70, 229, 322, 384
Wallace, Henry, 252–3

Waller, R. P., 116
Walpole, Horace, 66
Walsh, David, 36
War Cabinet, British, 19, 21–6, 61, 68, 103, 107, 198, 228, 244–5, 250, 291, 413, 448, 454; Amery's views on, 410–11; Arcadia and, 193; Atlantic Committee of, 160; Battle of Britain and, 77; Battle of France and, 5, 21–4, 26, 28, 31, 44, 45, 47, 50, 51, 54; Beveridge's views on, 201; Billancourt raid and, 209; Chiefs of Staff at meetings of, 122, 123; Cripps and, 200, 205, 278; Defence Committee of, *see* Defence Committee, British; French warship issue and, 66; Greek policy and, 113, 115; Ironside's views on, 122; opposition to Beaverbrook's inclusion in, 76; Overlord and, 353, 387; Placentia Bay meeting and, 168, 169; as policy-making body, 122; rationing and, 172; Second Front and, 253; settlement with Hitler advocated in, 31, 33–4, 37, 40–1; Soviet policy and, 132, 259, 342, 462; Turkey and, 293, 294; U.S. aid and, 34, 36
War Cabinet Joint Planning Staff, 463
Ward, Orlando, 289
War Department, U.S., 36, 139, 159, 286
Wardlaw-Milne, John, 245, 250, 251
War Information Office, U.S. (OWI), 437, 443
War Office, British, 22, 41, 77, 80, 101–2, 103, 129, 224, 279; Aegean and, 324; Brooke at, 179, 184, 258; invasion threats and, 136; Overlord and, 319, 324, 386; resistance movements and, 364–5; Soviet Union and, 137–8, 309
Warsaw rising (1944), 381–2, 406, 411, 414, 416
Washington, D.C., 184–97, 315; British embassy in, 149–50, 197, 239, 243–4, 384, 429, 431; British military mission in, 197, 427
Washington conference (Arcadia; 1941), 182–97
Washington conference (Trident; 1943), 303–7, 314, 315

Washington Post, 188, 189, 348, 428
Watt, D. C., 152
Waugh, Evelyn, 38–9
Wavell, Archibald, 85, 104–7, 109–17, 119, 179, 217, 271; Churchill's relationship with, 105, 112–13, 121, 278; Churchill's sacking of, 121; Far East and, 200, 202–3; Soviet policy and, 171, 255, 262, 264; Syria involvement opposed by, 120
Webb, Beatrice, 205
Wedemeyer, Albert, 159, 291, 313
Wehrmacht, 65, 118, 146, 166, 371, 460; in Balkans, 110; Battle of France and, 11, 20, 56; British Army vs., 56, 129, 222, 312; invasion threat and, 76, 87, 88; Operation Unthinkable and, 6; Red Army vs., 135, 305, 312; U.S. Army vs., 254, 293, 312
Weichs, Maximilian von, 376
Welles, Sumner, 48–9
Wellington, Duke of, 32, 223
Wells, H. G., 426–7
Wesson, Charles, 159
Western Desert, 105, 107, 217
Western Task Force, U.S., 276
Weygand, Maxime, 28, 29, 30, 43, 48, 50, 52, 55
"What Has Happened in Libya?" (Wintringham), 221–2
Wheeler, Burton K., 139
White, Harry Dexter, 259
White House, 193; Churchill at, 184, 186, 188, 190–1, 192, 194–5, 196, 240–1, 245, 306, 307, 317; food at, 190; Molotov at, 236, 237
Williams, Edgar, 272
Willkie, Wendell, 157, 165, 243, 256
Wilson, Charles, *see* Moran, Charles Wilson, Lord
Wilson, Woodrow, 36, 152, 158
Winant, John (Gil), 138, 153, 157, 158, 170, 180, 253
Windsor, 158
Windsor, Duke of (formerly King Edward VIII), 16, 76, 93, 207
Wingate, Orde, 347
Wintringham, Tom, 221–2
Wolff, Karl, 457

Wood, Kingsley, 19, 51, 79, 121, 122, 155, 320
Woodhouse, Monty, 373, 374, 375
Woodring, Harry, 36
Woolton, Lord, 172, 402
working class, 8, 205, 226–9, 248, 321–2, 384
World War I, 20, 55, 56, 62, 105, 157, 242, 326; British Army in, 218, 221, 222; British losses in, 252–3; Churchill in, 12, 16, 19, 100–1, 102, 339, 357, 455; Dardanelles campaign in, 339, 357; decision-making shift in, 123; Eden in, 112; Gallipoli campaign in, 11, 12, 16; Germany in, 101, 405; World War II compared with, 122, 123
Wrigley, Chris, 5
Wrong, Humphrey Hume, 271–2

Yalta Agreement, 450, 456–7, 462, 465
Yalta conference (1945), 438, 441–50
Yates, Andrew, 246
Yeo-Thomas, Edward, 370
Yugoslavia, 346, 363, 408, 415, 416, 424, 458; Communism in, 294, 349, 423, 464; Germans in, 110, 113, 114, 294, 355, 374; resistance movements in, 294, 364, 370, 372, 374–81, 383; Trieste and, 469–70, 471

Zeppelin, 376
Zervas, Napoleon, 373–4
Zhukov, Georgy, 292, 449, 456–7, 462–3, 473, 475
Zog, King of Albania, 416, 438
Zorab, Phillip, 429

ILLUSTRATION CREDITS

INSERT I

Churchill in Whitehall with Halifax in March 1938 *(Getty Images)*

Churchill outside Downing Street in May 1940 *(Getty Images)*

German columns advancing through France in May 1940 *(Imperial War Museum RML193)*

Churchill in Paris on May 31, 1940, with Dill, Attlee and Reynaud *(Getty Images)*

British troops awaiting evacuation at Dunkirk *(Imperial War Museum NYP68075)*

Dead British soldier at Dunkirk *(ECPAD, France)*

Churchill inspecting a roadblock *(Imperial War Museum H2653)*

French warships blaze at Mers-el-Kebir *(Musée National de Marine)*

The Battle of Britain: Hurricane pilots scramble *(Time & Life Pictures/Getty Images)*

The filter room at RAF Fighter Command, Bently Priory *(MOD Air Historical Branch)*

A Luftwaffe Heinkel over the London docks in September 1940 *(Imperial War Museum C5422)*

The blitz street scene *(Popperfoto/Getty Images)*

Churchill by Cecil Beaton *(Courtesy of the Cecil Beaton Studio Archive at Sotheby's)*

INSERT 2

Blazing shore facilities on Crete in May 1941 *(Imperial War Museum E31040E)*

A Russian soldier surrenders *(BA-MA Koblenz)*

Harry Hopkins and Churchill outside Downing Street *(Getty Images)*

Roosevelt and Churchill at Placentia Bay *(Imperial War Museum H12739)*

British troops advance through a minefield *(Imperial War Museum E1591)*

Italian prisoners during Operation Compass *(Imperial War Museum)*

George King *(Courtesy of Judith Avery)*

Sir John Kennedy *(National Portrait Gallery, London)*

Sir Alexander Cadogan *(Press Association Images)*

Harold Nicholson *(Getty Images)*

Charles Wilson, Lord Moran *(National Portrait Gallery, London)*

Hugh Dalton *(National Portrait Gallery, London)*

Leo Amery *(Getty Images)*

Cuthbert Headlam *(Press Association Images)*

Oliver Harvey *(Press Association Images)*

Lt. Gen. Sir Henry Pownall *(Imperial War Museum FE556)*

Churchill working on his train *(Imperial War Museum H10874)*

Churchill viewing new aircraft with Lindemann, Portal and Pound
(Imperial War Museum H10306)

Jock Colville's farewell to Downing Street *(Harriet Bowes-Lyon)*

Churchill at the controls of Boeing Clipper *(Imperial War Museum
H16645)*

One of the Second Front rallies 1942–43 *(Imperial War Museum D4593)*

INSERT 3

The Cairo conference, August 1942 *(AP/Press Association Images)*

Harriman and Churchill with Molotov *(Imperial War Museum MOI
FLM115)*

Dieppe after the August 1942 raid *(Imperial War Museum HU1904)*

Soviet troops advance towards Stalingrad *(The Archive of the Panoramic
Museum of the Battle of Stalingrad)*

The British advance at El Alamein *(Imperial War Museum E18807)*

American war leaders at Casablanca, January 1943
(© Bettmann/Corbis)

Aneurin Bevan *(Getty Images)*

Stafford Cripps *(Getty Images)*

Clement Attlee *(Getty Images)*

Ernest Bevin *(Getty Images)*

Lord Beaverbrook *(Getty Images)*

Churchill with General Anderson at Carthage, May 1943 *(Imperial
War Museum NA3253)*

U.S. troops advance through Italy *(NARA)*

Beaufighters attack German shipping off Kos *(Hansjurgen
Weissenborn/Anthony Rogers Collection)*

German troops land on Kos *(Imperial War Museum HU67424)*

Algiers, June 1943 *(Imperial War Museum NA3286)*

Churchill with Clementine, August 1943 *(Imperial War Museum
H32954)*

The "Big Three" at Tehran *(Imperial War Museum E26640)*
The Anzio landing *(Time & Life Pictures/Getty Images)*

INSERT 4

French *maquisards (Getty Images)*
SOE mission in occupied Yugoslavia *(Imperial War Museum HU67565)*
American troops approaching Normandy beaches *(Imperial War Museum EA25641)*
Operation Overlord *(Imperial War Museum EA29655)*
Churchill with Alexander in Italy *(Imperial War Museum NA18041)*
Churchill with De Gaulle *(Imperial War Museum BU1294)*
Churchill meeting the Greek factions in Athens *(Imperial War Museum NAM163)*
King, Brooke, Ismay and Marshall at Yalta in February 1945 *(Liddell Hart Centre for Military Archives)*
Victorious Russian soldiers in Sofia *(Courtesy of the Central Museum of the Armed Forces, Moscow)*
Churchill with Brooke and Montgomery *(Liddell Hart Centre for Military Archives)*
On the balcony of Buckingham Palace with the royal family on VE Day *(Imperial War Museum MH21835)*
Churchill broadcasts from Downing Street *(Imperial War Museum H41846)*
Churchill with Truman and Stalin at Potsdam *(Getty Images)*

Max Hastings is the author of more than twenty books. He has served as a foreign correspondent and as the editor of Britain's *Evening Standard* and *Daily Telegraph* and has received numerous British Press and literary awards. In 2008 the Royal United Services Institute awarded him its Duke of Westminster Medal for his lifetime contribution to military literature. He lives outside London.

A NOTE ON THE TYPE

This book was set in Janson, a typeface made by Nicholas Kis (1650–1702), a Hungarian, who most probably learned his trade from the master Dutch typefounder Dirk Voskens. The type is an excellent example of the influential and sturdy Dutch types that prevailed in England up to the time William Caslon (1692–1766) developed his own incomparable designs from them.

COMPOSED BY NORTH MARKET STREET GRAPHICS,
LANCASTER, PENNSYLVANIA
PRINTED AND BOUND BY BERRYVILLE GRAPHICS,
BERRYVILLE, VIRGINIA
BOOK DESIGN BY ROBERT C. OLSSON